A New Star-Rating System & Other Exciting News from Frommer's®!

In our continuing effort to publish the savviest, most up-to-date, and most appealing travel guides available, we've added some great new features.

Frommer's guides now include a new **star-rating system.** Every hotel, restaurant, and attraction is rated from 0 to 3 stars to help you set priorities and organize your time.

We've also added **seven brand-new features** that point you to the great deals, in-the-know advice, and unique experiences that separate travelers from tourists. Throughout the guide, look for:

Finds	Special finds—those places only insiders know about
Fun Fact	Fun facts—details that make travelers more informed and their trips more fun
Kids	Best bets for kids—advice for the whole family
Moments	Special moments—those experiences that memories are made of
Overrated	Places or experiences not worth your time or money
Tips	Insider tips—some great ways to save time and money
Value	Great values—where to get the best deals

We've also added a **"What's New"** section in every guide—a timely crash course in what's hot and what's not in every destination we cover.

Here's what the critics say about Frommer's:

"Excellent island-by-island information by Bill Goodwin, a writer who has been there and done his homework."
—*Chicago Tribune*

"Amazingly easy to use. Very portable, very complete."
—*Booklist*

"Detailed, accurate, and easy-to-read information for all price ranges."
—*Glamour Magazine*

"Hotel information is close to encyclopedic."
—*Des Moines Sunday Register*

"Frommer's Guides have a way of giving you a real feel for a place."
—*Knight Ridder Newspapers*

Other Great Guides for Your Trip:

Frommer's Australia
Frommer's New Zealand
Frommer's Southeast Asia

Frommer's®

South Pacific
8th Edition

by Bill Goodwin

Wiley Publishing, Inc.

About the Author

Bill Goodwin was an award-winning newspaper reporter before becoming a legal counsel and speechwriter for two U.S. senators, Sam Nunn of Georgia and the late Sam Ervin of North Carolina. In 1977 he sailed a 41-foot yacht from Annapolis, Maryland, to Tahiti; he then spent a year exploring French Polynesia and the rest of the South Pacific. Now based in northern Virginia, he returns to paradise as often as possible. He is also the author of *Frommer's Virginia* and coauthor of *Frommer's Florida* and *Frommer's Florida from $70 a Day.*

Published by:

Wiley Publishing, Inc.

909 Third Avenue
New York, NY 10022

ISBN 0-7645-6644-X
ISSN 1535-4490

Editor: Kitty Wilson Jarrett
Production Editor: Donna Wright
Photo Editor: Richard Fox
Cartographer: John Decamillis
Production by Wiley Indianapolis Composition Services

For information on our other products and services or to obtain technical support, please contact our Customer Care Department within the U.S. at 800-762-2974, outside the U.S. at 317-572-3993 or fax 317-572-4002.

Wiley also publishes its books in a variety of electronic formats. Some content that appears in print may not be available in electronic formats.

Manufactured in the United States of America

5   4   3   2

Contents

9   Introducing Fiji   224

10   Viti Levu   257

11   Northern Fiji   324

12   Samoa   342

13 American Samoa 384

14 The Kingdom of Tonga 398

Appendix: The South Pacific in Depth 444

Index 458

List of Maps

To my father,
with love, and thanks for the loans.

Acknowledgments

I wish to thank the many individuals and organizations without whose help this book would have been impossible to write. You will become acquainted with many of them in these pages, and with any luck at all you will meet them in the islands.

I am particularly grateful to the friendly and enormously helpful staffs of the South Pacific tourist information offices: Brigitte Vanizette, Merehani Parker, Al Keahi, Tracey Klem, and Kathy Maye of Tahiti Tourisme; Sitiveni Yaqona, Anare Senibulu, and Adeline Lee of the Fiji Visitors Bureau; Chris Wong, and Papatua Papatua of the Cook Islands Tourism Corporation; Fu'a Hazelman, Fasitau Ula, and Oscar Netzler of the Samoa Visitors Bureau; Virginia F. Samuelu of the American Samoa Office of Tourism; and Sione Finau Moala-Mafi, Viliami Halapua, and Sandradee Fonua of the Tonga Visitors Bureau.

My deep personal thanks go to Suzanne McIntosh, Nancy Monseaux, Max Parrish, Mark Miller, Curtis and Judy Moore, and Bill and Donna Wilder, whose generosity over the years have made this book possible; to my sister, Jean Goodwin Santa-Maria, who has consistently given much-needed moral support; to Hina Kaptain, my companion at many a happy hour on Moorea; and to Dick Beaulieu, always a font of information, advice, and ice-cold Fiji Bitters.

I am truly blessed to have friends and relatives like these.

An Invitation to the Reader

In researching this book, we discovered many wonderful places—hotels, restaurants, shops, and more. We're sure you'll find others. Please tell us about them so that we can share the information with your fellow travelers in upcoming editions. If you were disappointed with a recommendation, we'd love to know that, too. Please write to:

Frommer's South Pacific, 8th Edition
Wiley Publishing, Inc. • 909 Third Ave. • New York, NY 10022

An Additional Note

Please be advised that travel information is subject to change at any time—and this is especially true of prices. We therefore suggest that you write or call ahead for confirmation when making your travel plans. The authors, editors, and publisher cannot be held responsible for the experiences of readers while traveling. Your safety is important to us, however, so we encourage you to stay alert and be aware of your surroundings. Keep a close eye on cameras, purses, and wallets, all favorite targets of thieves and pickpockets.

New! Frommer's Star Ratings & Icons

Every hotel, restaurant, and attraction listing in this guide has been ranked for quality, value, service, amenities, and special features using a star-rating scale. In country, state, and regional guides, we also rate towns and regions to help you narrow down your choices and budget your time accordingly. Hotels and restaurants in the Very Expensive and Expensive categories are rated on a scale of one (highly recommended) to three stars (exceptional). Those in the Moderate and Inexpensive categories rate from zero (recommended) to two stars (very highly recommended). Attractions, towns, and regions are rated according to the following scale: zero stars (recommended), one star (highly recommended), two stars (very highly recommended), and three stars (must-see).

In addition to the rating system, we also use seven icons to highlight insider information, useful tips, special bargains, hidden gems, memorable experiences, kid-friendly venues, places to avoid, and other useful information:

| Finds | Fun Fact | Kids | Moments | Overrated | Tips | Value |

The following abbreviations are used for credit cards:

AE American Express	DISC Discover	V Visa
DC Diners Club	MC MasterCard	

FROMMERS.COM

Now that you have the guidebook to a great trip, visit our website at **www.frommers.com** for travel information on nearly 2,500 destinations. With features updated regularly, we give you instant access to the most current trip-planning information available. At Frommers.com, you'll also find the best prices on airfares, accommodations, and car rentals—and you can even book travel online through our travel booking partners. At Frommers.com, you'll also find the following:

- Online updates to our most popular guidebooks
- Vacation sweepstakes and contest giveaways
- Newsletter highlighting the hottest travel trends
- Online travel message boards with featured travel discussions

What's New in the South Pacific

Here's a recap of important changes affecting travelers that occurred in the South Pacific islands between 1999, when the previous edition of this book was prepared, until this edition went to press early in 2002.

FRENCH POLYNESIA For complete information on French Polynesia, see chapters 3 through 7.

On **Tahiti,** the city of **Papeete** revamped its waterfront. A new cruise-ship terminal and a new public park highlighted the improvements. The local government also decided to replace **Le Trucks**—the island's famous flatbed trucks with brightly painted wooden passenger compartments—with modern air-conditioned buses.

The Outrigger Hotel Tahiti changed its name to the **Sheraton Hotel Tahiti,** and the Tahiti Beachcomber Parkroyal switched to the **Tahiti Beachcomber Inter-Continental Resort.** The **Hotel Royal Papeete** wasn't so lucky; it went out of business.

One of Tahiti's best chefs, known simply as Acajou, opened **Le Rubis,** a vineyard-themed restaurant in Vaima Centre, the city's prime shopping plaza. He closed the outdoor **Restaurant Parc Bougainville.** See chapter 4 for more specifics on Tahiti.

On **Moorea,** the **Club Med Moorea** closed after the September 11, 2001, terrorist attacks and is not expected to reopen until 2004. Meanwhile, it is being renovated. The **Sheraton Moorea Lagoon Resort & Spa,** Moorea's best-equipped hotel, opened in 2000 on a beachside site between Cook's and Opunohu bays. The Moorea Beachcomber Parkroyal changed its name to **Moorea Beachcomber Inter-Continental Resort.** See chapter 5 for more specifics on Moorea.

Bora Bora's nagging water shortages went away when it built a huge desalinization plant. Now there's ample fresh water for both drinking and showering.

The **Sofitel Coralia Marara** was to get a much-needed renovation. Its sister property, the more luxurious **Sofitel Coralia Motu,** opened in 2000 on a small, rocky islet just offshore. The island's best midrange hotel, **Le Maitai Polynesia,** added more rooms and more overwater bungalows. See chapter 6 for more specifics on Bora Bora.

American anthropologist Paul Atallah started **Island Eco Tours,** giving in-depth guided tours of **Huahine's** historic Polynesian temples. The American-owned **Huahine Nui Pearls & Pottery** began offering a glimpse of how black pearls are produced. **Eden Parc,** a botanical garden, began using organically grown fruits and vegetables for its exotic lunches.

Also on Huahine, **Relais Mahana** remained open while it was being renovated and upgraded.

A **cruise-ship terminal** was built on the waterfront at Uturoa on **Raiatea.** The modern building holds a welcoming hall, restaurants, and shops. Next door, handcraft dealers sell their wares in Polynesian-style thatch huts.

On **Rangiroa,** the moderately priced **Les Relais de Josephine** opened in 2001, providing bed-and-breakfast accommodation with views of dolphins playing in one of the passes into Rangiroa's lagoon.

The luxurious **Tikehau Pearl Beach Resort** opened on **Tikehau** in 2001, on this nearly round atoll, Rangiroa's smaller neighbor. See chapter 7 for more specifics on Huanine and the other islands of French Polynesia.

THE COOK ISLANDS For complete information on these islands, see chapter 8.

Built by the government in 1977, **The Rarotongan Beach Resort** got a remarkable restoration from its new owner, Harvard-trained Cook Islander Tata Crocombe. **Edgewater Resort,** already Rarotonga's largest hotel, added 24 luxury suites. New on the scene: American Elliott Smith's **Shangri-La Beach Cottages,** a small motel within a few feet of lovely Muri Beach.

Noted chef Sue Curruthers sold **The Flame Tree,** one of the South Pacific's finest restaurants, and opened **Ambala Gardens,** which offers exciting Africa and Indian items for lunch. Also opening was **S.S. Maitai Café,** a chic coffeehouse in downtown Avarua. **Sails Brasserie & Bar** reopened in the **Rarotonga Sailing Club,** which was rebuilt after a fire.

The **Aitutaki Pearl Beach Resort,** the finest hotel in the Cook Islands, added the country's first overwater bungalows. **Are Tamanu** opened in 2001 beside Aitutaki's best beach; Aitutaki's second best hotel, it has 12 bungalows, all with kitchens. **Paradise Cove Guest House** added six A-frame bungalows with kitchens, a step up from its backpacker origins.

The Aitutaki Pearl Beach Resort bought Ralphie's Bar & Grill and turned it into **Fletcher's Cocktail Bar & Grill,** named for manager Steve Christian's ancestor, Lt. Fletcher Christian of the mutiny on HMS *Bounty.* **Samade Beach Bar & Restaurant** added a big thatch ceiling over its sand

floor, making it a poor person's version of Bora Bora's famous Bloody Mary's Restaurant & Bar. See chapter 8 for more specifics on the Cook Islands.

FIJI In May 2000 Fiji survived an insurrection that overthrew its first Indo-Fijan government, when its supreme court restored the country's constitution. The Fijian majority then elected one of its own as prime minister in 2001. For complete information on Fiji, see chapters 9 through 11.

On **Viti Levu, Sonaisali Island Resort** reopened after replacing its main structure, destroyed by fire in 1999. Offshore in the Mamanuca Islands, Naitasi Resort was renovated and reopened as **Malolo Island Fiji, Matamanoa Island Resort** went to an adults-only format, and **Musket Cove Resort** added several bungalows and a second pool.

Several new backpackers' resorts opened in the Yasawa Islands, including the "luxurious" **Oarsman's Bay Lodge,** on one of Fiji's finest beaches. **Turtle Airways** and **South Sea Cruises** began cut-rate fares to the Yasawas.

On the Coral Coast, the **Outrigger Reef Fiji** opened in 2000, on the site of the former Reef Resort. Only the lack of a good beach keeps it from ranking among Fiji's top hotels. Demonstrating traditional Fijian life, the **Kalevu Cultural Museum** opened opposite Shangri-la's Fijian Resort.

The unusual **Raintree Lodge** opened in a rain forest in the hills above **Suva.** Downtown, chef Eugene Gomes began offering fine cuisine at Suva versions of his **Chefs The Restaurant, The Edge,** and **The Corner,** all long established in Nadi. For more information on Viti Levu, see chapter 10.

In Savusavu in **northern Fiji,** tourism pioneer Dan Costello turned a former church camp into **Beachcomber Driftwood Village,** a version of his ever-popular Beachcomber Island Resort off Nadi. New American owners upgraded the former Kontiki Resort into **Koro Sun Resort,** which lacks a beach but has an unusual spa beside a rain forest cascade. Motivational speaker Anthony Robbins added an air-conditioned bowling alley and other toys at his luxurious **Namale Resort.**

On **Taveuni,** Dive Taveuni became **Taveuni Island Resort,** catering primarily to honeymooners instead of the tanks-and-regulator crowd. For more information on northern Fiji, see chapter 11.

SAMOA As part of an economic renaissance that saw new buildings pop up in Apia, Ian and Lyvia Black, owners of the excellent Sails Restaurant and Bar, opened **Cappuccino Vineyard,** a chic coffeehouse and cafe in the heart of the business district. For complete information on Samoa, see chapter 12.

AMERICAN SAMOA Efforts were ongoing to have the government sell the **Rainmaker Hotel** to private interests, who would restore the dilapidated resort. Also, plans for a new hotel near the airport were announced. The territory was still hurting for dining options, especially since **Sadie's Restaurant** closed. All was not lost, however, for the **DeLuxe Cafe** began serving good breakfasts and lunches in a quintessential American diner setting. For complete information on these islands, see chapter 13.

THE KINGDOM OF TONGA Long lacking quality accommodations, the capital Nuku'alofa got some relief with the opening of **Seaview Lodge** by the owners of the excellent Seaview Restaurant. **The Lagoon Lodge** also helped by building modern townhouse-style apartments beside Fanga'uta Lagoon. The situation should get even better because the government sold 49% of the long-neglected **International Dateline Hotel** to Chinese interests, who announced plans to renovate.

On Vava'u, the Italian owners of the **Hilltop Hotel** deserted its backpacker clientele in favor of building the island's best hotel rooms. They also opened the **Sunset Restaurant,** with pizzas and other Italian fare. Tongan interests built the simple **Twin View Motel** high on a ridge overlooking the island's two harbors. American, Carter Johnson, for years a colorful character on Vava'u, sold the **Paradise International Hotel** to another American. Down on Neiafu's waterfront, the **Mermaid Bar & Grill** metamorphosed from fine dining into a lively open-air pub. For complete information on Tonga, see chapter 14.

1

The Best of the South Pacific

The magical names of Tahiti, Rarotonga, Fiji, Samoa, and Tonga have conjured up romantic images of an earthly paradise since European explorers brought home tales of their tropical splendor and uninhibited people more than two centuries ago. And with good reason, for these are some of the most beautiful islands in the world—if not *the* most beautiful. Here you can relax at remote resorts perched on some of most gorgeous beaches the planet has to offer. Offshore are some of the globe's most fabulous diving and spectacular snorkeling.

Picking the best of the South Pacific is no easy task. I cannot, for example, choose the most friendly island, for the people of Tahiti and French Polynesia, the Cook Islands, Fiji, Samoa, American Samoa, and the Kingdom of Tonga are among the friendliest folks on earth. Their fabled history has provided fodder for famous books and films, their storied culture inspires hedonistic dreams, and their big smiles and genuine warmth are prime attractions everywhere in the South Pacific. Personally, I like all the islands and all the islanders, which further complicates my chore to no end.

In this chapter, I point out the best of the best—not necessarily to pass qualitative judgment, but to help you choose among many options. I list them here in the order in which they appear in the book.

Your choice of destination will depend on why you are going to the islands. You can scuba dive to exhaustion or just sit on the beach with a trashy novel. You can share a 300-room hotel with package tourists or get away from it all at a tiny resort on a remote island. Even out there, you can be left alone with your lover or join your fellow guests at lively dinner parties. You can totally ignore the Pacific Islanders around you or enrich your own life by learning about theirs. You can listen to the day's events on CNN or see what the South Seas were like a century ago. Those decisions are all yours.

For a preview of each South Pacific country, see "The Islands in Brief" in chapter 2.

1 The Most Beautiful Islands

"In the South Seas," Rupert Brooke wrote in 1914, "the Creator seems to have laid himself out to show what He can do." How right the poet was, for all across the South Pacific lie some of the world's most dramatically beautiful islands. In my opinion, the best of the lot have jagged mountain peaks plunging into aquamarine lagoons. Here are some that you see on the travel posters and in the brochures:

- **Moorea** (French Polynesia): I think Moorea is the most beautiful island in the world. Nothing to my mind compares with its sawtooth ridges and the great dark-green hulk of Mount Rotui separating glorious Cook's and Opunohu bays. The view from Tahiti of Moorea's dinosaur-like skyline is unforgettable. See chapter 5.

- **Bora Bora** (French Polynesia): James Michener thinks that Bora Bora is the most beautiful island in the world. Although tourism has turned this gem into sort of an expensive South Seas Disneyland since Michener's day, development hasn't altered the incredible beauty of Bora Bora's basaltic tombstone towering over a lagoon ranging in color from yellow to deep blue. See chapter 6.

- **Rarotonga** (Cook Islands): Only 32km (20 miles) around, the capital of the Cook Islands boasts the beauty of Tahiti—with hints of Moorea—but without the development and the high prices of French Polynesia. See chapter 8.

- **Aitutaki** (Cook Islands): A junior version of Bora Bora, Aitutaki sits at the apex of a shallow, colorful lagoon, which from the air looks like a turquoise carpet laid on the deep blue sea. See "Aitutaki" in chapter 8.

- **The Yasawa Islands** (Fiji): *Unspoiled* is the best description for this chain of long, narrow islands off the northwest coast of Viti Levu, Fiji's main island. Blue Lagoon Cruises goes out there, and the hilly islands have a few small resorts, but mostly the Yasawas are populated by Fijians who live in traditional villages beside some of the region's great beaches. See "Island Escapes from Nadi" and "Cruising in the Yasawa Islands" in chapter 10.

- **Ovalau** (Fiji): The sheer cliffs of Ovalau kept the town of Levuka from becoming Fiji's modern capital, but they create a dramatic backdrop to an old South Seas town little changed in the past century. Ovalau has no good beaches, which means it has no resorts to alter its landscape. See chapter 10.

- **Qamea and Matagi Islands** (Fiji): These little jewels off the northern coast of Taveuni are lushly beautiful, with their shorelines either dropping precipitously into the calm surrounding waters or forming little bays with idyllic beaches. See "Resorts Offshore from Taveuni" in chapter 11.

- **Upolu** (Samoa): Robert Louis Stevenson was so enraptured with Samoa that he spent the last 5 years of his life in the hills of Upolu. The well-weathered eastern part of the island is ruggedly beautiful, especially in Aliepata, where a cliff virtually drops down to one of the region's most spectacular beaches. See "Exploring Apia & the Rest of Upolu" in chapter 12.

- **Savai'i** (Samoa): One of the largest Polynesian islands, this great volcanic shield slopes gently on its eastern side to a chain of gorgeous beaches. There are no towns on Savai'i, only traditional Samoan villages interspersed among rain forests, which adds to its unspoiled beauty. See "Savai'i" in chapter 12.

- **Tutuila** (American Samoa): The only reason to go to American Samoa these days is to see the physical beauty of Tutuila and its magnificent harbor at Pago Pago. If you can ignore the tuna canneries and huge stacks of shipping containers, this island is right up there with Moorea. See chapter 13.

- **Vava'u** (Tonga): One of the South Pacific's best yachting destinations, hilly Vava'u is shaped like a jellyfish, with small islands instead of tentacles trailing off into a quiet lagoon. Waterways cut into the center of the main island, creating the picturesque and perfectly protected Port of Refuge. See "Vava'u" in chapter 14.

2 The Best Beaches

Because all but a few South Pacific islands are surrounded by coral reefs, there are few surf beaches in the region. Tahiti has a few, but they all have heat-absorbing black volcanic sand. Otherwise, most islands (and all but a few resorts) have bathtublike lagoons that lap on coral sands draped by coconut palms. Fortunately for the environmentalists among us, some of the most spectacular beaches are on remote islands and are protected from development by the islanders' devotion to their cultures and villages' land rights. Here are a few that stand out from the many.

- **Temae Plage Publique** (Moorea, French Polynesia): The northeastern coast of Moorea is fringed by an nearly uninterrupted stretch of white sand beach which commands a glorious view across a speckled lagoon to Tahiti sitting on the horizon across the Sea of the Moon. See "Exploring Moorea" in chapter 5.

- **Matira Beach** (Bora Bora, French Polynesia): Beginning at the Hotel Bora Bora, this fine ribbon of sand stretches around skinny Matira Point, which forms the island's southern extremity, all the way to the Club Med. The eastern side has views of the sister islands of Raiatea and Tahaa. See "Exploring Bora Bora" in chapter 6.

- **Relais Mahana's beach** (Huahine, French Polynesia): My favorite resort beach is at Relais Mahana, a small hotel near Huahine's south end. Trees grow along the white beach, which slopes into a lagoon deep enough for swimming at any tide. The resort's pier goes out to a giant coral head, a perfect and safe place to snorkel, and the lagoon here is protected from the trade winds, making it ideal for sail- and paddleboats. See "Where to Stay on Huahine" in chapter 7.

- **Muri Beach** (Rarotonga, Cook Islands): Wrapping for 14km (8½ miles) around Rarotonga's southeastern corner, Muri Beach faces little islets out on the reef and the island's best lagoon for boating. The sand rather than the road serves as the main avenue among the Muri Beach resorts and restaurants. See "Exploring Rarotonga" in chapter 8.

- **Beach on One Foot Island** (Aitutaki, Cook Islands): The sands on most beaches covered in this book are a tannish coral color, but on the islets surrounding Aitutaki, they are pure white, like talcum. Tiny One Foot Island has the best beach here, with part of it along a channel whose coral bottom is scoured clean by strong tidal currents, another running out to a sandbar known as Nude Island—a reference not to clothes but to a lack of vegetation. See "Exploring Aitutaki" in chapter 8.

- **Yasawa Island** (Fiji): One of the most spectacular beaches I've ever seen is on the northern tip of Yasawa Island, northernmost of the gorgeous chain of the same name. This long expanse of deep sand is broken by a teapotlike rock outcrop, which also separates two Fijian villages, whose residents own this land. Blue Lagoon Cruises and oceangoing cruise ships stop here; otherwise, the Fijians keep it all to themselves. There are other good beaches on Yasawa, however, all within reach of the Yasawa Island Resort. See "Island Escapes from Nadi" and "Cruising in the Yasawa Islands" in chapter 10.

- **Natadola Beach** (The Coral Coast, Fiji): Fiji's main island of Viti Levu doesn't have the high-quality beaches found on the country's small islands, but Natadola is an exception. Until recently this long stretch was spared development, but hotels and restaurants are coming. So far the locals haven't permitted buildings right on the beach. See "The Coral Coast" in chapter 10.

- **Vatulele Island Resort beach** (Vatulele Island, Fiji): Nearly a kilometer (½ mile) of deep white sand fronts the deluxe Vatulele Island Resort, off the south shore of Viti Levu, Fiji's main island. Guests can have dinner out on the beach, or get a bird's-eye view from a private gazebo overlooking the sands. See "Where to Stay on Vatulele Island" in chapter 10.

- **Namenalala Island beaches** (Namenalala Island, Fiji): Home to the charming Moody's Namena resort, the remote, dragon-shaped Namenalala has one large sandy strip with a deep lagoon plus three other small beaches tucked away in rocky coves. See "A Resort Off Savusavu" in chapter 11.

- **Horseshoe Bay** (Matagi Island, Fiji): Home of one of the region's best small resorts, Matagi is an extinct volcano whose crater fell away on one side and formed picturesque Horseshoe Bay. The half-moon beach at its head is one of the finest in the islands, but you will have to be on a yacht or a guest at Matangi Island Resort to enjoy it. See "Resorts Offshore from Taveuni" in chapter 11.

- **Aleipata Beach** (Upolu, Samoa): On the eastern end of Upolu, a clifflike mountain forms a dramatic backdrop to the deep sands of Aleipata Beach, which faces a group of small islets offshore. On a clear day you can see American Samoa from here. See "Exploring Apia & the Rest of Upolu" in chapter 12.

- **Return to Paradise Beach** (Upolu, Samoa): This idyllic stretch of white sand and black rocks overhung by coconut palms gets its name from *Return to Paradise,* the 1953 Gary Cooper movie that was filmed here. Surf actually pounds on the rocks. See "Exploring Apia & the Rest of Upolu" in chapter 12.

- **'Atata Island beach** (Tonga): A gorgeous, wide beach wraps around the "tail" of tadpole-shaped 'Atata, off Tonga's capital of Nuku'alofa and home of Royal Sunset Island Resort. The narrow peninsula protects a colorful, coral-speckled lagoon on its western side. See "Where to Stay on Tongatapu" in chapter 14.

3 The Best Honeymoon Destinations

Whether you're on your honeymoon or not, the South Pacific is a marvelous place for romantic escapes. After all, romance and the islands have gone hand-in-hand since the bare-breasted young women of Tahiti gave rousing welcomes to the European explorers in the late 18th century.

I've never stayed anywhere as romantic as a thatch-roof bungalow built on stilts over a lagoon, with a glass panel in its floor for viewing fish swimming below you and steps leading from your front deck into the warm waters below. You'll find lots of these in French Polynesia and a handful more in the Cook Islands and in Samoa.

One caveat is in order: Most overwater bungalows are relatively close together, meaning that your honeymooning next-door neighbors will be within earshot if not eyeshot. ("It can be like watching an X-rated video," a hotel manager once confessed, "but without the video.") If you're seeking a high degree of privacy and seclusion, therefore, they won't be your best choice.

On the other hand, the South Pacific's small, relatively remote offshore resorts offer as much privacy as you are likely to desire. These little establishments would also fall into another category: The Best Places to Get Away from It All. They are so romantic that a friend of mine says her ideal wedding would be to rent an entire small resort in Fiji, take her wedding party with her, get married in Fijian costume beside the beach, and make the rest of her honeymoon a diving vacation. Most resorts covered in this book are well aware of such desires, and they offer wedding packages complete with traditional ceremony and costumes. Choose your resort, and then contact the management for details about their wedding packages.

Meantime, here's what the two best honeymoon destinations have to offer:

• **French Polynesia:** The resorts here have the region's best selection of overwater bungalows. Invariably these are the most expensive style of accommodation in French Polynesia.

On Tahiti, which most visitors now consider a way station to the other islands, the **Tahiti Beachcomber Inter-Continental Resort** has overwater bungalows that face the dramatic outline of Moorea across the Sea of the Moon. See p. 111. Some of those at **Le Meridien Tahiti** also have this view. See p. 110.

On Moorea, some overwater units at the **Sofitel Coralia Ia Ora** actually face Tahiti across the Sea of the Moon, and they're built over Moorea's most colorful lagoon. See p. 134. There's actually a bar out on the pier leading to those at the new **Sheraton Moorea Lagoon Resort & Spa.** See p. 133. The **Moorea Beachcomber Inter-Continental Resort** has bungalows that are partially built over the lagoon. See p. 136.

On Bora Bora, the overwater bungalow dominates. A few of those at the **Hotel Bora Bora** look directly out to tombstonelike Mount Otemanu, rising across the famous lagoon; along with Cook's Bay on Moorea, this is one of the most photographed scenes in the entire South Pacific. Other bungalows sit right on the edge of the clifflike reef, making for superb snorkeling right off your front deck. Ashore, the Hotel Bora Bora has large, luxurious bungalows that boast their own courtyards with swimming pools; they are the most private quarters in all of French Polynesia. See p. 151.

Almost as private are the garden units at the **Bora Bora Pearl Beach Resort;** you can cavort to your heart's content in their wall-enclosed patios, which have sun decks and splash pools. See p. 150. The **Sofitel Coralia Marara** itself is not as charming or luxurious as other resorts on Bora Bora, but about five of its bungalows are the most private overwater units in French Polynesia, and they have large, partially covered decks. See p. 152. Bungalows at Sofitel Coralia Marara's sister resort, the **Sofitel Coralia Motu,** have great views of Mount Otemanu's tombstone face from the resort's own motu (little island). See p. 152. Out on an island, the **Bora Bora Lagoon Resort** has 50 rather closely packed bungalows over its reef, some with great views of Bora Bora's "other" peak, the more rounded Mount Pahia. See p. 150. The units at the friendly **Bora Bora Pearl Beach Resort,** which also sits on a motu, are spacious and nicely decorated. Some of the beachside units at the Pearl Beach have fence-surrounded private patios. See p. 150.

On Huahine, units at the **Te Tiare Beach Resort** have the largest decks of any overwater bungalows (one side is completed shaded by a thatch roof). See p. 164. The **Hotel Sofitel Heiva Coralia** has six bungalows with views of the mountainous main part of that island. See p. 163.

Out in the Tuamotu archipelago, the huge atoll known as Rangiroa, **Kia Ora Village** has bungalows over the world's second-largest lagoon. See p. 173. On the adjacent atoll, overwater bungalows at the new **Tikehau Pearl Beach Resort** actually sit over the rip tides in a pass that lets the sea into the lagoon. See p. 175. On Manihi atoll, units at the **Manihi Pearl Beach Resort** are cooled by the almost constantly blowing trade winds. Isolated on their own islets, the Pearl Beach resorts on Tikihau and Manihi more closely approximate Fiji's offshore resorts than any others in French Polynesia. See p. 175.

• **Fiji:** Fiji has one of the world's finest collections of small offshore resorts. These little establishments have two advantages over their French Polynesian competitors. First, they have only 3 to 15 bungalows each, instead of the 40 or more found at the French Polynesian resorts, which means they are usually more widely spaced than their Tahitian cousins. Second, they are on islands all by themselves. Together, these two advantages multiply the privacy factor several fold.

Off Nadi, the atmosphere at **Turtle Island Resort** and the **Vatulele Island Resort,** both of which are in the luxurious, super-expensive category, are active, with guests given the choice of dining alone in their bungalows or at lively dinner parties hosted by the engaging owners. See p. 287 and 289. **Yasawa Island Resort** sits on one of the prettiest beaches and has a very low-key, friendly ambiance. It has 16 very large bungalows, the choice being the secluded honeymoon unit, which sits by its own beach. If you can't get that, be sure to reserve one of the newer units because a communal pathway runs just outside the bedroom windows of the older bungalows. See p. 288.

In central Fiji off Suva, **The Wakaya Club** has the largest bungalows in Fiji, plus a palatial mansion with its own pool, perched high atop a ridge. The staff leaves the guests to their own devices. You might see a movie star or two relaxing at Wakaya. See p. 312.

Out in northern Fiji, motivational speaker Anthony Robbins has equipped **Namale Resort** with some of Fiji's most romantic honeymoon bungalows, with double-sized chaise lounges strewn with pillows, mosquito nets hanging over heavy bamboo-poster beds, and huge bathrooms with Jacuzzi tubs and ceiling fans. See p. 330.

On a dragon-shaped island all by itself in the Koro Sea off Savusavu, **Moody's Namena** is the most remote of all South Pacific resorts. You won't get a lot of amenities at Moody's, but one of its hexagonal bungalows is perched treehouse-like on a ridge, providing both privacy and stunning sea views. OCCUPIED/ UNOCCUPIED signs warn guests that someone else is already cavorting on four of the island's five private beaches. See p. 332.

Off Taveuni, **Matangi Island Resort** is one of the region's best values for both honeymooners and families. One of its widely spaced bungalows is built 20 feet up in a Pacific almond tree, and two more are carved into the side of a cliff (they are reserved for honeymooners). See p. 340. Among my favorite places to stay are the charming, old South Seas–style bungalows and stunning central building at **Qamea Beach Club.**

Kerosene lanterns romantically light the 52-foot-high thatch roof of Qamea's main building, and each bungalow has its own hammock strung across the front porch. See p. 341.

4 The Best Family Vacations

There are no Disney Worlds or other such attractions in the islands. That's not to say that children won't have a fine time here, but they will enjoy themselves most if they like being around the water.

A family can vacation in style and comfort at large resorts like the two Sheraton resorts in Fiji, or Shangri-la's Fijian Resort, but here are some of the best smaller establishments that welcome families with children.

- **Moorea Beachcomber Inter-Continental Resort** (Moorea, French Polynesia): Most resorts in French Polynesia are designed for romance, not children. The one notable exception is the Moorea Beachcomber, which has an attractive pool, a calm lagoon, the widest selection of water sports in French Polynesia, and a kids' program. See p. 136.
- **Muri Beachcomber** (Rarotonga, Cook Islands): There is no restaurant at the Muri Beachcomber premises—several dining options are a short walk away along lovely Muri Beach—but what you do get here are one-bedroom apartments facing a pool, so the folks can keep a sharp eye on the kids taking a dip. Or you can opt for one of three houses equipped with all the modern amenities at this little resort. The lagoon here is peaceful, shallow, and safe. See p. 205.

- **Castaway Island Resort** (Mamanuca Islands, Fiji): One of Fiji's oldest but thoroughly refurbished resorts, Castaway has plenty to keep both adults and children occupied, from a wide array of watersports to a kids' playroom and a nursery. There's even a nurse on duty. See p. 283.
- **Jean-Michel Cousteau Fiji Islands Resort** (Savusavu, Fiji): The South Pacific's finest family resort requires parents to enroll their kids in an environmental education program. It keeps the youngsters both educated and entertained from sunup to bedtime. See p. 328.
- **Matangi Island Resort** (Northern Fiji): Born as a hard-core dive base, this low-key, family run resort has adjusted to divers who want to bring the youngsters along. Parents do their two dives—or go snorkeling—in the morning, while the parents who stay behind help the staff keep the kids busy building sand castles. The children have their own mealtimes, but everyone is welcome to make visits to Fijian villages, go on picnics to the fabulous Horseshoe Bay, or hike up to Bouma Falls on Taveuni. See p. 340.

5 The Best Cultural Experiences

The South Pacific Islanders are justly proud of their ancient Polynesian and Fijian cultures, and they eagerly inform anyone who asks about both their ancient and modern ways. Here are some of the best ways to learn about the islanders and their lifestyles.

- **Tiki Theatre Village** (Moorea, French Polynesia): Built to resemble a pre-European Tahitian village, this cultural center on Moorea has demonstrations of handcraft making and puts on a nightly dance show and feast. It's a bit commercial, and the staff isn't always fluent in English, but this is the only place in French Polynesia where one can sample the old ways. See "Exploring Moorea" in chapter 5.

- **Rarotonga** (Cook Islands): In addition to offering some of the region's most laid-back beach vacations, the people of Rarotonga go out of their way to let visitors know about their unique Cook Islands way of life. A morning spent at the **Cook Islands Cultural Village** and on a **cultural tour** of the island is an excellent educational experience. For a look at flora and fauna of the island, and their traditional uses, **Pa's Cross-Island Mountain Trek** cannot be topped. See "Exploring Rarotonga" in chapter 8.

- **Fijian Village Visits** (Fiji): Many tours from Nadi and from most offshore resorts include visits to traditional Fijian villages, whose residents stage welcoming ceremonies (featuring the slightly narcotic drink kava) and then show visitors around and explain how the old and the new combine in today's villages. See "Cultural Tours" in chapter 10.

- **Samoa:** The entire country of Samoa is a cultural storehouse of *fa'a Samoa*, the old Samoan way of doing things. Most Samoans still live in villages featuring oval *fales,* some of which have stood for centuries (although tin roofs have replaced thatch). The island of Savai'i is especially well preserved. A highlight of any visit to Savai'i should be a **tour** with Warren Jopling, a retired Australian geologist who has lived on Samoa's largest island for many years. Not only does he know the forbidding lava fields like the back of his hand, but everyone on Savai'i knows him, which helps make his cultural commentaries extremely informative. See "Savai'i" in chapter 12.

- **Tongan National Centre** (Nuku'alofa, Tonga): Artisans turn out classic Tongan handcrafts, and a museum exhibits Tongan history, including the robe worn by Queen Salote at the coronation of Queen Elizabeth II in 1953; and the carcass of Tui Malila, a Galápagos turtle that Capt. James Cook reputedly gave to the king of Tonga in 1777, and which lived until 1968. The center also has island-night dance shows and feasts of traditional Tongan food. See "Exploring Tongatapu" in chapter 14.

6 The Best of the Old South Seas

Many South Pacific islands are developing rapidly, with modern, fast-paced cities replacing what were sleepy backwater ports, such as those at Papeete in French Polynesia and Suva in Fiji. However, there are still many remnants of the old South Sea days of coconut planters, beach bums, and missionaries.

- **Fare** (Huahine, French Polynesia): Of the French Polynesian islands frequented by visitors, Huahine has been the least affected by tourism. As on Aitutaki, agriculture is still king on Huahine, which makes it the "Island of Fruits." There are ancient *marae* temples to visit, and the only town, tiny Fare, is little more than a collection of Chinese shops fronting the island's wharf, which comes to life when ships pull in. See "Huahine" in chapter 7, "Huahine & the Other Islands of French Polynesia."

- **Aitutaki** (Cook Islands): Noted for its crystal-clear lagoon, the little island of Aitutaki is very much old Polynesia, with most of its residents still farming and fishing for a living. See "Aitutaki" in chapter 8, "The Cook Islands."

- **Levuka** (Ovalau Island, Fiji): No town has remained the same after a century as has Levuka, Fiji's first European-style town and its original colonial capital in the 1870s. The dramatic cliffs of Ovalau Island hemmed in the town and prevented growth, so the government moved to Suva in 1882. Levuka looks very much as it did then, with a row of clapboard general stores along picturesque Beach Street. See "A Side Trip to Levuka" in chapter 10, "Viti Levu."

- **Taveuni Island** (Northern Fiji): Like Savai'i, Fiji's third-largest and most lush island has changed little since Europeans started coconut plantations there in the 1860s. With the largest remaining population of indigenous plants and animals of any South Pacific island, Taveuni is a nature lover's delight. See "Taveuni" in chapter 11, "Northern Fiji."

- **Apia** (Samoa): Despite a sea wall along what used to be a beach, and two large high-rise buildings sitting on reclaimed land, a number of clapboard buildings and 19th-century churches make Apia look much as it did when German, American, and British warships washed ashore during a hurricane here in 1889. See "Exploring Apia & the Rest of Upolu" in chapter 12, "Samoa."

- **Savai'i** (Samoa): One of the largest of all Polynesian islands, this great volcanic shield also is one of the least populated, with the oval-shaped houses of traditional villages sitting beside freshwater bathing pools fed by underground springs. See "Savai'i" in chapter 12, "Samoa."

- **Neiafu** (Vava'u, Tonga): Although Nuku'alofa, the capital of Tonga on the main island of Tongatapu, still has a dusty, 19th-century ambience, the little village of Neiafu on the sailor's paradise of Vava'u has remained untouched by development. Built by convicted adulteresses, the Road of the Doves still winds above the dramatic Port of Refuge, just as it did in 1875. See "Vava'u" in chapter 14, "The Kingdom of Tonga."

7 The Best Food

You won't be stuck eating island-style food cooked in an earth oven (see "Feast from Underground Ovens" in the appendix), nor will you be limited to the rather bland tastes of New Zealanders and Australians, which predominate at many restaurants. Wherever the French go, fine food and wine are sure to follow, and French Polynesia is no exception. The East Indians brought curries to Fiji, and chefs trained there have spread those spicy offerings to the other islands. Many chefs in Tonga are from Germany and Italy and specialize in their own "native" food. Chinese cuisine of varying quality can be found everywhere.

Wine connoisseurs will have ample opportunity to sample the vintages from nearby Australia, where abundant sunshine produces renowned full-bodied, fruit-driven varieties, such as chardonnay, semillon, Riesling, shiraz, Hermitage, cabernet sauvignon, and merlot. New Zealand wines are also widely available, including distinctive whites, such as chenin blanc, sauvignon blanc, and soft merlot. Freight and import duties drive up the cost of wine, so expect higher prices than at home.

- **Auberge du Pacifique** (Papeete, Tahiti): Award-winning chef Jean Galopin has been blending French and Polynesian cuisines at his lagoonside restaurant—with a removable roof to let in starlight—since 1974. He's even written a cookbook about Tahitian cooking. See p. 114.

- **Le Lotus** (Papeete, Tahiti): The most romantic setting of any South Pacific restaurant is in this overwater dining room at the Tahiti Beachcomber Inter-Continental Resort. Even if the food weren't gourmet French and the service highly efficient and unobtrusive, the view of Moorea on a moonlight night makes an evening here special. See p. 114.

- **Te Honu Iti (Chez Roger)** (Moorea, French Polynesia): You can dine right beside awesomely beautiful Cook's Bay at award-winning chef Roger Iqual's snack bar-cum-restaurant, where he gives some delightful twists to seafood prepared in the classic French fashion. See p. 138.

- **Bloody Mary's Restaurant & Bar** (Bora Bora, French Polynesia): The chargrilled seafood and steaks aren't reason enough alone to come to Bloody Mary's, but this place offers the most unique and charming dining experience in the islands. And after eating heavy French fare elsewhere for a few days, the sauceless fish from the grill will seem downright refreshing. See p. 155.

- **Chefs The Restaurant** (Nadi, Fiji): Perhaps the best restaurant in the islands, chef Eugeme Gomes's establishment has gourmet cuisine, excellent service, and lots of little touches that make for a fine dining experience. There's a branch in Suva, too. See p. 277.

- **Vilisite's Seafood Restaurant** (The Coral Coast, Fiji): This seaside restaurant, owned and operated by a friendly Fijian woman named Vilisite, doesn't look like much from the outside, but it offers a handful of excellent seafood meals to augment a terrific view along Fiji's Coral Coast from the veranda. See p. 298.

- **Old Mill Cottage** (Suva, Fiji): Diplomats and government workers pack this old colonial cottage at breakfast and lunch for some of the region's best and least expensive local fare. Offerings range from English-style roast chicken with mashed potatoes and peas to sweet Fijian-style *palusami* (fresh fish wrapped in taro leaves and steamed in coconut milk). See p. 314.

- **Sails Restaurant and Bar** (Apia, Samoa): Ian and Lyvia Black have turned Robert Louis Stevenson's first Samoan home into one of the South Pacific's best casual restaurants, complete with tables on an upstairs veranda overlooking historic Beach Road and Apia Harbour. You'll never forget the Commodore Sashimi. See p. 377.

- **Seaview Restaurant** (Nuku'alofa, Tonga): In a country where restaurants come and go, this German-owned establishment in an old waterfront home has for years provided Nuku'alofa's best cuisine. Tonga is the last island nation with an abundance of spiny tropical lobsters, so go for one here. See p. 430.

- **Ocean Breeze Restaurant** (Vava'u, Tonga:): A native of Tonga, Amelia Dale learned to cook curries while living in

London, and hers are the best in the islands (and that includes Fiji, where the population is almost half East Indians). In fact, I've never had better, even in India or Pakistan. See p. 440.

8 The Best Island Nights

Don't come to the South Pacific islands expecting opera and ballet, or Las Vegas–style floor shows, either. Other than "pub crawling" to bars and nightclubs with music for dancing, evening entertainment here consists primarily of island nights, which invariably feature feasts of island foods followed by traditional dancing.

In the cases of French Polynesia and the Cook Islands, of course, the hip-swinging traditional dances are world famous. They are not as lewd and lascivious today as they were in the days before the missionaries arrived, but they still have plenty of suggestive movements to the primordial beat of drums. By contrast, dancing in Fiji, Tonga, and the Samoas is much more reserved, with graceful movements, terrific harmony, and occasional action in a war or fire dance.

- **French Polynesia:** Hotels are the places in which to see Tahitian dancing here. The resorts rely on village groups to perform a few times a week. The very best shows are during the annual *Heiva i Tahiti* festival in July; the winners then tour the other islands in August for minifestivals at the resorts. See "Island Nights" in chapters 4 through 6.
- **The Cook Islands:** Although the Tahitians are more famous for their dancing than the Cook Islanders, many of their original movements were quashed by the missionaries in the early 19th century. By the time the French took over in 1841 and allowed dancing again, the Tahitians had forgotten much of the old movements. They turned to the Cook Islands, where

dancing was—and still is—the thing to do when the sun goes down. In the Cooks the costumes tend to be more natural and less colorful than in the Tahitian floor shows, but the movements tend to be more active, suggestive, and genuine. There's an island night show every evening except Sunday on Rarotonga. The best troupes usually perform at the Edgewater Resort and the Rarotongan Beach Resort, but ask around. The best public performances are during the annual Dancer of the Year contest in April and the Constitution Week celebrations in August. See "Island Nights on Rarotonga" in chapter 8.

- **Samoa:** Among the great shows in the South Pacific are *fiafia* nights in the magnificent main building at Aggie Grey's Hotel in Apia. This tradition was started in the 1940s by the late Aggie Grey, who at the show's culmination personally danced the graceful *siva*. Daughter-in-law Marina Grey now plays that role, and the show has been expanded to include a rousing fire dance around the adjacent pool. See "Island Nights on Upolu" in chapter 12.
- **Tonga:** The weekly shows at the Tongan National Centre are unique, for this museum provides expert commentary before each dance, explaining its movements and their meanings. That's a big help, since all songs throughout the South Pacific are in the native languages. See "Island Nights on Tongatapu" in chapter 14.

9 The Best Buys

Take some extra money along, for you'll spend it on handcrafts, black pearls, and tropical clothing.

For the locations of the best shops, see in chapters 3 through 14.

- **Black Pearls:** Few people will escape French Polynesia or the Cook Islands without buying at least one black pearl. That's because the shallow, clear-water lagoons of French Polynesia's Tuamotu archipelago and the Manihiki and Penrhyn atolls in the Cook Islands are the world's largest producers of the beautiful dark orbs. The seemingly inexhaustible supply has resulted in fierce competition by vendors ranging from market stalls to high-end jewelry shops. See chapters 3 through 7.

- **Handcrafts:** Although many of the items you will see in island souvenir shops are actually made in Asia, locally produced handcrafts are the South Pacific's best buys. The most widespread are hats, mats, and baskets woven of *pandanus* or other fibers, usually by women who have maintained this ancient art to a high degree. Tonga has the widest selection of woven items, although Samoa and Fiji are making comebacks. The finely woven mats made in Tonga and the Samoas are still highly valued as ceremonial possessions and are seldom for sale to tourists. See chapters 9 through 12 and 14.

Before the coming of European traders and printed cotton, the South Pacific islanders wore garments made from the beaten bark of the paper mulberry tree. The making of this bark cloth, widely known as *tapa,* is another preserved art in Tonga, Samoa (where

it is known as *siapo*), and Fiji (where it is known as *masi*). The cloth is painted with dyes made from natural substances, usually in geometric designs whose ancestries date back thousands of years. Tapa is an excellent souvenir because it can be folded and brought back in a suitcase. See chapters 9 through 12 and 14.

Woodcarvings are also popular. Spears, war clubs, knives made from sharks' teeth, canoe prows, and cannibal forks are some examples. Many carvings, however, tend to be produced for the tourist trade and often lack the imagery of bygone days, and some may be machine-produced today. Carved tikis are found in most South Pacific countries, but many of them resemble the figures of the New Zealand Maoris rather than figures indigenous to those countries. The carvings from the Marquesas Islands of French Polynesia are the best of the lot today. See chapter 3.

- **Tropical Clothing:** Colorful hand-screened, hand-blocked, and hand-dyed fabrics are very popular in the islands for making dresses or the wraparound skirt known as *pareu* in Tahiti and Rarotonga, *lavalava* in the Samoas and Tonga, and *sulu* in Fiji. Heat-sensitive dyes are applied by hand to gauzelike cotton, which is then laid in the sun for several hours. Flowers, leaves, and other designs are placed on the fabric, and as the heat of the sun darkens and sets the dyes, the shadows from these objects leave their images behind on the finished product. See chapters 3 through 14.

10 The Best Diving & Snorkeling

All the islands have excellent scuba diving and snorkeling, and all but a few of the resorts either have their own dive operations or can easily make arrangements with a local company. Here are the best:

- **Rangiroa and Manihi** (French Polynesia): Like those surrounding most populated islands, many lagoons in French Polynesia have been relatively "fished out" over the years. That's not to say that diving in such places as Moorea and Bora Bora can't be world class, but the best is now at Rangiroa and Manihi in the Tuamotu Archipelago, both famous more for their abundant sea life, including sharks, than colorful soft corals. Go to Rangiroa to see sharks; to Manihi to see more fish than you imagined ever existed. See "Rangiroa" and "Manihi" in chapter 7.

- **Fiji:** With nutrient-rich waters welling up from the Tonga Trench offshore and being carried by strong currents funneling through narrow passages, Fiji is famous for some of the world's most colorful soft corals. This is especially true of the Somosomo Strait between Vanua Levu and Taveuni in northern Fiji, home of the Rainbow Reef and the Great White Wall. The Beqa Lagoon is also famous for having plentiful soft corals. See "Taveuni" in chapter 11 and "Pacific Harbour" in chapter 10.

- **Tonga:** The north shore of the main island of Tongatapu fronts a huge lagoon, where the government has made national parks of the Hakaumama'o and Malinoa reefs. The best diving in Tonga, however, is around unspoiled Ha'apai and Vava'u. See "Ha'apai" and "Vava'u" in chapter 14.

11 The Best Sailing

One would think that the South Pacific is a yachting paradise, and it certainly gets more than its share of cruising boats on holiday from Australia and New Zealand or heading around the world (the region is on the safest circumnavigation route). However, the reefs in most places make sailing a precarious undertaking, so yachting is not that widespread. It has only recently gained a toehold in Fiji. There are only two places where you can charter a yacht and sail it yourself:

- **Raiatea** (French Polynesia): Firms have charter fleets based in Raiatea in the Leeward Islands of French Polynesia. Raiatea shares a lagoon with Tahaa, a hilly island indented with long bays that shelter numer-

ous picturesque anchorages. Boats can be sailed completely around Tahaa without leaving the lagoon, and both Bora Bora and Huahine are just 32km (20 miles) away over blue water. See "Raiatea & Tahaa" in chapter 7.

- **Vava'u** (Tonga): The second most popular yachting spot, Vava'u is virtually serrated by well-protected bays like the nearby Port of Refuge. Chains of small islands trail off the south side of Vava'u like the tentacles of a jellyfish, creating large and very quiet cruising grounds. Many anchorages are off deserted islands with their own beaches. See "Vava'u" in chapter 14.

12 The Best Offbeat Travel Experiences

Some cynics might say that a visit to the South Pacific itself is an offbeat experience, but there are a few things to do that are even more unusual.

- **Getting Asked to Dance** (everywhere): I've seen so many traditional South Pacific dance shows that I now stand by the rear door, ready to beat a quick escape before those lovely young women in grass skirts can grab my hand and force me to make a fool of myself trying to gyrate my hips up on the stage. It's part of the tourist experience at all resorts, and it's all in good fun.

- **Swimming with the Sharks** (Bora Bora, French Polynesia): A key attraction in Bora Bora's magnificent lagoon is to snorkel with a guide, who actually feeds a school of sharks as they thrash around in a frenzy. I prefer to leave this one to the Discovery Channel. See "Exploring Bora Bora" in chapter 6.

- **Riding the Rip** (Rangiroa and Manihi, French Polynesia): Snorkelers will never forget the flying sensation as they ride the strong currents ripping through a pass into the lagoons at Rangiroa and Manihi. See "Rangiroa" and "Manihi" in chapter 7.

- **Sleeping in a Beach Fale** (Samoa): If you like to camp, you'll enjoy every minute spent in one of Samoa's beach fales—little thatch-roof buildings perched beside one of that country's lovely beaches. Forget privacy, since they're all open-sided in traditional Samoan fashion, but why block the view with unnecessary walls? And the neighbors you meet could become lifetime friends. See "Where to Stay on Upolu" and "Where to Stay & Dine on Savai'i" in chapter 12.

- **Worshipping with the King** (Nuku'alofa, Tonga): It's not every day you get to see a real-life king, but you can in Tonga. In fact, you can even go to church with him on Sunday, or perhaps watch him go by on his bicycle other days of the week. See "Surviving Sunday in Tonga" in chapter 14.

- **Cave Swimming** (Samoa and Tonga): Boats can go right into Swallows Cave on one of the small islands that make up beautiful Vava'u, but you have to don masks and snorkels and follow a guide underwater into Mariner's Cave, whose only light comes from the passage you just swam through. See "Exploring Vava'u" in chapter 14. You also have to swim underwater into the Piula Cave Pool in Samoa. See "Exploring Apia & the Rest of Upolu" in chapter 12.

2

Planning Your Trip to the South Pacific

Although they are similar in many respects, Tahiti and French Polynesia, the Cook Islands, Fiji, Samoa, American Samoa, and the Kingdom of Tonga have their own sources of information, entry requirements, currency, government, customs, laws, internal transportation, styles of accommodation, and food. Because the South Pacific can hold some surprises, wise planning is essential to get the most out of your time and money spent in this vast and varied modern paradise. This chapter gives a brief description of the islands and tells you how to plan your trip in general. It augments, but is not a substitute for, the information contained in the chapters devoted to each destination.

1 The Islands in Brief

The islands covered in this book are variations on an overall cultural theme, for most are part of the great Polynesian Triangle, which extends across the Pacific from Hawaii to Easter Island to New Zealand. Each has carved its own identity, yet each is fundamentally Polynesian. Only Fiji is significantly different. Living on the border between Polynesia and the Melanesian islands to the west, the indigenous Fijians look more like African Americans than their Polynesian neighbors. Their distinctly Fijian culture blends elements from both Polynesia and Melanesia. The Fijians also share their islands with East Indians, who add a starkly contrasting culture to the mix.

Let's make a quick tour to see what each island country or territory contributes to this smorgasbord.

FRENCH POLYNESIA

If there is a "major league" of dramatically beautiful islands, then Tahiti and its French Polynesian companions dominate it. This is especially true of **Moorea** and **Bora Bora,** which

provide Hollywood with many of its choice "stock shots" of glorious tropical settings. Moorea's jagged, shark's-teeth ridges serrate the horizon like the back of some primordial dinosaur resting on the sea just 20km (12 miles) west of Tahiti.

High and well watered, **Tahiti** is the largest of the French Polynesian islands and was the first to be discovered by European explorers in the late 18th century. A great majority of the territory's population lives on Tahiti, especially in and around **Papeete,** the capital. Today this busy little city is so overrun by cars, trucks, and motor scooters that it can take up to 2 hours to commute to work from the outlying regions. A building boom has drastically changed Papeete's face in the past 25 years, and the town has lost much of its old charm. So I will say from the outset: If you're going to travel this far, don't just stop on Tahiti.

Old Polynesia exists on the territory's third most beautiful island, **Huahine,** which locals call "wild" because of its undeveloped status. It's not all wild, however, for you can stay at a fine resort while exploring some of the region's most important archaeological sites. Nearby, the adjacent islands of **Raiatea** and **Tahaa** are even more natural. Raiatea has no beaches, and Tahaa has no resorts, but they are French Polynesia's prime sailing grounds.

Off to the northeast, the line of atolls known as the **Tuamotu Archipelago** boasts French Polynesia's top scuba diving destinations. **Rangiroa,** which encloses the world's second largest lagoon, is known for its remarkably clear waters, which are home to thousands of sharks. Sitting next to Rangiroa, **Tikehau** is considerably smaller, and its one international-standard resort sits on an islet all to itself. Also much smaller and shallower than the lagoon at Rangiroa, the fish-filled lagoon at **Manihi** makes it the world's largest producer of black pearls.

THE COOK ISLANDS

About 805km (500 miles) west of Tahiti, the tiny Cook Islands have much in common with French Polynesia. Barely 32km (20 miles) around, **Rarotonga** is a miniature Tahiti in terms of its mountains, beaches, and reefs—and in terms of development, it's like Tahiti was some 50 years ago. Yet no other South Pacific destination has as many hotels, restaurants, daytime activities, and nightclubs packed into so small a space as Rarotonga. Unlike Papeete, however, the capital of the Cook Islands, **Avarua,** remains a quiet little backwater, a picturesque village without a stoplight. Among the outer islands, **Aitutaki** bears the same relationship to Rarotonga as Bora Bora does to Tahiti, with a small central island surrounded by a shallow but spectacular aquamarine lagoon. It's worth a side trip to Aitutaki just to take a lagoon excursion out to the little islands fringing the reef. The beaches out there have the region's only pure white, talcumlike sand.

The Cook Islanders share with the Tahitians a fun-loving lifestyle, many of the old Polynesian legends and gods, and about 60% of their native language. The Cooks were a New Zealand territory from 1901 until 1965 and still are associated with New Zealand. Consequently, Cook Islanders speak English fluently, which makes it easy for English-speaking travelers to take advantage of the South Pacific's most informative cultural tours and exhibits.

FIJI

Because its international airport at Nadi is the region's major transportation hub, Fiji is a prime place with which to begin or end a trip to the South Pacific. In fact, twice as many people of every income bracket visit Fiji each year as come to any other South Pacific island destination.

This lush country of 300-plus islands has something for everyone to do—from lying on some of the region's best beaches to scuba diving on some of the world's most colorful reefs, from cruising to intriguing outer islands to hiking into the mountainous interior.

Although it's primarily a stop to and from more beautiful parts of Fiji, the **Nadi** area has two of the country's largest resorts and is awash with activities. From Nadi you can ride or trek into the tropical highlands or cruise out to the **Mamanuca** and **Yasawa** islands, all little specks of land which are home to fine beaches, a host of watersports, and a wide range of unpretentious offshore resorts. Or you can take the Queen's Road south to the **Coral Coast,** Fiji's first resort area, and on to **Pacific Harbour,** known for its challenging golf course; great deep sea fishing; and diving in the nearby Beqa Lagoon.

The Queen's Road leads on to Fiji's cosmopolitan capital city, **Suva.** Although known for its rainy climate, Suva gives a glimpse of the bygone era

The South Pacific

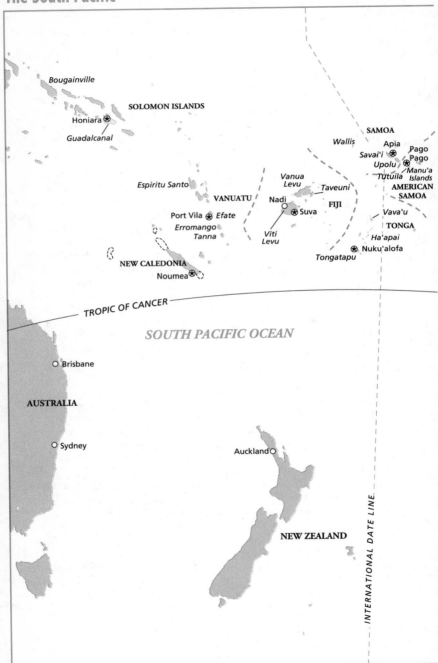

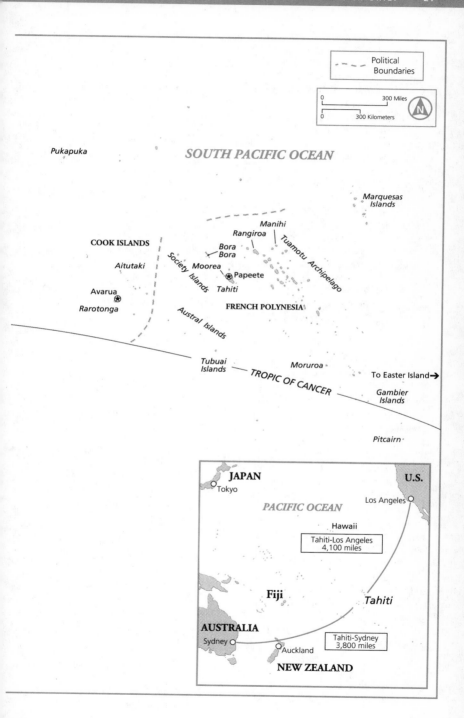

Easter Island: Where the Statues Reign

The great Polynesian migration across the Pacific Ocean reached its easternmost outpost around A.D. 400, when a small band of islanders settled on **Rapa Nui,** about halfway between Tahiti and South America (it's the most remote inhabited island in the world). Known by Westerners as **Easter Island,** this tiny spec of land is the most fascinating archaeological site in the Pacific, for it was here that the islanders erected the huge, mysterious statues known as *moai.*

Chiseled out of volcanic rock to represent the likeness of high chiefs and other important ancestors, the statues ranged in height from 2m to 10m (6 ft.–30 ft.) and stood on stone platforms known as *ahu* at the shoreline of each village. They were all toppled during tribal fighting in the late 17th century, when the carving abruptly stopped. Set upright by recent archaeological expeditions, a few gaze once again at the rolling grasslands covering most of the 72.5-square-km (45-square-mile) island. Several hundred remain eerily unfinished at the quarry on the slopes of Rano Raraku volcano. How the islanders, who knew nothing of the wheel, moved them from the quarry to the shoreline and then stood them upright is a mystery.

LanChile Airlines (© 800/735-5526; www.lanchile.com) flies twice a week between Easter Island and Santiago, Chile.

when Great Britain ruled here. A 10-minute flight from Suva will whisk you to the island of **Ovalau,** where the country's first European-style town, **Levuka,** still looks like it did in the late 1800s, before the government pulled up stakes and moved to Suva.

Up in Northern Fiji, the large islands of **Vanua Levu** and **Taveuni** will transport you back in time to the Fiji of colonial coconut plantations. Between the two islands lies the **Somosomo Strait,** home to the Great White Wall, the Rainbow Reef, and other world-class dive sites.

Fiji has the South Pacific's most fascinating mix of peoples. A bit more than half are extremely friendly, easygoing Fijians, most of whom still live in traditional villages surrounded by vegetable gardens. About 44% are industrious—and sometimes abrasive—East Indians whose ancestors came to work the sugarcane plantations that make Fiji the most self-

sufficient of the South Pacific countries. Although the contrasting Fijian-Indian cultures has resulted in political unrest and three coups since 1987, it also makes this an interesting place to get into a conversation.

THE SAMOAS

Known until 1997 as Western Samoa, independent **Samoa** is like a cultural museum, especially when compared with its much smaller cousin, **American Samoa.** The peoples of both are related by family and tradition, if not by politics. Samoan culture still exists in the American islands, and it is preserved to a remarkable degree in Samoa, relatively unchanged by modern materialism. Traditional Samoan villages, with their turtle-shaped houses, rest peacefully along the coasts of the two main western Samoan islands, **Upolu** and **Savai'i.** Although Samoa is experiencing an economic boom, time seems to have forgotten the weather-beaten, clapboard

All of the island's 3,500 residents live in Hangaroa, its only town. There are a few comfortable if not deluxe hotels and a score of guesthouses. The pick of the lot is the motel-style **Hotel Iorana** (© 32/ **100-608**; fax 32/100-312; iroana@entelchile.net), which has a spectacular view from a bluff about a 20-minute walk south of town. The best in the center of town is **Hotel Otai** (© **32/100-022**; fax 32/100-482; otairapanui@entelchile.net), whose owner, Nikko Hao, spent 12 years in the United States.

All hotels will arrange guided tours, which are the best way to see the island. I was impressed with **Kia Koe Tours** (© **32/100-852**; fax 100-282; www.kiakoetour.co.cl), whose chief guide, Yan Araki, grew up in England.

For more information click on the **Easter Island Home Page** at www.netaxs.com/~trance/rapanui.html. Another excellent source is the California-based **Easter Island Foundation,** whose site at www.island heritage.org is loaded with background information. You can also contact the **Chile National Tourist Board,** Providencia Avenue, Santiago, Chile (© **56/731-8300**; fax 56/251-8469; www.sernatur.cl), or check the website of the **Chile Tourism Promotion Corporation,** at www.visit-chile.org.

buildings that distinguish **Apia,** the country's picturesque capital. Although tourism is not a major industry, the country has two luxury beach resorts and modern hotels from which you can fan out and meet the friendly Samoans. Experiencing their unique culture and visiting their truly remarkable and undeveloped beaches (one of which was the setting for the Gary Cooper movie *Return to Paradise*) are highlights of any visit.

Tutuila, the main island in American Samoa, rivals the dramatic beauty of Moorea and Bora Bora in French Polynesia. The mountains drop straight down into fabled **Pago Pago,** the finest harbor in the South Pacific and the main reason that the United States has had a presence there since 1890. This American presence has resulted in a blend of cultures: the Samoan emphasis on extended families and communal ownership of property, especially land, and the

Western emphasis on business and progress. The result of the latter is that Pago Pago harbor is dominated—and polluted—by two large tuna canneries, and large stacks of shipping containers often block the splendid views. The road around the harbor is often clogged with vehicles as American Samoans rush past their traditional villages on their way to American-style shopping centers.

TONGA

From his Victorian palace in **Nuku'alofa,** King Taufa'ahau Tupou IV of Tonga—all 300-plus pounds of him—rules over a nobility that carries European titles but is in reality a pure Polynesian system of high chiefs. Despite considerable grumbling among his commoner subjects in recent years, the king, his family, and the nobles control the government and all the land, of which they are obligated to give 8½ acres to every Tongan adult male.

While the relatively flat main island of **Tongatapu** offers little in the way of dramatic scenic beauty, and accommodations here are below international standard, the adjacent lagoon provides excellent boating, snorkeling, fishing, and diving. On the other hand, hilly **Vava'u** in the north presents long and narrow fjords and a plethora of deserted islands, which make it one of the South Pacific's leading yachting centers. **Neiafu,** the only town on Vava'u, is a reminder of the old days of traders and beach bums.

Indeed, Tonga is the heart of the South Pacific "Bible Belt." Things are slow on Sunday in most island countries, but they stop completely in Tonga—for picnics at the beautiful beaches and escapes to resorts on tiny islets offshore.

2 Visitor Information

The best sources for data about the specific island countries are their tourist information offices (see the individual country chapters).

A good source for general information is the **Tourism Council of the South Pacific (TCSP),** P.O. Box 13119, Suva, Fiji Islands (© **679/ 304177;** fax 679/301-995; www.tcsp. com).

Another general source is the **Pacific Asia Travel Association (PATA),** an industry trade association based in Bangkok, Thailand. It has a North American office in the Latham Square Building, 1611 Telegraph Ave., Suite 1515, Oakland, CA 94612 (© **510/625-2055;** fax 510/625-2044; www.pata.org). PATA's Pacific Division Office, P.O. Box 645, Kings Cross, NSW 1340, Australia (© **02/ 332-3599;** fax 02/331-6592), directly handles the island countries. The association's website is linked to the home pages of each island country's visitors bureau.

The U.S. Department of State maintains a 24-hour **Travel Advisory** (© **202/647-5225**) to keep you abreast of political or other problems throughout the world and posts travel warnings and other timely information on its website, www.travel. state.gov.

The East-West Center at the University of Hawaii gathers news from throughout the islands on its **Pacific Islands Report** website, http://pidp. eastwestcenter.org/pireport. It's the best single source for breaking news stories, and it has links to newspapers, news services, universities, and other useful sites.

3 Entry Requirements & Customs

ENTRY REQUIREMENTS

All South Pacific countries require each new arrival to have a **passport** that will be valid for the duration of the visit, as well as an onward or return airline ticket. Your passport should be valid for 6 months beyond the date you expect to return home.

The South Pacific countries and territories do not require citizens of the United States, Canada, Australia, New Zealand, Japan, and the European Community countries to have visas for stays of 30 days or less. At press time, those visitors could stay in Fiji for 4 months. Samoa and Tonga will let visitors stay until the dates of their departing airline flights. See the individual country chapters for details.

The only vaccination required to enter the South Pacific countries is for yellow fever, and then only if you're coming from an infected area of South America or Africa. It's a good idea, however, to have your tetanus,

---

> **Tips Getting Hitched**
>
> Getting married in the islands is easy only in Fiji and the Cook Islands, where many resorts have wedding packages that include a traditional Fijian or Polynesian ceremony. They will tell you what documents you need to bring and what local formalities you need to execute before your wedding. Frankly, the formalities are so complicated that you're better off having your wedding at home and honeymooning in the islands.

---

typhoid fever, polio, diphtheria, hepatitis-A, and hepatitis-B vaccinations up to date.

Safeguard your passport in an inconspicuous, inaccessible place and keep a copy of the critical pages, with your passport number, in a separate place. If you lose your passport, you can go to a U.S. embassy in Fiji or Samoa, or the governor of American Samoa can issue a temporary replacement passport. Australia, New Zealand, and the United Kingdom have high commissioners in Fiji, Samoa, and Tonga.

GETTING A PASSPORT

RESIDENTS OF THE UNITED STATES If you're applying for a first-time passport, you need to do it in person at a U.S. passport office; a federal, state, or probate court; or a major post office. For general information, call the **National Passport Agency** (✆ 202/647-0518). To find your regional passport office, either check the U.S. State Department website (www.travel.state.gov) or call the **National Passport Information Center** (✆ 900/225-5674); the fee is 35¢ per minute for automated information and $1.05 per minute for operator-assisted calls.

American Passport Express (✆ 800/841-6778; www.american passport.com) will process your passport for you in a week for $50, plus the cost of the passport itself ($75 for a renewal; $95 for a first-time or lost passport). If you need the passport in 3 to 4 days, the fee is $100, and for a $150 fee you can receive your passport in 24 hours.

RESIDENTS OF CANADA Canadian citizens should contact the **Passport Office, Department of Foreign Affairs and International Trade,** Ottawa, ON K1A 0G3 (✆ **800/ 567-6868;** www.dfait-maeci.gc.ca/ passport). Processing takes 5 to 10 days if you apply in person, or about 3 weeks by mail.

RESIDENTS OF THE UNITED KINGDOM To pick up an application for a 10-year passport (the Visitor's Passport has been abolished), visit a passport office, major post office, or travel agency. You can also contact the **United Kingdom Passport Service** at ✆ **0870/571-0410** or search its website at www.ukpa.gov.uk. Passports cost £30 for adults and £16 for children under 16.

RESIDENTS OF IRELAND You can apply for a 10-year passport at the **Passport Office,** Setanta Centre, Molesworth Street, Dublin 2 (✆ **01/ 671-1633;** www.irlgov.ie/iveagh). You can also apply at 1A South Mall, Cork (✆ **021/272-525**), or at the counter of almost any main post office.

RESIDENTS OF AUSTRALIA You can apply at a post office or passport office or search the website www.passports.gov.au. The **Australia State Passport Office** can be reached at ✆ **131-232;** travelers must schedule an interview to submit passport application materials.

> **Tips   Be Careful What You Buy**
>
> Some South Pacific governments restrict the export of antique carvings and other artifacts of historic value. If a piece looks old, check before you buy. Jewelry made of shells and of pink or black coral is available in many countries, as is scrimshaw, but be careful when you shop, for items made of black coral and whalebone cannot legally be brought back to the United States and most other Western countries.

RESIDENTS OF NEW ZEALAND

You can pick up a passport application at any travel agency or Link Centre. For more info, contact the **Passport Office,** Dept. of Internal Affairs, P.O. Box 10-526, Wellington (② **0800/ 225-050;** www.passports.govt.nz).

CUSTOMS

Each country or territory has its own customs laws. See the individual country chapters for more information.

WHAT YOU CAN TAKE HOME

Returning **U.S. citizens** who have been away for at least 48 hours are allowed to bring back, once every 30 days, $400 worth of merchandise duty-free. You'll be charged a flat rate of 4% duty on the next $1,000 worth of purchases. These amounts double for American Samoa, provided you stay there more than 48 hours. Be sure to have your receipts handy. On mailed gifts, the duty-free limit is $100 ($200 for American Samoa). You cannot bring fresh foodstuffs into the United States; tinned foods, however, are allowed. For more information, contact the **U.S. Customs Service,** 1300 Pennsylvania Ave. NW, Washington, DC 20229 (② **877/ 287-8867**), and request the free pamphlet *Know Before You Go*. It's also available at www.customs.gov. (Click on "Traveler Information," then "Know Before You Go Brochure".)

For a clear summary of **Canadian** rules, get the booklet *I Declare,* from the **Canada Customs and Revenue Agency** (② **800/461-9999** in Canada, or 204/983-3500; www.ccra-adrc.gc.ca). Canada allows its citizens a Can$750 exemption, and you're allowed to bring back duty-free one carton of cigarettes, one can of tobacco, 40 imperial ounces of liquor, and 50 cigars. In addition, you're allowed to mail gifts to Canada valued at less than Can$60 a day, provided they're unsolicited and don't contain alcohol or tobacco (write on the package "Unsolicited gift, under $60 value"). All valuables should be declared on the Y-38 form before departure from Canada, including serial numbers of valuables you already own, such as expensive foreign cameras. *Note:* The Can$750 exemption can be used once a year and only after an absence of 7 days.

U.K. citizens have a customs allowance of 200 cigarettes; 50 cigars; 250g of smoking tobacco; 2 liters of still table wine; 1 liter of spirits or strong liqueurs (over 22% volume); 2 liters of fortified wine, sparkling wine or other liqueurs; 60ml perfume; 250ml of toilet water; and £145 worth of all other goods, including gifts and souvenirs. People under 17 are not entitled to the tobacco and alcohol allowances. For more information, contact **HM Customs & Excise,** Passenger Enquiry Point, 2nd Floor Wayfarer House, Great South West Road, Feltham, Middlesex, TW14 8NP (② **0181/910-3744;** from outside the U.K. 44/181-910-3744; www.hmce. gov.uk), or consult the website www.open.gov.uk.

The duty-free allowance in **Australia** is A$400 for adults and A$200 for those under 18. Personal property mailed back from the islands should be marked "Australian goods returned" to avoid payment of duty. Upon returning to Australia, citizens can bring in 250 cigarettes or 250g of loose tobacco, and 1,125ml of alcohol. If you're returning with valuable goods you owned before your trip to the South Pacific, such as foreign-made cameras, you should file form B263. A helpful brochure, available from Australian consulates or Customs offices, is *Know Before You Go.* For more information, contact **Australian Customs Service,** GPO Box 8, Sydney NSW 2001 (© **02/9213-2000;** www.customs.gov.au).

The duty-free allowance for **New Zealand** is NZ$700. Citizens over 17 can bring in 200 cigarettes, or 50 cigars, or 250g of tobacco (or a mixture of all three if their combined weight doesn't exceed 250g); plus 4.5 liters of wine and beer, or 1.125 liters of liquor. New Zealand currency does not carry import or export restrictions. You should fill out a certificate of export, listing the valuables you are taking out of the country; that way, you can bring them back without paying duty. Most questions are answered in a free pamphlet available at New Zealand consulates and Customs offices: *New Zealand Customs Guide for Travellers, Notice no. 4.* For more information, contact **New Zealand Customs,** 50 Anzac Ave., P.O. Box 29, Auckland (© **09/359-6655;** www.customs.govt.nz).

4 Money

CURRENCIES

The Cook Islands use New Zealand dollars, and American Samoa spends U.S. greenbacks. Otherwise, each South Pacific country has its own currency (see the individual country chapters). U.S., Australian, and New Zealand dollars are accepted widely in the islands, and the local banks will change most other major currencies. The major banks have exchange booths at the international airports with the same rates as in the cities and towns, so don't bother changing currency before leaving home.

To find exchange rates, go to **www.xe.com** and keep clicking at the bottom of the currency options boxes until all the world's currencies are displayed. There you can find the present exchange rates for French Pacific francs, Fiji dollars, Samoan tala, Tongan pa'anga, and the New Zealand dollar.

It's best to exchange currency or traveler's checks at a bank, not a currency exchange, hotel, or shop.

ATMS

Banks in all the main towns have **automated teller machines (ATMs),** at which you can use your Visa or MasterCard to withdraw local currency against your credit card or check (debit) card account. Check your card

---

Reader's Recommendation: Small Change

When you are leaving an island and want to get rid of your local currency, use it to pay part of your hotel bill. Every place we stayed, they allowed us to pay part of the bill like that and then we would put the rest on our credit card. It beat getting the crummy exchange rate at the airport.

—Laurie P. Floyd, Freehold, New Jersey

Fun Fact "Island Time"

There's an old story about a 19th-century planter who promised a South Pacific islander a weekly wage and a pension if he would come to work on his copra plantation. *Copra* is dried coconut meat, from which oil is pressed for use in soaps, cosmetics, and other products. Hours of back-breaking labor are required to chop open the coconuts and extract the meat by hand.

When the planter approached the islander, the latter was sitting in the shade, eating the fruit he had gathered while hauling in one fish after another from the lagoon.

"Do I understand correctly?" asked the islander. "You want me to break my back working for you for 30 years, and then you'll pay me a pension so I can spend the rest of my life sitting here in the shade, eating my fruit, and fishing in the lagoon? I may not be sophisticated, but I am not stupid."

The islander's response reflects an attitude still prevalent in the South Pacific, for here life moves at a much slower pace than what you might be accustomed to at home. The locals call it "island time."

The service rendered in most hotels and restaurants is not slothful inattention; it's just the way things are done here. Your drink will come in due course. If you must have it immediately, order it at the bar. Otherwise, relax with your friendly hosts and enjoy their charming company.

member agreement for charges, since Visa and MasterCard tack on a 1% currency conversion fee, and some banks add up to 5% to the transaction. You can avoid some of these fees by using your debit card (as opposed to a credit card). When I use my debit card, I get a rate of exchange up to 5% better than if I had changed traveler's checks, and I avoid the local banks' fees for changing traveler's checks (see below).

TRAVELER'S CHECKS

Traveler's checks are something of an anachronism from the days before the ATM, but I carry a few hundred dollars' worth in case the ATMs are broken, have run out of cash, or for some reason won't accept my credit or debit card (which is more likely in French Polynesia than elsewhere in the islands). Banks in all the main towns will cash, and most major hotels, resorts, restaurants, and car-rental firms will accept, traveler's checks

issued by American Express, Thomas Cook, Visa, Bank of America, Citicorp, and MasterCard. You won't necessarily be able to cash traveler's checks on many outer islands, which often have limited, if any, banking facilities, so read the applicable "Fast Facts" section in each of the following chapters before heading to an outer island. Also note that banks in French Polynesia and some other countries charge fees of up to $5 per transaction.

You can get traveler's checks at almost any bank or from an **American Express** office. You'll pay a service charge ranging from 1% to 4%. You can also get American Express traveler's checks over the phone by calling ⓒ **800/221-7282** (www.american express.com); Amex gold and platinum cardholders who use this number are exempt from the 1% fee. AAA members can obtain checks without a fee at most AAA offices.

Visa offers traveler's checks at Citibank locations nationwide, as well as at several other banks. The service charge ranges between 1.5% and 2%. Call © **800/732-1322** (www.visa.com) for information. **MasterCard** also offers traveler's checks. Call © **800/223-9920** (www.mastercard.com) for a location near you.

CREDIT CARDS

Most hotels, car-rental companies, restaurants and large shops accept Visa and MasterCard, and some accept American Express. Only the major hotels and car rental firms accept Diners Club. Leave your Discover card at home; it isn't accepted anywhere in the islands. Always ask first, and when you're away from the main towns, don't count on putting anything on plastic.

WHAT TO DO IF YOUR WALLET GETS STOLEN

Be sure to block charges against your account the minute you discover that a card has been lost or stolen. Then be sure to file a police report, since your credit card company or insurer may require a police report number or record of the theft.

Almost every credit card company has an emergency number to call if your card is stolen. Yours might be able to wire you a cash advance off your credit card immediately, and it might even be able to deliver an emergency credit card to you in a day or two. **American Express** has full-service representatives in Tahiti and Fiji.

The issuing bank's emergency numbers are usually on the back of your credit card—though of course, if your card has been stolen, that won't help you unless you recorded the number elsewhere. Be sure to jot down the regular phone numbers, since the U.S. toll-free numbers don't work from the South Pacific countries.

If you carry traveler's checks, be sure to keep a record of their serial numbers, and keep the record separate from your checks. You'll get a refund faster if you know the numbers.

WHAT WILL A TRIP TO THE SOUTH PACIFIC COST?

Granted, it costs a fair sum to fly cross the thousands of miles of ocean to the South Pacific islands, but from a cost standpoint, many destinations—including Hawaii—have caught up with the South Pacific in recent years. Some resorts in French Polynesia and Fiji can set you back more than $1,000 a day, some hotels nick you $20 or more for their breakfast buffets, and a beer in some Tahitian nightclubs can run more than $10. But you can have a fine time here without paying more for food and lodging than you would on a comparable vacation elsewhere. Cost-conscious travelers can get excellent value throughout the islands.

The South Pacific has a wide range of hotels, in both quality and price. Even in French Polynesia, dining out should be no more expensive than in most U.S. cities, provided that you eat somewhere other than in the big resort hotels, whose restaurants and dining rooms charge a premium. (This is a good reason not to buy a package tour that includes meals.)

All the islands impose duty on imported goods, including foodstuffs, so you will find many items in grocery and other stores to be more expensive than you might be used to at home. This is especially true in French Polynesia.

TIPPING & TAXES

In the South Pacific, tipping is considered contrary to the Polynesian and Melanesian traditions of hospitality and generosity. That's not to say that some small gratuity isn't in order for truly outstanding service, or that you won't get that "Where's-my-tip?" look from a porter as he delays leaving your room, but American-style tipping is officially discouraged throughout the islands. Nor will you be socked with a service charge on your hotel and restaurant bills. So for the most part, you can forget that hidden 15% or more your vacation could cost in the United States.

Hotel rooms are subject to an additional levy everywhere, and most countries impose a hidden "value-added tax," but direct sales taxes aren't added to your restaurant, bar, shopping, and other bills as they are in the United States.

5　When to Go

THE CLIMATE

The South Pacific islands covered in this book lie within the tropics. Compared to the pronounced winters and summers of the temperate zones, there is little variation from one island group to the next: They are warm and humid all year. Although local weather patterns have changed in the past 20 years, making conditions less predictable, local residents recognize two distinct seasons, which may bear on when you choose to visit.

A cooler and more comfortable **dry season** occurs during the austral winter, from May to October. The winter trade wind blows fairly steadily during these months, bringing generally fine tropical weather throughout the area. Daytime high temperatures reach the delightful upper 70s (24°C–27°C) to low 80s (28°C–30°C) in French Polynesia, Samoa, and Fiji, with early morning lows in the high 60s (18°C–20°C). Rarotonga in the Cook Islands and Tongatapu in Tonga are farther from the equator and see cooler temperatures, with the highs in the 60s or low 70s (15°C–23°C). Breezy wintertime nights can feel downright chilly in those islands.

The austral summer from November through April is the warmer and more humid **wet season.** Daytime highs climb into the upper 80s (30°C–33°C) throughout the islands, with nighttime lows around 70°F (21°C). Low-pressure troughs and tropical depressions can bring several days of rain at a time, but usually heavy rain showers are followed by

periods of very intense sunshine. An air-conditioned hotel room or bungalow will feel like heaven during this humid time of year. This is also the season for tropical cyclones (hurricanes), which can be devastating and should never be taken lightly. Fortunately, they usually move fast enough that their major effect on visitors is a day or two of heavy rain and wind. If you're caught in one, the hotel employees are experts on what to do to ensure your safety.

Another factor to consider is the part of an island that you'll visit. Because the moist trade winds usually blow from the east, the eastern sides of the high, mountainous islands tend to be wetter all year than the western sides.

Also bear in mind that the higher the altitude, the lower the temperature. If you're going up in the mountains, be prepared for much cooler weather than you'd have on the coast.

THE BUSY SEASON

July and August are the busiest tourist season in the South Pacific. That's when Australians and New Zealanders visit the islands to escape the cold back home. It's also when residents of Tahiti head to their own outer islands, in keeping with the traditional July-August holiday break in France. Many Europeans also visit the islands during this time.

There also are busy miniseasons at school holiday time in Australia and New Zealand. These periods vary, but in general they are from the end of March through the middle of April, 2 weeks in late May, two more weeks at

Moments When the Moon Is Full

The islands are extraordinarily beautiful anytime, but the play of moonlight on the lagoons and ocean and the black silhouettes the mountains cast against the sky make them magical when the moon is full.

the beginning of July, two more in the middle of September, and from mid-December until mid-January. You can get a list of Australian holidays at **www.oztourism.com.au**; for New Zealand go to **www.tourism.org.nz**.

With a few exceptions, South Pacific hoteliers do not raise their rates during the busy periods.

From Christmas through the middle of January is a good time to get a hotel reservation in the South Pacific, but airline seats can be hard to come by, since thousands of islanders fly home from overseas.

HOLIDAYS & SPECIAL EVENTS

The chapters of this book list each country's festivals and special events, which can change the nature of a visit to the South Pacific. The annual *Heiva I Tahiti* in French Polynesia, the King's Birthday in Tonga, and the week of Constitution Day in Rarotonga are just three examples, and every country has at least one such major celebration. These are the best times to see traditional dancing, arts, and sporting events. Be sure to make your reservations well in advance if you want to visit at celebration time, for hotel rooms and airline seats can be in short supply.

6 Insurance, Health & Safety

TRAVEL INSURANCE AT A GLANCE

Hospitals and clinics are widespread in the South Pacific, but the quality varies a great deal from place to place. You can get a broken bone set and a coral scrape tended, but treating more serious ailments likely will be beyond the capability of the local hospital everywhere except in Tahiti. For this reason, it's a good idea to buy a travel insurance policy that includes medical evacuation.

Check your existing insurance policies before you buy travel insurance to cover trip cancellation, lost luggage, medical expenses, or car-rental insurance. You're likely to have partial or complete coverage. But if you need coverage, ask your travel agent about a comprehensive package. The cost of travel insurance varies widely, depending on the cost and length of your trip, your age and overall health, and the type of trip you're taking. Insurance

for extreme sports or adventure travel, for example, will cost more than coverage for a cruise. Some insurers provide packages for specialty vacations, such as skiing or backpacking. Especially dangerous activities may be excluded from basic policies.

Also note that the travel insurance industry made a number of changes to its policies in the wake of the terrorist attacks of September 11, 2001. Some have stopped covering travelers whose trips are interrupted or canceled because an airline, cruise line, or tour company went bankrupt. Others will not cover trips offered by certain airlines, cruise lines, tour operators, and other firms. It is imperative, therefore, to read all the fine print before you buy a policy.

For information, contact one of the following popular insurers:

• **Access America** (© **800/284-8300;** www.accessamerica.com)

- **Travel Guard International** (© **800/826-1300;** www.travel guard.com)
- **Travel Insured International** (© **800/243-3174;** www.travel insured.com)
- **Travelex Insurance Services** (© **800/228-9792;** www.travelex-insurance.com)

TRIP-CANCELLATION INSURANCE (TCI)

There are three major types of trip-cancellation insurance—one, in the event that you prepay a cruise or tour that gets canceled, and you can't get your money back; a second when you or someone in your family gets sick or dies, and you can't travel (but beware that you may not be covered for a preexisting condition); and a third, when bad weather makes travel impossible. Some insurers provide coverage for events like jury duty; natural disasters close to home, like floods or fire, and even the loss of a job. A few have added provisions for cancellations due to terrorist activities. Always check the fine print before signing on, and don't buy TCI from the tour operator that may be responsible for the cancellation; buy it only from a reputable travel insurance agency. Don't overbuy. You won't be reimbursed for more than the cost of your trip.

MEDICAL INSURANCE

Most health insurance policies cover you if you get sick away from home, but they are not likely to provide for medical evacuation in case of life-threatening injury or illness. Given the state of healthcare in all the islands except Tahiti, I always buy a travel insurance policy that provides for **emergency medical evacuation.** If you have to buy a one-way same-day ticket home and forfeit your nonrefundable round-trip ticket, you may be out big bucks. And the cost of a flying ambulance could wipe out your life's savings.

Check with your insurer, particularly if you're insured by an HMO, about the extent of its coverage while you're overseas. With the exception of certain HMOs and Medicare/Medicaid, your medical insurance should cover medical treatment—even hospital care—overseas. However, most out-of-country hospitals make you pay your bills up front, and they send you a refund after you've returned home and filed the necessary paperwork.

Some credit cards (American Express and certain gold and platinum Visa and MasterCards, for example) offer automatic flight insurance against death or dismemberment in case of an airplane crash if you charged the cost of your ticket.

If you require additional insurance, try one of the following companies:

- **MEDEX International** (© **888/ MEDEX-00** or 410/453-6300; fax 410/453-6301; www.medex assist.com)
- **Travel Assistance International,** (© **800/821-2828;** www.travel assistance.com)
- **The Divers Alert Network** (DAN) (© **800/446-2671** or 919/684-8181; www.diversalert network.org)

LOST-LUGGAGE INSURANCE

On domestic flights, checked baggage is covered up to $2,500 per ticketed passenger. On international flights (including U.S. portions of international trips), baggage is limited to approximately $9 per pound, up to approximately $635 per checked bag. If you plan to check items that are more valuable than the standard liability, you may purchase "excess valuation" coverage from the airline, up to $5,000. Be sure to take any valuables or irreplaceable items with you in your carry-on luggage.

If you file a lost luggage claim, be prepared to answer detailed questions

(Tips) Lather Up

The sun in these latitudes can burn your skin in a very short period of time—even on what seems like a cloudy day. Limit your exposure to the sun, especially during the first few days of your trip and, thereafter, be careful from 11am to 2pm. Use sunscreen with a high protection factor (SPF 30 or more) and apply it liberally.

about the contents of your baggage, and be sure to file a claim immediately, as most airlines enforce a 21-day deadline. An inventory of all packed items and a rough estimate of the total value will help ensure that you're properly compensated if your luggage is lost. You will only be reimbursed for what you lost, no more. Once you've filed a complaint, persist in securing your reimbursement; there are no laws governing the length of time it takes for a carrier to reimburse you.

If you arrive at a destination without your bags, ask the airline to forward them to your hotel or to your next destination; most airlines will usually comply. If your bag is delayed or lost, the airline may reimburse you for reasonable expenses, such as a toothbrush or a set of clothes, but the airline is under no legal obligation to do so.

Lost luggage may also be covered by your homeowner's or renter's policy. Many platinum and gold credit cards cover you as well. If you choose to purchase additional lost-luggage insurance, be sure not to buy more than you need. You should buy in advance from the insurer or a trusted agent (prices will be much higher at the airport).

CAR-RENTAL INSURANCE (LOSS/DAMAGE WAIVER OR COLLISION DAMAGE WAIVER)

If you hold a private auto insurance policy, you probably are covered in the United States, but not abroad, for loss or damage to the car and liability in case a passenger is injured. The credit card you used to rent the card also may provide some coverage. Check your own auto insurance policy, the rental company policy, and your credit card coverage for the extent of coverage.

Even if you have such coverage, rental car companies in the islands are likely to require that you pay for any damages on the scene and sort it out with your insurer or credit card company when you get home. Given the hassles this can cause, I always buy the collision damage waiver and liability policies offered by the local companies. It adds to the cost, but it's a relatively small price to pay for peace of mind.

STAYING HEALTHY

The South Pacific islands covered in this book pose no major health problem for most travelers. If you have a chronic condition, however, you should check with your doctor before visiting the islands. For conditions like epilepsy, diabetes, or heart problems, wear a **MedicAlert Identification Tag** (© 800/825-3785; www.medicalert. org), which will immediately alert doctors to your condition and give them access to your records through MedicAlert's 24-hour hot line.

Pack **prescription medications** in your carry-on luggage, and carry prescription medications in their original containers. Also bring along copies of your prescriptions in case you lose your pills or run out. Carry the generic name of prescription medicines, since local pharmacies primarily carry medications manufactured in France, Australia, and New Zealand, and the brand names might be different there than in the United States.

Tips Insects & Other Critters

"You will find that we Cook Islanders are among the friendliest people in the South Pacific," the Aitutaki Pearl Beach Resort advises its guests. "Amongst all the friendly people we also have the friendliest ants, roaches, geckos, crabs, and insects, who are all dying to make your acquaintance."

Indeed, every South Pacific island has more than its share of mosquitoes, roaches, ants, houseflies, and other insects. Don't be frightened by those little **geckos** (lizards) crawling around the rafters of even the most expensive bungalows. They're harmless to us humans but lethal to insects. **Ants** are omnipresent here and will quickly invade if you leave crumbs lying around your room. Many beaches and swampy areas also have invisible **sand flies**—the dreaded "no-see-ums" or "no-nos"—which bite the ankles around daybreak and dusk.

Insect repellent is widely available in island shops. Good local brands are Dolmix Pic in French Polynesia and Rid, an excellent Australian brand sold elsewhere. American brands such as Off also are widely available. The most effective skin repellents contain a high percentage of "deet" (N,N-diethyl-m-toluamide).

I light a mosquito coil in my non-air-conditioned rooms at dusk in order to keep the pests from flying in, and I start another one at bedtime. Grocery stores throughout the islands carry these inexpensive green coils. Although they are more difficult to find than others, I have found the Fish brand coils to work best; they're made by the Blood Protection Company.

Also, don't be surprised to see a multitude of dogs, chickens, pigs, and squawking mynah birds, even in the finest restaurants.

And don't forget **sunglasses** and an extra pair of **contact lenses** or **prescription glasses.** You can easily replace your contacts and prescription lenses only in French Polynesia, the Cook Islands, and Fiji.

Among minor illnesses, the islands have the common cold and occasional outbreaks of influenza and conjunctivitis ("pink eye"). From time to time the islands will experience an outbreak of **dengue fever,** a viral disease borne by the *Aëdes aegypti* mosquito, which lives indoors and bites only during daylight hours. Dengue seldom is fatal in adults, but you should take extra precautions to keep children from being bitten by mosquitoes if the disease is present.

Cuts, scratches, and all open sores should be treated promptly in the tropics. I always carry a tube of antibacterial ointment and a small package of adhesive bandages such as Band-Aids.

Throughout the islands, sexual relations before marriage—heterosexual, homosexual, and bisexual—are more or less accepted behavior (abstinence campaigns fall on deaf ears here). Both male and female prostitution is common in the larger towns, such as Papeete and Suva. The **AIDS** virus is present in the islands, so if you intend to engage in sex with strangers, you should exercise *at least* the same caution in choosing them, and in practicing "safe sex," as you would at home.

Special precautions should be taken if you are traveling with **children.** See "Tips for Travelers with Special Needs," below.

Malaria is not present in the islands covered in this book. If you're going on to Vanuatu or the Solomon islands, check with your doctor well in advance of departure so that you can start antimalarial medication a week before you arrive.

SMOKING LOWDOWN

Although antismoking campaigns and hefty tobacco taxes have reduced the practice to some degree, cigarette smoking is still widespread in the islands. The airlines are smoke-free, but nonsmoking sections in restaurants are virtually nonexistent, and not all hotels have nonsmoking rooms. **Tap water** is safe to drink in the city of Papeete on Tahiti, on the island of Bora Bora, on Rarotonga in the Cook Islands, and in Fiji. Elsewhere you can buy bottled spring water in most grocery stores. See "Fast Facts" in the following chapters for particulars.

STAYING SAFE

Although the islands are among the world's safest destinations, they have seen increasing property theft in recent years, including occasional break-ins at hotel rooms and resort bungalows. Although street crimes against tourists are still relatively rare, friends of mine who live here don't stroll off Papeete's busy boulevard Pomare after dark, and they don't wander away from Suva's Victoria Parade at anytime. For that matter, you should stay alert wherever you are after dusk.

Don't leave valuable items in your hotel room, in your rental car, or unattended anywhere.

Women should not wander alone on deserted beaches any time, since some Polynesian men may consider such behavior to be an invitation for instant amorous activity.

7 Tips for Travelers with Special Needs

TRAVELERS WITH DISABILITIES

Unfortunately, the sensibilities that have led to ramps, handles, accessible toilets, automatic opening doors, telephones at convenient heights, and other helpful aids in Western countries have not made serious inroads in the islands.

Usually shy, the islanders traditionally have felt ashamed when something was "wrong" with them and were dreadfully afraid of being made fun of because of it. Even today, many islanders will stay home from work rather than have anyone know they have anything as simple as pink eye. This may explain the lack of political support in most island countries to provide programs and facilities for the disabled.

That's not to say that some hoteliers haven't taken it upon themselves to provide rooms specially equipped for people with disabilities. Such improvements are ongoing; I have pointed out some of them in this book, but inquire when making a reservation whether such rooms are available.

The major international airlines make special arrangements for disabled persons. Be sure to tell them of your needs when you make reservation. Most local interisland airlines, on the other hand, use small planes that are not equipped for disabled passengers.

GAY & LESBIAN TRAVELERS

Although homosexuality is officially frowned upon by local laws and by some religious leaders, and only Fiji has a gay-friendly hotel, an old Polynesian custom makes the South Pacific a friendly destination for gay men.

In the islands, many families with a shortage of female offspring rear young boys as girls, or at least relegate them to female chores around the home and village. These males-raised-as-girls are known as *mahus* in Tahiti, *magus* in Samoa, and *fakaleitis* in Tonga. Some of them grow up to be heterosexual; others become homosexual or bisexual and, often appearing publicly in women's attire, actively seek the company of tourists. Some dance the female parts in traditional island night shows. You'll see them throughout the islands; many hold jobs in hotels and restaurants.

On the other hand, women were not considered equal in this respect in ancient times, and lesbianism was discouraged.

The International Gay & Lesbian Travel Association (IGLTA) (© 800/448-8550 or 954/776-2626; fax 954/776-3303; www.iglta.org) links travelers with gay-friendly hoteliers, tour operators, and airline and cruise-line representatives. It offers monthly newsletters, marketing mailings, and a membership directory that's updated once a year. Membership is $150 yearly, plus a $100 administration fee for new members.

SENIOR TRAVELERS

Children are cared for communally in the South Pacific's extended family systems, and so are senior citizens. Most islanders live with their families from birth to death. Consequently, the local governments don't provide programs and other benefits for persons of retirement age. You won't find many senior citizen discounts. Children get them; seniors don't.

Nevertheless, mention the fact that you're a senior citizen when you first make your travel reservations. All major airlines and many hotels offer discounts for seniors. Members of **AARP** (formerly known as the American Association of Retired Persons), 601 E St. NW, Washington, DC 20049 (© 800/424-3410 or 202/434-2277; www.aarp.org), get discounts on hotels, airfares, and car rentals. AARP offers members a wide range of benefits, including *Modern Maturity* magazine and a monthly newsletter. Anyone over 50 can join.

The Alliance for Retired Americans, 8403 Colesville Rd., Suite 1200, Silver Spring, MD 20910 (© 301/578-8422; www.retiredamericans. org), offers a newsletter six times a year and discounts on hotel and auto rentals; annual dues are $13 per person or couple. *Note:* Members of the former National Council of Senior Citizens receive automatic membership in the Alliance.

Elderhostel, 75 Federal St., Boston, MA 02110-1941 (© 877/426-8056; www.elderhostel.org), arranges study programs for those aged 55 and over (and a spouse or companion of any age) in the United States and in more than 80 countries around the world, including occasional trips to the Cook Islands and Fiji. Most courses last 5 to 7 days in the U.S. (2–4 weeks abroad), and many include airfare, accommodations in university dormitories or modest inns, meals, and tuition.

TRAVELING FAMILIES

The islanders adore infants and young children, but childhood does not last as long in the South Pacific as it does in Western societies. As soon as they are capable, children are put to work, first caring for their younger siblings and cousins and helping out with household chores, later tending the village gardens. It's only as teenagers, and then only if they leave their villages for town, that they know unemployment in the Western sense. Accordingly, few towns and villages have children's facilities, such as playgrounds, outside school property.

On the other hand, the islanders invariably love children and are very good at babysitting. Just make sure you get one who speaks English. The hotels can take care of this for you.

Some hotels, such as **Jean-Michel Cousteau Fiji Islands Resort** and **Matangi Island Resort** in Fiji (see chapter 11), welcome children and have special programs to keep them safely occupied while their parents go diving. Most French Polynesian resorts welcome children, although most are oriented for couples. Others do not accept children at all; I point those out in the establishment listings, but you should ask to make sure.

Also ask whether the hotel can provide cribs, bottle warmers, and other needs. Because tourism in French Polynesia has traditionally focused on couples, most restaurants there don't have children's menus, and you may have to ask for one in the hotel dining rooms.

Disposable diapers, cotton swabs (known as Buds, not Q-Tips), and baby food are sold in many main-town stores, but you should take along a supply of such items as children's aspirin, a thermometer, adhesive bandages, and any special medications. Make sure your children's vaccinations are up to date before you leave home. If your children are very small, perhaps you should discuss your travel plans with your family doctor.

Remember to protect youngsters with ample sunscreen.

Some other tips: Some tropical plants and animals may resemble rocks or vegetation, so teach your youngsters to avoid touching or brushing up against rocks, seaweed, and other objects. If your children are prone to swimmer's ear, use vinegar or preventive drops before they go swimming in freshwater streams or lakes. Have them shower soon after swimming or suffering cuts or abrasions.

Rascals in Paradise, 2107 Van Ness Ave., Suite 403, San Francisco, CA 94107 (© **800/872-7225** or 415/921-7000; fax 415/921-7050; www.rascalsinparadise.com), specializes in organizing South Pacific tours for families with kids, including visits with local families and children.

STUDENT TRAVELERS

You won't find any student discounts in the islands, but you'd be wise to arm yourself with an **international student I.D. card,** which offers substantial savings on plane tickets. It also provides you with basic health and life insurance and a 24-hour help line. The card is available for $22 from the **Council on International Educational Exchange** (CIEE; © **800/40-STUDY;** www.ciee.org). The CIEE's travel branch, **Council Travel Service** (© **800/226-8624;** www.counciltravel.com), is the biggest student travel agency in the world. If you're no longer a student but are still under 26, you can get a **GO 25 card** from the same people; it entitles you to insurance and some discounts (but not on museum admissions). **STA Travel** (© **800/781-4040;** www.statravel.com) is another travel agency that caters especially to young travelers, although its bargain-basement prices are available to people of all ages.

In Canada, **Travel CUTS** (© **800/667-2887** or 416/614-2887; www.travelcuts.com), offers similar services. In London, **Campus Travel** (© **0171/730-3402;** www.campustravel.co.uk), opposite Victoria Station, is Britain's leading specialist in student and youth travel.

The Hanging Out Guides (www.frommers.com/hangingout), published by Frommer's, is the top student travel series for today's students, covering everything from adrenaline sports to the hottest club and music scenes.

WOMEN TRAVELERS

The South Pacific islands are relatively safe for women traveling alone, but don't let the charm of warm nights and smiling faces lull you into any less caution than you would exercise at home. *Do not* wander alone on deserted beaches. In the old days this was an invitation for sex. If that's what you want today, then that's what you're likely to get. Otherwise, it could result in your being raped.

And don't hitchhike alone, either.

Women Welcome Women World Wide (5W) (© **203/259-7832**; www.womenwelcomewomen.org.uk) works to foster international friendships by enabling women of different countries to visit one another (men can come along on the trips; they just can't join the club). It's a big, active organization, with more than 3,000 members from all walks of life in some 70 countries.

The Women's Travel Club (© **800/ 480-4448**; www.womenstravelclub. com) was designed by a woman in search of female travel companions because her husband preferred work to travel. Now the group organizes 25 to 30 tours a year, with an emphasis on foreign culture, scenery, and safety.

SINGLE TRAVELERS

Having traveled alone through the South Pacific for more years than I care to admit, I can tell you it's a great place to be unattached. After all, this is the land of smiles and genuine warmth toward strangers. The attitude soon infects visitors: All I've ever had to do to meet my fellow travelers is wander into a hotel bar, order a beer, and ask the persons next to me where they are from and what they have done in Fiji, Tahiti, and so on.

The islands have three playgrounds especially suited to singles. Two are the **Club Méditerranées** on Moorea and Bora Bora in French Polynesia. The other is rocking **Beachcomber Island Resort** in Fiji.

Unfortunately, the solo traveler is often forced to pay a punishing "single supplement" charged by many resorts, cruise lines, and tours for the privilege of sleeping alone.

Travel Companion Exchange (TCE) (© **631/454-0880**; www. travelcompanions.com) is one of the nation's oldest roommate finders for single travelers. Register with TCE and find a travel mate who will split the cost of the room with you and be around as little, or as often, as you like during the day.

Travel Buddies Singles Travel Club (© **800/998-9099**; www.travel buddiesworldwide.com) runs small, intimate, single-friendly group trips and will match you with a roommate free of charge and save you the cost of single supplements.

TravelChums (© **212/799-6464**; www.travelchums.com) is an Internet-only travel-companion matching service hosted by respected New York–based Shaw Guides travel service.

The Single Gourmet Club (© **212/980-8788**; www.single gourmetny.com) is the charter club of an international social, dining, and travel club for singles of all ages, with offices in 21 cities in the United States and Canada. Membership costs $75 for the first year; $40 to renew.

Outdoor Singles Network (P.O. Box 781, Haines, AK 99827; http:// kcd.com/ci/osn) is a quarterly newsletter for outdoor-loving singles, ages 19 to 90. The network will help you find a travel companion, pen pal, or soul mate. A subscription is $55, and your own personal ad is printed free in the next issue. Current issues are $15.

---

8 Getting There & Getting Around

BY PLANE

A few cruise ships visit the islands, but today all but a handful of visitors arrive by plane. Because populations are small and the distances are great (7½ hr. flying time from Los Angeles to Tahiti, 10 hr. or more to Fiji), flights are not nearly as frequent to

---

> ### *Tips* Always Reconfirm
>
> *Always* reconfirm your return flight as soon as you arrive on an outer
> island, primarily so that the local airline will know where to reach you in
> case of a schedule change. Avoid booking a return flight from an outer
> island on the same day you international flight is due to leave for home;
> give yourself plenty of leeway in case the weather or mechanical or
> scheduling problems prevent the plane from getting to and from the
> outer island on time.

---

and among the islands as Westerners are accustomed to at home. There may be only one flight a week between some countries, and flights that are scheduled today may be wiped off the timetables tomorrow.

Once you arrive in the islands, most of the outer-island airports are unlighted, so there are few connecting flights after dark. Accordingly, it's wise to consult a travel agent or contact the airlines to see what's happening at present.

Also, you might be limited to 10 kilograms (22 lb.) of baggage on small interisland planes, as opposed to 20 kilograms (44 lb.) on international flights (see "Baggage Allowances," below).

THE AIRPORTS

Most flights to the islands from North America depart from Los Angeles International Airport (LAX, in airline parlance). Australians and New Zealanders can get there from Auckland, Wellington, Christchurch, Sydney, Melbourne, or Brisbane, depending on the carrier.

If you don't live in a city where flights to the South Pacific originate, then you will have to pay to get there in order to make a connection. Some carriers offer "feeder" or "add-on" fares to cover the connecting flights. Be sure to ask about them.

Each island country has just one main international airport: **Papeete** on Tahiti in French Polynesia; **Rarotonga** in the Cook Islands; **Nadi** (and in a few cases **Suva**) in Fiji; **Apia** in

Samoa; **Pago Pago** in American Samoa; and **Tongatapu,** the main island in Tonga. Only Nadi (pronounced and sometimes spelled "Nandi") has enough international traffic to be considered a regional hub.

THE AIRLINES

- **Air New Zealand** ★★★ (© 800/ 262-1234 or 310/615-1111; www.airnewzealand.com) has the most extensive network to and from the islands. Consistently rated as one of the world's top airlines, it has several flights a week between Los Angeles and its home base in Auckland that stop in Tahiti, Fiji, the Cook Islands, Samoa, and Tonga. Within the islands, it has two flights a week that directly link Tahiti, the Cook Islands, and Fiji over its famous "Coral Route" (see below), From Vancouver, Canada, it has joint service to Fiji with Air Canada, and it flies to several Australian cities, so Aussies can reach most of the South Pacific islands through Auckland. It links Japan, Hong Kong, Singapore, Seoul, and Taipei to Auckland, with connections from there to the islands. It is a member of the Star Alliance, which includes United Airlines, Air Canada, and Lufthansa, and means you can get to the islands from most cities in the United States, Canada, and Europe on an Air New Zealand ticket.
- **Air Pacific** ★★★ (© 800/ 227-4446; www.airpacific.com),

Fiji's fine international airline, has several weekly Boeing 747 nonstop flights between Los Angeles and Fiji. At least one of these leaves about 3:30pm Los Angeles time and arrives in Nadi 10 hours later (about 9pm Fiji time the next day, because it crosses the International Dateline). Air Pacific also flies between Honolulu and Nadi once a week. It links Nadi to Sydney, Brisbane, and Melbourne in Australia. From New Zealand, it has nonstop service to Fiji from Auckland, Wellington, and Christchurch (some flights go directly to Suva). It provides nonstop service between Fiji and Tokyo in Japan. Within the region, it offers several flights per week linking Nadi to Samoa and Tonga, and it goes west to Vanuatu and Solomon Islands. Given its frequent and convenient flights and special deals for visitors from North America and Europe (see "Flying for Less: Tips for Getting the Best Airfare," below), traveling on Air Pacific is one of the most convenient and economical ways to get around the South Pacific. All Qantas Airways passengers bound for Fiji actually travel on Air Pacific (see below).

- **Air France** (© 800/321-4538; www.airfrance.com) flies to Tahiti from Paris, Los Angeles, and Tokyo.
- **Air Tahiti Nui** ★★ (© 877/824-4846; www.airtahitinui-usa.com), which is owned and operated by French Polynesians, flies between Tahiti and Los Angeles four times a week, with two of its flights departing early afternoon California time. That means you arrive in Papeete in time to connect to Moorea that same evening. Two of the return trips leave Tahiti at 8am; although the others are overnight, you arrive in

Los Angeles in time to make convenient connections. Air Tahiti Nui also links Tokyo and Auckland to Tahiti, and at press time was planning to inaugurate Paris-Papeete service.

- **Corsair Airlines** (© 800/677-0720; www.corsair.fr), a French carrier, flies to Tahiti from Paris via Los Angeles and San Francisco. Although primarily a charter airline, individuals can buy seats, though not necessarily at the charter price.
- **Hawaiian Airlines** (© 800/367-5320 in the continental U.S., Alaska, and Canada, or 808/838-1555 in Honolulu; www.hawaiianair.com) flies from Los Angeles, San Francisco, Portland, and Seattle to Tahiti and Pago Pago, connecting in Honolulu.
- **Polynesian Airlines** (© 800/264-0823; www.polynesianairlines.com), the national carrier of Samoa, connects its home base at Apia to Honolulu, New Zealand, Australia, Tonga, Fiji, and Tahiti. Its Polypass fare is good value (see "Flying for Less: Tips for Getting the Best Airfare," below).
- **Qantas Airways** (© 800/227-4500; www.qantas.com), the Australian carrier that owns a piece of Air Pacific, flies between Los Angeles, Tahiti, and Sydney. All its passengers fly to Fiji on Air Pacific planes, whether from Los Angeles or Australia.
- **Samoa Air** (© 684/699-9106; www.samoaair.com) flies its small planes between Pago Pago and Vava'u in Tonga.

BAGGAGE ALLOWANCES
A "weight system" applies on international flights, except to or from the United States and its territories (such as American Samoa). First-class and business-class passengers are limited to 30 kilograms (66 lb.) of checked

baggage and economy-class passengers to 20 kilograms (44 lb.).

A "piece system" applies to all flights to or from the United States and its territories. All passengers are limited to two checked bags without regard to weight but with size limitations: when added together, the three dimensions (length, height, depth) of any one first- or business-class bag must not exceed 158 centimeters (62 in.) in length. Economy-class passengers may check two bags whose total measurements do not exceed 270 centimeters (106 in.), with the larger of the two not more than 158 centimeters (62 in.).

For example, if you fly Los Angeles–Papeete-Fiji-Honolulu–Los Angeles, the piece system applies only on the Los Angeles–Papeete, Fiji-Honolulu, and Honolulu–Los Angeles segments. The weight system applies to Papeete-Rarotonga and Rarotonga-Fiji. In other words, pack according to the weight restrictions.

In addition to a small handbag or purse, all international passengers are permitted one carry-on bag with total measurements not exceeding 115 centimeters (45 in.).

Note: Many domestic air carriers in the islands limit their baggage allowance to 10 kilograms (22 lb.). Check with the individual airlines to avoid showing up at the check-in counter with too much luggage. Most hotels in the main towns have storage facilities where you can safely leave your extra bags during side trips.

NEW AIR TRAVEL SECURITY MEASURES

In the wake of the terrorist attacks of September 11, 2001, the airline industry began implementing sweeping security measures in airports. Expect a lengthy check-in process and extensive delays. Although regulations vary from airline to airline, you can expedite the process by taking the following steps:

- **Arrive early.** Arrive at the airport at least 2 hours before your scheduled flight.
- **Try not to drive your car to the airport.** Parking and curbside access to the terminal may be limited. Call ahead to check.
- **Don't count on curbside check-in.** Some airlines and airports have stopped curbside check-in altogether, and others offer it on a limited basis. For up-to-date information on specific regulations and implementations, check with your airline. There is no curbside check-in at the island airports.
- **Be sure to carry plenty of documentation.** A government-issued photo ID (federal, state, or local) is required (don't forget your passport!). You might need to show this at various checkpoints. And be sure that your ID is **up to date:** An expired driver's license, for example, may keep you from boarding the plane altogether, and an expired passport won't get you into any of the island countries.
- **Know what you can carry on and what you can't.** Travelers in the United States are now limited to one carry-on bag, plus one personal bag (such as a purse or a briefcase). The FAA has also issued a list of newly restricted carry-on items; see the box "What You Can Carry On—And What You Can't," below, for more information.
- **Prepare to be searched.** Expect spot-checks. Electronic items, such as laptops and cellphones, should be readied for additional screening. Limit the metal items you wear on your person.
- **Don't make jokes.** When a check-in agent asks if someone other than you packed your bag, don't decide that this is the time to

be funny. The agents will not hesitate to call an alarm.

- **No ticket, no gate access.** Only ticketed passengers will be allowed beyond the screener checkpoints, except for people with specific medical or parental needs.

FLYING FOR LESS: TIPS FOR GETTING THE BEST AIRFARE

The Pacific Ocean hasn't shrunk since it took 10 days and more than 83 hours in the air for Australian aviator Charles Kingsford Smith to become the first person to fly across it in 1928. Even though you can now board a jetliner in Los Angeles in the evening and be strolling under the palm trees of Tahiti or Fiji by the crack of dawn, the distances still run into the thousands of miles. Consequently, transportation costs may be the largest single expense of your trip to the South Pacific.

Be sure to shop all the airlines mentioned above to see who has the best deals. Keep calling and checking the websites if no attractive fare is available at first, because wholesalers and groups often reserve blocks of low-cost seats in advance but release some of them near the date of departure. Occasionally a carrier will hold a last-minute sale to get rid of unused seats, so always ask for the *lowest* fare.

SEASONAL & PROMOTIONAL FARES Depending on the carrier, the South Pacific has four airfare seasons: High, or "peak," season is from December through February. One "shoulder" season includes March and April; a second runs from September through November. The least expensive or "basic" season runs from May through August (when the weather is at its finest in the islands). Fares can vary by as much as 25%, depending on the season. Check the travel section of your Sunday newspaper for advertised discounts, and call the airlines directly or check their websites to see if any special seasonal fares are available.

Note: The lowest-priced fares are often nonrefundable, require advance purchase of 1 to 3 weeks and a certain

---

Tips What You Can Carry On—And What You Can't

In the United States, the Federal Aviation Administration (FAA) has devised new restrictions on carry-on baggage, not only to expedite the screening process but to prevent potential weapons from passing through airport security. Passengers are now limited to bringing just one carry-on bag and one personal item onto the aircraft (previous regulations allowed two carry-on bags and one personal item, like a briefcase or a purse). For more information, go to the FAA's website, **www.faa.gov**. The FAA has released a new list of items passengers are not allowed to carry onto an aircraft:

Not permitted: knives and box cutters, corkscrews, straight razors, metal scissors, metal nail files, golf clubs, baseball bats, pool cues, hockey sticks, ski poles, ice picks.

Permitted: nail clippers, tweezers, eyelash curlers, safety razors (including disposable razors), syringes (with documented proof of medical need), walking canes, and umbrellas (must be inspected first). The airline you fly may have additional restrictions on items you can and cannot carry on board. Call ahead to avoid problems.

length of stay, and carry penalties for changing dates of travel.

SPECIAL FARES & PASSES   The airlines set aside a certain number of seats for discounted promotional sale; these are usually the least expensive fares available and must be purchased from 2 weeks to a month in advance. Always ask what special deals the airlines are offering when you want to fly. Ask for their *lowest* fare, not just the best deal.

Several special fares offer savings if you're going to more than one South Pacific country, and if you can live with the restrictions that apply to each (always ask about restrictions).

On a regular basis, Air New Zealand has a discounted **Coral Route fare,** which includes stops at Tahiti, the Cook Islands, and Fiji (one of my recommended itineraries) as well as Honolulu. Air New Zealand has only one flight a week in each direction between the Cook Islands and Fiji, so you'll want to book this route as far in advance as possible.

Ask Air Pacific about its **Boomerang Pass,** which is sold in North America on a "sector" basis—a sector being one flight. One-way flights between Fiji, Samoa, Tonga, Australia, and New Zealand cost between $160 and $200 each. Air Pacific primarily flies "spoke" routes among the islands; like the spokes of a wheel, most of its planes fly from Nadi or Suva to another country, then turn around and come back. Among the restrictions, you must buy at least two sectors before departure from North America.

The Polynesian Airlines **Polypass** permits unlimited travel for 45 days among Samoa, American Samoa, Fiji, and Tonga, plus one round-trip to the islands from Los Angeles, Honolulu, Sydney, Melbourne, Auckland, or Wellington. A Polypass costs about $1,699 from North America ($1,874 if Tahiti is included), and $1,099 from Australia or New Zealand.

DISCOUNTERS & CONSOLIDATORS

Known as "discounters," many travel agents buy airline seats and hotel rooms at wholesale prices and then pass on some of their commissions to you. There are scores of them in the United States and abroad. Many of them run small ads in the Sunday travel sections of newspapers. You can find an up-to-date list of them—plus information about current discount fares worldwide—on the Web at **www.etn.nl/discount.htm#disco**.

Discover Wholesale Travel, Inc. ★★★ (© **800/576-7770** or 949/ 833-1136; www.discoverwholesale travel.com), is one of the few discounters specializing in the islands. Its discounted fares often are more than $100 off the lowest regular fare. It also discounts hotel rooms (see "Tips on Accommodations," below). By all means give this firm a try.

Many discounters—as well as some full-service travel agents—sell tickets provided by **consolidators,** which are sometimes called "bucket shops." Consolidators buy and resell seats on the major international carriers that otherwise would go unfilled, especially during the slow seasons. Consolidator deals can be riskier than direct buys from a carrier, but they can result in substantial savings on tickets that have fewer restrictions than you would get with an advance-purchase ticket bought directly from an airline. Generally it's best to ask a travel agent to comparison shop for you. Always compare the deals he or she comes up with to those offered directly by the airlines, inquire about any and all restrictions there may be, and pay by credit card.

Council Travel (© **800/226-8624;** www.counciltravel.com) and **STA Travel** (© **800/781-4040;** www.sta travel.com) cater especially to young travelers, but their bargain-basement prices are available to people of all ages. **TravelHUB** (© **888/AIR-FARE;** www.travelhub.com) represents nearly 1,000 travel agencies, many of which offer consolidator and discount fares. Other reliable consolidators include **1-800-FLY-CHEAP** (www.1800flycheap.com); **TFI Tours International** (© **800-745-8000** or 212/736-1140; www.lowestprice. com), which serves as a clearinghouse for unused seats; and "rebators" such as **Travel Avenue** (© **800/333-3335;** www.travel-avenue.com) and **Smart Traveller** (© **800/448-3338** in the U.S., or 305/448-3338), which rebate part of their commissions to you.

PACKAGE TOURS

Often a package tour will result in savings, not just on airfare but on hotels and other activities as well. You pay one price for a package that varies from one tour operator to the next. Airfare, transfers, and accommodations are always covered, and sometimes meals and specific activities are as well. The costs are kept down because wholesale tour operators (known as "wholesalers" in the travel industry) can make volume bookings on the airlines and at the hotels. The packages are usually then sold through retail travel agents, although some wholesalers deal directly with the public. It's worth a phone call to find out.

There are some drawbacks: The least expensive tours may put you up at a bottom-end hotel. And because the lower costs depend on volume, some more expensive tours could send you to a large, impersonal property. You might find that once you're in the islands, you want to shift to that cozy bungalow down the road; if you do, you might lose the accommodation portion of the money you've already paid. Some hoteliers will endorse your vouchers to another property if you're unhappy with theirs; others will not. And because the tour prices are based on double occupancy, the single traveler is almost invariably penalized. You

could end up traveling with strangers who become friends for life; they could also be loudmouthed bores.

Most tour companies require payment to be made well in advance of travel. If possible, pay by credit card, which will give you some protection in case the company doesn't come through with the tour. Also consider buying both trip cancellation and trip interruption insurance (see "Insurance, Health & Safety," earlier in this chapter).

If you decide to go for a package, read the fine print carefully. You might not want all the "extras" that are included, such as all meals (why pay in advance for all meals in places like French Polynesia, where dining out can be a major extracurricular activity?). And don't think the free manager's welcoming party is any big deal; you might be invited anyway, even if you're not on the tour.

Here are some reputable companies that specialize in selling package tours for the islands:

- **Air New Zealand Destinations** (© **800/262-1234** or 310/615-1111; www.airnewzealand.com) offers a variety of packages to Australia and New Zealand as well as to the South Pacific islands.
- **Brendan Tours** (© **800/421-8446** or 818/785-9696; www. brendantours.com) provides packages to Fiji for Air Pacific Holidays. Some of its recent basic season packages have started as low as $1,100 for a week, including air and hotel.
- **Islands in the Sun** (© **800/828-6877** or 310/536-0051; www.islandsinthesun.com), the largest and oldest South Pacific specialist, offers packages to all the islands. It was started in the 1960s by the late Ted Cook, who later sold the firm.
- **Jetset Tours** (© **800/638-3273;** www.jetsettours.com), an Aus-

tralian-based firm with offices in the United States, offers luxury trips to Tahiti, including round-trip airfare and accommodation in over-the-water bungalows.

- **Pacific Destination Center** (© 800/227-5317; www.pacific-destinations.com) is owned and operated by Australian-born Janette Ryan, who offers some good deals in Tahiti, the Cook Islands, Fiji, Samoa, and Tonga.
- **Pacific Navigator** (© 725504 in Fiji; www.pacificnavigator.com) is an offshoot of the Fiji-based Rosie Tours, which sells packages to the islands only via the Internet. It specializes in out-of-the-way islands.
- **PADI Travel Network** (© 800/729-7234; www.padi.com) puts together packages for divers of all experience levels.
- **Pleasant Tahitian Holidays** (© 800/742-9244; www.2tahiti.com), a huge company best known for its Pleasant Hawaiian and Pleasant Mexico operations, offers packages to French Polynesia.
- **Solace** (© 800/548-5331; www.solace1.com) specializes in trips to Tahiti and French Polynesia, offering fares and rates below those published by the airlines and hotels.
- **South Pacific Holidays** (© 800/940-1712; www.spac.com), based in Vancouver, Washington, offers packages to high-end resorts and less expensive diving destinations in Fiji.
- **Sunspots International** (© 800/334-5623 or 503/666-3893; www.sunspotsintl.com), based in Portland, Oregon, is expert on the Cook Islands and Samoa and can arrange an itinerary for you anywhere else in the islands.
- **Tahiti Legends** (© 800/200-1213; www.tahiti-legends.com) is run by former officials of Islands

in the Sun. It specializes in French Polynesia.

- **Tahiti Vacations** (© 800/553-3477 or 310/337-1040; www.tahitivacation.com) offers packages to French Polynesia, the Cook Islands, and Fiji. The company is a subsidiary of Air Tahiti, French Polynesia's domestic airline.
- **Travel Arrangements Ltd.** (© 800/392-8213; www.travelarrange.co.nz) is a New Zealand company whose North American representative is Fiji-born Ron Hunt, a veteran South Pacific travel agent. He sells packages to Tahiti, the Cook Islands, Fiji, Samoa, and Tonga but specializes in designing itineraries (and weddings) to suit your whims and pocketbook.

HOW TO HAVE AN (ALMOST) FIRST-CLASS EXPERIENCE IN COACH

If you're not accustomed to long, overnight flights (all flights to and from the South Pacific are long, and you're bound to get at least one overnighter between North America and the islands), here are a few tips to help make an otherwise cramped coach experience more comfy:

- For more legroom, check in early and ask for an aisle seat in an emergency-exit row or bulkhead.
- To have two seats for yourself, try for an aisle seat in a center section toward the back of coach.
- To sleep, avoid the last row or the row in front of the emergency exit, as these seats are the least likely to recline. You might also want to reserve a window seat so that you can rest your head and avoid being bumped in the aisle.
- If you're traveling with a companion, book an aisle and a window seat. Middle seats are usually booked last, so chances are good you'll end up with three seats to

yourselves. And in the case that a third passenger is assigned the middle seat, they'll probably be more than happy to trade for a window or an aisle.

- Unless you love noise, avoid seats in the very back or near toilets and pantries.

Try these tips to make yourself comfortable during your flight (and reduce jet lag while you're at it):

- Wear comfortable, low-heeled shoes and dress in loose-fitting layers that you can remove as cabin temperature fluctuates. Shorts and sleeveless blouses will be fine once you reach the islands, but airline cabins can be notoriously chilly, and blankets may be unavailable, so wear enough clothes to stay warm. Also wear breathable natural fabrics instead of synthetics.
- Hydrate before, during, and after your flight, to combat the lack of humidity in airplane cabins—which can be as dry as the Sahara Desert. Bring a bottle of water on board.
- Preorder a special meal. The airlines' vegetarian and kosher meals are usually fresher than standard plane fare. Or brown-bag your own meal.
- Get up and walk around whenever you can or perform stretching exercises in your seat to keep your blood flowing.
- Bring a toothbrush and moisturizer to stay fresh.
- If you're flying with kids, don't forget a deck of cards, toys, extra bottles, pacifiers, diapers, and chewing gum to help them relieve ear pressure buildup during ascent and descent. Let each child pack his or her own backpack with favorite toys.
- If you're flying with a cold or chronic sinus problems, use a decongestant 10 minutes before ascent and descent, to minimize pressure buildup in the inner ear.
- Try to acclimate yourself to the local time as quickly as possible. Stay up as long as you can the first day, and then try to wake up at a normal hour the next morning.

COPING WITH JET LAG

Except for Air Pacific's and Air Tahiti Nui's afternoon departures from Los Angeles bound for the islands (see "The Airlines," earlier in this chapter), flights from North America leave after dark, which means you will fly overnight and cross at least two time zones—and this invariably translates into jet lag. There are probably as many theories about what to do for jet lag as there are travelers. Some people advise trying to adjust to destination time before leaving home by getting up early or sleeping late. Others say you shouldn't eat or drink alcoholic beverages on the plane. Still others advise not sleeping during the flight. Air New Zealand says you should drink lots of nonalcoholic fluids to counter the dehydration that takes place at high altitudes, eat lightly, and exercise occasionally by walking up and down the aisle (all those fluids may send you to the rear of the plane, whether you're in the mood to exercise or not).

I live in Virginia, and I try to break my transpacific trips by stopping in either Los Angeles or Honolulu for at least one good night's sleep. I also make an effort to schedule flights during the daylight hours whenever possible. When I fly overnight, I eat lightly, and I try to sleep as much as possible, comforted by visions of lazing the next morning away on a South Pacific beach.

Here are some other tips for combating jet lag:

- **Reset your watch** according to your destination time before you board the plane.

- **Avoid drinking alcohol** or ingesting other depressants, such as motion sickness drugs, before and during your flight.
- **Be healthy.** Exercise, sleep well, and eat especially healthy foods during the few days before your trip.
- **Eat more lightly** than you would, both before and during your flight.
- When you reach your destination, **don't sleep longer than you normally would** to try to "catch up."
- **Push yourself** to stay as active as you can when you reach your destination, until the normal bedtime there. Likewise, wake at the same hours that locals do. The more you expose your body to daily rhythms in your destination, the faster your body will adjust.
- **Some doctors recommend melatonin** 2 hours before bedtime. A natural, sleep-inducing hormone, it's thought that melatonin will trick your body into thinking night has fallen earlier and help you adjust to a new time zone.
- Remember that eating **carbohydrates** (such as pasta or whole-grain bread) **before bedtime** will allow you to sleep better. High-protein foods—such as meats, fish, eggs, and dairy products—eaten before bedtime will give you energy.

BY SHIP

Although the days of the great ocean liners are long gone, occasionally it may be possible to cross the Pacific on a cruise ship making an around-the-world voyage or being repositioned, say, from Alaska to Australia. Most of them, however, steam through the islands for a week or two at a time from a home port such as Papeete or Sydney. They are usually under way at night, with visits to the islands during the day.

Passengers fly to the home port, enjoy the cruise, and fly home, which means cruises are no longer only for the idle rich with time on their hands. The cruise companies usually offer some form of reduced airfare on these "fly-and-cruise" vacations, so you'll save over the cost of booking the air and cruise separately. Many operators also offer land packages that enable their passengers to stay over for a few days or a week at a hotel at or near the home port, usually for a reduced rate.

The cruise price ordinarily includes all meals and double-occupancy stateroom or cabin, and the fares vary with the size and position of the quarters. You can save money by booking one of the smaller interior cabins on the lower decks. You won't have a porthole, but I can tell you from having served in the U.S. Navy that the lower amidships cabins tend to ride more smoothly than those on the outside of the upper decks.

The top local cruise ships are the Radisson Seven Seas *Paul Gauguin* in French Polynesia (see chapter 3) and the **Blue Lagoon Cruises** ships in Fiji (see chapter 10).

Most other cruise ships visiting the region sail from ports in Australia and New Zealand to islands in the western South Pacific such as Vanuatu, Fiji, and Tonga. Their itineraries tend to change from season to season, and there's not space here to describe every possibility and price.

You can get information from the major companies, which are likely to have ships in the South Pacific. Most sell tickets through travel agents, although some now offer them directly to the public on their websites. Operators include **Cunard Line** (© 800/528-6273; www.cunard line.com), whose ships include the *Queen Elizabeth II;* **Orient Lines** © 800/333-7300; www.orientlines. com); and **Princess Cruises** (© 800/

774-6237 or 904/527-6660; www. princesscruises.com). In addition, **Abercrombie & Kent** (© **800/ 323-7308;** www.abercrombiekent.

com), an upmarket travel packager, offers nature- and culture-oriented cruises, some to the islands.

9 Planning Your Trip Online

Researching and booking your trip online can save time and money. Then again, it might not. It is simply not true that you always get the best deal online. Most booking engines do not include schedules and prices for budget airlines, and from time to time you'll get a better last-minute price by calling the airline directly, so it's best to call the airline to see if you can do better before booking online.

On the plus side, Internet users today can tap into the same travel-planning databases that were once accessible only to travel agents—and do it at the same speed. Sites such as **Frommers.com, Travelocity.com, Expedia.com,** and **Orbitz.com** allow consumers to comparison shop for air-fares, access special bargains, book flights, and reserve hotel rooms and rental cars.

But don't fire your travel agent just yet. Although online booking sites offer tips and hard data to help you bargain shop, they cannot endow you with the hard-earned experience that makes a seasoned, reliable travel agent an invaluable resource, even in the Internet age. And for consumers with a complex itinerary, a trusty travel agent is still the best way to arrange the most direct flights to and from the best airports.

Still, there's no denying the Internet's emergence as a powerful tool in researching and plotting travel time. The benefits of researching your trip online can be well worth the effort.

Last-minute specials, such as weekend deals or Internet-only fares, are offered by airlines to fill empty seats. Most of these are announced on Tuesday or Wednesday and must be purchased online. They are only valid for travel that weekend, but some can be booked weeks or months in advance. Sign up for weekly e-mail alerts at airline websites or check mega-sites that compile comprehensive lists of last-minute specials, such as **Smarter Living** (www.smarterliving. com) and **WebFlyer** (www.webflyer. com).

 Frommers.com: The Complete Travel Resource

For an excellent travel planning resource, try **Arthur Frommer's Budget Travel Online** (www.frommers.com). You'll find the travel tips, reviews, monthly vacation giveaways, and online-booking capabilities indis-pensable. Among the special features are **Arthur Frommer's Daily Newsletter,** for the latest travel bargains and insider travel secrets; the electronic version of Frommer's travel guides, including expert travel tips, hotel and dining recommendations, and recommended sights in more than 2,000 destinations worldwide; and guidebook updates. When your research is done, the **Online Reservation System** (www.frommers.com/booktravelnow) takes you to Frommer's favorite sites for booking your vacation at affordable prices.

Tips Get a Paper Ticket

Electronic tickets (e-tickets) were conceived as a fast and easy ticket-free alternative to paper tickets. In the past, they allowed passengers to avoid long lines at airport check-in, while saving the airlines money on postage and labor. With the increased security measures in airports, however, an e-ticket no longer guarantees an accelerated check-in. You often can't go straight to the boarding gate, even if you have no bags to check. You'll probably need to show your printed e-ticket receipt or confirmation of purchase, as well as a photo ID, and sometimes even the credit card with which you purchased your e-ticket. Furthermore, most local airlines in the islands are not computerized to the extent that your e-ticket will be recognized on their flights. The long and the short of it: Even if you buy online, get a paper ticket for your South Pacific trip.

Some sites, such as Expedia.com, will send you **e-mail notification** when a cheap fare becomes available to your favorite destination. Some will also tell you when fares to a particular destination are lowest.

TRAVEL PLANNING & BOOKING SITES

Because several airlines are no longer willing to pay commissions on tickets sold by online travel agencies, these agencies may either add a $10 surcharge to your bill if you book on that carrier or neglect to offer those carriers' schedules.

The list of sites below is selective, not comprehensive. Some sites will have evolved or disappeared by the time you read this:

- **Travelocity** (www.travelocity.com or www.frommers.travelocity. com) and **Expedia** (www. expedia.com) are among the most popular sites, each offering an excellent range of options. Travelers search by destination, dates, and cost.
- **Orbitz** (www.orbitz.com) is a popular site launched by United, Delta, Northwest, American, and Continental airlines. (Stay tuned: At press time, travel-agency associations were waging an antitrust battle against this site.)

- **Qixo** (www.qixo.com) is a powerful search engine that allows you to search for flights and accommodations from some 20 airline and travel-planning sites (such as Travelocity) at once. Qixo sorts results by price.
- **Priceline** (www.priceline.com) lets you "name your price" for airline tickets, hotel rooms, and rental cars. For airline tickets, you can't say what time you want to fly or on what airline—you have to accept any flight between 6am and 10pm on the dates you've selected, and you may have to make one or more stopovers. Tickets are nonrefundable, and no frequent-flyer miles are awarded.

SMART E-SHOPPING

The savvy traveler is armed with insider information. Here are a few tips to help you navigate the Internet successfully and safely:

- **Know when sales start.** Last-minute deals may vanish in minutes. If you have a favorite booking site or airline, find out when last-minute deals are released to the public.
- **Shop around.** If you're looking for bargains, compare prices on different sites and airlines—and against a travel agent's best fare.

Try a range of times and alternative airports before you make a purchase.

- **Stay secure.** Book only through secure sites (some airline sites are not secure). Look for a key icon (Netscape) or a padlock (Internet Explorer) at the bottom of your web browser before you enter credit card information or other personal data.
- **Avoid online auctions.** Sites that auction airline tickets and frequent-flier miles are the number-one perpetrators of Internet fraud, according to the National Consumers League.
- **Maintain a paper trail.** If you book an e-ticket, print out a confirmation, or write down your confirmation number, and keep it safe and accessible—or your trip could be a virtual one!

ONLINE TRAVELER'S TOOLBOX

Veteran travelers usually carry some essential items to make their trips easier. Following is a selection of online tools to bookmark and use:

- **Visa ATM Locator** (www.visa. com), for locations of Plus ATMs worldwide, or **MasterCard ATM Locator** (www.mastercard.com), for locations of Cirrus ATMs worldwide.
- **Foreign Languages for Travelers** (www.travlang.com). Learn basic terms in more than 70 languages and click on any underlined phrase to hear what it sounds like. *Note:* Free audio software and speakers are required.
- **Intellicast** (www.intellicast.com) and **Weather.com** (www.weather. com). Give weather forecasts for all 50 states and for cities around the world.
- **Mapquest** (www.mapquest.com). This best of the mapping sites lets you choose a specific address or destination, and in seconds, it will return a map and detailed directions.
- **Cybercafes.com** (www.cybercafes. com) or **Net Café Guide** (www. netcafeguide.com/mapindex.htm). Locate Internet cafes at hundreds of locations around the globe. Catch up on your e-mail and log onto the Web for a few dollars per hour.
- **Universal Currency Converter** (www.xe.net/currency). See what your money is worth in more than 100 other countries.
- **U.S. State Department Travel Warnings** (www.travel.state.gov/ travel_warnings.html). Reports on places where health concerns or unrest might threaten U.S. travelers. It also lists the locations of U.S. embassies around the world.

10 Tips on Accommodations

The South Pacific has a wide range of accommodations, from deluxe resort hotels on their own islands to mom-and-pop guesthouses and dormitories with bunk beds.

TYPES OF ROOMS

My favorite type of hotel accommodates its guests in individual bungalows set in a coconut grove beside a sandy beach and quiet lagoon; if that's not the quintessential definition of the South Seas, then I don't know what is!

Some of these in French Polynesia, the Cook Islands, and Samoa are superromantic bungalows that actually stand on stilts out over the reef (although I should point out that these overwater units tend to be close together and thus less private than bungalows ashore elsewhere). Others are as basic as tents. In between they vary in size, furnishings, and comfort. In all, you enjoy your own place, one usually built or accented with thatch and other native materials but containing

Tips Internet Access Away from Home

E-mail is as much a part of life in the South Pacific as it is anywhere else these days. There is only one problem: Your local Internet service provider (ISP) will not have a local access number in the islands, so you can't just plug in your laptop and go online as you would at home. You can easily (if not inexpensively) use your own computer from any hotel room with a phone in French Polynesia, and you can sign up for local Internet access elsewhere (see "Fast Facts" in the destination chapters). There are also a number of ways to get your e-mail on the Web, using any computer, such as at your hotel or at a cybercafe:

• Your **ISP** may have a Web-based interface that lets you access your e-mail on computers other than your own. Just find out how it works before you leave home.

• You can open an account on a free, Web-based **e-mail provider** before you leave home, such as Microsoft's **Hotmail** (www.hotmail. com) or **Yahoo! Mail** (www.mail.yahoo.com). Your home ISP may be able to forward your home e-mail to the Web-based account automatically.

• Check out **www.mail2web.com**. This free service allows you to type in your regular e-mail address and password and retrieve your e-mail from any Web browser, anywhere, so long as your home ISP (such as America Online) hasn't blocked it with a firewall.

most of the modern conveniences. An increasing number of these accommodations are air-conditioned, which is a definite plus during the humid summer months from November through March. All but a few bungalows have ceiling fans, which usually will keep you comfortable during the rest of the year. Hotels of this style are widespread in the South Pacific.

With the exception of French Polynesia, the major tourist markets for the island countries are Australia and New Zealand. Accordingly, the vast majority of hotels are tailored to Aussie and Kiwi tastes, expectations, and uses of the English language.

Unlike the usual U.S. hotel room, which likely has two humongous beds, the standard Down Under room has a double or queen-size bed and a single bed that also serves as a settee. The room may or may not have a bathtub but always has a shower. There may be

no washcloths (bring your own), but there will be tea and instant coffee and an electric "jug" to heat water for same. Televisions are becoming more numerous but are not yet universal, but most hotels have radios whose selections are limited to the one, two, or three stations on the island.

Rooms are known to South Pacific reservation desks as "singles" if one person books them, regardless of the number and size of beds they have. Singles are slightly less expensive than other rooms. A unit is a "double" if it has a double bed and is reserved for two persons who intend to sleep together in that bed. On the other hand, a "twin" had two twin beds; it is known as a "shared twin" if two unmarried people book them and don't intend to sleep together. Third and fourth occupants of any room are usually charged a few dollars on top of the double or shared twin rates.

Some hotel rooms, especially in Rarotonga and the Cook Islands, have kitchenettes equipped with a small refrigerator (the "fridge"), hot plates (the "cooker"), pots, pans, crockery, silverware, and cooking utensils. Establishments with cooking facilities but no restaurants often call themselves "motels" rather than hotels, especially in the Cook Islands. Having a kitchenette can result in quite a saving on breakfasts and light meals.

MONEY-SAVING TIPS

The rates quoted in this book are known in the hotel industry as **rack rates,** or published rates; that is, the maximum a property charges for a room. Hotels pay travel agents and wholesalers 30% or more of their rack rates for sending clients their way, and they may even sell blocks of rooms at even more of a discount during slow periods. Some hotels may give you the benefit of at least part of this commission if you book directly instead of going through an airline or travel agent. Most also have "local" rates for islanders, which they may extend to visitors if business is slack. It never hurts to ask politely for a discounted or local rate.

You can also save on hotel rooms by booking them through the airlines or a discounter. One example is **Air New Zealand's "As You Please"** ★★★ program, which offers reduced rates at a number of establishments everywhere that airline flies. For example, it recently offered harbor-view rooms at the Tahiti Beachcomber Inter-Continental Resort for about $82 per double, more than $140 less than the hotel's published rates. You book and pay for the rooms ahead through Air New Zealand's offices and agents (see "The Airlines," earlier in this chapter). Ask the airline for an Air New Zealand Destinations brochure that lists the hotels and rates.

Some discount travel agents also deal in hotel rooms. **Discover Wholesale Travel, Inc.** (② **800/576-7770** or 949/833-1136; www.discoverwhole saletravel.com), for example, was recently selling rooms in Tahiti for $100 less than the published rate. This firm also discounts airfares (see "Discounters & Consolidators," earlier in this chapter).

Just as consolidators pare the price of airline tickets by selling unused seats, so do hotel brokers get rid of rooms hoteliers don't think they can sell at full price. The brokers may not offer the best deals you can find, but they're worth calling. These outfits usually work as consolidators, buying up or reserving rooms in bulk and then dealing them out to customers at a profit. They do garner special deals that range from 10% to 50% off; but remember, these discounts apply to rack rates, inflated prices that people rarely end up paying. You're probably better off dealing directly with a hotel, but if you don't like bargaining, this is certainly a viable option. Most of them offer online reservation services as well. Here are a few of the more reputable providers:

- **Accommodations Express** (② **800/950-4685;** www.accom modationsexpress.com)
- **Hotel Reservations Network** (② **800/715-7666;** www.hotel discounts.com)
- **Quikbook** (② **800/789-9887,** includes fax-on-demand service; www.quikbook.com)

Online, try booking your hotel through **Arthur Frommer's Budget Travel** (www.frommers.com). **Microsoft Expedia** (www.expedia.com) features a "Travel Agent" that will also direct you to affordable lodgings.

LANDING THE BEST ROOM

Somebody has to get the best room in the house. It might as well be you.

Tips **Using a Cellphone on Your Trip**

Most wireless companies in North America do not provide roaming services overseas, and since the islands use European GSM 900 mobile phones, which are incompatible with the American system, it's unlikely that you'll be able to use your own cellphone in the South Pacific. It's beyond me why you would want to have a cellphone during your get-away in the islands, but if you must, the most sensible way is to **rent one** in the United States or in the islands (most hotels will make the arrangements for you).

You can give **InTouch USA** (© **800/872-7626;** www.intouchusa.com) your itinerary, and they will tell you which wireless products and services you need. InTouch will also evaluate your own phone's international calling capabilities before you leave home. For this free evaluation, call © **703/222-7161** between 9am and 4pm.

Always ask about a corner room. They're often larger and quieter, with more windows and light, and they often cost the same as standard rooms.

When you make your reservation, ask if the hotel is renovating; if it is, request a room away from the construction. Ask about nonsmoking rooms, rooms with views, rooms with twin, queen-, or king-size beds. If you're a light sleeper, request a quiet room away from vending machines, elevators, restaurants, bars, and discos. Ask for one of the rooms that has been most recently renovated or redecorated. If you aren't happy with your room when you arrive, talk to the front desk. If they have another room, they may be willing to accommodate you. Join the hotel's frequent visitor club; you may qualify for upgrades.

In resort areas, particularly in warm climates, there are some other questions to ask before you book a room:

- What's the view like? If you're a cost-conscious traveler, you might be willing to pay less for a back room facing the parking lot, especially if you don't plan to spend much time in the room.
- Does the room have air-conditioning or just ceiling fans?
- Do the windows open?
- What is the noise level outside the room? If the climate is warm, and nighttime entertainment takes place alfresco, you might want to find out when show time is over.
- What's included in the price? Your room may be moderately priced, but if you're charged for beach chairs, towels, sports equipment, and other amenities, you could end up spending more than you bargained for.
- Is there a hotel pool, and is it fresh- or saltwater?
- Are airport transfers included in the price?
- If it's off-season, will any facilities be shut down while you're there?
- If you're single, ask if there's a singles program. If it's off-season, inquire about the occupancy rate. If you're with a partner and looking for quiet, an empty resort might be fine; but if you're single and looking for fun, you might want to find a place that's a little more bustling.
- What programs are available for kids?
- How far is the room from the beach?

- What is the dining plan? European Plan (EP; no meals), American Plan (AP; three meals), or Modified American Plan (MAP; breakfast and dinner)? You don't want to pay for three meals if you plan to eat out a lot.
- What is the cancellation policy?

11 Suggested Itineraries

People often ask where I would go on a vacation in the South Pacific. It's a difficult question for me to answer. I am fond of the dramatic, breathtaking scenery of French Polynesia, the liveliness of the Cook Islanders, the ancient cultures of Samoa and Tonga, the great variety of things to do in Fiji, and the enormously friendly people everywhere.

If you want to see it all, give yourself several busy months of island hopping. If you have only 1 week, then your time will best be spent in just one island country. Several companies offer attractively priced packages to individual countries, so you can save that way (see "Package Tours," earlier in this chapter). If you have 2 or 3 weeks, here are some suggestions to consider.

FIJI–RAROTONGA–TAHITI

One of the easiest and least expensive ways to sample the South Pacific is to fly with Air New Zealand over its **Coral Route,** from Tahiti to Rarotonga to Fiji, or vice versa. Air New Zealand pioneered this route in the days of flying boats, and its jets now fly it twice a week. I highly recommend this itinerary because it gives a good sampling of Melanesia and the transplanted Indian culture in Fiji, of English-speaking Polynesia in the Cook Islands, and of Polynesia with a French overlay in Tahiti and its islands.

For a 3-week trip, spend 1 week each in Fiji, the Cook Islands, and French Polynesia. Depending on flight connections, you can shorten your stays. As a variation, you can cut out Tahiti altogether and reduce your time in the Cook Islands by flying directly to Rarotonga from Los Angeles, Honolulu, or Auckland. See "The Airlines," earlier in this chapter, for information about Air New Zealand's excellent excursion fare over this route.

THE SAMOAS & TONGA

A tour through the "Bible Belt" of Polynesia includes Samoa, nearby American Samoa, and the Kingdom of Tonga. All three are very conservative, but by being so, they have maintained their traditional Polynesian cultures.

You can tour American Samoa in a day, so make your base in Samoa with its relatively unchanged Polynesian way of life. Tonga is worth a visit just to see all 300-plus pounds of King Tupou IV.

Air New Zealand flies directly to Samoa and Tonga from Los Angeles via Honolulu, or you can go on Air Pacific's Pacific Pass, Polynesian Airline's Polypass, or on the Visit South Pacific Pass offered by Polynesian and Royal Tongan airlines.

FIJI–TONGA–THE SAMOAS

Fiji, Tonga, and the Samoas offer diversity, friendly people, fine beaches, reefs, and tropical scenery. Fiji is by far the largest, so give yourself more time there.

Air Pacific's Boomerang Pass makes visits combining Fiji, Tonga, and Samoa attractive, as do each country's reasonably priced accommodations and restaurants. The most expeditious routing is Fiji-Tonga on Air Pacific, Tonga-Apia on Polynesian Airlines, and Apia-Fiji on Air Pacific or Polynesian Airlines.

THE BACKPACKING TRAIL

Backpackers will have lots of company while traveling the islands on a shoestring, just as I did back in the 1970s: Young Australians and New Zealanders frolic on school breaks, Canadians go or come from work Down Under, and Europeans go out to see the world. Except in Fiji, which is well equipped for low-budgeteers, the number of low-end properties is limited. The result: A narrow "trail" of backpackers traveling through the islands. Once on the trail, you will very quickly meet fellow travelers coming from the opposite direction who will clue you in on which places are clean and friendly, who's offering the best scuba diving prices, and so on.

The most popular low-budget journey is via Tahiti, Rarotonga, and Fiji—essentially the itinerary described above. Because Tahiti is the most expensive South Pacific destination, most budget travelers spend less time there before moving on for a week or two in the Cooks, then on to Fiji, where prices for accommodation, food, and transportation are the South Pacific's least expensive.

Another popular route includes stops in the Samoas and Tonga between the United States and New Zealand or Australia.

12 Recommended Reading

Rather than list the hundreds of books about the South Pacific, I have picked some of the best that are likely to be available in the United States and Canada, either in bookstores or at your local library. A number of out-of-print island classics have been reissued in paperback by **Mutual Publishing Company,** Mezzanine B, 1127 11th Ave., Honolulu, HI 96816 (© **808/ 732-1709;** fax 808/734-4094; www. mutualpublishing.com).

GENERAL

If you have time for only one South Pacific book, read *The Lure of Tahiti* (1986). Editor A. Grove Day, himself an islands expert, includes 18 short stories, excerpts of other books, and essays. There is a little here from many of the writers mentioned below, plus selections from captains Cook, Bougainville, and Bligh.

The National Geographic Society's book *The Isles of the South Pacific* (1971), by Maurice Shadbolt and Olaf Ruhen, and Ian Todd's *Island Realm* (1974) are somewhat out-of-date coffee-table books but have lovely color photographs. *Living Corals* (1979), by Douglas Faulkner and Richard Chesher, shows what you will see under water.

HISTORY & POLITICS

Several of the early English and French explorers published accounts of their exploits, but *The Journals of Captain James Cook* stand out as the most exhaustive and evenhanded. Edited by J. C. Beaglehole, they were published in three volumes (one for each voyage) in 1955, 1961, and 1967. A. Grenfell Price edited many of Cook's key passages and provides short transitional explanations in *The Explorations of Captain James Cook in the Pacific* (1971).

The explorers' visits and their consequences in Tahiti, Australia, and Antarctica are the subject of Alan Moorehead's excellent study *The Fatal Impact: The Invasion of the South Pacific, 1767–1840* (1966), a colorful tome loaded with sketches and paintings of the time.

Three other very readable books trace Tahiti's postdiscovery history. *Tahiti: Island of Love* (1979), by Robert Langdon, takes the island's story up to 1977. *Tahiti: A Paradise Lost* (1985), by David Howarth, covers more thoroughly the same early ground covered by Langdon but stops with France's taking possession in 1842. *The Rape of Tahiti* (1983), by

---

Fun Fact **Mutiny on the Bounty**

The most famous movies about the South Pacific are two *Mutiny on the Bounty* films based on the novel by Charles Nordhoff and James Norman Hall. The 1935 version starred Clark Gable as Fletcher Christian and Charles Laughton as a tyrannical Captain Bligh. (It actually was the second film to be based on the *Bounty* story; the first was an Australian production, starring Errol Flynn in his first movie role.) Although the 1935 version contained background shots of 40 Tahitian villages, most of the movie was filmed on Santa Catalina, off the California coast; neither Gable nor Laughton visited Tahiti. The 1962 remake with Marlon Brando and Trevor Howard in the Gable and Laughton roles, however, was actually filmed on Tahiti. It was the beginning of Brando's tragic real-life relationship with Tahiti. A 1984 version, *The Bounty,* not based on Nordhoff and Hall, was filmed in Opunohu Bay on Moorea and featured Mel Gibson as Christian and Anthony Hopkins as a more sympathetic (and historically accurate) Bligh.

Edward Dodd, covers the island from prehistory to 1900.

Mad About Islands (1987), by A. Grove Day, follows the island exploits of literary figures Herman Melville, Robert Louis Stevenson, Jack London, and W. Somerset Maugham. Also included are Charles Nordhoff and James Norman Hall, coauthors of the so-called "Bounty Trilogy" and other works about the islands (see "Fiction," below). *A Dream of Islands* (1980), by Gavan Dawes, tells of the missionary John Williams as well as of Melville, Stevenson, and the painter Paul Gauguin, who spent the final years of his life in French Polynesia.

Former *New York Times* reporter Robert Turnbull traveled the islands in the 1970s and reported his findings in *Tin Roofs and Palm Trees* (1977).

PEOPLES & CULTURES

Some of the most interesting accounts of island life were written by persons who lived among the islanders. Perhaps the most famous is *Coming of Age in Samoa* (1928), in which Margaret Mead tells of her year studying promiscuous adolescent girls in the Manu'a islands of American Samoa. The book created quite a stir when it was published in a more modest time than the present. Her interpretation of Samoan sex customs was taken to task by New Zealander Derek Freeman in *Margaret Mead and Samoa: The Making and Unmaking of an Anthropological Myth* (1983).

The late Bengt Danielsson, a Swedish anthropologist who arrived in Tahiti on Thor Heyerdahl's *Kon Tiki* raft in 1947 and spent the rest of his life there, painted a much broader picture of Polynesian sexuality in *Love in the South Seas* (1986). Heyerdahl tells his tale and explains his theory of Polynesian migration (since debunked) in *Kon Tiki* (1950; translated by F. K. Lyon). In 1936, Heyerdahl and his wife lived for a year in the Marquesas. The resulting book, *Fatu-Hiva: Back to Nature* (1975), provides an in-depth look at Marquesan life at the time.

Two Americans gave unscholarly but entertaining accounts of Polynesian island life during the 1920s. Robert Dean Frisbie spent several years as a trader in the Cook Islands and told about it charmingly in *The Book of Puka-Puka* (1928; reprinted by Mutual in 1986). Robert Lee Eskridge spent a year on Mangareva in

French Polynesia; his equally charming book is titled, appropriately, *Manga Reva* (1931; reprinted by Mutual in 1986).

TRAVELOGUES

Although the novelist Robert Louis Stevenson composed very little fiction about the South Pacific during his years in Samoa (see chapter 13), he wrote articles and letters about his travels and about events leading to Germany's acquisition of the islands in 1890. Many of them are available in two collections: *In the South Seas* (1901) and *Island Landfalls* (1987). The latter includes three Stevenson short stories with South Seas settings: "The Bottle Imp," "The Isle of Voices," and "The Beach at Falesá."

Sir David Attenborough, the British documentary film producer, traveled to Papua New Guinea, Vanuatu, Fiji, and Tonga in the late 1950s to film, among other things, Tongan Queen Salote's royal kava ceremony. Sir David entertainingly tells of his trips in *Journeys to the Past* (1983).

The noted travel writer and novelist Paul Theroux took his kayak along for a tour of the South Pacific and reported on what he found in *The Happy Isles of Oceania: Paddling the Pacific* (1992). The book is a fascinatingly frank yarn, full of island characters and out-of-the-way places. The king of Tonga reportedly was so upset with what Theroux had to say that he has banned him from returning to the kingdom.

FICTION

Starting with Herman Melville's *Typee* (1846) and *Omoo* (1847)—semifictional accounts of his adventures in the Marquesas and Tahiti, respectively—the South Pacific has spawned a wealth of fiction. (Though set in the South Pacific Ocean, Melville's 1851 classic, *Moby-Dick* does not tell of the islands.)

After Melville came Julian Viaud, a French naval officer who fell in love with a Tahitian woman during a short sojourn in Tahiti. Under the pen name Pierre Loti, he wrote *The Marriage of Loti* (1880; reprinted by KPI in 1986), a classic tale of lost love.

W. Somerset Maugham's *The Moon and Sixpence* (1919) is a fictional account of the life of Paul Gauguin. Maugham changed the name to Charles Strickland and made the painter English instead of French. (Gauguin's own novel, *Noa Noa*, was published in English in 1928, long after his death.) Maugham also produced a volume of South Pacific short stories, *The Trembling of a Leaf* (1921; reprinted by Mutual in 1985). The most famous is "Rain," the tragic story of prostitute Sadie Thompson and the fundamentalist missionary she led astray in American Samoa. My favorite is "The Fall of Edward Bernard," about a Chicagoan who forsakes love and fortune at home for "beauty, truth, and goodness" in Tahiti.

Next on the scene were Charles Nordhoff and James Norman Hall (more about them in chapters 3 and 4). Together they wrote the most famous of all South Pacific novels, *Mutiny on the Bounty* (1932). They immediately followed that enormous success with two other novels: *Men Against the Sea* (1934), based on

---

Impressions

I have often been mildly amused when I think that the great American novel was not written about New England or Chicago. It was written about a white whale in the South Pacific.

—James A. Michener, *Return to Paradise*, 1951

Captain Bligh's epic longboat voyage after the mutiny; and *Pitcairn's Island* (1935), about Lt. Fletcher Christian's demise on the mutineers' remote hideaway.

Nordhoff and Hall later wrote *The Hurricane* (1936), a novel set in American Samoa that has been made into two movies filmed in French Polynesia. Hall also wrote short stories and essays, collected in *The Forgotten One* (1986).

The second most famous South Pacific novel appeared just after World War II—*Tales of the South Pacific* (1947), by James A. Michener. A U.S. Navy historian, Michener spent much of the war on Espiritu Santo, in the New Hebrides (now Vanuatu), which is the setting for most of the book. Richard Rodgers and Oscar Hammerstein turned the novel into the musical *South Pacific,* one of the most successful Broadway productions ever; it was later made into the blockbuster movie.

Michener toured the islands a few years later and wrote *Return to Paradise* (1951), a collection of essays and short stories. The essays are particularly valuable because they describe the islands as they were after World War II but before tourists began to arrive via jet aircraft—in other words, near the end of the region's backwater, beachcomber days. His piece on Fiji predicts that country's Fijian–Indian problems.

3

Introducing French Polynesia

The largest and most heavily populated island in French Polynesia, Tahiti has evoked the magical image of an idyllic tropical paradise since canoe loads of young Tahitian *vahines* gave uninhibited, bare-breasted receptions to European explorers of the late 1700s. Today its name is often used synonymously with this overseas country of France.

Don't be surprised to find noise and traffic jams on Tahiti, and especially in the territory's bustling capital of Papeete. A freeway runs across the mountains to a wealthy suburb along Tahiti's west coast, and tract houses scale the flanks of the island's serrated ridges. Papeete's sleazy bars that once made the town a den of iniquity are long gone. Chic bistros and high-rise shopping centers have replaced its stage-set wooden Chinese stores, and glass and steel of luxury resorts on the edge of town have supplanted its cheap waterfront hotels. A huge chunk of the postnuclear-testing economic restructuring fund has gone into refurbishing its waterfront, including a new cruise-ship welcoming terminal and a classy new park where families gather and the city celebrates its festivals.

Beyond Papeete, the awesome beauty of these islands is unsurpassed anywhere in the world. On Moorea, Bora Bora, Huahine, and Tahiti's other companion islands, you will witness the other worldly mountain peaks, multihued lagoons, and palm-draped beaches that have come to symbolize the South Pacific.

1 French Polynesia Today

French Polynesia sprawls over an area of 2 million square miles in the eastern South Pacific. That's about the size of Europe, excluding the former Soviet Union, or about two-thirds the size of the continental United States. The 130 main islands, however, consist of only 1,500 square miles, an area smaller than Rhode Island, with a population of 230,000 or so.

THE ISLANDS

The territory's five major island groups differ in terrain, climate, and to a certain extent, people. With the exception of the Tuamotu Archipelago, an enormous chain of low coral atolls northeast of Tahiti, all but a few are high islands, the mountainous tops of ancient volcanoes that have been eroded into jagged peaks, deep bays, and fertile valleys. All have fringing or barrier coral reefs and blue lagoons worthy of postcards.

The most strikingly beautiful and most frequently visited are the **Society Islands,** so named by Capt. James Cook because they lay relatively close together. These include **Tahiti** and its nearby companion **Moorea,** which also are known as the Windward Islands because they sit to the east, the direction of the prevailing trade wind. To the northwest lie **Bora Bora, Huahine, Raiatea, Tahaa, Maupiti,** and several smaller islands. Because they are downwind of Tahiti, they also are called the Leeward Islands.

To the late James A. Michener's eye, Bora Bora was the most beautiful island in the world. Others give that title to Moorea, in a close race. It's all a matter of degree, for these definitely are the world's most dramatically beautiful islands.

Across the approaches to Tahiti from the east, the 69 low-lying atolls of the **Tuamotu Archipelago** run for 1,159km (720 miles) on a line from northwest to southeast. The early European sailors called them the "Dangerous Archipel-ago" because of their tricky currents and because they virtually cannot be seen until a ship is almost on top of them. Even today they are a wrecking ground for yachts and interisland trading boats. Two of them, Moruroa and Fangataufa, were used by France to test its nuclear weapons between 1966 and 1996. Oth-ers provide the bulk of Tahiti's well-known black pearls. **Rangiroa,** the world's second-largest atoll and the territory's best scuba diving destination, is the most frequently visited. Neighboring **Tikehau,** with a much smaller and shallower lagoon, also has a modern resort hotel, as does **Manihi,** the territory's major pro-ducer of black pearls.

The **Marquesas,** a group of 10 high islands, sit beyond the Tuamotus some 1,208km (750 miles) northeast of Tahiti. They are younger than the Society Islands, and protecting coral reefs have not enclosed them. As a result, the surf pounds on their shores, there are no encircling coastal plains, and the people live in a series of deep valleys that radiate out from central mountain peaks. The Marquesas have lost their once-large populations to 19th-century disease and the 20th-century economic lure of Papeete; today their sparsely populated, cloud-enshrouded valleys have an almost haunted air about them.

The seldom-visited **Austral Islands** south of Tahiti are part of a chain of high islands that continues westward into the Cook Islands. The people of the more temperate Australs, which include Rurutu, Raivavae, and Tubuai, once pro-duced some of the best art objects in the South Pacific, but these skills have passed into time.

Far on the southern end of the Tuamotu Archipelago, the **Gambier Islands** are part of a semisubmerged, middle-aged high island similar to Bora Bora. The hilly remnants of the old volcano are scattered in a huge lagoon, which is par-tially enclosed by a barrier reef marking the original outline of the island before it began to sink. The largest of these remnant islands is Mangareva.

GOVERNMENT

In 2000 French Polynesia shifted its status from an "overseas territory" of France to an "overseas country" of France. The islanders now have considerable auton-omy over their internal affairs. They are free to create their own citizenship and choose their own flag, national anthem, and even a name for themselves ("Tahiti-Nui" and other alternatives to "French Polynesia" have been proposed).

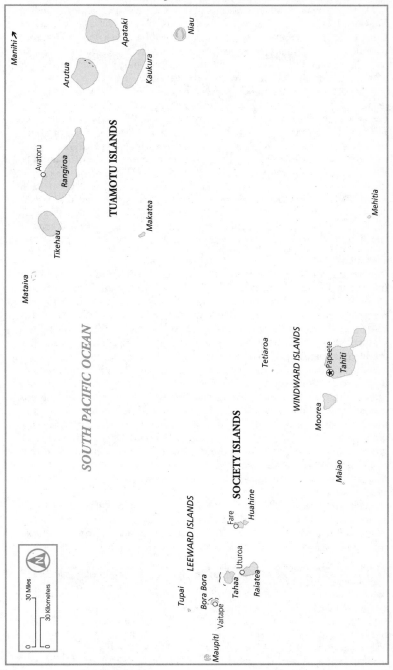

The Society Islands & the Northern Tuamotus

Manihi ↗

Apataki

Niau

Arutua

Kaukura

TUAMOTU ISLANDS

Avatoru

Rangiroa

Makatea

Mehitia

Tikehau

Mataiva

SOUTH PACIFIC OCEAN

Tetiaroa

WINDWARD ISLANDS

Papeete

Tahiti

Moorea

SOCIETY ISLANDS

Maiao

Fare

Huahine

LEEWARD ISLANDS

Uturoa

Tupai

Bora Bora

Tahaa

Vaitape

Raiatea

Maupiti

N

30 Miles

30 Kilometers

0

0

Nevertheless, Paris still controls about 30% of the islanders' affairs, including foreign affairs, defense, justice, internal security, and currency. The city of Papeete and a few other *communes* have their own local police forces, but they have limited authority. French *gendarmes* control law enforcement. The man wearing the round de Gaulle hat who stops you for riding a motorbike without a helmet is as likely to be from Martinique as from Moorea.

Local voters cast ballots in French presidential elections and choose two elected deputies and a senator to the French parliament in Paris. They also elect 49 members of a Territorial Assembly, the majority party of which selects a president, the territory's highest-ranking local official. The Assembly and its Council of Ministers decide all issues that are not reserved to the metropolitan French government.

A small movement would like to see the territory completely free of France. The village of Faaa, which is adjacent to the airport on Tahiti, is a hotbed of such proindependence sentiment. You'll see more English used in Faaa than anywhere else in French Polynesia, as evidenced by stores with American-sounding names such as "Cash and Carry," "Magic City," and "Home Center." Despite the movement's vociferousness, it has been unable to win a majority in the Territorial Assembly, which is solidly controlled by the proautonomy party of Pres. Gaston Flosse.

THE ECONOMY

The territory would be bankrupt were it not for billions of francs poured in by the French government in Paris. The money tap was turned on when France established its nuclear testing facility in the islands in 1963, and it has continued posttesting through an economic restructuring fund intended to foster self-sufficiency by developing local industries. The fund will continue until 2006.

Although many islanders gripe about the French, most Tahitians have readily accepted the largesse Paris has sent their way to pay for modern schools, roads, hospitals, airports, and other public projects. The result has been both a grossly inflated economy and the most modern infrastructure in the South Pacific islands.

In reality, French Polynesia has only two industries: tourism and black pearls (upward of $200 million worth of pearls are exported annually). In addition to using the restructuring fund to expand the islands' tourism facilities, the government is actively promoting tuna fishing. Otherwise, little is produced or grown locally, including most foodstuffs. However, professionals and government employees earn Parisian-level salaries. For ordinary workers, the minimum wage is about US$7 a hour—compared to US$1 or less in most other South Pacific islands.

Although prices are high for everyone, there's one saving grace for visitors: There is neither tipping nor a sales tax here, which can add 25% to your bill elsewhere. Consequently, you should find meals at most nonhotel restaurants to cost about the same as at comparable restaurants in U.S. cities.

2 History 101

Surely Capt. Samuel Wallis of HMS *Dolphin* could hardly believe his eyes when he arrived on the high, lush island in 1767. An army of large brown-skinned men paddled more than 500 canoes across the lagoon at Matavai Bay to greet him, many of

Dateline

- 6th century A.D. Polynesians arrive (estimated time).
- 1595 Alvaro de Mendaña discovers the Marquesas Islands.
- 1606 Pedro Fernández de Quirós sails through the Tuamotus.

them loaded with pigs, chickens, coconuts, fruit, and topless young women "who played a great many droll and wanton tricks" on his scurvy-ridden crew. Secretly sent by King George III to find *terra australis incognita*—the mysterious southern continent that theorists said was necessary to keep the earth in balance—Wallis had instead discovered Tahiti.

The French explorer Louis Antoine de Bougainville was similarly greeted when he arrived at Hitiaa a year later. Bougainville noted that one young woman "carelessly dropped the cloth which covered her and appeared to the eyes of all beholders much as Venus showed herself to the Phrygian shepherd—having indeed the form of that goddess." With visions of Aphrodite, the Greek goddess of love, Bougainville promptly named his discovery New Cythère in honor of Aphrodite's hometown. It has ever since been known as The Island of Love.

Bougainville stayed at Hitiaa only 10 days, but he took back to France a young Tahitian named Ahutoru, who became a sensation in Paris as living proof of Jean-Jacques Rousseau's theory that man was at his best a "noble savage." Indeed, Bougainville and Ahutoru gave Tahiti a hedonistic image that has survived to this day.

The real Venus played a role in Tahiti's history when Capt. James Cook arrived in 1769, on the first of his three great voyages of discovery to the South Pacific. Cook's job was to measure the transit of the planet across the face of the sun, which if successful would enable navigators for the first time to accurately measure longitude on the earth's surface. Cook set up an observation point on a sandy spit on Tahiti's north shore, a locale he appropriately named Point Venus. His measurements were of little use, but Cook remained in Tahiti for 6 months. His studies of the island contributed greatly to the world's understanding of Polynesian cultures.

- 1765 Searching for *terra australis incognita,* Capt. John Byron on HMS *Dolphin* finds some Tuamotu islands but misses Tahiti.
- 1767 Also on HMS *Dolphin,* Capt. Samuel Wallis discovers Tahiti, claims it for King George III.
- 1768 French Capt. Antoine de Bougainville discovers Tahiti.
- 1769 Capt. James Cook arrives to observe the transit of Venus on the first of his three voyages of discovery.
- 1788 HMS *Bounty* under Capt. William Bligh arrives and then takes breadfruit to the Caribbean.
- 1789 Lt. Fletcher Christian leads the mutiny on the *Bounty.*
- 1797 London Missionary Society emissaries arrive, looking for converts.
- 1827 Queen Pomare IV succeeds to the throne.
- 1837 Protestants deny French Catholic priests permission to land. Irate France demands full reparations.
- 1838 Queen reluctantly signs ultimatum of French Adm. du Petit-Thouars.
- 1841 French traders trick Tahitian chiefs into asking for French protection. They later disavow it.
- 1842 Tahiti becomes a French protectorate. Herman Melville jumps ship, spends time in the *Calaboosa Beretane* (British jail). He later writes *Omoo* about his adventures.
- 1844–48 Tahitians wage guerrilla war against the French.
- 1847 Queen Pomare acquiesces to full French protection.
- 1862 Irish adventurer William Stewart starts a cotton plantation at Atimaono.
- 1865 The first 329 Chinese people arrive from Hong Kong to work Stewart's plantation, which fails. Most of the Chinese people stay.
- 1872 Pierre Loti (Julian Viaud) spends several months on Tahiti. His *The Marriage of Loti* is published 8 years later.
- 1877 Queen Pomare IV dies at age 64.
- 1880 King Pomare V abdicates in return for pensions for him, his family, and mistress. Tahiti becomes a French colony.
- 1888 Robert Louis Stevenson spends 2 months at Tautira on Tahiti Iti.

continued

Cook used Tahiti as a base during his two subsequent voyages, during which he disproved the southern continent theory, discovered numerous islands, and charted much of the South Pacific.

THE MUTINY ON THE *BOUNTY*

Capt. William Bligh, one of Cook's navigators, returned to Matavai Bay in 1788 in command of HMS *Bounty* on a mission to procure breadfruit as cheap food for plantation slaves in Jamaica. One of Bligh's handpicked officers was a former shipmate, Fletcher Christian.

Delayed by storms off Cape Horn, Bligh missed the breadfruit season and had to wait on Tahiti for 6 months until his cargo could be transplanted. Christian and some of the crew apparently didn't want to leave, so much had they enjoyed the island's women and easygoing lifestyle. For whatever reason, the *Bounty's* 1,015 breadfruit plantings made it only to Tonga before Christian staged a mutiny on April 28, 1789. He set Bligh and 18 of his loyal officers and crewmen adrift in a longboat with a compass, a cask of water, and a few provisions.

Christian sailed the *Bounty* back to Tahiti, where he put ashore 25 other crew members who were loyal to Bligh. After searching unsuccessfully for a hiding place, the mutineers returned to Tahiti for the last time. Christian, eight mutineers, their Tahitian wives, and six Tahitian men then disappeared.

In one of the epic open-boat voyages of all time, Bligh and his crew miraculously made it back to England via the Dutch East Indies, thence to England, whereupon the Royal Navy sent HMS *Pandora* to Tahiti to search for the *Bounty*. It found only the crewmen still there. Four eventually were acquitted. Three were convicted but pardoned; one of these three was Peter

- 1891 "Fleeing from civilization," the painter Paul Gauguin arrives.
- 1903 Paul Gauguin dies at Hiva Oa in the Marquesas. All of eastern Polynesia becomes one French colony.
- 1914 Two German warships shell Papeete, sink the French navy's *Zélée*.
- 1917 W. Somerset Maugham spends several months on Tahiti.
- 1933 Charles Nordhoff and James Normal Hall publish *Mutiny on the Bounty,* an instant best-seller.
- 1935 Clark Gable and Charles Laughton star in the movie *Mutiny on the Bounty.*
- 1942 U.S. Marines build the territory's first airstrip on Bora Bora.
- 1960 Tahiti-Faaa International Airport opens, turning Tahiti into a jet-set destination. Marlon Brando arrives to film a second movie version of *Mutiny on the Bounty.*
- 1963 France chooses Mururoa as its nuclear testing site.
- 1966 France explodes the first nuclear bomb above ground at Mururoa.
- 1973 Infamous Quinn's Bar closes, is replaced by a shopping center.
- 1977 France grants limited self-rule to French Polynesia.
- 1984 Local autonomy statute enacted by French parliament.
- 1992 France halts nuclear testing, hurting local economy.
- 1995 Conservative French Pres. Jacques Chirac permits six more underground nuclear explosions; antinuclear riots in Papeete; Japanese boycott Tahiti tourism.
- 1996 France halts nuclear testing, signs Treaty of Rarotonga (declaring South Pacific to be nuclear-free), and tells French Polynesia to start earning its own way.
- 1997 Spurred by economic restructuring funds from Paris, several new hotels are built, Papeete waterfront is reconstructed.
- 1999 Local officials propose increased autonomy from France.
- 2000 French Polynesia becomes an "overseas country" of France, and locals assume more local control.
- 2001 Proautonomy party of Pres. Gaston Flosse wins election, continues in control of local government.

Heywood, who wrote the first English-Tahitian dictionary while awaiting court martial. Three others were hanged.

The captain of an American whaling ship that happened upon remote Pitcairn Island in 1808 was astonished when some mixed-race teenagers rowed out and greeted him not in Tahitian but in perfect English. They were the children of the mutineers, only one of whom was still alive.

Bligh collected more breadfruit on Tahiti a few years later, but his whole venture went for naught when the slaves on Jamaica insisted on rice.

THE FATAL IMPACT The discoverers brought many changes to Tahiti, starting with iron, which the Tahitians had never seen, and barter, which they had never practiced. The Tahitians figured out right away that iron was much harder than stone and shells and that they could swap pigs, breadfruit, bananas, and the affections of their young women for it. Iron cleats, spikes, and nails soon took on a value of their own, and so many of them disappeared from the *Dolphin* that Wallis finally restricted his men to the ship out of fear it would fall apart in Matavai Bay. A rudimentary form of monetary economy was introduced to Polynesia for the first time. The English word *money* soon entered the Tahitian language as *moni*.

Wars were fought hand-to-hand with sticks and clubs until the *Bounty* mutineers hiding on Tahiti loaned themselves and their guns to rival chiefs, who for the first time were able to extend their control beyond their home valleys. With the mutineers' help, Chief Pomare II came to control half of Tahiti and all of Moorea.

A much more devastating European import was diseases such as measles, influenza, pneumonia, and syphilis, to which the islanders had no resistance. Captain Cook estimated Tahiti's population at some 200,000 in 1769. By 1810 it had dropped to fewer than 8,000.

CONVERTS & CLOTHES The "opening" of the South Pacific coincided with a fundamentalist religious revival in England, and it wasn't long before the London Missionary Society (LMS) was on the scene in Tahiti to save the souls of the "heathens" discovered by Wallace and Cook. The first LMS missionaries, who arrived in the ship *Duff* in 1797, were the first Protestant missionaries to leave England for a foreign country. They chose Tahiti because there "the difficulties were least."

They toiled for 15 years before making their first convert, and even that was only accomplished with the help of Chief Pomare II. The missionaries thought he was king of Tahiti, but in reality Pomare II was locked in battle to extend his rule and to become just that. He converted to Christianity primarily to win the missionaries' support, and with it, he quickly gained control of the entire island. The people then made the easy intellectual transition from their primary god Taaroa to the missionaries' supreme being. They put on clothes and began going to church.

The Protestant missionaries had a free hand on Tahiti for almost 30 years. There were few ordained ministers among them, for most were tradesmen sent to Tahiti to teach the natives useful Western skills, which the London Missionary Society considered essential for the Tahitians' successful transition to devout, industrious Christians in the mold of working-class Englishmen and women. Some of the missionaries stayed and went into business on their own (some island cynics say they "came to do good and stayed to do well").

THE TRICKED QUEEN The Protestant monopoly ended when the first Roman Catholic priests arrived on the scene from France in the 1830s. The

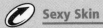 **Sexy Skin**

The United States isn't the only home of trendy tattoos. With their increasing interest in the ancient Polynesian ways, many young Tahitian men and women are getting theirs—but not with the modern electric needles used elsewhere.

Tattooing was unknown in Europe when the 18th-century explorers arrived on Tahiti. They were shocked, therefore, to find many Polynesians on Tahiti and throughout the South Pacific to be covered from face to ankle with a plethora of geometric and floral designs. In his journal, Capt. James Cook described in detail the excruciatingly painful tattoo procedure, in which natural dyes are hammered into the skin by hand. The repetitive tapping of the mallet gave rise to the Tahitian word *tatau,* which became *tattoo* in English.

Any Tahitian with plain old skin was rejected by members of the opposite sex, which may explain why members of Cook's crew were so willing to endure the torture to get theirs. At any rate, they began the tradition of the tattooed sailor.

Appalled at the sexual aspects of tattoos, the missionaries stamped out the practice on Tahiti in the early 1800s. Although the art continued in the remote Marquesas and in Samoa, by 1890 there were no tattooed natives left in the Society Islands.

When a British anthropologist undertook a study of tattooing in 1900, the only specimen he could find was in the Royal College of Surgeons. It had been worn by a Tahitian sailor, who died in England in 1816. Before he was buried, an art-loving physician removed his skin and donated it to the college.

Protestants immediately saw a threat, and in 1836 they engineered the interlopers' expulsion by Queen Pomare IV, the illegitimate daughter of Pomare II, who by then had succeeded to the throne created by her father.

When word of this outrage reached Paris, France sent a warship to Tahiti to demand a guarantee that Frenchmen would thereafter be treated as the "most favored foreigners" in Tahiti. Queen Pomare politely agreed, but as soon as the warship left Papeete, she sent a letter to Queen Victoria, asking for British protection. Britain declined to interfere, which opened the door for a Frenchman to trick several Tahitian chiefs into signing a document requesting that Tahiti be made a protectorate of France. The French were in fact interested in a South Pacific port, and when word of the document reached Paris, a ship was dispatched to Papeete. Tahiti became a French protectorate in 1842.

Unaware of the document signed by the chiefs, Queen Pomare continued to resist. Her subjects launched an armed rebellion against the French troops, who surrounded her Papeete palace and forced her to retreat to Raiatea. The fighting continued until 1846, when the last Tahitian stronghold was captured and the remnants of their guerrilla bands retreated to Tahiti Iti, the island's eastern peninsula. A monument to the fallen Tahitians now stands beside the round-island road near the airport at Faaa, the village still noted for its strong proindependence sentiment.

Giving up the struggle in 1847, the queen returned to Papeete and ruled as a figurehead until her death 30 years later. Her son, Pomare V, who liked the bottle more than the throne, ruled 3 more years, until abdicating in return for a sizable French pension for himself, his family, and his mistress. Tahiti then became a full-fledged French colony. In 1903 all of eastern Polynesia was consolidated into a single colony known as French Oceania, which it remained until 1957, when its status was changed to the overseas territory of French Polynesia.

A BLISSFUL BACKWATER   Except for periodic invasions by artists and writers, French Polynesia remained an idyllic backwater from the time France took complete possession until the early 1960s.

French painter Paul Gauguin gave up his family and his career as a Parisian stockbroker and arrived in 1891; he spent his days reproducing Tahiti's colors and people on canvas until he died in 1903 on Hiva Oa in the Marquesas Islands. Stories and novels by writers such as W. Somerset Maugham, Jack London, Robert Louis Stevenson, and Rupert Brooke added to Tahiti's romantic reputation during the early years of the 20th century. In 1932 two young Americans—Charles Nordhoff and James Norman Hall—published *Mutiny on the Bounty,* which quickly became an enormous bestseller. Three years later MGM released an even more successful movie version, with Clark Gable and Charles Laughton in the roles of Christian and Bligh, respectively.

The book and movie brought fame to Tahiti, but any plans for increased tourism were put on hold during World War II. Local partisans sided with the Free French, who gave permission for the United States to use the islands in the war against Japan. In 1942 some 6,000 U.S. sailors and marines quickly built the territory's first airstrip on Bora Bora and remained there throughout the war. A number of mixed-race Tahitians are descended from those American troops.

MOVIES & BOMBS   Even after the war, the islands were too far away and too difficult to reach to attract more than the most adventurous or wealthy travelers who arrived by ocean liner or seaplane. Then two early 1960s events brought rapid changes to most of French Polynesia.

First, Tahiti's new international airport opened at Faaa in late 1960. Shortly thereafter, Marlon Brando and a movie crew arrived to film a remake of *Mutiny on the Bounty.* This new burst of fame, coupled with the ability to reach Tahiti overnight on the new long-range jets, transformed the island into a jet-set destination, and hotel construction began in earnest.

Second, France established the *Centre d'Experimentation du Pacifique,* its nuclear testing facility in the Tuamotus, about 1,127km (700 miles) southeast of Tahiti. A huge support base was constructed on the eastern outskirts of Papeete.

Together, tourism and the nuclear testing facility brought a major boom to Tahiti almost overnight. Thousands of Polynesians flocked to Papeete to take the new construction and hotel jobs, which enabled them to earn good money and experience life in Papeete's fast lane.

In addition, some 15,000 French military personnel and civilian technicians swarmed into the territory to run the new nuclear testing facility, all of them with money and many with an inclination to spend it on the local girls. The Tahitians struck back, brawls erupted, and for a brief period in the 1960s the island experienced one of its rare moments of open hostility between the Tahitian majority and the French.

That's not to say that there weren't hard feelings all along. An independence movement had existed since the guerrilla skirmishes of the 1840s, and by the

---

Impressions

I was pleased with nothing so much as with the inhabitants. There is a mildness in the expression of their countenances which at once banishes the idea of a savage, and an intelligence which shows that they are advancing in civilization.

—Charles Darwin, 1839

1970s it forced France to choose between serious unrest or granting the territory a much larger degree of control over its internal affairs. In 1977 the French parliament created the elected Territorial Assembly with powers over the local budget. A high commissioner sent from Paris, however, retained authority over defense, foreign affairs, immigration, the police, civil service, communications, and secondary education. Additional grants of local control followed in 1984, and in 2000 the islands shifted from a an "overseas territory" of France (essentially a colony) to an "overseas country."

3 The Islanders

About 70% of French Polynesia's population of 230,000 or so are pure Polynesian. About 4% are of Asian descent (primarily Chinese), and some 14% are of mixed races. The rest are mostly French and a few other Europeans, Americans, Australians, and New Zealanders.

Members of the Polynesian majority are known as Tahitians, although persons born on the other islands do not necessarily consider themselves to be Tahitians, and sometimes gripe about this overgeneralization. They are all called Tahitians, however, because more than 70% of the territory's population lives on Tahiti and because the Polynesian language originally spoken only on Tahiti and Moorea has become the territory's second official language (French is the other).

Of the approximately 150,000 persons who live on Tahiti, some 120,000 reside in or near Papeete. No other village in the islands has a population in excess of 4,000.

THE TAHITIANS

Many Tahitians now refer to themselves as *Maohi* (the Tahitian counterpart of *Maori*), a result of an increasing awareness of their unique ancient culture. Their ancestors came to Tahiti as part of a great Polynesian migration that fanned out from Southeast Asia to much of the South Pacific (see "The Islanders" in the appendix). These early settlers brought along food plants, domestic animals, tools, and weapons. By the time Capt. Samuel Wallis arrived in 1767, Tahiti and the other islands were lush with breadfruit, bananas, taro, yams, sweet potatoes, and other crops. Most of the people lived on the fertile coastal plains and in the valleys behind them, each valley or district ruled by a chief. Wallis counted 17 chiefdoms on Tahiti alone.

TAHITIAN SOCIETY   Tahitians were highly stratified into three classes: chiefs and priests, landowners, and commoners. Among the commoners was a subclass of slaves, mostly war prisoners. One's position in society was hereditary, with primogeniture the general rule. In general, women were equal to men, although they could not act as priests.

A peculiar separate class of wandering dancers and singers, known as the *Arioi*, traveled about the Society Islands, performing ritual dances and shows—some of

Sex & the French Polynesian

The puritanical Christian missionaries who arrived in the South Pacific during early 19th century convinced the islanders that they should clothe their nearly naked bodies. They had less luck, however, when it came to sex. To the islanders, sex was as much a part of life as any other daily activity, and they uninhibitedly engaged in it with a variety of partners from adolescence until marriage.

Even today, they have a somewhat laissez-faire attitude about premarital sex. Every child, whether born in or out of wedlock, is accepted into one of the extended families that are the bedrock of Polynesian society. Mothers, fathers, grandparents, aunts, uncles, and cousins of every degree are all part of the close-knit Polynesian family. Relationships sometimes are so blurred that every adult woman within a mile is known as a child's "auntie"—even the child's mother.

Male transvestitism, homosexuality, and bisexuality are facts of life in Polynesia, where families with a shortage of female offspring will raise young boys as girls. Some of these youths grow up to be heterosexual; others become homosexual or bisexual and, often appearing publicly in women's attire, actively seek out the company of tourists. In Tahitian, these males are known as *mahus;* in Samoan, *magus;* and in Tongan, *fakaleitis.*

them sexually explicit—and living in a state of total sexual freedom. Family values were the least of their concerns; in fact, members immediately killed any children born into their clan.

The Polynesians had no written language, but their life was governed by an elaborate set of rules that would challenge modern legislators' abilities to reduce them to writing. Most of these rules were prohibitions known as *tabu,* a word now used in English as "taboo." The rules differed from one class to another.

A HIERARCHY OF GODS   The ancient Tahitians worshipped a hierarchy of gods. At its head stood Taaroa, a supreme deity known as Tangaroa in the Cook Islands and Tangaloa in Samoa. Below him, Tane was the god of all good and the friend of armies, and Tu was more or less the god of the status quo. *Mana,* or power, came down from the gods to each human, depending on his or her position in society. The highest chiefs had so much mana that they were considered godlike, if not actually descended from the gods. They lived according to special rules and spoke their own vocabularies. No one could touch them other than high-ranking priests, who cut their hair and fed them. If a high chief set foot on

Impressions
He had once landed [in the Marquesas], and found the remains of a man and a woman partly eaten. On his starting and sickening at the sight, one of Moipu's young men picked up a human foot, and provocatively staring at the stranger, grinned and nibbled at the heel.
—Robert Louis Stevenson, 1890

a plot of land, that land automatically belonged to him or her; consequently, servants carried them everywhere they went. If they uttered a word, that word became sacred and was never used again in the everyday language. When the first king of Tahiti decided to call himself Pomare, which means "night cough," the word for night—*po*—became tabu for a time. It isn't anymore.

The Tahitians worshipped their gods on *marae* (an ancient temple or meeting place) built of stones and rocks. Every family had a small marae, which served the same functions as a chapel would today, and villages and entire districts—even islands—built large marae that served not only as places of worship but also as meeting sites. Elaborate religious ceremonies were held on the large central marae. Priests prayed that the gods would come down and reside in carved tikis and other objects during the ceremonies (the objects lost all religious meaning afterward). Sacrifices were offered to the gods, sometimes including humans, most of whom were war prisoners or troublemakers. Despite the practice of human sacrifice, cannibalism apparently was never practiced on Tahiti, although it was fairly widespread in the Marquesas Islands.

The souls of the deceased were believed to be taken by the gods to Hawaiki, the homeland from which their Polynesian ancestors had come. In all Polynesian islands, Hawaiki always lay in the direction of the setting sun, and the souls departed for it from the northwest corner of each island.

THE CHINESE

The outbreak of the American Civil War in 1861 resulted in a worldwide shortage of cotton. In September 1862 an Irish adventurer named William Stewart founded a cotton plantation at Atimaono, Tahiti's only large tract of flat land. The Tahitians weren't the least bit interested in working for Stewart, so he imported a contingent of Chinese laborers. The first 329 of them arrived from Hong Kong in February 1865.

Stewart ran into difficulties, both with finances and with his workers. At one point, a rumor swept Tahiti that he had built a guillotine, practiced with it on a pig, and then executed a recalcitrant Chinese laborer. That was never proved, although a Chinese immigrant, Chim Soo, was the first person to be executed by guillotine in Tahiti. Stewart's financial difficulties, which were compounded by the drop in cotton prices after the American South resumed production after 1868, led to the collapse of his empire.

Nothing remains of Stewart's plantation at Atimaono (a golf course now occupies most of the land), but many of his Chinese laborers decided to stay. They grew vegetables for the Papeete market, saved their money, and invested in other businesses. Their descendants and subsequent immigrants from China now influence the economy far in excess of their numbers. They run nearly all of French Polynesia's grocery and general merchandise stores, which in French are called *magasins chinois,* or Chinese stores.

4 Language

French is the official language, although efforts are being made to make **Tahitian** a coequal. With the exception of some older Polynesians, everyone speaks French. **English** is also taught as a third language in many schools (especially those operated by the Chinese community), and many young Tahitians are eager to learn it, if for no other reason than to understand the lyrics of American songs, which dominate the radio airwaves in French Polynesia. Accordingly, English is widely spoken in shops, hotels, restaurants, and other businesses frequented by travelers; you're as likely to hear Europeans speaking to local residents in English as in French. Once you get off the beaten path, however, some knowledge of French or Tahitian is very helpful.

TAHITIAN PRONUNCIATION

Tahitian is still spoken in many homes in the Society Islands, although French is the predominate language used by young folk. The old local dialects are used on a daily basis in the far outer islands. Only after the Tahitians gained control over their own internal affairs in 1984 was their native tongue taught in the schools. This is one reason many proindependence Tahitians view French as a symbol of colonial control over their islands.

No Polynesian language was written until Peter Heywood jotted down a Tahitian vocabulary while awaiting trial for his part in the mutiny on the *Bounty.* The early missionaries who later translated the Bible into Tahitian decided which letters of the Roman alphabet to use to approximate the sounds of the Polynesian languages. These tended to vary from place to place. For example, they used the consonants *t* and *v* in Tahitian. In Hawaiian, which is similar, they used *k* and *w.* The actual Polynesian sounds are somewhere in between.

The consonants used in Tahitian are *f, h, m, n, p, r, t,* and *v.* There are some special rules regarding their sounds, but you'll be understood if you say them as you would in English.

The Polynesian languages, including Tahitian, consist primarily of vowel sounds, which are pronounced in the Roman fashion—that is, *ah, ay, ee, oh,* and *ou,* not *ay, ee, eye, oh,* and *you,* as in English. Almost all vowels are sounded separately. For example, Tahiti's airport is at Faaa, which is pronounced Fah-*ah*-ah, not Fah. Papeete is Pah-pay-*ay*-tay, not Pa-pee-tee. Paea is Pah-*ay*-ah.

Westerners have had their impact, however, and today some vowels are run together. Moorea, for example, technically is Moh-oh-*ray*-ah, but nearly everyone says Mo-*ray*-ah. The Punaauia hotel district on Tahiti's west coast is pronounced Poo-*nav*-i-a.

Look for *Say It in Tahitian,* by D. T. Tryon, in bookshops and hotel boutiques. This slim volume will teach you more Tahitian than you can use in one vacation.

USEFUL WORDS

To help you impress the local residents with what a really friendly tourist you are, here are a few Tahitian words you can use on them:

English	Tahitian	Pronunciation
hello	**ia orana**	ee-ah oh-*rah*-na (sounds like "your honor")
welcome	**maeva**	mah-*ay*-vah
goodbye	**parahi**	pah-*rah*-hee
good	**maitai**	*my*-tie
very good	**maitai roa**	*my*-tie-*row*-ah
thank you	**maruru**	mah-*roo*-roo
thank you very much	**maruru roa**	mah-*roo*-roo *row*-ah
good health!	**manuia**	mah-*new*-yah
woman	**vahine**	vah-*hee*-nay
man	**tane**	*tah*-nay
sarong	**pareu**	pah-*ray*-oo

continued

English	Tahitian	Pronunciation
small islet	**motu**	*moh*-too
take it easy	**hare maru**	*ha*-ray *mah*-roo
fed up	**fiu**	few

5 Visitor Information & Entry Requirements

VISITOR INFORMATION

The best source of up-to-date information in advance is **Tahiti Tourisme,** B.P. 65, Papeete, French Polynesia (℃ **50.57.00;** fax 43.66.19; www.tahiti-tourisme.com).

You can also contact Tahiti Tourisme's overseas offices:

- **United States:** 300 N. Continental Blvd., Suite 160, El Segundo, CA 90245 (℃ **310/414-8484;** fax 310/414-8490; www.gototahiti.com)
- **Australia:** 12 Ann St., Surry Hills, NSW 2010 (℃ **02/9281-6020;** fax 02/9211-6589)
- **New Zealand:** 26 Ponsonby Rd., Auckland (℃ **09/360-8880;** fax 09/360-8891; lolac@tahiti-tourisme.co.nz)
- **France:** 28, bd. Saint Germain, 75005 Paris (℃ **01/55426434;** fax 01/55426120)
- **Germany:** Bockenheimer Landstr. 45, D-60325 Frankfurt/Main (℃ **69/971-484;** fax 69/729-275; www.tahititourisme.de)
- **Italy:** Piazza Castello 3, 20 124 Milano (℃ **02/66-980317;** fax 02/66-92648)
- **Chile:** Av. 11 de Septiembre 2214, OF-116, Box 16057, Santiago 9 (℃ **251-2826;** fax 233-1787; tahiti@cmet.net)
- **Japan:** Sankyo Bldg. (no. 20) 8F-802, 3-11-5 Ildabashi, Chiyoda Ky, Tokyo 102 (℃ **3/3265-0468;** fax 3/3265-0581; tahityo@mail.fa2.so-net.ne.jp)

Once you're in Papeete, you can get maps, brochures, and other information at the **Tahiti Manava visitors bureau** (℃ **50.57.12;** www.tahiti-manava.pf), in the cruise-ship welcoming center on the waterfront on boulevard Pomare at the foot of rue Paul Gauguin. The staff members all speak English and are very helpful to visitors, especially in providing such information as when trading boats will leave for the distant island groups. Hours are 7:30am to 5pm Monday to Friday, 8am to noon on Saturday and holidays.

Be sure to pick up the *Tahiti Beach Press,* a free weekly English-language newspaper that lists special events and current activities. Copies also are available in most hotel lobbies.

Tips **Converting in Your Head**

Local residents think of 100CFP as US$1 and often express prices that way to visitors. If the price of something is 1,000CFP, they might say it costs $10. Using their method, you can make a quick conversion without a calculator by thinking of 100CFP as $1, 500CFP as $5, 1,000CFP as $10, and so on. That is, drop the last two zeros, then add or subtract the percentage difference between the actual rate and 100CFP. In the case of $1 = 135CFP, for example, you would subtract 25%.

The CFP & the U.S. Dollar

As a rule of thumb, $1 = approximately 135CFP, is the rate of exchange used to calculate the U.S. dollar prices given in this book. This rate has fluctuated widely and may not be the same when you visit. Therefore, use the following table only as a guide.

CFP	US$	CFP	US$
100	75¢	1,000	7.50
150	1.12	1,500	11.25
200	1.50	2,000	15.00
300	2.25	3,000	22.50
400	3.00	4,000	30.00
500	3.75	5,000	37.50
600	4.50	6,000	45.00
700	5.25	7,000	52.50
800	6.00	8,000	60.00
900	6.75	9,000	67.50
1,000	7.50	10,000	75.00

Low-budget travelers can request lists of all of French Polynesia's less expensive "unclassified" hotels, pensions, and campgrounds. These are compiled by island, so ask for the lists applicable to your specific destinations. Most owners of these establishments don't speak English, so some French on your part will be very helpful if you stay with them.

Local tourism committees have information booths on Moorea, Bora Bora, and Huahine.

ENTRY REQUIREMENTS

All visitors except French nationals are required to have a **passport** that will be valid for six months beyond their intended stay, as well as a **return or ongoing ticket.** French citizens must bring their national identity cards.

Citizens and nationals of the United States, Canada, New Zealand, Argentina, Bermuda, Brunei, South Korea, Croatia, Hungary, Japan, Malaysia, Mexico, Poland, the Czech Republic, Singapore, Slovakia, Slovenia, Uruguay, Bolivia, Chile, Costa Rica, Equator, Estonia, Guatemala, Honduras, Latvia, Lithuania, Nicaragua, Panama, Paraguay, and El Salvador may visit for up to 1 month without a visa.

Nationals of Australia, the European Union countries, Belgium, Luxembourg, Monaco, Switzerland, Andorra, the Vatican, Cyprus, Iceland, Liechtenstein, Malta, Norway, and St. Martin can stay up to 3 months without a visa.

Citizens from all other countries (including foreign nationals residing in the United States) must get a visa before leaving home. French embassies and consulates overseas can issue visas valid for stays of between 1 and 3 months, and they will forward applications for longer visits to the local immigration department in Papeete. *Note:* Such visas do not entitle you to visit Tahiti without being stamped "*valable pour la Polynésie Française*"—valid for French Polynesia.)

In the United States, the **Embassy of France** is at 4102 Reservoir Road NW, Washington, DC 20007 (© **202/944-6000;** www.info-france-usa.org), and there are French consulates in Boston, Chicago, Detroit, Houston, Los Angeles, New York, Miami, San Francisco, and New Orleans.

Your initial visa can be extended to 6 months (in 3-month increments) if you still have your return air ticket and sufficient funds, aren't employed in French Polynesia, and have stayed out of trouble. Applications for extensions must be made at the immigration office in the Tahiti-Faaa International Airport terminal building. Work and residency permits are difficult to obtain unless you are a French citizen.

No **vaccinations** are required unless you are coming from a yellow fever, plague, or cholera area.

Customs allowances are 200 cigarettes or 50 cigars, 2 liters of spirits or 2 liters of wine, 50 grams of perfume, 2 still cameras and 10 rolls of unexposed film, one video camera, one cassette player, and sports and camping equipment. Narcotics, dangerous drugs, weapons, ammunition, and copyright infringements (that is, pirated video- and audiotapes) are prohibited. Pets and plants are subject to stringent regulations.

6 Money

French Polynesia uses the **French Pacific franc (CFP)**, whose value is pegged to the European euro at a rate of **1 = 119.33CFP.** The CFP comes in coins up to 100CFP and in colorful notes ranging from 500CFP into the millions.

The value of the CFP against the U.S. dollar fluctuates. I have used the rate of **$1 = 135CFP** (or 100CFP = about U.S. 75¢) to compute the equivalent U.S. dollar prices given in parentheses after the CFP prices in this book.

No decimals are used with Pacific franc units, so prices at first can seem even more staggering than they really are.

Don't bargain in French Polynesia, for to haggle over a retail price is to offend the integrity of the seller, especially if he or she is a Polynesian.

HOW TO GET LOCAL CURRENCY Banque de Polynésie, Banque Socredo, and Banque de Tahiti have offices on the main islands. For specific locations and banking hours, see "Fast Facts" in the following chapters. All banks charge at least 450CFP ($3.25) per transaction to cash traveler's checks, regardless of the amount, so you should change large amounts each time to minimize this bite.

You can obtain cash advances by using your Visa and MasterCard credit and check cards at automatic teller machines (ATMs) at Tahiti-Faaa International Airport and at Banque Socredo and Banque de Tahiti offices on Tahiti, Moorea, Bora Bora, Huahine, and Raiatea. The simple operating instructions are given in both French and English. As noted in chapter 2, by using my Visa check card at an ATM, I got more than the exchange rate for traveler's checks, and I avoided the bank's service charge. You will need your personal identification number (PIN). See "Money" in chapter 2 for more information.

Readers' Recommendation: Low-Season Bargains

Because of the low season, we were upgraded at the Sofitel Coralia Ia Ora in Moorea and also at Le Meridien Bora Bora. Travelers wanting a bargain should consider coming here in the off-season of February/March.

—Hal and Dorsey Holappa, Lynnfield, Mass.

You will probably get a better rate if you change your money in French Polynesia rather than before leaving home.

CREDIT CARDS   MasterCard and Visa are widely accepted on the most visited islands, and American Express cards are taken by most hotels and car-rental firms and by many restaurants. Don't count on using your Diners Club card except at the major hotels. Discover cards are not accepted in the islands.

7 When to Go—Climate, Holidays & Events

There is no bad time to go to French Polynesia, but some periods are better than others. The weather is at its best—comfortable and dry—in July and August, but this is the prime vacation and festival season, so book your air tickets and hotel rooms as far in advance as possible. For the best combination of weather and availability of hotel rooms, the months of May, June, September, and October are best.

CLIMATE

Tahiti and the rest of the Society Islands have a balmy tropical climate. November through April is the summer **wet season,** when the average maximum daily temperature is 86°F (30°C) and rainy periods can be expected. Nighttime lows are about 72°F (22°C). May through October is the austral winter **dry season,** when midday maximum temperatures average a delightful 82°F (28°C), with early morning lows of 68°F (20°C) often making a blanket necessary. Some winter days, especially on the south side of the islands, can seem quite chilly when a strong wind blows from Antarctica. Tropical showers can pass overhead at any time of the year. Humidity averages between 77% and 80% throughout the year.

Average Daytime Temperatures in Tahiti

	Jan	Feb	Mar	Apr	May	June	July	Aug	Sept	Oct	Nov	Dec
Temp °F	80.6	80.8	81.3	80.8	79.5	77.4	76.5	76.3	77	78.1	79.3	79.9
Temp °C	27	27.1	27.4	27.1	26.4	25.2	24.7	24.6	25	25.6	26.3	26.6

The central and northern Tuamotus have somewhat warmer temperatures and less rainfall. Since there are no mountains to create cooling night breezes, they can experience desertlike hot periods between November and April. The Marquesas are closer to the equator, and temperatures and humidity tend to be slightly higher than in Tahiti. The climate in the Austral and Gambier islands is more temperate.

French Polynesia is on the far eastern edge of the South Pacific cyclone (hurricane) belt, and storms can occur between November and March.

PUBLIC HOLIDAYS

Public holidays are New Year's Day, Good Friday and Easter Monday, Ascension Day (40 days after Easter), Whitmonday (the seventh Mon after Easter), Missionary Day (Mar 5), Labor Day (May 1), Pentecost Monday (the first Mon in June), Bastille Day (July 14), Internal Autonomy Day (Sept 8), All Saints Day (Nov 1), Armistice Day (Nov 11), and Christmas Day.

From a visitor's standpoint, July is the busiest month because of the *Heiva i Tahiti* festival (see "French Polynesia Calendar of Events," below). Hotels on the outer islands are at their fullest during August, the traditional French vacation month, when many Papeete residents head for the outer islands to get away from it all.

Tahiti Tourisme publishes an annual list of the territory's leading special events on its website (see "Visitor Information & Entry Requirements," above).

FRENCH POLYNESIA CALENDAR OF EVENTS

January

Chinese New Year. Parade, musical performances, demonstrations of martial arts, Chinese dances, and handcrafts. Between mid-January and mid-February.

February

Tahiti Nui Marathon. Prizes worth up to $15,000 entice some of the world's best runners to trot 42km (26 miles) around Moorea. Second Saturday.

March

Arrival of First Missionaries. Gatherings on Tahiti commemorate the anniversary of the arrival of the London Missionary Society. March 5.

May

Te Tana Oa Nui Hoe. Traditional outrigger canoes race across the sea between the Marquesas Islands. First weekend.

Tahiti Pro WQS. World-class surfers compete on the big waves off Teuhupo'o on Tahiti Iti. First full week.

June

Tahiti Cup Regatta. Cruising yachts sail among Raiatea, Tahaa, Huahine, and Bora Bora. First 10 days.

Miss Tahiti, Miss *Heiva,* Miss Moorea, and Miss Bora Bora Contests. Candidates from around the islands vie to win the titles. Among the biggest annual events on outer islands. Early to mid-June.

Heiva Vaevae. A parade along bd. Pomare in Papeete celebrates the 1984 French law granting local autonomy. June 29.

July

Heiva i Tahiti ★★★. This is the festival to end all festivals in French Polynesia. It was originally a celebra-tion of Bastille Day on July 14, but the islanders have extended the shindig into a month-long blast (it is commonly called *Tiurai,* the Tahitian word for July). They pull out all the stops, with parades, outrigger canoe races, javelin-throwing contests, fire walking, games, carnivals, festivals, and reenactments of ancient Polynesian ceremonies at restored marae. Highlight for visitors: An extraordinarily colorful contest to determine the best Tahitian dancing troupe for the year—never do the hips gyrate more vigorously. Airline and hotel reservations are difficult to come by during July, so book early and take your written confirmation with you. Last weekend in June through July.

August

Mini Fêtes. Winning dancers and singers from the *Heiva i Tahiti* perform at hotels on the outer islands. All month.

Tahiti International Golf Open. Local and international golfers vie at Atimaono Golf Course, Tahiti. Midmonth.

September

Tourism Days. Islanders pay homage to overseas visitors, who get discounts. Last weekend.

October

Aitoman (Iron Man) Moorea Tri-athalon. Top-shape athletes swim, bike, and run on Moorea. First Saturday.

Hawaiki Nui Va'a. Local and international outrigger canoe teams race from Tahiti to the Leeward Islands. Third weekend.

Tahiti Carnival. Parades, floats, and much partying on the Papeete waterfront. Last week.

Tips **The Best Seats & Something to Eat**

For the best views of the islands, try to sit on the left side of the Air Tahiti aircraft when you're flying from Papeete to the outer islands. Sit on the right side when returning to Tahiti. And make sure you have your camera and a lot of film at the ready.

Most hotel dining rooms open for breakfast at 7am and close by 9:30am, so if you're catching an early morning flight to another island, stock up on some munchies and something to drink the night before, and bring them along on the plane.

November

All Saints Day. Flowers are sold everywhere to families who put them on graves after whitewashing the tombstones. November 1.

December

Tiare Tahiti Flower Festival. Everyone on the streets of Papeete and in the hotels receives a *tiare Tahiti,* the fragrant gardenia that is indigenous to Tahiti. Dinner and dancing later. First week in December.

New Year's Eve. A big festival in downtown Papeete leads territory-wide celebrations. December 31.

8 Getting There & Getting Around

GETTING TO FRENCH POLYNESIA

Air New Zealand, Air France, Air Tahiti Nui, Corsair Airlines, and **Hawaiian Airlines** link Tahiti to North America. **Qantas Airways** flies between Sydney and Tahiti. See "Getting There & Getting Around" in chapter 2 for details.

All arrive at **Tahiti-Faaa International Airport** on Tahiti's northwest corner, about 11km (7 miles) from downtown Papeete. See "Arriving & Getting Around" in chapter 4 for information about the airport and local transportation on Tahiti.

GETTING AROUND
BY PLANE

TO MOOREA   Air Tahiti (© **800/553-3477** in the U.S., or 86.42.42 in Papeete; fax 86.40.69; www.airtahiti-vt.com) has daily morning flights between Papeete and Moorea and evening flights which link up with Air Tahiti Nui arrivals from Los Angeles. The daytime flights go on to Huahine and Bora Bora. Air Tahiti charges about 3,400 CFP ($25) one way, 6,400CFP ($47) round-trip, but you get to fly in its comfortable 42- or 72-seat turbo-prop planes. Air Tahiti's terminal is on the west end of Tahiti-Faaa International Airport—that's to the right as you exit Customs.

Air Moorea (© **86.41.41;** fax 86.42.99) provides shuttle service between Tahiti-Faaa International Airport and Temae Airport on Moorea. Its small planes (and I do mean small) leave Faaa on the hour and half hour daily from 6 to 9am, then on the hour from 10am to 3pm, and on the hour and half-hour again from 4 to 6pm. Each plane turns around on Moorea and flies back to Tahiti. There are no flights after dark or before dawn. The fare is about 2,700CFP ($20) each way. Air Moorea's little terminal is on the east end of Tahiti-Faaa International Airport (that's to the left as you come out of Customs). Air Moorea will take you from the airport to your Moorea hotel for 500CFP ($3.75) each way.

Pack carefully, for the **baggage limit** on both of these airlines is 20 kilograms (44 lb.) per person if you're connecting with an international flight within 7 days, and it's 10 kilograms (22 lb.) per person if you're not. You will face a substantial extra charge for excess weight. You can leave your extra belongings in the storage room at your hotel or at Tahiti-Faaa International Airport (see "Arriving & Getting Around" in chapter 4).

TO THE OTHER ISLANDS   Air Tahiti (*©* **800/553-3477** in the U.S., or 86.42.42 in Papeete; fax 86.40.99; www.airtahiti.pf) provides service to more than 40 islands beyond Moorea. It has daily flights between Papeete and all the main islands, at least two daily to and from Bora Bora. Nevertheless, it's wise to reserve your seats as early as possible.

Air Tahiti's central downtown walk-in reservations office on boulevard Pomare (*©* **43.39.39**) is on the second level (the French call it the first floor, or *premier étage)* of Fare Tony, the building just west of the Vaima Centre. Its airport office is in the west end of Tahiti-Faaa International Airport.

One-way adult fares on the usual visitor's circuit (double the fare for round-trips between any two islands, half them for children) are as follows:

Papeete to Moorea	3,400CFP ($25)
Moorea to Huahine	12,400CFP ($92)
Huahine to Raiatea	5,000CFP ($37)
Raiatea to Bora Bora	5,800CFP ($43)
Bora Bora to Papeete	14,000CFP ($104)
Bora Bora to Rangiroa	23,300CFP ($173)
Rangiroa to Papeete	15,300CFP ($113)

Visitors can save by buying **passes** over the popular routes. For example, Air Tahiti's Bora Bora Pass permits travel over the popular Papeete-Moorea-Huahine-Raiatea–Bora Bora–Papeete route for 30,500CFP ($226), which is 10,100CFP ($75) less than the full adult fares. Rangiroa, Tikihau, and Manihi can be added to the pass, for a total of 45,500CFP ($337). Other passes permit travel to the Marquesas and Austral islands. All travel must be completed within 28 days of the first flight, and other restrictions apply.

An alternative to taking Air Tahiti's scheduled flights is to charter a plane and pilot from **Air Moorea, Air Tahiti,** or **Wan Air** (*©* **85.55.54;** fax 85.55.56; www.wanair.pf). **Heli-Pacific** (*©* **85.668.00;** fax 85.68.08) and **Heli-Inter Polynesia** (*©* **81.99.00;** fax 81.99.99) both charter helicopters and pilots. When the total cost is split among a large enough group, the price per person could be less than airfare on a commercial airline.

BY FERRY TO MOOREA

Three companies run several fast ferries from the Papeete waterfront to Moorea. The *Arimiti* (*©* **42.88.88** on Tahiti, or 56.31.10 on Moorea) and the *Moorea Jet* (*©* **42.37.42** on Tahiti, or 56.54.65 on Moorea) both land at Vaiare, a small bay on Moorea's east coast. They take about 30 minutes to cover the 19km (12 miles) between the islands. The *Ono Ono* (*©* **45.35.35**) takes a bit longer, but it goes to Paopao village in Cook's Bay. Fares are about 1,100CFP ($8) each way.

All are sleek, air-conditioned catamarans with bars that sell snacks and libations. In general, one or another of them departs Papeete about 6:25am, 7am, 9am, noon, 1:30pm, 3pm, and 5pm, with extra voyages on Friday and Monday (Moorea is a popular weekend retreat for Papeete residents).

Buses meet all ferries except the 1:30pm departures from Papeete to take you to your hotel or other destination on Moorea for 200CFP ($1.50) per person.

From Vaiare, they take about 1 hour to reach the Club Med area on the oppo-site side of Moorea.

BY SHIP TO THE OUTER ISLANDS

Several cargo ships journey to the Leeward, Tuamotu, Marquesas, Gambier, and Austral groups, including the excellent cargo/cruise vessel *Aranui* (see "Seeing the Islands by Cruise Ship & Yacht," below).

Two cargo ferries, the **Vaeanu** (© **42.25.35;** fax 41.24.34) and the **Hawaiki Nui** (© **45.23.24;** fax 45.24.44), make three voyages a week between Motu Uta in Papeete and Huahine, Raiatea, Tahaa, and Bora Bora. They depart Papeete about 5pm, arrive at Huahine about 3am the next morning, and then go on to the other Leeward Islands. Both have passenger cabins.

Boats to the outer islands keep schedules in terms of weeks or even months, not days. Their primary mission is trade—retail goods for fresh produce and copra (dried coconut meat)—with passenger traffic a secondary source of income. Accordingly, they leave an island when the cargo is loaded, not neces-sarily when their schedules dictate. They also are at the mercy of the weather and mechanical breakdowns.

There is a charm to riding these small ships. The sea is an incredible shade of royal blue, and the sun setting through the clouds splits the horizon into colors spanning the spectrum. Your fellow passengers are the salt of the Polynesian earth, with straw sleeping mats and cardboard suitcases. On the other hand, many pas-sengers (perhaps even you) spend the entire voyage with seasick heads slung over the rail. You often experience choking diesel fumes, and you seldom escape the acrid stench coming from sacks of copra. Your shipmates may include cock-roaches seemingly large enough to steal the watch off your wrist, and some of the cabins—if you can get one—could pass for outhouses. In other words, you need lots of flexible time, tolerance born of adversity, and the patience of Job.

If you're still interested, ask Tahiti Tourisme for a list of interisland schooners, their fares, and approximate schedules. Purchase tickets at least a day in advance of scheduled departure. Make sure you have obtained a 3-month visa to stay in French Polynesia. I once met a young Australian who took a boat to Rapa in the Austral Islands, expecting to return with it in a few weeks to Papeete. The ship broke down and went into the repair yard on Tahiti, stranding him for 3 months on Rapa, where he survived on coconuts and the generosity of the local residents.

BY RENTAL CAR

Avis and Hertz have rental-car agencies (*locations de voiture* in French) on Tahiti, Moorea, and Bora Bora. Europcar is present on all the main islands. See "Get-ting Around" in following chapters for details.

A valid **driver's license** from your home country will be honored in French Polynesia.

Service stations are fairly common on Tahiti, but only in the main villages on the other islands. Expect to pay about four times as much for a gallon of gaso-line as in the United States.

DRIVING RULES   **Driving is on the right-hand side of the road,** as in North America and continental Europe.

All persons in a vehicle **must wear seat belts.**

Helmets (*casques,* pronounced "casks") are mandatory if you drive or ride on a scooter or motorbike.

Speed limits are 40kmph (24 mph) in the towns and villages and 80kmph (48 mph) on the open road. The limit is 60kmph (36 mph) for 8km (5 miles) on either side of Papeete. The general rule on the Rte. 5 freeway between Papeete and Punaauia, on Tahiti's west coast, is 90kmph (54 mph), although there is one short stretch going down a hill where it's officially 110kmph (66 mph).

Drivers on the main rural roads have the right of way. In Papeete, priority is given to vehicles entering from the right side, unless an intersection is marked with a traffic light or a stop or yield sign. This rule differs from those of most other countries, so be especially careful at all intersections, especially those marked with a *priorité à droite* (priority to the right) sign, and give way accordingly.

Drivers are required to **stop for pedestrians** on marked crosswalks, but on busy streets, don't assume that drivers will politely stop for you when you try to cross.

Traffic lights in Papeete may be difficult to see, since some of them are on the far left-hand side of the street instead of on the driver's side of the intersection.

9 Seeing the Islands by Cruise Ship & Yacht

The Society Islands are ideal grounds for cruise ships, since it's barely an hour's steam from Tahiti to Moorea, half a day's voyage on to Huahine, and less than 2 hours each among Huahine, Raiatea, Tahaa, and Bora Bora. That means the ships spend most days and nights at anchor in lovely lagoons, allowing passengers plenty of time to explore the islands and play in the water.

Likewise, these are wonderful places to charter a yacht and set sail on your own. Major yacht companies are based in Raiatea, which shares a lagoon with Tahaa, the only French Polynesian island which can be circumnavigated entirely within a protective reef. From Raiatea or Tahaa, short blue-water cruises will take you to Huahine in one direction, to Bora Bora in the other.

TAKING A CRUISE

As we went to press, two 700-passenger ships formerly operated in the islands by the now-defunct Renaissance Cruise Lines as the *R3 and R4,* had been taken over by **Princess Cruises** (② **800/774-6237** or 904/527-6660; www.princess-cruises.com), which announced plans for one-week cruises through the islands from Papeete. One will operate full time in French Polynesia; the other will sail the islands for four months out of each year.

THE *ARANUI* ✶✶✶

The working cargo ship *Aranui* is the most interesting way to visit the out-of-the-way Marquesas Islands. Comfortably outfitted for 90 passengers, this 103m (343-ft.) freighter makes regular 15- to 16-day round-trips from Papeete to 6 of the 10 Marquesas Islands, with stops on the way at Rangiroa and Takapoto in the Tuamotus. While the crew loads and unloads the ship's cargo, passengers spend their days ashore experiencing the islands and islanders. Among the activities: picnicking on beaches, snorkeling, visiting villages, and exploring archaeological sites. Experts on Polynesian history and culture accompany some voyages.

Accommodation is in five air-conditioned deluxe cabins with their own showers and toilets, 40 air-conditioned first-class cabins (some of which share showers and toilets), and an air-conditioned dormitory-style cabin with 22 bunk beds (that also share showers and toilets). The ship has a restaurant and bar, boutique, library, video lounge, and swimming pool.

Fares for the complete voyage range from about $1,980 for a dormitory bunk to $3,950 for deluxe cabins. All meals are included, but you have to pay your own bar bill and your airfare to and from French Polynesia.

Tips Getting Online

If you brought a laptop, you can connect to MANA Internet, the territory's sole Internet provider, directly from your hotel room—provided that it has a phone, of course. The charge is 35CFP (26¢) per minute for access time and the cost of the local call is also billed to your room. It's not cheap, but it is a convenient way to send and receive e-mail. Here's how to set up your computer in Windows 95, 98, 2000, or Me:

- Double click **My Computer** on your Desktop.
- Double click **Dial-Up Networking.**
- Double click **Make New Connection.**
- Name the new connection anything you want ("Tahiti" will do).
- Click **Configure** and set the maximum speed of your modem to not more 57,600kbps. Click **OK.**
- Leave the Area Code box blank and type **0,368888** as the Telephone Number (0 is the number you dial to reach an outside line in all hotels). Don't change the Country box. Click **OK.**
- After you have created your new Tahiti connection, double-click **My Computer, Dial-Up Networking,** and the icon for your new connection. Click **Connect.** When the connection is made, enter *both* your name and your password as **ANONYMOUS,** in all capital letters.
- From then on, you can double-click **My Computer, Dial-Up Networking,** your Tahiti connection icon, and **Connect.** After the connection is made, load your browser, and you're online.

For more information or reservations, contact **Compagnie Polynésienne du Transport Maritime,** B.P. 220, Papeete, Tahiti (© **42.62.40;** fax 43.48.89; www.aranui.com). The company has an office in San Francisco (© **800/ 972-7268** or 650/574-2575; fax 650/574-6881).

THE *PAUL GAUGUIN* ★★★

Its interior trimmed with glistening chrome and polished teak, the sleek luxury liner *Paul Gauguin* spends most of its year making 7-day cruises through the Society Islands. Twice a year it goes on 2-week voyages to the Tuamotu and Marquesas islands, and it may even steam up to Hawaii and back during the Christmas season.

Built in 1997, this 156.5m (513-ft.), 318-passenger vessel has a crew of 206, including French officers and an international hospitality staff. Adding local flavor, eight young Tahitian women known as *Les Gauguins* serve as guides and stage cultural shows in the ship's semicircular Grand Salon entertainment venue.

The *Paul Gauguin* spends its time at anchor: one day at Huahine or Tahaa, one at Raiatea, and two each at Bora Bora and Moorea, in that order. Its two swift tenders will whisk you ashore for the same excursions described elsewhere in this book, but there's plenty to keep you occupied without leaving the ship. From a stern platform, you can swim, snorkel, dive, water ski, or kayak in the lagoons. There's even an onboard PADI dive certification program. Up on the top deck, you can order lunch or a drink from the al fresco Le Grill, grab the rays on the sun deck, take a dip in the swimming pool, or shoot a round of minigolf. Inside, there's a fully equipped spa, a library of books and videos, a board games room, a casino with roulette and blackjack, and boutiques offering black pearls and perfumes, among other high-end merchandise.

Before dinner, you can take in the view over a glass of fine wine and a Cuban stogie from the comfy, air-conditioned Connoisseurs Club. Superb French and Italian cuisines are provided in the formal L'Etoile and relaxed La Veranda dining rooms, both with big windows wrapping around the ship's fantail. After dinner, you can dance the night away at La Palette nightclub.

All of the ship's seven suites and about half of its 152 staterooms have private verandas or balconies (the least expensive lower-deck units have windows or portholes). All are luxuriously appointed with minibars, TVs and VCRs, direct-dial phones, and marble bathrooms with full-size tubs. Most have queen-size beds, although some have two twins. The staff provides 24-hour room service.

Per-person double-occupancy fares for the 1-week Society Islands cruises range from $3,095 to $5,695 for staterooms, and from $6,995 to $10,395 for suites. Add about $1,000 for single occupancy. Fares include all meals, wine with lunch and dinner, soft drinks, most onboard activities, and airfare to and from Los Angeles.

For information and reservations, contact **Radisson Seven Seas Cruises,** 600 Corporate Dr., Suite 410, Fort Lauderdale, FL 33334 (© **800/333-3333** or 904/776-6123 in the U.S., 54.51.00 in Papeete; www.rssc.com).

THE *WIND SONG*

Just before this book went to press, Windstar Cruises announced plans to reposition its four-masted sail cruiser *Wind Song* to Tahiti, where it would make 1-week voyages from Papeete to Huahine, Raiatea, Tahaa, Bora Bora, and Moorea. It was to be a return to paradise for this luxurious, 132m-long (440-ft.) ship, which operated here during the early 1990s. She carries up to 148 passengers in 74 spacious cabins. You won't get your hands chaffed hauling lines, however, for all sails are set mechanically. For more information contact **Windstar Cruises,** 300 Elliott Ave. West, Seattle, WA 98119 (© **800/258-7245** or 206/281-3535 in the U.S.; fax: 206/286-3229; www.windstarcruises.com).

THE *HAUMANA*

More along the lines of Blue Lagoon Cruises in Fiji (see chapter 10), the 33.5m (110-ft.), 42-passenger catamaran *Haumana* makes 7-night cruises among Bora Bora, Raiatea, Tahaa, and Huahine. It's considerably smaller and less luxurious than the other ships plying the Society Islands.

The unpretentious *Haumana* goes into shallow parts of the lagoons for swimming and snorkeling excursions, shark feeding, and even for breakfasting one morning while seated at tables waist deep in the Tahaa lagoon. Other activities include visits to villages and a vanilla plantation. Scuba diving can be arranged at an extra cost. On board, the crew of 14 provides handcraft demonstrations.

A main deck restaurant serves international fare, and a comfortable indoor lounge and fantail bar on the second deck supply evening entertainment and libation.

Each of the 21 air-conditioned cabins has large windows or portholes, a queen bed, a sofa or settee, a minibar, a TV, a VCR, a phone, and a shower-only bathroom with a hair dryer. Although they have the largest windows, the cabins along the front of the vessel are rather cramped.

The cruises cost about $2,000 per person double occupancy, including meals, tours, and excursions. Add about $500 for single occupancy.

Fun Fact Phoning Like a Local

In French Polynesia, the local phone numbers are presented as three two-digit numbers—for example, 42.29.17. If you ask someone there for a number, he or she will say it like this: *"quarante-deux, vingt-neuf, dix-sept"* in French or "forty-two, twenty-nine, seventeen" in English.

For information or reservations, contact **Bora Bora Pearl Cruises,** B.P. 9254, 98715 Papeete (C **43.43.03;** fax 45.10.65; www.boraborapearlcruises.com).

CHARTERING A YACHT

Boating enthusiasts can charter their own yachts—with or without skipper and crew—and knock around some of the French Polynesian islands as the wind and their own desires dictate.

The Moorings ★★★, a well-respected yacht charter company based in Florida (C **800/535-7289** or 727/535-1446; www.moorings.com), operates a fleet of sailboats based at **Apooti Marina** on Raiatea's northern coast (C **66. 35.93;** fax 66.20.94; moorings@mail.pf). That's a few minutes' sail to Tahaa, and depending on the wind, Bora Bora and Huahine are easy blue-water trips away. Depending on the size of the boat—they range from 11m to 15m (36 ft.–50 ft.) in length—and the season, daily bareboat rates (that is, you rent the "bare" boat without skipper or crew) range from about $285 to $1,185 per vessel. Provisions are extra. The agency will check you out to make sure you and your party can handle sailboats of these sizes; otherwise, you must pay extra for a skipper.

Stardust Yacht Charters (C **800/772-3500** or 207/253-5400 in the U.S., 66.23.18 on Raiatea; fax 66.23.19; www.sunyachts.com) also has a fleet of 11m to 15m (37 ft.–51 ft.) yachts based at Faaroa Bay on Raiatea. Its bareboat rates range from about $1,900 to $6,440 a week per boat, depending on size and season, plus provisions, skipper, and cook if you need them.

The French-owned **Tahiti Yacht Charter,** B.P. 608, Papeete (C **45.04.00;** fax 45.76.00; tyc@mail.pf), has 11m to 14m (35 ft.–48 ft.) yachts based at Papeete. It designs cruises throughout the territory, including day trips to Tetiaroa and lengthy voyages to the Tuamotus and Marquesas. So does **Archipel Croisiers,** B.P. 1160, Papetoai, Moorea (C **56.36.39;** fax 56.35.87; www.archipels.com).

SUGGESTED ITINERARIES

If You Have 1 Day

Some visitors have a 1-day layover in Tahiti between flights. If this is your case, spend at least half of it on Moorea. Head into downtown Papeete for breakfast and an early morning look at the Municipal Market. Take the 9am ferry to Moorea. Tour Moorea (including a trip to the Belvédère overlook) by rental car or scooter, or simply by riding the bus from the ferry landing to the Club Méditerranée area. Return to Papeete in the afternoon. Make a walking tour of downtown, with some shopping thrown in. In the late afternoon make your way to the Tahiti Beachcomber Parkroyal for sunset over Moorea from the hotel's Le Lotus restaurant and bar. Catch a Tahitian dance show in the evening.

If You Have 2 Days

Day 1 Take an early morning ferry to Moorea. Drive or take a tour around the island, including the Belvédère overlook. After lunch and some beach time, have a sunset drink at the Club Bali Hai, where the views of Cook's Bay are unparalleled. Overnight on Moorea.

Day 2 Return to Papeete on an early ferry or flight and go straight to the *Marché Municipale* (Municipal Market). After breakfast take a walking tour of downtown. Have lunch, and then spend the afternoon on a tour around Tahiti, either by car or with an organized tour. End the day by watching the sunset over Moorea from a hotel on the west coast, then attending a Tahitian dance show.

If You Have 7 Days

Day 1 & 2 Tour Tahiti and Moorea, as suggested above.

Day 3 Spend an extra day on Moorea.

Day 4 Fly to Huahine. Tour the island and its historical maraes in the afternoon. Spend some time looking around the village of Fare; it has lots of old South Seas charm.

Day 5 Fly to Raiatea. Tour the island, including the great Taputapuatea marae, and Uturoa, French Polynesia's second-largest town.

Day 6 Fly to Bora Bora. Tour the island and take a trip on the lagoon.

Day 7 Return to Papeete for your flight home.

 FAST FACTS: **French Polynesia**

The following facts apply to French Polynesia in general. For more specific information, see the "Fast Facts" sections in chapters 4 through 7.

American Express The territory's one full-service representative is in Papeete. See "Fast Facts" in chapter 4."

Bookstores Only Tahiti and Moorea have well-stocked bookstores (see "Fast Facts" in chapters 4 and 5). Many hotel boutiques sell colorful picture books of the islands.

Business Hours Although many shops in downtown Papeete stay open over the lunch period, general shopping and business hours are from 7:30 to 11:30am and from 2 to 5pm Monday to Friday, 8am to noon on Saturday. In addition to regular hours, most grocery stores also are open from 2 to 6pm Saturday and from 6 to 8am on Sunday.

Camera/Film Photographic film and color-print processing are widely available. You can bring 10 rolls with you duty-free.

Climate See "When to Go—Climate, Holidays & Events," earlier in this chapter.

Clothing Evening attire for men is usually a shirt and slacks; and for women, a long, brightly colored dress (slacks or long skirts help to keep biting sand flies away from your ankles). Women sunbathe topless at most beaches. Shorts are acceptable during the day almost everywhere. Outside Papeete, the standard attire for women is the colorful wraparound sarong known in Tahitian as a *pareu*, which can be tied in a multitude of ways into dresses, blouses, or skirts.

Drug Laws Possession and use of dangerous drugs and narcotics are subject to heavy fines and jail terms.

Electricity Electrical power is 220 volts, 50 cycles, and the plugs are the French kind with two round, skinny prongs. Most hotels have 110-volt outlets for shavers only, so you will need a converter and adapter plugs for your other appliances. Some hotels, especially those on the outer islands, have their own generators, so ask at the reception desk what voltage is supplied.

E-mail The government controls all communications, so no overseas Internet service provider has a local access number here. You can go to cyber-cafes on Tahiti, Moorea, Raiatea, Bora Bora, and Rangiroa (see "Fast Facts" in chapters 4 through 7), and many hotel and resort staffs can check it for you. Getting online is easy if you bring a laptop (see the box "Getting Online," below).

Embassies/Consulates The nearest full-service U.S. embassy is in Suva, Fiji (see chapter 9). Australia, Austria, Belgium, Chile, Denmark, Finland, Germany, Italy, Monaco, New Zealand, Norway, the Netherlands, South Korea, Sweden, and the United Kingdom have honorary consulates in Papeete. Tahiti Tourisme has their phone numbers (see "Visitor Information & Entry Requirements," earlier in this chapter).

Emergencies/Police If you are in a hotel, contact the staff. Otherwise, the emergency **police** phone number is © **17** throughout the territory.

Etiquette Even though many women go topless and wear the skimpiest of bikini bottoms at the beach, the Tahitians have a sense of propriety similar to what you find in any Western nation. Don't offend them by engaging in behavior that would not be permissible at home.

Firearms All weapons except bush knives (machetes) and BB guns are prohibited, but don't try to bring either into the territory.

Gambling You can play "Lotto," the French national lottery.

Healthcare Highly qualified specialists practice on Tahiti, where some clinics possess state-of-the-art diagnostic and treatment equipment; nevertheless, public hospitals tend to be crowded with local residents, who get their care for free. Most visitors use private doctors or clinics. English-speaking physicians are on call by larger hotels. Each of the smaller islands has at least one infirmary (see "Fast Facts" in chapters 4 through 7). American health insurance plans are not recognized, so remember to get receipts at the time of treatment.

Hitchhiking Thumbing rides is possible in the rural parts of Tahiti and on the outer islands. Women traveling alone should be extremely cautious.

Insects There are no dangerous insects in French Polynesia. The only real nuisances are mosquitoes and tiny, nearly invisible sand flies known locally as "no-nos," which appear at dusk on most beaches here. Wear trousers or long skirts and plenty of insect repellant (especially on the feet and ankles) to ward off the no-nos. If you forget to bring insect repellent along, look for the Off or Dolmix Pic brands at the pharmacies.

Liquor Laws Regulations about where and when you can drink are liberal, and some bars stay open until the very wee hours on weekends. Official *conventionné* restaurants and hotels pay reduced duty on imported alcoholic beverages, so they will cost less there than at local bars and nightclubs.

Mail Letters usually take about a week to 10 days to reach overseas destinations in either direction.

Mailing addresses in French Polynesia consist of post office boxes (*boîtes postales* in French, or B.P. for short) but no street numbers or names. Local addresses now have postal codes, which are written in front of the city or town.

Maps Tahiti Tourisme distributes free maps of each island. The most useful one is of downtown Papeete. Each weekly edition of the free *Tahiti Beach Press* carries artistic island and Papeete maps. Librairie Vaima, a large bookstore in Papeete's Vaima Centre, carries several *cartes touristiques.* The most detailed map is *Tahiti: Archipel de la Société,* published by the Institut Géographique National. It shows all the Society Islands in detail, including all roads and topographic features, and costs about 1,000CFP ($7.50). The full-color *Guide Toristique de Tahiti et ses Isles* shows the precise locations of all hotels and pensions on its 45 maps. It also costs about 1,700CFP ($12.50) and is a useful tool if you're hunting for cheap hotels.

Newspapers/Magazines The *Tahiti Beach Press,* an English-language weekly tabloid devoted to news of Tahiti's tourist industry, runs features of interest to tourists and advertisements for hotels, restaurants, real estate agents, car-rental firms, and other businesses that cater to tourists and have English-speaking staffs. Establishments that buy ads in it give away copies free. The daily newspapers, *La Dépêche de Tahiti* and *Les Nouvelles,* are in French. Le Kiosk in front of the Viama Centre on boulevard Pomare in Papeete carries the *International Herald Tribune, Time,* and *Newsweek.*

Pets If you bring your pet, it will spend your entire vacation in quarantine.

Radio/TV French Polynesia has government-operated AM radio stations with programming in French and Tahitian. Several private AM and FM stations in Papeete almost exclusively play American and British musical numbers in English; the announcers, however, speak French. Two government-owned and one private television station broadcast entirely in French and Tahitian. The government-owned radio and TV stations can be received throughout the territory via satellite. Canal+, a cablelike broadcast channel on Tahiti and Moorea, occasionally shows movies and sporting events in English. Moorea has an American-style cable system with CNN, ESPN, and HBO, all in English, and some hotels pick up ESPN and CNN's international programs (they're not the same as the channels in the U.S.).

Safety French Polynesia has seen increasing property theft in recent years, including break-ins of hotel rooms and resort bungalows, so don't leave valuables in your hotel room or unattended anywhere. Street crimes against tourists are still rare, and you should be safe after dark in the busy parks along boulevard Pomare on Papeete's waterfront. Friends of mine who live here, however, don't stroll away from the boulevard after dark. For that matter, stay alert everywhere after dusk. Women should not wander alone on deserted beaches any time, since some Polynesian men may still consider such behavior to be an invitation for instant amorous activity.

Taxes In addition to the stiff duties imposed on most imported goods, the government levies a value-added tax (VAT, or *TVA* in French) on most goods and services, including restaurant and hotel bills. Unlike in Europe, you can't get the VAT refunded when you leave. The territory adds 6% tax to hotel bills, and the Tahiti, Moorea, and Bora Bora communes tack on another 100CFP to 200CFP (75¢–$1.50) per night.

Telephone/Fax Direct international dialing is available to all telephone and fax numbers in French Polynesia. The international country code is **689**. There are no domestic area codes.

International calls can be placed through your hotel, though with a surcharge, which can more than double the fee. It's much less expensive to dial them directly from a pay phone, using a *télécarte*, a credit card required to make any call from a public pay phone (coin phones are history here). The cards are sold at all post offices and by most hotel front desks and many shops in 1,000CFP, 2,000CFP, and 5,000CFP ($7.50, $15, and $37.50) sizes. I buy a 1,000CFP or 2,000CFP version and keep it with me during my visit.

The direct-dial charge for all international calls is 100CFP (75¢) per minute, which is very reasonable by South Pacific standards.

To call overseas, dial **00**, then the country code (**1** for the U.S. and Canada), followed by the area code and phone number. Dial **19** if you need assistance making an overseas call. For directory information (*service des renseignements*), dial **12**. Both the international and information operators speak English.

Public pay phones are located at all post offices and are fairly numerous elsewhere on Tahiti, less so on the other islands. Local calls on Tahiti cost 50CFP (37¢) for the first 5 minutes. Calls to Moorea cost about 30CFP (22¢) per minute. Calls to the other islands cost at least 100CFP (75¢) per minute.

Your American mobile phone probably won't work in French Polynesia. If you must have one, try **Vini** (*©* **48.13.13**), a subsidiary of the Office of Posts and Telecommunications, which rents cellphones.

Time Local time in the most visited islands is 11 hours behind Greenwich mean time. I find it easier to think of it as 5 hours behind U.S. eastern standard time or 2 hours behind Pacific standard time. Translated: When it's noon in California, it's 10am in Tahiti. When it's noon on the U.S. East Coast, it's 5am in Tahiti. Add 1 hour to the Tahiti time during daylight saving time.

The Marquesas Islands are 30 minutes ahead of the rest of the territory.

French Polynesia is on the east side of the international date line; therefore, Tahiti has the same date as the United States, the Cook Islands, and the Samoas, and is one day behind Australia, New Zealand, Fiji, and Tonga.

Tipping Despite inroads made by uninformed American tourists (TIPPING IS NOT FORBIDDEN, reads a sign in one Papeete restaurant), tipping is considered contrary to the Polynesian custom of hospitality. In other words, tipping is not expected unless the service has been truly beyond the call of duty. Some hotels accept contributions to the staff Christmas fund.

Water Tap water is consistently safe to drink only in the city of Papeete and on Bora Bora, but you can buy bottled mineral water at every grocery. Derived from a spring on Tahiti, Vaimato is the purest of the local brands, which are much less expensive than imported French waters. Well water in the Tuamotus tends to be brackish; rainwater is used there for drinking.

Weights/Measures French Polynesia is on the metric system.

4

Tahiti

Tahiti's status as a large, abundant island centrally located in the eastern South Pacific made it a gateway and natural base for the early European explorers. It was from Tahiti that most of the rest of the South Pacific was explored and added to the world maps in the 18th century. In later years, the capital city, **Papeete,** became a major shipping crossroads. Located on Tahiti's northwest corner, Papeete curves around one of the South Pacific's busiest and most picturesque harbors.

Vehicles of every sort now crowd boulevard Pomare, the broad avenue along Papeete's waterfront, and the four-lane freeway linking the city to the trendy suburban districts of Punaauia and Paea on the west coast. Indeed, suburbs are creeping up the mountains overlooking the city and sprawling for miles along the coast in both directions. The island is so developed and so traffic clogged that many Tahitians commute up to 2 hours in each direction on weekdays. Many are moving to Moorea, a mere 30-minute ferry ride away.

There wasn't even a village where Papeete now stands until the 1820s, when Queen Pomare set up headquarters along the shore and merchant ships and whalers began using the harbor in preference to the less protected Matavai Bay to the east. A claptrap town of stores, bars, and billiard parlors sprang up quickly, and between 1825 and 1829 it was a veritable den of iniquity. It grew even more after the French made it their headquarters upon taking over Tahiti in 1842. A fire nearly destroyed the town in 1884, and waves churned up by a cyclone did severe damage in 1906. In 1914 two German warships shelled the harbor and sank the French navy's *Zélée*.

For many, the watershed in Papeete's transition from a backwater port to a modern city was not the building of the airport and the nuclear testing facility in the early 1960s. It was the tearing down of Quinn's, a quintessential South Seas bar, and its replacement by modern retail stores in 1973.

If you're a city-lover, Papeete's frantic pace, chic shops, busy Municipal Market, and lively mix of French, Polynesian, and Chinese cultures are sure to invigorate you. If you're looking for old-time Polynesia, you will find it on Tahiti's rural east and south coasts and on its peninsula, Tahiti Iti. Even if you plan to leave immediately for Moorea, Bora Bora, Huahine, and the other less developed islands, you will have to spend at least a few hours here, since all international flights land at Faaa on Tahiti's northwest coast. So make the most of this legendary and still very beautiful island.

1 Arriving & Getting Around

ARRIVING & DEPARTING

ARRIVING

All international flights arrive at **Tahiti-Faaa International Airport,** 7km (4 miles) west of downtown Papeete. Once you've cleared Customs, you will see a

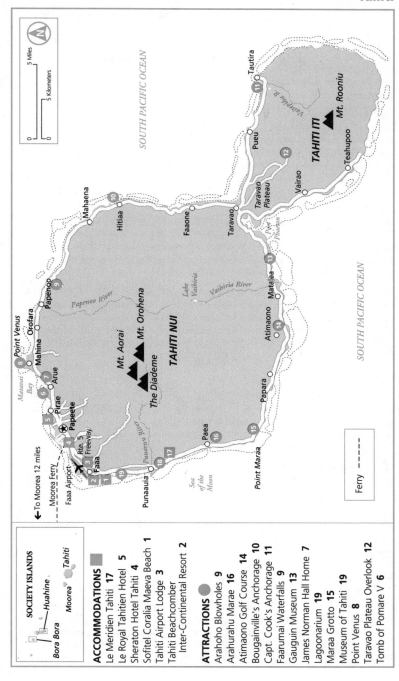

SOCIETY ISLANDS

Huahine

Bora Bora

Moorea — Tahiti

ACCOMMODATIONS
Le Meridien Tahiti **17**
Le Royal Tahitien Hotel **5**
Sheraton Hotel Tahiti **4**
Sofitel Coralia Maeva Beach **1**
Tahiti Airport Lodge **3**
Tahiti Beachcomber
Inter-Continental Resort **2**

ATTRACTIONS
Arahoho Blowholes **9**
Arahurahu Marae **16**
Atimaono Golf Course **14**
Bougainville's Anchorage **10**
Capt. Cook's Anchorage **11**
Faarumai Waterfalls **9**
Gauguin Museum **13**
James Norman Hall Home **7**
Lagoonarium **19**
Maraa Grotto **15**
Museum of Tahiti **19**
Point Venus **8**
Taravao Plateau Overlook **12**
Tomb of Pomare V **6**

booth straight ahead that is usually staffed by **Tahiti Manava,** the local tourist information office. Start there for maps and other information. Group tour operators will be holding signs announcing their presence. **Banque de Polynésie** has a currency exchange booth to the left as you exit Customs, and **Banque Socredo** is to the right. Both have ATMs.

A **snack bar** to the right is open around the clock. (The upstairs cafeteria is expensive and not that good.)

GETTING TO YOUR HOTEL   Unless you're on a package tour, your only choice of transportation to your hotel between 10pm and 6am will be a **taxi.** A large board mounted near the taxi area gives the official fares. From 8pm to 6am they are 1,500CFP ($11) to the hotels on the west coast; 2,500CFP ($18.50) to downtown. Add 100CFP (75¢) for each bag.

If you arrive any other time and are in good physical condition, you can haul your baggage across the parking lot in front of the terminal, climb the stairs to the main road, and flag down a local bus (see "Getting Around," below).

If you're driving a rental car (see "Getting Around," below), take Route 1 west to the Tahiti Beachcomber Inter-Continental Resort, the Sofitel Coralia Maeva Beach, or Le Meridien Tahiti. If you're going to downtown, watch for the Route 5 signs directing you to the freeway that connects Papeete to the west coast. Route 1 east goes to the Sheraton Hotel Tahiti.

BAGGAGE STORAGE   To the right of the Air Tahiti terminal, the airport's **baggage storage room** is open Monday to Friday from 6am to 7pm, Saturday and Sunday from 6am to noon and from 1:30 to 6:30pm, and 2 hours before every international flight departs. Charges range from 395CFP ($3) per day for regular-size bags to 1,040CFP ($7.75) for large items such as surfboards and bicycles. Every hotel will keep your baggage for free.

DEPARTING

Check-in time for departing international flights is 90 minutes before flight time; for domestic flights, be there 1 hour in advance. There is no airport departure tax for either international or domestic flights.

Note: There is no bank or currency exchange bureau in the departure lounge, so change your money before clearing immigration.

GETTING AROUND

Except for the Route 5 freeway between Papeete and Punaauia, the island's highway system consists primarily of a paved road running for 116km (72 miles) around Tahiti Nui and halfway down each side of Tahiti Iti. From the isthmus, a road partially lined with trees wanders up to the high, cool Plateau of Taravao, whose pastures and pines give it an air more of provincial France than of the South Pacific.

Impressions

Edward called for him in a rickety trap drawn by an old mare, and they drove along a road that ran by the sea. On each side of it were plantations, coconut and vanilla; now and then they saw a great mango, its fruit yellow and red and purple among the massy green of the leaves, now and then they had a glimpse of the lagoon, smooth and blue, with here and there a tiny islet graceful with tall palms.
—W. Somerset Maugham, "The Fall of Edward Bernard," 1921

Tips Around Tahiti by Bus

No local bus goes completely around Tahiti, so you have to walk across the Taravao isthmus to make a circumnavigation of the island. If you're adventurous enough to try it, go clockwise. Take an early morning east-bound long-distance bus to Taravao, walk across the isthmus—about 2km (1¼ miles)—and hail a returning west coast bus to Papeete. More buses run along the west coast than along the east, and there are more hitch-hiking possibilities in case you get stranded. Bear in mind, however, that hitchhiking is not a reliable means of transport on Tahiti, and women traveling alone or with other women should exercise extreme caution.

BY BUS

Although it might appear from the number of vehicles scurrying around Papeete that everyone owns a car or scooter, the average Tahitian gets around by local bus. There might still be a few of the famous *le trucks* running around Papeete, but modern buses are slated to replace all these colorful vehicles, called "trucks" because the passenger compartments are gaily painted wooden cabins mounted on the rear of flatbed trucks.

You can catch buses at official stops (called *arrêt le bus* in French).

Most buses begin their initial runs before the crack of dawn (about 5am) from their owners' residences and proceed to the market in Papeete. Successive runs are made from the market to the end of the route and back during the course of the day. The villages or districts served by each bus are written on the sides and front of the bus.

Buses going west line up on rue du Maréchal-Foch behind the Municipal Market. They travel along rue du Général-de-Gaulle, which becomes rue du Commandant-Destremeau and later route de-l'Ouest, the road that circles the island. There is frequent service from dawn to 10pm along this route as far as the Continent shopping center south of the Sofitel Coralia Maeva Beach. Buses labeled Faaa, Maeva Beach, and Outuamaru will pass the airport and the Sheraton Hotel Tahiti and Tahiti Beachcomber Inter-Continental Resort.

Buses going east line up in the block west of the Banque de Polynésie on boulevard Pomare, opposite the cruise ship terminal and near the Municipal Market and rue Paul Gauguin. They proceed out of town via avenue du Prince-Hinoi, passing the Hotel Royal Tahitien cutoff on their way to Pirae, Arue, and Mahina. They run frequently from 6am to 5pm as far as the Royal Matavai Bay Hotel Resort (formerly the Hyatt Regency Tahiti), less so between 5 and 10pm.

In general, the last long-distance runs of the day leave their villages about midday for Papeete, then depart the market shortly after everyone gets off work at 5pm.

Confused? Never fear, for all you really have to do to ride the bus is to show up at stations near the market and look like a tourist who wants a ride to your hotel. The drivers or their assistants will find you and tell you which vehicle to get in.

Fares are 120CFP (90¢) until 6pm and 200CFP ($1.50) thereafter. A trip to the end of the line in either direction costs about 600CFP ($4.50).

BY TAXI

Papeete has a large number of taxis, although they can be hard to find during the morning and evening rush hours, especially if it's raining. You can flag one down on the street or find them gathered at one of several stations. The largest gathering points are on boulevard Pomare near the market (© **42.02.92**) and at the Centre Vaima (© **42.60.77**). Most taxi drivers understand some English.

Taxi fares are set by the government and are posted in the main concourse at Tahiti-Faaa International Airport and on a board at the Centre Vaima taxi stand on boulevard Pomare. Few cabs have meters, so be sure that you and the driver have agreed on a fare before you get in. Note that *all fares are increased by at least 20% from 8pm to 6am.* A trip anywhere within downtown Papeete during the day starts at 1,000CFP ($7.50) and goes up 120CFP (90¢) for every kilometer after the first one. As a rule of thumb, the fare from the Papeete hotels to the airport or vice versa is about 1,700CFP ($12.50) during the day; from the west coast hotels to the airport, about 1,000CFP ($7.50). A trip to the Gauguin Museum on the south coast costs 1,000CFP ($75) one way. The fare for a 4-hour journey all the way around Tahiti is about 16,000CFP ($119). Drivers may charge an extra 50CFP to 100CFP (37¢–75¢) per bag of luggage.

BY RENTAL CAR

International car-rental firms on Tahiti are **Avis** (© **800/331-1212** or 41.93.93; www.avis.com), **Hertz** (© **800/654-3131** or 42.04.72; www.hertz.com), and **Europcar** (© **800/227-7368** or 45.24.24; www.europcar.com). At press time, Avis was the only company that could make reservations on the other islands by computer, which saves your having to do it yourself. Europcar is slightly less expensive than the others, with rates starting at 1,875CFP ($14) a day plus 41CFP (30¢) per kilometer, or 8,100CFP ($60) a day with unlimited kilometers. Consider the unlimited kilometer rate if you intend to drive around the island, since the round-island road is 114km (72 miles) long, not counting side trips on Tahiti Iti.

DRIVING HINTS In Papeete priority is given to vehicles entering an intersection from the right side. This rule does not apply on the four-lane boulevard Pomare along the waterfront, but be careful everywhere else because drivers on your right will expect you to yield the right of way at intersections where there are no stop signs or traffic signals. Outside of Papeete, priority is given to vehicles that are already on the round-island road.

PARKING People park everywhere in downtown Papeete, including on the sidewalks. Therefore, finding a parking space can be difficult. Some large buildings, such as the Centre Vaima, have garages in their basements. If I'm not staying downtown, I usually leave my car at the hotel and take a bus into the city.

 FAST FACTS: **Tahiti**

The following facts apply specifically to Tahiti. For more information, see "Fast Facts: French Polynesia" in chapter 3.

American Express The full-service American Express representative is **Tahiti Tours,** on rue Jeanne-d'Arc (© **54.02.50**; fax 42.25.15), across from the Centre Vaima in downtown Papeete. The mailing address is B.P. 627, Papeete, Tahiti, French Polynesia.

Bookstores **Librairie Vaima,** on the second level of the Centre Vaima (© **45.57.57**), has some English-language novels and a wide selection of books on French Polynesia, many of them in English and some of them rare editions. It also sells the excellent *Carte Touristique,* or Tourist Map, published by the Institut Géographique Nationale, showing geographical features (in topographical relief) and the system of roads and trails on all the Society Islands. **Le Kiosk** in front of the Centre Vaima sells the *International Herald Tribune, Time,* and *Newsweek.*

Business Hours Although some shops stay open over the long lunch break, most businesses are open from 8 to 11:30am and 2 to 5pm, give or take 30 minutes. Saturday hours are 8 to 11:30am, although some shops in the Centre Vaima stay open Saturday afternoon. The Papeete Municipal Market is a roaring beehive from 5 to 7am on Sunday, and many of the nearby general stores are open during those hours. Except for some small groceries, most other stores are closed on Sunday.

Camera/Film Film and 1-hour color print processing are available at several stores in downtown Papeete. One of the best is **Tahiti Photo,** in the Centre Vaima (© **42.97.34**), where you can get help in English.

Currency Exchange **Banque de Polynésie, Banque de Tahiti,** and **Banque Socredo** each has at least one branch on boulevard Pomare and in many suburban locations where you can cash traveler's checks. They all charge a fee of at least 500CFP ($3.75) for each transaction. You can also get cash advances against your Visa or MasterCard or use your debit card to withdraw funds at their automatic teller machines (ATMs). The instructions are in both French and English.

   Banking hours on Tahiti are generally 8 to 11:45am and 1:30 to 4:30pm Monday to Friday.

Drugstores **Pharmacie du Vaima,** on rue du Général-de-Gaulle at rue Georges La Garde behind the Centre Vaima (© **42.97.73**), is owned and operated by English-speaking Nguyen Ngoc-Tran, whose husband runs Pharmacie Tran on Moorea. Pharmacies rotate night duty, so ask your hotel staff to find out which one is open after dark.

E-mail **Tiki Soft Café,** on rue Paul Gauguin at the Rond Point de L'Est traffic circle (© **88.93.98**), 3 blocks inland from boulevard Pomare, has computer terminals where you can send and receive e-mail or surf the Internet while sipping a cup of French roast java. Access costs 250CFP ($1.85) for 15 minutes, 1,000CFP ($7.50) for an hour. Open Monday to Friday from 7:30am to 1am, Saturday from 2pm to 1am. The owners speak English.

Emergencies/Police Consult with your hotel staff. The emergency police telephone number is © **17** (but don't expect the person on the other end of the line to speak English). The **central gendarmerie** is at the inland terminus of avenue Bruat (© **42.02.02**).

Eyeglasses **Optique Vaima** (© **42.77.52**) is in the Centre Vaima.

Hairdressers/Barbers The staffs of the beauty salons in the Sofitel Coralia Maeva Beach and the Tahiti Beachcomber Inter-Continental Resort speak English.

Healthcare Both **Clinque Cardella** (© **42.80.10**), on rue Anne-Marie-Javouhey, and **Clinic Paofai** (© **43.77.00**) on boulevard Pomare, have highly trained specialists and some state-of-the-art equipment. They are open 24 hours.

Libraries The **Office Territorial D'Action Culturelle** (Territorial Cultural Center) on boulevard Pomare, west of downtown Papeete (© **42.88.50**), has a small library of mostly French books on the South Pacific and other topics. Hours are 8am to 5pm Monday to Friday, except on Wednesday when it closes at 4pm.

Post Office The main post office is on boulevard Pomare a block west of the Centre Vaima. The main desks on the second floor (take the escalators) are open from 7am to 3pm Monday through Friday, but there's also one postal clerk downstairs who is on duty from 7am to 6pm Monday through Friday, from 8 to 11am Saturday. Mail, which is held for a maximum of 2 weeks, can be picked up at the *poste restante* counter on the ground floor next to the international telephone counter. The branch post office at the Tahiti-Faaa International Airport terminal is open from 6 to 10:30am and noon to 2pm Monday through Friday, and from 6am to 9am on Saturday, Sunday, and holidays.

Restrooms The cruise-ship terminal on the waterfront at rue Paul Gauguin has free and clean public toilets.

Safety Papeete has seen increasing street crime. The busy parks on boulevard Pomare along the waterfront generally are safe, but be very careful if you wander onto the side streets after dark.

Telephone/Fax The cruise-ship terminal on the waterfront has a bank of pay phones, where you can use a *télécarte* to make international calls. The telephone, telegraph, and telex desks on the first floor of the main post office on boulevard Pomare are open Monday to Friday from 7am to 6pm and Saturday from 8 to 11am. The desks on the second floor are open from 7am to 3pm Monday through Friday. See "Fast Facts" in chapter 3 for more information about pay phones and international calls.

Water You can drink the tap water in Papeete and its nearby suburbs, which includes all the hotels, but not out in the rural parts of Tahiti. Bottled water is available in all grocery stores.

2 Exploring Tahiti

Tahiti is shaped like a figure eight lying on its side. The "eyes" of the eight are two extinct, eroded volcanoes joined by the flat Isthmus of Taravao. The larger, western, part of the island is known as Tahiti Nui ("Big Tahiti" in Tahitian), and the smaller eastern peninsula beyond the isthmus is named Tahiti Iti ("Little Tahiti"). Together they comprise about 670km (416 square miles), about two-thirds the size of the island of Oahu in Hawaii.

Tahiti Nui's volcano has been eroded over the eons so that now long ridges, separating deep valleys, march down from the crater's ancient rim to the coast far below. The rim itself is still intact, except on the north side, where the Papenoo River has cut its way to the sea. The highest peaks, **Mount Orohena** 2,206m (7,353 ft.) and **Mount Aora** 2,045m (6,817 ft.), tower above Papeete. Another peak, the toothlike Mount Te Tara O Maiao, or **the Diadème** 1,308m (4,360 ft.), can be seen from the eastern suburb of Pirae but not from downtown.

With the exception of the east coast of Tahiti Iti, where great cliffs fall into the lagoon, and a few places where the ridges end abruptly at the water's edge,

> **Impressions**
>
> *To those who insist that all picturesque towns look like Siena or Strat-*
> *ford-on-Avon, Papeete will be disappointing, but to others who love*
> *the world in all its variety, the town is fascinating. My own judgment:*
> *any town that wakes each morning to see Moorea is rich in beauty.*
> —James A. Michener, *Return to Paradise*, 1951

the island is skirted by a flat coastal plain. Tahiti's residents live on this plain, in the valleys, or on the hills adjacent to the plain.

THE TOP ATTRACTIONS

Arahurahu Marae ★★ Arahurahu is the only *marae*—an ancient temple or meeting place—in all of Polynesia that has been fully restored, and it is maintained like a museum. This particular temple apparently had no special historical importance, but it was restored in 1954, complete with exhibit boards explaining the significance of each part. For example, the stone pens near the entrance were used to keep the pigs to be sacrificed to the gods. Arahurahu is used for the reenactment of old Polynesian ceremonies during the July *Heiva i Tahiti* celebrations.

Paea, 22.5km (14 miles) west of Papeete. No phone. Free admission. Open daily 24 hr.

James Norman Hall Home ★★ James Norman Hall, coauthor with Charles Nordhoff of *Mutiny on the Bounty,* lived most of his adult life in Arue, which is now a suburb of Papeete. Nordhoff and Hall served together in World War I, moved to Tahiti to write, and produced three novels on the mutiny (*Men Against the Sea* and *Pitcairn's Island* are the others) and several more books about French Polynesia. His original house fell into disrepair, and the territorial government replaced it with this exact replica in 2001. Hall is buried on the hill above the house. A poem he wrote is engraved on the gravestone: "Look to the Northward, stranger / Just over the hillside there / Have you in your travels seen / A land more passing fair?" You'll see his typewriter and other family heirlooms.

Arue, 5.5km (3½ miles) east of Papeete. ℂ 50.01.60. Admission 600CFP ($4.50). Tues–Sun 9am–4pm.

Lagoonarium You don't have to be a snorkeler or diver to enjoy the deep, for this underwater viewing room is surrounded by pens containing reef sharks, sea turtles, and many colorful species of tropical fish. It's part of the Captain Bligh Restaurant and Bar (see "Where to Dine," below), and has a terrific view of Moorea.

Punaauia, 12km (7 miles) west of Papeete. ℂ 43.62.90. Admission 500CFP ($3.75) adults, 300CFP ($2.25) children under 12. Daily 9am–5:30pm.

Marché Municipale (Municipal Market) ★★★ An amazing array of fruits, vegetables, fish, meat, handicrafts, and other items are sold under the big tin pavilion of Papeete's bustling public market. Unwritten rules dictate that Tahitians sell fruits and traditional vegetables, such as taro and breadfruit, Chinese sell European and Chinese vegetables, and Chinese and Europeans serve as butchers and bakers. If your stomach can handle it, look for hogs' heads hanging in the butcher stalls. The market is busiest early in the mornings, but it's like a carnival here from 5 to 7am every Sunday, when people from the outlying areas of Tahiti, and even from the other islands, arrive to sell their produce.

(*Note:* By 8am the pickings are slim.) A Tahitian string band plays during lunch at the upstairs snack bar, which purveys inexpensive island chow.

Papeete, between rue du 22 Septembre and rue François Cardella, 1 block inland from bd. Pomare. No phone. Free admission. Mon–Fri 5am–6pm, Sat 5am–1pm, Sun 4–8am.

Musée de Tahiti et Ses Isles (Museum of Tahiti and Her Islands) ★★★

Set in a lagoon-side coconut grove with a gorgeous view of Moorea, this ranks as one of the best museums in the South Pacific. On display is the geological history of the islands; their sea life, flora, and fauna; and the history and culture of their peoples. Exhibits are devoted to traditional weaving, tapa-cloth making, early tools, body ornaments, tattooing, fishing and horticultural techniques, religion and maraes, games and sports, warfare and arms, deaths and funerals, writers and missionaries. Most, but not all, of the display legends are translated into English.

Punaauia, 15km (9 miles) west of Papeete. ℰ 58.34.76. Admission 600CFP ($4.50) adults, free for children. Tues–Sun 9:30am–5:30pm. Turn toward the lagoon at the Total station and follow the signs.

Musée Gauguin (Gauguin Museum) ★★★

This museum/memorial to Paul Gauguin, the French artist who lived in the Mataiea district from 1891 until 1893, owns some of his sculptures, wood carvings, engravings, and a ceramic vase. It has an active program to borrow his major works, however, and one might be on display during your visit. Otherwise, the exhibits are dedicated to his life in French Polynesia. It's best to see them clockwise, starting at the gift shop, which sells excellent reproductions of his works. The museum sits in lush **Harrison W. Smith Botanical Gardens,** which were started in 1919 by Harrison Smith, an American who left a career teaching physics at the Massachusetts Institute of Technology and moved to Tahiti. He died here in 1947. His gardens, which now belong to the public, are home to a plethora of tropical plants from around the world, as well as "Romeo" and "Juliet," two giant tortoises from the Galapagos Islands. This is the wettest part of Tahiti, so bring an umbrella.

Mataiea, 51km (32 miles) west of Papeete. ℰ 57.10.58. Museum admission 600CFP ($4.50) adults, 300CFP ($2.25) children. Gardens admission 430CFP ($3.25) per person. Daily 9am–5pm.

Point Venus ★★★

Capt. James Cook observed the transit of the planet Venus in 1769 at Point Venus, Tahiti's northernmost extremity. The low, sandy peninsula covered with ironwood (casuarina) trees is about 2km (1¼ miles) from the main road. Captains Wallis, Cook, and Bligh landed here after anchoring their ships offshore, behind the reef in Matavai Bay. Captain Cook made his observations of the transit of Venus across the sun in 1769 from a point between the black-sand beach and the meandering river that cuts the peninsula in two. The beach and the parklike setting around the tall white lighthouse, which was completed in 1868 (notwithstanding the 1867 date over the door), are popular for picnics. There are a snack bar, a souvenir and handcraft shop, and toilets.

Mahina, 10km (6 miles) east of Papeete. No phone. Free admission. Open daily 24 hr.

WALKING TOUR   **PAPEETE**

Start:	Tahiti Manava visitors bureau.
Finish:	Papeete Town Hall.
Time:	2 hours.
Best Time:	Early morning or late afternoon.
Worst Time:	Midday, or Sunday when most establishments are closed.

Begin at Tahiti Manava visitors bureau at the cruise-ship dock, at the foot of rue Paul Gauguin. The paved park and new visitor center were constructed in 2000, with funds intended to diversify French Polynesia's economy. Stroll westward along Boulevard Pomare. Opposite the tuna boat dock stands Centre Vaima.

① Centre Vaima

The chic shops here are a mecca for Papeete's French and European communities (the Municipal Market still attracts mostly Tahitians). The infamous Quinn's Bar stood in the block east of the Centre Vaima, where the Noa Noa boutique is now. The Centre Vaima takes its name from the Vaima Restaurant, everyone's favorite eatery in those days, which it replaced.

Across the four-lane boulevard from the Vaima is the wooden boardwalk along the Quay.

② The Quay

Cruising yachts from around the world congregate here from April to September, and resident boats are docked here all year. Beyond them, on the other side of the harbor, is **Motu Uta,** once a small natural island belonging to Queen Pomare but now home of the wharves and warehouses of Papeete's shipping port. The reef on the other side has been filled to make a breakwater and to connect Motu Uta by road to **Fare Ute,** the industrial area and French naval base to the right. The interisland boats dock alongside the filled-in reef, and their cargoes of copra (dried coconut meat) are taken to a mill at Fare Ute, where coconut oil is extracted and later shipped overseas to be used in cosmetics.

Walk west along the waterfront, past the main post office, next to which is Parc Bougainville.

③ Parc Bougainville

This shady park is named for the French explorer who found Tahiti a little too late to get credit for its discovery. Two naval cannons hang over the sidewalk: The one nearest the post office was on the *Seeadler,* Count von Luckner's infamous World War I German raider, which ran aground in the Cook Islands after terrifying the British and French territories of the South Pacific. The other was on the French navy's *Zélée.* Bougainville's statue stands between the guns.

Walk halfway around the traffic circle at the end of avenue Bruat to the Pacific Battalion Monument.

④ Pacific Battalion Monument

This monument is a tribute to the French Polynesians who fought with Gen. Charles de Gaulle's Free French forces during World War II. The territory quickly went over to the free French side after the fall of France to Nazi Germany in 1940, and it permitted the Allies to build an airstrip on Bora Bora in 1942. Later, the majority of French Polynesians supported de Gaulle as president of France, and the conservative Gaullist party has been an important force in local politics ever since.

Keep going west along the waterfront, to rue l'Arthémise, where you can't miss the big beige church on the mountain side of the boulevard.

⑤ Eglise Evangélique

An impressive steeple sits atop Eglise Evangélique, the largest Protestant church in French Polynesia. The local evangelical sect grew out of the early work by the London Missionary Society. Today the pastors are Tahitian. Sleek outrigger racing canoes are kept on the shady black sand beach across the boulevard. They can be seen cutting the harbor during lunchtime and in the late afternoons (canoe racing is Tahiti's national sport). Embedded in the stone gateway are the twin hulls of the *Hokule'a,* a traditional voyaging canoe that toured the South Pacific in the 1980s, setting off a wave of Polynesian pride.

Continue west along boulevard Pomare for 6 more blocks. You'll see the canoes and harbor on one side and a few remaining stately old colonial homes across the boulevard. On the harbor side you will come to Place Toata.

⑥ Place Toata

Another recent project funded by the economic restructuring fund, Place Toata is a park built on landfill, and it is a favorite gathering place for office workers during the day and families at night. They come to stroll, take in the view, and dine at inexpensive, open-air snack bars that are comparable to *les roulottes* (see "Where to Dine," below). This is a good place to have a cold drink or an ice cream cone, and there are clean public restrooms here. Place Toata turns into an outdoor amphitheater for the national dance competition during the huge *Heiva i Tahiti* festival in July. Next door, on the banks of Tipaerui River, stands the *Office Territorial d'Action Culturelle,* Tahiti's cultural center and library.

Turn around and backtrack east on boulevard Pomare to Parc Bougainville (see number 3, above), cut through the park, and proceed east along rue du Général-de-Gaulle. To the right as you walk back toward Centre Vaima are the spacious grounds of Place Tarahoi.

⑦ Place Tarahoi

Place Tarahoi, Papeete's governmental center, was royal property in the old days and site of Queen Pomare's mansion, which the French used as their headquarters after 1842. Her impressive home is long gone but is replicated by the Papeete Town Hall (see number 10, below). As you face the grounds, the buildings on the right house the French government and include the home of the president of French Polynesia. The modern building on the left is the Territorial Assembly. You can walk around hallways of the Assembly building during business hours. In front stands a monument to Pouvanaa a Oopa (1895–1977), a Tahitian who became a hero fighting for France in World War I and then spent the rest of his life battling for independence for his homeland.

During the 1960s and '70s he spent 15 years in prison in France, but he returned home in time to see more local autonomy granted to the territory. In fact, his fellow Tahitians promptly sent him back to Paris as a member of the French Senate.

Continue 2 more blocks along rue du Général-de-Gaulle, past the rear of Centre Vaima, to Cathédrale de l'Immaculée Conception.

⑧ Cathédrale de l'Immaculée Conception

Tahiti's oldest Catholic church, Cathédrale de l'Immaculée Conception houses a series of paintings of the Crucifixion. It's a very cool, quiet, and comforting place to worship or just to contemplate.

Rue du Général-de-Gaulle becomes rue du Maréchal-Foch past the church. Follow it for a block. Bear left at rue Colette and continue until you come to *Marché Municipale.*

⑨ Marché Municipale

Take a stroll under the large tin pavilion of Papeete's Municipal Market and examine the multitude of fruits and vegetables offered for sale (see "The Top Attractions," above).

After sampling the market and the marvelous handcrafts stalls along its sidewalk and upstairs, walk along rue Colette 2 more blocks, until you come to Papeete Town Hall.

⑩ Papeete Town Hall

This is a magnificent replica of Queen Pomare's mansion, which once stood at Place Tarahoi. This impressive structure, with its wraparound veranda, captures the spirit of the colonial South Pacific. This *Hôtel de Ville* or *Fare Oire* (French and Tahitian, respectively, for "town hall") was dedicated in 1990 by French Pres. François Mitterand, during an elaborate celebration. Walk up the grand entrance steps to catch a cool breeze from the broad balconies.

From here you can find your way back to Vaima Centre and some much-needed refreshment at its open-air cafes (see "Where to Dine," below).

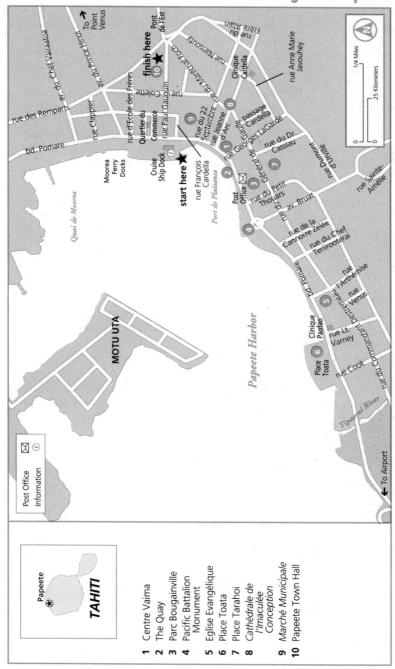

To
Point
Venus

finish here ★ ⑩

Pont
de l'Est

rue Colette

rue du Maréchal Foch

rue Nansouty

rue du
Frère Alain

Clinique
Cardella

⑧

rue Anne Marie
Javouhey

av. du Prince Hinoi

av. du Chef Vairaatoa

rue des Remparts

rue Clappier

rue d'Ecole des Frères

rue Paul Gauguin

Quartier du
Commerce

⑨

rue du 22
Septembre

rue Jeanne
d'Arc

①

rue Georges LaGarde

rue de Gaulle

passage
Cardella

⑧

bd. Pomare

Moorea
Ferry
Docks

Cruise
Ship Dock

start here ★

rue François
Cardella

②

Post
Office ✉

③

général de

rue du Dr.
Cassiau

⑦

rue du Petit
Thouars

rue Dumont
d'Urville

rue Sainte-
Amélie

Quai de Moorea

Port de Plaisance

④

av. Bruat

rue de la
Cannorre Zélée

rue du Chef
Teriirooterai

MOTU UTA

rue
l'Arthémise

rue
Venus

⑤

Papeete Harbor

Clinique
Paofao

⑥

Place
Toata

rue Lt.
Varney

bd. Pomare

rue Cook

rue du Commandant

Tipaerui River

To Airport

1/4 Miles
25 Kilometers

✉ Post Office
ⓘ Information

TAHITI

Papeete

1 Centre Vaima
2 The Quay
3 Parc Bougainville
4 Pacific Battalion
   Monument
5 Eglise Evangélique
6 Place Toata
7 Place Tarahoi
8 Cathédrale de
   l'Imaculée
   Conception
9 Marché Municipale
10 Papeete Town Hall

THE CIRCLE ISLAND TOUR ★★

Known locally as the **Circle Island Tour,** a drive around Tahiti is a popular way to see the island's outlying sights and a bit of old Polynesia away from Papeete's bustle. It takes less than a day and can be done even if you're staying on Moorea (take an early-morning ferry over and a late-afternoon boat back to Moorea).

The road around the island is 114km (72 miles) long, not counting side trips on Tahiti Iti. It's 54km (32 miles) from Papeete to Taravao along the east coast and 60km (40 miles) back along the west coast. If your car has a trip meter, reset it to zero; if it doesn't, make note of the total kilometers on the odometer at the outset.

On the land side of the road are red-topped concrete **kilometer markers** (*pointes kilomètres* in French, or "PK" for short), which tell the distance in kilometers between Papeete and the isthmus of Taravao. The markers give the distance from Papeete to Taravao in each direction—not the total number of kilometers around the island. The large numbers facing the ocean are the number of kilometers from Papeete; the numbers facing you as you drive along are the number of kilometers you have to go to Papeete or Taravao, depending on your direction. Distances between the PKs are referred to in tenths of kilometers; for example, PK 35.6 would be 35.6km from Papeete.

For a more detailed description of the tour than given here, buy a copy of Bengt Danielsson's *Tahiti: Circle Island Tour Guide.* French and English editions are available in the local bookstores.

THE NORTH & EAST COASTS OF TAHITI NUI

Proceeding clockwise from Papeete, you'll leave town by turning inland off Boulevard Pomare and following the broad **avenue du Prince-Hinoi,** the start of the round-island road.

FAUTAUA VALLEY, LOTI'S POOL & THE DIADEME   It's not worth the side trip, but at PK 2.5, a road goes right into the steep-walled Fautaua Valley and the **Bain Loti,** or Loti's Pool. Julien Viaud, the French merchant mariner who wrote under the pen name Pierre Loti, used this pool as a setting for his novel *The Marriage of Loti,* which recounted the love of a Frenchman for a Tahitian woman. Now part of Papeete's water-supply system, the pool is covered in concrete. Try to safely pull over near the bridge for a look up the valley to **the Diadème,** a rocky outcrop protruding like a crown from the interior ridge (I think it looks like a single worn molar sticking up from a gum). The road goes into the lower part of the valley and terminates at the beginning of a hiking trail up to the **Fautaua Waterfall,** which plunges over a cliff into a large pool 300m (985 ft.) below. The all-day hike to the head of the valley is best done with a guide (see "Golf, Watersports & Other Outdoor Activities," below).

TOMB OF POMARE V ★★   At PK 4.7 turn left at the sign and drive a short distance to a Protestant churchyard commanding an excellent view of Matavai Bay to the right. The tomb with a Grecian urn on top was built in 1879 for

---

Tips Avoid Rush Hour & Check on Road Work

If you drive yourself around Tahiti, avoid getting snarled in morning and evening weekday rush hours. Landslides between PK 44 and PK 45 on the east coast can close the round-island road, so ask the car rental agent or the staff at the Tahiti Manava visitors bureau if it is open all the way around.

Impressions

*The air was full of that exquisite fragrance of orange blossom and gar-
denia which is distilled by night under the thick foliage; there was a
great silence, accentuated by the bustle of insects in the grass, and that
sonorous quality, peculiar to night in Tahiti, which predisposes the lis-
tener to feel the enchanting power of music.*

—Pierre Loti (Julien Viaud), *The Marriage of Loti,* 1880

Queen Pomare. Her remains were removed a few years later by her son, King
Pomare V, who abdicated in return for a French pension and later died of too
much drink. Now he is buried there, and tour guides like to say the urn is not
an urn at all but is a liquor bottle, which makes it a monument not to Pomare
V but to the cause of his death.

JAMES NORMAN HALL HOME ★★   At PK 5.4, on the mountain side of
the road just east of the small bridge, stands an exact replica of the home of
James Norman Hall, coauthor with Charles Nordhoff of *Mutiny on the Bounty.*
It's a museum commemorating his life. See "The Top Attractions," above.

ONE TREE HILL ★★   At PK 8, you'll come to the top of One Tree Hill, so
named by Capt. James Cook because a single tree stood on this steep headland
in the late 1700s. For many years it was the site of a luxury hotel, now closed.
Pull into the round-about at the entrance and stop for one of Tahiti's most magnificent vistas. You'll look down on the north coast all the way from Matavai Bay
to Papeete, with Moorea looming on the far horizon.

POINT VENUS ★★★   At PK 10, turn left at Super Marché Venus Star and
drive to Point Venus, Tahiti's northernmost point, where Capt. James Cook
observed the transit of the planet Venus in 1769 (see "The Top Attractions,"
above).

OROFARA LEPER COLONY   At PK 13.2 begins the entrance to Orofara
Valley, which the French colonial administration made a leper colony in 1914.
Leprosy once was a fairly common disease throughout Polynesia, and until then,
those afflicted were sent into the hills. Today leprosy is curable with sulfa drugs,
and patients can remain at home with their families.

PAPENOO VALLEY   At PK 17.1, Tahiti's longest bridge crosses its longest
river at the end of its largest valley at one of its largest rural villages—all named
Papenoo. The river flows down to the sea through the only wall in Tahiti Nui's
old volcanic crater. Four-wheel-drive vehicles go up the valley on their excursions across the island (see "Safari Expeditions," below).

ARAHOHO BLOWHOLES   At PK 22, the surf pounding against the headland at Arahoho has formed overhanging shelves with holes in them. As waves
crash under the shelves, water and air are forced through the holes, resulting in
a geyserlike phenomenon. An overlook with free parking and toilets is west of
the sharp curve.

FAARUMAI WATERFALLS ★★   At PK 22.1, a sign on the right just past the
blowhole marks a paved road that leads 1.5km (1 mile) up a small valley to the
Cascades de Faarumai, Tahiti's most accessible waterfalls. Park near the stand of
bamboo trees and follow the signs. Vaimahuta falls are an easy walk; Haamaremare
Iti and Haamaremarerahi falls are a 45-minute climb up a more difficult trail.

> **Finds Take a Break**
>
> After you've looked around the black sand beach and lighthouse, head back to the main road for a refreshment stop at **Chez Kennedy** (*C* **48.35.97**), a small snack bar opposite the Point Venus turnoff. Its juicy, Australian-style hamburgers are among Tahiti's best.

Vaimahuta falls plunge straight down several hundred feet from a hanging valley into a large pool. Bring insect repellent.

MAHAENA BATTLEFIELD   At PK 32.5, the Tahitian rebellion came to a head on April 17, 1844, when 441 French troops charged several times and many poorly armed Tahitians dug in near the village of Mahaena. The Tahitians lost 102 men and the French, 15. It was the last set battle of the rebellion.

BOUGAINVILLE'S ANCHORAGE ⊛   At PK 37.6, a plaque mounted on a rock on the northern end of the bridge at Hitiaa commemorates Bougainville's landing. The French explorer anchored just offshore when he arrived in Tahiti in 1768. The two small islands on the reef, Oputotara and Variararu, provided slim protection against the prevailing trade winds, and Bougainville lost six anchors in 10 days trying to keep his ships off the reef. Tahitians recovered one and gave it to the high chief of Bora Bora, who in turn gave it to Captain Cook in 1777.

FAATAUTIA VALLEY   At PK 41.8 begins a view of Faatautia Valley, which looks so much like those in the Marquesas that in 1957 director John Huston chose it as a location for a movie version of *Typee,* Herman Melville's novelized account of his ship-jumping adventures among the Marquesans in the 1840s. The project was scrapped after another of Huston's Melville movies, *Moby-Dick,* bombed at the box office. The uninhabited valley surely looks much today as it did 1,000 years ago.

TARAVAO   At PK 53, after passing the small-boat marina, the road climbs up onto the Isthmus of Taravao. At the top are the stone walls of Fort Taravao, which the French built in 1844 to bottle up what was left of the rebellious Tahitians on the Tahiti Iti peninsula. Germans stuck on Tahiti during World War II were interned there. It is now used as a French army training center. The village of Taravao with its shops, suburban streets, and churches has grown up around the military post. Its snack bars are a good place for a refueling stop.

TAHITI ITI

Taravao joins the larger Tahiti Nui to its smaller conjoined twin, the peninsula of Tahiti Iti. The latter is much more sparsely populated, and paved roads dead-end about halfway down its north and its south sides. A series of cliffs plunges into the sea on Tahiti Iti's rugged east end.

TARAVAO PLATEAU   If you have to chose one of three roads on Tahiti Iti, take the one by the school and stadium (look for the flashing yellow traffic signal).

Impressions

It came upon me little by little. I came to like the life here, with its ease and its leisure, and the people, with their good-nature and their happy smiling faces.
—W. Somerset Maugham, "The Fall of Edward Bernard," 1921

It dead-ends high up into the rolling pastures of the Taravao Plateau. It begins at the traffic signal on the north coast road to Tautira and runs up through cool pastures reminiscent of rural France, with huge trees lining the narrow paved road. At more than 360m (1,200 ft.) high, the plateau is blessed with a refreshing, perpetually spring-like climate. Near the end of the road you'll come to the **Taravao Plateau Overlook,** where you'll have a spectacular view of the entire isthmus and down both sides of Tahiti Nui.

THE NORTH COAST   The road on the north coast of Tahiti Iti goes for 18km (11 miles), to the sizable village of **Tautira,** which sits on its own little peninsula. Captain Cook anchored in the bay off Tautira on his second visit to Tahiti in 1773. His ships ran aground on the reef while the crews were partying one night. He managed to get them off but lost several anchors in the process. One of them was found in 1978 and is now on display at the Museum of Tahiti and Her Islands, which we will come to on the west side of the island.

A year after Cook landed at Tautira, two Franciscan priests were put ashore there by the *Aguila,* a Spanish ship from Peru, whose captain claimed the island for Spain. It was the third time Tahiti had been claimed for a European power. The *Aguila* returned a year later, but the priests had had enough of Tahiti and sailed back to Peru.

When you enter the village, bear left and drive along the scenic coast road as far as the general store, where you can buy a cold soft drink and snack.

THE SOUTH COAST   The picturesque road along the south coast of Tahiti Iti skirts the lagoon, passing through small settlements. Novelist Zane Grey had a deep-sea-fishing camp at PK 7.3, near the village of Toahotu from 1928 to 1930. He caught a silver marlin that was about 4m (14 ft.) long and weighed more than 1,000 pounds—even after the sharks had had a meal on it while Grey was trying to get it aboard his boat. He wrote about his adventures in *Tales of Tahitian Waters.*

According to Tahitian legends, the demigod Maui once made a rope from his sister Hina's hair and used it to slow down the sun long enough for Tahitians to finish cooking their food in their earth ovens (a lengthy process). He accomplished this feat while standing on the reef at a point 8.5km (5 miles) along the south coast road, and his footprints are still there. Beyond Maui's alleged footprints, the Bay of Tapueraha provides the best natural harbor on Tahiti and was used as a base by a large contingent of the French navy during the above-ground nuclear tests at Moruroa atoll in the 1960s. Some of the old mooring pilings still stand just offshore.

THE SOUTH COAST OF TAHITI NUI

As you leave Taravao, heading back to Papeete along Tahiti's south coast, note that the PK markers begin to decrease the nearer you get to Papeete. The road rims casuarina-ringed Port Phaeton, which cuts nearly halfway across the isthmus. Port Phaeton and the Bay of Tapueraha to the south are Tahiti's finest

---

(**Fun Fact**   R. L. S. Was Here

Robert Louis Stevenson spent 2 months at Tautira in 1888, working on *The Master of Ballantrae,* a novel set not in Tahiti but in Scotland. Stevenson's mother was with him in Tautira. After she returned to London, she sent the local Protestant church a silver communion service, which is still being used today. See chapter 12 for more about Stevenson's South Pacific adventures.

The Moon & Six Million

In 1891 a marginally successful Parisian painter named Paul Gauguin left behind his wife and six children and sailed to Tahiti. He wanted to devote himself to his art, free of the chains of civilization.

Instead of paradise, however, Gauguin found a world that suffered from some of the same maladies as did the one from which he fled. Poverty, sickness, and frequent disputes with church and colonial officials marked his decade in the islands. He had syphilis, a bad heart, and an addiction to opium.

Gauguin disliked Papeete and spent his first 2 years in the rural Mataiea district, on Tahiti's south coast, where a village woman asked what he was doing there. Looking for a girl, he replied. The woman immediately offered her 13-year-old daughter Tehaamana, first of Gauguin's early teenage Tahitian mistresses. One of them bore him a son in 1899.

Tehaamana and the others figured prominently in Gauguin's impressionistic masterpieces, which brought fame to Tahiti but did little for his own pocketbook. After 649 paintings and a colorful career, immortalized by W. Somerset Maugham in *The Moon and Sixpence*, Gauguin died penniless in 1903.

At the time of his death, in the Marquesas Islands, a painting by Gauguin sold for 150 French francs. Today, on the rare occasion when one comes on the market, it fetches far in excess of $6 million.

harbors, yet European settlement and most development have taken place on the opposite side of the island, around Papeete. The shrimp you'll order for dinner come from the aqua farms in the bay's shallow waters.

PAPAEARI   At PK 52 stands Tahiti's oldest village. Apparently the island's initial residents recognized the advantages of the south coast and its deep lagoons and harbors, for word-of-mouth history says they came through the Hotumatuu Pass in the reef and settled at Papeari sometime between A.D. 400 and 500. Robert Keable, author of *Simon Called Peter*, a best-selling novel about a disillusioned clergyman, lived here from 1924 until he died in 1928 at the age of 40. His home, now a private residence, stands at PK 55. Today Papeari is a thriving village whose residents often sell fruit and vegetables at stands along the road.

GAUGUIN MUSEUM ✮✮✮   At PK 51.2 is the entrance to the museum/memorial to Paul Gauguin, who lived near here from 1891 until 1893 (see "The Top Attractions," above). The museum sits in lush **Harrison W. Smith Botanical Gardens,** started in 1919 by American Harrison Smith. The museum and gardens are open daily from 9am to 5pm. There's a snack bar here, but your best bet is to continue west.

VAIHIRIA RIVER   At PK 48 the main road crosses the Vaihiria River. An unpaved Jeep track beside the bridge leads inland to Lake Vaihiria. At 450m (1,500 ft.) above sea level, Tahiti's only lake is noted for its freshwater eels. Cliffs up to 900m (3,000 ft.) tall drop to the lake on its north side. The road from Papenoo on the north coast follows a water supply tunnel through the rim of the volcano and emerges above the lake. It's the favorite cross-island route for four-wheel-drive excursions (see "Safari Expeditions," below).

ATIMAONO   At PK 41 begins the largest parcel of flat land on Tahiti, site of **Atimaono Golf Course,** French Polynesia's only links. Irishman William Stewart started his cotton plantation here during the American Civil War. Nothing remains of the plantation, but it was Stewart who brought the first Chinese indentured servants to Tahiti.

DORENCE ATWATER'S GRAVE   At PK 36, on the lagoon side of the road in Papara village, stands a Protestant church in whose paved yard is buried Dorence Atwater, American consul to Tahiti after the Civil War. Atwater had been a Union Army soldier held as a prisoner of war by the Confederates. He was assigned to the hospital at the infamous Confederate prisoner-of-war camp at Andersonville, Georgia, where he surreptitiously recorded the names of Union soldiers who died while in captivity. He later escaped and brought his lists to the federal government, thus proving that the Confederacy was keeping inaccurate records. His action made him a hero in the eyes of the Union Army. He later moved to the south coast of Tahiti, married the daughter of a chief of the Papara district, and at one time invested in William Stewart's cotton venture.

MARAA GROTTO   At PK 28.5, on Tahiti's southwest corner, the road turns sharply around the base of a series of headlands, which drop precipitously to the lagoon. Deep into one of these cliffs goes the Maraa Grotto, also called the Paroa Cave. It usually has a lake inside and goes much deeper into the hill than appears at first glance. The mouth of the cave is clearly visible from the road. Park in the parking lot, not along the road.

THE WEST COAST OF TAHITI NUI

North of Maraa the road runs through the Paea and Punaauia suburbs of Papeete. The west coast is the driest part of Tahiti, and it's very popular with Europeans, Americans, and others who have built homes along the lagoon and in the hills overlooking it and Moorea. It's so populated that local officials are extending the Route 1 freeway as far south as the Punaruu River, just north of the Museum of Tahiti and Her Islands. But we'll stay on Route 1, the old road.

ARAHURAHU MARAE ★★   At PK 22.5 a small road on the right of Magasin Laut leads to a narrow valley, on the floor of which sits the restored Arahurahu Marae (see "The Top Attractions," above). It's worth a stop here to see one of the best examples of ancient Polynesian temples and meeting places.

MUSÉE DE TAHITI ET SES ISLES ★★★   At PK 15.1, turn left at the gas station and follow the signs through a residential area to the lagoon and the *Musée de Tahiti et Ses Isles* (Museum of Tahiti and Her Islands), one of the South Pacific's best museums (see "The Top Attractions," above).

⟨**Finds**⟩ **Take a Break**

The circle island tour buses deposit their passengers for lunch at the lagoon-side **Restaurant du Musée Gauguin,** at PK 50.5, which is worth a stop just for its phenomenal view of Tahiti Iti. Owner Roger Gowan, a transplanted Englishman, and his French Polynesian wife, Juliette, offer a buffet for 2,350CFP ($17.50) per person. Sandwiches are available for 500CFP to 700CFP ($3.75–$5.25). The restaurant is open daily from noon to 3pm. For reservations, call ⓒ **57.13.80.**

> (*Moments* **Watching the Sun Paint Moorea**
>
> I was born to see sights, and no matter how many times I visit French Poly-
> nesia, I never tire of its incredible natural beauty. I always spend sunset of
> my first day on Tahiti's west coast, burning up film as the sun paints
> another glorious red and orange sky over Moorea's purple ridges.

PUNARUU VALLEY   On a cloudless day you will have a view up the Punaruu
Valley to the Diadème as you drive from the museum back to the main road.
Power lines mar the view, but it's worth stopping to take a look. Tahitian rebels
occupied the valley during the 1844–48 war, and the French built a fort to keep
them there (the site is now occupied by a television antenna). Later the valley
was used to grow oranges, most of which were shipped to California. Villagers
sell the now-wild fruit at roadside stands during July and August.

You'll come to a traffic circle on the north side of the Punaruu River. The first
exit will take you up into the valley. If you're in a hurry, take the second exit onto
the new four-lane bypass road, which will whisk you to the Lagoonarium. The
third exit takes you to the old and more scenic coastal road.

LAGOONARIUM   At PK 11.4, the Captain Bligh Restaurant and Bar has a
terrific view of Moorea and is home to *Le Lagoonarium de Tahiti,* an underwater viewing room (see "The Top Attractions," above).

After the Lagoonarium, the road passes shopping centers and marinas in
Punaauia. It splits just before the Sofitel Coralia Maeva Beach. The left lanes
feed into the Route 5 freeway, which roars back to Papeete. The right lanes takes
you along Route 1, the old road that goes past the west coast hotels and the
Tahiti-Faaa International Airport before returning to town.

ORGANIZED TOURS AROUND THE COASTAL ROAD

Several companies offer tours around the coastal road. Expect to pay about
4,500CFP ($34), for a half-day tour, 7,500CFP ($56) for all day, plus entrance
fees to the museums and other attractions and lunch at the Restaurant du Musée
Gauguin.

Among the tour group guides, English-speaking William Leteeg of **Adventure Eagle Tours** (✆ **77.20.03**) lends his experiences growing up on the island
to his commentaries.

For a private tour without a group, contact **Joel Hart,** B.P. 1368, Papetoai,
Moorea (✆ **56.59.78** or 20.55.95; joel.hart@mail.pf). Joel grew up in French
Polynesia but has lived in the United States. He often shows television and
movie crews the best locations. Joel's all-day tour around the island in his air-
conditioned Oldsmobile costs 20,000CFP ($150) for up to five persons.

Other circle island tour operators with English-speaking guides are **Tahiti
Tours** (✆ **42.78.70**; www.tahiti-tours.com), **Tahiti Nui Travel** (✆ **42.68.03**;
www.tahiti-nui.com), and **Marama Tours** (✆ **82.08.42**; www.maramatours.
com). They have reservations desks in several hotels.

SAFARI EXPEDITIONS ✰✰✰

So-called safari expeditions into Tahiti's interior offer a very different view of the
island—and some spectacular views at that. Riding in the back of open, four-
wheel-drive vehicles, you follow narrow, unpaved roads up over the mountains
from one coast to the other, usually via the breathtaking Papenoo Valley.
Weather permitting, you'll ride through a water supply tunnel cut through the

---

Tips **Pick a Clear Day**

The safari expeditions do not go into the mountains when the weather is bad, and even if it's not raining, clouds atop the mountains can obscure what would otherwise be some fantastic views. It's best, therefore, to pick as clear a day as possible for this thrilling outing. Your best chance for that will be during the drier austral winter, June through early September.

---

island's steep interior ridge, and from there down a track to Lake Vaihiria and on along Vaihiria River to the south coast. You'll stop for a refreshing swim in the chilly. The cool temperatures at the higher elevations are refreshing.

Patrice Bordes's **Tahiti Safari Expedition** (© **42.14.15;** www.tahiti-safari. com) is the best. **Marama Tours** (© **83.96.50**) is also good. Both charge about 5,000CFP ($37) per person for a half-day trip, 7,500CFP ($56) for a full day. Reservations can be made at most hotel activities desks.

3 Golf, Watersports & Other Outdoor Activities

GOLF   The 18-hole, 6,950-yard **Atimaono Golf Course,** PK 40.2 (© **57. 43.41**), sprawls over the site of William Stewart's cotton plantation. A clubhouse, pro shop, restaurant, bar, locker rooms, showers, a swimming pool, a spa pool, and a driving range are on the premises. The club is open daily from 8am to dark. Greens fees are about 5,300CFP ($40). **Marama Tours** (© **83.96.50**) has an all-day golf outing for about 14,000CFP ($104) per person; it includes greens fees, equipment, and transportation to and from the course.

HIKING   Tahiti has a number of hiking trails, such as the cross-island Papenoo Valley–Lake Vaihiria route. Another ascends to the top of Mount Aorai, and another skirts the remote and wild eastern coast of Tahiti Iti. None of these should be undertaken without the proper equipment and a guide. Downpours can occur in the higher altitudes, swelling the streams that most trails follow, and the nights can become bitterly cold and damp. Which side of the island is the rainy side can shift from one day to the next, depending on which way the wind blows. In addition, the quick-growing tropical foliage can quickly obscure a path that was easily followed a few days before. Permits are required to use some trails that cross government land.

You can check with the **Tahiti Manava visitors bureau** in Papeete (© **50. 57.12;** www.tahiti-manava.pf) for the names of guides and hiking clubs.

WATERSPORTS   Based at the Tahiti Beachcomber Inter-Continental Resort, **Tahiti Aquatique** (© **53.34.96**) offers a comprehensive list of watersports activities. Some sample prices (per person, unless otherwise indicated): scuba diving, per dive including equipment and a guide, 5,500CFP ($41); introductory dive, 6,000CFP ($45); snorkeling gear rental, 1,000CFP ($7.50); snorkeling trips, 3,300CFP ($24); water-skiing, 4,500CFP ($33); and kayak rental, 1,600CFP ($12) per hour.

4 Shopping

There's no shortage of things to buy in Tahiti, especially in Papeete. Black pearls, both French and Tahitian fashions, and handcrafts are some of the items that might tempt you. The selection and prices on some items may be better on Moorea.

If you just can't live without visiting a modern shopping mall, head for the **Centre Moana Nui,** on the main road in Punaauia about ¼ mile south of the Sofitel Coralia Maeva Beach. Here you'll find a huge Continent supermarket, several boutiques, a snack bar with excellent hamburgers for 400CFP ($3), and a post office (open Mon–Fri 8am–5pm, Sat 8am–noon). The local **Centre Artisinant** stands across the parking lot, under a teepee-shaped roof.

Duty-free shopping is very limited, with French perfumes the best deal. **Duty Free Tahiti** (© 42.61.61), on the street level, water side of the Centre Vaima, is the largest duty-free shop. Its specialties are Seiko, Lorus, and Cartier watches and Givenchy, Yves St. Laurent, Chanel, and Guerlain perfumes. The **airport departure lounge** has two duty-free shops.

BLACK PEARLS ★★★

French Polynesia is the world's largest producer of cultured black pearls. In fact, so many are being produced that competition is fierce among the islands' shops, some of which (or their agents—commissioned tour guides and bus and taxi drivers) will bombard you with sales pitches almost from the moment you arrive. Some stalls in Papeete's Municipal Market even sell pearls, but give them a miss and buy yours from an experienced, reputable dealer.

Most of the territory's pearls are grown at farms in the lagoons of the Tuamotu Archipelago east of Tahiti, with Manihi being the most productive (see chapter 7).

Pearls are cultured by implanting a small nucleus into the shell of a live oyster, which then coats it with nacre, the same lustrous substance that lines the mother-of-pearl shell. The nacre of the oysters used in French Polynesia, the *Pinctada margaritifera,* produces dark pearls that are known as "black" but whose actual color ranges from black with shades of rose or green, which are the rarest and most valuable, to slightly grayer than white. The bulk of the crop is black with bluish or brownish tints. Most range in size from 10 millimeters to 17 millimeters (slightly less than ½ in. to slightly less than ¾ in.).

Size, color, luster, lack of imperfections, and shape determine a pearl's value. No two are exactly alike, but the most valuable are the larger ones that are most symmetrical and have few dark blemishes, and whose color is dark with the shades of a peacock showing through a bright luster. A high-quality pearl 13 millimeters or larger will sell for $10,000 or more, but there are thousands to choose from in the $300 to $1,000 range. Some small, imperfect-but-still-lovely pearls cost much less.

National Geographic carried very informative articles on cultured pearls in its August 1985 and June 1997 issues, so dig them out of the attic before heading off to Tahiti.

With most tourists now spending minimum time on Tahiti in favor of the other islands, you might find pearl prices in Papeete to be lower than on Moorea and Bora Bora. That's not always the case, so you should look in **Island Fashion Black Pearls** on Moorea or **Matira Pearls** on Bora Bora before making a purchase in Papeete (see "Shopping" in chapters 5 and 6). You're also more likely to get a salesperson over there who speaks English fluently.

The city has scores of *bijouteries* (jewelry shops) that carry black pearls in a variety of settings. Most of these stores are in or around the Centre Vaima, along boulevard Pomare, and in the Quartier du Commerce, the narrow streets off boulevard Pomare between rue Paul Gauguin and rue d'Ecole des Frères north of the Municipal Market.

Tips **Don't Pay Full Price!**

With so many black pearls flooding the market, discounting them is the rule of the day throughout French Polynesia. Despite the general rule to avoid haggling in French Polynesia, you shouldn't pay the price marked on a pearl or a piece of jewelry until you have politely asked for a discount.

Your beginning point should be the **Musée de la Perle Robert Wan,** on the rue Jeanne d'Arc side of the Centre Vaima (✆ **45.21.22**). Named for Robert Wan, the man who pioneered the local industry back in the 1960s, this museum explains the history of pearls from antiquity, the method by which they are cultured, and the things to look for when making your selection. The museum is open Monday to Saturday from 8am to 7pm, Sunday from 9am to 7pm. Admission is 600CFP ($4.50) for adults, 300CFP ($2.25) for children. Call for a free ride from local hotels.

Adjoining the museum, **Tahiti Perles** (✆ **45.05.05**) carries only excellent-quality pearls and uses only 18-karat gold for its settings, so the prices tend to be high.

On the second level of the Centre Vaima, **Sibani Perles Joallier** (✆ **41. 36.34**) carries the jewelry line of Didier Sibani, another pioneer of the local industry. European-style elegance is the theme here and at the other Sibani outlets throughout the islands.

HANDCRAFTS ★

Many local residents, especially on the outer islands, produce a wide range of jewelry made from seashells, homemade quilts, rag dolls, needlework, and straw hats, mats, baskets, and handbags.

The most popular item by far, however, is the cotton *pareu,* or wraparound sarong, which is screened, blocked, or printed by hand in the colors of the rainbow. The same material is made into other tropical clothing and various items, such as bedspreads. Pareus are sold virtually everywhere a visitor might wander.

The **Papeete Municipal Market** is the place to shop (see "The Top Attractions," above). It has stalls both upstairs and on the surrounding sidewalk, where local women's associations offer a wide selection of handcrafts at reasonable prices. The market is one of the few places where you can regularly find pareus for 1,000CFP ($7.50), bedspreads made of the colorful tie-dyed and silk-screened pareu material, and *tivaivai,* the colorful appliqué quilts stitched together by Tahitian women as their great-grandmothers were shown by the early missionaries. By and large, cloth goods are sold at the sidewalk stalls; those upstairs have a broader range of shell jewelry and other items.

Several villages have *centres artisanats,* where local women display their wares. The one in Punaauia, in the Continent Centre Commercial parking lot just south of the Sofitel Coralia Maeva Beach, is the best place to look for tivaivai quilts, which sell for about 35,000CFP ($260).

For finer-quality handcrafts, such as woodcarvings from the Marquesas Islands, shell chandeliers, tapa lamp shades, or mother-of-pearl shells, try **Manuia Curios** (✆ **42.04.94**) on place Notre Dame opposite the Catholic cathedral. Manuia Curios carries some artifacts from several South Pacific countries, including some from the Sepik River area of Papua New Guinea. **Tamara Curios** (✆ **42.54.42**), on rue du Général-de-Gaulle in Fare Tony, has a wide range of quality shell jewelry, wood carvings, place mats, and local pineapple jam made with rum.

Impressions

It's a comfort to get into a pareu when one gets back from town . . . I should strongly recommend you to adopt it. It's one of the most sensible costumes I have ever come across. It's cool, convenient, and inexpensive.
        —W. Somerset Maugham, "The Fall of Edward Bernard," 1921

TROPICAL CLOTHING

You've arrived in Tahiti and you notice that everyone under the sun is wearing printed sundresses or flowered aloha shirts. Where do you go to get yours?

Each hotel has at least one boutique that carries tropical clothing, including pareus. The prices there reflect the heavy tourist traffic, but they aren't much worse than at the stores in Papeete. Clothing, to put it bluntly, is dear in French Polynesia.

On boulevard Pomare, stop in **Marie Ah You** (*©* **42.03.31**) and **Aloha Boutique** (*©* **42.87.52**), both in the block west of the Centre Vaima. Their selections for women are trendy and a bit expensive.

Tahiti Art (*©* **42.97.43**), in Fare Tony on boulevard Pomare just west of the Centre Vaima, specializes in block-printed traditional designs (as opposed to the swirls and swooshes with leaves and flowers that are popular on most pareus). Tahiti Art was block printing long before this became the most popular style throughout the South Pacific, and its designs are among the most unique in town.

5 Where to Stay

If you can't get a room at the hotels I recommend below, try downtown Papeete, which has several properties that are convenient to the Moorea Ferry docks. Most charge between 12,000CFP and 18,000CFP ($90–$135) for a double room.

Hotel Tiare Tahiti, B.P. 2359, Papeete (*©* **43.68.48;** fax 43.68.47), an upstairs, five-story facility on boulevard Pomare a block west of the Centre Vaima, was built in 1996 and is modern and clean. The rooms are minimally furnished, however, and can be noisy, since most face directly onto the busy boulevard (request one on the upper floors). A saving grace if you're a TV addict: The sets have CNN and ESPN in English.

The Chinese-accented **Hotel Le Mandarin,** B.P. 302, Papeete (*©* **53.33.50;** fax 42.16.32; chris.beaumont@mail.pf), enjoys a somewhat quieter location than Hotel Tiare Tahiti, on rue Collette opposite the Town Hall. It's popular with business types from the outer islands.

In Tipaeru, a 10-minute walk west of downtown, the 1970s vintage **Matavai Hotel, Resort & Sports Centre,** B.P. 32, Papeete (*©* **42.67.76;** fax 42.36.90; www.hotelmatavai.pf), is a former Holiday Inn. The refurbished American-style rooms are clean and comfortable. The public areas have seen better days, however, and there's no Polynesian ambience afoot. Many New Zealanders on low-cost package tours stay here. The Matavai is the only hotel here that is allowed to pick you up at the airport—and that's a 2,500CFP ($19) savings each way at night. The "sports center" is a public recreation complex out front, with tennis, squash, and other diversions.

VERY EXPENSIVE

Le Meridien Tahiti ★★   Two blocks from the Museum of Tahiti and Her Islands, this luxury resort opened in 1998, alongside Tahiti's only stretch of white-sand beach. It's an excellent choice—provided you don't have to get to Tahiti-Faaa International Airport to catch a flight during the weekday morning traffic jam, when the usual 15-minute ride can take up to 2 hours. The Melanesian-inspired architecture is stunning, with swayback shingle roofs evoking the "spirit houses" of Papua New Guinea. Imported sand surrounding the wade-in pool compensates for the pebbly beach and shallow lagoon here.

The best accommodations are 12 overwater bungalows with either glass floors or steps into the lagoon from their porches. Try to get a north-facing unit because these have Moorea views. The luxuriously appointed guest rooms occupy 2-, 3-, and 4-story buildings flanking the main activities area. All rooms have balconies. On the ends of the buildings, "senior suites" add a separate bedroom and larger balcony, and entry to each "junior suite" is through a triangular lanai rather than from an interior hallway. Rooms on one floor are designated as nonsmoking, and some units are equipped for travelers with disabilities.

B.P. 380595, Tamanu 98718, Tahiti (Punaauia, 15km/9 miles south of Papeete, 8km/5 miles south of the airport). ✆ **800/225-5843** or 47.07.07. Fax 47.07.08. www.lemeridien-tahiti.com. 150 units. 35,000CFP–48,400CFP ($259–$359) double, 48,000CFP ($356) bungalow. AE, DC, MC, V. **Amenities:** 2 restaurants (French), 2 bars; outdoor pool; tennis court; exercise room; watersports equipment rentals; concierge; activities desk; car-rental desk; limited room service; babysitting; laundry service. In room: A/C, TV, dataport, minibar, coffeemaker, hair dryer, iron, safe.

Sheraton Hotel Tahiti ★★

An easy walk to downtown and a quick drive to the airport, this state-of-the-art hotel (formerly the Outrigger Hotel Tahiti) was built from scratch in 1998–99 on the site of the old Hotel Tahiti, whose massive thatch-roofed public areas hosted many a local soiree. A lagoon-side terrace with sand-bordered horizon pool is the focal point here, since there's no beach, only a shoreline bulkhead. The well- if not luxuriously equipped guest rooms are in four- and five-story shingle-roofed hotel blocks. Except for 10 suites, which have one or two bedrooms, the spacious units are all identical except for the vistas off their private balconies (rates increase from harbor to ocean to Moorea view).

B.P. 416, Papeete (1km/½ mile west of downtown, 6km/3½ miles east of the airport). ✆ **800/325-3535** or 86.48.48. Fax 86.48.40. www.sheraton.com. 200 units. 31,600CFP–37,500CFP ($234–$278) double, 55,000CFP–75,000CFP ($407–$556) suite. AE, DC, MC, V. **Amenities:** 1 restaurant (French), 1 bar; outdoor pool; health club; exercise room; concierge; activities desk; car-rental desk; business center; spa; salon; limited room service; massage; babysitting; laundry service. In room: A/C, TV, dataport, minibar, coffeemaker, hair dryer, iron, safe.

Tahiti Beachcomber Inter-Continental Resort ★★★

This extraordinarily well-managed property, formerly known as the Tahiti Beachcomber Parkroyal, is consistently Tahiti's best all-around hotel. Known here simply as "The Beachcomber," it sits at Tataa Point on the island's northwest corner, from whence souls supposedly leaped to the ancient Polynesian homeland in pre-Christian days. Today's guests get one of Tahiti's best views of Moorea, especially from romantic overwater bungalows that directly face the sister island. The Beachcomber was born in the 1960s as a Travelodge, so don't expect large rooms in its original wings. On the other hand, you'll have plenty of space in one of the 60 deluxe "Panoramic" rooms built in 1999 on the south end of the property. Whatever the vintage, all units here have private patios or balconies with a Moorea view through the coconut palms dotting the property. The resort doesn't have a natural beach (nor is the lagoon here as clear as those on the outer islands), but bulkheads separate the sea from white imported sand. Or you can frolic in two pools, one in a large complex, sitting lagoon side before the main building or in another smaller pool with water cascading over its horizon (and apparently into the lagoon). The latter is adjacent to the romantic Le Lotus restaurant, one of the South Pacific's best (see "Where to Dine," below). A special feature here is a 24-hour lobby bar, where you can get a snack and cup of coffee after your overnight flight.

B.P. 6014, Faaa, Tahiti (Faaa, 8km/5 miles west of Papeete). $\mathcal{C}$ 800/327-0200 or 86.51.10. Fax 86.51.30. www.interconti.com. 214 units. 30,084CFP–43,818CFP ($223–$325) double, 47,088CFP–59,950CFP ($348–$444) bungalow. AE, DC, MC, V. **Amenities:** 2 restaurants (French), 2 bars; 2 outdoor pools; tennis courts; health club; spa; Jacuzzi; watersports equipment rentals; concierge; activities desk; car-rental desk; salon; 24-hr. room service; massage; babysitting; laundry service; coin-op washers and dryers. *In room:* A/C, TV, dataport, minibar, coffeemaker, hair dryer, iron, safe.

EXPENSIVE

Sofitel Coralia Maeva Beach   Designed like a modern version of a terraced Mayan pyramid, this high-rise building sits beside Maeva Bay and a half-moon, dark-sand beach of the same name. Built in the late 1960s, it was in need of the refurbishment scheduled for 2002. The murky lagoon off the beach isn't as good for swimming and snorkeling as for anchoring numerous yachts, whose masts slice the beach's view of Moorea. The smallish, European-style rooms open to balconies; those on the upper floors on the north (or "beach") side have commanding views of Moorea, and those on the garden side look south along Tahiti's west coast.

B.P. 6008, Papeete, Tahiti (Punaauia, 7.5km/4 miles west of Papeete). $\mathcal{C}$ 800/221-4542 or 86.66.00. Fax 41.05.05. www.accorhotels.com. 230 units. 22,300CFP–29,000CFP ($165–$215) double, 42,500CFP ($315) suite. AE, DC, MC, V. **Amenities:** 2 restaurants (French/Japanese), 2 bars; outdoor pool; tennis courts; watersports equipment rentals; concierge; activities desk; car-rental desk; limited room service; babysitting; laundry service. *In room:* A/C, TV, minibar, coffeemaker, hair dryer, iron.

MODERATE

Le Royal Tahitien Hotel ★★ *Value*   One of the best values in French Polynesia, this American-owned hotel is the only moderately priced place on the island that has its own beach, a stretch of deep black sand from which its suburban neighbors fish and swim. And Australian-born manager Lionel Kennedy and his English-speaking staff are Tahiti's best when it comes to friendly, personalized service. Sitting in an expansive lawn and lush garden traversed by a small stream, a swimming pool sports a waterfall cascading over rocks, under which is built a daytime snack bar. The spacious guest rooms are in contemporary two-story wood and stone buildings that look like an American condominium complex. They have a Scandinavian ski lodge ambience, with Danish-style furniture and stonelike brick walls. The tropics pervade the fine beachside restaurant under a 1937-vintage thatch ceiling. Both the restaurant and adjacent bar are popular with local businesspeople, since they are one of the few beachside establishments on Tahiti. A local band plays on Friday and Saturday evenings. Your fellow guests are likely to be businesspersons living on the other islands and travelers who have made their own arrangements (that is, few groups stay here).

B.P. 5001, Pirae, Tahiti (Pirae, 4km/2½ miles east of downtown). $\mathcal{C}$ 818/843-6068 or 50.40.40. Fax 50.40.41. royalres@mail.pf. 40 units. 17,000CFP ($126) double. AE, DC, MC, V. Take a Mahina bus or follow av. Prince Hinoi to the Total and Mobil stations opposite each other; turn left, follow lane to Maire de Pirae, then turn into parking lot. **Amenities:** 1 restaurant (French), 1 bar; outdoor pool; laundry service. *In room:* A/C, TV, fridge, coffeemaker.

INEXPENSIVE

Tahiti Airport Lodge   Perched on the side of a hill in the Cité de l'Air housing development above the airport, Charlie and Margarite Bredin's simple but clean and friendly bed-and-breakfast commands a spectacular view of Moorea

Cost-Conscious Travelers Be Warned

There's is a huge difference in quality between French Polynesia's moderate and inexpensive accommodations. The latter are very basic, roof-over-your-head establishments. In fact, no establishment in the entire territory is comparable in price or quality to the inexpensive motels that are so common in the United States, Canada, Australia, and New Zealand. Nor will you get the same value-for-money as in the other South Pacific countries.

Tahiti Tourisme has a list of "nonclassified" pensions, private homes, and camping facilities (see "Visitor Information & Entry Requirements" in chapter 3). If you decide to go this route, a knowledge of French will be very helpful—if not essential.

from its lovely, open-air guest lounge. Unfortunately you won't get this view from any of the rather dark rooms, which range from ample motel-size with king beds and private bathrooms down to tiny share-bathroom units barely big enough to accommodate a double bed. All rooms have fans and electric mosquito deterrents, and all showers dispense hot water. The house is a steep, 5-minute climb from the round-island road, but Charlie will pick you up from the airport or the bus stop. He will also take you on beach picnics for an extra fee. The Bredins speak English as well as French, so communication shouldn't be a problem here.

B.P. 2580, Faaa (at P.K. 5.5, opposite Tahiti-Faaa International Airport). ✆ **82.23.68.** Fax 82.25.00. 10 units (4 with bathroom). 6,000CFP–8,000CFP ($45–$60) double. Rates include breakfast, taxes, and airport transfers. No credit cards. *In room:* No phone.

6 Where to Dine

Tahiti has a plethora of excellent French, Italian, and Chinese restaurants. The ones recommended below are but a few of many; don't hesitate to strike out on your own.

MA'A TAHITI The Tahitians have adopted many Western and Chinese dishes, but *ma'a Tahiti* (Tahitian food) remains highly popular. Like their Polynesian counterparts elsewhere, Tahitians still cook meals in an earth oven, known here as an *himaa.* Pork, chicken, fish, shellfish, leafy green vegetables such as taro leaves, and root crops such as taro and yams are wrapped in leaves, placed on a bed of heated stones, covered with more leaves and earth, and left to steam for several hours. When all is done, the earth is removed, the food unwrapped, and everyone proceeds to eat with his or her fingers. Results of the himaa are quite tasty, since the steam spreads the aroma of one ingredient to the others, and liberal use of coconut cream adds a sweet richness.

Most of Tahiti's big resort hotels have at least one *tama'ara'a* (Tahitian feast) a week; phone them to see when one will be offered. They usually run about 6,500CFP ($48) a head, but most include a Tahitian dance show after the meal (see "Island Nights," below). Another good sampling is at the Sunday buffet at the Captain Bligh Restaurant and Bar (see below).

Many restaurants whose cuisine may otherwise be French, Italian, or Chinese also offer Tahitian dishes. One you will see on almost every menu is *poisson cru,* French for "raw fish"; it's a Tahitian-style salad of fresh tuna or mahimahi marinated in lime juice, cucumbers, onions, and tomatoes, all served in coconut cream. (Red chilis are added to spice up a variation known as "Chinese poisson cru.") Another is local freshwater shrimp—they're grown in ponds on Moorea—sautéed and served in a sweet sauce of curry and coconut cream.

SNACK BARS   Downtown Papeete has a McDonald's, at the corner of rue du Général-de-Gaulle and rue du Dr. Cassiau behind Centre Vaima, but locals still prefer their plethora of snack bars, which they call simply "snacks." You can get a hamburger and usually poisson cru, but the most popular item is the *casse-croûte*, a sandwich made from a crusty French baguette and ham, tuna, *roti* (roast pork), *hachis* (hamburger), lettuce, tomatoes, and cucumbers—or even spaghetti. A *casse-croûte* usually costs 200CFP ($1.50) or less. **Place Toata,** the new waterfront park near the western end of boulevard Pomare, has half a dozen excellent snack bars, all with outdoor seating (see "Walking Tour: Papeete," above).

MONEY-SAVING TIPS   You can save at regular restaurants by taking advantage of *plats du jour* (daily specials), especially at lunch, and *prix-fixe* (fixed priced) menus, sometimes called "tourist menus" by Tahiti's restaurants. These three- or four-course offerings are usually made from fresh produce direct from the market and provide a significant savings over ordering from the menu.

Restaurants *Conventionné* get breaks on the government's high duty on imported alcoholic beverages, so wine and mixed drinks in these establishments cost significantly less than elsewhere. You can also order *vin ordinaire* (table wine), served in a carafe, to save money. The chef buys good-quality wine in bulk and passes the savings on to you.

You can make your own snacks or perhaps a picnic lunch to enjoy at the beach. Every village has at least one Chinese-owned grocery store (*magasin chinoise*). In downtown Papeete, the large **Champion** supermarket is on rue du Général-de-Gaulle in the block west of the Eglise Evangélique. On the west coast, head for the huge **Continent** supermarket south of the Sofitel Coralia Maeva Beach. Fresh sticks of French bread cost about 50CFP (37¢) each everywhere, and the markets carry cheeses, deli meats, vegetables, and other sandwich makings, many items imported from France.

Locally brewed Hinano beers sell for about 150CFP ($1) in grocery stores, versus 350CFP ($2.50) or more at the hotel bars, and bottles of decent French wine cost a fraction of restaurant prices.

VERY EXPENSIVE

Auberge du Pacifique ✦✦✦   TRADITIONAL FRENCH/TAHITIAN This lagoon-side restaurant has been among Tahiti's finest since 1974. Owner Jean Galopin was named a Maître Cuisinier (Master Chef) de France in 1987, in large part because of his unique blending of French and Tahitian styles of cooking. His *fafa* (chicken and taro leaves steamed in coconut milk) is in marked contrast with what comes out of a local himaa on Sunday afternoon. Jean has shared many of his techniques in a popular cookbook, *La Cuisine de Tahiti et des Iles.* The roof over his main dining room opens to reveal the twinkling stars above, while a second, air-conditioned salon sports a mural by noted local artist François Revello. Guests are welcome to visit Tahiti's only air-conditioned wine cellar and choose from among excellent French vintages. A special tourist menu features poisson cru and main courses such as a light mahimahi soufflé.

PK 11.2, Punaauia (3.7km/2¼ miles south of Sofitel Coralia Maeva Beach on the round-island road; take a Paea bus during the day, a taxi at night). (C) **43.98.30.** Reservations recommended, especially on weekends. 2,000CFP–3,650CFP ($15–$27). AE, MC, V. Wed–Mon 11:30am–2pm and 6:30–9:30pm.

Le Lotus ✦✦✦   FRENCH/CONTINENTAL   With two round, thatch-roof dining rooms extending over the lagoon and enjoying an uninterrupted view of

---

Value **Don't Miss *Les Roulottes***

Prices in some hotel dining rooms here can be shocking, but you don't have to spend a fortune to eat well in French Polynesia. In fact, the best food bargains in Papeete literally roll out after dark on the cruise ship docks: portable meal wagons known as *les roulottes.*

Some owners set up charcoal grills behind their trucks and small electric generators in front to provide plenty of light for the diners, who sit on stools along either side of the vehicles. A few operate during the daytime, but most begin arriving about 6pm. The entire waterfront soon takes on a carnival atmosphere, especially on Friday and Saturday nights.

The traditional menu includes charbroiled steaks or chicken with french fries (known, respectively, as *steak frites* and *poulet frites),* familiar Cantonese dishes, poisson cru, and *salade russe* (Russian-style potato salad, tinted red by beet root juice) for 800CFP to 1,100CFP ($6–$8) per plate. Glassed-in display cases along the sides of some trucks hold actual examples of what's offered at each (not exactly the most appetizing exhibits, but you can just point to what you want rather than fumbling in French). You'll find just as many trucks specializing in crepes, pizzas, couscous, and waffles (*gaufres*). So many tourists eat here that most truck owners understand some English.

Even if you don't order an entire meal at *les roulottes,* stop for a crepe or waffle and enjoy the scene.

Moorea, Le Lotus has the best setting of any restaurant in the South Pacific. The widely spaced tables are all at the water's edge (a spotlight between the two dining rooms shines into the lagoon, attracting fish in search of a handout). The gourmet French fare and attentive but unobtrusive service more than live up to this romantic scene. You'll have a choice at lunchtime of grazing an extensive buffet or picking a three-course meal. Rather than ordering a la carte at dinner, you can pick from two-, three-, or four-course set meals. Your choices will depend on which of Europe's top master chefs has accepted the resort's invitation to take a month-long working vacation here. Whomever is in residence, you're in for a gastronomic delight.

In Tahiti Beachcomber Inter-Continental Resort, Faaa (7km/4 miles west of Papeete). © **86.51.10**, ext. 5512. Lunch buffet 2,680CFP ($20), fixed-price lunch 3,820CFP–4,640CFP ($28–$35); fixed-priced dinners 7,100CFP–8,500CFP ($53–$63). AE, DC, MC, V. Daily noon–2:30pm; Tues–Sat 7–9:30pm.

EXPENSIVE

Captain Bligh Restaurant and Bar ★ TRADITIONAL FRENCH   One of Tahiti's most unusual restaurant settings, this large thatch-roofed building extends over the lagoon (you can toss bread crumbs to the fish swimming just over the railing), or you can stroll along a pier to a tiny man-made island and dine al fresco under the stars. The pier goes out to the Lagoonarium (see "The Top Attractions," above). Specialties of the house are grilled steaks and lobster, plus other seafood dishes such as whiskey shrimp and mahimahi under a creamed pepper sauce. The Captain Bligh usually stages Tahitian dance shows Friday and Saturday at 8:30pm, and it has a *ma'a Tahiti* buffet Sunday at noon.

PK 11.4, Punaauia, at the Lagoonarium (3.9km/2½ miles) south of Sofitel Coralia Maeva Beach on the round-island road; the Paea trucks go by it during the day; take a taxi at night). $\textcircled{C}$ **43.62.90.** Reservations recommended on weekends. Main courses 1,700CFP–3,200CFP ($13–$24). AE, MC, V. Daily 11am–2:30pm and 6:30–10pm; bar 9am–10pm.

Casablanca Cocktail Restaurant ★★ FRENCH/MEDITERRANIAN

Perched beside the yachts moored in Marina Taina, this casual restaurant is very popular with local residents, especially on weekends, when live music is featured (make Fri and Sat reservations at least 2 days in advance). Couscous night, Wednesday, also draws a crowd. The main menu features French and Mediterranean treatments of local seafood, and the value-priced "Cowboy" (grilled rib-eye steak) or "Marina" (grilled mahimahi) options come with a salad and french fries or rice, plus ice cream for dessert. Only the dessert menu is written in English, but the friendly staff will help you decipher *le carte*.

P.K. 9, Punaauia, at Marina Taina. $\textcircled{C}$ **43.91.35.** Reservations recommended. Main courses 1,600CFP–3,300CFP ($12–$25); fixed-price dinner 4,300CFP ($32). AE, MC, V. Daily noon–2pm and 7–10pm. Heading south, turn right into marina after first traffic circle.

Le Belvédère ★★ (Finds FRENCH/FONDUE

Dinner at Le Belvédère is a highlight of Tahiti for many visitors, for this innlike establishment has a spectacular view of the city and Moorea from its perch 600m (2,000 ft.) up in the cool hills above Papeete. The restaurant provides round-trip transportation from your hotel up the narrow, one-lane, winding, switchback road that leads to it (I don't encourage anyone to attempt this drive in a rental car). The 5pm pickup reaches the restaurant in time for a sunset cocktail. The specialty of the house is fondue Bourguignonne served with six sauces. Other choices are mahimahi grilled with butter, steak in green-pepper sauce or "any way you like it," shish kebab, and chicken with wine. The price includes three courses, wine, and transportation, so it is a reasonably good value. The quality of the cuisine doesn't match the view, however, so treat the evening as a sightseeing excursion, not as a fine dining experience.

Fare Rau Ape Valley (perched high on a ridge overlooking Papeete and Moorea; transportation provided by restaurant from your hotel). $\textcircled{C}$ **42.73.44.** Reservations required. 4,900CFP ($36) adults, 2,500CFP ($19) children, including full meal, wine, and transportation. AE, MC, V. Thurs–Tues 11:30am–2pm and 6–9:30pm.

Le Rubis ★★ TRADITIONAL FRENCH/REGIONAL

The latest creation of a noted local chef who goes by the nickname Acajou ("The Turtle"), this restaurant has an elegant garden ambience. Faux grape vines (*rubis* in French) hang from the ceilings, and the mat-lined walls are adorned with numerous paintings of wine bottles and vineyards. The decor will get you in the mood to select from one of Tahiti's most extensive lists of French vintages, many of them offered by the glass. Acajou helps you out by suggesting a match for each menu item. He was a pioneer in developing the wonderful local dish shrimps in a sweet, slightly curried coconut cream sauce, and that is the star here. Or you can opt for the same sauce over fresh tuna. Salmon in puff pastry and traditional French versions of steak, veal, lamb, and duck are all tasty. Less expensive weeknight specials include seafood spaghetti, roast lamb, and curried coconut chicken.

16 rue Jeanne d'Arc, in Vaima Centre. $\textcircled{C}$ **43.25.55.** Reservations recommended. Main courses 1,600CFP–3,500CFP ($12–$26). AE, DC, MC, V. Mon–Thurs 12:15–1:45pm and 5:30–9:30pm, Fri 12:15–1:45pm and 5:30–10pm, Sat 5:30–10pm.

MODERATE

L'Api'zzeria ITALIAN ★

Although a notch below Lou Pescadou (see below), this restaurant in a grove of trees across from the harbor has been serving very good pizza and pasta since 1968. Most guests prefer tables outside under the trees rather than inside, which resembles an Elizabethan waterfront tavern accented with nautical relics such as a ship's brass compass in one corner and a large pilot wheel used as a table divider. The food, on the other hand, is definitely Italian. Both the pizzas and tender steaks are cooked in a wood-fired oven. The menu also features spaghetti, fettuccine, lasagna, steak Milanese, veal in white or marsala wine sauce, and grilled homemade Italian sausage.

Bd. Pomare, between rue du Chef Teriirooterai and rue l'Arthémise. ✆ **42.98.30.** Reservations not accepted. Pizzas and pastas 400CFP–1,500CFP ($3–$11); meat courses 1,500CFP–2,350CFP ($11–$17). MC, V. Mon–Sat 11:30am–10pm.

Les 3 Brasseurs FRENCH   This sidewalk microbrewery is one of Papeete's trendiest pubs and a fine place to wait for the Moorea ferry. You can sip the home brew at tables under a canvas awning out on the sidewalk or just inside the open-front, dark-wood tavern. The tabloid menu is all in French, but wait staffers speak enough English to explain the offerings. Choose from sandwiches, salads, half a roast chicken served hot or cold, and grilled steaks, mahimahi, tuna plain or with optional French sauces, and *jarret de porc*, smoked ham hocks served with sautéed potatoes and sauerkraut. The best deal here is the *croque brasseurs*, a ham sandwich served under melted Gruyère cheese and accompanied by a glass of beer and a green salad with excellent vinaigrette dressing, all for 900CFP ($7).

Bd. Pomare, between rue Prince Hinoi and rue Clappier, opposite Moorea ferry docks. ✆ **50.60.25.** Reservations not accepted. Sandwiches and salads 700CFP–1,500CFP ($5–$11); main courses 1,150CFP–2,400CFP ($8.50–$18). MC, V. Daily 9am–1am.

Lou Pescadou ⭐⭐ *Value* ITALIAN   A lively young professional clientele usually packs this quintessential Italian trattoria (red-and-white-checked tablecloths, dripping candles on each table, Ruffino bottles hanging from every nook and cranny). They come for good, fresh, and tasty Italian fare at reasonable prices (be prepared to wait for a table). The individual-size pizzas are cooked in a wood-fire oven range, and the pasta dishes include lasagna and spaghetti and fettuccine under tomato, carbonara, and Roquefort sauces.

Rue Anne-Marie Javouhey at passage Cardella. ✆ **43.74.26.** Reservations not accepted. Pizzas and pastas 600CFP–1,350CFP ($4.50–$10); meat courses 1,650CFP–2,450CFP ($12–$18). MC, V. Mon–Sat 11:30am–2pm and 6:30–11pm. Take the narrow passage Cardella, a 1-block street that looks like an alley, directly behind Centre Vaima.

INEXPENSIVE

L'Oasis du Vaima SNACK BAR   You'll find me having a breakfast of a small quiche or a tasty pastry with strong French coffee at this kiosklike building on the southwest corner of Centre Vaima. In addition to dishing out ice cream and milkshakes to passersby at a sidewalk counter, it serves up a variety of goodies, from crispy *casse-croûtes* to two delicious *plats-du-jour* selections each day, on a covered dining terrace and in an air-conditioned dining room upstairs. A special treat for Papeete: You can make a light meal from the salad bar.

Rue du Général-de-Gaulle at rue Jeanne d'Arc (at the corner of Centre Vaima, opposite Cathédrale de l'Immaculée Conception). ✆ **45.45.01.** Sandwiches, burgers, quiches, small pizzas 300CFP–1,000CFP ($2–$7.50); meals 1,300CFP–1,700CFP ($10–$13). No credit cards. Mon–Sat 5am–6pm.

Le Retrot FRENCH/ITALIAN/SNACKS   You'll find better food elsewhere, but this Parisian-style sidewalk cafe is a popular place to grab a quick bite, a drink, or an ice cream while watching the world pass along the quay. A diverse selection of salads, sandwiches, pizzas, and pasta gets attention from the cafe

A Very Indecent Dance

The young girls when ever they can collect 8 or 10 together dance a very indecent dance which they call Timorodee singing most indecent songs and useing most indecent actions in the practice of which they are brought up from their earlyest Childhood.
—Capt. James Cook, after seeing his first Tahitian dance show in 1769

Before the great explorer arrived, the Tahitians would stage a *heiva* (festival) for almost any reason, from blessing the harvest to celebrating a birth. After eating meals cooked in their earth ovens, they would get out the drums and nose flutes and dance the nights away. Some of the dances involved elaborate costumes, and others were quite lasciviously and explicitly danced in the nude or seminude, which added to Tahiti's reputation as an island of love.

The puritanical Protestant missionaries got laws enacted in the early 1820s to end all dancing. Of course, strict prohibition never works, and Tahitians—including a young Queen Pomare—would sneak into the hills to dance. Only after the French took over in 1842 was dancing permitted again, and then only with severe limitations on what the dancers could do and wear. A result of these various restrictions was that most of the traditional dances performed by the Tahitians before 1800 were totally forgotten within 100 years.

You'd never guess that Tahitians ever stopped dancing, for after tourists started coming in 1961, they went back to the old ways. Today traditional dancing is a huge part of their lives—and of every visitor's itinerary. No one goes away without vivid memories of the elaborate and colorful costumes, the thundering drums, and the swinging hips of a Tahitian *tamure* in which young men and women provocatively dance around each other.

The *tamure* is one of several dances performed during a typical dance show. Others are the *o'tea,* in which men and women in spectacular costumes dance certain themes, such as spear throwing, fighting, or love; the *aparima,* the hand dance, which emphasizes everyday themes, such as bathing and combing one's hair; the *hivinau,* in which men and women dance in circles and exclaim *"hiri haa haa"* when they meet each other; and the *pata'uta'u,* in which the dancers beat the ground or their thighs with their open hands. It's difficult to follow the themes without understanding Tahitian, but the color and rhythms (which have been influenced by faster, double-time beats from the Cook Islands) make the dances thoroughly enjoyable—and leave little doubt as to the temptations that inspired the mutiny on the *Bounty.*

crowd. There's also a tapas bar to one side and a good ice cream stand on the corner. Tahitian musicians usually entertain on Friday and Saturday nights and at midday Sunday.

Bd. Pomare, front of Centre Vaima, on waterfront. (*C*) **42.86.83.** Salads 400CFP–1,200CFP ($3–$9); sandwiches and burgers 500CFP–800CFP ($4–$6); pizza and pastas 700CFP–1,300CFP ($5–$10); main courses 1,650CFP–2,150CFP ($12–$16). AE, MC, V. Daily 6am–midnight.

Jugglers, dancers and an assortment of acrobats fill the street.

She shoots you a wide-eyed look as a seven-foot cartoon character approaches.

What brought you here was wanting the kids

to see something magical while they still believed in magic.

America Online Keyword: Travel

With 700 airlines, 50,000 hotels and over 5,000 cruise and vaca-

tion getaways, you can now go places you've always dreamed of.

Travelocity.com
A Sabre Company
Go Virtually Anywhere.

"WORLD'S LEADING TRAVEL WEB SITE, 5 YEARS IN A ROW." WORLD TRAVEL AWARDS

I HAVE TO CALL THE TRAVEL AGENCY AGAIN. DARN, OUT TO LUNCH. NOW I HAVE TO CALL THE AIRLINE. I HATE CALLING THE AIRLINES. I GOT PUT ON HOLD AGAIN. "INSTRUMENTAL TOP-40" ... LOVELY. I HATE GETTING PUT ON HOLD. TICKET PRICES ARE ALL OVER THE MAP. HOW DO I DIAL INTERNATIONALLY? OH SHOOT, FORGOT THE RENTAL CAR. I'M STILL ON HOLD. THIS MUSIC IS GIVING ME A HEADACHE. I WONDER IF SOMEONE ELSE HAS CHEAPER FLIGHTS. FORGET IT, CAN'T TAKE IT ANYMORE ... I'M HANGING UP.

YAHOO! TRAVEL
100% MUZAK-FREE

Booking your trip online at Yahoo! Travel is simple. You compare the best prices. You click. You go have fun. Tickets, hotels, rental cars, cruises & more. Sorry, no muzak.

YAHOO!
Travel
travel.yahoo.com

Pacific Burger (Value) SNACK BAR   Cost-conscious guests at Le Meridien Tahiti resort walk next door to this open-air snack bar for good, reasonably priced salads, poisson cru, sashimi, pizzas from a wood-fired oven, burgers (beef, chicken, or fish), and grilled rib-eye steaks, and fish with or without sauce. A big tarp covers plastic patio tables and chairs in front of the fast-food-style counter. The friendly staff will hand you menu in English as soon as they figure out you're a tourist. The Tahiti museum is a few blocks away, so this is a good place to stop for refreshment on your round-island tour.

P.K. 15, Punaauia. (C) **42.40.84.** Reservations not accepted. Burgers 400CFP–850CFP ($3–$6); pizza 700CFP–1,400CFP ($5–$10.50); main courses 1,300–1,800CFP ($10–$13.50). MC, V. Tues–Sun 10am–3pm and 5:30–9pm.

7 Island Nights

A 19th-century European merchant wrote of the Tahitians, "Their existence was in never-ending merrymaking." In many respects this is still true, for after the sun goes down, Tahitians like to make merry as much today as they did in the 1830s, and Papeete has lots of good choices for visitors who want to join in the fun.

TAHITIAN DANCE SHOWS ★★★

Traditional Tahitian dancing isn't as indecent as it was in Captain Cook's day (see the box "A Very Indecent Dance," above), but seeing at least one show should be on your agenda. You'll have plenty of chances, since nightlife on the outer islands consists almost exclusively of dance shows at the resorts, usually in conjunction with a feast of Tahitian food.

Each of Tahiti's big resort hotels has shows at least 1 night a week. Not to be missed is the **Grande Danse de Tahiti** troupe, which usually performs at the Tahiti Beachcomber Inter-Continental Resort ((C) **86.51.10**) on Friday and Saturday evenings. Call the resort to make sure. Another good place to catch a show is the **Captain Bligh Restaurant and Bar** ((C) **43.62.90**), which usually has them on Friday and Saturday at 8:30pm.

PUB CRAWLING

Papeete has a nightclub or watering hole to fit anyone's taste, from upscale private (*privé*) discotheques to down-and-dirty bars and dance halls where Tahitians strum on guitars while sipping on large bottles of Hinano beer (and sometimes engage in a fisticuffs after midnight). If you look like a tourist, you'll be allowed into the private clubs. Generally, everything gets to full throttle after 9pm (except on Sun, when most pubs are closed). None of the clubs are inexpensive. Expect to pay at least 1,000CFP ($7.50) cover charge, which will include your first drink. After that, beers cost at least 500CFP ($3.75), with most mixed drinks in the 1,000CFP to 1,500CFP ($7.50–$11) range.

Before you head out, stroll over to the Municipal Market, where you will find Tahitian women weaving flower crowns, traditional headgear for Papeete's female merrymakers. Buy one if you want to look the part. The Tahitians will love you for it; everyone else will think you're a silly tourist.

The narrow rue des Ecoles is the heart of Papeete's mahu district, where male transvestites hang out. The **Piano Bar** ((C) **42.88.24**) is the most popular of the "sexy clubs" along this street, especially for its late-night strip shows featuring female impersonators. When you've seen enough, go next door to **Lido Nightclub** ((C) **42.95.84**). Both are open daily from 3pm to 3am. The multistory **Mana Rock Cafe,** at the corner of boulevard Pomare and rue des Ecoles ((C) **48.36.36**), draws a more mixed crowd to its bars and discotheque.

Impressions

They have several negative comments on the beachcombing life in Tahiti: Not much cultural life. No intellectual stimulus. No decent library. Restaurant food is disgraceful . . . But I noticed that Saturday after Saturday they turned up at Quinn's with the most dazzling beauties on the island. When I reminded them of this they said, "Well that does compensate for the poor library."

—James A. Michener, *Return to Paradise,* 1951

8 An Easy Excursion to Tetiaroa

Marlon Brando did more than star in the remake of *Mutiny on the Bounty* when he came to Tahiti in 1962. He fell in love with his beautiful Tahitian costar, Tarita Terepaia, who became his wife and the mother of two of his children. He also fell for Tetiaroa, an atoll 42km (25 miles) north of Tahiti and Moorea.

In the old days, this cluster of 12 flat islets surrounding an aquamarine lagoon was the playground of Tahiti's high chiefs, who were frequently joined by the *Arioi,* those traveling bands of sexually explicit entertainers and practitioners of infanticide. High-ranking women would spend months on Tetiaroa, resting in the shade to lighten their skins and gouging on starchy foods to broaden their girths. Chiefly men and women were said to possess *mana,* and the bigger the body, the more the *mana.*

For a time, a British dentist who married into the royal family owned Tetiaroa, but the island was abandoned when Brando bought it in 1966. He turned one of his islets into a refuge for Tetiaroa's thousands of seabirds. He built a retreat for himself on a second islet and a small, rather rustic resort on a third. Guests at the resort would seldom see the actor, on whose waistline Tetiaroa worked its expansive magic. During the day he would stay at home in the shade, playing with his radios and computers. At night he would go fishing and lobstering.

A series of hurricanes almost blew his resort away in 1983, and Brando's relationship with Tahiti turned to human disaster a decade later, when his son Christian shot and killed his sister's Tahitian boyfriend in Hollywood. Marlon's distraught daughter later committed suicide on Tahiti.

Brando's ex-wife Tarita still operates the resort, which is once again a local playground, especially on weekends. **Hotel Tetiaroa,** B.P. 2418, Papeete, Tahiti (© **82.63.02;** fax 85.00.51), has a booth in the Air Moorea terminal at Tahiti-Faaa International Airport, where you can book day trips for 24,800CFP ($184) per person, including airfare, lunch, and a boat trip to Bird Island. Overnight stays cost 32,900CFP ($244) for one person or 56,600CFP ($419) per couple, including air, hotel, and meals.

5

Moorea

Most visitors to French Polynesia soon grab the ferry to Moorea, and with very good reason. Only 20km (12 miles) from Tahiti, Moorea is an island so stunningly beautiful that Hollywood often uses stock shots of its jagged mountains, deep bays, and emerald lagoons to create a South Seas setting for movies that don't even take place in French Polynesia. This still is a surprisingly peaceful island, where a hint of old Polynesia coexists with modern resort hotels and fine restaurants. Compared to the noisy city across the Sea of the Moon, Moorea is a rural paradise. (An increasing number of Moorea residents take the ferry to work in Papeete each weekday morning—and ride your bumper in their haste to get there.) And it's a clean and tidy paradise, thanks to a mayor who sends out crews to pick up roadside trash.

Geologists attribute Moorea's rugged beauty to a great volcano, the northern half of which either fell into the sea or was blown away in a cataclysmic explosion, leaving the heart-shaped island we see today. The remaining rim of the old crater has eroded into the jagged peaks and spires that give the island its haunting, dinosaur-like profile. Cathedral-like Mount Mouaroa—Moorea's trademark "Shark's Tooth" or "Bali Hai Mountain"—shows up on innumerable postcards and on the 100CFP coin. Mount Tohiea has a hole in its thumblike top, made by the legendary hero Pai when the god of thieves attempted to steal Mount Rotui in the middle of the night. Legend says Pai threw his spear from Tahiti and pierced the top of Mount Tohiea. The noise woke up Moorea's roosters, which alerted the citizenry to put a stop to the dastardly plan.

Mount Rotui stands alone in the center of the ancient crater, its black cliffs and stovepipe buttresses dropping dramatically into Cook's Bay and Opunohu Bay, two dark blue fingers that cut deep into Moorea's interior. If not the world's most gorgeous bodies of water, these mountain-shrouded bays are certainly among the most photographed.

A paved road climbs to the base of the cliffs of the crater's wall to the Belvédère overlooking both bays, Mount Rotui, and the jagged old crater rim curving off to left and right. It is one of the South Pacific's most awesome views.

An offshore coral reef around Moorea encloses a calm blue lagoon, making the island ideal for swimming, boating, snorkeling, and diving. Unlike the black sands of Tahiti, white beaches stretch for miles on Moorea.

There are no towns on Moorea, which adds to its charm. Most of the island's 12,000 or so residents live on its fringing coastal plain, many of them in small settlements where lush valleys meet the lagoon. Vanilla was the island's big crop early in the 20th century, and clapboard "vanilla houses" built with the profits still stand, surrounded by wide verandas trimmed with Victorian fretwork.

Impressions

From Tahiti, Moorea seems to have about forty separate summits: fat thumbs of basalt, spires tipped at impossible angles, brooding domes compelling to the eye. But the peaks which can never be forgotten are the jagged saw-edges that look like the spines of some forgotten dinosaur.
—James A. Michener, *Return to Paradise*, 1951

Tourism is the base of Moorea's economy today, but vegetables, pineapples, and copra are still grown and are shipped to market in Papeete.

1 Getting Around

Except for the *Ono Ono,* which docks in Cook's Bay, the ferries from Papeete land at Vaiare, 5km (3 miles) south of **Temae Airport** on Moorea's east coast (see "Getting There & Getting Around" in chapter 3).

Buses meet most ferries at Vaiare to carry passengers to their final destinations. Tell the drivers where you're going; they will show you which vehicle is going to your hotel. The trip from Vaiare to the end of the line at the Club Med, on Moorea's northwest corner, takes about 1 hour. These buses also return to Vaiare prior to each departure, starting at the Club Med. They stop at the hotels and can be flagged down along the road elsewhere. The one-way fare is 200CFP ($1.50), regardless of direction or length of ride.

BY TAXI Moorea's taxis are owned by individuals who don't run around looking for customers. The only **taxi stands** are at the airport (© **56.10.18**) and Club Med (© **56.33.10**). The airport stand is staffed daily from 6am to 6pm. The hotel desks can call one for you, or phone **Pero Taxis** (© **56.14.93**) or **Albert Tours** (© **56.13.53**). Make advance reservations for service between 6pm and 6am.

Fares are 600CFP ($4.50) plus 110CFP (30¢) per kilometer. They double from 8pm to 6am. Expect to pay about 2,000CFP ($15) one way from the ferry or airport to the Cook's Bay area, about 3,500CFP ($26) one way from the airport or Cook's Bay to the Club Med area, less for stops along the way. Be sure that you understand what the fare will be before you get in.

BY RENTAL CAR & SCOOTER Avis (© **800/331-1212** or 56.32.68; www.avis.com) has a booth at the airport, and **Europcar** (© **800/227-7368** or 56.34.00; www.europcar.com) has booths at the Vaiare ferry wharf, opposite Club Med, and elsewhere on Moorea. Europcar is the more widespread and the less expensive of the two, with daily rates starting at 8,100CFP ($60). Europcar also rents little "Fun Cars" (noisy, open-air buglike contraptions with two seats and three wheels) starting at 4,300CFP ($32) for 4 hours. The local firm **Albert Rent-a-Car** (© **56.13.53**) has unlimited-kilometers rates starting at 8,000CFP ($60) for a day. Insurance is included in all rates, but gasoline is not.

Europcar also rents scooters and mopeds starting at 4,500CFP ($33) for 4 hours and 5,500CFP ($41) for 24 hours, including gasoline, full insurance, and unlimited kilometers. Albert Rent-a-Car's scooter prices are about 500CFP ($3.75) less.

Making reservations for cars and scooters is a very good idea, especially on weekends, when many Tahiti residents come to Moorea for a day or two.

BY BICYCLE The 60km (36-mile) road around Moorea is relatively flat. The two major hills are on the west side of Cook's Bay and just behind the Sofitel Coralia Ia Ora (the latter is worth the climb, since it has a stupendous view of Tahiti). **Europcar** (see above) rents mountain bikes for about 1,500CFP ($11) for 8 hours, 2,000CFP ($15) if you keep a bike overnight.

 ## FAST FACTS: Moorea

The following facts apply specifically to Moorea. For more information, see "Fast Facts: French Polynesia" in chapter 3.

Bookstores **Kina Maharepa** (© 56.22.44) in the Maharepa shopping center has English novels and magazines. **Supersonics** (© 56.14.96) in Le Petit Village shopping center opposite Club Med carries some English-language magazines and newspapers.

Camera/Film The hotel boutiques, **Kina Maharepa** (© 56.22.44) in the Maharepa shopping center, and **Supersonics** (© 56.14.96) in Le Petit Village opposite the Club Med all sell film.

Currency Exchange **Banque Socredo, Banque de Tahiti,** and **Banque de Polynésie** have offices in or near the Maharepa shopping center near the Hotel Bali Hai. **Banque de Polynésie** also is in Le Petit Village opposite the Club Med, and Banque Socredo has an office at Vaiare. Banque Socredo and Banque de Polynésie have ATMs at their branches. Banks are open Monday to Friday from 8am to noon and 1:30 to 4:30pm.

Drugstores **Pharmacie Tran** (© 56.10.51) is in Maharepa. The owner, Tran Thai Thanh, is a Vietnamese refugee who speaks English. It's open Monday to Friday from 7:30am to noon and 2 to 5pm; Saturday from 7:30am to noon; and Sunday and holidays from 8 to 11am. In case of emergency, knock on the door.

E-mail **C.Y.M.** (© 55.01.45), in Le Petit Village opposite the Club Med, has computers with Internet connections. Access time costs 25CFP (19¢) a minute. Open daily from 9am to 7pm.

Emergencies/Police The emergency police telephone number is © 17. The telephone number for the **gendarmerie** in Cook's Bay is © 56.13.44. Local police have offices at **Pao Pao** (© 56.13.63) and at **Haapiti** (© 56.10.84), near Club Med.

Hairdressers/Barbers **Harmony Coiffure** (© 56.18.04) is in Centre Noha in Maharepa, opposite the post office.

Healthcare **Dr. Christian Joinville** (© 56.32.32) has an office in Centre Noha, opposite the post office in Maharepa. He has lived on Moorea many years, speaks English fluently, and has treated many visitors, including me. The island's **infirmary,** which has an ambulance, is at Afareaitu on the southwest coast (© 56.24.24).

Information The local **Comité du Tourisme,** B.P. 1121, Papetoai, Moorea (© 56.29.09), has an office at Le Petit Village shopping center opposite the Club Med. Hours are Monday to Saturday from 8am to 5pm (more or less; they sometimes change). The committee has a booth at the airport, where you can pick up maps and brochures any time.

Post Office Moorea's main post office is in the shopping center at Maharepa. It's open Monday to Thursday 7:30am to noon and 1:30 to 3pm, Friday to 3pm, and Saturday 7:30 to 9:30am. You place long-distance and international telephone calls at the counter. A new post office in Papetoai village will be open by the time you get here.

Taxes Moorea's municipal government adds 100CFP to 150CFP (75¢–$1) per night to your hotel bill. Don't complain: The money keeps the island litter-free.

Water Tap water on Moorea is not safe to drink, so buy bottled water at any grocery store. Some hotels filter their water; ask if it's safe before drinking from the tap.

2 Exploring Moorea

The sights of Moorea may lack great historical significance, but the physical beauty of the island makes a tour—at least of the north shore, around Cook's and Opunohu bays—a highlight of any visit here. There are few places on earth this gorgeous.

As on Tahiti, the round-island road is marked every kilometer with a PK post. Distances are measured between the intersection of the airport road with the main round-island coastal road and the village of Haapiti on Moorea's opposite side. In other words, the distances indicated on the PKs increase from the airport in each direction, reaching 30km near Haapiti. They then decrease as you head back to the airport.

THE CIRCLE ISLAND TOUR ★★★

The hotel activities desks offer tours around Moorea and up to the Belvédère lookout in the interior. **Albert Tours** (② **56.13.53**) and **Moorea Explorer** (② **56.12.86**) have half-day round-island tours, including the Belvédère, for about 2,500CFP ($19) per person. The tour buses all stop at one black pearl shop or another (guess who gets a commission when you buy the pearl of your dreams?). I suggest you look at more than one establishment before making a purchase because quality, settings, and prices vary from store to store (see "Shopping," below).

MAHAREPA   Begin at the airport on Moorea's northeast corner and head counterclockwise around the island. The airstrip is on the island's only sizable area of flat land. At one time it was a *motu*, or small island, sitting on the reef by itself. Humans and nature have since filled the lagoon except for Lake Temae, which you can see from the air if you fly to Moorea. Head west from the round-island road/airport road junction.

Temae, 1km (½ mile) from the junction, supplied the dancers for the Pomare dynasty's court and is still known for the quality of its performers. Herman Melville spent some time here in 1842 and saw the famous, erotic *upaupa*, which he called the "lory-lory," performed clandestinely, out of sight of the missionaries.

The relatively dry north shore between the airport and the entrance to Cook's Bay is known as **Maharepa.** The road skirts the lagoon and passes the Hotel Bali Hai and the shopping center and other businesses that have grown up around it.

Moorea

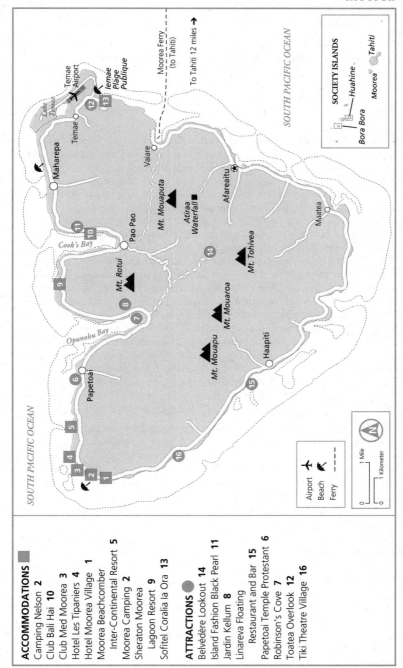

SOCIETY ISLANDS

Huahine
Moorea
Tahiti
Bora Bora

SOUTH PACIFIC OCEAN

SOUTH PACIFIC OCEAN

Moorea Ferry
(to Tahiti)

To Tahiti 12 miles →

Temae
Airport
Temae

Lake
Temae

Maharepa

Temae

Teavaro

Iemae
Plage
Publique

Viaire

Maatea

Afareaitu

Atiraa
Waterfall

Mt. Mouaputa

Mt. Tohivea

Mt. Rotui

Pao Pao

Cook's Bay

Opunohu Bay

Mt. Mouaroa

Mt. Mouapu

Haapiti

Papetoai

Airport
Beach
Ferry

0   1 Mile
0   1 Kilometer

ACCOMMODATIONS

Camping Nelson **2**
Club Bali Hai **10**
Club Med Moorea **3**
Hotel Les Tipaniers **4**
Hotel Moorea Village **1**
Moorea Beachcomber
  Inter-Continental Resort **5**
Moorea Camping **2**
Sheraton Moorea
  Lagoon Resort **9**
Sofitel Coralia la Ora **13**

ATTRACTIONS

Belvédère Lookout **14**
Island Fashion Black Pearl **11**
Jardin Kellum **8**
Linareva Floating
  Restaurant and Bar **15**
Papetoai Temple Protestant **6**
Robinson's Cove **7**
Toatea Overlook **12**
Tiki Theatre Village **16**

Moments   Riding Around Moorea

Few things give me as much pleasure as riding around Moorea, its magnificent peaks hanging over my head one minute and plunging into its two great bays the next. I've done it by bicycle, scooter, car, and foot, and I always have trouble keeping my eyes on the road, so dramatically beautiful are the surroundings.

COOK'S BAY ★★★   As the road curves to the left, you enter **Cook's Bay,** the fingerlike body of water virtually surrounded on three sides by the jagged peaks lining the semicircular "wall" of Moorea. **Mount Tohiea** is the large thumb with a small hole in its top made by Pai's spear. **Mount Mouaroa,** the "Shark's Tooth," is the cathedral-like mountain buttressed on its right by a serrated ridge. It comes into view as you drive farther along the bay.

Huddled along the curving beach at the head of the bay, the village of **Pao Pao** is one of Moorea's economic centers. The *Marché Municipale* (Municipal Market) is open Monday to Saturday from 5am to 5pm and Sunday from 5 to 8am. Unlike Papeete's market, this one has slim pickings. The paved road that seems to run through the school next to the bridge cuts through the valley between Cook's Bay and Opunohu Bay. Its surface soon turns to dirt, but it intersects with the main road between Opunohu Bay and the Belvédère lookout.

The small **St. Joseph's Catholic Church** sits on the shore on the west side of Cook's Bay, at PK 10 from the airport. Inside is a large mural that artist Peter Heyman painted in 1946 and an altar decorated with mother-of-pearl. From the church, the road climbs up the side of the hill, offering some fine views, and then descends back to the lagoon's edge. Here you'll pass the University of California's **Gump Biological Research Station** and then a road leading to the **Moorea Distillery and Fruit Juice Factory** (© 56.22.33), which turns the island's produce into the Rotui juices sold throughout French Polynesia.

OPUNOHU BAY ★★★   Towering over you is jagged **Mount Rotui,** the huge green-and-black rock separating Moorea's two great bays. Unlike Cook's Bay, Opunohu is virtually devoid of development, a testament to efforts by local residents to maintain the natural beauty of their island (they have ardently resisted efforts to build a luxury resort and golf course here). As soon as the road levels out, you can look through the trees to yachts anchored in **Robinson's Cove,** one of the world's most photographed yacht anchorages. Stop here and put your camera to work.

JARDIN KELLUM ★★   From the cove, you can walk along the shore to **Jardin Kellum** (© 56.18.52), at PK 17.5 on the round-island road, an extraordinary bay-side botanical garden started by the late Medford and Gladys Kellum, an American couple that once owned all of Opunohu Valley. The Kellums arrived here in 1925, aboard his parents' converted lumber schooner, and they lived for 65 years in their clapboard colonial-style house, which still looks

---

Impressions

Seen for the first time by European Eyes, this coast is like nothing else on our workaday planet; a landscape, rather, of some fantastic dream.
—Charles Nordhoff and James Norman Hall, *Mutiny on the Bounty,* 1933

Moments **The View from Belvédère Lookout**

If the view from Le Belvédère restaurant on Tahiti doesn't thrill me enough, the scene from the Moorea lookout of the same name certainly does. I never tire of standing at the base of that cliff and watching dramatic Mount Rotui separate the deep blue fingers of Cook's and Oponohu bays.

---

out over the bay. Today their daughter, Marimari Kellum, will give you a personalized tour of the house and garden and explain (in French or English) the 100-plus species of tropical plants growing here. She charges 500CFP ($3.75) per person and offers tours Tuesday to Saturday, preferably in the mornings. Just show up and ring the cowbell by the road.

From the garden, the road soon curves right along a beach backed by shade trees and the valley at the head of Opunohu Bay. The beach was turned into Matavai Bay on Tahiti for the 1983 production of *The Bounty*, starring Mel Gibson and Anthony Hopkins.

BELVÉDÈRE LOOKOUT ★★★   After the bridge by the beach, a paved road runs up Moorea's central valley through pasture land, across which Warren Beatty and Annette Benning strolled in the movie *Love Affair* (the scenes with Katherine Hepburn were filmed in the white house on the hill to your right). The road then climbs steeply up the old crater wall to the restored **Titiroa Marae,** which was part of a concentration of marae and other structures. Higher up you'll pass an archery platform used for competition (archery was a sport reserved for high-ranking chiefs and was never used in warfare in Polynesia). A display in the main *marae* parking lot explains the history of this area. You can walk among the remains of the temples, now shaded by towering Tahitian chestnut trees that have grown up through the cobblestone-like courtyards.

The narrow road then ascends to **Belvédère Lookout,** whose awesome panorama of the valley and the bays on either side of Mount Rotui is unmatched in the South Pacific. You won't want to be without film here. There's a snack bar in the parking lot, so grab a cold drink or ice cream while you take in this remarkable vista.

PAPETOAI   Back on the coastal road, the sizable village of **Papetoai,** which has more than its share of vanilla houses, was the retreat of the Pomare dynasty in the 1800s and the base from which Pomare I launched his successful drive to take over all of Tahiti and Moorea. It was also headquarters for the London Missionary Society's work throughout the South Pacific, and the road to the right, past the new post office, leads to the octagonal **Papetoai Temple Protestant,** built on the site of a *marae* dedicated to Oro, son of the supreme Taaroa and the god of war. The original church was constructed in the 1820s, and although advertised as the oldest European building still in use in the South Pacific, the present structure dates from the late 1880s.

HAAPITI   From Papetoai, the road runs through the Club Med hotel district on the northwest corner and then heads south through the rural parts of Moorea. The 300-bungalow Club Med and the businesses it has generated, including Le Petit Village shopping center across the road, dominate the northwest corner of the island.

The Club Med area is your last chance to stop for refreshment before you travel the sparsely populated southern half of Moorea. There are several choices here (see "Where to Dine," below).

About 4km (2½ miles) beyond Club Med, look for the **Tiki Theatre Village** ⭐⭐⭐, a cultural center that consists of thatch huts on the coastal side of the road. It's the only place to see what a Tahitian village looked like when Captain Cook arrived, so pull in. See "Tiki Theatre Village," below, for details.

When the first Europeans arrived, the lovely, mountain-backed village of **Haapiti** was home of the powerful Marama family, which was allied with the Pomares. It became a center of Catholic missionary work after the French took over the territory, and it is one of the few villages whose Catholic church is as large as its Protestant counterpart. Stop here and look up behind the village for a view of Mount Mouaroa from a unique perspective.

THE SOUTH COAST South of Haapiti, just as the road curves sharply around a headland, is a nice view of a small bay with the mountains towering overhead (there's no place to park on the headland, so stop and walk up for the view). In contrast to the more touristy north shore, the southeast and southwest coasts have retained an atmosphere of old Polynesia.

The village of **Afareaitu,** on the southeast coast, is the administrative center of Moorea, and the building that looks like a charming hotel across from the village church actually is the island's *mairie,* or town hall.

About half a kilometer (¼ mile) beyond the town hall, opposite an A-frame house on the shore, an unpaved road runs straight between several houses and then continues uphill to the **Atiraa Waterfall** ⭐⭐. A favorite stop on four-wheel-drive safari expeditions, the falls plunge more than 32m (100 ft.) down a cliff, into a small pool. You can drive partway to the falls, then walk 20 minutes up a steep, slippery, and muddy trail. Wear shoes or sandals that have good traction if you make this trek, for in places the slippery trail is hacked into a steep hill; if you slip, it's a long way down to the rocks below. Villagers will be waiting at the beginning of the footpath to extract an access fee of 200CFP ($1.50) per person.

Beyond Afareaitu, the small bay of **Vaiare** is a beehive of activity when the ferries pull in from Papeete.

Just past the Sofitel Coralia Ia Ora, the road climbs a hill. At the top is the **Toatea Overlook** ⭐⭐⭐. Here you'll have a magnificent view of the hotel, the green lagoon flecked with brown coral heads, the white line of the surf breaking on the reef, the deep blue of the Sea of the Moon, and all of Tahiti rising magnificently from the horizon. There's a parking area at the overlook, so stop and burn up some film.

The unpaved road to the right at the bottom of the hill leads to the **Temae Plage Publique** ⭐⭐, Moorea's finest stretch of public beach. Follow the left fork through the coconut grove to the lagoon. This is a continuation of the Sofitel

---

⌒Moments Tahiti in All Its Glory

My neck strains every time I cross the hill behind Moorea's Sofitel Coralia Ia Ora, for there across the Sea of the Moon sits Tahiti in all its green glory. What amazement the early explorers must have felt when those mountains appeared over the horizon!

Impressions

Nothing on Tahiti is so majestic as what faces it across the bay, for there lies the island of Moorea. To describe it is impossible. It is a monument to the prodigal beauty of nature.

—James A. Michener, *Return to Paradise,* 1951

Coralia Ia Ora's beach, except that here you don't have a staff to rake the leaves and coral gravel from the sand. Locals often sell snacks and souvenirs here, especially on weekends. Bring insect repellent if you do your beaching here.

SAFARI TOURS ★★

You can see the sights and learn a lot about the island on a four-wheel-drive excursion through Moorea's mountainous interior. Among several tour operators, I think Alex and Gheslaine Haamatearii's **Inner Island Safari Tours** (© **56.20.09**) is the best. They will take you through the valleys, up to Belvédère Lookout, and then down to a vanilla plantation in Opunohu Valley. They explain the island's flora and fauna along the way. The trip ends with a drive around Moorea's south coast and a hike up to Atiraa Waterfall for a refreshing swim (see "The South Coast," under "The Circle Island Tour," above). Alex and Gheslaine charge 4,500CFP ($33) per person for a half-day tour, 6,000CFP ($45) for a full day.

American Derek Grell of **Tefaarahi Safari Tours** (© **56.41.24**) can take you up to see ancient petroglyphs he has discovered on land he owns up in the highlands. Derek charges the same as Inner Island Safari Tours.

You can book these safari tours at any hotel activities desk.

LAGOON EXCURSIONS ★★★

One of the best ways to experience Moorea is on a half- or full-day boat trip out on the lagoon. The full-day version of these excursions invariably includes a "motu picnic"—a lunch of grilled fresh fish, poisson cru, and salads served on one of the little islets out on the reef. Quite often the fresh fish is caught on the way to the motu. You'll have an opportunity to snorkel in the lagoon, and the staff will show you how to husk a coconut.

Based at the Club Bali Hai in Cook's Bay, Hiro Kelley's **Moorea Tours** (© **56.13.68**) offers snorkeling and glass-bottom-boat trips in addition to lagoon excursions. His motu picnic features a leisurely ride along the north shore, past both bays, in a thatched-roof vessel equipped with two outboard motors. You'll walk from the boat to the motu—a small island near Club Med—so wear shoes you don't mind getting wet. Hiro's trips range in price from 2,500CFP ($19) for a glass-bottom-boat ride to 5,000CFP ($37) for either the motu picnic (including the libation) or a shark-feeding expedition. Call for schedule and prices.

A variation on the motu picnic theme is a **Coconut Cookout** with Maco Roometua, a gregarious, English-speaking Tahitian based at the Sofitel Coralia Ia Ora (© **55.03.55** or 56.36.05 at home; mooreablue@mail.pf). Maco takes you out to a small island off Moorea's southeast coast in the *A'a Katiki Nui,* a traditional Tahitian sailing outrigger. You can snorkel (bring your own gear) and watch Maco and the staff feed the sharks. You can take a less exciting snorkel while Maco's crew grills fish and chicken for a picnic lunch on the beach. Maco usually voyages on Tuesday and Friday from 9am to 3:30pm and charges

7,500CFP ($56) a head, including lunch, soft drinks, beer, and wine. (*Note:* Unlike Moorea Tours, Maco combines the picnic and shark-feeding trips into one, hence, the higher price.)

TIKI THEATRE VILLAGE ★★★

The best cultural experience in all of French Polynesia is at **Tiki Theatre Village,** 2km (1¼ miles) south of Club Med (© **56.18.97;** www.tikivillage.pf). Built in the fashion of ancient Tahitian villages, this cultural center has old-style *fares* (houses) in which the staff demonstrates traditional tattooing, tapa-cloth making and painting, wood and stone carving, weaving, cooking, and making costumes, musical instruments, and flower crowns. There's even a "royal" house floating out on the lagoon, where you can learn about the modern art of growing black pearls.

Tiki Theatre Village will even arrange a traditional beachside wedding. The bride is prepared with flowery *monoi* oil like a Tahitian princess, and the groom is tattooed (with a wash-off pen). Both wear traditional costumes.

The village is open Tuesday to Saturday from 11:30am to 3pm. Admission and a guided tour costs 2,000CFP ($15).

The village also stages a terrific evening Tahitian feast and dance show (see "Island Nights," below).

3 Dolphin-Watching, Hiking, Watersports & Other Outdoor Activities

Local residents have successfully fought various proposals to build a golf course on Moorea, so for the time being, stay on Tahiti if you must play. Moorea also has no public tennis courts, so pick a hotel that has them if tennis is important to you.

DOLPHIN- & WHALE-WATCHING   Among the many activities at the Moorea Beachcomber Inter-Continental Resort (see "Watersports," below), by far the most popular is **Dolphin Quest** ★★ (© **55.19.48;** www.dolphinquest. org). These encounters with the intelligent sea mammals are sure to excite young and old alike. Children as young as 5 years old can wade in shallow water with the dolphins, which live in a fenced area (Dolphin Quest is dedicated to their care and conservation). Kids 12 and older can join adults in snorkeling with the mammals in deeper water. The wading excursions cost 16,500CFP ($122) for adults, 7,500CFP ($56) for children 5 to 12, and snorkeling with the dolphins costs 18,700CFP ($139) for kids and adults. Adults can also don a diving helmet and walk with the dolphins for 15,000CFP ($111). Call for reservations.

More educational are the dolphin- and whale-watching excursions led by American marine biologist **Dr. Michael Poole** ★★★ (© **56.28.44**). An expert on sea mammals, Dr. Poole will take you out beyond the reef to meet some of the 150 acrobatic spinner dolphins he has identified as regular Moorea residents. In calm conditions you can don snorkeling gear and swim with them. You'll also be on the lookout for pilot whales that swim past year-round and giant humpback whales that frequent these waters from July to October. The half-day excursions cost about 5,000CFP ($37) per person, including pickup at most hotel docks.

FISHING   Chris Lilley, an American who has won several sportfishing contests, takes guests onto the open ocean in search of big game on his *Tea Nui* (© **55.19.19,** ext. 1903, or 56.15.08 at home). You can go out for half a day for about 16,000CFP ($119) per person, or charter the boat for a whole day for about 63,000CFP ($467). In keeping with South Pacific custom, you can keep the little fish you catch; Chris sells the big ones. Chris is based at the Moorea Beachcomber Inter-Continental Resort.

HIKING   You won't need a guide to hike from the coast road up the Opunohu Valley to Belvédère Lookout. Up and down will take most of a day. It's a level but hot walk along the valley floor and steep approaching the lookout. Bring lots of water.

Tropic Escape (② and fax **56.42.49**), offers guided hikes ranging from a 2-hour stroll to a waterfall to an 8-hour climb to the summit of Mount Rotui. Prices range from 3,000CFP to 5,000CFP ($22–$37) per person. The activities center at the **Moorea Beachcomber Inter-Continental Resort** (② **55.19.19**) also has guided half- and full-day hikes at 3,200CFP and 4,200CFP ($24 and $31) per person, respectively.

HORSEBACK RIDING   Landlubbers can go horseback riding along the beach and into the interior with **Tiahura Ranch** (② **56.28.55**), west of Club Med, or with **Pegasus Ranch** (② **56.34.11**) in Maharepa. Rates are about 3,500CFP ($26) for a 1-hour ride.

SCUBA DIVING   Although Moorea's lagoon is not in the same league with those at Rangiroa and Bora Bora, its outer reef has some decent sites for viewing coral and sea life. The island's best diving operator is **TOPdive** (② **56. 17.32;** www.topdive.com), with bases in Cook's Bay and at the Sheraton Moorea Lagoon Resort & Spa. On the northwest coast, the Moorea Beachcomber Inter-Continental Resort is home to **Bathy's Club Moorea** (② **55. 19.19,** ext. 1139), and **Scubapiti Moorea** (② **56.30.38**) resides at Hotel Les Tipaniers. All charge about 5,500CFP ($41) for one dive, including equipment (gauges are metric). Beginners' lessons cost about 6,500CFP ($48).

WATERSPORTS   Most hotels have active watersports programs for their guests, such as glass-bottomed-boat cruises and snorkeling in, or sailing on, Moorea's beautiful lagoon. Of the resort hotels, the Sofitel Coralia Ia Ora and Club Med have the best lagoons for water sports.

By far the most extensive array of sporting activities is at the **Moorea Beach-comber Inter-Continental Resort** (② **55.19.19**), whose facilities can be used by both guests and visitors who are willing to pay. In addition to Bathy's Club Moorea scuba diving (see above), these facilities include parasailing (magnificent views of the bays, mountains, and reefs from up there hanging from a parachute); water-skiing; sailboarding; scooting about the lagoon and Opunohu Bay on jet skis; viewing coral and fish from Aquascope boats; walking on the lagoon bottom while wearing diving helmets; sailing on a 38-foot catamaran; viewing coral from a glass-bottom boat; line fishing; and speedboat rentals. Nonguests can also pay to use the pool, snorkeling gear, and tennis courts, and to be taken over to a small islet. Call the hotel for prices, schedules, and reservations, which are required.

4 Shopping

THE SHOPPING SCENE

Of Moorea's many boutiques and other shops, I mention those that have been in business for many years and that I have found to give good value for your money.

Every village has at least one Chinese grocery store. **Chez Toa** supermarket at Vaiare is by far the island's largest. All the staff speak English at **Chez Are**, a modern establishment on Cook's Bay in Pao Pao.

A one-stop place to shop is in front of Club Med, where numerous stores sell pareus, T-shirts, souvenirs, and some Marquesan wood carvings. The neocolonial buildings of **Le Petit Village** shopping center anchor this area. A **Sibani Perles** outlet occupies about a third of the center (see below), and **Supersonics** (ⓒ **56.29.73**) carries film, watch and camera batteries, stamps, magazines, and other items; **Tahiti Parfum** (ⓒ **56.17.12**) sells French perfumes; and **Arts Polynésiens** purveys wood carvings from the Marquesas Islands (see separate listing below). There's also a branch of Chez Toa supermarket here.

ART

Galerie A.P.I.   Take the gravel road on the eastern edge of Club Med to find Patrice Bredel's beachside art gallery and home. A long-time Moorea resident, he sells works by noted local artists. One museum-like room displays such artifacts as 18th-century stone carvings from the Marquesas, ancient hair decorations made of human bone, and intricately carved canoe paddles from the Austral Islands. Haapiti, east side of Club Med. ⓒ **56.13.57.** Tues–Sat 10am–noon and 2:30–5:30pm.

Galerie van der Heyde   Dutch artist Aad van der Heyde has lived and worked on Moorea since 1964. One of his bold impressionist paintings of a Tahitian woman was selected for French Polynesia's 100CFP postage stamp in 1975. Aad will sell you an autographed lithograph of the painting. Some of his works are displayed on the gallery's garden wall. He also has a small collection of pearls, wood carvings, tapa cloth, shell and coral jewelry, and primitive art from Papua New Guinea. East side of Cook's Bay. ⓒ **56.14.22.** Mon–Sat 8am–5pm.

Sculpture Par Woody   American Woody Howard was studying horticulture at the University of Hawaii when he came to Moorea in 1982 to work on Hotel Bali Hai's plantation. Like so many others, he stayed. Today you can visit his lagoon-side workshop and watch him carving award-winning wooden images of dolphins, fish, women, and other Polynesian wildlife. He also has reasonably priced selection of black pearls. Papetoai, between village and Moorea Beachcomber Inter-Continental Resort. ⓒ **56.37.00** or 56.17.73. Mon–Sat 8am–5pm.

BLACK PEARLS

Equipped with the chain's bamboo-trimmed display cases, the local branch of the upmarket **Sibani Perles** (ⓒ **56.14.62**) is in Le Petit Village shopping center, opposite Club Med. Near the center, **Herman Perles** (ⓒ **56.42.79**) is noted for the crystal and gold settings surrounding its black pearls. It also carries a collection of Marquesan wood carvings and a few duty-free perfumes.

Island Fashion Black Pearls *Value*   Ron Hall sailed from Hawaii to Tahiti with the actor Peter Fonda in 1974; Peter went home, Ron didn't. Now Ron runs this air-conditioned Moorea retail outlet, which he has decorated with old photos of Tahiti, including one of the infamous Quinn's Bar and an original Leeteg painting of a Tahitian vahine (Ron's wife, Josée, was herself a championship Tahitian dancer when they met in the 1970s). In 15 minutes of "pearl school," Ron will show you the basics of picking a pearl. He will also have your selection set in a mounting of your choice, and his prices are fair. In addition to stylish pearls, Island Fashions has one of Moorea's best selections of bathing suits, aloha shirts, and T-shirts. East side of Cook's Bay. ⓒ **56.11.06.** Mon–Sat 9am–6pm.

CLOTHING & SOUVENIRS

Arts Polynésiens   This shop sells a host of souvenir items plus tapa cloth and Marquesan wood carvings. Also for sale are paintings by local artists. Haapiti, in Le Petit Village opposite Club Med. ⓒ **56.39.42.** Mon–Sat 9am–6pm.

La Maison Blanche (The White House)   It's worth a stop here just to see this whitewashed vanilla planter's house with railing enclosing a magnificent front veranda. Today it houses this shop carrying an array of pareus, tropical dresses, aloha shirts, bathing suits, T-shirts, shell jewelry, and other handcrafts. Prices reflect the high quality of the merchandise. Mararepa. © **56.13.26.** Mon–Sat 8:30am–5pm, Sun 9am–noon.

5 Where to Stay

Most of Moorea's hotels and restaurants are grouped in or near Cook's Bay or in the Haapiti district on the northwest corner of the island. With the exception of the Sofitel Coralia Ia Ora Coralia, those in or near Cook's Bay do not have the best beaches on the island, but their views of the mountains are unsurpassed in the South Pacific. Those on the northwest corner, on the other hand, have generally fine beaches, lagoons like giant swimming pools, and unobstructed views of the sunset, but not of Moorea's mountains. The two areas are relatively far apart, so you might spend most of your time near your hotel unless you rent a vehicle or otherwise make a point to see the sights. An alternative is to split your stay between the two areas.

All Moorea hotels provide watersports activities, Tahitian string bands nightly, and dance shows at least 1 night a week.

HOTELS IN THE COOK'S BAY AREA

Club Bali Hai *(Value*   The last property operated by Moorea's two surviving Bali Hai Boys (see the box "The Bali Hai Boys," below), this basic hotel has an incredible view of Moorea's ragged mountains across Cook's Bay, a scene that epitomizes the South Pacific. Taking in the full scope of the view, the thatch-roof bay-side bar is one of the South Pacific's best, and it's one of my favorite gathering places for a sundowner and the Wednesday night Tahitian dance show is worth catching, too (see "Island Nights," below). You can get continental breakfast and daytime snacks at the bar, but no other meals are served. A swimming pool with a rock waterfall helps compensate for the very small beach here. Most guest rooms are part of a time-share operation, but that means they come equipped with cooking facilities, which is a plus for budget-minded travelers. The overwater bungalows are the least expensive in French Polynesia. Most other units are in one- or two-story motel-style buildings. They are simply but comfortably furnished. This is good value if you don't need a phone in your room or other such luxuries. On the other hand, the view is worth a million bucks.

B.P. 8, Maharepa, Moorea. © **56.13.68.** Fax 56.13.27. www.clubbalihai.com. 44 units. $85–$185 double, $245 bungalow. AE, DC, MC, V. **Amenities:** 1 bar; outdoor pool; activities desk; coin-operated washers and dryers. *In room:* A/C (rooms only), kitchen, fridge, coffeemaker, no phone.

Sheraton Moorea Lagoon Resort & Spa ★★   Moorea's newest resort opened in 2000 on the site of the old Moorea Lagoon Resort, on the north coast about halfway between Cook's and Opunohu bays. It's not particularly convenient to restaurants and activities, but the resort provides shuttles to the Tiki Village Theatre and the Vaiare ferry dock. Two stunning, conical thatch roofs cover the reception area and a French restaurant overlooking a decent if not exceptional beach. Steps lead down to a beachside pool, where a free massage will get you in the mood to pay for some serious pampering in the resort's full-service spa. All the guest bungalows are identical except for their location. A Y-shaped

The Bali Hai Boys

Californians Jay Carlisle, Don "Muk" McCallum, and the late Hugh Kelley gave up their budding business careers as stockbroker, lawyer, and sporting goods salesman, respectively, and in 1960 bought an old vanilla plantation on Moorea. Much to their chagrin, the vanilla boom had gone bust in the 1920s. Simply put, there was no money to be made in vanilla.

So instead of planting, they refurbished an old beachfront hotel that stood on their property. Taking a page from James A. Michener's *Tales of the South Pacific*, they renamed it the Bali Hai and opened for business in 1961. With construction of Tahiti-Faaa International Airport across the Sea of the Moon that same year, their timing couldn't have been better. With Jay managing the money, Hugh doing the building, and Muk overseeing the entertainment, they quickly had a success on their hands. Travel writers soon dubbed them the "Bali Hai Boys."

Supplies and fresh produce weren't easy to come by in those days, so they put the old vanilla plantation to work producing chickens, eggs, and milk. It was the first successful poultry and dairy operation on the island.

Only the inexpensive Club Bali Hai remains of their hotels, but we can thank Jay, Muk, and Hugh for the overwater bungalow—cabins sitting on pilings over the lagoon with glass panels in their floors so that we can watch the fish swim below us. They built the first one in 1968 on Raiatea. A novelty at the time, their romantic invention has spread throughout French Polynesia and even to the Cook Islands and Samoa.

pier—with its own bar—leads to half of them out over the lagoon. These all have glass floor panels for fish-viewing and decks with steps down into the clear, 4-foot-deep water. The others are situated in a coconut grove by the beach. Every unit is equipped with niceties such as CD players, complimentary snorkeling gear, plush robes, and claw-foot bathtubs, in addition to walk-in showers. Reasonable prices and a wide selection make the two-story, air-conditioned boutique here a good place to shop. A lack of good service prevents me from giving this resort top rating. I hope this problem is resolved by the time you arrive, for the public areas and guest quarters here are the most luxurious on Moorea.

B.P. 416, Papeete (between Cook's and Opunohu bays). © 800/325-3535 or 68.48.48 in Papeete. Fax 86.48.40. www.sheraton.com. 106 units. 39,000CFP–65,000CFP ($289–$482). AE, DC, MC, V. **Amenities:** 2 restaurants (French), 3 bars; outdoor pool; 2 tennis courts; health club; spa; watersports equipment rentals; bike rentals; concierge; activities desk; car-rental desk; business center; 24-hr. room service; massage; babysitting; laundry service. *In room:* A/C, TV, CD player, dataport, minibar, coffeemaker, hair dryer, iron, safe.

Sofitel Coralia Ia Ora ★   On the island's northeast coast, south of the airport, this resort was built in the 1960s beside one of the South Pacific's best lagoons and a long, lovely beach over which grape-leaf and casuarina trees hang. It's also the only hotel with a view of Tahiti, whose green, cloud-topped mountains seem to climb out of the horizon beyond the reef. Most of the Ia Ora's thatch-roofed bungalows stand in a long coconut grove, but 20 are over the lagoon. The overwaters and 10 deluxe beachfront models—all built in the mid-1990s—are air-conditioned, while the rest have ceiling fans. Five of the 10 deluxe bungalows, most of the older beachfront units, and those perched on a ridge above the trees have unobstructed views of Tahiti. Most of the overwater units, however, face the lagoon rather than Tahiti. Unfortunately, many guests have complained about the smaller beachfront bungalows dating from the 1960s, since these are not fully screened and are thus liable to be invaded by mosquitoes and other critters. Their beds are draped by mosquito nets, and scheduled renovations should cure this problem. Nevertheless, if you can't afford one of the new overwater or beachfront units, you'll be better off to sacrifice the view and take one of the larger garden bungalows here.

B.P. 28, Maharepa, Moorea (Temae, on the northeast coast, facing Tahiti). ✆ 800/763-4835, 55.03.55, or 41.04.04 in Papeete. Fax 41.05.05. www.accorhotels.com. 110 units. 28,000CFP–56,000CFP ($207–$415) bungalow. AE, DC, MC, V. **Amenities:** 2 restaurants (French); 1 bar; outdoor pool; 2 tennis courts; watersports equipment rentals; bike rentals; activities desk; car-rental desk; massage; babysitting; laundry service. *In room:* A/C, TV, minibar, coffeemaker, hair dryer, iron, safe.

HOTELS ON THE NORTHWEST COAST

A major landmark 27km (17 miles) west of the airport, the 350-bungalow **Club Med** (✆ **800/528-3100** or 55-00-00; www.clubmed.com) has been the center of activity on the northwest corner of Moorea for more than 3 decades. It shut its doors in 2001 for a thorough, $23 million renovation and is scheduled to reopen in 2004.

Hotel Les Tipaniers ★★ *Value*   Moorea's best value, this friendly, French-owned establishment sits in a coconut grove beside the same sandy beach as Club Med. The widely spaced bungalows stand back in the trees, which gives the small complex an open, airy atmosphere. They also are far enough from the road to be quiet. Well worth the extra cost, each of the larger "standard superior" bungalows has an L-shaped settee facing sliding glass doors to covered porches. Behind the settee is a raised sleeping area with a queen-size bed, and behind that, a fully tiled bathroom has a sizable shower and vanity space. To the rear of the property, other bungalows are equipped with kitchens and can sleep up to five persons. Also back there is a building that houses four small hotel-style rooms equipped with twin beds (you can push them together), reading lights, and ample tiled bathrooms with showers. Okay for couples, these rooms are the least expensive yet comfortable place to stay on Moorea. Unlike the others, however, they do not have phones, fridges, or safes. All units here have ceiling fans. A pleasant restaurant with a deck over the beach is open daily for breakfast, lunch, and snacks. The hotel is also home to the excellent Restaurant Les Tipaniers, which is known for its Italian fare (see "Where to Dine," below). Guests can make free use of snorkeling gear, canoes, and bicycles, or pay for kayaking, water-skiing, motu trips, and diving with Scubapiti, which is based here.

B.P. 1002, Papetoai, Moorea (in Haapiti, east of the Club Med). ✆ 800/521-7242 or 56.12.67. Fax 56.29.25. www.lestipaniers.com. 22 units. 5,800CFP ($43) double, 10,500CFP–12,500CFP ($78–$93) bungalow without kitchenette, 12,800CFP–15,900CFP ($95–$118) double with kitchenette. AE, DC, MC, V. **Amenities:** 2 restaurants (French/Italian), 2 bars; watersports equipment rentals; free snorkeling gear, canoes, and bicycles; babysitting; laundry service. *In room:* Kitchen (6 units), fridge (18 units), safe (18 units).

Hotel Moorea Village   This basic resort attracts Americans and Europeans on low-end package tours. Its 75 simply furnished bungalows are closely packed on a grassy lawn under coconut palms, within walking distance of Club Med and nearby restaurants and shops. All but 10 consist of one room and a bathroom under a peaked thatch roof that extends out over a covered, semicircular front porch equipped with plastic table and chairs. Each of these unit has two platform double beds plus a single bed that serves as a settee, two chairs and a small drink table, refrigerators and hot pots (bring your own tea and coffee), and cramped bathrooms with skinny shower stalls and thin towels. The other 10 units are larger and have kitchens. Beachside bungalows are worth the extra cost. Avoid the garden units by the noisy round-island road. Breakfast, lunch, and libations are served on a long porch that hangs over the sand along the lagoon side of the restaurant. The Tahitian feast here at midday Sunday is one of the most authentic in the islands (see "Where to Dine," below).

P.O. Box 1008, Papetoai, Moorea (in Haapiti, 1km west of Club Med). ℂ **56.10.02.** Fax 56.22.11. moorea village@mail.pf. 75 units. 10,000CFP–12,500 ($75–$93) double without kitchen; 17,000CFP–21,000CFP ($126–$156) double with kitchen. AE, MC, V. **Amenities:** 1 restaurant (French), 1 bar, outdoor pool, 2 tennis courts, watersports equipment rentals, bike rentals, laundry service. *In room:* TV (in kitchen units only), no phone.

Moorea Beachcomber Inter-Continental Resort ★★★ *Kids* Although relatively isolated about 2.5km (1½ miles) east of the Club Med area, Moorea's best all-around resort has plenty to keep its house guests busy. The beach and sometimes murky lagoon here aren't Moorea's best, but the resort has the widest range of watersports activities on the island—all of them available both to guests and to nonguests who are willing to pay (see "Dolphin-Watching, Hiking, Watersports & Other Outdoor Activities," earlier in this chapter). A well-organized children's program makes this the best family vacation resort in French Polynesia. The large, airy central building with a shingle roof opens to a large pool area surrounded by an ample sunning deck. Most of the guest bungalows extend partially over the water from man-made islands. They are of European construction, but mat walls and rattan furnishings lend tropical ambience. They also are air-conditioned, which the less expensive garden bungalows are not. A curving two-story building holds 52 spacious, air-conditioned hotel rooms; they all have patios or balconies facing the beach and combination tub-showers, a rarity on Moorea. The Tahitian weekly dance show on the beach is one of Moorea's most colorful.

B.P. 1019, Papetoai, Moorea (between Papetoai and Haapiti). ℂ **800/327-0200** or 55.19.19. Fax 55.19.55. www.interconti.com. 52 units, 102 bungalows. 30,956CFP ($229) double; 33,790CFP–53,519CFP ($250–$396) bungalow. AE, DC, MC, V. **Amenities:** 1 restaurant (French), 1 bar; outdoor pool; tennis courts; watersports equipment rentals; bike rentals; children's programs; concierge; activities desk; car-rental desk; limited room service; babysitting; laundry service. *In room:* A/C, TV, minibar, coffeemaker, hair dryer.

HOSTELS & CAMPING

Camping Nelson All guests share adequate toilets, cold-water showers, and communal kitchen facilities at this campground and hostel in a beachside coconut grove about 200 yards west of the Club Med. In addition to camping space on a shadeless lawn, very basic accommodations here include small bungalows for couples, four blocks of small dorm rooms (two bunks each), and four other thatch-roofed hostel bungalows down the road (and still on the beach).

PK 27.1, Tiahura, Moorea (in Haapiti, west of Club Med). ℂ and fax **56.15.18.** 32 dorm beds, 5 cabins, 4 bungalows. 1,000CFP ($7.50) per camper; 1,200CFP–1,500CFP ($9–$11) dorm bed; 2,600CFP–4,000CFP ($19–$30) per cabin; 2,800CFP–3,000CFP ($21–$22) bungalow. Lower rates for stays of more than 1 night. 2-night minimum required for camping. AE, DC, MC, V. *In room:* No phone.

Moorea Camping You pay slightly more to camp here than at Camping Nelson (see above), but this establishment in a coconut grove has much more shade and a better beach for swimming. A beachside pavilion covers picnic tables and a communal kitchen. Two long plywood houses—actually little more than permanent tents—contain eight rooms with foam mattresses. One bungalow can accommodate up to four persons. The showers dispense cold water.

PK 27.5, Tiahura, Moorea (in Haapiti, west of Club Med). ℂ **56.14.47.** Fax 56.30.22. 20 tent sites, 20 beds, 8 units, 5 bungalows. 1,000CFP–1,200CFP ($7.50–$9) per camper; 1,200CFP–1,800CFP ($9–$13) dorm bed; 2,400CFP–3,400CFP ($18–$25) per person in rooms; 4,500CFP–6,000CFP ($33–$45) single or double per bungalow. Lower rates for stays of more than 1 night. No credit cards. *In room:* No phone.

6 Where to Dine

The restaurant scene changes quickly on Moorea, but the ones I recommend below have been in business several years and offer very good value. As on Tahiti, you can save by eating at snack bars for breakfast, lunch, or an early dinner.

RESTAURANTS IN COOK'S BAY

The Maharepa area near Club Bali Hai has several restaurants where you pay from 1,500CFP to 2,500CFP ($11–$19) for main courses. Expatriates from France operate most of them, so expect heavy traditional French sauces such as béarnaise, Roquefort, creamy black or green pepper, and *vanille* (vanilla) over fresh local fish or New Zealand steaks.

Local French residents flock to **Le Cocotier** (ℂ **56.12.10**), which offers a variety of nightly specials. **La Case** (ℂ **56.42.95**) proffers Swiss as well as French dishes. Actually in Cook's Bay, **Caprice des Isles** (ℂ **56.44.24**) occupies a large thatch-roof building made of coconut logs.

At least one inexpensive *roulotte* sets up shop at the municipal market in Paopao each evening. See "Where to Dine" in chapter 4 for more information about these meal wagons.

Alfredo's ★ *Value* ITALIAN Gregarious French restaurateur Christian Boucheron, who worked at hotels in northern Virginia for 19 years, will make you feel right at home in this old building, formerly a Chinese grocery store. In fact, Christian's white patio tables with green-and-red tablecloths are usually packed, mostly with Americans and other English-speaking visitors who come here for some of the finest Italian fare in the islands. (French residents tired of their own traditional heavy sauces flock here, too.) The wonderfully sweet tomato sauce used on pizzas and pastas is the result of adding local honey to the recipe. Start with the carpaccio, made with fresh, sashimi-quality yellowfin tuna marinated in olive oil, lime juice, and crushed garlic. In season, the big tank in the middle of the dining room holds live local lobsters. Call for free dinner transportation from as far away as Club Bali Hai (Alfredo's will pay half the taxi fare from the Sofitel Coralia Ia Ora or the Moorea Beachcomber Inter-Continental Resort). Club Bali Hai guests can charge meals to their rooms here.

Pao Pao, near Club Bali Hai. ℂ **56.17.71.** Reservations recommended. Pizzas 1,350CFP ($10); main courses 1,350CFP–2,400CFP ($10–$18). MC, V. Tues–Sun 11am–2:30pm and 5:30–9:30pm.

⌒ *Value* **Call for Transportation**

Most Moorea restaurants will either come get you or pay half if not all of your taxi fare if you make reservations for dinner. Although they restrict this service to nearby restaurants, depending on the size of your group, it usually pays to call ahead.

(*Finds*) **The Best Tahitian Feasts**

The **Tiki Theatre Village** ★★★, at PK 31 in Haapiti (*€* **55.02.50**), provides French Polynesia's most authentic Tahitian feast on Tuesday, Wednesday, Friday, and Saturday nights. You watch the *himaa* being opened about dusk, then choose your fare from the goodies laid out on several buffet tables in the beachside, thatch-roof dining room. The combined feast and show cost 6,900CFP ($51). See "Tiki Theatre Village," earlier in this chapter, for information about the village, and "Island Nights," below, for details about the evening show.

Also authentic is the Sunday feast at **Hotel Moorea Village** (*€* **56. 10.02**) in Haapiti (see "Where to Stay," above). You can watch the dirt being removed from atop the *himaa* shortly after noon, then sit down about 1pm at long tables in the beachside dining room. The succulent food is served in the traditional Tahitian way, family style without silverware. That's right. You eat with your fingers. Dancers from a nearby village put on a short show after the feast. It's a bargain at 3,900CFP ($29) per person, which includes wine. It's a popular event with locals, some of whom hang around after the show to drink at the bar. They can reportedly become rowdy later in the afternoon.

Chez Jean-Pierre CANTONESE When my body tells me to eat my vegetables, I head for this plain but clean Chinese family restaurant beside Cooks' Bay. In addition, you can try chicken with sweet Moorea pineapple. The house specialty, a crispy whole reef fish fresh from the lagoon, isn't listed on the menu, but ask for it. Saturday night features Tahitian-style roast pig with coconut cream. Everything's fresh and tasty here.

Pao Pao, near Municipal Market. *€* **56.18.51.** Main courses 1,150CFP–1,950CFP ($8.50–$14.50). MC, V. Mon–Tues and Thurs–Sat 11:15am–2:30pm; Thurs–Tues 6:15–9:30pm.

Le Mahogany ★★ (*Value*) FRENCH/CHINESE French chef François Courtien spent 30 years cooking at the former Hotel Bali Hai before joining Tahitian Blondine Agnia at her pleasant little dining spot next to the local gym. It's a favorite with local expatriates who appreciate value and friendly service. Polished mahogany tables, mat walls, and a window opening to a garden provide tropical ambience. A rich and tasty avocado and shrimp cocktail is a good way to start, as is a bowl of lobster bisque, which will leave a spicy pepper aftertaste on your tongue. Daily specials feature the likes of Moorea-grown shrimp with curry, garlic, or whiskey sauce, and shrimp and scallops in a puff pastry with a light cream sauce. The Cantonese main courses are as good as those at any Chinese restaurant here. End with a *tarte tatin*, a caramelized apple pie served with vanilla ice cream. Lunchtime snacks include salads, omelets, burgers, and grilled mahimahi or steak.

Maharepa. *€* **56.39.73.** Reservations recommended. Snacks (lunch only) 900CFP–1,550CFP ($7–$11.50); main courses 1,200CFP–2,400CFP ($9–$18). DC, MC, V. Thurs–Tues 11am–2:30pm and 6–9:30pm.

Te Honu Iti (Chez Roger) ★★★ CLASSICAL FRENCH This extraordinary restaurant is the home of owner-chef Roger Iqual, who won the *Concours National de la Poêle d'Or* (Golden Pot Contest) in Cannes for a sea-bass concoction. The scenic setting beside Cook's Bay is worthy of Roger's cuisine. He works his magic on fresh seafood, prepared in the classical French fashion but with some delightful twists, such as lightly smoking sashimi-thin slices of yellowfin tuna and serving them over a piquant potato salad. Roger's chalkboard menu often features his delicate mahimahi mousse, which is a local favorite. A special tourist menu lets you choose from among three main courses, plus salad, dessert, and a glass of wine, a beer, or a soft drink for 2,800CFP ($21).

Pao Pao, north of Municipal Market. ℂ 56.19.84. Reservations recommended. Main courses 1,900CFP– 2,500CFP ($14–$19). MC, V. Daily 11:30am–2pm and 6:30–10pm.

SNACK BARS IN COOK'S BAY

Le Sylesie Patisserie PATISSERIE/SNACKS   This largest of the Le Sylesie branches has a wider selection of pastries, crepes, pizzas, salads, omelets, quiches, burgers, sandwiches, fruit plates, ice cream, sundaes, and other goodies than its sister in Haapiti (see below). The patio tables here are set in a cool, shady spot for a full, American-style breakfast (served all day) or tasty lunch, but you can get sunburned while eating outside in the late afternoon.

Maharepa, next to the post office. ℂ 56.15.88. Reservations not accepted. Breakfasts 500CFP–1,500CFP ($3.75–$11); snacks and light meals 400CFP–1,500CFP ($3–$11). MC, V. Daily 6am–6pm.

Snack L'Ananas Bleu SNACKS/CREPES   "Top Burger" says the roadside sign in front of Matahi Hunter's little front-porch restaurant, and indeed you can get a big juicy beef, fish, or teriyaki one accompanied by french fries here. Continental or cooked breakfasts are served all day, or you can join the French in partaking of a substantial serving of steak, beef curry, shrimp in garlic or curry sauce, or grilled fish for lunch. Ice cream, sundaes, and fruit drinks provide relief from the midday heat.

Pao Pao, opposite Club Bali Hai. ℂ 56.12.06. Reservations not accepted. Breakfast 550CFP–1,400CFP ($4–$10); burgers and sandwiches 700CFP–1,150CFP ($5–$8.50); main courses 1,500CFP–1,800CFP ($11–$13). MC, V. Daily 7:30am–2:30pm.

Snack Rotui SNACK BAR   Located on the shore of Cook's Bay, this walk-up "snack" is run by a Chinese family, and for about 400CFP ($3) you can get a *casse-croûte* sandwich, a soft drink, and a slice of delicious homemade cake topped with chocolate pudding. Forget the daily plate lunches, usually a Chinese dish with rice, which are prepared earlier in the day and served without refrigeration. A few tables under a roof beside the beach catch the breezes off the bay.

Pao Pao, west of the bridge at the head of Cook's Bay. ℂ 56.18.16. Reservations not accepted. Sandwiches 130CFP–200CFP ($1–$1.50). No credit cards. Tues–Sun 7am–6pm.

RESTAURANTS ON THE NORTHWEST COAST

Restaurants come and go in La Petit Village shopping center opposite Club Med, but the reasonably priced **Lagon Cafe** (ℂ **56.39.41**) has been around a while, offering breakfast, lunch, afternoon sandwiches and salads, and French cuisine at dinner. It's open Monday to Saturday from 8am to 10pm.

Budgeteers will find a *roulotte* or two stationed outside Club Med each evening. See "Where to Dine" in chapter 4 for more information about these meal wagons.

Linareva Floating Restaurant and Bar ★★★ FRENCH SEAFOOD You'll pay a price to have dinner here, but Eric Lussiez's restaurant and bar is consistently Moorea's finest restaurant. It's also the most unusual: It occupies of the original *Tamarii Moorea*, the first ferry to ply between Papeete and Moorea.

Eric completely rebuilt the old vessel (twice, actually, for it sank at its dock due to a plumbing error after the job was finished). He outfitted the dining room with polished wood, large windows, and plenty of bright brass and other nautical decor. The menu changes with availability of local seafood such as shark and emperor fish, most expertly prepared with traditional French sauces. Tour groups stop here for lunch, when dinnertime prices are almost cut in half. Ask about discounted transportation from Haapiti-area hotels when you make your reservation.

Haapiti (7km/4 miles south of Club Med). $\bigcirc$ **56.15.35.** Reservations strongly recommended for dinner. Main courses 1,800CFP–3,250CFP ($13–$24). MC, V. Daily 11am–4pm and 5:30–9pm.

Restaurant Les Tipaniers ★★ ITALIAN/FRENCH   This romantic, thatch-roofed restaurant is popular with both visitors and Moorea's permanent residents, who come here for delicious pizzas with a variety of toppings and homemade spaghetti, lasagna, tagliatelle, and gnocchi served with Bolognese, carbonara, or seafood sauce. French dishes include pepper steak and filets of mahimahi in butter or vanilla sauce. Discounted transportation is available for guests staying at Haapiti-area hotels.

Haapiti, at Hotel Les Tipaniers, east of Club Med. $\bigcirc$ **56.12.67.** Reservations recommended. Pasta and pizza 1,000CFP–1,450CFP ($7.50–$11); main courses 1,600CFP–2,300CFP ($12–$17). AE, DC, MC, V. Daily 7–9:15pm.

SNACK BARS ON THE NORTHWEST COAST

Le Motu Pizza Grill SNACK BAR   You can get a *roulotte*-style grilled steak with french fries at this open-air restaurant (a small air-conditioned dining room is open during hot weather), but it's best known for excellent sandwiches and hamburgers, including a monster size hamburger-filled baguette. Pizzas also are offered. Light fare includes salads, crepes, and soft ice cream, and you can choose from a wide selection of soft drinks, beer, and wine.

Haapiti, opposite Club Med. $\bigcirc$ **56.16.70.** Reservations not accepted. Burgers and sandwiches 500CFP–800CFP ($3.75–$6); pizza 1,050CFP–1,300CFP ($8–$10). MC, V. Daily 9:30am–9pm.

Le Sylesie Patisserie SNACKS/BREAKFAST   Like Le Sylesie in Maharepa (see above), this little shop serves croissants and coffee or full American-style breakfasts all day, plus crepes, burgers, sandwiches, small pizzas, quiches, and pastries. The low-slung building has six tables under cover in front.

Haapiti, west of the Club Med. $\bigcirc$ **56.20.45.** Breakfasts 500CFP–1,500CFP ($3.75–$11); sandwiches, salads, burgers 400CFP–900CFP ($3–$7). No credit cards. Daily 6:30am–5pm.

7 Island Nights

No one has gone to Moorea for its nightlife since the One Chicken Inn, Moorea's colorful version of Quinn's infamous Tahitian-style bar in Papeete, bit the dust in Pao Pao 2 decades ago. The island's evening entertainment is now limited to the hotels, with a few exceptions.

Remember that the hotels' schedules change, so do your detective work. Call ahead before striking out. Most charge 4,500CFP to 6,500CFP ($33–$48) per person for dinner and a Tahitian dance show.

Tiki Theatre Village ★★★ ($\bigcirc$ **55.02.50**) in Haapiti, 2km (1¼ miles) west of the Club Med, stages the island's most authentic feast and dance show on Tuesday, Wednesday, Friday, and Saturday. They pick you up from your hotel and deposit you on the beach for a rum punch and sunset. After the staff uncovers the earth oven, they take you on a tour the village. A buffet of both Tahitian

---

Moments Sunsets & Drinks at Club Bali Hai

If I'm on Moorea, you'll find me on Tuesday having a sunset drink beside Cook's Bay at the **Club Bali Hai** (© **56.13.68**). Many of the island's English-speaking expatriate residents show up between 6 and 7pm to take advantage of reduced-price drinks. It's one of the greatest vistas in the South Pacific; you'll want to become a modern Paul Gauguin in order to capture the changing colors as the sunset paints the bay, sky, and the jagged mountains. Club Bali Hai also has a Tahitian dance show, usually on Wednesday night.

---

and Western foods is followed by an energetic 1½-hour dance show with some of the most elaborate yet traditional costumes to be seen in French Polynesia. The performers can number more than 70 if overseas troupes are visiting the island. The dinner and show cost 6,900CFP ($51) per person, or you can come for the 9pm show for 3,300CFP ($25). Add 1,000CFP ($7.50) in either case for round-trip transportation. See "Tiki Theatre Village," earlier in this chapter, for more about Tiki Theatre Village.

Chez Billy (© **56.43.82**), on the beach west of Hotel Moorea Village in Haapiti, offers a chance to dance, drink, and occasionally fight with the locals on Friday and Saturday nights. Billy kicks off at 8pm and roars on into the wee hours. Expect to pay a 1,000CFP ($7.50) cover charge and 350CFP ($2.50) and up for drinks.

Sofitel Coralia Ia Ora (© **56.12.90**) usually has its main dance show at 8pm on Saturday. **Moorea Beachcomber Inter-Continental Resort** (© **55.19.19**) has a barbecue and Tahitian dance show twice a week, with Saturday's performed under the stars on the beach.

Hotel Moorea Village (© **56.10.02**) stages a barbecue with a pareu fashion show on Saturdays at 7:30pm.

Bora Bora

Because of its fame and beauty, little Bora Bora has become a playground for the well-to-do and occasionally the famous. It has seen an explosion of hotel construction in recent years, with piers and overwater bungalows reaching out like tentacles over its gorgeous lagoon. Indeed, some travel industry professionals think that Bora Bora is already overbuilt and overpriced. Despite development, you'll still appreciate why James A. Michener wrote that this half-atoll/half-mountain is the world's most beautiful island.

Lying 230km (143 miles) northwest of Tahiti, Bora Bora is a middle-aged island that consists of a high center completely surrounded by a lagoon, enclosed by coral reef. What makes it so beautiful is the combination of sand-fringed motus (small islets) sitting on the outer reef, the multihued lagoon cutting deep bays into the central high island, and the basaltic tombstone known as Mount Otemanu towering over it all.

Be first to board the plane, for all this will be visible from the left side of the aircraft as you fly up from Papeete and descend to Bora Bora's airport on Motu Mute, a flat island on the northern edge of the barrier reef. Beyond Motu Mute the lagoon turns deep blue, where it's deep enough for the U.S. Navy to have used Bora Bora as a way station during World War II. The airstrip you land on is another legacy of that war, built by the U.S. Navy as part of Operation Bobcat, during which 6,000 American sailors and soldiers were stationed on this tiny island. Bora Bora never saw combat during World War II, but it was a major refueling base on the America-to-Australia supply line.

You'll get to see the lagoon close up soon after landing, for all passengers are ferried across it from the airport, some directly to their hotels but most to **Vaitape,** the main village on the west coast, sitting opposite Teavanui Pass, the only entrance through the reef into the lagoon.

As is the case on Tahiti and Moorea, a road runs around the shoreline of Bora Bora, cutting in and out of the bays and skirting what seem like 1,000 white-sand beaches lapped by the waters of the lagoon. The best of the beaches—in fact, one of the best beaches in French Polynesia—stretches for more than 3km (2 miles) around a flat, coconut-studded peninsula known as **Matira Point.**

The island is so small that the road around it covers only 32km (19 miles) from start to finish. All the 4,500 or so Bora Borans live on a flat coastal strip that quickly gives way to the mountainous interior. The highest point on the island is the unusual slab, **Mount Otemanu** (725 m; 2,379 ft.), Bora Bora's trademark. Next to it is the more normal **Mount Pahia** (660 m; 2,165 ft.). These two mountains never seem quite the same from any two different viewpoints. Mount Otemanu can look like a tombstone from one direction, a needle from another. Because these mountains are relatively low, Bora Bora doesn't get as much rain as the taller Tahiti,

Moorea, and Raiatea. Water shortages can occur, especially during the drier months from June through September (consequently, most hotels have their own desalinization facilities).

1 Getting Around

Buses going to the hotels meet Air Tahiti's airport launches when they land at Vaitape. They also wait for the interisland ferries, which dock at the Farepiti wharf, at the mouth of Faanui Bay about 1.5km (1 mile) north of the village. See "Getting There & Getting Around" in chapter 3 for more information. At either location, get in the truck with the name of your hotel painted on the side. Fares to the Matira Point hotel district are about 300CFP ($2.25) from Vaitape and 500CFP ($3.75) from Farepiti.

There is no public transportation system on Bora Bora. The larger hotels get their guests to Vaitape and back, but the frequency can vary depending on how many tourists are on the island. Some restaurants pick up dinner guests who call for reservations.

BY RENTAL CAR, SCOOTER & BICYCLE

Avis (© **800/230-4898** or 67.74.34; www.avis.com), **Europcar** (© **800/227-7368** or 67.70.15; www.europcar.com), and a local firm, **Fare-Piti Rent a Car** (© **76.65.28**), all have offices at Vaitape wharf. Avis and Fare-Piti also rents scooters, and all three have bicycles for hire. All charge about 7,000CFP ($52) a day for their smallest cars, including unlimited kilometers and insurance. Bikes cost about 1,200CFP ($9) for 2 hours and 1,800CFP ($13) for all day. Scooters cost about 6,500CFP ($48) per day.

The 32km (19 miles) of road around Bora Bora are paved, with the exception of a short stretch on the east coast. Most of it is flat, but be very cautious on the unpaved portion, which climbs a steep hill. Always drive or ride slowly and carefully and forever be on the lookout for pigs, chickens, pedestrians, and dogs.

BY TAXI

No taxis patrol Bora Bora looking for passengers, but several firms have "transport" licenses, which means they can come get you if someone calls. The hotel desks and restaurants will do that for you, or you can phone **Charley Taruoura** (© **67.64.37** or 78.27.71), **Otemanu Tours** (© **67.70.49**), **Jeanine Buchin** (© **67.74.14**), or **Jacques Isnard** (© **67.72.25**). Fares between Vaitape and the Matira Point hotel district are at least 1,000CFP ($7.50) from 6am to 6pm and 1,500CFP ($11) from 6pm to 6am; a ride between Vaitape and Anau village on the east coast costs 5,000CFP ($37) anytime. The vehicles aren't metered, so make sure you and the driver agree on a fare before setting out.

Impressions

I saw it first from an airplane. On the horizon there was a speck that became a tall, blunt mountain with cliffs dropping sheer into the sea. And about the base of the mountain, narrow fingers of land shot out, forming magnificent bays, while about the whole was thrown a coral ring of absolute perfection. . . . That was Bora Bora from aloft. When you stepped upon it the dream expanded.

—James A. Michener, *Return to Paradise*, 1951

If you're staying at a resort out on an islet and don't want to wait for the next shuttle boat, you can call **René et Maguy Water Taxi Motu** (© **67.60.61**). The ride to the main island costs about 1,600CFP ($12).

 ***FAST FACTS:* Bora Bora**

The following facts apply specifically to Bora Bora. For more information, see "Fast Facts: French Polynesia" in chapter 3.

Babysitters The hotels can arrange for English-speaking babysitters, or you can contact **Robin Teraitepo** at Chez Ben's (© **67.74.54**).

Camera/Film **Camera Shop,** in the Le Jardin Gauguin shopping center north of the Hotel Bora Bora (© **67.76.93**), offers professional photo services and overnight processing of color print film. It also has a branch at the Vaitape wharf. Some hotel boutiques will send your film here for you.

Currency Exchange **Banque de Tahiti, Banque Socredo,** and **Banque de Polynésie** have branches in Vaitape; all are open Monday through Friday from 8 to 11:45am and from 2 to 4pm, but beyond that, each has its own business hours. Banque de Tahiti has an ATM.

Drugstores **Pharmacie de Bora Bora** (© **67.70.30**), north of the town wharf in Vaitape, is open Monday through Friday from 8 to noon and 3:30 to 6pm, Saturday from 8 to noon and 5 to 6pm, Sunday and holidays from 9 to 9:30 am.

E-mail **L'Appetisserie,** in the Centre Commercial Le Pahia just north of the Vaitape wharf (© **67.78.88**), has a computer terminal for e-mail, which costs 40CFP (30¢) per minute of online time. See "Where to Dine," below, for more about this pastry shop.

Emergencies/Police The emergency police telephone number is © **17**. The **gendarmerie** (© **67.70.58**) is opposite the Vaitape wharf.

Healthcare The island's **infirmary** is in Vaitape (© **67.70.77**), as are the offices of **Dr. Azad Roussanaly** (© **67.77.95**). For dental service, see **Dr. J. F. Macouin,** in the Centre Commercial Le Pahia, north of the wharf (© **67. 70.55**).

Post Office The **Vaitape post office** is open Monday from 8am to 3pm, Tuesday through Friday from 7:30am to 3pm, and Saturday from 8 to 10am.

Visitor Information The **Bora Bora Comité du Tourisme** (© and fax **67. 76.36**) has an office in the large building on the north side of the Vaitape wharf. It's not always staffed, but hours are posted as Monday to Thursday from 8am to 4pm, Friday 8am to 3pm, and weekends if cruise ships are in port. The address is B.P. 144, Vaitape, Bora Bora.

Water Bora Bora recently built a huge desalinization plant, so the tap water here is safe to drink.

2 Exploring Bora Bora

THE CIRCLE ISLAND TOUR ★★

Because the round-island road is only 32km (19 miles) long, many visitors see it by bicycle (give yourself at least 4 hr.), scooter, or car. Some of those sights

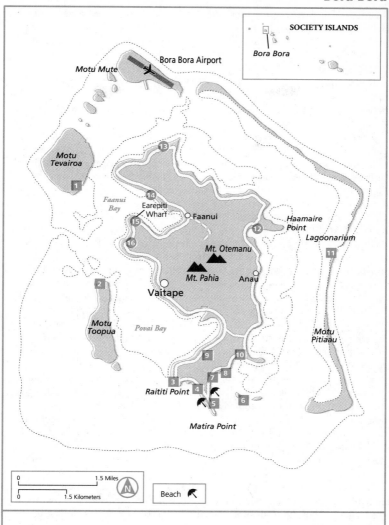

SOCIETY ISLANDS

Bora Bora

Motu Mute

Bora Bora Airport

Motu Tevairoa

1

Faanui Bay

13

14
Earepiti Wharf

○ Faanui

15

Haamaire Point

16

12

Lagoonarium

11

▲▲ *Mt. Otemanu*

▲ *Mt. Pahia*

Anau ○

2

○ **Vaitape**

Motu Toopua

Povai Bay

Motu Pitiaau

9

10

3

7 **8**

Raititi Point **4**

5

6

Matira Point

| 0 | 1.5 Miles |
| 0 | 1.5 Kilometers |

Ⓝ

Beach 🏖

ACCOMMODATIONS
Bora Bora
  Lagoon Resort **2**
Bora Bora Pearl
  Beach Resort **1**
Club Med Bora Bora **10**
Hotel Bora Bora **3**
Hotel Matira **4**
Le Maitai Polynesia **7**

Le Meridien
  Bora Bora **11**
Moana Beach
  Inter-Continental Resort **5**
Sofitel Coralia Marara **8**
Sofitel Coralia Motu **6**
Village Pauline **9**

ATTRACTIONS
Aehautai Marae **12**
Marotetini Marae **15**
Old Hyatt Site **13**
U.S. Wharf **14**
U.S. Guns **16**

mentioned below may not be easy to find, however, so consider taking a guided sightseeing tour around the island. **Otemanu Tours** (© **67.70.49**) still uses one of the traditional, open-air "le truck" vehicles, which adds an extra dimension to its trips. You can book them at any hotel activities desk. They charge about 2,500CFP ($19) per person.

If you do it yourself, begin at the **wharf in Vaitape,** where there's a monument to French yachtsman Alain Gerbault, who sailed his boat around the world between 1923 and 1929 and lived to write a book about it (thus adding to Bora Bora's fame).

From the wharf, head counterclockwise around the island. The road soon curves along the shore of **Povai Bay,** where mounts Otemanu and Pahia tower over you. Take your time along this bay; the views here are the best on Bora Bora. When you reach the area around Bloody Mary's Restaurant, stop for a killer view back across the water at Mount Otemanu.

The road climbs the small headland, where a huge banyan tree marks the entrance to the Hotel Bora Bora on **Raititi Point,** then runs smoothly along curving **Matira Beach** ★★★, one of the South Pacific's finest. You can do some good snorkeling just off the end of the beach closest to the hotel. When the road curves sharply to the left, look for a narrow paved road to the right. This leads to **Matira Point,** the low, sandy, coconut-studded peninsula that extends out from Bora Bora's south end. Down this track about 50 yards is a **public beach** on the west side of the peninsula, opposite the Moana Beach Inter-Continental Resort. The lagoon is shallow all the way out to the reef at this point, but the bottom is smooth and sandy. When I first came to Bora Bora in 1977, I camped a week on Matira Point; the Moana Beach Inter-Continental Resort is only one of many structures in what was then a deserted coconut grove completely surrounded by unspoiled beach.

Up the east coast, you'll pass through the island's busy hotel and restaurant district before climbing a steep hill above Club Med. A trail cuts off to the right on the north side of the hill and goes to the **Aehautai Marae,** one of several old temples on Bora Bora. This particular one has a great view of Mount Otemanu and the blue outlines of Raiatea and Tahaa islands beyond the motus on the reef.

You will go through a long stretch of coconut plantations before entering **Anau,** a typical Polynesian village with a large church, a general store, and tin-roofed houses crouched along the road.

The road goes over two hills at Point Haamaire, the main island's easternmost extremity, about 4km (2½ miles) north of Anau village. Between the two hills on the lagoon side of the road stands **Aehautai Marae,** a restored temple. Out on the point is **Taharuu Marae,** which has a great view of the lagoon. The Americans installed more naval guns in the hills above the point.

On the deserted northwest coast you will ride through several miles of coconut plantations pockmarked by thousands of holes made by the land crabs known as *tupas.* After turning at the northernmost point, you pass a group of overwater bungalows and another group of houses, which climb the hill. Some of these are expensive condominiums; the others are part of defunct project that was to have been a Hyatt resort. Across the lagoon are Motu Mute and the airport.

Faanui Bay was used during World War II as an Allied naval base. It's not marked, but the U.S. Navy's Seabees built the concrete wharf on the north shore as a seaplane ramp. Just beyond the main shipping wharf at the point on

> (*Moments* Like Flying Underwater
>
> Shining with every hue on the blue end of the color spectrum, Bora Bora's watery playground is one of my favorite snorkeling spots. Hotel Bora Bora has bungalows sitting right on the edge of a reef that drops precipitously to dark depths. I experience the exhilaration of flying when I glide out over that underwater cliff.

the south side of Faanui Bay is the restored **Marotetini Marae,** which in pre-European days was dedicated to navigators. In his novel *Hawaii,* James Michener had his fictional Polynesians leave this point to discover and settle the Hawaiian Islands. Nearby are tombs in which members of Bora Bora's former royal family are buried. If you look offshore at this point, you'll see the only pass into the lagoon. The remains of two **U.S. guns** that guarded it stand on the hill above but are best visited on a safari tour (see "Safari Tours," below).

As you enter Vaitape, **Magasin Chin Lee** is a major gathering place for local residents. It's a good place to soak up some island culture while trimming your thirst with a cold bottle of Eau Royale. Opposite the store is the modern **Centre Commercial Le Pahia,** with a patisserie, hairdresser, a branch of Sibani Perles, a bookstore, and other shops.

SAFARI TOURS ★★

The regular tours stick to the shoreline, but some head into the hills in open-air four-wheel-drive vehicles for panoramic views and visits to the old U.S. Navy gun sites. The mountain roads are mere ruts in places, so you could get stuck if it has been raining. Dany Leverd's **Tupuna Four-Wheel Drive Expeditions** (© 67.75.06) is the best. Book at any hotel activities desk. Dany charges about 6,500CFP ($48) per person.

LAGOON OUTINGS ★★★

Bora Bora has one of the world's most beautiful lagoons, and getting out on it, snorkeling and swimming in it, and visiting the islands on its outer edge are absolute musts. Most lagoon tours take you out in fast outrigger canoes and include shark-feeding demonstrations (the guide feeds reef sharks while you watch from a reasonably safe distance while snorkeling). **Shark-feeding** ★ is likely to be one of your most indelible memories of this island. Your hotel will book you on one of these trips, which you must try.

Some excursions go to the **Bora Bora Lagoonarium** (© 67.71.34), a fenced-in underwater area off a motu near Le Meridien Bora Bora, where you can swim with (and maybe even ride) the manta rays and observe the sharks (which are on the other side of the fence here). The Lagoonarium is open Sunday to Friday. Your hotel will arrange transfers or a rental boat.

A much drier way to see the underwater delights is in the semisubmersible vessels *Aquascope Moana View* (© 67.61.92) and *Spirit of Polynesia* (© 67.64.00), which operate along the outer edges of the lagoon and along the reef outside the pass. The 50-minute voyages cost about 4,000CFP ($30) for adults, 3,000CFP ($22) for children 4 to 12. The transfer boats leave Vaitape wharf several times a day, but call for reservations.

3 Diving, Fishing & Watersports

SCUBA DIVING ★★

Certified and noncertified divers alike can swim among the coral heads, sharks, rays, eels, and some 1,000 species of colorful tropical fishes out in the lagoon here. Every resort has a scuba diving program. Both 30-minute introductory courses and one-tank lagoon dives cost about 6,500CFP ($48), and open-water and night dives are priced at 8,000CFP ($60).

Based adjacent to Hotel Bora Bora, friendly dive operators Michel and Anne Condesse offer morning, afternoon, and evening dives from their **Bora Diving Center** (© 67.71.84; fax 67.74.83; www.boradive.com). They provide buoyancy compensators, fins, snorkels, wetsuits, regulators, and all other equipment, which my traveling companion found to be in excellent condition (but be prepared for the metric system; depth and pressure gauges display measurements in meters and kilograms). They also teach PADI certification courses.

The island's other major dive operator, **TOPdive Bora Bora** (© 60.50.50; fax 60.50.51; www.topdive.com), also has top-of-the line equipment and some of the best dive boats in French Polynesia. Its base is on the northern outskirts of Vaitape.

SPORT FISHING

For combined sailing and fishing, American Richard Postma's **Tara Vana** (© 949/650-7175 in the U.S., or 67.77.79; www.taravana.com) is the world's first sail-powered luxury game fishing boat. This 50-footer is available for day trips or overnight charters to the other Leeward Islands. Sailing or fishing costs from 90,000CFP ($667) for a half day, to 120,000CFP ($889) for a full day, including food but not alcoholic beverages. You can go on a nonfishing sunset cruise for about 6,500CFP ($48) per person. Among Richard's first guests were actors Dennis Quaid and Meg Ryan (when they were still a couple). Former *Baywatch* star Pamela Anderson Lee came along later.

For regular offshore fishing, contact American **Kirk Pearson** (© 67.79.59 or 79.17.49; mokalei11@hotmail.com), who has lived on Bora Bora for many years. Kirk spends most of his time these days as an accomplished furniture maker, but he will rip himself away from his saws and sanders to take you fishing for $600 a day.

OTHER WATERSPORTS

Every hotel has some water toys for its guests to use, and hotel activities desks can arrange fishing, diving, and other watersports. You don't have to stay at the **Sofitel Coralia Marara** (© 67.70.46) to use its equipment and facilities, but you do have to pay a fee; you can go water-skiing, sail on Hobie Cats, paddle canoes, and get a bird's-eye view of the lagoon while hanging below a parasail.

Based at Village Pauline (see "Where to Stay," below), **Bora Bora Kayaks** (© 67.72.16; www.boraborakayak.com) rents one- and two-person sea kayaks ranging from 1,000CFP ($7.50) for 1 hour to 3,500CFP ($26) for a whole day. These quality boats were made in the United States and come equipped with snorkeling and fishing gear.

4 Shopping

Local artisans display their straw hats, pareus, and other handcraft items at **Bora Bora I Te Fanau Tahi** (no phone), in the large hall at the Vaitape wharf. It's always open when cruise ships are in the lagoon. The local **Bora Bora Comité**

du Tourisme (📞 **67.76.36**) has its offices on the waterfront side of the building and can tell you when cruise ships are due.

Art du Pacific One of several boutiques in Le Jardin Gauguin shops near Bloody Mary's restaurant, this shop carries exquisite paintings on tapa cloth and sports the island's best collection of wood carvings from the Marquesas Islands. The carvings are very expensive, but it's worth stopping here just to have a look at the museum-quality pieces. Povai Bay, 1.5km (1 mile) north of Hotel Bora Bora. 📞 **67. 63.85.** Mon–Sat 9am–5:30pm.

Boutique Bora Bora Catering to the cruise ship crowd, this store has more T-shirts and pareus than most others here, plus it sells wood carvings, books, calendars, curios, and a few black pearls. It's a good place to stock up on Hinano beer glasses. Vaitape, opposite the ferry wharf. 📞 **67.79.72.** Mon–Sat 9am–5:30pm.

Boutique Gauguin In a white house next to Le Jardin Gauguin, 1.5km (1 mile) north of Hotel Bora Bora, Boutique Gauguin offers a selection of handcrafts, clothing, and black pearls, in addition to curio items such as ashtrays and coasters featuring the works of Paul Gauguin. Some of its pareus are particularly artistic. Povai Bay. 📞 **67.76.67.** Daily 8am–5:30pm.

Matira Pearls _Value_ One of the best places on the islands to shop for black pearls, this store is operated by two Americans—Steve Fearon, whose family once owned a piece of Hotel Bora Bora, and Steve Donnatin, who's been living here since 1984. Set and loose black pearls start at $100. Unlike other stores, the customized settings here are designed to emphasize the pearl, not the gold. The shop also has a selection of bathing suits, aloha shirts, and T-shirts. East side of Matira Point. 📞 **67.79.14.** Mon–Sat 9am–5pm, Sun 10am–5pm.

Moana Arts & Pearls In addition to black pearls and wood carvings, this store carries some of the dramatic works of noted photographer Erwin Christian, who settled in the islands in the 1960s. You will inevitably see Erwin's photos in numerous books and on many postcards. Raititi Point, near Hotel Bora Bora. 📞 **67.70.33.** Mon–Sat 9am–5:30pm.

Sibani Perles This swanky shop offers the designs of Didier Sibani, one of the pioneers of the black pearl industry. His elegant and pricey designs are displayed in bamboo cases. Vaitape, in Centre Commercial le Pahia. 📞 **67.72.49.** Mon–Sat 9am–5:30pm.

5 Where to Stay

Bora Bora has some of the South Pacific's finest—and most expensive—resorts. In light of how many have been built in the past few years, it may also have a few too many of them for the time being. As a result, you should shop around and ask for discounts during the off-season—it just might pay off.

As noted in chapter 1, most bungalows here don't provide a great deal of privacy. The high cost of labor and land means that a resort must have at least 40 units in order to be economically viable, and therefore bungalows are likely to be close together. Except for the bungalows with private patios at Hotel Bora Bora and the Bora Bora Pearl Beach Resort, and a few overwaters at the Sofitel Coralia Marara, the offshore resorts described in chapters 9 through 11 offer a higher level of seclusion than the ones here.

Except at Club Med, guests pay extra for everything except their rooms. If you're going to dine exclusively at your hotel, add about 8,000CFP ($59) per person per day for a meal plan.

Keep in mind that mosquitoes and sand flies love to feast on guests on Bora Bora's motus, so you'll want a good supply of mosquito coils and insect repellent if you opt for one of the offshore resorts.

VERY EXPENSIVE

Bora Bora Lagoon Resort ✿   Speed boats shuttle 23 times a day from the Vaitape wharf to this posh resort on Motu Toopua, a hilly island facing the rounded peak of Mount Pahia (not Mount Otemanu's tombstone). It opened to much fanfare in 1996 but never quite lived up to the hype. Orient Express Hotels bought it in 2001, however, and undertook renovations and improvements, including adding air-conditioners to all guest bungalows. The main building, under three interlocking thatch roofs, holds a reception area, a bar, and a gourmet restaurant. To the rear, an expansive stone deck surrounds one of French Polynesia's largest swimming pools, where you'll find another bar and restaurant. Long piers with hand-carved railings lead to the 50 overwater bungalows, and 30 more sit ashore in tropical gardens. All of the 528-square-foot units are identical. Three of the beachside bungalows—one of which has a Jacuzzi tub—interconnect to form suites. Although they are luxurious, the units are so close together that you can overhear your neighbor's favorite TV show (not to mention certain amorous activities).

B.P. 175, Vaitape, Bora Bora (on Motu Toopua, 1km/½ mile off Vaitape). © 800/830-2409 or 60.40.00. Fax 60.40.01. www.boraboralagoonresort.orient-express.com. 80 units. 50,000CFP–79,000CFP ($370–$585) bungalow. Rates include full breakfast and airport transfers. AE, DC, MC, V. **Amenities:** 2 restaurants (French), 2 bars; large outdoor pool; 2 tennis courts; exercise room; game room; watersports equipment rentals; concierge; activities desk; limited room service; laundry service. *In room:* A/C (in overwater bungalows), TV, dataport, minibar, coffeemaker, hair dryer, safe.

Bora Bora Pearl Beach Resort ✿✿   Owned and operated by local interests, this is the most traditionally Polynesian resort on Bora Bora. It sits beside a white sand beach on Motu Tevairoa, the largest of the islands dotting the outer reef, and it has better views of Mount Otemanu across the lagoon than does the Bora Bora Lagoon Resort to its south (see above). Free boats run between the resort and the Farepiti wharf (it's a 20-min. walk if you don't catch the bus). Covered by interconnected conical thatch roofs, the open-air restaurant, main bar, and library stand on a raised earthen platform, which enhances their views across Bora Bora's largest freshwater swimming pool to the lagoon and mountains. Guests can also enjoy splashing or snorkeling in the natural sand-bottom lagoon (the beach sand is subject to erosion, but dredges replenish it as needed). Gilles Petrie, one of French Polynesia's top dive operators, is in charge of the shop here. Long, curving piers extend out to 50 spacious overwater bungalows, all of which are identical except for the views. They are smaller than those at the Bora Bora Lagoon Resort but have more Polynesian charm. The 15 "premium" units are worth paying extra for, because they are more private than the others and enjoy unimpeded views of Bora Bora. If privacy is more important than the sound of water lapping under your bungalow, consider one of the garden bungalows, which have private courtyards with sun decks and splash pools. If you bring the kids, opt for a beachside bungalow with a separate bedroom. As at all Pearl Beach resorts, the Tahitian staff here is friendly and English-fluent, and management is sensitive to North American likes and dislikes.

B.P. 169, Vaitape, Bora Bora (on Motu Tevairoa, 1km/½ mile off Farepiti). © 800/841-4145 or 60.52.00. Fax restaurants (French), 2 bars; outdoor pool; tennis courts; exercise room; watersports equipment rentals; game room; concierge; activities desk; limited room service; massage; babysitting; laundry service. *In room:* A/C (beachfront and garden bungalows), TV, dataport, minibar, coffeemaker, hair dryer, iron, safe.

Hotel Bora Bora ★★★   This venerable institution has been the finest resort in French Polynesia since the day it opened in 1961. A few years ago, its owners, the luxury-laden Amanresorts, gave it some serious upgrading, which also put an emphasis on expediency rather than laid-back Polynesian service. Left alone during the renovations was the thatch-roofed central building that has always been a key part of the resort's charm. It sits atop Point Raititi, a low headland overlooking the start of magnificent Matira Beach, whose coral gardens provide some of the best snorkeling of any hotel in the territory. Down below, one of the best beach bars in the South Pacific rests right on those white sands. The entire complex faces west, presenting glorious sunsets over the lagoon and hilly Motu Toopua.

The comfortable Tahitian-style bungalows sit among the palm trees on the flat shoreline on either side of the headland. On the north, some of the 15 over-water bungalows are actually perched right on the reef's edge, where coral gives way to a deep blue lagoon (snorkeling off their porches is like flying off a canyon wall). A few others enjoy views of Mount Otemanu's tombstone across Povai Bay. Most of the bungalows are smaller than those at Bora Bora Lagoon Resort, but not the hotel's huge L-shaped units known as villas. Virtual houses, the villas all have separate bedrooms, and the "garden" versions even have their own small swimming pools, surrounded by rock walls for privacy. Each villa and overwater bungalow has a four-poster king-size bed with a romantic mosquito net. Furnishings throughout are top of the line, with some Oriental antique pieces here and there. All units have oak-trimmed claw-foot bathtubs in addition to showers. Three of the villas are air-conditioned and have Jacuzzis.

The only serious drawback here is the neighboring round-island road, which can send the noise of Bora Bora's innumerable scooters into some units at the crack of dawn. Also note that you will find no satisfaction here if you need to splash around in a swimming pool or watch TV in your room.

B.P. 1, Vaitape, Bora Bora (Matira Point, 7km/4½ miles from Vaitape). (C) 800/421-1490 or 60.44.11. Fax 60.44.22. www.amanresorts.com. 54 units. US$450–US$850. AE, DC, MC, V. Amenities: 1 restaurant (French), 2 bars; tennis courts; exercise room; watersports equipment rentals; bike rentals; game room; concierge; activities desk; car-rental desk; limited room service; massage; babysitting; laundry service. In room: A/C (in villas), stereo, dataport, fridge, minibar, coffeemaker, hair dryer, iron, safe.

Le Meridien Bora Bora ★   Located on the northern tip of an atoll-like island stretching 10km (6 miles) along the southeastern side of the outer reef, Le Meridien is the most unusual of Bora Bora's new resorts. Most obvious is its Melanesian architecture, like its sister property on Tahiti (see "Where to Stay," in chapter 4). The architects also created a seawater-fed, lakelike lagoon, in which you can swim if you tire of the real lagoon or the resort's small freshwater pool. There's scant shade on this wind-swept islet, so you'd better love sand and sun if you stay here. And note that the hotel's launch shuttles to Anau village, which is an expensive taxi ride from Vaitape (see "Getting Around," earlier in this chapter). Of the 100 identical guest units, 85 are built overwater. Only a few of these have views of Mt. Otemanu, whose tombstone is seen from its narrow end out here. Standing over waist-deep water, they are primarily notable for their huge glass floors, which make it seem as if you're walking on air (maids cover the glass with carpets at evening turndown). All units here are smaller than those at Bora Bora's other resorts, however, and you could stumble over too much furniture for the space available (shins have been skinned on the pointed ends of the lengthy, canoe-shaped coffee tables). Only the ten otherwise identical "beach" bungalows, which actually sit beside the manmade lake, are air-conditioned.

B.P. 190, Vaitape, Bora Bora (on Motu Pitiaau, 1km/½ mile off Anau village). (© **800/225-5843** or 60.51.51. Fax 60.51.10. www.lemeridien-tahiti.com. 100 units. 60,000CFP–70,000CFP ($444–$519). AE, DC, MC, V. **Amenities:** 2 restaurants (French), 1 bar; small outdoor pool; watersports equipment rentals; game room; concierge; activities desk; 24-hr. room service; babysitting; laundry service. *In room:* A/C (in beach units), TV, dataport, minibar, coffeemaker, hair dryer, safe.

Moana Beach Inter-Continental Resort ★★   The former Moana Beach Parkroyal, this deluxe resort went under the knife for some serious renovation in 2001. All of the resort's overwater bungalows—the first in which you could remove the tops of the glass coffee tables and actually feed the fish swimming in the turquoise lagoon below—were remodeled. Ashore, 11 beachside bungalows are less enchanting, but like the overwater units, they have Raiatea and Tahaa in their lagoon views. Also beside the beach, a circular thatch-roofed building surrounding a small courtyard houses the reception area, a lounge complete with a TV that is equipped to play any type of videotape, and the restaurant and bar, both with outdoor seating. The airy, beachside dining room offers very fine French selections, with an emphasis on seafood.

B.P. 156, Vaitape, Bora Bora (east side of Matira Point). (© **800/327-0200** or 60.49.00. Fax 60.49.99. www. interconti.com. 41 units. 62,130CFP–89,380CFP ($460–$662). AE, DC, MC, V. **Amenities:** 1 restaurant (French), 1 bar; outdoor saltwater pool; watersports equipment rentals; bike rentals; concierge; activities desk; car-rental desk; limited room service; massage; babysitting; laundry service. *In room:* A/C, TV, dataport, minibar, coffeemaker, hair dryer, iron, safe.

Sofitel Coralia Marara   Italian movie producer Dino De Laurentis built this resort in 1977, to house star Mia Farrow and the crew working on his box-office bomb *Hurricane*. A beehive-shaped central building houses the restaurant and bar, both of which open to a swimming pool sunken into a deck built out over Matira Beach and the lagoon. The beach sports the island's largest array of watersports activities, which are available to both guests and nonguests who are willing to pay for them. The Marara is not as luxurious as the other major resorts on Bora Bora, but its bungalows aren't far behind. Facing a curving beach of white sand, the land-based bungalows have views of the lagoon and Raiatea and Tahaa on the horizon. A long pier leads to 21 overwater units, which have Bora Bora's largest overwater decks. Overwater bungalows 51, 52, 62, 63, and 64 are the island's most private, so try to get one of them. Many meals at the resort restaurant are served buffet style and leave much to be desired.

B.P. 6, Vaitape, Bora Bora (northeast of Matira Point). (© **800/763-4835** or 41.04.04 in Papeete, or 60.55.00 on Bora Bora. Fax 41.05.05 or 67.74.03. www.accorhotels.com. 64 units. 34,370CFP–54,200CFP ($255–$402). AE, DC, MC, V. **Amenities:** 1 restaurant (French), 1 bar; outdoor pool; 1 tennis court; watersports equipment rentals; bike rentals; concierge; activities desk; car-rental desk; limited room service; babysitting; laundry service. *In room:* A/C, TV, dataport, minibar, coffeemaker, hair dryer, iron, safe.

Sofitel Coralia Motu ★★   More exclusive and private than its sister property, this intimate resort sits on a rocky, one-hill motu a 3-minute boat ride from the Sofitel Coralia Marara. Guests here can take the free on-demand shuttle boat and use all of the Marara's facilities. Marara guests, on the other hand, are allowed out here only for dinner. Unlike any other Bora Bora resort, this one has a gorgeous, picture-postcard view of Mount Otemanu's tombstone face (most but not all units enjoy the view, so ask for one that does). Perched on the side of the hill, the dining room serves much better French fare than does the Marara's restaurant, although it is a bit small for intimate dining. Often-steep stone pathways lead up and downhill to the guest bungalows; for this reason, I don't recommend the Motu to disabled travelers or to families with children. Most of the luxurious if not overly spacious units are overwater. Those that are ashore extend on stilts from the side of the hill, rendering great lagoon views. Several small beaches are equipped with hammocks and easy chairs, and one has a shower mounted on a tree.

B.P. 516, Vaitape, Bora Bora (on Piti Uuuta, .5km/½ off Matira Beach). © 800/763-4835 or 41.04.04 in Papeete, or 60.56.00 on Bora Bora. Fax 41.05.05 or 60.56.66. www.accorhotels.com. 30 units. 55,500CFP–70,300CFP ($411–$521). AE, DC, MC, V. **Amenities:** 1 restaurant (French), 1 bar; watersports equipment rentals; activities desk; limited room service; massage; babysitting; laundry service. *In room:* A/C, TV, dataport, minibar, coffeemaker, hair dryer, safe.

EXPENSIVE

Club Med Bora Bora *Value* Lush tropical gardens provide the setting for this Club Med beside a good beach in a little half-moon-shaped bay north of Matira Point. Behind it, the round-island road climbs up the interior hills, which provide a backdrop. The focus of attention is a large thatch-roofed beachside pavilion, which houses a reception area, bar, buffet-oriented dining room, and nightclub. Guests pay extra for scuba diving, but a wide range of watersports activities are included in the rates. Considering the prices elsewhere on Bora Bora, this makes Club Med a good value. The accommodations are in a mix of standalone and duplex bungalows and two-story, motel-style buildings. The air-conditioned beachfront bungalows are the preferred choice here, especially for honeymooners and others seeking a degree of privacy. The rooms are comfortably if minimally furnished (their most interesting feature: lights shining up from their tile floors). If you don't have a roommate, one of the same sex may be assigned.

B.P. 34, Vaitape, Bora Bora (northeast of Matira Point). © 800/258-2633, 60.46.04, or 42.96.99 in Papeete. Fax 42.16.83. www.clubmed.com. 150 units. 21,300CFP ($158) per person double, 25,200CFP ($187) per person bungalow. Rates include all meals, with wine, and most activities. AE, DC, MC, V. **Amenities:** 1 restaurant (French), 1 bar; 2 tennis courts; bike rentals; salon; massage; activities desk; car-rental desk; coin-op washers and dryers. *In room:* A/C, TV, hair dryer, safe.

Hotel Matira The reception desk for Hotel Matira is just inside Matira Bar and Restaurant (see "Where to Dine," below), which serves as headquarters for this collection of bungalows on and near the beach. Imported from Indonesia, the teak units have thatch roofs, porches on one corner, shower-only bathrooms, and pairs of double beds. You'll get a fridge and coffeemaker, but forget amenities like TVs, phones, and hair dryers. What you get here is an essentially unscreened cottage, so keep your insect repellent handy. The four "standard" units on the beach adjacent to the restaurant are subject to road noise. The "deluxe" models are about 500 meters away on Matira Point, a much more preferable location. Ask for a discount if you book directly with the hotel.

B.P. 31, Vaitape, Bora Bora (on Matira Beach, south of Hotel Bora Bora). © 67.70.51 or 67.78.58. Fax 67.77.02. www.hotelmatira.com. 20 units. 20,090CFP–37,730CFP ($149–$280). AE, MC, V. **Amenities:** 1 restaurant (Chinese/French), 1 bar; bike rentals; activities desk; car-rental desk. *In room:* Fridge, coffeemaker, no phone.

Le Maitai Polynesia ★★ *Value* In the early 1990s, I spoke with Pauline Youseff, who back then had her Village Pauline hostel and campground on this spot (see below). Pauline looked over her prime location, right on Matira Beach between the Moana Beach Inter-Continental Resort and Sofitel Coralia Marara resorts, and promised to put up a moderately priced hotel (moderate by Bora Bora's inflated standards, that is). She moved the campground in 1996, and with help from investors taking advantage of French Polynesia's hotel-promoting tax laws, she opened this comfortable establishment in 1998. The round-island road runs through the property, separating the beach and bungalows from the thatch-roofed main building and hotel rooms. Wedged between the shore and a cliff, the grounds are cramped but festooned with tropical plants.

The 56 moderate-size, air-conditioned hotel rooms occupy two-story blocks behind the main building. Units on the upper floor have at least partial lagoon views from their balconies, but downstairs you'll be looking at the hotel's kitchen. Worth asking for, upstairs rooms in a new wing completed in 2000 have spectacular lagoon views. Across the road, the virtually identical beach and overwater bungalows are smaller than those at the more expensive resorts, but they are packed with Polynesian decor. About 300 yards north of the property, 10 "villa suites" are actually thatch-roofed houses with separate bedrooms and kitchens with doors opening to covered porches. The villas aren't on the beach, but they are well suited for small families. You'll have to do without face towels, which aren't provided here.

B.P. 505, Vaitape, Bora Bora (northeast of Matira Point). © **60.30.00.** Fax 67.66.03. www.hotelmaitai.com. 84 units. 25,500CFP ($189) double; 31,200CFP–45,000CFP ($231–$333) bungalow or villa. AE, DC, MC, V. **Amenities:** 2 restaurants (French), 2 bars; watersports equipment rentals; bike rentals; activities desk; car-rental desk; babysitting; laundry service. In room: A/C (hotel rooms only), TV, dataport, kitchen (in villas), mini-bar, coffeemaker (in villas), hair dryer.

HOSTELS & CAMPING

It's difficult to get a reservation here because local French residents love its beachside location on the peninsula leading to Matira Point, but the pension-style **Chez Nono,** B.P. 282, Vaitape, Bora Bora (© **67.71.38;** fax 67.74.27), has simple rooms, bungalows, and an apartment starting at 6,000CFP ($45) for a double. Expect to share a bathroom here.

Although inconveniently located near Anau village on the east coast, **Chez Stillo,** B.P. 267, Vaitape, Bora Bora (© **67.71.32**), has the island's only beach-side campsites.

Village Pauline   Pauline Youseff has a variety of no-frills accommodations at her very popular place, one of the better hostels in the South Pacific. It sits in tropical gardens across the road from a beach and, except for the Sofitel Coralia Motu and a few units at the Hotel Bora Bora, is the only accommodation here in any price range with a view of Mount Otemanu's tombstone, albeit through towering palms. Pauline's five small bungalows have hot-water showers, kitchens, and front porches with tables and chairs, and the one larger bungalow also has a TV and kitchen. Budget travelers can pitch a tent in the yard, sleep in an eight-bed dormitory building, or try a simple garden room with a window; they all share communal toilets, cold-water showers, and a kitchen. All buildings have thatched roofs. A restaurant provides inexpensive meals and libations.

B.P. 215, Vaitape, Bora Bora (1km/½ mile north of Hotel Bora Bora). © **67.72.16.** Fax 67.78.14. vpauline@ mail.pf. 30 tent sites, 8 dorm beds, 7 units (none with bathroom), 6 bungalows. 2,300CFP ($17) tent site; 3,000CFP ($22) dorm bed; 7,000CFP ($52) double room; 15,000CFP ($111) bungalow. MC, V. **Amenities:** 1 restaurant (French), 1 bar; bike rentals. In room: TV (in large bungalow), kitchen (in large bungalow), no phone.

6 Where to Dine

The local *roulottes* roll out on and near the Vaitape wharf after dark. See "Where to Dine" in chapter 4 for details about these food wagons, which offer the only inexpensive meals on Bora Bora.

Bloody Mary's and a few other restaurants provide free transportation to guests who make reservations, so call ahead.

EXPENSIVE

Bamboo House FRENCH/SEAFOOD   That's exactly what this little establishment is: It's a bamboo house, and it's a charming one at that. The entire building is made of varnished split bamboo, and lots of dried bamboo leaves are stacked or hung here and there to render a jungly effect. Prime tables are on a small front porch, where you can watch the passing scene on the main road. The menu depends on what seafood is caught in local waters but usually features parrot fish, tuna, and shrimp, all well prepared in French sauces. Like Bloody Mary's (see below), it has a rouges' gallery of famous faces pasted on a roadside board.

Povai Bay, 1.5km (1 mile) north of Hotel Bora Bora. ℂ **67.76.24.** Reservations recommended. Main courses 2,000CFP–2,700CFP ($15–$20). AE, MC, V. Daily 11:30am–2pm and 6:30–8:30pm.

Bloody Mary's Restaurant & Bar ★★★ SEAFOOD/STEAKS   Having a few drinks and a slab of barbecued fish at this charming structure is as much a part of the Bora Bora experience as is taking a lagoon excursion. Ceiling fans, colored spotlights, and stalks of dried bamboo dangle from a large thatch roof over a floor of fine white sand (it's perfectly all right to take off your shoes). The butcher-block tables are made of coconut-palm lumber, and the seats are sections of palm trunks cut into stools. Just don't expect gourmet cuisine, for Bloody Mary's is essentially an American-style barbecued seafood and steak joint—which can be a welcomed relief after a diet of lard-laden French sauces. You'll be shown the fish and beef laid out on a bed of ice. The chef will charbroil your selection to order and serve it with a salad, vegetables, and your choice of sauce on the side. The cozy bar, cut from a beautifully polished litchi tree, is the only place on Bora Bora where the island's American expatriate residents hang out (if he's on the island, American owner Dexter Hewitt will be on his regular stool by the big tree trunk). Offered when cruise ships are in port, the lunch menu consists of burgers, fish and chips, and salads, which are not served at dinner. Come here for an evening of fun, as many famous souls have done (their photos are on a board out by the road).

Povai Bay, 1km (½ mile) north of Hotel Bora Bora. ℂ **67.72.86.** Reservations strongly recommended. Lunch 900CFP–1,400CFP ($7–$10); dinner main courses 2,500CFP–6,000CFP ($19–$45). MC, V. Lunch 11am–3pm (cruise ship days only); Mon–Sat 6–9pm. Bar Mon–Sat 9am–11pm.

TOPdive Restaurant ★★★ NEW FRENCH   Sitting beside the lagoon, a soaring thatch roof covers this excellent restaurant, Bora Bora's most romantic place to have dinner. Chef Phillipe Bachman oversees the kitchen, which produces wonderful nouvelle cuisine renditions of fresh seafood, some of it flown in from New Zealand. For example, you might start with the bacon-wrapped kiwi scallops served with a parsley vinaigrette. You might think you've had enough vanilla sauce before you get here, but the mahimahi steamed with taro spinach in vanilla won't be anything like the versions you've been offered at innumerable other restaurants. The fixed-price tourist menu offers a choice of starters, a main course, and a dessert. You'll need both an appetizer and a main course here because the portions are as small as they are extraordinarily well presented.

Vaitape, 1km (½ mile) north of wharf. ℂ **60.50.50.** Reservations recommended. Main courses 2,000CFP–3,400CFP ($15–$25); tourist menu 5,500CFP ($41). AE, MC, V. Daily 11:30am–2pm and 6:30–9pm. Bar daily 11:30am–9pm.

MODERATE

Chez Ben's SNACK BAR/PIZZA   Bora Bora–born Ben Teraitepo and his Oklahoma-born wife, Robin, hold fort at this lunch and afternoon snack spot, under a lean-to tin roof just across the road from a shady portion of Matira

---

Beach. Ben's fresh tuna salad sandwiches, pizzas and pastas, unusually spicy poisson cru, tacos, and fajitas are homemade and substantial, although Ben and Robin's company is the main reason to hang out here. They will shoo the dogs and cats away if they bother you.

Matira, between Hotel Bora Bora and Matira Point. © 67.74.54. Sandwiches and salads 500CFP–900CFP ($3.75–$7); pizzas and meals 1,000CFP–1,900CFP ($7.50–$14). AE. Daily 9am–5pm.

La Bounty ⭐ *Value* FRENCH/ITALIAN   Chef Eric Fadier has been providing the island's best pizza and other reasonably priced Italian (and French) fare under this L-shaped thatch roof since 1993. A pie makes an ample meal for one person or can be shared as an appetizer. The spaghetti and tagliatelle are tasty, too, with either smoked salmon, carbonara, Alfredo, Neapolitan, blue cheese, or seafood sauce. Steaks and fish are served under French sauces such as mustard or creamy vanilla. I was pleased with local shrimp in a whiskey sauce made piquant by thinly sliced onions. Pizzas are served quickly here, but everything else is prepared to order and takes longer. It's excellent quality for the price, however, so the wait is worth it.

Matira, east side, in hotel district. © 67.70.43. Reservations recommended. Pizza and pasta 950CFP–1,500CFP ($7–$11); main courses 1,200CFP–1,950CFP ($9–$14). MC, V. Tues–Sun 11:30am–2pm and 6:30–9pm.

Matira Bar and Restaurant CANTONESE/FRENCH   Literally hanging over the beach, this restaurant is an excellent place to have a lagoon-side lunch, a sunset drink, or a good Chinese meal without completely breaking the bank. The menu offers a selection of beef, pork, chicken, duck, and seafood dishes done in the Cantonese fashion, with Hakka overtones (Tahiti's first Chinese immigrants came from the Hakka region of the mainland).

In Hotel Matira, on Matira Beach. © 67.70.51. Breakfast 800CFP–1,800CFP ($6–$13); main courses 1,150CFP–1,550CFP ($9–$12). AE, MC, V. Daily 7–10am, 11am–2pm, and 6–9pm.

INEXPENSIVE

L'Appetisserie *Value* FRENCH/PASTRIES   French pastry chef Marc André was trying to sell this popular spot during my last visit, but if he's still here, you'll get fabulous croissants, tarts, quiches, sandwiches, pizzas by the slice, or a French-style *plat du jour,* all at extraordinarily reasonable prices for the high quality. Order at the counter and the staff will deliver to tables inside the shop or to tables under umbrellas on the shopping center sidewalk. You can use the computer terminal here to check your e-mail (see "Fast Facts: Bora Bora," earlier in this chapter).

North of the Vaitape wharf, in Centre Commercial le Pahia. © 67.78.88. Reservations not accepted. Pastries and sandwiches 200CFP–750CFP ($1.50–$5.50); meals 1,400CFP ($10.50). No credit cards. Mon–Sat 6am–6pm.

7 Island Nights

As on Moorea, things are really quiet on Bora Bora after dark (this is, after all, one of the world's most beautiful honeymoon destinations, not a place to practice your dance steps). You might want to listen to a Tahitian band playing at sunset or watch the furious hips in a Tahitian dance show, which all the resorts have at least 1 night a week. The schedules change, so call ahead.

Even if you're not staying at the **Club Med Bora Bora** (© **60.46.04**), you can have dinner there and watch the nightclub show staged by its staff. The full meal, wine, and show together cost 5,900CFP ($44). Call for reservations.

La Récife Discothèque (© **67.73.87**), about 1km (½ mile) north of Vaitape, is the island's one nightclub, and it opens only on Fridays and Saturdays at 11pm (that's right, 11pm) and closes at 3am (or later) the following morning. The clientele are mostly Tahitians between 18 and 24 years, and fights have been known to break out at that late hour. Admission is about 500CFP ($3.75), although women get in free on Friday. Beers cost at least 500CFP ($3.75) each.

7

Huahine & the Other Islands of French Polynesia

To catch a glimpse of "the way Tahiti used to be," as they say in these parts, you should stop at Huahine, the third most beautiful island in French Polynesia (behind Moorea and Bora Bora). Agriculture still far outweighs tourism on Huahine, and unless a cruise ship is in port, you'll have it almost to yourself. The friendliness of the people is unmatched anywhere in French Polynesia.

Huahine is famous for its ancient archaeological sites, as is nearby Raiatea, once the most important Polynesian island and today the administrative center of the Leeward Islands. Neither Raiatea nor Tahaa, the smaller island with which it shares a lagoon, has beaches, which takes them off the usual tourist circuit. But the deep-water lagoon here is the territory's charter yacht center. You can spend a lazy week or more circumnavigating Tahaa without venturing onto the open ocean.

The atolls of the Tuamotus offer a very different kind of experience. This immense archipelago, stretching across the northeastern approaches to Tahiti, consists not of high, mountainous islands but of low-lying necklaces of islets enclosing crystal clear lagoons. Rangiroa, Tikehau, and Manihi provide both excellent diving and tours of black pearl farms, the territory's second-largest industry.

1 Huahine ★★

The first of the Leeward Islands northwest of Tahiti, mountainous Huahine, known as the "Island of Fruits," is notable for its Bora Bora–like beaches and Mooreaesque bays and basaltic thumbs sticking up atop steep cliffs. It also has ancient maraes, a picturesque main town, and independent-spirited residents whose main livelihood is farming. As the least developed of the islands with luxury hotels and comfortable hostels, Huahine offers one of the territory's best opportunities to observe Polynesian life relatively unchanged by fast-paced Western civilization.

Pronounced "Wa-ee-nee" by the French and "Who-a-hee-nay" by the Tahitians, Huahine is actually two islands enclosed by the same reef and joined by a bridge. About 5,400 people live on the two islands, and most of them earn a living growing cantaloupes and watermelons and harvesting copra for the Papeete market. Huahine was not annexed by France until 1897—more than 50 years after Tahiti was taken over—and its friendly people are still independent in spirit. At the time that the first Europeans arrived, Huahine was governed as a single chiefdom and not divided into warring tribes as were the other islands, and this spirit of unity is still strong. Pouvanaa a Oopa, the great leader of French Polynesia's independence movement, was born on Huahine.

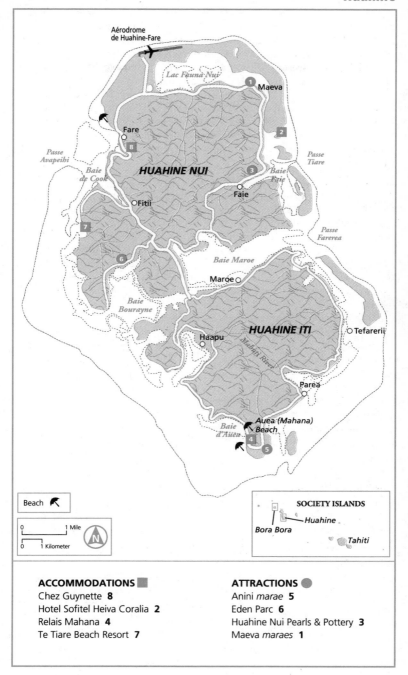

Aérodrome
de Huahine-Fare

Lac Fauna Nui

1 Maeva

Fare

2

*Passe
Avapeihi*

*Baie
de Cook*

8

HUAHINE NUI

3 *Baie
Faie*

*Passe
Tiare*

○Faie

○Fitii

*Passe
Farerea*

7

Baie Maroe

6

Maroe ○

*Baie
Bourayne*

HUAHINE ITI

○ Tefarerii

Haapu
○

Mahuti River

Parea
○

*Baie
d'Aïten*

Auea (Mahana)
Beach

4

5

Beach ☚

0 _____ 1 Mile
0 _____ 1 Kilometer

N

SOCIETY ISLANDS

Huahine

Bora Bora

Tahiti

ACCOMMODATIONS ■
Chez Guynette **8**
Hotel Sofitel Heiva Coralia **2**
Relais Mahana **4**
Te Tiare Beach Resort **7**

ATTRACTIONS ●
Anini *marae* **5**
Eden Parc **6**
Huahine Nui Pearls & Pottery **3**
Maeva *maraes* **1**

The ancient chiefs built a series of *maraes* on the shores of **Lake Fauna Nui,** which separates the north shore from a long, motulike peninsula, and on Matairea Hill above the lakeside village of **Maeva.** These have been restored and are some of the most impressive *maraes* in French Polynesia.

Hardly more than a row of Chinese stores opposite a wharf, the main village of **Fare** is nestled alongside the lagoon on the northwest shore, opposite the main pass in the reef. When the interisland boats put in from Papeete, Fare comes to life long before the crack of dawn. Trucks and buses arrive from all over Huahine with passengers and cargo bound for the other islands. The rest of the time, however, Fare lives at the lazy, slow pace of the South Seas of old, as a few people amble down its tree-lined main street and browse through the Chinese general stores facing the town wharf.

GETTING AROUND HUAHINE

The airport is on the peninsula paralleling the north side of the island, 3km (2 miles) from Fare. Unless you have previously reserved a rental car or are willing to walk into Fare, take your hotel minibus. At other times, **Enite's Taxi** (© **68.82.37**) will carry you around.

Avis (© **800/230-4898** or 68.73.34; www.avis.com), **Europcar** (© **800/227-7368** or 68.82.59; www.europcar.com), and the local firm **Huahine Locations** (© **68.67.85**) have offices in Fare. All three rent scooters and bicycles.

You can also rent **bicycles** at **Photo JoJo** (© **68.89.16**), on Fare's main street, opposite the wharf.

The island's only **gasoline stations** are in the center of Fare.

Each district has **local buses,** which run into Fare at least once a day, but the schedules are highly irregular. If you take one from Fare to Parea, for example, you might not be able to get back on the same day.

FAST FACTS : Huahine

The following facts apply specifically to Huahine. For more information, see "Fast Facts: French Polynesia" in chapter 3.

Currency Exchange **Banque Socredo** is in Fare, on the road that parallels the main street and bypasses the waterfront. Banque de Tahiti and most other businesses are along Fare's waterfront. Both have ATMs.

Drugstore The pharmacist at the drugstore opposite the town wharf speaks English (© **68.80.90**). It's Open Monday to Friday from 7:30 to 11:30am and 2 to 5pm, Saturday from 7:30 to 11:30am.

Emergencies/Police The emergency **police** telephone number is © **17.** The phone number of the **gendarmerie** in Fare is © **68.82.61.**

Healthcare The **government infirmary** is in Fare (© **68.82.48**). Ask you hotel for the name of doctors and dentists in private practice.

Post Office The colonial-style post office is in Fare, on the bypass road north of the waterfront area. Hours are Monday to Thursday from 7:30am to 3pm, Friday from 7am to 2pm.

Safety Campers have reported thefts from their tents on Huahine, so don't camp.

Telephone There are *télécarte* phones outside the post office, on the veranda.

Visitor Information On Fare's main street opposite the wharf, **Manava Huahine Visitors Bureau** (© and fax **68.78.81**) is open Monday to Saturday from 7:30 to 11:30am.

Water You shouldn't drink the tap water on Huahine except at the two major resorts.

EXPLORING HUAHINE
TOURING THE *MARAES* ★★★

The village of **Maeva,** beside the pass where Lake Fauna Nui flows toward the sea, was a major cultural and religious center before Europeans arrived in the islands. All of Huahine's chiefly families lived here. More than 200 stone structures have been discovered between the lakeshore and **Matairea Hill,** which looms over Maeva, including some 40 *maraes* (the others were houses, paddocks, and agricultural terraces).

You can see them on your own, but you will learn a lot more with Paul Atallah of **Island Eco Tours** ★★ (© **68.79.67;** islandecotours@msn.com). Paul is an American who graduated from the University of Hawaii with a major in anthropology and a minor in Polynesian Island archaeology. He is married to a Tahitian and has lived in French Polynesia for more than a decade. His is more than a typical safari expedition, for he gives in-depth commentary about the Maeva *marae* and other historical sites. He charges 5,000CFP ($37) for either morning or afternoon trips. The 4-hour trips depart daily at 8am and 1pm. He will pick you up at your hotel. Paul can also guide you to the *maraes* on Matairea Hill by special arrangement. He gives his commentary only in English.

If you want to see the *maraes* on your own, start west of Maeva village at **Fare Potee,** the large, reed-sided meeting house that extends out over Lake Fauna Nui. A small museum in the fare is open Monday to Saturday from 8:30am to 4pm. Admission is free. The stones sitting at the lake's edge and scattered through the adjacent coconut grove were family *maraes.*

Six *maraes* and other structures sit on Matairea Hill; some were built as fortifications during the 1844–48 French-Tahitian war. The track up the hill can be muddy and slippery during wet weather, and the steep climb is best done in early morning or late afternoon.

⸢Fun Fact⸣ Adzes, Fishhooks & Ornaments

When construction began on the now-defunct Hotel Bali Hai Huahine on the north side of Fare in 1973, workers discovered some artifacts while excavating the lily ponds. Dr. Yoshiko of the Bernice P. Bishop Museum in Honolulu just happened to be on the island and took charge of further excavations. During the next 2 years the diggers uncovered adzes, fishhooks, and ornaments that had been undisturbed for more than 1,000 years, according to radiocarbon dating of a whale bone found with the other items. So far, it's the earliest evidence of habitation found in the Society Islands.

> ## ⌒ *Finds* Fruit Juice & an Exotic Lunch
>
> On your way back to Fare from Huahine Iti, turn off the main road toward Bourayne Bay to **Eden Parc** (*©* **68.86.58**), a lush tropical garden where you can get freshly squeezed fruit juice or enjoy an "exotic" lunch made from produce organically grown on the premises. It's a hot and steamy site, and insect repellent is necessary, but the fruit and vegetables are as fresh as they can possibly be. The park is open Monday to Saturday from 7am to 5pm, with lunch served from 9am to 4pm.

Easier to reach, the large **Manunu Marae** stands on the beach about 1km (½ mile) across the bridge on the east end of Maeva. To find it, follow the left fork in the dirt road after crossing the bridge. The setting is impressive.

From the bridge you will see several stone fish traps, which were restored by Dr. Yoshiko H. Sinoto, the chairman of the anthropology department of the Bernice P. Bishop Museum in Honolulu and the man responsible for restoring many maraes throughout Polynesia. The traps work as well today as they did in the 16th century, trapping fish as the tide ebbs and flows in and out of the narrow passage separating the lake from the sea.

TOURING THE ISLAND

You can rent a vehicle and tour both parts of Huahine in half a day. The main roads around both parts of the island are about 32km (20 miles) long. Most of Huahine's roadways are paved, but there are some gravel sections, where you should drive very carefully. You should be especially careful on the *traversière,* which traverses the mountains from Maroe Bay to Faie Bay on the east coast. Except during periods of heavy rain, this road is passable, but it is very steep and rough; travelers have died trying to ride bicycles down it.

Heading clockwise from **Fare,** you skirt the shores of Lake Fauna Nui and come to the *maraes* just outside Maeva village (see "Touring the *Maraes,*" above).

From Maeva the road heads south until it turns into picturesque Faie Bay. There you'll pass the landing for **Huahine Nui Pearls & Pottery** ⌒ (*©* **78. 30.20**), a pearl farm and pottery studio operated by American Peter Owen. He offers free tours daily from 10am to 4pm, with the boat leaving Faie Bay every 15 minutes. If you aren't going to the Tuamotus, this is a good place to see how black pearls are grown in the shallow waters of the lagoon.

Once you're past Faie village at the head of the bay, the road starts uphill across the unpaved *traversière* (see above), so be especially careful. If you make it, you'll be rewarded with a view down across Mooreaesque **Maroe Bay,** which splits Huahine into two islands.

Turn right at the dead-end by the bay and drive west to the main west-coast road. Turn left and follow it across the bridge over the narrow pass separating Huahine Nui from Huahine Iti. A right turn past the bridge will take you along the winding west coast road to **Auea Bay,** where Relais Mahana (see "Where to Stay on Huahine," below) sits beside one of the South Pacific's greatest beaches. It's an excellent place to stop for refreshment.

Sitting at the end of the peninsula at the south end of Huahine Iti, **Anini Marae** presents a glorious view of the island's southern coast. Nearby, **Parea** is one of Huahine's largest villages and should soon be home to a moderately priced resort. From Parea you'll face several kilometers of gravel road, until you come to the village of **Tefarerii,** on the east coast. From there it's an easy drive back to the Maroe Bay bridge.

LAGOON EXPEDITIONS

You'll get a good look at Huahine while you're learning a lot about island's past with Paul Atallah of **Island Eco Tours** (see "Touring the *Maraes*," above).

As on Moorea and Bora Bora, one of the most enjoyable ways to see the island is on a lagoon excursion including snorkeling and a picnic on an islet out on the reef. **Poetaina Cruises** (no phone; book at any hotel desk) charges 7,000CFP ($52) per person for its all-day trips, which include a visit to Huahine Nui Pearls & Pottery (see "Touring the Island," above).

HORSEBACK RIDING, DIVING & OTHER OUTDOOR ACTIVITIES

La Petite Ferme ("The Little Farm"; ✆ **68.82.98**), on the main road north of Fare, just before the airport turnoff, has Marquesas-bred horses that can be ridden with English or Western saddles along the beach and around Lake Fauna Nui. Prices start at 6,000CFP ($45) for half a day. You can also go on a 2- or 3-day horseback camping trip into Huahine's interior.

Pacific Blue Adventure (✆ **68.87.21;** fax 68.80.71; www.divehuahine.com), Didier Forget's scuba dive operation, has an office on the Fare wharf. Didier charges 5,400CFP ($40) for a one-tank dive, during which he often feeds the sharks and pets the moray eels.

You can go for a half- or full-day cruise on Huahine's lagoon in a 15m (50-ft.) yacht with **Sailing Huahine Voile** (✆ and fax **68.72.49;** www.sailinghuahine.com). Half day's sailing costs 6,000CFP ($45) per person; a whole day, 12,000CFP ($89). The boat is also available for 1- or 2-week cruises in the Leeward or Tuamotu islands.

For lagoon or deep-sea fishing, contact **Huahine Marine Transports** (✆ **68. 84.02;** hua.mar.trans@mail.pf), a company owned by American expatriate Rich Shamel, who has lived on Huahine for many years and who runs the transfer boats for Te Tiare Beach Resort (see "Where to Stay on Huahine," below). Rich charges $400 for half a day and $650 for a full day of fishing on his 11m (36-ft.) Hatteras sportfishing boat. He lives and works at the resort's transfer base, just across the bridge on the south side of Fare.

WHERE TO STAY ON HUAHINE
RESORTS

Hotel Sofitel Heiva Coralia   This resort sits at the end of Maeva Motu, the flat almost-island joined to the mainland by the one-lane bridge at Maeva village. A large, airy, thatch-roofed central building opens to adult and children's swimming pools, which are necessary here since erosion has taken away much of the white-sand beach. Still, the property enjoys views of the speckled lagoon and Huahine's green mountains beyond. The best choice from among the spacious duplex or standalone bungalows are the six overwater models joined to the shore by a curving pier; they have glass panels for fish watching and balconies with steps to the lagoon. Although they are in long buildings and not as private, the less expensive rooms are as spacious and well equipped as the bungalows (try to get in numbers 39–45, which are only a row of bungalows removed from the beach).

B.P. 38, Fare, Huahine (on Maeva Motu, 10km/6 miles from airport). ✆ **800/763-4835** or 68.85.86; 41.04.04 in Papeete. Fax 41.05.05. www.accorhotels.com. 53 units. 24,500CFP ($181) double; 34,200CFP–62,700CFP ($253–$464) bungalow. AE, DC, ME, V. **Amenities:** 1 restaurant (French); 1 bar; outdoor pool; watersports equipment rentals; bike rentals; activities desk; car-rental desk; limited room service; babysitting; laundry service. *In room:* Coffeemaker, hair dryer, safe.

Relais Mahana ⭐ *Value*   This relatively remote property offers one of the South Pacific's best beach-lagoon combinations, for it sits right on the long white beach stretching down the peninsula on Huahine's south end. A pier from the main building runs out over a giant coral head, around which fish and guests swim. The peninsula blocks the brunt of the southeast trade winds, so the lagoon is usually as smooth as glass. Just climb down off the pier and swim with the fishes. The original bungalows are of the Motel 6 variety (minus the TVs and phones), but they were on the verge of being ripped down and replaced by more luxurious models during my recent visit. Theses new bungalows should have TVs, phones, and other niceties except phones. It was all part of an improvement project undertaken by new owners Elmer Daves, a retired judge from Tennessee, and his Swiss-born partner, Olivier Davinm, who lived in Los Angeles. They already had upgraded the beachfront restaurant. Even if you get one of the original, amenity-starved bungalows, it will be a bargain for the quality of beach here.

B.P. 30, Fare, Huahine (on Avera Bay, near Huahine's south end). ℂ 68.81.54. Fax 68.85.08. www.relais mahana.pf. 22 units. 19,184CFP–21,364CFP ($142–$158). AE, DC, MC, V. **Amenities:** 1 restaurant (French), 1 bar; outdoor pool; tennis court; watersports equipment rentals; game room; bike rentals; activities desk; car-rental desk; babysitting; laundry service; coin-op washers and dryers. *In room (new bungalows only):* A/C, TV (in some units), dataport, coffeemaker, hair dryer, safe, no phone.

Te Tiare Beach Resort ⭐⭐⭐   Rudy Markmiller made a fortune in the overnight courier business in California and then spent more than a decade—and a sizable chunk of his loot—building this luxury resort, one of French Polynesia's finest. A land dispute blocks road access, so guests are ferried here from Fare, which makes this seem like a remote offshore resort. You will land at a thatch-roofed, overwater structure housing reception, lounge, bar, and dining room. A long pier connects this central complex to a westward-facing, white-sand beach with gorgeous sunsets over Raiatea and Tahaa out on the horizon. The lagoon gets deep quickly here, making for excellent swimming and snorkeling over coral heads close to shore. You can use canoes, paddle boats, and kayaks, or cool off in a beachside swimming pool equipped with its own bar. You can pay to go diving, sailing, fishing, picnicking on a motu, horseback riding, or touring the maraes. Jet skis and water-skiing are available but not in front of the resort.

The 41 spacious bungalows are as luxuriously appointed as any in French Polynesia. You won't have a fishing-viewing glass panel in the floor, but you can step out to huge L-shaped decks, one half of them under the shade of thatch roofs. Steps lead into the lagoon from the decks of the 16 overwater bungalows, which have spa tubs in their bathrooms. Other bungalows sit beside the beach, but the garden units (the least expensive here) don't have unimpeded views of the lagoon.

B.P. 36, Fare, Huahine (in Fiiti District, 10 min. by boat from Fare). ℂ 888/841-4145 or 60.60.50. Fax 60.60.51. www.tetiarebeach.com. 41 units. US$285–US$650 double. AE, DC, MC, V. **Amenities:** 1 restaurant (French), 2 bars; outdoor pool; watersports equipment rentals; activities desk; car-rental desk; limited room service; babysitting; laundry service. *In room:* A/C, TV, minibar, coffeemaker, hair dryer, safe.

HOSTELS

Chez Guynette *Value*   Marty and Moe Temahahe (wife Marty is American; Moe is Tahitian) operate this friendly hostel facing the Fare waterfront. A corridor runs down the center of the building to the kitchen and lounge at the rear.

The simple but clean rooms and dorms flank the hallway to either side. The rooms are screened and have ceiling fans and bathrooms with cold-water showers. The dorms also have ceiling fans; they share two toilets and showers. Marty and Moe offer breakfast and lunch (sandwiches, salads, poisson cru on their street-side patio, plus wine and beer). It's the best place in Fare to slake a thirst and get into a good conversation—in English.

B.P. 87, Fare, Huahine (opposite the town wharf). © **68.83.75.** chezgynette@mail.pf. 7 units (all with bathroom), 8 bunks. 1,500CFP–1,700CFP ($11–$13) dorm bed; 4,700CFP–5,700CFP ($35–$42) double (higher rates apply to 1-night stays). MC, V. **Amenities:** 1 restaurant (French), 1 bar. *In room:* No phone.

WHERE TO DINE ON HUAHINE

The best poisson cru in town is served at **Snack Te Manava,** at the north end of the wharf (© **68.89.31**), which is open for lunch from Sunday to Friday.

Huahine's version of *les roulottes* gather on the Fare wharf when boats are in port. See "Where to Dine" in chapter 4 for more information about these meal wagons.

Definitely try to have breakfast or lunch at the patio at **Chez Guynette** (see "Where to Stay on Huahine," above).

Restaurant Tiare Tipanie *Value* FRENCH   On the veranda of a converted house, this restaurant is the best of the slim pickings on the island. It offers good home-cooked French fare such as poisson cru, sashimi, and steak or fish in pepper sauce. The special three-course dinners, which include a bottle of beer or ⅛ liter of house wine, are a good value.

Fare, north end between wharf and bypass road. © **68.80.52.** Main courses 1,450CFP–1,960CFP ($11–$14.50); 3-course dinner 2,060CFP ($15). MC, V. Tues–Sat 11:30am–1:45pm; Mon–Sat 6–8:45pm.

2 Raiatea & Tahaa ★

The mountainous clump of land you can see on the horizon from Huahine or Bora Bora is actually two islands, Raiatea and Tahaa, which are enclosed by a single barrier reef. Cruising yachts can circumnavigate Tahaa without leaving the lagoon, and Huahine and Bora Bora are relatively easy hauls from here. Accordingly, this is one of the South Pacific's two great yacht-chartering centers. There are no beaches on either Raiatea or Tahaa, and except for sailing and cruise-ship visits, tourism is not an important part of their economies, which are based on agricultural produce and, in the case of Raiatea, government salaries.

Raiatea, the largest of the Leeward Islands, is by far more important than Tahaa, both in terms of the past and the present. In the old days it was the religious center of all the Society Islands, including Tahiti. Polynesian mythology has it that Oro, the god of war and fertility, was born in **Mount Temehani,** the extinct flat-top volcano that towers over the northern part of Raiatea. **Taputapuatea,** on its southeast coast, was at one time the most important marae in the islands. Legend also has it that the great Polynesian voyagers who discovered and colonized Hawaii and New Zealand left from there. Archaeological discoveries have substantiated the link with Hawaii.

Today Raiatea (pop. 8,000) is still important as the economic and administrative center of the Leeward Islands. Next to Papeete, the town of **Uturoa** (pop. 3,500) is the largest settlement and is one of the most important transportation hubs in French Polynesia. Uturoa's waterfront has undergone a major transformation of late, with a big new cruise-ship terminal and welcome center now dominating the town wharf.

Tahaa (pronounced "*Tah*-ah-ah") is much smaller than Raiatea in terms of land area, population (about 1,500), and the height of its terrain. It's a lovely island, with a few very small villages sitting deep in bays that cut into its hills. Other than sailors, few visitors see it, and most of those who do see it on day tours from Raiatea.

GETTING AROUND RAIATEA & TAHAA

The Raiatea airstrip is 3km (2 miles) north of Uturoa. You have to rent a vehicle or take a taxi, for there is no regular public transportation system on Raiatea and no public transport whatsoever on Tahaa. There is no airport on Tahaa.

The passenger ferry *Temarii Tahaa* (© 65.67.10) runs between Uturoa's waterfront and Patio on Tahaa's northern coast, and it departs from Uturoa from Monday to Friday, usually at 10:45am, and Saturday at 11am. You had best make sure it will return to Uturoa on the same day it leaves. Fares are about 800CFP ($6) one way, 1,200CFP ($9) return. Water-taxi service is available at the waterfront (© 65.66.64); rides cost about 1,500CFP ($11).

Avis (© 800/230-4898 or 66.34.35; www.avis.com) and **Europcar** (© 800/ 227-7368 or 66.34.06; www.europcar) both have rental-car offices here. Prices start at 7,600CFP ($56) a day, including insurance and unlimited kilometers. Europcar also has an office on Tahaa (© 65.67.00), so you can take the ferry there, rent a car, and drive around the island. You must take a water taxi back to Uturoa.

There is a taxi stand near the cruise-ship terminal in Uturoa, or you can contact **René Guilloux** (© 66.31.40), **Marona Teanini** (© 66.34.62), or **Apia Tehope** (© 66.36.41). Fares are about 600CFP ($4.50) from the airport to town and 1,200CFP ($9) to the Raiatea Pearl Resort.

 FAST FACTS: **Raiatea & Tahaa**

The following facts apply specifically to Raiatea and Tahaa. For more information, see "Fast Facts: French Polynesia" in chapter 3.

Bookstores **Librairie d'Uturoa** (© 66.30.80) on the inland side of the main street, in the center of town, carries French books and magazines.

Currency Exchange French Polynesia's three banks have offices on Uturoa's main street. All have ATMs. There is no bank on Tahaa.

Drugstores **Pharmacie de Raiatea** (© 66.34.44) in Uturoa carries French products.

E-mail **Phenix,** halfway between Uturoa and the airport (© 66.20.66), has computers with Internet access for 15CFP (11¢) a minute. It's open Monday to Friday 8am to noon and 2 to 5pm, Saturday 8am to noon.

Emergencies/Police The emergency police telephone number is © **17.** The telephone number of the **Uturoa gendarmerie** is © **66.31.07.** The **Tahaa gendarmerie** is at Patio, the administrative center, on the north coast (© **65.64.07**).

Healthcare Opposite the post office, the **hospital** at Uturoa (© **66.32.92**) serves all the Leeward Islands. Tahaa has an **infirmary** at Patio (© **65. 63.31**). Private **physicians** and **dentists** practice in Uturoa; ask your hotel for a recommendation.

Information There might be a local tourist information desk at the cruise-ship terminal by the time you arrive.

Post Office The post and telecommunications office is in a modern build-ing north of Uturoa on the main road (as opposed to a new road that runs along the shore of reclaimed land on the north side of town) and is open Monday to Thursday from 7:30am to 3pm Friday from 7am to 2pm, and Saturday from 8 to 10am.

Telephone There are *télécarte* phones outside the post and telecommu-nications office.

Water Don't drink the tap water on either Raiatea or Tahaa.

EXPLORING RAIATEA & TAHAA

Highlights of a visit to Raiatea include day trips to and around Tahaa, picnics on small islands on the outer reef, canoe adventures up the Faaroa River (French Polynesia's only navigable river), and four-wheel-drive excursions into the mountains to see the *tiare apetahi*, a one-sided white flower found nowhere else on earth. Legend says that the five delicate petals are the fingers of a beautiful Polynesian girl who fell in love with a prince but couldn't marry him because of her low birth. Just before she died, heartbroken, in her lover's arms, she prom-ised to give him her hand to caress each day throughout eternity. At daybreak each morning, accordingly, the five petals pop open.

TAPUTAPUATEA MARAE ★★★

On the outskirts of Opoa village 29km (18 miles) south of Uturoa, the **Taputa-puatea Marae** is one of the most sacred locations in all of Polynesia, for legend says that Te Ava Moa Pass offshore was the departure point for the discovery and settlement of both Hawaii and New Zealand. The large *marae* on the site was actually built centuries later by the Tamatoa family of chiefs. Vying for supremacy, the Tamatoas mingled religion with politics by creating Oro, the ferocious god of war and fertility supposedly born on Mount Temehani, and by spreading his cult. It took almost 200 years, but Oro eventually became the most important god in the region. Likewise, the Tamatoas became the most powerful chiefs. They were on the verge of conquering all of the Society Islands when the missionaries arrived in 1797. With the Christians' help, Pomare I became king of Tahiti, and the great *marae* the Tamatoas built for Oro was soon left to ruin, replaced by the lovely Protestant church in nearby Opoa village.

The *marae* was restored in the 1960s, and the Tahiti Museum began an even more extensive rehabilitation in 1994. The museum's archaeologists have dis-covered human bones under some of the structures, apparently the remains of sacrifices to Oro. The *marae*'s huge *ahu*, or raised altar of stones for the gods, is more than 50 yards long, 10 yards wide, and 3½ yards tall. Flat rocks, used as backrests for the chiefs and priests, still stand in the courtyard in front of the ahu. The entire complex is in a coconut grove on the shore of the lagoon, oppo-site a pass in the reef, and legend says that bonfires on the *marae* guided canoes through the reef at night.

Taputapuatea is worth a visit not only for the *marae* itself but for the scenery there and along the way. The road skirts the southeast coast and follows Faaroa Bay to the mouth of the river, then back out to the lagoon.

WALKING AROUND UTUROA

Once an example of what Papeete must have been like a few generations ago, the town of Uturoa has seen a major transformation in recent years. A number of Chinese stores still line the main street, which parallels the waterfront a block inland, but Raiatea now has a glistening new **Gare Maritime,** a cruise-ship terminal built with money from France's economic restructuring fund. You can't miss this big Mediterranean-style building, which houses three restaurants, a black pearl shop, a large meeting room, and public restrooms. Handcraft and souvenir vendors occupy a number of small thatch buildings next door. Needless to say, the waterfront is packed when a cruise ship puts into port.

Just north of downtown Uturoa, the street to the left as you face the gendarmerie leads to a trail that ascends to the television towers atop 291m (970-ft.) **Papioi Hill.** (Be sure to close the gates, which keep the cows out of the station.) From the top you can see Uturoa, the reef, and the islands Tahaa, Bora Bora, and Huahine. Another trail begins with a Jeep track about 200 yards south of the bridge, at the head of Pufau Bay on the northwest coast. It leads up to the plateau atop **Mount Temehani.** The mountain itself is actually divided in two by a deep gorge.

ORGANIZED TOURS & SAFARI EXPEDITIONS

Try to avoid days when cruise ships are in port, since their passengers can monopolize all shore-based activities here.

American Bill Kolans of **Almost Paradise Tours** ★★★ (② **66.23.64**) has lived on Raiatea since sailing his boat down from Hawaii in 1979. He leads road expeditions to Taputaputea and other archaeological sites, and provides very informative commentary about the history and culture of the islands (his is the only such English-language tour here). His 3-hour island tour costs 4,000CFP ($30) per person.

Take your pick between **Raiatea 4×4** (② **66.24.16**) and **Jeep Safari Raiatea** (② **66.15.73**), two French-owned companies that will take you into the island's interior via four-wheel-drive Jeep. Each has two trips a day, requires reservations a day in advance, and charges about 5,000CFP ($37) per person.

LAGOON OUTINGS, DIVING, SAILING ★★★ & OTHER OUTDOOR ACTIVITIES

If you can put together your own group (because a minimum of four persons is required), you can take a variety of **lagoon excursions** and see firsthand the Raiatea-Tahaa lagoon, one of the most beautiful in French Polynesia. All trips include snorkeling, and most include picnics on tiny islets sitting on the outer reef; unlike the mainland part of Raiatea, they have beautiful white-sand beaches.

Book at your hotel or call Roselyne and Andrew Brotherson at **Manava Excursions** (② **66.28.26;** fax 66.28.26; maraud@mail.pf). They charge 5,500CFP ($41) per person for an all-day trip to Tahaa, including visits to a vanilla plantation and pearl farm, a picnic on a motu, and snorkeling over a coral garden. They also offer a half-day lagoon trip with a motu picnic for 1,200CFP ($9) per person, and a boat trip up the Faaroa River and on to the Taputapuatea *marae* for 3,300CFP ($24) per person. Roselyne speaks pretty good English; Andrew's is passable.

Faaroa River Cruises (② **66.32.70**) also has half-day cruises up the river, at 5,000CFP ($37) per person. Its Tahaa trips cost 6,000CFP ($44) for half-day and 8,000CFP ($59) for a full day per person; the full-day trip includes a motu picnic.

The Moorings (© 800/535-7289 or 727/535-1446; www.moorings.com) and **Stardust Yacht Charters** (© 800/772-3500 or 207/253-5400 in the U.S., or 66.23.18 on Raiatea; fax 66.23.19; www.sunyachts.com), which are based on Raiatea, charter sailboat operators (see "Seeing the Islands by Cruise Ship & Yacht," in chapter 3). If a boat is available, it can be chartered on a daily basis. Arrangements for longer charters ordinarily should be made before leaving home.

Raiatea may not have beaches, but the reef and lagoon are excellent for scuba diving. Based at Apooiti Marina, **Hémisphère Sub Raiatea** (© 66.12.49; fax 66.28.63; www.multimania.com/diveraiatea) takes divers on one-tank excursions for about 6,000CFP ($44).

You can go horseback riding with **Kaoha Nui Ranch** (© 66.25.46; kaohanui@ mail.pf), which charges 2,500CFP ($19) for a half day.

WHERE TO STAY ON RAIATEA & TAHAA
HOTELS

Raiatea Pearl Resort ★   Still referred to by its former name, the Hotel Hawaiki Nui (and before that the Hotel Bali Hai Raiatea), the island's best hotel sits on narrow site wedged between the road and lagoon. The friendly and helpful staff all speak English, but the ambience is definitely French. Like everywhere else on Raiatea, there is no beach, but eight overwater bungalows extend out over the clifflike reef face. The other bungalows, some of which have two units under their thatch roofs, are either along the seawall or in the gardens beyond. The least expensive units here are hotel rooms, which have the same amenities as the bungalows. A pier extends out to a dock from which you can climb into the water and get the sensation of flying as you snorkel along the face of the reef.

B.P. 43, Uturoa, Raiatea (2km/1¼ miles south of town). © 800/841-4145 or 66.20.23. Fax 66.20.20. www.pearlhotels.com. 32 units. 15,000CFP ($111) double; 20,000CFP–34,000CFP ($148–$252) bungalow. AE, DC, MC, V. **Amenities:** 1 restaurant (French), 1 bar; outdoor pool; tennis court; bike rentals; activities desk; car-rental desk; babysitting; laundry service. *In room:* TV, fridge, coffeemaker, hair dryer, safe.

Sunset Beach Motel *Value*   One of the best values in French Polynesia for guests wanting to do their own cooking, this is not a motel but a collection of cottages in a coconut grove on a peninsula sticking out west of the airport. The cottages sit in a row just off a palm-draped beach. The lagoon here is very shallow, but the beach enjoys a gorgeous westward view toward Bora Bora, and a long pier stretches to deep water (guests can paddle free kayaks from it). Of European construction rather than Polynesian, the modern bungalows are spacious, comfortably furnished, and have fully equipped kitchens and large covered verandas facing the sea. Part of the grove is set aside for campers, who have their own building with toilets, showers, and kitchen (bring your own tent and 1,100CFP/$8 per person per night). Manager Eliane Boubée and her manager son Moana both speak English.

B.P. 397, Uturoa, Raiatea (in Apooiti, 5km/3 miles northwest of Uturoa). © 66.33.47. Fax 66.33.08. www. raiatea.com/sunsetbeach. 22 units. 8,600CFP ($64) double bungalow. MC, V. *In room:* TV, kitchen, no phone.

HOSTELS & CAMPING

Pension Manava   Roselyne and Andrew Brotherson rent two rooms in their house and have four simple bungalows in their gardens, across the road from the lagoon. The two rooms share a bathroom and the Brothersons' kitchen. The bungalows have corrugated tin roofs, louvered windows, double and single beds, and large bathrooms with hot-water showers. Two also have kitchens. Roselyne will cook breakfast and provide free dinner transportation to town on request.

B.P. 559, Uturoa, Raiatea (6km/3½ miles south of town). ℂ **66.28.26.** www.manavapension.com. 6 units. 4,200CFP ($31) double (no bathroom); 6,600CFP ($49) bungalow with kitchen; 5,500CFP ($41) bungalow without kitchen. No credit cards.

Peter's Place   Backpackers will find a home in Peter Brotherson's simple and basic rooms in a plywood building, or they can pitch a tent in his expansive front yard across the road from the lagoon (it's worth the extra money to camp at Sunset Beach Motel; see above). Everyone shares communal toilets, hot-water showers, and a kitchen under its own thatch-line tin roof. Peter organizes tours to the *marae,* and guests get free use of canoes.

Avera, Raiatea (6km/3¾ miles south of Uturoa). ℂ **66.20.01.** 8 units. 1,300CFP–1,500 CFP ($10–$11) per person in units; 900CFP ($7) per person camping (higher rates for stays of 1 night). No credit cards. **Amenities:** Free use of canoes.

WHERE TO DINE ON RAIATEA & TAHAA

Raiatea's *les roulottes* congregate after dark in the middle of Uturoa's business district. They stay open past midnight on Friday and Saturday.

Brasserie Maraamu (Value) CHINESE/TAHITIAN   Before it moved into the new cruise-ship center, this restaurant occupied a waterfront shack and was widely known for its simple but good Chinese dishes, poisson cru, and fried chicken and steaks served with french fries. The chow is still good, as witnessed by the number of local office workers who head here for lunch. This also is the best place in town for breakfast (business types like to hang out here over strong cups of morning coffee).

In Gare Maritime, Uturoa waterfront. ℂ **66.46.64.** Reservations not accepted. Main courses 900CFP–1,500CFP ($7–$11). MC, V. Mon–Fri 7am–2pm and 6–10pm, Sat 6am–10pm.

Club House FRENCH   You'll find yachties sipping cold brews under this big, L-shaped Polynesian-style building next to the boats moored in Apooiti Marina, the local base for The Moorings charter company. An outrigger canoe hanging from the ceiling and lights inside bamboo Tahitian fish traps help set a romantic mood for seafood and steaks in French sauces. A snack menu offers salads and omelets, or you can order simple grilled chicken served with french fries.

Apooiti Marina (4.5km/3 miles north of Uturoa). ℂ **66.11.66.** Reservations recommended for dinner. Snacks 570CFP–1,250CFP ($4–$9); main courses 1,450CFP–3,200CFP ($11–$24). MC, V. Daily 9am–2pm and 5–10:30pm.

Seahorse Restaurant (★★) CHINESE   Proprietor Alphonse Léogite lived in the United States for 15 years before returning home to Raiatea and opening this excellent establishment in Uturoa's cruise-ship terminal. Varnished wood furniture, potted plants, and linen tablecloths set a tropical ambience for very good Chinese cuisine. Most items on the menu will be familiar, but you can also try delicacies such as sea cucumber steamed with ginger and served with pork and vegetables. If that's not on hand, try seafood prepared with shredded taro.

In Gare Maritime, Uturoa waterfront. ℂ **66.16.34.** Reservations recommended weekend evenings. Main courses 900CFP–1,800CFP ($7–$13). MC, V. Tues–Sun 10am–1:30pm and 6–9:30pm.

Snack Moemoea (★) SNACKS/FRENCH/CHINESE   This old corner storefront has tables both outside on the sidewalk and inside on the ground floor or on a mezzanine platform. The menu includes *casse-croûte* sandwiches, fine hamburgers, grilled fish and steaks, and excellent poisson cru.

Waterfront, Uturoa (in Toporo Bldg.). ℂ **66.39.84.** Reservations not accepted. Sandwiches 300CFP–550CFP($2.25–$4); main courses 1,100CFP–1,600CFP ($8–$12). No credit cards. Mon–Fri 6am–5pm, Sat 6am–2pm.

3 Rangiroa ⭐⭐

The largest and most often visited of the Tuamotu atolls, Rangiroa lies 312km (194 miles) northeast of Tahiti. It consists of a ring of low, skinny islets enclosing a tadpole-shaped lagoon more than 70km (43 miles) long and 26km (16 miles) wide. That's wide enough so that when you stand on one side of the lagoon, you cannot see the other. In fact, the entire island of Tahiti could be placed in Rangiroa's lagoon, with room to spare.

Like all the atolls, the islets here are so low—never more than 3m (10 ft.) above sea level, not including the height of the coconut palms growing all over them—that ships can't see them until they're a few kilometers away. For this reason, Rangiroa and its Tuamotu sisters are also known as the Dangerous Archipelago. Hundreds of yachts and ships have been wrecked on these reefs, either unable to see them until it was too late or dragged ashore by tricky currents.

Schools of dolphins usually play early mornings and late afternoons in Rangiroa's two navigable passes into its interior lagoon. Currents of up to 6 knots race through the passes as the tides first fill the lagoon and then empty it during their never-ending cycle. Even at slack tide, watching the coral rocks pass a few feet under your yacht is a tense experience. Once inside the lagoon, however, you anchor in a huge bathtub whose crystal-clear water is stocked with an incredible variety of sea life (including a multitude of large sharks and manta rays).

Most visitors come to Rangiroa primarily for the territory's best scuba diving and snorkeling. Others venture across the lagoon to Rangiroa's islets, where they can literally get away from civilization at a very remote resort.

GETTING AROUND RANGIROA

Rangiroa's airstrip and most of its hotels and pensions lie on a perfectly flat, 11km-long (7-mile) island on the north side of the lagoon. The airport is about equidistant from the village of Avatoru on the west end and Tiputa Pass on the east. The hotels and pensions send buses or vans to meet their guests.

Europcar (ℂ **800/227-7368** or 96.08.28; www.europcar.com) has an agency near Avatoru and a desk at the Kia Ora Village (see "Where to Stay on Rangiroa," below). Scooters and open-air "Fun Cars" (the most you'll need here) cost about 6,500CFP ($48) for a day (which is longer than you'll need to see the islet). Bicycles rent for 900CFP ($7) for half a day, 1,500CFP ($11) for a full day.

 FAST FACTS: Rangiroa

The following facts apply specifically to Rangiroa. For more information, see "Fast Facts: French Polynesia" in chapter 3.

Currency Exchange **Banque de Tahiti** has a branch in Avatoru. It's open Monday, Wednesday, and Friday from 8 to 11am and 2 to 4pm, Tuesday and Thursday from 8am to 4:30pm. *Note:* There is no ATM on Rangiroa.

E-mail **Taaroa Web,** on the eastern side of the Kia Ora Village (ℂ **96. 03.04**), charges 250CFP ($2) for 15 minutes of Internet access. It's open daily 8am to 8pm. The modem usually occupies the phone line here, so just drop by.

Emergencies/Police The emergency **police** telephone number is ✆ **17.** The phone number of the **gendarmerie** on Rangiroa is ✆ **96.03.61.**

Healthcare **Dr. Guy Thirouard** has an office in Avatoru (✆ **96.04.44** or 96.04.33). There are **infirmaries** at Avatoru (✆ **96.03.75**) and across the pass at Tiputa (✆ **96.03.96**).

Photographic Needs For film, check the boutique at the **Kia Ora Village hotel.** You won't get overnight processing here.

Post Office The small post office in Avatoru is open Monday to Thursday from 7am to 3pm, Friday 7am to 2pm.

Telephone Public pay phones are at the post office in Avatoru and at the dock on the eastern end of the island.

Water Except at Kia Ora Village, the tap water is brackish. Don't drink it.

LAGOON EXCURSIONS & SCUBA DIVING ★★★

Except for walks around Avatoru and Tiputa, typical Tuamotuan villages with whitewashed churches and stone walls lining the main streets, plan on either doing nothing or enjoying the fantastic lagoon. The hotels and pensions either have or can arrange lagoon excursions by boat. One favorite destination is the **Lagon Bleu** (Blue Lagoon), a small lagoon within the big lagoon on the far eastern side of the island. It's full of colorful corals and plentiful sea life. **Les Sables Rose** (The Pink Sands), on the eastern end, is another popular destination. These trips are not inexpensive—plan on paying 10,000CFP ($75) or more for a full day's outing. You're looking at an hour's boat ride in each direction to reach the Blue Lagoon or The Pink Sands.

Close to home, snorkelers and scuba divers can **"ride the rip"** tide through the passes, one of the most exhilarating waterborne experiences French Polynesia has to offer. These so-called drift snorkeling trips cost about 4,200CFP ($31) and are worth it—if you've got a strong heart.

The same operators also have **dolphin-watching** cruises, usually for about 4,300CFP ($32) per person, but you can ride or walk to the public park at the western side of Tiputa Pass and watch them play for free.

The best **scuba diving** here is from December to March, when huge hammerhead sharks gather off Tiputa Pass for their mating season, and when the manta rays look for mates between July and October. You can see gray and black-tipped sharks all year. But be aware that dives here are deep and long compared to American standards, so bring a buddy and be prepared to stretch the limits of the dive tables in order to see the magnificent sea life. Divers must be certified in advance and bring their medical certificates.

Any of the hotels or pensions can arrange scuba dives. The best operator is **Blue Dolphins** (✆ **96.03.01;** www.bluedolphinsdiving.com), which operates from the Hotel Kia Ora Village (see "Where to Stay on Rangiroa," below). One-tank day dives cost 6,000CFP ($44), while night dives cost 7,500CFP ($56). Other operators here include **The Six Passengers** (✆ **96.02.60**), which allows only six divers on its boat at any one time; **Raie Manta Club** (✆ **96.04.80**); and **Rangiroa Paradive** (✆ **96.05.55**).

Impressions

At Rangiroa you pick up a hundred natives with pigs, guitars, breadfruit and babies. They sleep on deck, right outside your bunk, and some of them sing all night.

—James A. Michener, *Return to Paradise*, 1951

At press time, the Louisiana-based **Aggressor Fleet, Ltd.** (© 800/348-2628 or 985/385-2628; fax 985/384-0817; www.aggressor.com) had announced plans to place the 32m (106-ft.), 16-passenger live-aboard dive boat *Tahiti Aggressor* at Rangiroa for 1-week cruises through the northern Tuamotus. Contact the firm for prices and reservations.

WHERE TO STAY ON RANGIROA

Kia Ora Sauvage   This outpost offers one of the South Pacific's most remote Robinson Crusoe–like escapes. Guests are transferred daily by a 1-hour speedboat ride from Kia Ora Village, which manages this retreat. Once you're out on tiny, triangle-shaped Avearahi motu, you will find a thatched main building, where the Tahitian staff cooks up the day's catch, often caught during the guests' lagoon excursions. Accommodation is in five comfortable bungalows built entirely of native materials. They have their own modern bathrooms, but they are not screened. Nor do they have electricity. Bring reef shoes, lots of insect repellent, and 60-factor sunblock.

B.P. 4607, Papeete, Tahiti (hotel is 1-hr. boat ride from airport). © 800/763-4845 or 96.02.22. Fax 96.02.02. www.hotelkiaora.com. 5 units. 34,000CFP ($252) double. Meals and drinks 7,600CFP ($56) per person per day. Round-trip boat transfers cost 7,500CFP ($56) per person. AE, DC, MC, V. **Amenities:** 1 restaurant (French), 1 bar. *In room:* No phone.

Kia Ora Village ★★   This romantic establishment has been Rangiroa's premier hotel for almost three decades, and it has gotten better in recent years. Its thatch-roofed buildings look like a Polynesian village set in a coconut grove directly on the lagoon. White sand has been hauled over from the ocean side of the island, but the beach still is a bit rocky; however, a long pier reaches out into deep water for excellent swimming, snorkeling, and sunset watching. Ten bungalows sit over the reef and share the sunsets. Recent additions include two-story beachside bungalows with air-conditioned bedrooms downstairs and up, and one-story models with only the downstairs bedroom. All these additions have Jacuzzi tubs set in their partially covered front decks, but they have not one iota of privacy. Some of the much smaller original bungalows have been left as less expensive "garden" models. Unlike the new and renovated bungalows, they do not have telephones or safes. Guests here are mainly European and Japanese couples, plus some American divers.

B.P. 4607, Papeete, Tahiti (3km/2 miles east of airport, near east end of island). © 800/763-4835 or 96.02.22. Fax 96.02.20. www.hotelkiaora.com. 58 units. US$200–US$550 double. Meals 9,900CFP ($73) per person per day. AE, DC, MC, V. **Amenities:** 1 restaurant (French), 1 bar; tennis court; watersports equipment rentals; bike rentals; activities desk; car-rental desk; babysitting; laundry service. *In room:* A/C, kitchen, minibar (in overwater units), fridge, coffeemaker, hair dryer, safe.

Les Relais de Josephine ★ *Value*   You can watch the dolphins frolic in Tiputa Pass from the front porch of your bungalow at this comfortable inn, the creation of Denise Thirouard, whose husband, Dr. Guy Thirouard, practices in Avatoru (see "Fast Facts," above). The bungalows flank a Mediterranean-style

> ⎛Tips⎞ **Come Up Here First**
>
> Unless you're a serious scuba diver, there isn't a lot to do in the Tuamotu Islands, which makes them great for resting and recovering from your long flight before tackling Tahiti, Moorea, and Bora Bora. So come here first for a little R&R, and then hit the more developed islands.

villa with an expansive veranda overlooking the pass. Guests can relax there or in a lounge equipped with a TV, VCR, and CD player. At night the veranda turns into the family style Le Dolphin Gourmand restaurant, which serves very good three-course French and Mediterranean meals for 3,500CFP ($26) per person (nonguests are welcome if they make reservations before noon). Furnished with reproductions of French colonial antiques, the bungalows have thatch roofs over solid white walls. Sliding doors open to the porches with high-quality wooden patio furniture. Neither the doors nor the prop-up windows are screened, but the queen-size beds are covered by tentlike mosquito nets. The substantial bathrooms have double sinks and walk-in showers.

B.P. 140, Avatoru, Rangiroa. ℭ and fax **96.02.00.** http://relaisjosephine.free.fr/englis/indexuk.htm. 3 units. 13,200CFP ($98) per person. Rates include breakfast and dinner. DC, MC, V. **Amenities:** 1 restaurant (French), 1 bar; bike rentals; laundry service. *In room:* Coffeemaker, safe, no phone.

WHERE TO DINE ON RANGIROA

A snack bar on the dock at Tiputa Pass is open for lunch and dinner Monday to Saturday, and don't forget Le Dolphin Gourmand restaurant at Les Relais de Josephine (see above). Outsiders also are welcome at the Kia Ora Village's dining room.

Vaimario Restaurant & Pizzeria ITALIAN/FRENCH One-person and large pizzas are the highlights at this restaurant in a thatch-roof house just west of the airport. You can dine inside but preferable tables are on the coral-floor veranda. The best main courses are grilled fresh fish with almond, Provençal, or mustard sauces. The wait staffers are good-natured about their limited knowledge of English.

Main road, west of airport. ℭ **96.04.69.** Pizza 1,350CFP ($10); main courses 850CFP–1,750CFP ($6–$13). MC, V. Tues–Sat 11:30am–1:30pm and 6:30–9pm; Sun 11:30am–2pm.

4 Tikehau ⍟

Separated from Rangiroa by a deep-water channel, Tikehau is a much smaller and less developed version of its big sister. Its nearly circular lagoon, 26km (16 miles) across, is dotted with islets such as Ohihi, which has a pink-sand beach, and Puarua and Oeoe, where noddy birds and snowy white fairy terns nest. The lagoon is no more than 30m (100 ft.) deep, which means you won't see rays and big sharks. A multitude of colorful tropical fish swim in the lagoon, which makes it great for snorkelers and novice divers, but Tikehau's best diving is in the ocean beyond the one pass in the reef.

Gilles Petrie's **Manihi Blue Nui Dive Center,** based at the Tikehau Pearl Beach Resort (see below), is the best in French Polynesia, with top-of-the-line equipment and hard-topped boats with ladders. It charges about 6,500CFP ($48) per one-tank dive, and it teaches PADI certification courses.

Famous for a riot of hibiscus, frangipani, bougainvillea, and other colorful flowers that seem to grow everywhere, Tikehau's only village, **Tuherahera,** is one of the most picturesque in the Tuamotus. It's also one of the wealthiest, since the 400 or so residents here make more money by trapping and shipping fish to Papeete than do from their four black pearl farms.

You'll find three grocery stores, a post office, and an infirmary in Tuherahera, but you won't find a bank. You can shop for shell jewelry and hand-painted bedspreads and pareus at **Artisana,** beside the village wharf (no phone). It's usually open Monday to Friday from 4 to 5:30pm, weekends from 3 to 5:30pm.

WHERE TO STAY & DINE ON TIKEHAU

Tikehau Pearl Beach Resort ★★   From a distance, rustic Tuamotu-style thatch disguises the luxuries awaiting at this resort, which occupies all of Motu Tiano, a small reef islet a 10-minute boat ride from the village and the airport. Other than a concrete patio separating the lagoon-side pool from the conical-roofed dining room and bar, everything about it is *tres* Polynesian, with *beaucoup* thatch, mats, and bamboo. Strong currents in a shallow pass rip in and out beneath the overwater bungalows here, which means you can't go swimming from their decks. As romantic as the overwaters may be, the currents make the widely spaced bungalows beside the beach the preferable choices here. Also, the beach here has considerably more white sand than you'll find on Rangiroa and Manihi. Every unit here is spacious and well appointed, and the beachside units have large outdoor bathrooms protected by high rock walls. The bungalows aren't screened, but the staff closes the windows and turns on the electric mosquito repellents while you're at dinner. Only five units were air-conditioned during my recent visit; ceiling fans and the trade winds usually provide plenty of ventilation, but ask for an air-conditioned bungalow if it's important to you. Guests get free use of snorkel gear, canoes, and kayaks. They pay for diving, fishing, and excursions to the pink sands and bird islets.

B.P. 20, Tuherahera, Tikehau. ✆ **800/841-4145** or 43.16.10 for reservations, or 96.23.00. Fax 43.17.86 for reservations, or 96.23.01. www.pearlhotels.com. 30 units. 38,000CFP–60,000CFP ($281–$444) double. Meals 9,500CFP ($70) per person per day. AE, DC, MC, V. **Amenities:** 1 restaurant (French/Mediterranean), 1 bar; outdoor pool; free use of snorkeling gear, canoes, and kayaks; watersports equipment rentals; bike rentals; activities desk; babysitting; laundry service. *In room:* A/C (in beach units), TV, dataport, fridge, coffeemaker, hair dryer.

5 Manihi ★

Known for its black pearl farms, Manihi lies 520km (312 miles) northeast of Tahiti in the Tuamotus. At 30km (16 miles) long by 5.6km (4 miles) wide, the clear lagoon is not nearly as large—nor as deep—as Rangiroa's, but it's better for diving among colorful tropical fish, as opposed to the multitudinous rays and sharks that make diving at Rangiroa so exciting. Tairapa Pass, the main entry into the lagoon, is wider and deeper than those at Ranigroa, but it has a strong enough current to make riding-the-rip snorkeling trips a highlight here.

French Polynesia's pearl farming industry started here in the late 1960s, and the farms seem to sit atop nearly every coral head dotting the lagoon. Most of the workers stay in Turipaoa, the only village here.

Note: There is no bank on Manihi, and the airport does not have restrooms.

As at Tikehau, Gilles Petrie's **Manihi Blue Nui Dive Center,** based at the Manihi Pearl Beach Resort (see below), provides top-of-the-line PADI diving. It charges about 6,500CFP ($48) per one-tank dive.

WHERE TO STAY & DINE ON MANIHI

Manihi Pearl Beach Resort ★★   This modern resort and the airstrip share a motu on the western end of Manihi's lagoon. Like at Rangiroa, the beach here is more pebbly than sandy, so most guests sun themselves on little islets equipped with palm trees and chaise longues or on a faux beach beside a lagoon-side horizon pool. A thatch-roof bar adjacent to the pool is cozy and conducive to meeting your fellow guests. In addition to diving, activities include swimming, snorkeling (you can ride the rip tide through the pass), canoeing, visiting pearl farms and the village, lagoon and deep-sea fishing, spending a day on a deserted motu, and cruising at sunset. The prevailing trade winds can generate a choppy lagoon under the 19 overwater bungalows here. Both the overwater and beachside units have mat-lined walls, natural wood floors, ceiling fans hanging from thatch roofs, king-size beds, writing tables, ample shower-only bathrooms, and covered porches with two recliners. Each beachfront unit also has a hammock strung between two palm trees out front, and the beachfront unit bathrooms are outdoors under thatch roofs and behind high wooden walls. Although a majority of guests here are European couples, the English-speaking Tahitian staff makes Americans feel at home.

B.P. 2460, Papeete, Tahiti. ⓒ **800/841-4145** or 43.16.10 for reservations, or 96.42.73. Fax 43.17.86 for reservations, or 96.42.72. www.pearlhotels.com. 41 units. 28,000CFP–54,000CFP ($207–$400) double. Meals 9,500CFP ($70) per person per day. AE, MC, V. **Amenities:** 1 restaurant (French), 1 bar; outdoor pool; watersports equipment rentals; game room; activities desk; babysitting; laundry service. *In room:* TV, dataport, fridge, minibar, coffeemaker, hair dryer, safe.

The Cook Islands

Perhaps it's the rugged beauty, rivaling that of the more famous Tahiti. Maybe it's the warmth and friendliness of the proud Polynesian people who love to talk about their islands, and do so in English. It could be the old South Seas charm of a small island nation whose little capital is like Papeete was a very long time ago. Whatever the reason, there are few old South Pacific hands who aren't absolutely enraptured with Rarotonga and the other Cook Islands.

The Cook Islanders have more than beautiful islands in common with the people of French Polynesia, which lies some 900km (550 miles) to the east. They share with the Tahitians about 60% of their native language, and their lifestyles and religions were similar in the old days. Like many Tahitians, Cook Islanders have a keen interest in their eastern Polynesian past, but they are better at showing it off, explaining to visitors the old ways and the new.

They also enjoy having a good time, and this lust for happiness very quickly rubs off on visitors. With tourism their primary industry, the Cook Islanders offer a surprising lot to do in their very small islands. Indeed, no other place in the South Pacific has so much to see and do in so small a space.

1 The Cook Islands Today

Rarotonga and the other 14 Cook Islands are tiny specks scattered between Tahiti and Samoa, in an ocean area about one-third the size of the continental United States, yet all together they comprise only 150 square km (93 square miles) of land. Rarotonga is by far the largest, encompassing 42 square km (26 sq. miles), yet it is only 32km (20 miles) around. A microcosm of modern Polynesia, Rarotonga has enough island activities to satisfy almost anyone, including snorkeling, shopping, sightseeing, and scuba diving. Its cultural tours are the best in the South Pacific.

THE NATURAL ENVIRONMENT   The Cook Islands are divided both geographically and politically into a Southern and a Northern Group. Most of the nine islands of the Southern Group, including Rarotonga, are volcanic, with lush mountains or hills. The islands of the remote Northern Group, except Nassau, are typical atolls, with circles of reef and low coral islands enclosing central lagoons. The sandy soil and scarce rainfall support coconut palms, scrub bush, and a handful of people. Although they can be reached by air, the remote Northern Group receives few visitors.

Rarotonga, the only high, mountainous island, is in many ways a miniature Tahiti: It has jagged peaks and steep valleys surrounded by a flat coastal plain, white sandy beaches, an azure lagoon, and a reef extending about ½km (¼ mile) offshore. In most places the shoreline consists of a slightly raised sandy bar backed by a swampy depression, which then gives rise to the valleys and mountains. Before the coming of missionaries in 1823, Rarotongans lived on the

---

Impressions

*If I could vacation on only one Pacific island I would choose Rarotonga.
It's as beautiful as Tahiti, much quieter, much stuffier and the food is even
worse. But the climate is better and the natives are less deteriorated.*
—James A. Michener, *Return to Paradise*, 1951

---

raised ground beyond the swampy flats, which they used for growing taro and
other wet-footed crops. They built a remarkable road, actually paved in part
with stones, from village to village almost around the island. That "back road"
still exists, although the paved round-island road now runs near the shore. The
area between the two roads appears to be bush but is in fact heavily cultivated
with a plethora of crops and fruit trees.

If Rarotonga masquerades as a small version of Tahiti, **Aitutaki** plays the role
of Bora Bora in the Cook Islands. Although lacking the spectacular mountains
that Bora Bora has, little Aitutaki is nearly surrounded by a large, shallow lagoon
whose multihued beauty and abundant sea life rival those of its French Polynesian counterpart and make this charming, atoll-framed outpost the second
most-visited of the Cooks.

The vegetation of the southern islands is typically tropical: The mountains
and hills are covered with native brush, while the valley floors and flat coastal
plains are studded with coconut and banana plantations and a wide range of
flowering trees and shrubs.

THE GOVERNMENT The Cook Islands are an independent country in
association with New Zealand, which provides for the national defense needs of
the islands and renders substantial financial aid. Cook Islanders hold New
Zealand citizenship, which means they can live there. New Zealanders, on the
other hand, are not citizens of the Cook Islands. There is an official New
Zealand "representative" (not an ambassador or consul) in Avarua. Although the
Cook Islands are technically independent, their ties with New Zealand deprive
the Cooks of a seat in the United Nations.

An effort had been afoot to reduce the number of parliamentarians, but at
press time the Cook Islands had a Westminster-style parliament with 25 elected
members, led by a prime minister chosen by members of the majority party. Parliament meets twice a year, in February and March and from July to September.
There is also a House of Ariki (that is, hereditary chiefs), which advises the government on matters of traditional custom and land tenure. Each island has an
elected island council and a chief administrative officer, who is appointed by the
prime minister.

THE ECONOMY The economy in the Cook Islands is based on tourism
(about half of the country's gross domestic product), black pearls (its number
one export), and agriculture, mainly tropical fruit and fruit juices. Some revenue
is derived from the Cook Islands' status as a tax-free haven. Without overseas
aid, cash sent home by islanders living abroad, and the money earned from
tourism, however, the country would be in serious financial trouble. In fact, it
ran into a great deal of difficulty in the mid-1990s, when the debt-ridden government failed to back its local currency with adequate New Zealand dollars,
thus rendering the local money worthless. When foreign lending organizations
forced the government to mend its ways (see "A Look at the Past," below),
expenditures were drastically reduced and more than half of all government

workers were fired. Before the cutbacks, more than 3,300 islanders—almost 20% of the total population—were civil servants. Some 4,500 Cook Islanders have since pulled up stakes and left for New Zealand, resulting in a decrease in the islands' population from approximately 22,500 to 18,000 (with some estimates as low as 13,800). The exodus has resulted in a shortage of labor, especially in the tourism industry (you're likely to see Australians and Fijians working alongside Cook Islanders at the major hotels these days).

2 A Look at the Past

Legend has it that the first Polynesians arrived in the Cook Islands by canoe from the islands of modern-day French Polynesia about A.D. 1200, although anthropologists think the first of them may have come much earlier. In any event, they discovered the Cook Islands as part of the great Polynesian migrations that settled all of the South Pacific, long before the Spanish explorer Alvaro de Mendaña laid the first European eyes on any of the Cook Islands when he "discovered" Pukapuka in 1595.

The Spanish at that time were more interested in getting from Peru to the riches of Manila than in general exploration. Thus, except for Rakahanga, which was "discovered" by Pedro Fernández de Quirós during a voyage along the same general route in 1606, the islands did not appear on European maps for another 170 years.

And then, as happened in so many South Pacific island groups, along came Capt. James Cook, who stumbled onto some of the islands during his voyages in 1773 and 1777; he named them the Hervey Islands. In 1824 the name was changed to the Cook Islands by the Russian cartographer John von Krusenstern.

Captain Cook sailed around the Southern Group but missed Rarotonga, which apparently was visited first by the mutineers of HMS *Bounty*, under Fletcher Christian. There is no official record of the visit, but oral history on Rarotonga has it that a great ship arrived offshore about the time of the mutiny. A Cook Islander visited the ship and was given some oranges,

Dateline

- A.D. 1200 First Polynesians arrive.
- 1595 Mendaña discovers Pukapuka.
- 1606 De Quirós finds Rakahanga.
- 1773–77 Capt. James Cook discovers more islands, names them the Hervey Islands.
- 1789 Capt. William Bligh finds Aitutaki shortly before the mutiny on the *Bounty*.
- 1790 *Bounty* mutineers probably visit Rarotonga.
- 1814 American sandalwood trader discovers Rarotonga.
- 1821 Tahitian missionaries convert Aitutaki to Christianity.
- 1823 Rev. John Williams rediscovers Rarotonga, lands missionaries.
- 1824 Missionaries divide Rarotonga into five villages.
- 1863 William Marsters starts unique family with three wives on Palmerston Island.
- 1888 Residents on Manihiki trick French warship into turning away; Britain declares protectorate.
- 1901 Cook Islands included in boundaries of newly independent New Zealand.
- 1942 U.S. troops build airstrip on Aitutaki.
- 1965 Cook Islands become independent in association with New Zealand. Sir Albert Henry elected first prime minister.
- 1974 Queen Elizabeth II dedicates new Rarotonga International Airport. Islands opened to tourists.
- 1978 Sir Albert Henry indicted, stripped of knighthood.
- 1989 Geoffrey Henry, Sir Albert's cousin, becomes prime minister.
- 1990 Rarotonga gets television.

continued

the seeds of which became the foundation for the island's citrus industry.

When the first Europeans arrived, the local Polynesians were governed by feudal chiefs, who owned all the land within their jurisdictions and held life-and-death power over their subjects. Like other Polynesians, they believed in a hierarchy of gods and spirits, among them Tangaroa, whose well-endowed carved image is now a leading handcraft item.

MORE MISSIONARIES The man who claimed to have discovered Rarotonga was the same man who brought Christianity to the Cook Islands, the Rev. John Williams of the London Missionary Society. Williams had come from London to Tahiti in 1818 as a missionary, and he soon set up a base of operations on Raiatea in the Society Islands, from which he intended to spread Christianity throughout the South Pacific. He set his sights on the Hervey Islands after a canoe load of Polynesians from there was blown by a storm to Raiatea. They were receptive to Williams's teachings and asked that missionaries be sent to the Herveys.

In 1821 Williams went to Australia and on the way dropped two teachers at Aitutaki. One of them was a Tahitian named Papeiha. By the time Williams returned 2 years later, Papeiha had converted the entire island. Pleased with this success, Williams and a new missionary named Charles Pitman headed off in search of Rarotonga. It took a few weeks, during which Williams stopped at Mangaia, Mauke, Mitiaro, and Atiu, but he eventually found it in July 1823. Until the day he died, years later in a cannibal's oven in Vanuatu, Williams insisted that he had discovered Rarotonga—nevermind the inconvenient fact that the *Bounty* mutineers were there or that an American sandalwood trader almost certainly stopped on the island in 1814.

Williams, Pitman, and Papeiha were joined in 1824 by Aaron Buzacott, another missionary. Pitman soon left for the village of Ngatangiia on the east coast, Papeiha went to Arorangi in the west, and Buzacott took over in Avarua in the north. Williams spent most of the next 4 years using forced native labor to build a new ship, *The Messenger of Peace,* and eventually sailed it west in search of new islands and more converts.

Meanwhile, the missionaries quickly converted the Cook Islanders. They overcame the powerful feudal chiefs, known as *ariki,* whose titles but not their power have been handed down to their present-day heirs. On Rarotonga, the missionaries divided the island into five villages and split the land into rectangular parcels, one for each family. Choice parcels were set aside for the church buildings and rectories. Rarotongans moved down from the high ground near their gardens and became seaside dwellers for the first time.

As was the case throughout the South Pacific, the missionaries taught a rock-ribbed, puritanical version of Christianity. They blamed the misdeeds of the people for every misfortune, from the epidemics of Western diseases that came with the arrival of more Europeans to the hurricanes that destroyed crops. For the most part, however, the transition to Christianity was easy, since in their old

- **1992** Rarotonga hosts South Pacific Arts Festival, adding public buildings and infrastructure.
- **1994** Sheraton Hotel project goes bust.
- **1995** Cook Islands dollar becomes virtually worthless in New Zealand.
- **1996** International lenders force reduction in number and pay of civil servants; economy nose dives.
- **1999** Despite winning a slim majority, Prime Minister Geoffrey Henry steps aside when party members join opposition.
- **2000** Under probusiness government, tourism reaches new record; economy booms.

Fun Fact On Her Merry Way

When the 19th-century missionaries would shear a woman's locks for mis-
behaving, she would appear in public wearing a crown of flowers and
continue on her merry way.

---

religion the Rarotongans, like most Polynesians, believed in a single, all-power-
ful Tangaroa, who ruled over lesser gods.

Out of the seeds planted by Williams and the London Missionary Society
grew the present-day Cook Islands Christian Church, to which about 60% of all
Cook Islanders belong. The churches, many of them built by the missionaries in
the 19th century, are the center of life in every village, and the Takamoa College
Bible school that the missionaries established in 1837 still exists in Avarua. The
Cook Islands Christian Church still owns the land under its buildings; the
churches of other denominations sit on leased property.

THE COMING OF THE KIWIS   It was almost inevitable that the Cook
Islands would be caught up in the wave of colonial expansion that swept across
the South Pacific in the late 1800s. The French, who had established Tahiti as a
protectorate, wanted to expand their influence west, and in 1888 a French warship was sent to Manihiki in the Northern Group of the Cooks. The locals
quickly sewed together a British Union Jack and ran it up a pole. The French
ship turned away. Shortly thereafter the British declared a protectorate over the
Cook Islands, and the Union Jack went up officially.

The islands were small and unproductive, and in 1901 Britain gladly acceded
to a request from New Zealand's prime minister, Richard Seddon, to include the
Cook Islands within the boundaries of his newly independent country. In addition to engineering the transfer, Seddon is best remembered in the Cook Islands
for his vehement hatred of the Chinese. He instituted the policy that has effec-
tively barred the Chinese—and most other Asians, for that matter—from the
Cooks to this day.

Otherwise, New Zealand, itself a former colony, was never interested in
becoming a colonial power, and the Kiwis never did much to exploit—or
develop—the Cook Islands or Samoa (over which they exercised a League of
Nations trusteeship from the end of World War I until 1962). For all practical
purposes, the Cook Islands remained a South Seas backwater for the 72 years of
New Zealand rule, with a brief interlude during World War II when U.S. troops
built and staffed an airstrip on Aitutaki.

SIR ALBERT GETS THE BOOT   The situation began to change after 1965,
when the Cook Islands became self-governing in association with New Zealand.
The first prime minister of the newly independent government was Sir Albert
Henry, one of the South Pacific's most colorful modern characters. He ruled for
a controversial 13 years, during which the Cook Islands were put back on the
map. In 1974, using aid from New Zealand, which wanted to provide an independent source of revenue for its former colony, the government enlarged Rarotonga's airport. Queen Elizabeth II was on hand for the new strip's grand
opening. Three years later The Rarotongan Beach Resort opened, and the Cook
Islands became an international destination.

All in the Family

The missionaries weren't the only English folk to have a lasting impact on the Cook Islands.

In 1863 a farmhand from Gloucester named William Marsters accepted the job as caretaker of tiny, uninhabited Palmerston Island, an atoll sitting all by itself northwest of Rarotonga. He took his Cook Islander wife and her sister with him. They were joined by a Portuguese sailor and his wife, who was a first cousin of Mrs. Marsters.

The Portuguese sailor skipped the island within a year, leaving his wife behind. Marsters then declared himself a minister of the Anglican church and married himself to both his wife's sister and her first cousin.

Marsters proceeded to start three families, one with each of his three wives. Within 25 years he had 17 children and 54 grandchildren. He divided the island into three parts, one for each clan, which he designated the "head," "tail," and "middle" families. He prohibited marriages within a clan (in a twist of logic, he apparently thought sleeping with your half-brother or half-sister wasn't incest).

Obviously there was a lot of marrying outside the clans, for today there are uncounted thousands of Marsters in the Cook Islands and New Zealand. All trace their roots to Palmerston Island, although only 50 or so live there.

William Marsters died in 1899 at the age of 78. He is buried on Palmerston near his finely crafted homestead.

Sir Albert ruled until the national elections in 1978. Even though his party won a majority, he and it were indicted for bribery. Allegedly, government funds had been used to pay for charter flights that ferried his party's voters home from New Zealand on election day. The chief justice of the high court agreed, and Sir Albert and his party were booted out of power. Queen Elizabeth then stripped him of his knighthood. He remained highly popular with his supporters, however, and many Cook Islanders still refer to him as "Sir Albert." When he died in 1981, his body was taken around Rarotonga on the back of a pickup truck; the road was lined with mourners.

MORE MONEY, NO MONEY Sir Albert was succeeded by Dr. Tom Davis, a Cook Islander who had worked in the United States for NASA until returning home. To avoid a repetition of the scandal that caught Sir Albert, he added a seat in Parliament for voters living overseas. The constitution was also amended to include a bill of rights. Davis ruled until 1987, when his own party deposed him in favor of Dr. Pupuke Robati.

The premiership returned to Henry hands in 1989, with the victory of Sir Geoffrey Henry, Sir Albert's cousin. Sir Geoffrey's tenure was marked by scandal, first when a long-planned and almost-completed Sheraton Hotel project was caught up in a Mafia scandal in Italy. Although there has been talk about reviving the project, the hotel's unfinished buildings stand hauntingly like ancient ruins-in-the-making. Sir Geoffrey also allowed too much Cook Islands currency to be printed, which left it valueless outside the country, and he caught severe criticism for signing letters guaranteeing billions of dollars in loans that the Cook Islands didn't make and can never repay. His government also doubled the government workforce, from some 2,000 employees to more than 3,600—nearly 60% of the total employment here.

International lending organizations cracked the whip in 1996, forcing the debt-strapped government to cuts expenses by laying off more than half of the bloated civil service and seriously cutting the salaries of those who remained on the government payroll. Many axed civil servants and other islanders left the country for New Zealand and Australia. Although the man everyone calls simply "Geoff" narrowly won an election in 1999, he stepped aside when members of his party defected to the opposition.

The new government under Dr. Terepai Maoate adopted probusiness policies, including loosing restrictions on overseas ownership of businesses. The economy boomed throughout 2000, with tourism reaching record arrival numbers. Although black pearls became the country's top export, many newly wealthy Cook Islanders began importing luxury Western goods, which resulted in a record trade deficit by 2001. Tourism was also severely affected by the terrorist attacks of September 11, 2001, and at press time, it was unclear whether it would recover to its 2000 levels.

3 The Islanders

About half of the 18,000 or so people who live in the Cook Islands reside on Rarotonga, and of these, about half live on the north coast in Avarua, the only town in the country. Some 80% to 85% of the entire population is of pure Polynesian descent. In culture, language, and physical appearance, this great majority is closely akin to both the Tahitians and the Maoris of New Zealand. Only on Pukapuka and Nassau atolls to the far northwest, where the residents are more like the Samoans, is the cultural heritage significantly different.

Modern Cook Islanders have maintained much of the old Polynesian way of life, including the warmth, friendliness, and generosity that characterize Polynesians everywhere. Like their ancestors, they put great emphasis on family life. Within the extended family it's share and share alike, and no one ever goes without a meal or a roof over his or her head. In fact, they may be generous to a fault: Many of the small grocery stores they run reputedly stay on the verge of bankruptcy.

Although not a matriarchy, Cook Islands culture places great responsibility on the wife and mother. The early missionaries divided all land into rectangular plots (reserving choice parcels for themselves and their church buildings, of course), and women are in charge of the section upon which their families live. They decide which crops and fruit trees to plant, they collect the money for household expenses, and, acting collectively and within the churches, they decide how the village will be run. The land cannot be sold, only leased, and when the mother dies, it passes jointly to her children. Many women prefer to build simple homes so as not to set off squabbles among their offspring when they pass away, so most houses provide basic shelter and are not constructed with an eye to increasing value. In fact, when a woman dies, the house is occasionally left vacant by succeeding generations.

The burial vaults you see in many front yards are the final resting places of the mothers who built the houses. Their coffins are sealed in concrete vaults both for sanitary reasons and because to shovel dirt on a woman's dead body is to treat her like an animal. (Likewise, striking a live woman is the quickest way for a Cook Islands man to wind up in prison.) The survivors care only for the graves of persons they knew in life, which explains the many overgrown vaults. Eventually, when no one remembers their occupants, the tops of the old vaults are removed and the ground is plowed for a new crop.

Cook Islanders have also live by the old Polynesian tradition known as "island time." The clock moves more slowly here, as it does in other South Pacific Islands. Everything will get done in due course, not necessarily now. So service is often slow by Western standards, but why hurry? You're on vacation.

In addition to those who are pure Polynesian, a significant minority in the Cook Islands are of mixed European-Polynesian descent. There are also a number of New Zealanders, Australians, Americans, and Europeans, most of whom live on Rarotonga and move to the beat of "island time." There are very few Chinese or other Asians in the Cook Islands—hence the scarcity of Asian cuisine here.

4 Language

Nearly everyone in the Cook Islands speaks English, which is an official language. All signs and notices are written in it. The other official language—and the everyday lingua for most people—is Cook Islands Maori, a Polynesian language similar to Tahitian and New Zealand Maori. A little knowledge of it is helpful, particularly because nearly all place names are Maori.

Cook Islands Maori has eight consonants and five vowels. The vowels are pronounced in the Roman fashion: *ah, ay, ee, oh, oo* instead of *a, e, i, o, u* as in English. The consonants used are *k, m, n, p, r, t,* and *v.* These are pronounced much as they are in English. There is also *ng,* which is pronounced as the *ng* in "ring." The language is written phonetically; that is, every letter is pronounced. If there are three vowels in a row, each is sounded. The name of Mangaia Island, for example, is pronounced "Mahn-gah-*ee*-ah."

Generally, Cook Islanders speak English to Americans and Europeans, but here are some helpful expressions with pronunciations:

English	Maori	Pronunciation
hello	**kia orana**	*kee*-ah oh-*rah*-nah
goodbye	**aere ra**	ah-*ay*-ray rah
thank you	**meitaki**	may-ee-*tah*-kee
how are you?	**peea koe**	*pay*-ay-ah *ko*-ay
yes	**ae**	*ah*-ay
no	**kare**	*kah*-ray
good luck	**kia manuia**	*kee*-ah mah-*nu*-ee-ah
European person	**Papa'a**	pah-*pah*-ah
wraparound sarong	**pareu**	*pah*-ree-oo
keep out	**tapu**	*tah*-poo
small island	**motu**	*moh*-too

5 Visitor Information & Entry Requirements

VISITOR INFORMATION

The helpful staff at the **Cook Islands Tourism Corporation** provide information upon request. The address is P.O. Box 14, Rarotonga, Cook Islands

(© **29-435;** fax 21-435; www.cook-islands.com). The main office and visitors center is just west of the traffic circle, in the heart of Avarua. Other offices are:

- **North America:** 280 Nelson St., Suite 202, Vancouver, BC V6B 2E2, Canada (© **604/301-1190;** fax 604/687-3454; cookislands@earthlink.net)
- **New Zealand:** 1/127 Symonds St. (P.O. Box 37391), Parnell, Auckland (© **09/366-1199;** fax 09/309-1876)
- **Australia:** P.O. Box H95, Hurlstone Park, NSW 2193 (© **02/9955-0446;** fax 02/9955-0447; mereana-cookisland@bingpond.com.au)
- **United Kingdom:** 48 Glentham Rd., Barnes, London SW13 9JJ (© **020/ 8741-6082;** fax 020/8741-6107; info@interfaceinternational.co.uk)
- **Germany:** Petersburgstrasse 94, 10247 Berlin (© **30/4225-6027;** fax 30/4225-6286; cooksrep@5-online.de)

When you get to Rarotonga, visit the Cook Islands Tourism Corporation office and pick up brochures and other current information. The office should have copies of *What's On in the Cook Islands,* the *Cook Islands Sun,* and *Jasons Passport Cook Islands,* three free tourist publications that are full of facts, advertisements, and excellent maps of the islands. The daily newspaper, the *Cook Islands News,* provides radio and TV schedules, weather forecasts, shipping information, and advertisements for island nights and other entertainment.

If you're heading to the outer islands, check the bookstores for Elliott Smith's guidebook, *Cook Islands Companion.* It's out of date but still has some useful information.

ENTRY REQUIREMENTS

Visas are not required for visitors, who can stay for 31 days if they have valid passports, onward or return air tickets (they will be examined at the immigration desk upon arrival), and sufficient funds. Extensions are granted on a month-to-month basis for up to 5 months beyond the initial 31-day visa upon application to the Immigration Department near the airport in Avarua. Visitors intending to stay more than 6 months must apply from their home country to the **Principal Immigration Officer,** Ministry of Labour and Commerce, P.O. Box 61, Rarotonga, Cook Islands (© **29-363**).

Customs allowances are 2 liters of spirits or wine, 200 cigarettes or 50 cigars, and NZ$250 ($113) in other goods. Arriving passengers can purchase items from the duty-free shop and change money before clearing Immigration. Firearms, ammunition, and indecent materials are prohibited. So are live animals, including pets (they will be placed in quarantine until you leave the country). Personal effects are not subject to duty. All food and other agricultural products must be declared and will be inspected.

(*Fun Fact* **Tangaroa & Her Highness**

No longer in use, the Cook Islands's colorful local notes and unusual coins, such as the triangular $2 piece and the famous Tangaroa dollar, are now collectors' items. One side of the dollar bore the likeness of the Polynesian god of fertility, Tangaroa—including his well-defined private part. On the other side was the image of Queen Elizabeth II, who was reportedly not at all pleased about sharing the coin with Tangaroa in all his glory.

---

6 Money

The New Zealand dollar is the medium of exchange in the Cook Islands. At the time of this writing, one New Zealand dollar is worth about US45¢, give or take a few cents. The exchange rate is carried in the business sections of most daily newspapers. You can also find the present rate on currency conversion websites such as **www.xe.net**.

HOW TO GET LOCAL CURRENCY   **Westpac Bank** has its main office west of the traffic circle on the main road in Avarua. It's open Monday to Friday from 9am to 3pm, Saturday from 9 to noon. Westpac does not charge a fee to cash traveler's checks.

ANZ Bank is next to the visitors' center, west of the traffic circle in Avarua. It's open Monday to Thursday from 9am to 3pm, Friday from 9am to 4pm. ANZ Bank charges NZ$2 (US90¢) per traveler's check transaction, regardless of the amount. ANZ has an ATM.

CREDIT CARDS   American Express, MasterCard, and Visa are widely accepted by hotels and restaurants on Rarotonga and Aitutaki. Only the major hotels and car-rental firms accept Diner's Club cards. Discover cards are not accepted anywhere in the islands. If you're going to Aitutaki or another outer island, your can use credit cards at the larger hotels and some restaurants, but not elsewhere. Therefore, you should carry cash or small-denomination traveler's checks, which you can cash at the post offices.

7 When to Go

THE CLIMATE

The islands of the Southern Group, which are about as far south of the equator as the Hawaiian Islands are north of it, have a very pleasant tropical climate. Even during the summer months of January and February, the high temperatures on Rarotonga average a comfortable 29°C (84°F), and the southeast trade winds usually moderate even the hottest day. The average high drops to 25°C (77°F) during the winter, from June to August, and the ends of Antarctic cold fronts can bring a few downright chilly nights during those months. It's a good idea to bring a light sweater or jacket for evening wear any time of the year.

December through April is both the cyclone (hurricane) and rainy season. There always is a chance that a cyclone will wander along during these months, but most of the rain comes in short, heavy cloudbursts that are followed by sunshine. Rain clouds usually hang around Rarotonga's mountain peaks, even during the dry season, from June to August.

In short, there is no bad time weatherwise to visit the Cook Islands, although the "shoulder" months of April, May, September, and October usually provide the best combination of sunshine and warmth.

HOLIDAYS & SEASONS

Legal holidays are New Year's Day, Anzac (Memorial) Day (Apr 25), Good Friday, Easter Monday, the Queen's Birthday (first Mon in June), Gospel Day (July 26 on Rarotonga only), Constitution Day (Aug 4), Christmas Day, and Boxing Day (Dec 26).

The busiest season is from late June through August, when New Zealanders and Australians escape their own winters. Make hotel reservations early for these months. Many Cook Islanders live in New Zealand and come home for Christmas;

The New Zealand Dollar & the U.S. Dollar

At this writing, **NZ$1** = approximately **US45¢** (or **US$1 = NZ$2.22**), the rate of exchange used to calculate the U.S. dollar prices given in this chapter. This rate may change by the time you visit, so use the following table only as a guide:

NZ$	US$	NZ$	US$
.25	.11	15	6.75
.50	.23	20	9.00
.75	.34	25	11.25
1	.45	30	13.50
2	.90	35	15.75
3	1.35	40	18.00
4	1.80	45	20.25
5	2.25	50	22.50
6	2.70	75	33.75
7	3.15	100	45.00
8	3.60	125	56.25
9	4.05	150	67.50
10	4.50	200	90.00

you can easily get a room, but airline seats are hard to come by during that holiday season.

THE COOK ISLANDS CALENDAR OF EVENTS

April

Anzac Day. Cook Islanders killed in the two World Wars are honored with parades and church services. April 25.

Dancer of the Year Contest ★★. This is one of the South Pacific's great traditional dance competitions; villages from all over the country send their young people to Rarotonga to compete for the coveted Dancers of the Year award. Late April and early May.

August

Constitution Week/Cultural Festival Week. ★★★ Honoring the attainment of self-government on August 4, 1965, this biggest Cook Islands celebration is highlighted by a weeklong Polynesian dance contest. The dancing is at its purest and most energetic as each village's team vies for the title of best in the country. There are also parades and sporting events. Begins August 4.

October

Round Rarotonga Road Run. Marathoners race completely around Rarotonga—all 32km (20 miles) of it. First week in October.

Tivaevae Exhibition. Traditional and modern quilts are showcased in month-long show. Mid-October to mid-November.

Gospel Day. Honors the arrival of the first missionaries and features outdoor religious plays known as *nuku*. Last Sunday in October.

November

All Souls Day. Colorful decorations and evening programs are held to remember deceased loved ones. November 1.

Tiare Week Festival. Shops and offices are ablaze with fresh floral arrangements, leading up to beauty contest, parade of flower-covered floats. Fourth week in November.

8 Getting to Rarotonga & Getting Around

GETTING TO RAROTONGA

Although the local government has been trying to get another carrier to serve the islands, at press time **Air New Zealand** had a monopoly on flights to and from the Cook Islands. It flies from Los Angeles to Rarotonga, via either Tahiti or Honolulu. It also has weekly service to Rarotonga from Tahiti and Fiji on its Coral Route, and it has several flights a week between Auckland and Rarotonga. For more information, see "Getting There & Getting Around" in chapter 2.

ARRIVING The small terminal at **Rarotonga International Airport,** the country's only gateway, is 2km (1⅛ miles) west of Avarua. Westpac Bank's terminal office is open 1 hour before and after all international flights; it has windows both inside and outside the departure lounge. Small shops in the departure lounge sell handcrafts, liquor, cigarettes, and stamps. Arriving passengers can purchase duty-free items before clearing Immigration. Air New Zealand has its Rarotonga offices in the terminal.

Transportation from the airport to all the hotels and hostels is by **Raro Tours** bus (© **25-325**), which costs NZ$10 ($4.50) per person. In general, taxi fares are NZ$3 ($1.35) per kilometer. See "By Taxi," below.

DEPARTING Raro Tours (© **25-325**) begins picking up departing passengers about 2 hours before each international flight. Your hotel or guest house can reserve a seat for you and tell you when it will arrive at your accommodation. A **departure tax** of NZ$25 ($11.25) for adults and NZ$12.50 ($5.60) for children between the ages of 2 and 12 is payable in New Zealand currency. You can pay this in advance at Westpac Bank in Avarua, or prior to clearing immigration at Westpac's airport booth. No tax is imposed for domestic departures.

GETTING AROUND RAROTONGA

BY PLANE **Air Rarotonga** (© **22-888**; www.airraro.com) has three flights per day (except Sun) to Aitutaki and one per day to Atiu, Mauke, Mangaia, and Mitiaro. Regular round-trip fares are about NZ$368 ($166) to Aitutaki, the most visited island, slightly less to the others in the Southern Group. You can save with Air Rarotonga's off-peak fares, which can be as little as NZ$246 ($111) round-trip to Aitutaki (you must buy your ticket in Rarotonga and fly on the early morning or late afternoon flights).

Moments **Swinging Hips**

I never visit the Cook Islands without watching the hips swing at a traditional dance show. Take my word for it: Had the crew of HMS *Bounty* seen the dancing on Rarotonga instead of Tahiti, even Captain Bligh might have stayed behind. The best time to see the best dancing is during the Dancer of the Year contest and during Constitution Week.

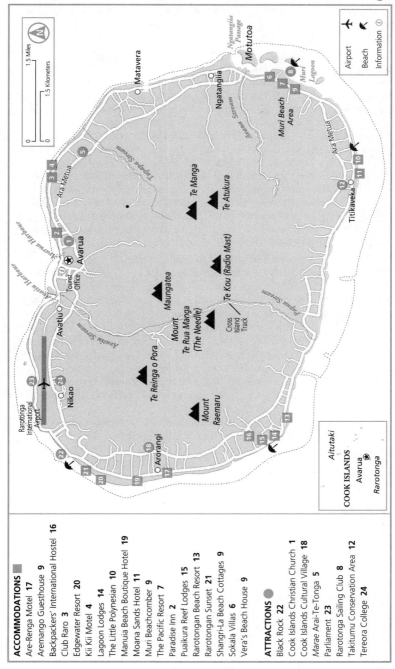

Rarotonga

ACCOMMODATIONS
Are-Renga Motel **17**
Aremango Guesthouse **9**
Backpackers' International Hostel **16**
Club Raro **3**
Edgewater Resort **20**
Kii Kii Motel **4**
Lagoon Lodges **14**
The Little Polynesian **10**
Manuia Beach Boutique Hotel **19**
Moana Sands Hotel **11**
Muri Beachcomber **9**
The Pacific Resort **7**
Paradise Inn **2**
Puaikura Reef Lodges **15**
Rarotongan Beach Resort **13**
Rarotongan Sunset **21**
Shangri-La Beach Cottages **9**
Sokala Villas **6**
Vera's Beach House **9**

ATTRACTIONS
Black Rock **22**
Cook Islands Christian Church **1**
Cook Islands Cultural Village **18**
Marae Arai-Te-Tonga **5**
Parliament **23**
Rarotonga Sailing Club **8**
Takitumu Conservation Area **12**
Tereora College **24**

Airport
Beach
Information

COOK ISLANDS
Avarua
Rarotonga
Aitutaki

Air Rarotonga will also book hotels and most activities on the other islands free of charge. You can save as much as NZ$100 ($45) by buying a package that includes airfare and accommodations.

Don't forget to reconfirm your return flight.

BY BUS When people say "catch the bus" on Rarotonga, they mean the **Cook's Island Bus** (℃ 25-512), which is actually two buses that leave the Cook's Corner shopping center in Avarua once an hour going clockwise and counterclockwise around the island, respectively. These buses have "Cook's Passenger Transport" painted on their sides and run Monday to Friday from 7am to 4pm and Saturday from 8am to 1pm, with less frequent, one-bus evening service Monday to Saturday from 6 to 10pm (to 1:30am on Fri night). The two buses each take 50 minutes to circle the island, arriving back in Avarua in time to start another trip. Get a schedule at the Cook's Corner bus stop or from the Cook Islands Tourism Corporation, or ask your hotel receptionist when a bus will pass. Elsewhere, just wave to get on board. Regardless of the length of the ride, daytime fares are NZ$2.50 ($1.15) one way, NZ$4 ($1.80) round-trip. You can buy one-day passes for NZ$6 ($2.70) or a 10-ride book of tickets for NZ$17 ($7.65). The buses cost NZ$4 ($1.80) at night.

BY RENTAL CAR & SCOOTER I usually rent a car or Jeep from Arthur Pickering and his friendly crew at **Budget Rent-A-Car** (℃ **800/527-0700** or 20-895; https://rent.drivebudget.com), whose vehicles are consistently clean and in excellent condition. The main Budget office is in Avarua, a block off the main road (behind Ronnie's Bar & Restaurant), or you can rent at a booth west of the traffic circle and at desks at the Edgewater Resort Hotel and Rarotongan Resort Hotel. Cars start at NZ$45 ($20.25) per day with unlimited kilometers. You will be responsible for the first NZ$1,000 ($450) of any damage. Budget provides free delivery and drop-off at the hotels or airport.

The other firms here are **Avis** (℃ **800/331-1212** or 21-901; www.avis.com); **Tipani Rentals** (℃ **22-327** or 22-328); **Rarotonga Rentals** (℃ **22-326**), and **Island Car & Bike Hire** (℃ **27-632**).

Cook Islanders are as likely to travel by motorbike or scooter as they are by automobile. **Polynesian Bike Hire Ltd.** (℃ **20-895**) and **Tipani Rentals** (℃ **22-327**) both rent motorbikes and scooters on a daily or weekly basis. Rates start at about NZ$25 ($11.25) per day. Polynesian Bike Hire Ltd. and Budget Rent-A-Car share offices (see above).

Visitors are required to have a valid Cook Islands driver's license before operating any motorized vehicle. To get one, go to Police Headquarters (on the main road just west of the Avarua traffic circle), present your valid overseas license, and pay NZ$10 ($4.50). It's valid for the same class of vehicles covered by your home-country license. If you want to rent a motorbike or scooter and you aren't licensed to drive them at home, you have to take a driving test and pay an additional NZ$5 ($2.25). All drivers must be at least 21 years old. (The laminated license with your photo makes a nice souvenir.) The license desk is open Monday to Friday from 8am to 3pm, Saturday and Sunday from 8am to noon.

Driving is on the left side of the road. The speed limit is 50kmph (30 mph) in the countryside and 25kmph (15 mph) in Avarua and the villages. Gasoline (petrol) is available from service stations in Avarua and at some village shops. During my recent visit, gasoline cost about NZ$1 (US45¢) a liter, the equivalent of about NZ$2.60 ($1.15) for an American-size gallon. The road around the island is paved but somewhat rough, and drivers must be on the alert at all times for dogs, chickens, potholes, and pigs.

BY BICYCLE   There are no hills on the round-island road, so touring by bicycle (or "push bikes," as they're called here) is a pleasure. Several hotels have bicycles available for their guests to use. **Polynesian Bike Hire Ltd.** (✆ **20-895**), **Tipani Rentals** (✆ **22-327**), and **Terekira Bike Rentals** (✆ **20-331**) rent them for NZ$8 ($3.60) per day. The latter is at Muri Beach, as is **The Internet Cafe** (✆ **27-242**), which rents bikes for NZ$7 ($3.15) per day.

BY TAXI   A number of cars and minibuses scurry around Rarotonga with TAXI signs on top. Service is available daily from 7am to midnight and whenever international flights arrive. As a rule of thumb, taxi fares should be about NZ$3 ($1.35) per kilometer, but the drivers are free to set their rates at will. Negotiate a fare before you get in. To call a taxi, phone **A's Taxi** (✆ **27-021**), **Ngatangiia Taxi** (✆ **22-238**), **BK Taxi** (✆ **20-019**), or **Muri Beach Taxi** (✆ **21-625**).

BY SHIP   *Adventures in Paradise,* the 1950s television series, may have glorified the South Pacific "copra schooners" that plied the South Seas, trading corned beef and printed cotton for copra, but today's ships operating in the Cook Islands keep erratic schedules. To put it bluntly, you can't count on getting anywhere by ship these days. If you want to see whether any are running, and if you don't really care when you get from place to place, check in with the Harbour Office at the wharf in Avatiu. The daily *Cook Islands News* prints the local shipping schedules each morning.

FAST FACTS: Rarotonga

American Express There is no American Express representative in the Cook Islands.

Babysitters Contact your hotel reception desk.

Baggage Storage **Raro Tours** (✆ **25-325**) will store your baggage at the airport (they're next to Air New Zealand's office) for NZ$2 (90¢) per piece per day. Most hotels and motels will keep your bags for free.

Bookstores **Bounty Bookshop** (✆ **22-660**), in the high-rise C.I.D.B. Building in Avarua, and the **Cook Islands Trading Corporation (C.I.T.C.)** (✆ **22-000**), on the waterfront, both sell paperback novels, maps of Rarotonga and Aitutaki, and books about the Cook Islands and the South Pacific in general. Bounty Bookshop carries the international editions of *Time* and *Newsweek,* the latter incorporated into the *Bulletin,* an Australian newsmagazine.

Business Hours Most shops on Rarotonga are open Monday to Friday from 8am to 4pm and Saturday from 8 to noon. Some small grocery stores in the villages are open in the evenings and for limited hours on Sunday.

Camera/Film A reasonable selection of color-print film is available at many shops in Avarua. One-hour processing of color-print film is available at **Cocophoto,** in the C.I.T.C. shopping center in Avarua (✆ **22-000**). Color slides are sent to New Zealand for processing.

Clothing Dress in the Cook Islands is informal. Shorts of respectable length (that is, not of the short-short variety) can be worn during the day by both men and women, but beach attire should stay at the beach. Nude or topless sunbathing is not permitted anywhere (although some European tourists do it anyway). The colorful wraparound pareu is popular with local women. Evenings from May to September can be cool, so trousers, skirts, light jackets, sweaters, or wraps are in order after dark. The only neckties to be seen are at church on Sunday.

Currency Exchange See "Visitor Information & Entry Requirements" and "Money," above.

Drug Laws Dangerous drugs and narcotics are illegal; possession can land you in a very unpleasant jail for a very long time.

Drugstores **C.I.T.C. Pharmacy** (© **29-292**), in the C.I.T.C. shopping center west of the traffic circle, dispenses prescription medications and carries toiletries. The clinics on the outer islands have a limited supply of prescription medications.

Electricity Electricity is 230 volts, 50 cycles, so converters are necessary in order to operate U.S. appliances. The plugs, like those of New Zealand and Australia, have two-angled prongs, so an adapter will also be needed. If your appliances or the table lamps in your room don't work, check to see whether the switch on the wall outlet is turned on.

E-mail In Avarua, **Telecom Cook Islands** (© **26-171**; www.telecom.co.ck) has Internet access in its main office (see "Telephone & Fax," below) and in its **TelePost** outlet in the C.I.T.C. shopping center (© **29-940**). The main office is open 24 hours a day. TelePost is open Monday to Friday from 8am to 4pm, Saturday from 8:30am to noon. Access at both costs NZ$1.75 (80¢) for each 5 minutes. At Muri Beach, **The Internet Cafe** (© **27-242**) charges NZ30¢ (15¢) a minute. It's open Monday to Saturday from 10am to 6pm, Sunday from noon to 6pm.

If you take your laptop, you can sign up for a "Temporary Oyster" access account at Telecom's main office. There's a one-time NZ$25 ($11.25) connection fee, plus NZ$7 ($3.15) per hour spent online, which can be billed to your American Express, Diners Club, MasterCard, or Visa credit card.

Embassies/Consulates The New Zealand government has a representative, whose office is at the traffic circle in Avarua, but no other foreign government maintains an embassy or consulate here. In case of a problem, seek advice from the travel facilitation and consular officer in the **Ministry of Foreign Affairs** (© **20-507**). The U.S. embassy in Wellington, New Zealand, has jurisdiction.

Emergencies/Police The emergency number for the **police** is © **999**; for an **ambulance** or the **hospital,** © **998**; for fire, © **996**. The nonemergency **police** number is © **22-499**.

Eyeglasses **Cook Islands Optics** (© **26-605**), in the Mana Court shopping center, west of the traffic circle, has single-prescription replacement lenses in stock (bifocal lenses must be ordered from New Zealand, which can take up to 2 weeks). The company can repair broken or damaged frames, and it sells contact lens solutions.

Firearms Don't even think about it—they're illegal.

Gambling There are no gambling casinos in the Cook Islands, but you can bet on the Australian and New Zealand lotteries at the C.I.T.C. shopping center.

Hairdressers/Barbers **Paradise Hair & Beauty,** in Panama between Avarua and the airport (② 22-774), is a full-service beauty salon.

Healthcare **Dr. Wolfgang Losacker** has a private practice in the Banana Court shops at the traffic circle in Avarua (② 23-306). His office hours are Monday to Friday from 10am to 1pm. Ask at your hotel desk for the name of a private **dentist** or go to the **Tupapa Outpatient Clinic** on the east end of Avarua, where hours are Monday to Friday from 8am to 4pm. The **hospital,** behind the golf course (② 22-664, or 998 in case of emergency), has a 24-hour emergency room.

Hitchhiking It's not illegal, but hitchhiking is frowned upon by the government.

Insects There are no poisonous insects in the Cook Islands. Mosquitoes are plentiful, especially during the summer months and in the inland areas, so bring a good repellent. Mosquito coils can be bought at most village shops.

Laundry/Dry Cleaning **Snowbird Laundry & Dry Cleaners** has 1-day laundry and dry cleaning service at its main plant in Arorangi (② 20-952) and a small laundry opposite Avatiu Harbour (② 21-952). It will wash, dry, and fold a load for NZ$9.50 ($4.30), and will pick up and deliver if you or your hotel staff call in advance.

Libraries The **Cook Islands Library and Museum,** in Avarua near the Cook Islands Christian Church (② 26-468), is open Monday to Friday from 9am to 1pm, Saturday 9:30am to 1pm, with additional hours on Tuesday from 4 to 8pm. The library has a fine collection of works on the South Pacific, including many hard-to-find books. If you want to check them out, you must pay NZ$25 ($11.25) to join plus a NZ$15 ($6.75) refundable deposit.

Liquor Laws The legal drinking age is 18. Bottled liquor, beer, and wine is available from several stores. Bars and nightclubs close promptly at midnight Saturday. The hotel bars can sell alcoholic beverages to their guests all day Sunday, and the restaurants can resume service on Sunday at 6pm.

Maps The best readily available maps of the islands are in the tourist publications *Jasons Passport Cook Islands, What's On in the Cook Islands,* and the *Cook Islands Sun.* Get copies at Cook Islands Tourism Corporation office (see "Visitor Information," above) or at most hotels.

Newspapers/Magazines The daily *Cook Islands News* (www.cinews.co.ck) contains local, regional, and world news; radio and TV schedules; shipping schedules; a weather map for the South Pacific; and notices of local events, including advertisements for "island nights" at the hotels. It even has two comic strips. Copies are available at the Bounty Bookshop and the large C.I.T.C. shopping center in the center of Avarua.

Post Office **Cook Islands Post** is located at the traffic circle in Avarua. Hours are Monday to Friday 8am to 4pm, Saturday 8am to noon. There's a branch office opposite Titikaveka College on Rarotonga's south coast, which is open Monday to Friday from 8am to noon and 1 to 3:30pm. Each of the other islands has a post office. There is no mail delivery, so every address includes a post office box.

Radio/TV Rarotonga has one AM radio station and one FM radio station. Programming is in both English and Maori. One TV channel broadcasts news, sports, and entertainment in English daily from about 6 to 11pm, later if there's a rugby game on.

Safety The streets here are safe. Property thefts can occur, so don't leave valuables in your hotel room or your belongings untended elsewhere.

Taxes The government imposes a **value-added tax (VAT),** which is included in the price of most goods and services. You should ask if the VAT is included in the rates quoted by the hotels and hostels, or whether it will be added to your bill when you leave. Unlike in Europe, the VAT here is not refunded at the end of your visit. The **departure tax** on international flights is NZ$25 ($11.25), which you can pay at the airport or in advance at Westpac Bank in Avarua.

Telephone/Fax Direct-dialed calls can be made into the Cook Islands from most parts of the world. The country code is **682.** There are no local area codes.

International telephone calls and fax messages can be made or sent from most hotels or from **Telecom Cook Islands,** on the street between the C.I.T.C. shopping center and the Cook's Corner shopping center in Avarua (© **26-171;** www.telecom.co.ck). The Telecom office is open 24 hours daily.

The easiest way to make both local and international calls is from a pay phone using a prepaid "Kia Orana" card, which is sold in NZ$5, NZ$10, NZ$20, and NZ$50 denominations at Telecom, any post office, and the C.I.T.C. shopping center in Avarua. For international calls, dial **00** followed by the country code (which is **1** for the U.S. and Canada) and the number you're trying to reach. A digital readout tells you how much money you have left during the call and warns you when to put in a fresh card. International calls cost NZ$2.98 ($1.35) per minute to North America, NZ$4 ($1.80) to the United Kingdom and Europe, and about half that to Australia and New Zealand.

You can have Telecom's staff place the calls at its headquarters, but there's an additional charge of NZ$8.50 ($3.85) for operator assistance. You can pay there by MasterCard or Visa credit cards if your charges total NZ$20 ($9) or more.

Some long-distance carriers have access numbers their customers can dial from within the Cook Islands to have international calls billed to their credit or prepaid cards, including **AT&T** (© **09111**) and **MCI** (© **09121**). You'll pay the regular local call charges on top of the international rates if you dial them from your hotel room.

Dial © **010** for local **directory assistance,** © **015** for an **international operator,** and © **020** for **calls to the outer islands.** Emergency numbers are listed under "Emergencies/Police," above.

Time Local time is 10 hours behind Greenwich mean time. That's 2 hours behind California during standard time, 3 hours behind California during daylight saving time. The Cook Islands are on the east side of the international date line, which puts them in the same day as the United States and a day behind New Zealand and Australia.

Tipping Tipping is considered contrary to the Polynesian way of life and is frowned upon.

Water Generally, the water on Rarotonga is safe to drink from the tap. It is filtered but not treated and can become slightly muddy after periods of heavy rain. Many hotels have their own filtration systems. If in doubt, boil it in the electric "jug" in your hotel room. The tap water on Aitutaki is not safe to drink.

Weights/Measures The Cook Islands use the metric system.

9 Exploring Rarotonga

The Cook Islands' capital can be seen on foot, since this picturesque little South Seas town winds for only a mile or so along the curving waterfront between its two harbors. Virtually every sight and most of the shops sit along or just off the main around-the-island road, which for this mile serves as Main Street.

A STROLL AROUND AVARUA

Let's start at the traffic circle in the heart of town at the old harbor, which is both the beginning and end of the round-island road. The rusty carcass on the reef offshore belonged to the **SS *Maitai***, a trading ship that went aground here in 1916. To the west, the low-slung building with a large veranda houses a restaurant, several shops, and **The Banana Court,** one of the South Pacific's most famous watering holes (see "Island Nights on Rarotonga" later in this chapter). The building actually began life as a hotel.

From the traffic circle, walk east to the modern **Beachcomber, Ltd.** This pearl and handcraft shop occupies a coral-block building erected in 1843 as a school for missionary children. The local legislative council met here from 1888 to 1901, but by 1968 it was condemned as unsafe. It was restored to its present grandeur in 1992 (see "Shopping on Rarotonga," below).

In a shady parklike setting across the road stands **Taputapuatea *Marae*** and the restored "palace" of Queen Makea Takau Ariki. Don't enter the grounds without permission, for they are *tabu* to us commoners. Queen Makea is long dead, but when she was around in the 19th century, the palace was reputedly a lively place.

Facing the palace grounds across the road running inland is the **Cook Islands Christian Church** ★★★. This whitewashed coral block structure was constructed in 1855. Just to the left of the main entrance is the grave of Sir Albert Henry, the late prime minister. A bust of Sir Albert sits atop the grave, complete with shell lei and flower crown. Robert Dean Frisbie, an American-born writer and colorful South Seas character, is buried in the inland corner of the graveyard, next to the road. (See "Recommended Reading" in chapter 2.)

To the right, near the end of the road, is the **Cook Islands Library and Museum** ★★ (© **26-468**). The museum is small but well worth a visit to see its excellent examples of Cook Islands handcrafts; a canoe from Pukapuka built in the old style, with planks lashed together; the island's first printing press (brought to Rarotonga by the London Missionary Society in the 1830s and used until the 1950s by the government printing office); and the bell and compass from the *Yankee,* a world-famous yacht that in 1964 wrecked on the reef behind the Beachcomber, where its forlorn skeleton rusted away for 30 years. The library and museum are open Monday to Friday from 9am to 1pm, Saturday 9:30am to 1pm, and on Tuesday from 4 to 8pm. Admission is NZ$2 (US90¢).

Farther up the inland road past the **Avarua School** stands **Takamoa Theological College,** opened in 1842 by the London Missionary Society. The original **Takamoa Mission House** still sits on the campus.

Walk a block east on Makea Tinerau Road in front of the library and museum to the **Sir Geoffrey Henry National Cultural Centre** (also known as *Te Puna Korero),* the country's showplace, built in time for the 1992 South Pacific Festival of the Arts. The large green building houses the Civic Auditorium, and the long yellow structures contain government offices as well as the **National Museum** and **National Library** (© 20-725). Exhibits at the National Museum feature contemporary and replicated examples of ancient crafts. The museum is open Monday to Friday from 9am to 4pm. Admission is by donation. The library is open when school is in session, Monday and Wednesday from noon to 8pm and Tuesday, Thursday, and Saturday from 9am to 4pm.

Opposite the national museum is the **Tupapa Sports Ground.** Like other South Pacific islanders formerly under New Zealand or Australian rule, the Cook Islanders take their rugby seriously. Although much of the action has shifted to the stadium at Tereora College behind the airport, Tupapa may still see a brawl or two on Saturday afternoons.

Walk back to the main road, turn left at the Paradise Inn, and head to downtown. You can take a break at one of the restaurants or snack bars along the way. From the traffic circle west is a lovely stroll, either by the storefronts or along the seafront promenade known as **Te Ara Maire Nui.** At the west end of town, stroll through **Punanga Nui Market,** where vendors sell clothing and souvenirs (see "Shopping on Rarotonga," below) and food stalls offer take-out food that you can munch at picnic tables under the shade of casuarinas whispering in the wind (see "Where to Dine on Rarotonga," below).

End your tour at **Avatiu Harbour,** which is Rarotonga's commercial port (the small anchorage at Avarua is strictly a small-boat refuge). **Rob's Paradise Bar** (© 29-879), under a large thatch cabana at the harbor, is the perfect place to recover with ice-cold refreshment.

THE CIRCLE ISLAND TOUR

Traveling completely around Rarotonga and seeing the sights should take about 4 hours, with the help of a motor; allow a full day if you go by bicycle.

The **Cook Islands Cultural Village** (see "Cultural Experiences," below), will take you around the island while explaining the cultural and historical aspects of Rarotonga. Book at any hotel activities desk. You can do the circle island tour independently by car or motorbike, but you'll miss the informative commentary.

Here's what you'll see, traveling clockwise from Avarua.

THE NORTH COAST

About 1km (½ mile) past the Kii Kii Motel, signs mark a small dirt road to the right. It leads to the **Marae Arai-Te-Tonga,** one of the most sacred spots on the island. Before the coming of Europeans, these stone structures formed a *koutu,* or royal court. The investiture of high chiefs took place here amid much pomp

---

Impressions

I have hunted long for this sanctuary. Now that I have found it, I have no intention, and certainly no desire, ever to leave it again.
—Robert Dean Frisbie, *The Book of Puka-Puka,* 1928

Finds **Take a Fruit Break**

Rarotonga's best snorkeling is in the Muri Lagoon on the southeast corner of the island. You can pull off the road, take a dip, and grab a fresh fruit juice or a smoothie at **Fruits of Rarotonga,** near The Little Polynesian (© **21-509**). This country store also sells jams, chutneys, relishes, and other fruit products, and it'll keep your bag while you're in the water. Open Monday to Friday 7:30am to 5pm, Saturday 9am to 5pm.

and circumstance; also, offerings to the gods and the "first fruits" of each season were brought here and presented to the local *ariki,* or chief. The basalt investiture pillar, the major remaining structure, stands slightly offset from a rectangular platform about 3.5m (12 ft.) long, 2m (7 ft.) wide, and 20cm (8 in.) high. Such temples, or *maraes,* are still considered sacred by some Cook Islanders, so don't walk on them.

The ancient Ara Metua road crosses by Arai-Te-Tonga and leads south a few yards to a small *marae* on the banks of **Tupapa Stream.** A trail follows the stream up to the peaks of Mounts Te Ikurangi, Te Manga, and Te Atukura, but these are difficult climbs; it's advisable to make them only with a local guide.

THE EAST COAST

Back on the main road, **Matavera** village begins about 2km (1¼ miles) beyond Tupapa Stream. Notable for the picturesque Cook Islands Christian Church and graveyard on the mountain side of the road, it's worth a stop for a photograph before continuing on to historic **Ngatangiia** village. Legend has it that a fleet of canoes left Ngatangiia sometime around A.D. 1350 and sailed off to colonize New Zealand, departing from a point across the road from where the Cook Islands Christian Church now stands in the center of the village. Offshore is **Ngatangiia Passage,** between the mainland and **Motutapu,** a low island, through which the canoes left on their voyage.

Ngatangiia also had its day in the sun in the early 1800s, when it was the headquarters of Charles Pitman, the missionary who came with the Rev. John Williams and later translated *The Pilgrim's Progress* into Cook Islands Maori. Unlike many of his fellow missionaries, Pitman carefully avoided becoming involved in local politics or business, and he objected strongly when Williams forced the Cook Islanders to build *The Messenger of Peace.* The **courthouse** across from the church was the first one built in the Cook Islands.

The shore at Ngatangiia, with three small islands sitting on the reef beyond the lagoon, is one of the most beautiful parts of Rarotonga. An old **stone fish trap** is visible underwater between the beach and the islands. Such traps were quite common throughout eastern Polynesia: Fish were caught inside as the tide ebbed and flowed through Ngatangiia Passage.

THE SOUTH COAST

South of Ngatangiia begins magnificent **Muri Beach** ★★★. The white sands here stretch for 14km (8 miles) around the southeast corner of Rarotonga. Sailboats glide across the crystal-clear lagoon, the island's best for boating. Muri Beach is the finest place to enjoy the beach and go for a swim in the lagoon and have resorts at your fingertips.

The Cook Islands Christian Church in the village of **Titikaveka** was built in 1841 of coral blocks hand-cut from the reef almost a mile away and carried to the building site. The lagoon at Titikaveka is the deepest on the island and the best for snorkeling.

Above the village, a part of the mountain is preserved in its natural state by the **Takitumu Conservation Area** ✦ (© **29-906;** kakerori@tca.co.ck). The area is the only home of the unique and endangered kakerori (*pomarea dimidiata*), a sparrow-size yellowish bird that is native to Rarotonga. The conservation program has raised the kakerori population from 29 in 1989 to more than 130 today. Rangers lead nature walks in the forest Tuesday to Friday from 9:30am to 1:30pm. They cost NZ$45 ($20.25) for adults, NZ$20 ($9) for children, including a light lunch.

From Titikaveka, the road runs along the south coast and passes the late Albert Henry's white beachside home. **Mount Te Rua Manga,** the rock spire also known as "The Needle," can be seen clearly from the main road between Liana's Restaurant and The Rarotongan Beach Resort. You also will pass what looks like a modern ruin; it's the site of the aborted and highly controversial Sheraton Hotel.

THE WEST COAST

The road turns at The Rarotongan Beach Resort and heads up the west coast to the low white walls of **Arorangi,** the coastal community founded as a peace-making "Gospel Village" by the missionary Aaron Buzacott when a dispute over land boundaries broke out in 1828. Arorangi replaced the old inland village, Puaikura, where the Tahitian missionary Papeiha went to teach Christianity after he had converted all of Aitutaki. Papeiha is buried in the yard of Arorangi's Cook Islands Christian Church, which was built in 1849. According to Polynesian legend, the canoes that left Ngatangiia in the 1300s stopped in Arorangi before heading off west to New Zealand. There is no reef passage near Arorangi, but the story enables the people on both sides of Rarotonga to claim credit for colonizing New Zealand.

The flat-topped mountain behind Arorangi is **Mount Raemaru.** Another legend says that mighty warriors from Aitutaki, which had no mountain, stole the top of Raemaru and took it home with them. There is a steep and somewhat dangerous trail to the top of Mount Raemaru.

The area north of Arorangi is well developed with hotels, restaurants, and shops. The shore just before the golf course is known as **Black Rock** because of the volcanic outcrop standing sentinel in the lagoon offshore. According to ancient Maori belief, the souls of the dead bid farewell to Rarotonga from this point before journeying to the fatherland, which the Cook Islanders called Avaiki.

There are two ways to proceed after passing the golf course. The main road continues around the west end of the **airport** runway (be careful; there are more road accidents on this sharp curve than anywhere else on Rarotonga). The New Zealand government built the original airstrip during World War II. It was enlarged in the early 1970s to handle jumbo jets, and Queen Elizabeth II officially opened the new strip, which was renamed Rarotonga International Airport, on July 29, 1974. The **Parliament** building is located on the shore about halfway along the length of the runway. Parliament meets from February to March and from July to September. Visitors can observe the proceedings from the gallery.

The other way to return to Avarua from Black Rock is to turn right on the first paved road past the golf course and then left at the dead-end intersection onto the Ara Metua, or "back road," as the section running from Black Rock to town is called. About halfway to town is **Tereora College,** established as a mission school in 1865. An international stadium was built on the college campus

---

Moments **Learning a Little Culture**

One of my fondest South Pacific memories was exploring Rarotonga with the entertaining and highly informative Exham Wichman. He told me much of what this chapter has to say about the Cook Islanders' lifestyle. Exham has retired from the tour business, replaced by the terrific Cook Islands Cultural Village's tour.

---

for the 1985 South Pacific Mini Games held on Rarotonga and is now the site of rock 'em, sock 'em rugby games on Saturday afternoons from June through August.

The short ride back to town concludes the circle island tour.

SAFARI EXCURSIONS

Hooking up with **Raro Safari Tours** ★★ (② **23-629** or 55-139) is the best way to see the island's mountainous interior without hiking. In fact, you'll get better views down over the reef and the sea from these 4-wheel-drive vehicles than you will on foot. The open-air trucks go up the Avatiu Valley on some unbelievably narrow tracks. Guides give often humorous commentary about the native flora and its uses, about ancient legends, and about what life was like in the old days when Rarotongans lived up in the valleys instead of along the coast. The 3½-hour tours depart Monday to Friday at 9am and 1:30pm, Sunday at noon. They cost NZ$60 ($27) per person.

CULTURAL EXPERIENCES ★★★

Given their use of English and their pride in their culture, the Cook Islanders themselves offer a magnificent glimpse into the lifestyle of eastern Polynesia. They are more than happy to answer questions put to them sincerely by inquisitive visitors. Some of them also do it for money, albeit in a low-key fashion, by offering some of the finest learning experiences in the South Pacific. Unless you sit on the beach and do nothing, you won't go home from the Cook Islands without knowing something about Polynesian culture, both of yesteryear and the present.

COOK ISLANDS CULTURAL VILLAGE ★★★

Plan an early visit to the **Cook Islands Cultural Village** (② **21-314**), on the back road in Arorangi, for it will enable you to understand what you will see during the rest of your stay here. The village consists of thatch huts featuring different aspects of life, such as the making of crafts, cooking, and even dancing. Guests are guided through the huts and then enjoy a lunch of island-style foods, music, and dancing. The tour begins Monday to Friday at 10am. Cost for the entire morning and lunch is NZ$48 ($21.50), or NZ$44 ($20) if you provide your own transportation to and from the village. The Cultural Village also does its own half-day circle island historical tour; it costs NZ$35 ($16) and includes transfers and lunch. A full day combining the village tour, lunch, and a trip around the island costs NZ$66 ($30) including transfers to and from the village.

PA'S NATURE WALKS ★★★

The best way to explore Rarotonga's mountainous interior on foot is in the company of a blond, dreadlocked Cook Islander named **Pa** (② **21-079**), who leads mountain and nature walks. Along the way he points out various wild plants, such as vanilla, candle nuts, mountain orchids, and the shampoo plant,

Moments   **Magnificent Harmony**

Nearly everyone in the Cook Islands puts on his or her finest white straw hat and goes to church on Sunday morning. Many visitors join them, for even though most sermons are in Maori, the magnificent harmony of Polynesian voices in full song will not soon be forgotten. Families have been worshiping together in the same pews for generations, but the ushers are accustomed to finding seats for tourists. Cook Islanders wear their finest to church, including neckties, but visitors can wear smart casual attire.

Sunday morning services at Rarotongan village churches usually begin at 10am; buses leave the hotels at 9:30am. Reserve at the activities desk, or just show up at any church on the island.

and their everyday and medicinal uses in the days before corned beef and pharmacies. Either Pa's Cross-Island Mountain Trek or Pa's Nature Walk costs NZ$50 ($22.50) for adults, NZ$25 ($11.25) for children under 12. Wear good walking or running shoes and bring a bathing suit (for a dip in an ancient pool once used by warriors). The nature walk takes 3½ hours. See "Fishing, Hiking, Diving & Other Outdoor Activities," below, for information about the cross-island hike. Reserve at any hotel activities desk, or call. You can also book at Bergman & Sons (The Black Pearl shop) west of the traffic circle.

10 Fishing, Hiking, Diving & Other Outdoor Activities

With tourism as its main business, Rarotonga has enough sporting and other outdoor activities to occupy the time of anyone who decides to crawl out of a beach chair and move the muscles. A couple of activities, such as Pa's Mountain Trek, are mentioned above, in "Cultural Experiences."

BOATING & SAILING   Captain Tama's AquaSports (© **27-350**) at the Rarotonga Sailing Club on Muri Beach, where the lagoon offshore is the island's best spot for swimming, snorkeling, and boating, rents a variety of watersports equipment, including beach kayaks, sailboats, Windsurfers, canoes, and snorkeling gear. Rental rates range from NZ$7 ($3.15) for an hour's use of a one-person kayak to NZ$25 ($11.25) to rent a Windsurfer for a day. You get a free beginner's Windsurfer lesson (on a simulator) with a rental or pay NZ$35 ($15.75) for a full course. Captain Tama's is open daily from 8am to 5pm.

FISHING   There have been some world-class catches of skipjack tuna (bonito), mahimahi, blue marlin, wahoo, and barracuda in Cook Islands waters. If the sea is calm enough for them to leave Rarotonga's relatively unprotected harbors, charter boats start deep-sea fishing as soon as they clear the reef. Several boat owners will take you out, but I recommend Elgin and Sharon Tetachuk's **Seafari Charters** (© **20-328**) and Wayne Barclay and Jenny Sorensen's **Pacific Marine Charters** (© **21-237**), which have ship-to-shore radios and safety equipment. They charge about NZ$100 ($45) per person for half a day's fishing, one of the lowest rates in the South Pacific. They like to have a day's notice, which you can probably give in person at the **Cook Islands Game Fishing Club** (© **21-419**), whose clubhouse is beside the lagoon 1km (½ mile) east of the traffic circle. Whether you fish or not, you'll be welcome to have snacks and drinks at the club while taking in the view and swapping a few tall tales.

Don't expect to keep your catch; fresh fish are expensive here and will be sold by the boat operator. Bring a camera.

GOLF   Visitors can take their shots at the radio towers and guy wires that create unusual obstacles on the nine holes of **Rarotonga Golf Club** (✆ 27-360). The course was once located on what is now the Rarotonga International Airport, but it had to move it when the runway was expanded. It now lies under Rarotonga's radio station antennae (balls that hit a tower or wire can be replayed). Greens fees are NZ$12 ($5.50). Rental equipment and drinks are available in the clubhouse. The club is open Monday through Saturday from 8am until dark.

HIKING   There are a number of hiking trails on Rarotonga, but the most popular by far is the **Cross-Island Track** ✯✯✯ from Avarua to the south coast. A landslide had closed the track during my recent visit, but if it has reopened (check with the Cook Islands Tourism Corporation), it's the best hike in the South Pacific. The trail begins in the Avatiu valley and follows the stream high up to the base of Mount Te Rua Manga ("The Needle"). It's a very steep and often slippery climb, but the trail is well marked. The best way to do it is with **Pa's Cross-Island Mountain Trek** (see "Cultural Experiences," above). For do-it-yourselfers, Cook Islands Tourism Corporation distributes a brochure detailing the cross-island and other hikes, and it has helpful brochures published by the Cook Islands Natural Heritage Project that explain what you will see.

LAGOON EXCURSIONS   **Captain Tama's Aquasports** (✆ 27-350), at the Rarotonga Sailing Club on Muri Beach, has glass-bottom boat excursions on Muri Lagoon which include fish-feeding, snorkeling, and lunch on one of the small offshore islands. Captain Tama charges NZ$60 ($27).

RUNNING & JOGGING   The Hash House Harriers organization meets once a week for a fun run and sponsors an annual Round Rarotonga Road Run in October. Really, all one has to do for a jog on Rarotonga is to run down the road or beach.

SCUBA DIVING   Rarotonga's lagoon is only 1m to 3m (4 ft.–10 ft.) deep, but depths easily reach 30m (100 ft.) outside the reef, and a drop-off starts at 24m (80 ft.) and descends to more than 3,600m (12,000 ft.). There are canyons, caves, tunnels, and many varieties of coral. Visibility usually is in the 30m to 60m (100 ft.–200 ft.) range. Two wrecks, and a 30m (100 ft.) fishing boat and a 45m (150 ft.) cargo ship, sit in depths of 24m (80 ft.) and 18m (60 ft.), respectively. Best of all for money-conscious travelers, the diving fees here are the lowest in the South Pacific.

Owner Barry Hill of **Dive Rarotonga** (✆ 21-873; fax 21-837; jbateman@ tumanu.co.ck), and his humorous mate Eric Bateman (of Tumanu Tropical Restaurant & Bar; see "Where to Dine on Rarotonga," below), make two dive trips daily. They charge NZ$45 ($20.25) per dive, including tank, air, weight belt, and boat; or NZ$55 ($24.75) including all equipment. Their office is roadside in Arorangi.

Greg Wilson of **Cook Island Divers**, P.O. Box 1002, Rarotonga (✆ 22-483; fax 22-484), operates out of his house in Arorangi (watch for the roadside signs) and from the Mana Court Dive Shop in Avarua. He charges NZ$75 ($33.75) for a one-tank dive, including all equipment.

At Muri Beach, Graham and Christine McDonald of **Pacific Divers** (✆ and fax 22-450; www.pacificdivers.co.ck) charge NZ$75 ($33.75) per dive, but two-tank dives for NZ$130 ($58.50) are their specialty. They also teach a beginner's lagoon dive for NZ$70 ($31.50).

Both Cook Island Divers and Pacific Divers teach PADI certification courses for NZ$485 ($218).

SWIMMING & SNORKELING   Getting into the water has to have high priority during a visit to the South Pacific, and Rarotonga is certainly no exception. The lagoon is deep enough for snorkeling off most hotels at high tide, but you'll do better walking on the west coast reef when the tide's out. Only in Titikaveka on the south coast is the lagoon deep enough for snorkeling at low tide; specifically, try snorkeling off the Fruits of Rarotonga shop (see the box "Take a Fruit Break," above), which will store your bag for you, and off The Little Polynesian and the Moana Sands Hotel (see "Where to Stay on Rarotonga," below). Muri Lagoon off The Pacific Resort & Villas is the best spot for boating, but the best snorkeling is just off the motu opposite the Muri Beachcomber.

Most hotels have snorkels, fins, and masks for their guests to use for free. You can rent them from the **Edgewater Resort** (© 25-435) or from **Dive Rarotonga** (© 21-873) on the west coast, or from **Captain Tama's AquaSports** (© 27-350) at the Rarotonga Sailing Club on Muri Beach. Cost is NZ$7 ($3.15) a day.

TENNIS   The **Edgewater Resort** (© 25-435) has four lighted, beachside Astro Grass courts, where pro Malcolm Kajer gives private lessons for NZ$30 ($13.50) per hour. You can rent court time here for NZ$15 ($6.75) per hour (Edgewater guests can play for free). Racquet rentals and balls are available.

11 Shopping on Rarotonga

Thanks to the New Zealand dollar being valued at less than its U.S. counterpart, Rarotonga offers some relatively good bargains for those who carry U.S. greenbacks—especially on black pearls, native handcrafts, and tropical clothing. For the most part, you can do your shopping during your visit to Avarua, for most stores line the town's waterfront on either side of the traffic circle. Some stores specialize in one particular item, but many carry a variety of pearls, handcrafts, and clothing.

Manihiki and Penrhyn atolls in the Northern Group of the Cook Islands produce a fair number of **black pearls.** You'll be offered pearls at small shops and even by street vendors, but stick to dealers who are members of the local Pearl Guild.

I strongly encourage anyone interested in buying black pearls in the South Pacific to do some research beforehand, perhaps starting with excellent articles in the August 1985 and June 1997 issues of *National Geographic.* Also see "Shopping" in chapter 4.

Cook Islanders may not produce island **handcrafts** in the same volume as Tongans (see "Shopping on Tongatapu" in chapter 14), but there is a fine assortment to choose from here, especially items made on the outer islands. Particularly good if not inexpensive buys are the delicately woven *rito* (white straw hats), which the women wear to church on Sunday, and the fine Samoan-style straw mats from Pukapuka in the Northern Group. Carvings from wood are plentiful, as is jewelry made from shell, mother-of-pearl, and pink coral. The most popular woodcarvings are small totems that represent the exhibitionist Tangaroa; they might be more appropriate for the nightstand than the coffee table.

The craze for block-printed, tie-dyed, and silk-screened **tropical clothing** swept from Tahiti to Rarotonga, where local artisans make colorful cotton pareus, shirts, blouses, dresses, swimwear, beach apparel, and other items. Some of the works are more artistically creative than those in French Polynesia, especially one-of-a-kind pareus and women's apparel.

For years the Cook Islands government has earned a considerable portion of its revenue from the sale of its **stamps** to collectors and dealers overseas. The **Philatelic Bureau,** next to Cook Islands Post, at the traffic circle in Avarua, issues between three and six new stamps each year. All are highly artistic and feature birds, shells, fish, flowers, and historical events and people, including the British royal family. For whatever reason—perhaps the remoteness of the islands or the beauty of the stamps—they are popular worldwide.

SHOPPING A TO Z

Beachcomber, Ltd.   This upscale establishment is worth a stop just to see the beautiful renovation of its 1843-vintage coral-block school house (see "A Stroll Around Avarua," above). Now owned by Bergman & Sons (see below), it has an excellent selection of black pearls, either loose or in exquisite settings designed and produced in the atelier behind the store. Also out back, a glass-blower artistically produces gorgeous vases and other items. You'll also find some of the best handcrafts available here, including woodcarvings, marvelous *tivaevae* quilts, black and pink coral jewelry, and exquisite rito hats. One section is devoted to paintings and other works by local artists. Avarua, east of traffic circle. ℂ **21-939.** Mon–Fri 9:30am–4pm, Sat 9:30am–noon.

Bergman & Sons (The Pearl Shop)   Mike and Marge Bergman and sons Trevor and Ben helped to pioneer the pearl industry in the Cook Islands, and their two shops (plus Beachcomber Ltd.) are the place to see Rarotonga's largest selection of natural and cultured pearls, whether loose or incorporated into jewelry. They carry small pearls still attached to their gold-trimmed shells and sold as necklaces. Avarua, in Cook's Corner, and next to Banana Court. ℂ **21-902.** Mon–Fri 9:30am–4pm, Sat 9:30am–noon.

Island Crafts   This large store next to Westpac Bank has been Rarotonga's best place to shop for handcrafts since 1943. It has the island's largest selection—including some pieces from other parts of the South Pacific—and a wide choice of carved wooden Tangaroa tikis in various sizes. You can even buy a 9-karat gold pendant of the well-endowed god. The shop carries some black pearls, some set as pendants and earrings. Avarua, in Centrepoint Building. ℂ **20-919.** Mon–Fri 8am–5pm, Sat 8:30am–1pm.

Maui Pearls *(Value*   Cook Islander Paka Worthington attended American University in Washington, D.C. He obviously stopped at the shops owned by his friends Ron Hall on Moorea and Steve Fearon on Bora Bora (see "Shopping" in chapters 5 and 6), for these two outlets bear a lot of similarities with those fine stores. Instead of teaching "pearl school," however, Paka lets a computer program explain all about the orbs. Specialties here are tension-set designs (where tension instead of a hole secures the pearl in place) and enhancers, which let you clip the pearl and setting on any chain or even a white pearl necklace. His prices are among the most reasonable here. Avarua, at C.I.T.C. shopping center and west of traffic circle next to Mana Court. ℂ **26-064.** Mon–Fri 8am–5pm, Sat 8:30am–noon.

The Perfume Factory   John Abbott's factory produces delightful perfumes, soaps, body oils, and after-shave lotions made of local gardenia, jasmine, aloe vera, and coconut oils. John also makes coffee, coconut, and vanilla liqueurs, some of them in souvenir bottles that replicate the Tangaroa tiki. Avarua, on the back road between the harbors. ℂ **22-690.** Mon–Sat 8am–4pm, Sun 10am–4:30pm.

Punanga Nui Market *(Value*   The vendor stalls in this waterfront municipal market are the best places to look for tie-dyed bedspreads and tablecloths. You can also find good prices on T-shirts, although some may be Chinese-made cottons that will shrink (buy a size larger than you usually wear). Saturday morning is market day here—the best time to shop. Avatiu Harbour. No phone. Mon–Fri 8am–5pm, Sat 8am–1pm.

TAV Ltd. Check out Ellena Tavioni's workshop for one of the island's best selections of block-printed swim wear, sundresses, and other items for men, women, and children. Ellena pioneered block printing here, and she exports her clothing to the United States, Europe, the United Kingdom, and the high-end boutiques in Fiji. Here she has Rarotonga's best selection in this lovely style. Her workshop can alter items for free or make them for you from scratch. Avarua, on 2nd road inland behind Ronnie's Bar & Restaurant. (✆) 21-802. Mon–Fri 8am–4pm, Sat 8am–noon.

12 Where to Stay on Rarotonga

Rarotonga may be a small island, but it's blessed with a wide range of accommodations. Although all of them are comfortable, this is not the place to come for superdeluxe resorts like those in French Polynesia and Fiji. Most of the properties here are small, owner-operated motels, whose friendly, hands-on management makes up for the lack of luxury. They call themselves "motels" because they're modeled after the typical New Zealand motel, in which each room has a small but quite complete kitchen, which compensates for the lack of restaurants on the premises. Whether motel or hotel, rooms in all except some of the least expensive establishments have electric "jugs" for making tea and coffee.

Accommodations here are grouped in three areas: the southeast, on or near **Muri Beach;** the **west coast,** especially near Arorangi; and in or near the town of **Avarua.** The southeast coast boasts the marvelous Muri Beach and a lagoon that's wider, deeper, and better for snorkeling and sailing than any other on Rarotonga. The prevailing southeast trade winds, however, can make this area chilly during the austral winter months of June through August. By the same token, these same winds provide nature's air conditioning during the warmer summer months. You get glorious sunsets on the west coast, which the mountains shield from the prevailing trade winds, thus making the west somewhat drier than Muri Beach—and hotter during the summer months of December to March. Much of the west coast beach has been eroded by recent storms, and the lagoon tends to be very shallow, especially at low tide. The hotels in or near Avarua are close to shops and restaurants, but the north coast is rocky, and its lagoons are perpetually shallow. Keep these factors in mind when making your choice.

Unless noted otherwise, every hotel or motel sits in a tropical garden complete with coconut palms and flowering plants. Telephones in the rooms are the exception here.

ACCOMMODATIONS AT MURI BEACH

The Little Polynesian (✿) Reminiscent of the small hotels on Moorea or Bora Bora but without the restaurant and bar, this establishment has an idyllic coconut grove location right on the beach near some of the deeper waters of Muri Lagoon. Owners/sisters Jeannine Peyroux and Dorice Reid have eight duplex units in four cottages, plus a smaller bungalow that stands by itself beside the beach. Each unit has a king-size bed, ceiling fan in case the trade winds die down, and cooking facilities. The lagoon-side bungalow also has its own veranda overlooking the beach. There's a small swimming pool surrounded by a rock ledge. This is a good choice for couples.

P.O. Box 366, Rarotonga (Titikaveka, 14km/8½ miles from Avarua). ℂ **24-280**. Fax 21-585. littlepoly@ beach.co.ck. 9 units. NZ$220–NZ$260 ($99–$117). MC, V. **Amenities:** Outdoor pool, free use of kayaks, bike rentals, babysitting, laundry service. *In room:* Kitchen, minibar, coffeemaker, no phone.

Moana Sands Hotel   Right on the beach at the deepest part of Muri Lagoon, this two-story motel-like structure has six rooms upstairs and six on the ground level. Each has a balcony or patio facing the lagoon, a ceiling fan, a cane table and chairs, a tiled shower-only bathroom, bright flower-print drapes and spreads, and a kitchenette with a microwave oven. Some units have single beds in addition to queens; others have only a queen-size bed. The hotel also has two rental houses, about .5km west of the main property. One of these hexagonal homes sits right beside the beach; the second is just behind the first. Each has three bedrooms, two bathrooms, a full kitchen, and a big porch. A small dining room provides breakfasts (brought to your room if you wish) and two- or three-course fixed menu dinners (eaten dinner party-style by the beach if weather permits). No lunch is served, but guests have access to the dining room and "honesty" bar at all times. The guest lounge has a small library and games and other distractions for children.

P.O. Box 1007, Rarotonga (Muri Beach, 14km/8½ miles from Avarua). ℂ **26-189**. Fax 22-189. www.moana sandshotel.co.ck. 12 units, 2 houses. NZ$225 ($101) double; NZ$395 ($178) house. AE, MC, V. **Amenities:** 1 restaurant (regional), 1 bar, scooter rentals, snorkeling and kayaking equipment, babysitting, laundry service. *In room:* Kitchen (houses only), hair dryer, safe, no phone (except in houses).

Muri Beachcomber ★★ *Value* *Kids*   One of my favorites places to stay on Rarotonga, this friendly motel sits right on Muri Beach and a short walk from The Pacific Resort, Sails Brasserie & Bar, and The Flame Tree restaurant, which more than make up for its lack of on-site dining and activities. Ten of the one-bedroom, full-kitchen units are in five duplex buildings built of brown timber, with yellow peaked roofs that evoke the tropics. They form two courtyards that open to the beach. Best suited for singles or couples, these spacious units have French doors opening from both living rooms and bedrooms to covered verandas with coffee tables and comfortable lawn chairs. Children under 12 are allowed only in the larger family units, which stand away from the beach but next to the pool, making it easy for parents to keep an eye on the kids from their shady verandas. Some of Rarotonga's best accommodations, the deluxe Watergarden Villas have stucco exteriors and huge wraparound verandas that make them look like coral-block colonial houses. Although they are behind and across a lily pond from the beachside units, they are more private and better equipped, with air-conditioned bedrooms, ceiling fans in bedrooms and living areas, phones, TVs, and VCRs.

P.O. Box 379, Rarotonga (Muri Beach, 11km/6½ miles from Avarua). ℂ **21-022**. Fax 21-323. www. beachcomber.co.ck. 18 units, 3 houses. NZ$250 ($112.50) double; NZ$330 ($148.50) house. AE, DC, MC, V. **Amenities:** Outdoor pool; bike rentals; babysitting; laundry service; coin-op washers and dryers. *In room:* A/C (in villas), TV/VCR (in villas), kitchen, coffeemaker, hair dryer, safe, no phone (except in villas).

The Pacific Resort & Villas ★★   Although it needs some improvements, especially to its beachside bar and restaurant, this resort sitting in a coconut grove alongside the island's best beach and lagoon comes closest of any Rarotonga property to capturing the appearance and ambience of French Polynesia's small resorts. The luxurious seaside "villas" have two bedrooms, private entertainment areas, full kitchens, laundry facilities, minibars, and TVs with VCRs. Most other units are in two-story buildings on either side of a tropical garden complete with a stream crossed by two foot bridges. More bungalow-like, the beachside and beachfront suites give the impression of having your own cottage.

P.O. Box 790, Rarotonga (Muri Beach, 11km/6½ miles from Avarua). ℂ **20-427.** Fax 21-427. www.pacific resort.com. 65 units, 7 houses. NZ$300–NZ$465 ($135–$209) double; NZ$640–NZ$690 ($288–$311) villa. Rates include continental breakfast. AE, DC, MC, V. **Amenities:** 1 restaurant (regional), 1 bar; outdoor pool; watersports equipment rentals; bike rentals; activities desk; car-rental desk; babysitting; laundry service; coin-op washers and dryers. *In room:* A/C (in villas), TV/VCR (in villas), kitchen, minibar (in villas), coffeemaker, no phone.

Shangri-La Beach Cottages   American expatriate Elliott Smith, who wrote the *Cook Islands Companion* guidebook, owns these adults-only cottages at Muri Beach. Although the cottages are not directly on the beach, which is about 25 yards away, each has a partial lagoon view from its veranda. The sailing club, The Pacific Resort & Villas, and the Muri restaurants are short walks away. The tropically attired cottages, which are of modern construction, are better equipped than most accommodations on Rarotonga; each unit has a shower as well as a two-person whirlpool tub. Screened doors and windows let in lots of light and fresh air. A counter separates the kitchen from the sleeping area, which has a queen-size bed. Ask about discounts if you book more than 30 days in advance.

P.O. Box 146, Rarotonga (Muri Beach, 11km/6¾ miles from Avarua). ℂ **22-779.** Fax 22-775. www.shangri-la. co.ck. 5 units. NZ$325 ($146.50) double. MC, V. 4-night minimum stay required. Children under 18 not accepted. **Amenities:** Outdoor pool; free use of snorkeling and kayaking equipment. *In room:* A/C, TV, kitchen, coffeemaker, hair dryer.

Sokala Villas   This unusual property sits in a small beachside casuarina-and-palm grove facing Motutapu islet across Ngatangiia Channel. Much of the thick vegetation has been left intact, obscuring the lagoon views but adding touches such as palms growing through the decks and tin roofs of some bungalows. Built entirely of New Zealand pine, they seem more like mountain cabins than tropical island retreats, with half-round log exteriors and knotty interior walls. Four two-story units have sleeping lofts that open to their own decks. Each single-floor cabin has a bedroom. Each unit has a deck that faces the beach, and five units have their own little swimming pools. Privacy is sparse, however, because the cabins are packed together on a small parcel of land. There is no restaurant, but The Flame Tree (see "Where to Dine on Rarotonga," below) is next door, and The Pacific Resort and Sails Brasserie & Bar are short walks away.

P.O. Box 82, Rarotonga (Muri Beach, 10km/6¼ miles from Avarua). ℂ **29-200.** Fax 21-222. www.sokala.com. 7 units. NZ$320–NZ$480 ($144–$216) double. MC, V. Children under 12 not accepted. **Amenities:** Free use of outrigger canoes, paddle boats, and snorkeling gear; laundry service. *In room:* Kitchen, coffeemaker, hair dryer.

ACCOMMODATIONS ON THE WEST COAST

Are-Renga Motel   This good budget choice is located in the village of Arorangi and is popular with Canadian travelers. The entire property enjoys a beautiful view of the mountains, and a path leads to the beach through a churchyard across the road. The Estall family runs this basic but clean establishment, and the spaciousness of the units makes up for a complete lack of frills. Nine units are in a motel-like block at the rear of the property. An older building has six units in which the bedroom is separated from the living and cooking area by a curtain; the three upstairs apartments share a large veranda, and a patio does double duty for the three apartments downstairs. All units have kitchen facilities. A small house has three bedrooms; houseguests share communal showers, toilets, kitchen facilities, lounge, and spacious veranda. Low-budget travelers can share a room in the house.

P.O. Box 223, Rarotonga (Arorangi village). ☎ **20-050.** Fax 29-22320. arerenga@oyster.net.ck. 20 units (3 without bathroom). NZ$50 ($22.50) double; NZ$20 ($9) per person shared unit. No credit cards. *In room:* Kitchen, no phone.

Edgewater Resort

The Edgewater has the most units of any resort on the island, and like The Rarotongan Beach Resort (see below), it is often full of visitors on package tours. Although thick tropical foliage helps make the grounds—just 4 beachside acres—seem less crowded, you won't have nearly as much room to roam here as at The Rarotongan Beach. Several concrete two- and three-story block structures hold most of the rooms here. Each has a bougainvillea-draped patio or balcony. Rooms in the 400 and 500 blocks are closest to the beach and farthest from the restaurant, bar, and swimming pool, which can be crowded and noisy when the house is full. Farther removed and much better appointed, the more expensive beachside executive suites are among Rarotonga's most luxurious accommodations. Rocks along the shoreline have been pushed back to create a small beach overlooked by the pool and expansive patio space for sunning and sitting.

P.O. Box 121, Rarotonga (Arorangi, 7km/4 miles from Avarua). ☎ **25-435.** Fax 25-475. www.edgewater.co.ck. 206 units. NZ$210–NZ$420 ($94.50–$189) double. AE, MC, V. **Amenities:** 2 restaurants (regional/Italian), 1 bar; outdoor pool; 2 tennis courts; watersports equipment rentals; bike rentals; game room; concierge; activities desk; car-rental desk; babysitting; laundry service; coin-op washers and dryers. *In room:* A/C, TV, fridge, coffeemaker, hair dryer.

Lagoon Lodges ★★ ⟨Value⟩

Those who agree with me that bungalow living is the way to go in the South Pacific will find it at these lodges, which are within an easy walk of The Rarotongan Beach Resort. Owners/managers Des and Cassey Eggelton have studio, one-, and two bedroom units. The two-story units have big decks facing the lagoon and two upstairs bedrooms. Even though some units are duplexes, there is a feeling of privacy. Guests have breakfast on a terrace whose architecture is reminiscent of Santa Fe (it's also the venue for popular Sun night barbecues). The tropical gardens contain a swimming pool, a grass tennis court, and a barbecue area, and the beach is just across the road. Lagoon Lodges also has two real houses: a three-bedroom villa with its own enormous veranda and private swimming pool on the premises and another at Muri Beach.

P.O. Box 45, Rarotonga (on southwest corner, near The Rarotongan Beach Resort, 13km/7¾ miles from Avarua). ☎ **22-020.** Fax 22-021. www.lagoonlodges.com. 21 bungalows, 1 house. NZ$165–NZ$195 ($74–$88) bungalows; NZ$245–$600 ($110–$270) house for up to 7 persons. Rates include breakfast. MC, V. **Amenities:** Outdoor pool; tennis court; bike and scooter rentals; babysitting; laundry service; coin-op washers and dryers. *In room:* Kitchen, coffeemaker, hair dryer, safe.

Manuia Beach Boutique Hotel ★

This intimate little establishment serves adults only. The 20 rooms are in 10 duplex bungalows set rather close together on a narrow rectangle of beachfront land. Tropical foliage helps give the garden units some semblance of privacy, but the more expensive beachfront units definitely are the choice here. Ceiling fans send breezes down over cool, white tile floors in all units, and sliding glass doors lead to semiprivate wooden verandas. Angled shower stalls in one corner and lavatories in another maximize space in the rather small bathrooms. Each beachfront unit has a king-size bed and a view of the reef across a kidney-shaped swimming pool. Each garden unit has a queen and a single bed. None of the rooms have kitchens, but you can amble down to the Right on the Beach Bar and dig holes in its white-sand floor while enjoying a bistro-style meal under a low-slung thatch roof.

P.O. Box 700, Rarotonga (Arorangi, 8km/5 miles from Avarua) ☎ **22-461**. Fax 22-464. www.manuia.co.ck. 20 units. NZ$255–NZ$420 ($115–$189). AE, MC, V. Children under 12 not accepted. **Amenities:** 1 restaurant (regional), 1 bar; outdoor pool; bike rentals; limited room service; laundry service. *In room:* A/C, fridge, coffeemaker, hair dryer.

Puaikura Reef Lodges *Value*

This modest but comfortable motel's units are in two one-story buildings facing a grassy lawn, pool, barbecue area, and honesty bar, across the road from a shady beachside park. Each unit has a double bed and two twins, plus a patio with table and chairs. In half the units, the bedroom is separate from the living area. If you can do without frills and are looking for a good value, try the clean and relatively spacious accommodations here.

P.O. Box 397, Rarotonga (southeast corner of island, 12km/7 miles from Avarua). ☎ **23-537**. Fax 21-537. www.puaikura.co.ck. 12 units. NZ$135 ($61) double. MC, V. **Amenities:** 1 bar; outdoor pool; bike and scooter rentals; laundry service. *In room:* Kitchen, coffeemaker, no phone.

The Rarotongan Beach Resort ★★ *Kids*

After years of neglect by the government, which built it in 1977, Rarotonga's flagship hotel has undergone a remarkable transformation under its present owner, Tata Crocombe, a Cook Islander who graduated from Harvard Business School. The dismal dark-brown color scheme has been replaced by lively pastels that make this seem as much Caribbean as South Pacific. All the guest units have been renovated and upgraded, including the addition of modern air conditioners—a vast improvement over the noisy old units that elicited numerous complaints in years past. There's even a full-service spa for grownups, and the children's program is the best on the island. A poolside stone patio and a large lagoon-side deck compensate for the eroded beach—a common condition at most west coast resorts. The choice units here are 30 beachfront deluxe suites, which are in one-story buildings staggered to make them seem like individual bungalows. Each of these spacious rooms has a bathroom with a whirlpool bathtub in addition to an outdoor shower; their sliding front doors open to wooden decks facing the beach. The other rooms here are in nine two-story, motel-style buildings linked to the central complex by covered walkways. About two-thirds of them face the beach, and a few have been turned into two-bedroom "garden suites" with kitchens and whirlpool bathtubs. Every room in the resort has either a patio or a balcony.

P.O. Box 103, Rarotonga (southwest corner of the island, 13km/8 miles from Avarua). ☎ **25-800**. Fax 25-799. www.rarotongan.co.ck. 156 units. NZ$315–NZ$579 ($142–$261) double; NZ$825–NZ$1,125 ($371–$507) suite. AE, DC, MC, V. **Amenities:** 2 restaurants (regional), 2 bars; outdoor pool; 2 tennis courts; spa; watersports equipment rentals; bike rentals; children's programs; game room; activities desk; car-rental desk; business center; limited room service; babysitting; laundry service; coin-op washers and dryers. *In room:* A/C, TV (in suites), kitchen (in garden suites), minibar, coffeemaker, hair dryer.

The Rarotongan Sunset ★★ *Value*

Nicholas Reeves's and Deborah Manley's little place has come a long way since I spent my first night ever on Rarotonga here in the mid-1980s. Tropical chairs and tables make the units look like they belong in the South Seas. Nicholas and Deborah have turned four of the beachfront units into three air-conditioned suites, one with a bedroom that's separate from the living quarters. The older units all have ceiling fans and bedrooms that are separate from the living quarters. Net curtains double as mosquito netting across the sliding glass fronts at night. Dense tropical foliage provides privacy on this closely packed property, but it also means that only the beachfront units have lagoon views from their verandas. Set away from the beach, an odd-shaped pool has a bridge over it and a shallow end for children; the adjacent Bird Cage Bar has colorful wooden parrots suspended from its peaked ceiling. Guests eat breakfast by the pool, and they and outsiders can attend lively Sunday evening poolside barbecues. Book early at this popular establishment.

P.O. Box 377, Rarotonga (Arorangi, 6.5km/3¾ miles from Avarua). ☎ 28-028. Fax 28-026. www.rarotongan sunset.com. 19 units. NZ$185–NZ$205 ($83–$92) double; NZ$345 ($155) suite. Rates include breakfast. AE, DC, MC, V. **Amenities:** 1 bar; outdoor pool; bike rentals; car rentals; babysitting; laundry service; coin-op washers and dryers. *In room:* A/C (in beachfront suites), TV, kitchen, coffeemaker, hair dryer, iron, safe.

ACCOMMODATIONS IN OR NEAR AVARUA

Club Raro (☎ 22-415; www.clubraro.co.ck), 2.5km (1½ miles) east of Avarua, is often the lowest-priced property offered as part of package tours. Lined up on either side of a main complex, the motel-style rooms (which have no cooking facilities) can be noisy. Club Raro does have popular Island Night buffets and dance shows.

Kii Kii Motel   Harry and Pauline Napa's lagoon-side motel is one of Rarotonga's best bargains if you don't need a beach with sand. Kii Kii has six units facing the lagoon, six facing the pool, eight older units with separate bedrooms, and four budget rooms. All are spacious and spotlessly maintained, and all have full kitchens. The pool helps compensate for the absence of sand on the rocky lagoon shore. The four budget rooms have the same amount of space as the newer units but do not have phones or TVs. There is no restaurant or bar on premises, but Club Raro is virtually next door. Ask about lower rates during the off-season.

P.O. Box 68, Rarotonga (3km/1½ miles east of Avarua). ☎ 21-937. Fax 22-937. www.kiikiimotel.co.ck. 24 units. NZ$90–NZ$160 ($40.50–$72) double. AE, DC, MC, V. **Amenities:** Outdoor pool; babysitting; laundry service. *In room:* TV, kitchen, coffeemaker.

Paradise Inn   Owner Diane Haworth liked vacationing at Rarotonga's most unusual accommodation so much that she bought it and moved here permanently. Until being converted into this innlike hotel in 1986, this warehouse-size pink building was a dance hall. Each room has a kitchenette, a lavatory, large glass doors that open out to a narrow walkway alongside the hotel, and a spiral staircase that leads to a sleeping lofts with a double bed. Two small budget rooms lack the lofts and have only single beds downstairs. One family unit is more like an apartment. The common areas at the rear of the building are split level, with an honesty bar and patio next to the rocky lagoon shore and an open-air lounge with a TV and VCR upstairs. Except for this common area, there are no grounds; the building occupies almost all of the hotel's land.

P.O. Box 674, Rarotonga (Avarua, east of traffic circle). ☎ 20-544. Fax 22-544. paradise@oyster.net.ck. 16 units. NZ$52–NZ$112 ($23.50–$50.50) double. AE, MC, V. **Amenities:** 1 bar; bike rentals; laundry service. *In room:* Kitchen, coffeemaker, no phone.

HOSTELS

Aremango Guesthouse   If you can't get into Vara's Beach House (see below), head to Aremango Guesthouse. The Tairea family constructed this modern, peaked-roof building specifically with backpackers in mind. A central hallway runs between the relatively spacious rooms, which have ceiling fans, screened windows, and two or three single beds that couples can push together. The communal kitchen is large enough so that everyone gets a cupboard, and the shared bathrooms have hot-water showers and are fully tiled (as are all the floors here). Guests can congregate in an indoor lounge, but most prefer the side porch with tables and chairs, the yard with lounge furniture under coconut palms, or Muri Beach, which is just a short walk away.

P.O. Box 714, Rarotonga (Muri Beach, 11km/7 miles east of Avarua). ☎ 24-362. 10 units (shared bathrooms). NZ$40 ($18) double; NZ$18 ($8) dorm bed. No credit cards. *In room:* No phone.

Backpackers' International Hostel   Bill Bates and family operate this backpackers' hostel a block from the beach on Muri Beach. One building holds 20 simple rooms, all of which share toilets and hot-water showers. The upstairs part of the other building is a dormitory with eight beds. The open-air downstairs has a TV lounge and communal kitchen. There's a weekly Cook Islands–style feast. Airport transfers cost NZ$5 ($2.25) each way.

P.O. Box 878, Rarotonga (Arorangi, 12km/7½ miles from Avarua). © 21-847. Fax 21-847. annabill@ backpackers.co.ck. 20 units (shared bathrooms), 8 dorm beds. NZ$16 ($7.25) per person in rooms; NZ$15 ($6.75) dorm bed. MC, V. *In room:* No phone.

Vara's Beach House   The most popular backpackers' hostel in the entire South Pacific, Vara's is usually packed with as many as 200 young travelers jammed into dorm bunks, five rooms, and two small cabins right on Muri Beach, or in five houses that climb the hill across the road. There seems to be a bed everywhere you step here (56 down by the beach, at least another 74 in the hillside houses), but no one seems to mind. The original beach house, a new lagoon-side dorm, and the five houses all have communal kitchens, toilets, and showers. Needless to say, reservations are absolutely essential here.

P.O. Box 434, Rarotonga (Muri Beach, 11km/6¾ miles east of Avarua). © 21-156. Fax 22-619. backpack@ varasbeach.co.ck. 25 units (11 with bathroom), 2 cabins (both with bathroom), 130 dorm beds (shared bathrooms). NZ$48 ($21.50) double room; NZ$20–NZ$25 ($9–$11.25) dorm bed. Higher rates for stays shorter than 4 nights. MC, V. **Amenities:** Scooter rentals; snorkeling gear rentals; e-mail access; coin-op washing machines. *In room:* No phone.

13 Where to Dine on Rarotonga

If you sampled the fare at French Polynesia's fine restaurants, then you may be disappointed in the Cook Islands. Most of the cuisine here is cooked to old-fashioned New Zealand tastes, which means the chefs go easy with the spices. By and large, fresh ingredients are limited to local fruits and vegetables. Aitutaki supplies some lobster and lagoon fishes, but most of the fresh (as opposed to frozen) seafood on Rarotonga will be tuna and an occasional mahimahi caught outside the reef—and even that may be unavailable if the weather has kept the local fishing boats in port. The island also occasionally may lack some imported ingredients such as butter and flour if a supply ship is late arriving. You'll get good, substantial meals here, but don't expect gourmet quality anywhere.

Like the hotels, above, I have arranged the restaurants by geographic location: Muri Beach, the west coast, and in or near Avarua.

WHERE TO DINE AT MURI BEACH

Ambala Gardens ★★★ INTERNATIONAL   Sue Curruthers, who grew up in Kenya and who founded The Flame Tree (see below), meant to retire to her lovely home in the hills above Muri Beach, but she couldn't stay out of the kitchen—at least for 3 days a week, when she serves breakfast and lunch on her veranda. You can start your day with plain eggs, corn fritters with avocado, waffles with fresh fruit and cream, or freshly baked muffins and fruit cakes. For lunch, Sue combines flavors with such flair that you'll have trouble choosing among her corn fritters with guacamole and tomato salsa, spiced lentil and pecan veggie burgers with yogurt mint sauce, and cannelloni with taro leaves, pumpkin and mushrooms with tomato basil sauce. Sue wrote *The Flame Tree Cookbook,* which is available here and at bookstores in Avarua.

Muri Beach, between Muri Beachcomber and The Little Polynesian. © 26-486. Breakfast NZ$5.50–NZ$11.50 ($2.50–$5.25); lunch NZ$12.50–NZ$14.50 ($5.50–$6.50). No credit cards. Thurs–Sat 9am–3pm.

Moments Don't Miss an Island Night Feast

Like their counterparts throughout Polynesia, in pre-European days the Cook Islanders cooked all their food in an earth oven—known here as an *umu*—and they still do for special occasions. The food (*umukai*) is as finger-licking good today as it was hundreds of years ago, although it's now eaten with knives and forks rather than fingers during "Island Nights" at Rarotonga's hotels, which include Cook Island dance shows (see "Island Nights on Rarotonga," below). The hotels provide a wide assortment of salads and cold cuts for those who are not particularly fond of taro, arrowroot, and *ika mata* (the local version of poisson cru—fish marinated in lime juice and mixed with coconut milk and raw vegetables).

Get a schedule of island nights from Cook Islands Tourism Corporation. Also check the daily *Cook Islands News* (especially the Thurs and Fri editions) or with the hotels to find out when the feasts are on. Most buffets cost less than NZ$50 ($22.50), an absolute steal compared to French Polynesia's prices. Some of them may charge a small admission fee to see the dance show if you don't have dinner.

The Flame Tree ★★★ INTERNATIONAL   Within walking distance of The Muri Beachcomber, The Pacific Resort, and Sokala Villas, this is one of the South Pacific's most interesting restaurants. Calling on the cuisines of Kenya, India, and other countries, it offers a range of selections such as an absolutely delightful fish served under coconut, chili, and peanut sauce. I particularly enjoyed one of the nightly specials: fresh parrot fish breaded, fried, and served over rice and under a mound of taro leaves sweetly cooked in coconut sauce. Smoking is allowed only outside, not inside the converted house.

Muri Beach, near The Pacific Resort (11km/6½ miles from Avarua). ✆ 25-123. Reservations strongly recommended. Main courses NZ$17.50–NZ$32 ($7.75–$14.50). AE, MC, V. Daily 6:30–9:30pm.

Maire Nui Gardens & Cafe ★ *Value* SALADS/SANDWICHES   You won't appreciate Hinano MacQuarie's sophisticated cafe from the road, but wait until you walk around the thatch-roof building to the big veranda and its terrific vista of the green mountains rising beyond the flowery botanical gardens. It's the perfect spot to break a round-island tour or stop in for breakfast, a light lunch, an afternoon snack, a fruit smoothie, or a cup of espresso, cappuccino, or fresh mint tea. Hinano's breakfast offerings include muffins, fresh fruit, and omelets. You'll have more choices from her lunch-and-afternoon blackboard menu. The lemon meringue cheesecake is well worth the calories.

Muri Beach, opposite The Little Polynesian. ✆ 22-796. Reservations not accepted. Most items NZ$9.50–NZ$13.50 ($4.25–$6). No credit cards. Mon–Fri 9am–4pm, Sat noon–4pm.

Sails Brasserie & Bar ★★ INTERNATIONAL   Occupying the main floor of the Rarotonga Sailing Club, this airy, nautically decorated restaurant is an excellent spot for an al fresco lagoonside lunch, and it's an excellent choice for dinner, too. The daytime menu offers a variety of salads, sandwiches, and "island fries"—sweet potato, taro, and banana. At dinner the chef turns his attention to fresh fish and vegetables, plus mussels and steaks flown in from New Zealand.

You might be offered tuna marinated in Asian spices, a spicy version of Thai curry chicken, or vegetarian lasagna. Saturday afternoon is especially lively here; club members gather to sail their radio-controlled miniature yachts out on the lagoon.

Muri Beach, in Rarotonga Sailing Club, between The Pacific Resort and Muri Beachcomber. ☎ 27-349. Reservations strongly recommended for dinner. Lunch NZ$7.50–NZ$22 ($3.50–$10); main courses NZ$17.50–NZ$30 ($7.75–$13.50). AE, MC, V. Daily noon–8:30pm.

WHERE TO DINE ON THE WEST COAST

Alberto's Steakhouse STEAKS/SEAFOOD   A New Zealander living on Rarotonga once said she appreciated the sacrifices of the Kiwis at home, since all their country's top-grade beef is exported rather than consumed at home. Some of those tender steaks end up at this roadside restaurant, where exposed dark beams, potted plants, and tables with candles help set a romantic scene. A big blackboard announces fresh local lobster in lemon butter and other nightly specials, including chargrilled tuna, wahoo, and mahimahi when available. Pastas are also on the menu. Quality wines are available by the glass.

Arorangi, near Edgewater Resort. ☎ 23-597. Main courses NZ$14–NZ$39 ($6.50–$17.50). MC, V. Mon–Sat 6–9pm (bar opens at 5:30pm).

Tumanu Tropical Restaurant & Bar REGIONAL   With its low-slung roof and lush outdoor gardens, this is the only restaurant and bar on Rarotonga that genuinely looks like it belongs in the South Seas. Julie and Eric Bateman's cozy place has subdued lighting inside, foreign flags hanging on split bamboo walls, and various paraphernalia stuck around the bar area, including old license plates from as far away as Texas, Oregon, Iowa, and Alaska. Colorful tablecloths help spice up otherwise plain dining room furniture. The menu is heavy on seafood, served braised or fried, but you can also get baked chicken or steaks in pepper or mushroom sauce. A special vegetarian platter includes fruit salad, vegetables, and cheese omelet. A caution is in order: The humor can get raunchy at Eric's lively bar. He spends the day diving, so if you want to eat here, you should stop by to leave your name on the reservations sheet just inside the entry.

Arorangi, near Edgewater Resort. ☎ 20-501. Reservations recommended. Main courses NZ$19.50–NZ$28 ($8.75–$12.50). AE, MC, V. Daily 6–10pm (bar stays open later).

Vaima Restaurant & Bar ⛨ INTERNATIONAL   Lots of islandy ambience prevails at this bamboo-clad beachside restaurant, which offers a wide range of exciting tastes, including a not-very-accurate but nevertheless spicy rendition of Cajun cooking. The menu also features the likes of spicy Thai-style chicken, or you can choose from the daily blackboard specials such as Indian beef vindaloo (which the chef will prepare mild as well as fiery, thank goodness). The walls of the main dining room feature works by local artists (they're for sale). There are a few tables on a veranda facing the beach, and there are picnic tables out by the sand.

Takitimu (1km/½ mile east of The Rarotongan Beach Resort). ☎ 26-123. Reservations recommended. Main courses NZ$17–NZ$26.50 ($7.50–$12). MC, V. Thurs–Tues 6:30–9pm.

WHERE TO DINE IN AVARUA

Blue Note Café SNACK BAR/REGIONAL   A fine place to take a town break and watch the traffic along the waterfront, this open-air snack bar occupies one end of the veranda of the Banana Court building. Breakfast is served all day, as are espresso, ice cream, milkshakes, and exotic cocktails. Sandwiches and big burgers are made to order for lunch. You can also try chicken or lamb curry, fish and chips, smoked fish, or barbecue pork.

Avarua, at the traffic circle. ℭ **23-236**. Breakfast NZ$7.50–NZ$16.50 ($3.50–$7.50); sandwiches, salads, and burgers NZ$10.50–NZ$13.50 ($4.75–$6); meals NZ$14.50–NZ$19 ($6.50–$8.50). MC, V. Daily 8am–6pm (Fri to midnight).

The Cafe ★★ SALADS/SANDWICHES/SNACKS   This cafe, which would grace Auckland's trendy Parnell district, is the best place to grab a latte and a papaya muffin before striking out on your tour of Avarua. And when you've finished your walk, you can retire here and select from daily specials such as veggie quiche, pan-seared tuna over a Greek salad, or a panini-style sandwich (pastrami, eggplant, and mustard is nicely piquant). Lots of natural wood and big canvas patio umbrellas hung from the ceiling create an outdoorsy ambience.

Avarua, east of traffic circle. ℭ **21-283**. Reservations not accepted. Breakfast NZ$3.50—NZ$12.50 ($1.50–$5.50); sandwiches and salads NZ$9–NZ$16 ($4–$7.25). AE, MC, V. Mon–Tues and Thurs–Fri 8am–4pm, Wed 7am–9pm, Sat 7:30am–2pm.

Cook's Corner Cafe SNACK BAR   You will find me having a cooked breakfast and reading the *Cook Island News* at this sidewalk cafe, where everyone waits for the bus (it begins its runs here). Maureen Young serves breakfast all day, as well as snacks, morning and afternoon teas, and light lunches, which include the likes of curry, fish and chips, and spicy roast chicken. You purchase your food at a counter and eat it on the covered sidewalk of the small shopping center.

Avarua, in Cook's Corner. ℭ **22-345**. Burgers and sandwiches NZ$3–NZ$8 ($1.35–$3.50); meals and breakfasts NZ$6–NZ$18.50 ($2.75–$8.50). No credit cards. Mon–Fri 6am–2:30pm, Sat 6am–1pm.

Portofino Restaurant ★ ITALIAN   This cozy old clapboard store dressed up with a cross between Mediterranean and Polynesian decor is the best place in town for pizza or pasta. An open-air pavilion to one side makes room for a few fresh-air tables. Spaghetti or penne is served with Neapolitan, Bolognese, Florentine, or Alfredo sauces, either as a heavy appetizer or as a main course. Tender charbroiled New Zealand–bred steaks are cooked plain or under chili, garlic, or pepper sauce.

Finds **Food Stalls & the Best Burgers in Town**

Just as *les roulottes* offer some of the best food bargains in French Polynesia (see "Where to Dine" in chapter 4), Rarotonga has its own version of these popular food trucks. Here they are the **food stalls** in Punanga Nui Market, just east of Avatiu Harbour. The best of the lot is **Moana Takeaways** (ℭ **22-536**), which offers everything from cold coconuts to slake a thirst to seafood platters to placate late-night hunger pangs. Prices range from NZ$3.50 to NZ$12.50 ($1.50–$5.50). Most food stalls are open Monday to Saturday from 9am to 6pm, and some stay open Monday to Thursday until 9pm, Friday until 2am, and Saturday until midnight. Guess where everyone goes after crawling the pubs Friday night?

Nearby at Avatiu Harbour, **Palace Takeaway** (ℭ **21-438**) serves the best juicy, slaw-laden hamburgers in town. It's open Monday to Saturday from 11am to 9pm, late into the night on Friday. Many pub-crawlers stop for a bite along the way or end their revelry here (see "Island Nights on Rarotonga," below).

Cook Islands Dancing

A New Zealander once told me, only partly in jest, that all Cook Islanders are deaf because they grow up 3 feet from a drum whose beats you can hear from 3 miles away.

Their Cook Islanders' hip-swinging **tamure** is very much like that in Tahiti, except it tends to be faster (which I found hard to believe the first time I saw it) and even more suggestive (which I had even more trouble believing). The costumes generally aren't as colorful as those in Tahiti but are more likely to be made in the traditional fashion, using natural materials as opposed to dyed synthetic fabrics.

Even though the dance shows at the hotels are tailored for tourists, the participants go at it with an enthusiasm that is too seldom seen in the French Polynesian hotel shows these days. Dancing is the thing to do in the Cook Islands, and it shows every time the drums start their tattoo.

Unadulterated Cook Islands dancing is best seen during the annual **Dance Week** in April or during the **Constitution Week** celebrations in late July and early August. In the absence of one of these celebrations, make do with an "Island Night" show or two at the hotels. There will be at least one performance every night except Sunday. A little detective work is required, but you'll easily find out where the next island night is being staged by asking at your hotel tour desks or Cook Islands Tourism Corporation or checking the daily *Cook Islands News.*

Daily specials feature such tempting dishes as seafood lasagna with fish, crabmeat, and smoked mussels. Pizzas and pastas are also available to carry out.

Avarua, east of traffic circle. (℃ **26-480.** Reservations recommended. Pizzas NZ$15 ($6.75); main courses NZ$15.50–NZ$35 ($7–$15.75). AE, MC, V. Mon–Sat 6:30–9pm.

S.S. Maitai Café ⭐ PIZZA/REGIONAL   Named for the wrecked freighter whose rusting smokestack still stands out on the reef, this trendy sidewalk cafe is the recent creation of Paka Worthington, owner of Maui Pearls (see "Shopping," above). The best food here is the smoky, wood-fired pizzas by the slice or by the pie, with mix-and-match toppings. You'll also find sandwiches, meat pies, and other fare, most of it displayed cafeteria-style, but watch for daily specials such as grilled fresh tuna or authentic Tahitian-style poisson cru. You can get a caffeine fix from a cappuccino, an espresso, or a latte, and you can fatten up on the creamy offerings of the Cook Islands Ice Cream Company.

Avarua, in C.I.T.C. shopping center. (℃ **22-215.** Pizza NZ$3.50–NZ$39 ($1.50–$17.50); sandwiches and salads NZ$2.50–NZ$5 ($1–$2.25); main courses NZ$10–NZ$15 ($4.50–$6.75). MC, V. Mon–Sat 9:30am–5:30pm and 6:30–10pm (Fri to midnight).

Trader Jack's Bar & Grill ⭐⭐⭐ SEAFOOD   You won't be on Rarotonga long before you hear about New Zealander "Trader Jack" Cooper's harbor-side joint, one of the South Pacific's great bars and Rarotonga's best place to dine. Local business types crowd in at happy hour Monday to Thursday and all of Friday and Saturday nights, when "The Trader" keeps a sharp eye peeled (that's him sitting at the bar, next to the ship's wheel). Floor-to-ceiling windows on three sides open to the water and giving nearly everyone in the bar, split-level dining area, and long lagoon-side deck a view of the harbor, the reef, and the sea and sunsets beyond. A regular printed menu plays second fiddle to the chalkboard specials, which feature the freshest fish served on the island. Snacks are offered from Monday to Saturday from 3 to 6pm and *kati-kati* ("bite-bite") snacks are available from midnight to closing on Friday. Fine musicians entertain every night.

Avarua, waterfront at traffic circle. ℂ 26-464. Reservations recommended for dinner. Main courses NZ$18–NZ$32 ($8–$14.50). AE, DC, MC, V. Mon–Sat noon–10pm, Sun 6–9pm. Bar Mon–Thurs and Sat 11am–midnight, Fri 11am–2am, Sun 6–10pm.

14 Island Nights on Rarotonga

Cook Islanders are some of the most fun-loving folks you will meet in the South Pacific, and you can easily catch their spirit. Every evening except Sunday is a party night, especially Friday, when the pubs stay open until 2am (they close promptly when the Sabbath strikes at Sat midnight). And as with their Tahitian cousins, the infectious sound of the traditional drums starts everyone dancing.

When Rarotongans aren't dancing in a show, they seem to be dancing with each other at some of the most colorful bars in the South Pacific. No one ever explained to me why they call their tour-de-pubs a *crawl.* I assume it's because crawling is one method of travel after a few too many of the locally brewed Cook's Lagers. All you have to do is walk along the Avarua waterfront east of the traffic circle after 10pm Friday; you'll hear the bands playing and can check it all out for yourself.

The Friday night crawl both begins and ends at **Trader Jack's Bar & Grill** ★★★ (ℂ **26-464**) at Avarua's old harbor, one of the best bars in all of the South Pacific. The island's affluent movers and shakers start boozing here after work. Pianist Garth Young usually appears at Jack's from Sunday to Wednesday, and bands take the stage other nights.

Heading east, a very young crowd dances at **TJ's** (ℂ **24-722**), and the Trader Jack's crowd wanders on the **Stair Case Restaurant & Bar** (ℂ **22-254**), an upstairs restaurant that has rock-and-roll music for dancing after 10pm.

Backtracking to the traffic circle, you'll come to **The Banana Court** (ℂ **23-397**), which for several generations was *the* place to do your drinking, dancing, and fighting. It was closed for several years but is now back in business on Friday nights. The NZ$3 ($1.35) cover charge helps keep rowdy young locals away from the tourists.

At Avatiu Harbour, **Rob's Paradise Bar** (ℂ **29-879**) is the second best joint for grownups (after Trader Jack's). The bar is under a big thatch roof; the bands play in the backyard. From there you can head toward the airport and the **RSA Club** (ℂ **20-590**), where the country's military veterans welcome everyone to drink and dance.

After the bewitching hour of 2am Saturday, many crawlers head to **Palace Takeaways** (ℂ **21-438**) at Avatiu Harbour and the food stalls at **Punanga Nui Market** (see the box under "Where to Dine on Rarotonga," above).

15 Aitutaki ★★★

The farther away visitors get from the South Pacific's international airports, the more likely they are to find an island and a way of life that have escaped relatively unscathed by the coming of Western ways—remnants of "old" Polynesia. This is certainly true of Aitutaki, the most frequently visited of the outer Cook Islands.

⟨ *Fun Fact* **Dropping Their Rocks**

Legend has it that in the beginning Aitutaki was completely flat, but then its warriors sailed to Rarotonga and stole the top of Mount Raemaru. Pitched battles were fought on the way home, and the warriors dropped some of their rocks into the sea: Black Rock, on Rarotonga's northwest point; Rapota and Moturakau islands, in the south of Aitutaki's lagoon; and the black rocks along Aitutaki's west coast. In the end, the Aitutakian warriors were victorious, and the top of Raemaru is now **Mount Maungapu,** the highest point on Aitutaki, at 122m (407 ft.).

Lying 225km (140 miles) north of Rarotonga, Aitutaki is often referred to as "the Bora Bora of the Cook Islands" because it consists of a small, hilly island at the apex of a triangular barrier reef dotted with skinny flat islands. This reef necklace encloses one of the South Pacific's most beautiful lagoons, which appears at the end of the flight up from Rarotonga as a turquoise carpet spread on the deep blue sea. The view from the air is memorable.

The central island, only 13 square km (8 sq. miles) in area, is dotted with the coconut, pineapple, banana, and tapioca plantations that are worked by most of the island's 2,500 residents. A few Aitutakians make their living at the island's hotels, but the land and the lagoon still provide most of their income. Aitutaki is a major supplier of produce and seafood to Rarotonga. Much of the fresh reef fish and lobsters consumed at Rarotonga's restaurants is harvested here.

The administrative center, most of the shops, and the main wharf are on the west side of the island at **Arutanga** village, where a narrow, shallow passage comes through the reef. Trading boats cannot get through the pass and must remain off-shore while cargo and passengers are ferried to land on barges. A network of mostly unpaved roads fans out from Arutanga to **Viapai** and **Tautu** villages on the east side and to the airport on a flat hook at the northern end of the island.

The uninhabited coconut-studded small islands out on the reef have white-sand beaches on their lagoon sides and pounding surf on the other; they're perfect for picnics and snorkeling expeditions, which are Aitutaki's prime attractions.

A LITTLE HISTORY According to ancient legend, the first Polynesians to reach Aitutaki came in through **Ootu Pass,** between the airport and **Akitua** island, site of today's Aitutaki Pearl Beach Resort (see "Where to Stay on Aitutaki," below). They were led by the mighty warrior and navigator Ru, who brought four wives, four brothers, and a crew of 20 young virgins from either Tubuai or Raiatea (the legend varies as to which one) in what is now French Polynesia. Akitua island, where they landed, was originally named *Urituaorukitemoana,* which means "where Ru turned his back on the sea."

The first European to visit Aitutaki was Capt. William Bligh, who discovered it in 1789, a few weeks before he was set adrift in Tonga by the mutinous crew of HMS *Bounty.* Just south of the post office in Arutanga is the **Cook Islands Christian Church,** the country's oldest church, built in 1839 of coral and lime-stone. The monument in front is to John Williams, the exploring missionary who came to Aitutaki in October 1821, and to Papeiha, the Tahitian teacher who came with him and stayed for 2 years, during which time he converted the entire island. Papeiha then went to Rarotonga and helped the missionaries do the same thing there. The interior of the church is unusual in that the altar is on one side rather than at one end. Worshippers from each village sit together during services, but visitors can take any vacancy during services at 10am on Sunday. An anchor suspended from the ceiling is a symbol of hope being a sure and steadfast anchor, as in Hebrews 6:19.

The volcanic part of Aitutaki is joined to the reef on the island's north end, and it was here that U.S. forces—with considerable help from the local residents—built the large airstrip during World War II. About 1,000 Americans were stationed at the strip, which was used as a refueling stop on the route between North America and New Zealand. Many present-day Aitutakians are reportedly the children and grandchildren of those U.S. sailors. The war ended before the Americans could complete a navigable channel from Arutanga to deep water. Today all cargo must be unloaded offshore and brought to the wharf by barge.

The late Sir Albert Henry was born and raised on Aitutaki, and the divided road to the wharf is named for him and his wife, Elizabeth (one lane for Sir Albert and one lane for Lady Elizabeth).

GETTING TO AITUTAKI

Air Rarotonga (© 22-888 on Rarotonga, or 31-888 on Aitutaki; www.air-raro.com) has several 50-minute flights a day from Monday to Saturday to and from Aitutaki. Regular round-trip fare is about NZ$368 ($166), but it drops to NZ$246 ($111) if you fly during off-peak times such as early morning or late afternoon. Air Rarotonga also has day trips to Aitutaki for about NZ$389 ($175), which includes round-trip airfare and a lagoon excursion with a barbecue lunch.

Air/hotel packages to Aitutaki can vary in price but always represent a savings over do-it-yourself arrangements, so check with Air Rarotonga or the travel agents in Avarua to see whether they have deals. **Island Hopper Vacations** (© 22-026), **Hugh Henry & Associates** (© 25-320), and **Stars Travel** (© 23-669) specialize in outer island trips.

Aitutaki's airport sits on the northeast corner of the island, and you will probably fly over the lagoon on the approach; you're likely to see more of the island from the left side of the aircraft.

GETTING AROUND AITUTAKI

The airport is about 7km (4 miles) from most hotels and guesthouses. Most hotels will pick up their guests, and the airline provides **airport transfers** for NZ$8 ($3.60) each way. Ask the hotel desk to reconfirm your return to Rarotonga. Air Rarotonga's office is in Ureia village, just north of Arutanga (© 31-888).

There is no **public transportation** system on Aitutaki.

All hotels and guest houses can arrange **car, scooter, and bike rentals,** or you can call **Rino's Rentals** (© 31-197) or **Swiss Rentals** (© 31-600), both north of Arutanga. Scooters go for NZ$20 ($9) per day, bikes for NZ$5 ($2.25) per day, cars for NZ$80 ($36) per day, and Jeeps for NZ$70 ($31.50) per day.

 FAST FACTS: Aitutaki

Currency Exchange Except at the hotels and guesthouses, don't rely on credit cards or traveler's checks. Westpac Bank's small agency here is open only Monday and Thursday, from 9:30am to 3pm.

Drugstores Some prescription drugs are available at the island's hospital near Arutanga. There is no private pharmacy on Aitutaki.

Emergencies In case of emergency, contact your hotel staff. The **police station** is in Arutanga (© **31-015**).

Healthcare Medical and dental treatment are available at the island's **hospital** (© **31-002**), near Arutanga.

Post Office The post office at Arutanga is open Monday to Friday 8am to 4pm.

Radio/Television The national radio stations can be received here, and a small privately owned TV station broadcasts the BBC world news several times a day.

Safety See "Fast Facts: Rarotonga," earlier in this chapter, for general warnings and precautions.

Telegrams/Fax The communications counter at the post office is open Monday to Friday from 8am to 4pm. It does not accept credit cards but you can use Kia Orana prepaid calling cards.

Visitor Information Cook Islands Tourism Corporation does not have an office on Aitutaki, so stop at its visitor center in Rarotonga before coming here—and bring at least one of the tourist publications that has a current map of Aitutaki.

Water Don't drink the tap water on Aitutaki unless you are sure it comes from a rainwater catchment. Ask first.

EXPLORING AITUTAKI

This is a very small island, perfect for seeing via scooter or bicycle. I describe the main attractions in the introduction to this section and in "A Little History," above, and they're all easy to find if you've brought a map with you from Rarotonga. You can tour the island in an open-air, Tahitian-style *le truck* with Mike Henry's **Island Tours** (© **31-339**) for NZ$15 ($6.75) per person.

LAGOON EXCURSIONS ★★★

The main reason to come to Aitutaki is to spend a day on the lagoon and one of the small islands out on the reef. The "standard" day trip begins at 9am and ends about 4pm. The boats spend the morning cruising and fishing on the lagoon. Midday is spent on one of the reef islands, where guests swim, snorkel, and sun while the crew cooks the day's catch and the local vegetables. The itinerary changes from day to day depending on the weather and the guests' desires.

A common destination is **Tapuaetai, or "One Foot," Island** and its adjacent sandbar, known as Nude Island (for its lack of foliage, not clothes). According to Teina Bishop, who runs one of the lagoon excursions, this tiny motu got its name when an ancient chief prohibited his subjects from fishing there on pain of death. One day the chief and his warriors saw two people fishing on the reef and gave chase. The two were a man and his young son. They ran onto the island, the boy carefully stepping in his father's footprints as they crossed the beach. The son then hid in the top of a coconut tree. The chief found the father, who said he was the only person fishing on the reef. After a search proved fruitless, the chief decided it must have been rocks he and his men saw on the reef. He then killed the father. Ever since, the island has been known as Tapuaetai (in the local dialect, *tapuae* means footprint, and *tai* is one).

Fun Fact Don't Get Burned

The boats all have canopies, but bring a hat and plenty of high-powered sunscreen on your Aitutaki lagoon outing—and use it! The sun out there on the water can blister you, even if you're under a canopy.

Those dark things that look like cucumbers dotting the bottom of the lagoon, by the way, are *bêches-de-mer* (sea slugs). Along with sandalwood, they brought many traders to the South Pacific during the 19th century because both brought high prices in China. Sea slugs are harmless—except in China, where they are considered to be an aphrodisiac.

Your hotel can book an excursion for you any day except Sunday with Teina Bishop and his **Bishop's Lagoon Cruises** (© 31-009; fax 31-493; bishop cruz@aitutaki.net.ck). He charges NZ$55 ($24.75) per person for the all-day excursions, including lunch, to both Maina and Tapuaetaiislands.

Kit Kat Cruises (© 31-418) charges NZ$45 ($20.25) for an excursion to Tapuaetai Island, where it has a bungalow that you can rent for NZ$150 ($67.50) per night.

If you come here on an Air Rarotonga day trip (see "Getting to Aitutaki," above), you'll cruise on a larger but slower boat equipped with a bar and toilet.

BOATING, GOLF, HIKING & SCUBA DIVING

BOATING   You can rent kayaks at **Samade Beach Bar & Restaurant** (© 31-526), on the lagoon (north) of the Aitutaki Pearl Beach Resort, for NZ$10 ($4.50) per hour to NZ$24 ($11) per day. Instead of going to the resort at the Y intersection, follow the dirt track to the west.

GOLF   Golfers who missed hitting the radio antennae and guy wires on the Rarotonga course can try again at the nine-hole course at the **Aitutaki Golf Club,** on the north end of the island between the airport and the sea. Balls hit onto the runway used to be playable, but broken clubs and increasing air traffic put an end to that. You can rent equipment at the clubhouse. The club has neither a phone nor regular hours, but the hotels and guesthouses can arrange rentals and tee times. Members are more likely to volunteer to mow the greens between May and August than during the wetter summer months.

HIKING   Hikers can take a trail to the top of Mount Maungapu, Aitutaki's highest point, at 124m (410 ft.). It begins about a mile north of the former Rapae Cottage Hotel (a well-known and often-used local landmark), across from the Paradise Cove Guest House. The trail starts under the power lines and follows them uphill for about a mile. The tall grass is sharp and can be soaked after a rain, but the track is usually well tramped and should be easy to follow. Nevertheless, wear trousers. The view from the top includes all of Aitutaki and its lagoon. Sunrise and sunset are the best times.

SCUBA DIVING   Divers can contact Neil Mitchell of **Aitutaki Scuba,** P.O. Box 40, Aitutaki (© 31-103; fax 31-310; scuba@aitutaki.net.ck), for underwater adventure over the edge of the reef. Neil operates from his home just south of the former Rapae Cottage Hotel. He charges NZ$85 ($38) per one-tank dive and will teach a 4-day PADI and NAUI certification course for NZ$550 ($248). Neil can also tell you how to go deep-sea fishing.

WHERE TO STAY ON AITUTAKI

A relative of Rarotonga's Pacific Resort & Villas (see "Where to Stay on Raro-tonga," above) was under construction during my recent visit. Check the resort's website (www.pacificresort.com) to see if it's up and running.

Aitutaki Lodges ⟨★⟩   Located on the east side of the island within a 10-minute drive of Arutanga, Wayne and Aileen Blake's immaculate A-frame-style bunga-lows are set into a hillside sloping to the edge of the lagoon. Although not as spa-cious as those at the Aitutaki Pearl Beach Resort or Are Tamanu (see below), they are the most secluded and private of any bungalows on Aitutaki. Quiet and pri-vate, each has a queen-size and a single bed, a ceiling fan, dinette booth, a kitch-enette, a show-only bathroom, and a porch that offers spectacular views across the lagoon to the islands and the reef (note, however, that the sliding doors do not have screens, and they directly face the morning sun). There is no beach here, and the lagoon in front of the hotel is too shallow for swimming, but the Blakes will customize lagoon cruises to fit your desires. There is a hilltop dining room and bar, from which guests have a grand view of the lagoon. Plans call for a swimming pool and several more luxuriously appointed units.

P.O. Box 70, Aitutaki (east side of island, between Vaipai and Tautu villages). ℂ **31-334**. Fax 31-333. www.ck/aitutakilodges. Rates include breakfast. 6 units. NZ$230 ($103.50). AE, MC, V. **Amenities:** 1 restau-rant (regional), 1 bar; bike and scooter rentals; activities desk; limited room service; babysitting; laundry service. *In room:* Minibar, coffeemaker, no phone.

Aitutaki Pearl Beach Resort ⟨★★★⟩   Owned and operated by the Pearl Beach hotels of French Polynesia, this is the top resort in the Cook Islands. It's reached by one-lane bridge across Ootu Pass to Akitua, a sandy islet south of the airport. The ocean surf breaks on one side of Akitua; on the other, the magnificent lagoon laps a white-sand beach, off which a channel has been dredged deep enough for swimming. The choice—and most expensive—units here are spacious overwater bungalows endowed with Polynesian charm. Although the lagoon off their decks is not as deep or as clear, they are on par with most overwater units in French Polynesia as far as amenities go. Their rears actually sit on land, and each has an outdoor shower in a private garden. Next best, and the farthest apart (and there-fore most private), are the deluxe beachfront bungalows, each of which has a raised sleeping area behind a sofa-equipped lounge that opens through sliding, wooden louvered doors to a lagoon-side deck. The remodeled versions of the more closely packed original bungalows that were here before Pearl Beach took over have solid walls on one side, which affords privacy at the expense of ventila-tion (air conditioners and ceiling fans calm the heat, but they operate only when you're in your room). Some of the original bungalows have been spruced up but not renovated; these have big window walls on two sides, which provide ventila-tion (if not privacy). Least expensive are three motel-style units attached to the central building, whose restaurant provides excellent international fare. Another restaurant and bar by the beach offers lunch and snacks.

P.O. Box 99, Aitutaki (on Akitua Island, 2km/1 mile south of airport, 9km5½ miles from Arutanga). ℂ and fax **20-234** for reservations, or 31-201. Fax 31-202. www.pearlhotels.com. 40 units. NZ$320 ($144) double; NZ$440–NZ$1,120 ($198–$505) bungalow. AE, DC, MC, V. **Amenities:** 2 restaurants (regional), 2 bars; out-door pool; watersports equipment rentals; bike rentals; activities desk; car-rental desk; limited room service (for overwater and deluxe bungalows); babysitting; laundry service. *In room:* A/C, minibar, coffeemaker, hair dryer, iron, safe (in overwater units).

Are Tamanu ⟨★★⟩   Aitutaki's second best hotel, Are Tamanu ("House of the Mahogany Tree") sits in a palm grove beside a powdery white-sand beach stretching along the entire northwestern shore of the island. Opened in 2001, it's the creation of Mike Henry, a grandson of the late Prime Minister Sir Albert Henry. The grounds are not nearly as spacious as those at the Aitutaki Pearl Beach, nor are the bungalows as private as those at Aitutaki Lodges, but the beach is better here, and a high fence around the property keeps uninvited guests away. Built of pine with tin roofs, the spacious guest bungalows face a courtyard that opens to the beach, where you'll find a snack cafe (Mike encourages his guests to dine out), a full bar, and a small pool surrounded by a deck with mahogany umbrella tables and chairs. Mahogany furniture also adorns the bungalows, each of which has queen-size bed, a full kitchen, and a shower only bathroom. All the bungalows are identical, except for the more private honeymoon unit, which has a larger veranda directly facing the beach (it's the top choice whether you're newly married or not). Mike can organize night snorkeling expeditions.

P.O. Box 59, Aitutaki (on west coast, 3km/2 miles from airport. (© **31-810.** Fax 32-816. www.aretamanu.com. 12 units. NZ$365–NZ$410 ($164–$185) bungalows. Rates include continental breakfast. AE, MC. V. Children under 12 not accepted. **Amenities:** 1 restaurant (snacks), 1 bar; small outdoor pool; free use of bikes; free use of snorkeling equipment; coin-op washers and dryers. In room: A/C, coffeemaker, hair dryer.

Maina Sunset Motel Although more inconveniently located than most other properties on Aitutaki, this little motel is on one of the prettiest stretches of beach on the island. Unfortunately, the lagoon here is extremely shallow, and an unattractive pier mars the fine view of Maina Island and glorious sunsets. The one-story, New Zealand–style motel units are built around a courtyard with a small pool. Four of the units have full kitchens and bedrooms that are separate from the living area; the others are like motel rooms with kitchens. All have verandas facing the pool, ceiling fans, and jalousie windows to permit ample cross-ventilation. A beachside dining room provides local-style breakfasts and dinners at moderate prices. The motel has its own supply of drinkable tap water.

P.O. Box 34, Aitutaki (on west coast, 6km/3¾ miles from airport, 1km/½ mile south of Arutanga). © **31-511.** Fax 31-611. solomon@oyster.net.ck. 13 units. NZ$165–NZ$195 ($74–$88) double. AE, DC, MC, V. **Amenities:** 1 restaurant (regional), 1 bar; small outdoor pool; bike rentals; laundry service. In room: Kitchen, coffeemaker, no phone.

Paradise Cove Guest House This hotel in a gorgeous beachside setting near Are Tamanu is the most popular hotel on Aitutaki among backpackers. Budget travelers are drawn to rooms in a European-style house (with communal kitchen and cold-water bathrooms) and to six tentlike huts—the only accommodations in the Cook Islands constructed of thatch and other natural materials. Low-slung thatch roofs over the huts cover just enough space for a bed and small refrigerator. They have electric lights and are fully screened. Far more comfortable are six new A-frame bungalows with kitchenettes, hot-water showers, and porches with great lagoon views.

P.O. Box 64, Aitutaki (1.5km/1 mile north of former Rapae Cottage Hotel). © **31-218.** Fax 31-293. mtl@aitutaki.net.ck. 17 units (11 with shared bathroom). NZ$35 ($15.75) double; NZ$50–NZ$150 ($22.50–$67.50) bungalow. MC, V. In room: Kitchen (in new bungalows), no phone.

Rino's Beach Bungalows The clean, comfortable New Zealand–style rooms and apartments here sit beside the beach north of Arutanga. The duplex apartments open to decks by the beach, and the standard rooms are in two-story buildings just behind them. Three larger apartments are on the other side of the road. All units have kitchens, table fans and walls of wood paneling and concrete blocks painted white, although some flowered fabrics lend an islandy touch.

P.O. Box 140, Aitutaki (Ureia Village, on west coast .5km north of Arutanga). ℂ **31-197**. Fax 31-559. rinos@aitutaki.net.ck. 11 units. NZ$111 ($50) double room; NZ$169–NZ$473 ($76–$213) apt. MC, V. **Amenities:** Coin-op washers and dryers. *In room:* Coffeemaker, no phone.

Sunny Beach Lodge   A palm grove sits between the beach and this modern, clean, and comfortable motel-style building. Entry to the spacious, U-shaped rooms is off a long porch equipped with plastic chairs. Each unit has a double bed, a dinette table and chairs, a full kitchen, and a shower-only bathroom. Big jalousie windows on the sides make the units on the ends of the buildings preferable.

P.O. Box 94, Aitutaki (Ureia Village, on west coast .5km north of Arutanga). ℂ and fax **31-446**. sunny beach@aitutaki.net.ck. 5 units. NZ$75 ($33.75) double. MC, V. *In room:* TV, coffeemaker, no phone.

WHERE TO DINE ON AITUTAKI

Some Aitutaki restaurants will come and get you at your hotel and take you back after dinner, so sure to ask about free transportation when you make reservations.

Coconut Crusher Bar 🗼 REGIONAL   Owner Teariki "Ricky" Devon makes this one of the most charming South Seas restaurant-bars I have ever been in. An entertainer who made his mark in Australia and Europe, Ricky and whomever he can round up take to the stage after dinner and entertain the rest of the night. "Ricky isn't a bar owner," said one guest. "He's a first-rate blues musician." You may soon forget the food—a buffet of salads and grilled local fish and New Zealand steaks—but you will long remember the music. Thursday is Island Night here, with a Cook Islands dance show after the buffet. Saturday sees a "backpacker's special" meal for NZ$12.50 ($5.50), and Sunday is roast night, for NZ$18.50 ($8.50).

Amuri, west coast. ℂ **31-283**. Reservations required. Main courses NZ$18.50–NZ$22.50 ($8.50–$10). MC, V. Mon–Wed and Fri–Sun 6–9pm (bar open till midnight), Thurs 6pm–2am.

Fletcher's Cocktail Bar & Grill REGIONAL   The Aitutaki Pearl Beach Resort had just taken over and renovated this joint, formerly known as Ralphie's Bar & Grill, during my recent visit. The resort's long-time manager, Steve Christian, renamed the place in honor of his direct ancestor, *Bounty* mutineer Fletcher Christian. Plans called for lunches of fish and chips, burgers, sandwiches, salads and other midday fare, and dinner was to see creative treatments of fresh fish, lobster, and other local foods.

Amuri, on west coast. ℂ **31-950**. Reservations recommended for dinner. Main courses NZ$17.50–NZ$28 ($7.75–$12.50). MC, V. Mon–Thurs and Sat 11am–9pm, Fri 11am–2am, Sun 6–9pm.

Samade Beach Bar & Restaurant *(Value* REGIONAL   On Ootu Beach, a 5-minute walk from the Aitutaki Pearl Beach Resort, this lagoon-side restaurant has a white-sand floor under a big tin roof lined with coconut mats to set the stage for hearty local-style meals. Indeed, this is a poor person's version of the famous Bloody Mary's Restaurant & Bar on Bora Bora. There's nothing fancy about the chow, but the parrot fish and other lagoon delicacies don't get any fresher, nor do the prices get more reasonable. The name Samade is from owner Sam Vakalahi and his Tongan wife, Adrian. They rent kayaks and other toys here during the day. Tuesday is island night here.

Ootu Beach, north of Aitutaki Pearl Beach Resort (turn west at the Y intersection). ℂ **31-526**. Reservations recommended. Main courses NZ$12.50–NZ$15 ($5.50–$6.75). No credit cards. Mon–Sat 11am–3pm and 7–9pm, Sun 1:30–5:30pm.

Tuano's Garden Cafe 🗼🗼 REGIONAL   This is not really a cafe but the home of Tuano and Sonja Raela, who organically grow the vegetables and fruits they use in their arrowroot bread, papaya soup, breadfruit chips, and fruit plates. They have no set menu, only daily specials culled from their plantation and the lagoon. I had a lunch of perfectly grilled mahimahi served with chilled cucumbers and mango chutney. Tuano and Sonja grow and roast their own coffee, which with an omelet and a slice of coconut cake makes for a tasty breakfast.

Amuri, on west coast. © 31-950. Reservations not accepted. Sandwiches and cakes NZ$4.50–NZ$7.50 ($2–$3.50); main courses NZ$12.50–NZ$15.50 ($5.50–$7). No credit cards. Mon–Sat 9am–6pm.

ISLAND NIGHTS

Island Night feasts and dance shows usually take place Tuesday at **Samade Beach Bar & Restaurant;** Thursday at the **Coconut Crusher Bar;** Friday at **Fletcher's Cocktail Bar & Grill** (see "Where to Dine on Aitutaki," above); and Saturday at the **Aitutaki Pearl Beach Resort** (see "Where to Stay on Aitutaki," above).

9

Introducing Fiji

If there is one thing every visitor remembers about Fiji, it's the enormous friendliness of the Fijian people. You'll see why as soon as you get off the plane, clear Customs and Immigration, and are greeted by a procession of smiling faces, all of them exclaiming an enthusiastic *"Bula!"* That one word—"health" in Fijian—expresses the warmest and most heartfelt welcome you'll receive anywhere.

This diverse country's great variety will also be immediately evident, for the taxi drivers who whisk you to your hotel are not Fijians of Melanesian heritage, but Indians whose ancestors migrated to Fiji from places like Calcutta and Madras. Now about 44% of the population, these "Indo-Fijians" have played major roles in making their country the most prosperous of the independent South Pacific island nations. But their presence has also resulted in racial animosity and political coups, most recently in 2000.

The political tensions exist primarily in the towns. In the countryside—and especially on Fiji's marvelous offshore islets—you'll find gorgeous white-sand beaches bordered by curving coconut palms, azure lagoons and colorful reefs offering world-class scuba diving and snorkeling, green mountains sweeping to the sea, and a tropical climate in which to enjoy it all.

For visitors, Fiji is an affordable paradise for every pocketbook. Its wide variety of accommodations ranges from deluxe resorts nestled in tropical gardens beside the beach to down-to-basics hostels that cater to the young and the young-at-heart. It has the largest and finest collection of remote, Robinson Crusoe–like offshore resorts in the entire South Pacific—if not the world. Regardless of where you stay, you are in for a memorable time. The Fijians will see to that.

1 Fiji Today

From their strategic position in the southwestern Pacific some 5,152km (3,200 miles) southwest of Honolulu and 3,156km (1,960 miles) northeast of Sydney, Fiji is the transportation and economic hub of the South Pacific islands. **Nadi International Airport** is the main connection point for flights going to the other island countries, and Fiji's capital city, **Suva,** is one of the region's prime shipping ports.

The archipelago forms a horseshoe around the reef-strewn **Koro Sea,** a body of water that's shallow enough for much of it to have been dry land during the last Ice Age some 18,000 years ago. There are more than 300 bits of land ranging in size from **Viti Levu** ("Big Fiji"), which is 10 times the size of Tahiti, to tiny atolls that barely break the surface of the sea. With a total land area of 11,300 square km (7,022 square miles), Fiji is slightly smaller than the state of New Jersey. Viti Levu has 4,171 of those square miles, giving it more dry land than all the islands of French Polynesia put together.

Viti Levu and **Vanua Levu,** the second-largest island, lie on the western edge of Fiji. The **Great Sea Reef** arches offshore between them and encloses a huge lagoon dotted with beautiful islands. Many scuba divers think of the coral reefs in this lagoon, the **Astrolabe Reef** south of Viti Levu, and the **Rainbow Reef** between Vanua Levu and Taveuni as the closest places on earth—or below it— to paradise.

GOVERNMENT   When the British granted independence to its former colony in 1970, they left behind a constitution that set up a parliamentary democracy. The majority Fijians retained control of most land, and the Indians were given a chance to gain political power. Indians outnumbered the indigenous Fijians by the mid-1980s, however, and in coalition with some of the more liberal Fijians, they formed a government in 1987. A month later the Fijian-dominated army stormed into parliament, staged the region's first military coup, and set up an interim government dominated by Fijians. In 1990 it promulgated a constitution giving the country a Fijian president and a parliament in which Fijians were guaranteed a majority and thus control of the government.

This arrangement lasted until 1998, when the country adopted a new multiracial constitution, creating a 65-member parliament of 19 Fijians, 17 Indians, 3 general electors (anyone who's not a Fijian or Indian), 1 Rotuman, and 25 open seats. The constitution also set up a relatively powerless senate chosen by the Great Council of Chiefs, whose members are Fiji's highest hereditary chiefs. In 1999 the country elected its first Indian prime minister. He was in office less than a year when a gang of thugs invaded parliament and held him and other parliamentarians hostage for 56 days. The army again stepped in an appointed an all-Fijian interim government. Fiji's supreme court reinstated the 1998 constitution, however, and in 2001 the Fijians won a solid majority in parliament and installed one of their own as prime minister. See "History 101," below.

ECONOMY   Despite its ups and downs in recent years, tourism is Fiji's largest and most profitable industry. Sugar has also had its problems but is still a close second to tourism. Grown primarily by Indian farmers, the cane is harvested between June and November and processed at five sugar mills operated by the government-owned Fiji Sugar Company. The Lautoka facility is the largest crushing mill in the Southern Hemisphere. There is no refining mill here, so most of the sugar served in Fiji is brown, not white.

The Emperor Gold Mine on northern Viti Levu makes an important contribution to the economy, as do fishing, copra, timber, garments, furniture, coffee (you'll get a rich, strong brew throughout the country), and other consumer goods produced by small manufacturers (the Colgate toothpaste you buy in Fiji is made here). Fiji is also a major transshipment point for goods destined for other South Pacific islands.

Even before the recent political instability hurt the economy, Fiji had a persistent problem with unemployment. More than half the population is under the age of 25, and there just aren't enough jobs being created for the youngsters coming into the workforce. By 2001, about 50% of all households were living below the official poverty line or just above it. As a consequence, the country has seen a marked increase in burglaries and other property crimes.

Thousands of Indo-Fijians fled the country in the aftermath of the political coups, resulting in a major brain drain (see "History 101," below). Many of them were highly skilled managers, doctors, nurses, teachers, and technical workers. Tourism dropped precipitously after the 2000 insurrection but had regained most of its business before the September 2001 terrorist attacks in the

Impressions

There is no part of Fiji which is not civilized, although bush natives prefer a more naked kind of life.
—James A. Michener, *Return to Paradise*, 1951

United States provided another setback. Further complicating matters, more than 1,200 land leases expired at the end of 2001, thus forcing many Indo-Fijian farmers off their sugar cane farms. Formerly self-sufficient, Fiji was experiencing a widening trade deficit in 2002.

2 History 101

The Dutch navigator Abel Tasman sighted some of the Fiji Islands in 1642 and 1643, and Capt. James Cook visited one of the southernmost islands in 1774, but Capt. William Bligh was the first European to sail through and plot the group. After the mutiny on HMS *Bounty* in April 1789, Bligh and his loyal crew sailed their longboat through Fiji on their way to safety in Indonesia. They passed Ovalau and sailed between Viti Levu and Vanua Levu. Large Fijian *druas* (speedy war canoes) gave chase near the Yasawas, but with some furious paddling, the help of a fortuitous squall, and the good luck to pass through a break in the Great Sea Reef, Bligh and his boat escaped to the open ocean.

Bligh's rough, handmade charts were amazingly accurate and shed the first European light on Fiji. For a while, Fiji was known as the Bligh Islands, and the passage between Viti Levu and Vanua Levu still is named Bligh Water.

The Tongans warned the Europeans who made their way west across the South Pacific about Fiji's ferocious cannibals, and the reports by Bligh and others of reef-strewn waters added to the dangerous reputation of the islands. Consequently, European penetration into Fiji was limited for many years to beach bums and convicts who escaped from the British penal colonies in Australia. There was a sandalwood rush between 1804 and

Dateline

- 1500 B.C. Polynesians arrive from the west.
- 500 B.C. Melanesians settle in Fiji, push Polynesians eastward.
- A.D. 1300–1600 Polynesians, especially Tongans, invade from the east.
- 1643 Abel Tasman sights some islands in Fiji.
- 1774 Capt. James Cook visits Vatoa.
- 1789 After the mutiny on the *Bounty*, Capt. William Bligh navigates his longboat through Fiji and is nearly captured by a war canoe.
- 1808 Swedish mercenary Charlie Savage arrives at Bau and supplies guns to Chief Tanoa in successful wars to conquer western Fiji.
- 1822 European settlement begins at Levuka.
- 1840 A U.S. exploring expedition under Capt. John Wilkes visits the islands.
- 1848 Prince Enele Ma'afu exerts Tongan control over eastern Fiji from outpost in Lau Group.
- 1849 U.S. Consul John Brown Williams's home is burned and looted during July 4 celebrations; he blames Cakobau, high chief of eastern Viti Levu.
- 1851 U.S. warship arrives, demands that Cakobau pay $5,000 for Williams's losses.
- 1853 Cakobau is installed as high chief of Bau, highest post in Fiji.
- 1855 United States claims against Cakobau grow to $40,000; U.S. warship arrives, claims some islands as mortgage.

continues

1813. Other traders arrived in the 1820s in search of *bêche-de-mer* (sea cucumber). This trade continued until the 1850s and had a lasting impact on Fiji because along with the traders came guns and whisky.

CAKOBAU RISES The traders and settlers established the first European-style town in Fiji at Levuka on Ovalau in the early 1820s, but for many years the real power lay on Bau, a tiny island just off the east coast of Viti Levu. With the help of a Swedish mercenary named Charlie Savage, who supplied the guns, High Chief Tanoa of Bau defeated several much larger confederations and extended his control over most of western Fiji. Bau's influence grew even more under Tanoa's son and successor, Cakobau, who rose to the height of power in the 1840s. Cakobau never ruled over all the islands, however, for Enele Ma'afu, a member of Tonga's royal family, moved to the Lau Group in 1848 and exerted control over eastern Fiji. Ma'afu brought along Wesleyan missionaries from Tonga and gave the Methodist church a foothold in Fiji.

Although Cakobau governed much of western Fiji, the chiefs under him continued to be powerful enough at the local level to make his control tenuous. The lesser chiefs, especially those in the mountains, also saw the Wesleyan missionaries as a threat to their power, and most of them refused to convert or even to allow the missionaries to establish outposts in their villages.

CAKOBAU FALLS Cakobau's slide from power is usually dated from July 4, 1849, when John Brown Williams, the American consul, celebrated the birth of his own nation. A cannon went off and started a fire that burned Williams's house. The Fijians promptly looted the burning building. Williams blamed Cakobau and demanded $5,000 in damages. Within 2 years an American warship showed

- 1858 Cakobau offers to cede Fiji to Britain for $40,000.
- 1862 Britain rejects Cakobau's offer.
- 1867 Unrest grows; Europeans crown Cakobau King of Bau; Rev. Thomas Baker is eaten.
- 1868 Polynesia Company buys Suva in exchange for paying Cakobau's debts.
- 1871 Europeans form central government at Levuka, make Cakobau king of Fiji.
- 1874 Cakobau's government collapses; he and other chiefs cede Fiji to Britain without price tag.
- 1875 Sir Arthur Gordon becomes first governor.
- 1879 First Indians arrive as indentured laborers.
- 1882 Capital moved from Levuka to Suva.
- 1916 Recruitment of indentured Indians ends.
- 1917 German Raider Count Felix von Luckner captured at Wakaya.
- 1917–18 Fijian soldiers support Allies in World War I.
- 1942–45 Fijians serve as scouts with Allied units in World War II; failure of Indians to volunteer angers Fijians.
- 1956 First Legislative Council established, with Ratu Sir Lala Sukuna as speaker.
- 1966 Fijian-dominated Alliance Party wins first elections.
- 1969 Key compromises pave way for constitution and independence. Provision guarantees Fijian land ownership.
- 1970 Fiji becomes independent; Alliance party leader Ratu Sir Kamisese Mara chosen as first prime minister.
- 1987 Fijian-Indian coalition wins majority; names Dr. Timoci Bavadra as prime minister with Indian-majority cabinet. Col. Sitiveni Rabuka leads two bloodless military coups, installs interim government.
- 1991 New constitution guaranteeing Fijian majority is promulgated.
- 1992 Rabuka's party wins election; he becomes prime minister.
- 1994 Second election cuts Rabuka's majority; he retains power in coalition with mixed-race general electors.
- 1995 Rabuka appoints constitutional review commission.

continues

up and demanded that Cakobau pay up. Other incidents followed, and U.S. claims against the chief totaled more than $40,000 by 1855. Another U.S. man-of-war arrived that year and claimed several islands in lieu of payment; the United States never followed up, but the ship forced Cakobau to sign a promissory note due in 2 years. In the late 1850s, with Ma'afu and his confederation of chiefs gaining power and disorder growing in western Fiji, Cakobau offered to cede the islands to Great Britain if Queen Victoria would pay the Americans. The British pondered his offer for 4 years and turned him down.

- 1998 Parliament adopts new constitution with 25 open seats holding balance of power.
- 1999 Labor union leader Mahendra Chaudhry is elected as Fiji's first Indian prime minister.
- 2000 Failed businessman George Speight leads insurrection, holds Chaudhry and other parliamentarians hostage. Military disbands constitution, appoints interim Fijian-led government. Army arrests Speight.
- 2001 Fiji's supreme court upholds 1998 constitution; Fijians win parliamentary majority in new elections, choose Fijian prime minister.

Cakobau worked a better deal when the Polynesia Company, an Australian planting and commercial enterprise, came to Fiji looking for suitable land after the price of cotton skyrocketed during the U.S. Civil War. Instead of offering his entire kingdom, Cakobau this time tendered only 200,000 acres of it. The Polynesia Company accepted, paid off the U.S. claims, and in 1870 landed Australian settlers on 23,000 acres of its land on Viti Levu, near a Fijian village known as Suva. The land was unsuitable for cotton and the climate was too wet for sugar, so the speculators sold their property to the government, which moved the capital there from Levuka in 1882.

THE BRITS TAKE OVER   The Polynesia Company's settlers were just a few of the several thousand European planters who came to Fiji in the 1860s and early 1870s. They bought land for plantations from the Fijians, sometimes fraudulently and often for whiskey and guns. Claims and counterclaims to land ownership followed, and with no legal mechanism to settle the disputes, Fiji was swept to the brink of race war. Things came to a head in 1870, when the bottom fell out of cotton prices, hurricanes destroyed the crops, and anarchy threatened. Within a year the Europeans established a national government at Levuka and named Cakobau king of Fiji. The situation continued to deteriorate, however, and 3 years later Cakobau was forced to cede the islands to Great Britain. This time there was no price tag attached, and the British accepted. The Deed of Cession was signed on October 10, 1874, at Nasovi village near Levuka.

Britain sent Sir Arthur Gordon as the new colony's first governor. As the Americans were later to do in their part of Samoa, he allowed the Fijian chiefs to govern their villages and districts as they had done before (they were not, however, allowed to engage in tribal warfare) and to advise him through a Great Council of Chiefs. He declared that native Fijian lands could not be sold, only leased. That decision has to this day helped to protect the Fijians, their land, and their customs, but it has helped fuel the bitter animosity on the part of the land-deprived Indians.

Gordon prohibited the planters from using Fijians as laborers (not that many of them had the slightest inclination to work for someone else). When the planters switched from profitless cotton to sugarcane in the early 1870s, Sir Arthur convinced them to import indentured servants from India. The first 463 East Indians arrived on May 14, 1879 (see "The Islanders," below).

Following Gordon's example, the British governed "Fiji for the Fijians"—and the European planters, of course—leaving the Indians to struggle for their civil rights. The government exercised jurisdiction over all Europeans in the colony and assigned district officers (the "D.O.s" of British colonial lore) to administer various geographic areas. There was a large gulf between the appointed civil servants sent from Britain and the locals.

PREPARING FOR INDEPENDENCE   One of the highest-ranking Fijian chiefs, Ratu Sir Lala Sukuna, rose to prominence after World War I. (*Ratu* means "chief" in Fijian.) Born of high chiefly lineage, Ratu Sukuna was educated at Oxford, served in World War I, and worked his way up through the colonial bureaucracy to the post of chairman of the Native Land Trust Board. Although dealing in that position primarily with disputes over land and chiefly titles, he used it as a platform to educate his people and to lay the foundation for the independent state of Fiji. As much as anyone, he was the father of modern, independent Fiji.

After the attack on Pearl Harbor began the Pacific war in 1941, the Allies turned Fiji into a vast training base. They built the airstrip at Nadi, and several coastal gun emplacements still stand along the coast.

Thousands of Fijians fought with great distinction as scouts and infantrymen in the Solomon Islands campaigns. Their knowledge of tropical jungles and their skill at the ambush made them much feared by the Japanese. The Fijians were, said one war correspondent, "death with velvet gloves."

Although many Indo-Fijians at first volunteered to join, they also demanded pay equal to that of the European members of the Fiji Military Forces. When the colonial administrators refused, they disbanded their platoon. Their military contribution was one officer and 70 enlisted men of a reserve transport section, and they were promised that they would not have to go overseas. Many Fijians to this day begrudge the Indo-Fijians for not doing more to aid the war effort.

THE BRITS QUIT   Ratu Sukuna continued to push the colony toward independence until his death in 1958, and although Fiji made halting steps in that direction during the 1960s, the road was rocky. The Indo-Fijians by then were highly organized, in both political parties and trade unions, and they objected to a constitution that would institutionalize Fijian control of the government and Fijian ownership of most of the new nation's land. Key compromises were made in 1969, however, and on October 10, 1970—exactly 96 years after Cakobau signed the Deed of Cession—the Dominion of Fiji became an independent member of the British Commonwealth of Nations.

Under the 1970 constitution, Fiji had a Westminster-style Parliament consisting of an elected House of Representatives and a Senate composed of Fijian chiefs. For the first 17 years of independence, the Fijians maintained a majority—albeit a tenuous one—in the House of Representatives and control of the government under the leadership of Ratu Sir Kamisese Mara, the country's first prime minister.

⸢ *Fun Fact*   **A Holy Meal**

The Viti Levu highlanders didn't take kindly to the Rev. Thomas Baker's attempt to convert them to Christianity in 1867. They killed him, threw his body into an earth oven, and made a meal of him.

> **Fun Fact** **The Count Confounded**
>
> In 1917 Count Felix von Luckner arrived at Wakaya Island off eastern Viti
> Levu in search of a replacement for his infamous World War I German
> raider, the *Seeadler,* which had gone aground in the Cook Islands after
> shelling Papeete on Tahiti. A local constable became suspicious of the
> armed foreigners and notified the district police inspector. Only Euro-
> peans—not Fijians or Indians—could use firearms, so the inspector took a
> band of unarmed Fijians to Wakaya in a small cattle trading boat. Think-
> ing he was up against a much larger armed force, von Luckner unwit-
> tingly surrendered.

Then, in a general election held in April 1987, a coalition of Indo-Fijians and
liberal Fijians voted Ratu Mara and his Alliance party out of power. Dr. Timoci
Bavadra, a Fijian, took over as prime minister, but his cabinet was composed of
more Indians than Fijians. Hard feelings immediately flared between some
Fijians and Indians.

RAMBO STAGES A COUP   Within little more than a month of the election,
members of the predominantly Fijian army stormed into Parliament and
arrested Dr. Bavadra and his cabinet. It was the South Pacific's first military
coup, and although peaceful, it took nearly everyone by complete surprise.

The coup leader was Col. Sitiveni Rabuka (pronounced "Rambuka"), whom
local wags quickly nicknamed Rambo. A Sandhurst-trained career soldier, the
38-year-old Rabuka was third in command of the army. A Fijian of nonchiefly
lineage, he immediately became a hero to his "commoner" fellow Fijians.
Rabuka at first installed a caretaker government, but in September 1987 he
staged another bloodless coup. A few weeks later he abrogated the 1970 constitution, declared Fiji to be an independent republic, and set up a new interim
government with himself as minister of home affairs and army commander.

In 1990 the interim government promulgated a new constitution guaranteeing Fijians a parliamentary majority—and rankling the Indians. Rabuka's pro-
Fijian party won the initial election, but he barely hung onto power in fresh
elections in 1994 by forming a coalition with the European, Chinese, and
mixed-race general-elector parliamentarians.

YET ANOTHER COUP   Rabuka also appointed a three-person Constitutional Review Commission, which proposed a new constitution that parliament
adopted in 1998. It created a parliamentary house of 65 seats, with 19 held by
Fijians, 17 by Indians, 3 by general-electors, 1 by a Rotuman, and 25 open to
all races.

A year later, with support from many Fijians who were disgruntled with their
own leaders because of the country's poor economy, rising crime, and deterio-
rating roads, labor union leader Mahendra Chaudhry's party won an outright
majority of parliament, and he became Fiji's first Indian prime minister.
Chaudhry had been minister of finance in the Bavadra government toppled by
Rabuka's coup in 1987.

Chaudhry quickly appointed several well-known Fijians to his cabinet. The
revered Ratu Mara encouraged his fellow Fijians to support the new administration. It didn't work, for in May 2000 a disgruntled Fijian businessman named
George Speight led a gang of armed henchmen into parliament. Demanding the

appointment of an all-Fijian government, they held Chaudhry and several members of parliament hostage for the next 56 days. While negotiating with Speight, the army disbanded the constitution and appointed an interim government headed by Laisenia Qarase, a Fijian banker. Speight released his hostages after being promised amnesty, but the army arrested him 2 weeks later and charged him with treason. He was due to be tried in 2002.

Fiji's supreme court then ruled that the 1998 constitution was still in effect and ordered fresh parliamentary elections to be held in 2001. Under the watchful eye of international observers, the Fijians won an outright majority, and caretaker leader Qarase became the legal prime minister. Chaudhry also was returned to parliament, but he refused to cooperate with Qarase in forming a coalition government.

Despite being held prisoner on Nukulau Island off Suva, Speight also won a seat. The army would not allow him to attend the sessions, however, and he was therefore expelled from parliament.

3 The Islanders

Fiji's population was officially 834,494 in 2000. Indigenous Fijians made up 51%, Indo-Fijians 44%, and other Pacific islanders, Chinese, and Europeans the other 5%. Thanks to a high Fijian birth rate, the overall population has been rising slightly despite the country's losing thousands of Indo-Fijians since the 1987 military coups.

It's difficult to imagine peoples of two more contrasting cultures living side by side. "Fijians generally perceive Indians as mean and stingy, crafty and demanding to the extent of being considered greedy, inconsiderate and grasping, uncooperative, egotistic, and calculating," wrote Professor Asesela Ravuvu of the University of the South Pacific. On the other hand, he said, Indians see Fijians as "jungalis," still living on the land, which they will not sell, poor, backward, naive, and foolish.

Given that these attitudes are not likely to change anytime soon, it is remarkable that Fijians and Indo-Fijians actually manage to coexist. Politically correct Americans may take offense at some things they could hear said in Fiji because racial distinctions are a fact of life here.

From a visitor's standpoint, the famously friendly Fijians give the country its laid-back South Seas charm while at the same time providing relatively good service at the hotels. For their part, the Indo-Fijians make this an easy country to visit by providing excellent maintenance of facilities and efficient and inexpensive services, such as transportation.

The 1998 constitution officially makes everyone here, regardless of his or her race, a "Fiji Islander."

THE FIJIANS

When meeting and talking to the smiling Fijians, it's difficult to imagine that less than a century ago their ancestors were among the world's most ferocious cannibals. Today the only vestiges of this past are the four-pronged wooden cannibal forks sold in handcraft shops (they make interesting conversation pieces when used at home to serve hors d'oeuvres). Yet in the early 1800s, the Fijians were so fierce that Europeans were slow to settle in the islands for fear of literally being turned into a meal—perhaps even being eaten alive. More than 100 white-skinned individuals ended up with their skulls smashed and their bodies baked in an earth oven. "One man actually stood by my side and ate the very eyes out of

Impressions

Many of the missionaries were eaten, leading an irreverent planter to suggest that they triumphed by infiltration.
—James A. Michener, *Return to Paradise,* 1951

a roasted skull he had, saying, '*Venaca, venaca,*' that is, very good," wrote William Speiden, the purser on the U.S. exploring expedition that charted Fiji in 1840.

Cannibalism was an important ritualistic institution among the Fijians, the indigenous Melanesian people who came from the west and began settling in Fiji around 500 B.C. Over time they replaced the Polynesians, whose ancestors had arrived some 1,000 years beforehand, but not before adopting much of Polynesian culture and intermarrying enough to give many Fijians lighter skin than that of most other Melanesians, especially in the islands of eastern Fiji near the Polynesian Kingdom of Tonga. (This is less the case in the west and among the hill dwellers, whose ancestors had less contact with Polynesians in ancient times.) Similar differences occur in terms of culture. For example, whereas Melanesians traditionally pick their chiefs by popular consensus, Fijian chiefs hold titles by heredity, in the Polynesian fashion.

FIJIAN SOCIETY

Ancient Fijian society was organized by tribes, each with its own language, and subdivided into clans of specialists, such as canoe builders, fishermen, and farmers. Powerful chiefs ruled each tribe and constantly warred with their neighbors, usually with brutal vengeance. Captured enemy children were hung by the feet from the rigging of the winners' canoes, and new buildings were sometimes consecrated by burying live adult prisoners in holes dug for the support posts. The ultimate insult, however, was to eat the enemy's flesh. Victorious chiefs were even said to cook and nibble on the fingers or tongues of the vanquished, relishing each bite while the victims watched in agony.

Fijians wouldn't dream of doing anything like that today, of course, but they have managed to retain much of their old lifestyle and customs, including their hereditary system of chiefs and social status. Most Fijians still live in small villages along the coast and riverbanks or in the hills, and you will see many traditional thatch *bures,* or houses, scattered in the countryside away from the main roads. Members of each tribe cultivate and grow food crops in small "bush gardens" on plots of communally owned native land assigned to their families. More than 80% of the land in Fiji is owned by Fijians.

A majority of Fijians are Methodists today, their forebears having been converted by puritanical Wesleyan missionaries who came to the islands in the 19th century. Along with the Great Council of Chiefs, the Methodist Church is a powerful political force in the country.

FIJIAN CULTURE

THE TABUA   The highest symbol of respect among Fijians is the tooth of the sperm whale, known as a *tabua* (pronounced "tambua"). Like large mother-of-pearl shells used in other parts of Melanesia, tabuas in ancient times played a role similar to that of money in modern society and still have various ceremonial uses. They are presented to chiefs as a sign of respect, given as gifts to arrange marriages, offered to friends to show sympathy after the death of a family member, and used as a means to seal a contract or another agreement. It is illegal to

A Bowl of Grog

Known as *kava* elsewhere in the South Pacific, the slightly narcotic drink Fijians call *yaqona* ("yong-gona") rivals the potent Fiji Bitter beer as the national drink. You will likely have half a coconut shell full of "grog" offered—if not shoved in your face—beginning at your hotel's reception desk. Fiji has more "grog shops" than bars.

And thanks to the promotion of *kavalactone*, the active ingredient, as a health-food answer to stress and insomnia in the United States and elsewhere, growing the root has become an important part of the economy here and elsewhere in the South Pacific. Fears have surfaced recently, however, that the health-food variety could be linked to liver disease. If that is true of the freshly ground variety used here, then there are very few healthy livers in Fiji!

Yaqona has always played an important ceremonial role in Fijian life. No significant occasion takes place without it, and a *sevusevu* (welcoming) ceremony is usually held for tour groups visiting Fijian villages. Mats are placed on the floor, the participants gather around in a circle, and the yaqona roots are mixed with water and strained through coconut husks into a large carved wooden bowl, called a *tanoa*.

The ranking chief sits next to the *tanoa* during the welcoming ceremony. He extends in the direction of the guest of honor a cowrie shell attached to one leg of the bowl by a cord of woven coconut fiber. It's extremely impolite to cross the plane of the cord once it has been extended.

The guest of honor (in this case your tour guide) then offers a gift to the village (a kilogram or two of dried grog roots will do these days) and makes a speech explaining the purpose of his visit. The chief then passes the first cup of yaqona to the guest of honor, who claps once, takes the cup in both hands, and gulps down the entire cup of sawdust-tasting liquid in one swallow. Everyone else then claps three times.

Next, each chief drinks a cup, clapping once before bolting it down. Again, everyone else claps three times after each cup is drained. Except for the clapping and formal speeches, everyone remains silent throughout the ceremony, a tradition easily understood considering kava's numbing effect on the lips and tongue.

export a tabua out of Fiji, and even if you did, the international conventions on endangered species prohibit your bringing them into the United States and most other Western countries.

FIRE WALKING   Legend says that a Fijian god once repaid a favor to a warrior on Beqa island by giving him the ability to walk unharmed on fire. His descendants, all members of the Sawau tribe on Beqa, still walk across stones heated to white-hot by a bonfire—but usually for the entertainment of tourists at the hotels rather than for a particular religious purpose.

Traditionally, the participants—all male—had to abstain from women and coconuts for 2 weeks before the ceremony. If they partook of either, they would suffer burns to their feet. Naturally a priest (some would call him a witch doctor) would recite certain incantations to make sure the coals were hot and the gods were at bay and not angry enough to scorch the soles.

Today's fire walking is a bit touristy but still worth seeing. If you don't believe the stones are hot, go ahead and touch one of them—but do it gingerly.

Some Indians in Fiji engage in fire walking, but it's strictly for religious purposes.

ETIQUETTE Fijian villages are easy to visit, but keep in mind that to the people who live in them, the entire village—not just the individual houses—is home. In your native land, you wouldn't walk into a stranger's living room without being invited, so find someone and ask permission before traipsing into a Fijian village. The Fijians are highly accommodating people, and it's unlikely they will say no; in fact, they may ask you to stay for a meal or perhaps stage a small yaqona ceremony in your honor. They are very tied to tradition, however, so ask first.

If you are invited to stay or eat in the village, a small gift to the chief is appropriate; F$10 ($4.50) per person or a handful of dried kava root from the local market will do. The gift should be given to the chief or highest-ranking person present to accept it. Sometimes it helps to explain that it is a gift to the village and not payment for services rendered, especially if it's money you're giving.

Only chiefs are allowed to wear hats and sunglasses in Fijian villages, so it's good manners for visitors to take theirs off. Shoulders must be covered at all times. Fijians go barefoot and walk slightly stooped in their bures. Men sit cross-legged on the floor; women sit with their legs to the side. They don't point at one another with hands, fingers, or feet, nor do they touch each other's heads or hair. They greet each other and strangers with a big smile and a sincere "*Bula.*"

THE INDO-FIJIANS

The *Leonidas* was a labor transport ship that arrived at Levuka from Calcutta on May 14, 1879, and landed 463 indentured servants destined to work the sugar cane fields.

As more than 60,000 Indians would do over the next 37 years, these first immigrants signed agreements (*girmits,* they called them) requiring that they work in Fiji for 5 years; they would be free to return to India after 5 more years. Most of them labored in the cane fields for the initial term of their *girmits,* living in "coolie lines" of squalid shacks hardly better than the poverty-stricken conditions most left behind in India. After the initial 5 years, however, they were free to seek work on their own. Many leased small plots of land from the Fijians and began planting sugarcane or raising cattle on their own. To this day most of Fiji's sugar crop, the country's most important agricultural export, is produced on small leased plots rather than on large plantations. Other Indo-Fijians went into business in the growing cities and towns and, joined in the early 1900s by an influx of business-oriented Indians, thereby founded Fiji's modern merchant and professional classes.

Impressions

It is doubtful if anyone but an Indian can dislike Fijians. . . . They are one of the happiest peoples on earth and laugh constantly. Their joy in things is infectious; they love practical jokes, and in warfare they are without fear.
—James A. Michener, *Return to Paradise,* 1951

Moments **Meeting the Friendly Fijians**

The indigenous Fijians are justly renowned for their friendliness to strangers, and many Indo-Fijians are as well educated and informed as anyone in the South Pacific. Together, these two peoples are fun to meet, whether it be over a hotel desk or while riding with them in one of their fume-belching buses.

Of the immigrants who came from India between 1879 and 1916, when the indenturing system ended, some 85% were Hindus, 14% were Muslims, and the remaining 1% were Sikhs and Christians. Fiji offered these adventurers far more opportunities than they would have had in caste-controlled India. In fact, the caste system was scrapped very quickly by the Hindus in Fiji, and, for the most part, the violent relations between Hindus and Muslims that racked India were put aside on the islands.

Only a small minority of the Indo-Fijians went home after their *girmits* expired. They tended then—as now—to live in the towns and villages, and in the "Sugar Belt" along the drier north and west coasts of Viti Levu and Vanua Levu. Hindu and Sikh temples and Muslim mosques abound in these areas, and places such as Ba and Tavua look like small towns on the Indian subcontinent. On the southern coasts and in the mountains, however, the population is overwhelmingly Fijian.

4 Languages

Fiji has three official languages. To greatly oversimplify the situation, the Fijians speak Fijian, the Indians speak Hindi, and they speak English to each other. Schoolchildren are taught in their native language until they are proficient in English, which thereafter is the medium of instruction. This means that English-speaking visitors have little trouble getting around and enjoying the country.

There is one problem for the uninitiated, however: the unusual pronunciation of Fijian names. For instance, Cakobau is pronounced "Thak-*om*-bau." There are many other names of people and places that are equally or even more confusing.

FIJIAN

As is the case throughout Melanesia, many native languages are spoken in the islands of Fiji, some of them similar, others quite different. Fijians still speak a variety of dialects in their villages, but the official form of Fijian—and the version taught in the schools—is based on the language of Bau, the small island that came to dominate western Fiji during the 19th century.

Fijian is similar to the Polynesian languages spoken in Tahiti, the Cook Islands, Samoa, and Tonga in that it uses vowel sounds similar to those in Latin, French, Italian, and Spanish: *a* as in b*a*d, *e* as in s*ay*, *i* as in b*ee*, *o* as in g*o*, and *u* as in kangar*oo*.

Some Fijian consonants, however, sound very different from their counterparts in English, Latin, or any other language. In devising a written form of Fijian, the early Wesleyan missionaries decided to use some familiar Roman consonants in unfamiliar ways. It would have been easier for English speakers to read Fijian had the missionaries used a combination of consonants—*th*, for example—for the Fijian sounds. Their main purpose, however, was to teach Fijians to read and write their own language. Because the Fijians separate all consonant sounds with vowels, writing two consonants together confused them.

The missionaries came up with the following usage: *b* sounds like *mb* (as in reme*mb*er), *c* sounds like *th* (as in *th*at), *d* sounds like *nd* (as in Su*nd*ay), *g* sounds like *ng* (as in si*ng*er), and *q* sounds like *ng* + *g* (as in fi*ng*er).

Here are some Fijian names with their unusual pronunciations:

Ba	mBah	**Labasa**	Lam-*ba*-sa
Bau	mBau	**Mamanuca**	Ma-ma-*nu*-tha
Beqa	*mBeng*-ga	**Nadi**	*Nan*-di
Buca	*mBu*-tha	**Tabua**	*Tam*-bua
Cakobau	Thack-*om*-bau	**Toberua**	Tom-*bay*-rua
Korotogo	Ko-ro-*ton*-go	**Tubakula**	Toom-ba-*ku*-la

You are likely to hear these Fijian words and phrases used during your stay:

English	Fijian	Pronunciation
hello	**bula**	*boo*-lah
hello (formal)	**ni sa bula**	nee sahm *boo*-lah
good morning	**ni sa yadra**	nee sah *yand*-rah
good night	**ni sa moce**	nee sah *mo*-thay
thank you	**vinaka**	vee-*nah*-kah
thank you very much	**vinaka vaka levu**	vee-n*ah*-kah *vah*-ka *lay*-voo
house/bungalow	**bure**	*boo*-ray
tapa cloth	**masi**	*mah*-see
sarong	**sulu**	*sue*-loo

FIJI HINDI

The common everyday language spoken among the Indo-Fijians is a tongue peculiar to Fiji. Although it is based on Hindustani, it is very different from that language as spoken in India. The Indo-Fijians, in fact, refer to it as *Fiji Bat* ("Fiji talk") because it grew out of the need for a common language among the immigrants who came from various parts of the subcontinent and spoke some of the many languages and dialects found in India and Pakistan. Thus it includes words from Hindi, Urdu, Tamil Nadu, a variety of Indian dialects, and even English and Fijian.

Unlike the Fijians, who are likely to greet you with "*Bula*," the Indo-Fijians invariably address visitors in English. If you want to impress them, try these phrases in Fiji Hindi:

English	Fiji Hindi	Pronunciation
hello and good-bye	**namaste**	na-*mas*-tay
how are you?	**kaise?**	ka-*ee*-say
good	**accha**	*ach*-cha
I'm okay	**Thik hai**	teak high
right or okay	**rait**	right

5 Planning Your Trip to Fiji

Given the size and diversity of the country, any trip to Fiji requires careful planning to avoid disappointment. You could spend your entire vacation in Nadi, and although the tourism industry provides a host of activities to keep you busy

---

Impressions

The question of what to do with these clever Indians of Fiji is the most acute problem in the Pacific today. Within ten years it will become a world concern.

—James A. Michener, *Return to Paradise,* 1951

---

there, you would miss the best parts of Fiji. After all, this is a country of more than 300 gorgeous islands, and not to experience more than one is a mistake. By and large, the main island of Viti Levu does not have the best beaches in Fiji, and where it does have good sands, the reef offshore is more walkable than swimmable, especially at low tide. In other words, look beyond Nadi for good beaches and the best diving.

FIJI'S REGIONS IN BRIEF

From a tourist's standpoint, Fiji is divided into several regions, each with its own special characteristics and appeal. Here's what each has to offer.

ON VITI LEVU ISLAND

NADI   Most visitors arrive at Nadi International Airport, a modern facility located among sugar cane fields on Viti Levu's dry western side. Known collectively as **Nadi,** this area is the focal point of much of Fiji's tourism industry, and it's where most tourists on package deals spend their time. There are a variety of hotels between the airport and hot, dusty, predominately Indian **Nadi Town,** whose main industry is tourism and where duty-free, souvenir, and handcraft merchants wait to part you from your dollars. None of the airport hotels are on the beach, and even at the Sheraton Fiji and Sheraton Royal Denarau Resort, the area's two large resorts, coastal mangrove forests make the beaches gray and the water offshore murky. There are many things to do in Nadi, but knowledgeable visitors with more than 1 or 2 days to spend in Fiji will consider it a transit stopover on the way to someplace else.

THE CORAL COAST   The **Queen's Road** runs around the south coast of Viti Levu through the resort area called the **Coral Coast.** Here you'll find comfortable hotels, luxury resorts, and fire-walking Fijians, but the beaches lead into very shallow lagoons, and most visitors staying on the "The Coast" these days are tourists on packages. It's still a good choice for anyone who wants on-the-beach resort living while being able to conveniently see some of the country. Offshore, the island of **Vatulele** has one of the world's finest small resorts. Farther south, **Kadavu** and its Astrolabe Reef hail scuba divers.

PACIFIC HARBOUR   About 48km (30 miles) west of Suva, Pacific Harbour was developed in the early 1970s as a resort complete with golf course, private residences, shopping center, cultural center, and a seaside hotel. Because this area is in Viti Levu's rain belt, the project never reached its full potential. Today Pacific Harbour is known primarily for excellent deep-sea fishing and the South Pacific's finest golf course. It's also the jumping-off point for the **Beqa Lagoon,** which attracts divers from around the planet.

NORTHERN VITI LEVU   An alternative driving route to Suva, the **King's Road** runs from Lautoka through the Sugar Belt of northern Viti Levu, passing through the predominately Indian towns of Ba and Tavua to **Rakiraki,** a Fijian village near the island's northernmost point and site of one of the country's few remaining colonial-era hotels. Jagged green mountains lend a gorgeous back-drop to the shoreline along the Rakiraki coast. Offshore, **Nananu-I-Ra Island** beckons backpackers.

All of the King's Road except about 50km (31 miles) through the central mountains is paved. East of Rakiraki, it turns into deep, mountain-bounded **Viti Levu Bay,** one of the most beautiful parts of Fiji. From the head of the bay, the road then twists and turns its way through the mountains, following the Wainbuka River until it emerges near the east coast at Korovou. A left turn there takes you to Natovi Wharf; and a right, to Suva. In other words, it's possible to drive or take buses all the way around Viti Levu via the Queen's and King's roads.

SUVA   The Queen's Road goes on to **Suva** (pop. 85,000), Fiji's busy capital and one of the South Pacific's most cosmopolitan cities. Steamy Suva houses a fascinating mix of atmospheres and cultures. Remnants of Fiji's century as a British possession and the presence of so many Indians give the town a certain air of the colonial "Raj"—as if this were Agra or Bombay, not the boundary between Polynesia and Melanesia. On the other hand, Suva has modern high-rise buildings and lives at as fast a pace as can be found in the South Pacific west of Tahiti; this is no surprise because in many respects it's the bustling economic center of the region. The streets are filled with a melting-pot blend of Indians, Chinese, Fijians, other South Pacific islanders, "Europeans" (a term used in Fiji to mean persons of white skin, regardless of geographic origin), and individuals of mixed race.

JUST OFF VITI LEVU
THE MAMANUCA ISLANDS   Beckoning off Nadi, the **Mamanuca Islands** offer day cruises and several offshore resorts of various sizes that appeal to a broad spectrum, from swinging singles to quieter couples and families. Generally speaking, they are in the driest part of Fiji, which means sunshine most of the time. Some are flat atolls so small you can walk around them in 5 minutes. Others are on hilly, grassy islands reminiscent of the Virgin Islands in the Caribbean. They are relatively close together, and most offer excursions to the others. They also are close to Nadi, so you don't have to spend much extra money or time to get there.

THE YASAWA ISLANDS   Some visitors join up with **Blue Lagoon Cruises** at its base in **Lautoka,** Fiji's second-largest city and its prime sugar-milling center. The cruises spend several days or a week in the **Yasawas,** a chain of gorgeous and unspoiled islands that shoot off north of the Mamanucas. Like Moorea and Bora Bora in French Polynesia, the Yasawas are often used as movie sets. Two versions of *The Blue Lagoon* were filmed here, the latest starring Brooke Shields as the castaway schoolgirl. The Yasawas have two deluxe resorts and several fine new establishments that cater to backpackers.

LEVUKA & OVALAU   Off Suva, the picturesque island of **Ovalau** is home to the historic town of **Levuka,** which has changed little in appearance since its days as a boisterous whaling port and the first capital of a united Fiji in the 1800s. Few places in the South Pacific have retained their frontier facade as has this living museum.

NORTHERN FIJI
Vanua Levu, Taveuni, and their nearby islands are known locally as "The North" because they comprise Fiji's Northern Province. Over on Vanua Levu, Fiji's

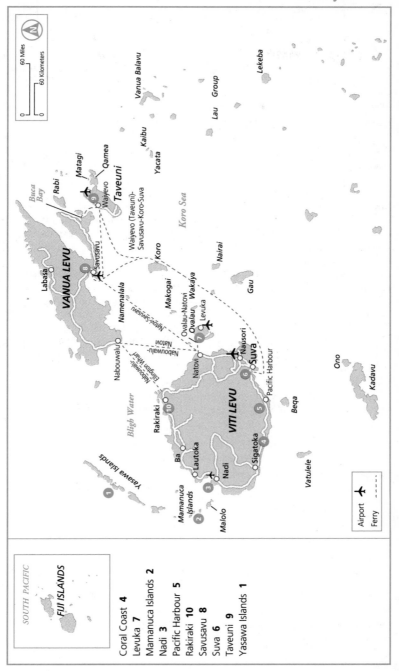

Coral Coast **4**
Levuka **7**
Mamanuca Islands **2**
Nadi **3**
Pacific Harbour **5**
Rakiraki **10**
Savusavu **8**
Suva **6**
Taveuni **9**
Yasawa Islands **1**

SOUTH PACIFIC

FIJI ISLANDS

Airport
Ferry

second largest island, a little town with the exotic name **Savusavu** lies nestled in one of the region's most protected deep-water bays. Savusavu and the "Garden Isle" of **Taveuni** are throwbacks to the old South Pacific, a land of copra plantations and small Fijian villages tucked away in the bush. Travelers looking for a do-it-yourself soft adventure trip into the past can take a local bus across Vanua Levu to Savusavu and a ferry on to Taveuni. Both Savusavu and Taveuni have excellent places to stay, and there are fine resorts off Vanua Levu and near Taveuni's north coast on **Matagi** and **Qamea.**

STAYING AT ONE OF FIJI'S OFFSHORE RESORTS

Fiji has one of the world's finest collections of offshore resorts, small establishments with islands all to themselves. They all have lovely beach settings and modern facilities, and without exception they are excellent places to get away from it all. The major drawback of any offshore resort, however, is that you've done just that. You won't see much of Fiji while you're basking in the sun on a tiny rock some 40km (25 miles) offshore. Consider them for what they have to offer, but not as bases from which to explore the country. I have included the offshore resorts in the following chapters, along with their nearest large islands. If you decide to stay at one of them, I suggest you read all of chapters 10 and 11 before making your choice of resort.

Pay close attention to what I say about the owners and managers, and especially the styles with which they run their operations. For example, if you don't enjoy getting to know your fellow guests at sometimes raucous dinner parties, you might not like Vatulele Island or Turtle Island resorts, but you might love The Wakaya Club or Yasawa Island Resort. If you like a large establishment with a lively, Club Med–like ambience, you might prefer Mana Island and Plantation Island resorts. Many other resorts offer peace, quiet, and few fellow guests. If you are taking the kids, Jean-Michel Cousteau Fiji Islands Resort and Matangi Island Resort are two of the best small family resorts in the South Pacific, but nearby Qamea Beach Club doesn't allow kids under 13. In other words, choosing carefully could mean the difference in a miserable week or a slice of heaven.

DIVING IN FIJI

Fiji is justly famous among divers as being the "Soft Coral Capital of the World" because of its enormous number and variety of colorful soft corals. These species grow well where moderate to heavy currents keep them fed. In turn, the corals attract a host of fish. As one example, more than 35 species of angelfish and butterfly fish swim in these waters.

Several of Fiji's most popular dive destinations are in Northern Fiji. The colorful **Rainbow Reef** and **Great White Wall** are both on Vanua Levu's barrier reef but within a few miles of Taveuni. The Great White Wall is covered from between 23m and 60m (75 ft. and 200 ft.) deep with pale lavender corals, which appear almost snow-white underwater. Near Qamea and Matagi, off Taveuni, are the appropriately named **Purple Wall,** a straight drop from 9m to 24m (30 ft.–80 ft.), and Mariah's Cove, a small wall as colorful as the Rainbow Reef. Also in the north, **Magic Mountain** on the Namena barrier reef around Moody's Namena has hard corals on top and soft ones on the sides, which attract an enormous number of small fish and their predators.

Another popular site is **Beqa Lagoon,** easily reached by boat from Pacific Harbour, about 48km (30 miles) west of Suva. The soft corals in Beqa's **Frigate Passage** seem to fall over one another, and **Side Streets** has unusual orange coral.

The relatively undeveloped island of Kadavu is surrounded by the famous **Astrolabe Reef,** where holes in the coral attract volumes of fish and other sea life.

Even the heavily visited **Mamanuca Islands** off Nadi have their share of good sites, including **The Pinnacle,** a coral head rising 18m (60 ft.) from the lagoon floor, and a W-shaped protrusion from the outer reef. A drawback for some divers is that they don't have the Mamanuca sites all to themselves.

All but a few resorts in Fiji have dive operations on site, as will be pointed out in the following chapters. Many of them have contacts in North America.

One of the best ways to dive a lot of reefs in Fiji, and especially the out-of-the-way sites, is on a live-aboard dive boat.

The *Princess II,* P.O. Box 9082, Nadi Airport (© **800/576-7327;** www.princessii.com), is owned and operated by Selwyn Douglas, brother of Noel Douglas at Matangi Island Resort (see "Resorts Offshore from Taveuni" in chapter 11). This 26m (85-ft.) luxury vessel does 6-night cruises from Ellington Wharf to the colorful reefs off Taveuni, with dives off northern Viti Levu, Wakaya, and Namena along the way. It can accommodate 12 divers in 6 cabins, each with its own air-conditioning unit and bathroom. The main lounge has a bar, sound system, and video players, and there's a darkroom on board. Rates range from about US$275 per person per day, including meals, diving, weights and tanks (bring your own gear).

Even more luxurious, the *Fiji Aggressor* makes weekly voyages from Levuka to the reefs off eastern Viti Levu. It is equipped with photo lab, video, and high-speed canopied dive boat. You'll dive for 5½ days out of the week, making at least two dives per day. Rates are about US$2,500 per person, including accommodations, meals, snacks, and unlimited diving, but not equipment. For information and reservations, contact **Aggressor Fleet** (© **800/348-2628** or 985/385-2628; fax 985/384-0817; www.aggressor.com).

SUGGESTED ITINERARIES

The following suggested itineraries are designed primarily with sightseeing in mind. Because Fiji is a relatively large country with much to see and do, your actual itinerary will obviously depend on your particular interests—watersports or cultural tours, lounging on a beach, or sightseeing.

Many people stop in Fiji for a few days on their way to or from Australia or New Zealand. If you're one of them, don't cut your visit too short. Give yourself at least enough time to learn something about the islands and their peoples.

If your ambition is to rest on a tropical beach and not do much else, choose an offshore resort rather than stay on the "mainland" of Viti Levu. The offshore resorts' beaches are better than what you will find on the big island.

The usual "circuit" goes something like this: Nadi; Coral Coast; Suva; day trip to Levuka, Taveuni, or Savusavu; return to Nadi. An option in the dry season (May–Sept) is to drive from Nadi to Suva on the King's Road around northern Viti Levu, overnight in Rakiraki, and then return to Nadi via the Queen's Road.

If You Have 1 Day

Visit your hotel desk early to see what's happening. If nothing catches your eye, spend the morning touring the Mamanuca Islands on the *Island Express.* Have lunch in Nadi, shop for handcrafts, and take the open-air local bus to Lautoka. The bus stops at the market, so look there first for handcrafts. Stroll around the business district, including the duty-free shops. During the evening, take in a *meke,* the traditional Fijian feast and dance, at one of the Nadi hotels. If shopping doesn't appeal to you, spend the entire day at a resort in the Mamanucas.

If You Have 3 Days

Unless you can afford a room at the Sheratons, which are on Denaru Beach (see "Where to Stay in Nadi" in chapter 10), consider staying one night in Nadi and then moving to the Coral Coast. You'll be on the beach and closer to Suva.

Day 1 Take a day cruise to one of the Mamanuca resorts, where you can snorkel, swim, play with the water toys, and have lunch.

Day 2 Take a day trip to Suva, which usually includes stops at the cultural center at Pacific Harbour. Do your handcraft shopping in Suva, and don't miss the Fiji Museum.

Day 3 Take a land excursion from Nadi, such as the Nausori Highlands.

If You Have 7 Days (Blue Lagoon Cruise)

Days 1–4 Take a Blue Lagoon Cruise through the Yasawa Islands. You will see a *meke* and eat Fijian food, so on night 4 (back in Nadi), eat curry.

Day 5 When you're rested up, drive to Suva. Tour the town, including the Fiji Museum. Do your handcraft shopping, and then spend the night in Suva.

Day 6 Take a day trip to Levuka, Fiji's first capital.

Day 7 Take a morning flight back to Nadi, followed by a day of rest or one of the tours described in chapter 10.

If You Have 7 Days (No Cruise)

Day 1 Do what I recommend above for a 1-day visit. Spend the night in Nadi.

Day 2 Make your way by bus, taxi, or rental car to the Coral Coast. Spend the night on the coast.

Day 3 Proceed to Suva in the morning; tour the town and the Fiji Museum. Spend the night in Suva.

Day 4 Take a day trip to Levuka, Fiji's first capital.

Days 5–7 Fly to Taveuni and spend the remainder of your holiday seeing the main island and relaxing at an offshore resort.

Day 7 Return to Nadi. If you have time, take one of the tours mentioned in chapter 10.

If You Have 7 Days & Want to Do Whirlwind Sightseeing

I did this 7-day whirlwind swing around Fiji once, so I know it can be done. You won't have much time to do much besides sightsee.

Day 1 Catch an early morning flight from Nadi to Savusavu. Tour the town in the morning; spend the afternoon swimming and relaxing. Spend the night in Savusavu.

Day 2 Take a morning flight to Taveuni (about 20 min.). Tour the island and have lunch. Spend the night on Taveuni or at Matangi Island Resort or Qamea Beach Club.

Day 3 Take a morning flight to Suva. Tour the city. Spend the night in Suva.

Day 4 Take a day trip to Levuka. Spend the night in Suva.

Day 5 Drive the Coral Coast, stopping off at Pacific Harbour Cultural Centre & Market Place. Spend the night on the Coral Coast.

Day 6 Spend the morning resting on the Coral Coast; drive to Nadi.

Day 7 Take the *Island Express* tour of the Mamanucas during the morning. Shop in Nadi Town or Lautoka during the afternoon.

If You Have 2 Weeks

Days 1–4 Take one of Blue Lagoon Cruises' short trips through the Yasawa Islands.

Day 5 Drive the Coral Coast, stopping off at the Pacific Harbour Cultural Centre. Spend the night on the Coral Coast.

Day 6 Spend the morning resting on the Coral Coast, and then drive to Suva (plan to arrive before dark).

Day 7 Tour Suva, including the Fiji Museum. Do your handcraft shopping.

Day 8 Take a day trip to Levuka, Fiji's first capital.

Day 9 Fly to Taveuni on a morning Air Fiji flight. Tour the island and have lunch. Spend the night on Taveuni or at Matangi Island Resort or Qamea Beach Club.

Day 10 Spend the day at leisure.

Day 11 Take a morning flight to Savusavu. Tour the town and spend the night there.

Day 12 Spend the day at leisure.

Day 13 Fly to Nadi and spend the night there.

Day 14 Take one of the Nadi tours mentioned in chapter 10 and complete any unfinished handcraft shopping.

6 Visitor Information & Entry Requirements

VISITOR INFORMATION

The **Fiji Visitors Bureau,** G.P.O. Box 92, Suva, Fiji Islands (© **0800/672 1721** from within Fiji, or 330 2433; fax 330 0970; www.bulafiji.com), provides maps, brochures, and other materials from the bureau's head office in a restored colonial house at the corner of Thomson and Scott streets in the heart of Suva. It also has a small office in the international arrivals concourse at Nadi International Airport (© **672 2433**), which is open for all arriving flights.

The bureau's award-winning website is a trove of up-to-date information (weather and currency exchange rates, for example) and is linked to the home pages of the country's airlines, tour operators, attractions, and hotels. It also has a directory of e-mail addresses.

Other Fiji Visitors Bureau offices are:

- **United States and Canada:** 5777 West Century Blvd., Suite 220, Los Angeles, CA 90045 (© **800/932-3454** or 310/568-1616; fax 310/670-2318; www.bula-fijiamericas.com)
- **Australia:** Level 12, St. Martins Tower, 31 Market St., Sydney, NSW 2000 (© **02/9264-3399;** fax 02/9264-3060; infosyd@bulafiji.au.com)
- **New Zealand:** 48 High St., 5th Floor (P.O. Box 1179), Auckland (© **09/373-2133;** fax 09/309-4720; www.bulafiji.co.nz)
- **Japan:** Noa Building, 14th Floor, 3-5, 2 Chome, Azabuudai, Minato-Ku, Tokyo 106 (© **03/3587-2038;** fax 03/3587-2563; www.tabi.or.jb/fvb)
- **Korea:** Room 808, Paiknam Bldg., 188-3 I-ka, Ulchiro Chung-ku, 100-191 Seoul (© **2/773-8559;** fax 2/752-6921; kabifj@unitel.co.kr)

The bureau also has marketing representatives in:

- **Germany:** Petersburger Strasse 94, 10247 Berlin (© **30/4225-6026;** fax 30/4225-6287).
- **United Kingdom:** 48 Grantham Rd., Barnes, London SW13 9J (© **0208/8741-5566;** fax 0208/741-6107; southpacific@iiuk.co.uk).

Other websites worth exploring include **www.fijivillage.com** and **www.fiji live.com**, both of which have current news, weather, and sports.

If you have a TV in your room, you can tune in to the advertiser-supported **Visitor Information Network (VIN),** usually on channel 10, for tips about what to do and where to dine.

ENTRY REQUIREMENTS

Visitor permits good for stays of up to 4 months are issued upon arrival to citizens of the United States; all Commonwealth countries; most European, South American, and South Pacific island nations; and Mexico, Japan, Israel, Pakistan, South Korea, Thailand, Tunisia, and Turkey. You must have a passport valid for 3 months beyond your visit, onward or return airline tickets, and enough money or proof of finances to support you during your stay.

Citizens of all other countries must apply for visas in advance from the Fiji embassies or consulates. In the United States, contact the **Embassy of Fiji,** 2233 Wisconsin Ave., Suite 240, NW, Washington, D.C. 20007 (© **202/337-8320;** fax 202/337-1996; fijiemb@earthlink.net). Other Fiji embassies or high commissions are in Ottawa, Canada; Canberra, Australia; Wellington, New Zealand; London, England; Brussels, Belgium; Tokyo, Japan; Kuala Lumpur, Malaysia; Port Moresby, Papua New Guinea; Hong Kong, China; and Tel-Aviv, Israel. Check your local phone book.

Persons wishing to remain longer than 4 months must apply for extensions from the **Immigration Department,** whose primary offices are at the Nadi International Airport terminal (© **672 2454**) and in the Labour Department building on Victoria Parade in downtown Suva (© **321 1775**).

Vaccinations are not required unless you have been in a yellow fever or cholera area shortly before arriving in Fiji.

Customs allowances are 500 cigarettes; 2 liters of liquor, beer, or wine; and F$400 ($180) worth of other goods in addition to personal belongings. Pornography is prohibited. Firearms and nonprescription narcotic drugs are strictly prohibited and subject to heavy fines and jail terms. Pets will be quarantined. Any fresh fruits and vegetables must be declared and are subject to inspection and fumigation.

7 Money

The national currency is the Fiji dollar, which is divided into 100 cents and trades independently on the foreign exchange markets. The Fiji dollar is abbreviated "FID" by the banks and airlines, but I use **F$** in this chapter. Some hotels and resorts quote their rates in U.S. dollars, indicated here by **US$.**

As we went to press, one Fiji dollar was worth about US45¢. The exchange rate is not published in U.S. newspapers, but you can check **www.xe.com,** a currency conversion site.

Like islanders elsewhere in the South Pacific, Fijians might take offense if you try to haggle over a price. On the other hand, many Indo-Fijian merchants expect you to haggle (see "Shopping in Nadi" in chapter 10).

HOW TO GET LOCAL CURRENCY An **ANZ Bank** branch in the international arrivals concourse at Nadi International Airport is open 24 hours a day, 7 days a week. It charges a F$2 (90¢) fee for each transaction over F$100 ($45), F$1 (45¢) if under that amount. Neither of ANZ's other branches nor any other bank charges such a fee. There's an ATM on the wall outside the branch, where you can draw Fijian currency by using MasterCard or Visa credit or debit cards.

ANZ Bank and **Westpac Bank** have offices throughout the country where currency and traveler's checks can be exchanged. Both have ATMs at their Nadi and Suva branches, but don't count on using an ATM on the outer islands. Banking hours nationwide are Monday to Thursday from 9:30am to 3pm and Friday from 9:30am to 4pm. You can also cash traveler's checks at **Thomas**

Tips Beware of Unofficial "Tourist Information Centres"

When you see "Tourist Information Centre" in Nadi or elsewhere, it is most likely a travel agent or tour operator, whose staff will invariably steer you to its products. The only official, nonprofit tourist information centers are operated by the Fiji Visitors Bureau, at the Suva and Nadi locations listed above.

Cook Travel Service offices in Nadi Town and Suva. See the "Fast Facts" sections in chapters 10 and 11 for specific currency exchange locations.

CREDIT CARDS American Express, MasterCard, and Visa are widely accepted by the hotels, car-rental firms, travel and tour companies, duty-free shops, and some restaurants. Don't count on using a Diners Club card outside the hotels, and don't even bring your Discover card to Fiji.

8 When to Go

THE CLIMATE

During most of the year, the prevailing southeast trade winds temper Fiji's warm, humid, tropical climate. Average high temperatures range from 83°F (28°C) during the austral winter (June–Sept) to 88°F (31°C) during the summer months (Dec–Mar). Evenings are in the warm and comfortable 70s (21°C–28°C) throughout the year.

The islands receive the most rain during the austral summer, but the amount depends on which side of each island the measurement is taken on. The north and west coasts tend to be drier (and warmer), and the east and south coasts wetter (and somewhat cooler but more humid). Nadi, on the west side of Viti Levu, gets considerably less rain than does Suva, on the southeast side (some 200 in. a year). Consequently, most of Fiji's resorts are on the western side of Viti Levu. Even during the wetter months, however, periods of intense tropical sunshine usually follow the rain showers.

Fiji is in the heart of the South Pacific cyclone belt and receives its share of hurricanes between November and April. Fiji's Meteorological Service is excellent at tracking hurricanes and issuing timely warnings, and the local travel industry is very adept at preparing for them. I've been through of a few Fiji cyclones, and I've never let the thought of one keep me from returning every chance I get.

HOLIDAYS & EVENTS

Unlike the other South Pacific island countries, Fiji has no grand national festivals around which to plan a visit. In fact, the Fiji Visitors Bureau doesn't even provide a calendar of events.

More likely to impact your visit is a seemingly interminable list of national holidays—so many of them, in fact, that in 2002 the government started paring the list in a effort to improve the national economy.

At press time, all banks, government offices, and most private businesses are closed for New Year's Day, Good Friday, Easter Saturday, Easter Monday, Ratu Sukuna Day (May 30 or the Mon closest thereto), The Prophet Mohammed's Birthday (a Mon in mid-July), Fiji Day (the Mon closest to Oct 10), Deepawali (an Indian festival in late Oct or early Nov), Christmas Day, and December 26 (Boxing Day).

The Fiji Dollar & the U.S. Dollar

At this writing, F$1 = approximately US45¢ (or US$1 = approximately F$2.22), the rate of exchange used to calculate the U.S. dollar prices given in chapters 9 through 11. This rate may change by the time you visit, so use the following table only as a guide:

F$	US$	F$	US$
.25	.11	15	6.75
.50	.23	20	9.00
.75	.34	25	11.25
1	.45	30	13.50
2	.90	35	15.75
3	1.35	40	18.00
4	1.80	45	20.25
5	2.25	50	22.50
6	2.70	75	33.75
7	3.15	100	45.00
8	3.60	125	56.25
9	4.05	150	67.50
10	4.50	200	90.00

Banks take an additional holiday on the first Monday in August, and some businesses also close for various Hindu and Muslim holy days. And if Fiji wins the annual Hong Kong Sevens rugby tournament, don't expect anyone to be at work the next day!

9 Getting There & Getting Around

GETTING THERE

Air New Zealand, **Air Pacific**, and **Qantas Airways** fly to Fiji from North America, Australia, and New Zealand. In addition, **Polynesian Airlines, Solomon Airlines, Air Nauru,** and **Air Calin** (the international airline of New Caledonia) have regional services from Australia and New Zealand to Fiji as well as among the South Pacific islands. See "Getting There & Getting Around" in chapter 2 for details.

ARRIVING & DEPARTING

ARRIVING AT NADI   Most international flights arrive at and depart from **Nadi International Airport,** about 11km (7 miles) north of Nadi Town. A few flights arrive from Auckland, Samoa, and Tonga at Nausori Airport, some 19km (12 miles) from Suva on the opposite side of the island. Both airports are used for domestic flights. They are the only lighted airstrips in the country, which means you don't fly domestically after dark. Because many international flights arrive during the night, at least a 1-night stay-over in Nadi will likely be necessary before you leave for another island.

Arriving passengers can purchase duty-free items at two shops in the baggage claim area before clearing Customs (imported liquor is expensive in Fiji, so if you drink, don't hesitate to buy two bottles here).

A large sign on the wall behind the Immigration counters lists all the hotels in the Nadi area, their present room rates, and the taxi fares to get to them.

After clearing Customs, you emerge onto an open-air concourse lined on both sides by airline offices, travel and tour companies, car-rental firms, and a 24-hour-a-day branch of the **ANZ Bank** (see "Money," above).

The **Fiji Visitors Bureau** has an office just to the left, and the friendly staff will give advice, supply information, and even make a hotel reservation for the cost of the phone call. Brochures from every hotel and activity in Fiji are on display. The bureau's airport office is open during regular business hours (see "Fast Facts: Fiji," below) and for at least an hour after the arrival of all major international flights.

Touts for the inexpensive hotels will be milling about, offering free transportation to their establishments. The larger hotels will also have transportation available for their guests.

Taxis will be lined up to the right outside the concourse (see the table in "Getting Around," below, for fares to the hotels).

Local buses to Nadi and Lautoka pass the airport on the Queen's Road every day. To get to one, walk straight out of the concourse, across the parking lot, and through the gate to the road. Driving in Fiji is on the left, so buses heading for Nadi and its hotels stop on the opposite side, next to Raffles' Gateway Hotel; those going to Lautoka stop on the airport side of the road. You will see the covered bus stands. See "Getting Around Nadi" in chapter 10 for details.

The Nadi domestic terminal and the international check-in counters are to the right of the arrival concourse as you exit Customs (or to the left, if you are arriving from the main road). A **snack bar** is located between the two terminals.

The Left Luggage counter at the far end of the departures concourse provides **baggage storage** for F\$3 to F\$6 (\$1.35–\$2.70) a day, depending on the size of the baggage. The counter is open 24 hours daily. The hotels all have baggage-storage rooms and will keep your extra stuff for free.

A **post office,** in a separate building across the entry road from the main terminal, is open Monday to Friday from 8am to 4pm.

ARRIVING AT SUVA   Suva is served by **Nausori Airport,** on the flat plains of the Rewa River delta about 19km (12 miles) from downtown. The small terminal has a snack bar but few other amenities. Taxis between Nausori and downtown Suva cost about F\$20 (\$9) each way.

DEPARTING   Passengers leaving the country must pay a **departure tax** of F\$20 (\$9) in Fiji currency (or by MasterCard or Visa credit cards at Nadi). Check in first at either airport, since you get your boarding pass stamped. There is no departure tax for domestic flights.

Nadi Airport has a modern, air-conditioned international departure lounge with a currency exchange counter, snack bar, showers, and the largest duty-free shops in the South Pacific. Duty-free prices, however, are higher here than you'll pay elsewhere in the country, and there is no haggling.

Nausori Airport near Suva has a small duty-free shop in its departure lounge. Some of Air Pacific's flights bound from Nadi to Western Samoa first stop at Nausori, where you will off and clear immigration before continuing to Apia.

GETTING AROUND

Fiji has an extensive and reliable transportation network of airlines, rental cars, taxis, ferries, and both long-distance and local buses. This section deals primarily with getting from one island or major area to another; see the "Getting Around" sections in chapters 10 and 11 for details on transportation within the local areas.

> **Tips   Avoid Backtracking**
>
> Most flights from Nadi to Taveuni stop in Savusavu going and coming, so don't let an uninformed travel agent book you back to Nadi or Suva in order to get from Taveuni to Savusavu.

BY PLANE & HELICOPTER

The easiest way to get around the country is on **Air Fiji** (© 888/234-5447 or 672 2521 in Nadi, 331 3666 in Suva; www.airfiji.net) and **Sun Air** (© 0800/ 772 5725 from anywhere in Fiji or 672 3016 in Nadi, 331 5755 in Suva; www. fiji.to). Both fly small planes from Nadi to the tourist destinations. Both have offices in the international concourse at Nadi International Airport and on Victoria Parade in Suva.

From Nadi, one-way **fares** on both Air Fiji and Sun Air are about F$51 ($23) to Malololailai Island (Plantation Island and Musket Cove resorts); F$64 ($29) to Mana Island; F$118 ($53) to Suva; F$178 ($80) to Savusavu; and F$220 ($99) to Taveuni.

Turtle Airways (© 877/732-75263 in the U.S., or 672 2988; www.turtleairways.com) flies small seaplanes from Wailoaloa Beach on Nadi Bay to the Mamanuca and Yasawa resorts. Fares are about F$150 ($67.50) per person each way. Turtle has a special F$79 ($35.50) one-way fare for backpackers staying at hostels in the Yasawa Islands. You can charter its planes and fly anywhere in Fiji for about F$800 ($360) per flying hour.

Pacific Islands Seaplanes (© 672 5643; pacisair@is.com.fj) provides service in its Canadian-built floatplanes, which use wheels to take off from Nadi airport and floats to land on water at the Mamanuca resorts. The one-way fare to the close-in resorts off Nadi is F$20 ($9) per person or F$110 ($49.50) per planeload.

Island Hoppers (© 672 0140; www.helicopters.com.fj) will whisk you out to the Mamanucas in one of its helicopters. If you have to ask how much these expensive rides cost, you can't afford them.

BY RENTAL CAR   Rental cars are widely available in Fiji. Each company has its own pricing policy, and you can frequently find discounts, special deals, and some give-and-take bargaining over long-term and long-distance use. All major companies, and a few not so major, have offices in the commercial concourse at Nadi International Airport, so it's easy to shop around. Most are open 7 days a week, some for 24 hours a day. Give careful consideration to how far you will drive; it's 197km (118 miles) from Nadi Airport to Suva, so an unlimited kilometer rate could work to your advantage if you plan to drive to Suva.

Avis (© 800/331-1212, or 672 2233 in Nadi; www.avis.com.fj) has more than 50% of the business here, and for good reason: The Toyota dealer is the local agent, so it has the newest and best-maintained fleet. Rates start at F$125 ($56) per day with unlimited kilometers. Add F$20 ($9) a day for liability insurance. In addition to the office at Nadi Airport, Avis can be found in Suva (© 331 3833), in Korolevu on the Coral Coast (© 653 0176), and at several hotels.

Thrifty Car Rental (© 800/367-2277, or 772 2935 in Nadi; www.thrifty. com), which is handled in Fiji by Rosie the Travel Service, is next best, with rates and cars comparable to Avis's.

Hertz (© 800/654-3131 or 672 3466; www.hertz.com) has offices at Nadi airport, Korolevu on the Coral Coast, Pacific Harbour, and Suva.

Budget Rent-A-Car (© 800/527-0700 or 672 2735; http://rent.drive budget.com) also has an agency here, but I have never been particularly pleased with its vehicles or service.

The largest and most reliable local company is **Khan's Rental Cars** (© 679 0617; rehnuma@is.com.fj). Others include **Roxy Rentals** (© 672 2763; roxy mplfj@is.com.fj) and **Central Rent-A-Car** (© 672 2711; centralrentals@ suva.is.com.fj). Be sure to "kick the tires"—in other words, check the cars thoroughly before renting from these companies.

Even though your home **insurance** policy might cover any damages that occur in Fiji, if you do have a mishap, you must pay out of your own pocket and file a claim when you get home. Since that can be an enormous hassle, I strongly recommend getting local coverage when you rent a car. Pay close attention to the insurance offered, however, for it may not cover damages that occur off the paved roads. Some policies even require you to pay the first F$500 ($225) or more of damages in any event.

All renters must be at least 21 years old, and a few companies require them to be at least 25.

DRIVING RULES   Your valid home driver's license will be honored in Fiji. **Driving is on the left-hand side of the road. Seat belts** are mandatory. **Speed limits** are 80kmph (48 mph) on the open road and 50kmph (30 mph) in the towns and other built-up areas.

Driving under the influence of alcohol or other drugs is a criminal offense in Fiji, and the police frequently throw up road blocks and administer Breathalyzer tests to all drivers.

You must **stop for pedestrians** in all marked crosswalks.

The Queen's and King's roads are paved all the way around Viti Levu. Most other roads can be impassable during periods of heavy rain, when landslides can close even the paved roads.

Gasoline (petrol) is readily available, even on Sunday, at Shell, Mobil, and BP service stations in all the main towns. Expect to pay about twice what you would pay in the United States and Canada, about the same as elsewhere.

BY BUS   Buses are plentiful and inexpensive in Fiji, and it's possible to go all the way around Viti Levu on them. I did it once by taking the Sunset Express from Nadi to Suva one morning, a local express to Rakiraki the next morning, and then another express to Lautoka and a local back to Nadi.

Fiji Express (© 672 3105) is the only air-conditioned "tourist class" express bus operating between Suva and Nadi Airport. It begins its daily run at the Centra Suva hotel at 7:30am. It stops at the major hotels along the Queen's Road

---

Tips Weigh Your Bag & Reconfirm Your Flight

Baggage allowances on domestic flights may be 10 kilograms (22 lb.) instead of the 20 kilograms (44 lb.) allowed on international flights. Check with the airlines to avoid showing up with too much luggage. And always reconfirm your domestic return flights as soon as possible after arriving at your destination. Also, check in when the airlines tell you to; planes sometimes arrive and depart a few minutes early.

before arriving at Nadi about noon. The return trip begins at 12:45pm, with arrival in Suva about 5:15pm. Fares run up to F$30 ($13.50), depending on how far you go. Book at any hotel tour desk or the Coral Sun Fiji office at Nadi Airport.

Sunset Express (© **672 0266** in Nadi, or 332 2811 in Suva) has non-air-conditioned buses that run twice a day between Lautoka and Suva, with stops at Nadi Airport and Sigatoka. These buses usually leave Nadi Airport daily about 9:50am and 3:35pm, with arrival in Suva about 1:35 and 7:20pm. The return trips depart Suva at 8:45am and 4pm, getting back to Nadi Airport at 12:30 and 7:50pm. The Nadi-Suva fare is F$11 ($5). Sunset Express has an office on the second floor of the Nadi Airport arrivals concourse.

Pacific Transport Ltd. (© **670 0044** in Nadi, or 330 4366 in Suva) has several express and local buses between Lautoka and Suva from Monday to Saturday via the Queen's Road. They all stop at the domestic terminal at Nadi Airport and the markets at Nadi Town, Sigatoka, and Navua. The Fiji Visitors Bureau usually has schedules at its offices. The express buses take about 4 hours between Nadi and Suva, compared to 5 hours on the local "stages." All these buses cater to local residents, do not take reservations, and have no air-conditioning. The Nadi-Suva fare is about F$10 ($4.50), express or local.

Sunbeam Transport Ltd. (© **666 2822** in Lautoka, or 338 2122 in Suva), **Reliance Transport Bus Service** (© **666 3059** in Lautoka, or 382296 in Suva), and **Akbar Buses Ltd.** (© **669 4760** in Rakiraki) have express and local service between Lautoka and Suva via the King's Road. The Fiji Visitors Bureau may have their schedules. If not, ask around the local markets. The Lautoka-Suva fare is about F$10 ($4.50).

Fume-belching **local buses** use the produce markets as their terminals, but they'll stop anywhere if you signal the driver from the side of the road. The older buses have side windows made of canvas panels that are rolled down during inclement weather (they usually fly out the sides and flap in the wind like great skirts). More and more modern models are being used all the time.

Buses run every few minutes along the Queen's Road between Lautoka and Nadi Town, passing the airport and most of the hotels and restaurants along the way (see "Getting Around Nadi" in chapter 10).

Tips   Watch Out for Cows, Horses & Road Humps!

Most roads in Fiji are narrow, poorly maintained, and crooked. Not all local drivers are well trained, experienced, or skilled, and some of them (including bus drivers) go much too fast for the conditions. Consequently, you should **drive defensively** at all times. Constantly be alert for potholes, landslides, hairpin curves, and various stray animals—cows and horses are a very real danger, especially at night.

Also keep an eye out for speed bumps known in Fiji as **road humps**. Most Fijian villages have them. Although big signs made to resemble traditional Fijian war clubs announce when you're entering and leaving villages on the Queen's Road, there are usually road humps between the clubs, *so slow down!* The humps are large enough to do serious damage to the bottom of a car, and no local rental insurance covers that.

Be very careful when coming down a hill on an unpaved road, as cars can easily skid on loose dirt and gravel.

<hr>

Tips **Keep an Eye on Your Beer Mug**

Bartenders in Fiji are taught to keep your beer mug full and your pockets empty—that is, they don't ask if you want another beer, they keep pouring until you tell them emphatically to stop.

<hr>

Minivans scoot along between the Nadi market and Rodwell Road, just around the corner from the Suva Municipal Market. These vehicles are not regulated by the government and should be considered unsafe.

BY TAXI Taxis are as abundant in Fiji as taxi meters are scarce. Some of the Nadi Airport taxi drivers have allegedly taken advantage of naive tourists, so make sure to settle on a fare to your destination before setting out (see the distance chart below). Some drivers will complain about short fares and will badger you for more business later on during your stay; politely ignore these entreaties.

Not to be confused with unlicensed minibuses, **"share taxis"** or "rolling taxis"—those not otherwise occupied—pick up passengers at bus stops and charge the bus fare. They are particularly good value on long-distance trips. A taxi returning to Suva, for example, will stop by the Nadi Town market and pick up a load of passengers at the bus fare rather than drive back to the capital empty. Ask around the local market bus stops if share taxis are available. You'll meet some wonderful Fijians that way.

The following are distances from Nadi International Airport via the Queen's Road and the official government-regulated taxi fares:

From Nadi Airport to:	km	Miles	Approx. Taxi Fare
Tanoa/Mocambo Hotels	1.3	0.8	F$3.00 ($1.35)
Skylodge Hotel	3.3	2.0	F$4.00 ($1.80)
Dominion/Sandalwood Inn/ West Motor Inn	5.2	3.1	F$5.00 ($2.25)
Sheratons/Denarau Island	15.0	9.3	F$20.00 ($9.00)
Nadi Town	9.0	5.4	F$7.00 ($3.15)
Fijian Resort	60.0	36.0	F$55.00 ($25.00)
Sigatoka	70.0	42.0	F$60.00 ($27.00)
Outrigger Reef Resort	78.0	46.8	F$65.00 ($29.00)
Hideaway Resort	92.0	55.2	F$68.00 ($30.50)
The Warwick Fiji	104.0	62.4	F$80.00 ($36.00)
Pacific Harbour	148.0	88.8	F$145.00 ($65.00)
Suva	197.0	118.2	F$165 ($74.00)

BY FERRY As an alternative to flying, you can take one of the ferries that run between the main islands. The schedules can change abruptly depending on the weather and the condition of the ships, so call the operators for the latest information. Double all one-way fares for round-trips.

The newest and most comfortable ship is the *Lagilagi,* operated by **Beach-comber Cruises (© 666 1500** in Lautoka, or 330 7889 in Suva). This speedy catamaran usually operates on Tuesday and Saturday between Nadi and Savusavu, with stops at Beachcomber Island Resort, Lautoka, Nananu-I-Ra, and Ellington Wharf. It normally leaves Denarau Island at 6am and arrives at

---

> ⌒ **Tips** **It Never Hurts to Bargain**
>
> In Nadi and on the Coral Coast, you will see the same taxi drivers stationed outside your hotel every day. Usually they are paid on a salaried rather than a fare basis, so they may be willing to spend more time than usual showing you around. Also, they might charge you less than the government-regulated fares for long-distance trips, such as from Nadi to the Coral Coast or Suva, because many would rather earn one big fare a day than several small ones. It never hurts to politely bargain.

Savusavu at noon, having done most of the passage on calm waters inside the reef (there's about a 40-min. stretch of rough water between Viti Levu and Vanua Levu, so bring your Dramamine). The one-way fare is about F$90 ($40.50).

Beachcomber Cruises also runs the clean and well-maintained *Adi Savusavu* between Suva and Savusavu three times a week, with extensions to Taveuni twice a week. Both first- and economy-class cabins are air-conditioned and have airline-style seats. The ship takes about 11 hours to steam between Suva and Savusavu, often an overnight voyage. Fares from Suva to Savusavu are about F$62 ($28) for first class and F$42 ($19) for economy; you pay slightly more to Taveuni. You can book at the Suva booking office in Suite 8, Epworth House, Nina Street.

 ***FAST FACTS:* Fiji**

The following facts apply to Fiji in general. For more specific information, see the "Fast Facts" sections in chapters 10 and 11.

American Express The full-service representative, **Tapa International Ltd.,** has offices in Nadi and Suva. See the "Fast Facts" sections in chapter 10 for details.

Business Hours Stores are generally open Monday to Friday from 8am to 4:30pm, although many close for lunch from 1 to 2pm, and some stay open until 5:30pm. Saturday hours are from 8:30am to noon in town, but many suburban stores stay open until 6pm and even 8pm. Shops in many hotels stay open until 9pm every day. Government office hours are Monday to Thursday from 8am to 1pm and 2 to 4:30pm, Friday from 8am to 1pm and 2 to 4pm.

Camera/Film **Caines Photofast,** the largest processor of Kodak films, has shops in the main towns.

Climate See "When to Go," earlier in this chapter.

Clothing Modest dress is the order of the day, particularly in the villages. As a rule, don't leave the hotel swimming pool or the beach in bathing suits or other skimpy attire. If you want to run around half naked, go to Tahiti, where the French think it's all right. The Fijians do not. Do not enter a Fijian village wearing a hat or sunglasses, or with your shoulders uncovered.

Fijian men and women wear *sulus,* the wraparound skirts known as *pareus* in Tahiti and the Cook Islands and *lavalavas* in the Samoas. Fijian women wear *chambas,* or hip-length blouses, over their *sulus.* Many Indian women wear saris, lengths of cloth wrapped and pleated around the body.

Drug Laws A lot of marijuana is grown illegally up in the hills, but one drive past the Suva Gaol will convince you not to get caught buying it— or smuggling narcotics or dangerous drugs into Fiji.

Drugstores The main towns have reasonably well-stocked drugstores. Their medicines are likely to be from Australia or New Zealand. The large Morris Hedstrom department stores throughout Fiji carry a wide range of toiletries, including Coppertone, Colgate, and many other brands that are familiar to Americans.

Electricity Electric current in Fiji is 240 volts, 50 cycles. Many hotels have converters for 110-volt shavers, but these are not suitable for hair dryers. The plugs are the angled two-prong types used in Australia and New Zealand. Outlets have separate on/off switches mounted next to them.

E-mail Many hotels and resorts will send and receive e-mail for their guests, and cybercafes in Nadi, Suva, and Savusavu have computer terminals, as does Telekom Fiji (the local phone company) in Suva. See the "Fast Facts" sections in chapter 10.

No U.S. Internet service provider has a local access number in Fiji. If you take your laptop, you can sign up for temporary Internet access through **Telekom Fiji** (© **330 0100**). You'll have to go to Telekom's offices in Nadi or on the Queen's Road in Namaka (next to Westpac Bank). In Suva, go to Telekom's Customer Care Center on Victoria Parade at Gladstone Road. The Nadi clerks may not be familiar with the procedures, so ask them to call the Suva office for instructions on setting up a "temporary Internet account" (those exact words are crucial). They must also fax your application to Suva, so be prepared to wait. There's a F$55 ($25) fee for 1 month's access, payable in cash. An additional F11¢ (5¢) a minute access fee will be billed to your hotel room. See the "Getting Online" box in chapter 3 for information on how to configure your computer.

Embassies/Consulates The **U.S. Embassy** is at 31 Loftus St., Suva (© **331 4466;** www.amembassy-fiji.gov). Other major diplomatic missions in Suva are **Australia,** 37 Princes Rd., Tamavua (© **338 2211**); **New Zealand,** 10th Floor, Reserve Bank of Fiji Bldg., Pratt St. (© **331 1422**); **United Kingdom,** Victoria House, 47 Gladstone Rd. (© **331 1033**); **Japan,** 2nd Floor, Dominion House, Thomson St. (© **330 2122**); **France,** 7th Floor, Dominion House, Thomson St. (© **331 2233**); **People's Republic of China,** 147 Queen Elizabeth Dr. (© **330 0215**); and **South Korea,** 8th Floor, Vanua House, Victoria Parade (© **330 0977**).

Emergencies The emergency telephone number for **fire** and **ambulance** is © **911** throughout Fiji. The **police** emergency number is **917.**

Firearms Guns are illegal in Fiji, and persons found with them could be fined severely and sentenced to jail.

Gambling There are no casinos in Fiji, but you can play Tattslotto and a newspaper numbers game known as "Fiji Sixes."

Healthcare Medical and dental care in Fiji are not up to the standards common in the industrialized world. The hospitals tend to be overcrowded and understaffed. Most hotels have private physicians on call or can refer one. Doctors are listed at the beginning of the White Pages section of the Fiji telephone directory, under the heading "Medical Practitioners." See the "Fast Facts" sections in chapters 10 and 11 for specific doctors.

Hitchhiking Local residents seldom hitchhike, so the custom is not widespread. Women traveling alone should never hitchhike in Fiji.

Insects Fiji has no dangerous insects, and its plentiful mosquitoes do not carry malaria. The only dangerous animal is the bolo, a venomous snake that is docile and rarely seen.

Liquor Laws The legal drinking age is 18. Both beer and spirits are produced locally and are considerably less expensive than imported brands, which are taxed heavily. If you drink quality brands of liquor, bring some with you. Fiji Bitter and Fiji Gold are the local beers. Fiji Bitter served in a bottle is known as a "Stubbie." Fiji Gold is a much lighter lager than Fiji Bitter. Most bars also sell Budweiser from the United States and most Australian and New Zealand beers.

Maps Most bookstores and hotel gift shops sell maps of Fiji.

Newspapers/Magazines Three national newspapers are published in English: the **Fiji Times** (www.fijivillage.com), the **Daily Post** (www.fijipost.com), and the **Fiji Sun** (www.sun.com.fj)—but note that the latter two may have merged by the time you arrive. All are tabloids and appear Monday to Saturday mornings (and Sun for the *Daily Post*). They carry the latest major stories from overseas. The international editions of *Time* and *Newsweek* (the latter in the rear of *The Bulletin,* an Australian newsmagazine) and the leading Australian and New Zealand daily newspapers are available at some bookstores and hotel shops. The latter usually are several days old before they reach Fiji. Published in Suva, the excellent **Pacific Magazine** (www.pacificislands.cc) covers South Pacific regional news.

Pets You will need advance permission to bring any animal into Fiji; if not, your pet will be quarantined.

Post Office All the main towns have post offices operated by Fiji Post, and there is a branch at Nadi International Airport, across the entry road from the terminal. Allow at least a week for delivery of airmail letters between Fiji and North America. Surface mail can take 2 months or more. Post offices usually are open Monday to Friday from 8am to 4pm. Mail will move faster if you use the country's official name—Fiji Islands—on all envelopes and packages sent here.

Radio/TV The Fijian government operates three nationwide radio networks whose frequencies depend on the location of the relay transmitters. Radio Fiji 1 carries programming in Fijian. Radio Fiji 2 is Hindi. Radio Fiji Gold broadcast in English and sounds very much like a popular-music station in Western countries. Radio Fiji 1 and Radio Fiji Gold both carry news bulletins on the hour and full world, regional, and local news reports and weather bulletins daily at 7am and 6pm. Several privately owned English-language FM stations can be heard in Suva and Nadi.

Fiji may expand its TV services, but at press time it had two broadcast channels—one government owned, the other a Christian station—which could be received around Suva, Nadi, and Lautoka. Headline news from the BBC is aired during the off-hours on the government channel, and the local news comes on at 6pm or 7pm daily, usually followed by world news from the BBC. The published schedules, carried in the local newspapers, are more or less reliable, but programs don't start crisply on the hour as they do in the United States. Some hotels have Sky TV, a pay system that airs live sports via ESPN during the afternoons.

Safety Fiji has experienced a serious increase in property crime in recent years ("Petty theft is a national pastime," says one local resident), and armed robberies have become more frequent. A tourist's chances of being robbed or assaulted in Fiji are lower than in the centers of most large American cities, but caution is advised. Stick to the main streets after dark, and take a taxi back to your hotel if you're out late at night. Some of the smaller hotels in Suva lock their front doors at 11pm, and the large resorts have checkpoints to monitor who comes and who goes. Do not leave valuables in your hotel room or unattended elsewhere, including in rental cars and tour buses.

Women should not wander alone on deserted beaches and should be extremely cautious about accepting an offer to have a few beers outside a bar or to be given a late-night lift back to their hotel or hostel.

Taxes Fiji imposes a 10% value added tax (VAT) on most goods and services. Businesses are technically required to include the tax in the prices they charge. These are known as "VAT-inclusive prices," or VIP for short. A few still add it like a sales tax, however, and hoteliers are not required to include it in the rates they quote outside Fiji. Therefore, be sure to ask whether a hotel room rate or other price includes the VAT. You will not be entitled to a VAT refund when you leave the country.

Visitors leaving the country by air must pay an airport departure tax of F$20 ($9) in Fijian currency (or by MasterCard or Visa) at Nadi International Airport.

Telephone/Fax International calls can be dialed directly into Fiji from most areas of the world. The international country code is **679.** There are no area codes within Fiji.

Several international long-distance carriers have access numbers their customers can call from within Fiji to reach their international networks: **AT&T** (© **00-48-901001**); **MCI** (© **00-48-901002**); **Sprint** (© **00-48-901003**); **Hawaii Telecom** (© **00-48-901004**); and **Teleglobe Canada** (© **00-48-901005**). These numbers can be dialed toll free from any Phonecard public phone (see below). Using an MCI prepaid calling card is the least expensive way to call the United States.

The numbers for **directory assistance** in Fiji are © **011** for domestic information, © **022** for international numbers.

Pay phones are located at all post offices and in many other locations. You can make local, domestic long-distance ("trunk"), or international calls without operator assistance from any of them.

Pay phones accept only Fiji Telecom **Phonecards,** not coins. Post offices and many shops (including the gift shops in the Nadi Airport terminal) sell

Phonecards in denominations up to F$50 ($22.50). Lift the receiver and slip the card into the slot, picture side up. A digital readout will tell you how much money you have left on the card at all times during your call. Calls to the United States cost about F$3 ($1.35) a minute when dialed directly. You *cannot* use your AT&T or other phone company credit cards from a Phonecard phone.

To call outside Fiji, dial **00** first, then the country code (**1** for the U.S. and Canada) and the area code and phone number. No prefix is required for domestic long distance calls.

Most post offices provide fax service.

Time Local time in Fiji is 12 hours ahead of Greenwich Mean Time from March 1 to October 31. Daylight saving time is in effect from November 1 to February 28, when local time is 13 hours ahead of GMT. Although the 180° meridian passes through Taveuni, all of Fiji is west of the international date line, so it's one day ahead of the United States and shares the same day with Australia and New Zealand. Translated: When it's 5am on Tuesday in Fiji, it's noon on Monday in New York and 9am on Monday in Los Angeles.

Tipping Tipping is discouraged throughout Fiji unless truly exceptional service has been rendered. That's not to say that the porter won't give you that where's-my-money look once he figures out you're an American.

Water Except during periods of continuous heavy rain, the tap water in the main towns and at the resorts is safe to drink. Bottled "Fiji" spring water is widely available at shops and hotels.

Weights/Measures Fiji uses the metric system.

10

Viti Levu

Viti Levu ("Big Fiji"), the largest island of Fiji, is 10 times the size of Tahiti. In fact, at 6,713 square km (4,171 sq. miles), it has more dry land than all the islands of French Polynesia put together. Two main roads, the Queen's and King's roads, go all the way around the island.

Most visitors to Fiji arrive at Nadi International Airport, a modern facility located among sugar cane fields on Viti Levu's dry western side. The **Nadi** area is the focal point of much of Fiji's tourism industry, and it's where many tourists on package deals spend their time. There are many things to do in Nadi, but knowledgeable visitors with more than 1 or 2 days to spend in Fiji will make it a transit stopover on the way to someplace else.

From Nadi, it's also easy to hop over to the pleasant resorts out in the little **Mamanuca Islands,** which have the beaches and clear lagoons the mainland lacks. Farther out, the even more beautiful and less developed **Yasawa Islands** have the best beaches in Fiji. Small, low-keyed cruise ships ply the Yasawas, which have two of Fiji's most luxurious offshore resorts and one of its best backpacker retreats.

South of Nadi along the Queen's Road, the **Coral Coast** has widely spaced resorts with gorgeous scenery and Fijian villages in between. Although its beaches are not as good as those on the offshore islands, the Coral Coast was Fiji's first major resort

area,. and it still attracts visitors in search of a beachside vacation on the "mainland."

On the Queen's Road between the Coral Coast and Suva, **Pacific Harbour** may have a rainy climate, but it has Fiji's best golfing, fine fishing, and great diving (in the Beqa Lagoon).

Suva, with a population of 85,000, is Fiji's busy capital and one of the South Pacific's most cosmopolitan cities. Remnants of Fiji's century as a British possession and the presence of so many Indians give the town a certain air of the colonial "Raj." On the other hand, Suva has modern high-rise buildings and lives at as fast a pace as can be found in the South Pacific west of Tahiti; this is no surprise because in many respects it's the bustling economic center of the region.

From Suva, it's a relatively easy side trip over to historic Levuka, Fiji's first Western-style capital on the beautiful island of Ovalau. Whereas Suva is very much a modern city, Levuka looks much like it did in the days when whalers and beach bums made it a den of iniquity in the 19th century.

From Suva, you can go the other way around back to Nadi, along the King's Road from Lautoka, through the waving sugar cane fields of **northern Viti Levu,** where Rakiraki beckons, with its charming colonial-era hotel.

1 Nadi

Although you won't see much of the "real" Fiji if you spend your entire vacation in Nadi, this area has more activities to keep you busy than any other part of the country. That's because Nadi's international airport and warm, dry climate make it the country's main tourist center.

Nadi, as the area around the international airport is known, is the fastest-growing part of Fiji. New homes, department stores, and shopping centers have been popping up all along the 9km (5½ miles) of the traffic-heavy Queen's Road between the airport and **Nadi Town,** a 7-block strip lined with a plethora of duty-free, handcraft, souvenir, and other shops. The predominately Indo-Fijian town has seen some improvement in recent years. The main drag has been spruced up with planter boxes, big stores now offer fixed prices and polite clerks, and restaurants provide some of the finest dining in the South Pacific.

Although the area has a multitude of activities to keep you busy, and it's home to the large Sheraton Fiji and Sheraton Royal Denarau resorts on Denarau Island, for many visitors Nadi is primarily a stop on the way to other, more beautiful, parts of Fiji. You can easily get to anywhere in Fiji from here, but the lagoon off Nadi is usually murky from runoff coming from the area's sugar cane fields, so this is not the best place in Fiji for a beach vacation.

From Nadi, it's an easy 33km (20-mile) trip to **Lautoka,** Fiji's second largest city, which offers a genteel contrast to tourist-oriented Nadi Town. It's also close to the **Mamanuca Islands** and the less developed **Yasawa Islands.**

GETTING AROUND NADI

All of Fiji's major international and local **car-rental** firms have offices in the international arrival concourse of Nadi International Airport. See "Getting There & Getting Around," in chapter 9.

Taxis gather outside the arrival concourse at the airport and are stationed at the larger hotels. Ask the reception desk to call you one. The aggressive drivers will find you in Nadi Town. See the taxi fare chart under "Getting There & Getting Around," in chapter 9.

Local buses ply the Queen's Road between the markets in Nadi Town and Lautoka, leaving each hour on the hour and on the half-hour between 6am and 8pm Monday to Saturday. The buses destined for Votualevu pass the Tanoa International and Fiji Mocambo hotels. You pay when you board. Tell the driver where you're going; he'll tell you how much to pay. Fares vary according to the length of the trip. About F50¢ (25¢) will get you around the Nadi area.

A cream-and-blue **Denarau Island bus** is the only bus between Nadi Town and the Sheraton resorts, running every 30 minutes daily from 6:30am to 6:30pm. It does not go up the Queen's Road to the airport.

 FAST FACTS: Nadi & Lautoka

The following facts apply specifically to Nadi and Lautoka. For more information, see "Fast Facts: Fiji" in chapter 9.

American Express **Tapa International Ltd. (© 672 2100 or 672 2325)** has full American Express services at its office in the arrival concourse of Nadi International Airport. The address is P.O. Box 9240, Nadi Airport, Fiji

Islands. It's open Monday to Friday from 8:30am to 4:30pm and Saturday from 9am to noon.

Bookstores "Bookshops" here are actually stationery stores. Hotel boutiques are the best places to buy magazines and books.

Camera/Film **Caines Photofast** has a film and 1-hour processing shop on Queen's Road in Nadi Town (✆ **670 1608**). Most of the hotel gift shops also sell film and do 1-day processing.

Currency Exchange **ANZ Bank** and **Westpac Bank** have offices on the Queen's Road in Nadi Town and in Lautoka. Both have ATM machines. ANZ Bank has a 24-hours-a-day branch in the arrivals concourse at Nadi International Airport. **Thomas Cook Travel Service** has a currency exchange office on the Queen's Road in Nadi Town next to the Mobil Station; it's open Monday to Friday from 8:30am to 5pm, Saturday from 8:30am to noon.

Drugstores There are three drugstores on the Queen's Road in Nadi Town. **Budget Pharmacy** (✆ **670 0064**) is the best stocked.

E-mail **Internet Planet,** on the Queen's Road in Martintar (✆ **672 5130**), has computer terminals for e-mail and web surfing. It's open Monday to Friday 8am to 9pm, Saturday and Sunday 9am to 9pm. The terminals at **Cybercafe,** in Nadi Town opposite the Mobil station (✆ **670 5111**), are more private. It's open Monday to Saturday 8am to 5:30pm. Both charge F20¢ (10¢) a minute.

Emergencies/Police The emergency phone number for **police** is ✆ **917.** For **fire** and **ambulance** dial ✆ **911.** The Fiji **police** have stations at Nadi Town (✆ **670 0222**) and at the airport terminal (✆ **672 2222**).

Eyeglasses For optical needs, try **Opticare,** 54 Naviti St. (near Vakabale St. and the market), Lautoka (✆ **666 3337**).

Hairdressers/Barbers **Tanoa International Hotel** (✆ **672 0277**) and the **Dominion International Hotel** (✆ **672 2255**) both have unisex hair salons (see "Where to Stay in Nadi," below).

Healthcare The government-operated **Lautoka Hospital** (✆ **666 3337**) is the region's main facility. There is a **government medical clinic** in Nadi Town (✆ **670 0362**). **Dr. Ram Raju,** 2 Lodhia St., Nadi Town (✆ **701769** or **976333** mobile), has treated many visitors, including me. Ask your hotel staff to recommend a **dentist** in private practice.

Information The **Fiji Visitors Bureau** (✆ **672 2433**) has an office in the arrivals concourse of Nadi International Airport. Other so-called Tourist Information Centres are in reality travel agents or tour operators.

Laundry/Dry Cleaning **Prabhat Steam Laundry** (✆ **672 3061**), on Northern Press Road between the airport and Nadi Town, has 1-day laundry and dry-cleaning service.

Post Office The Nadi Town post office, on Hospital Road near the south end of the market, is open Monday to Friday 7:30am to 5pm, Saturday 8 to 11am. It has a well-stocked stationery store in the lobby. A small airport branch is across the main entry road from the terminal (go through the gates and turn left) is open Monday to Friday 8am to 4pm.

Water The tap water is safe to drink.

SIGHTSEEING & CULTURAL TOURS

Most Coral Coast and Pacific Harbour tours and activities are available from Nadi, since the operators provide transportation. Accordingly, I have included all activities available from Nadi in this and the following sections. It can take 1 hour or more to reach the Coral Coast and 2 hours to get to Pacific Harbour, so be prepared for some long days.

All but a few hotels have tour desks that can make reservations or arrangements for all the activities mentioned below, and the reception-desk staffs of the others will do so. Like travel agents, the activities desks get a percentage of the proceeds; their services cost you nothing extra. Round-trip bus transportation from the Nadi area hotels is included in the price of the tours and outings; a bus usually will pick you up within 30 minutes of the scheduled departure time. Children under 12 years of age pay half fare on most of the activities.

The major tour operators are **United Touring Fiji (UTC)** (© **672 2811**), **Road Tours of Fiji** (© **672 2935**), and **Sun Tours of Fiji** (© **672 2666**). They have decades of experience, their vehicles are clean and air-conditioned, and their staffs are knowledgeable.

SIGHTSEEING TOURS

Several companies operate tours on air-conditioned buses to various destinations near Nadi, on the Coral Coast, and to Suva. Their rates are about the same, but some shopping around could pay off. Talk to more than one hotel activities desk, most of which are operated by the tour companies and will steer you to their own trips. Here are some of the key sightseeing tours.

CORAL COAST RAILWAY ✮   The *Fijian Princess* (© **925 8731**), a restored sugar cane locomotive, pulls you from Shangri-La's Fijian Resort on the Coral Coast to lovely Natadola Beach, where you swim (bring your own towel) and have lunch at a restaurant on the beach. These outings cost about F$83 ($37.50) from the Nadi hotels and F$73 ($33) from those on the Coral Coast, including lunch. Occasionally there's a shopping run to Sigatoka.

Once at Natadola Beach, you can take a sailboat ride out to **Robinson Crusoe Island** for swimming, snorkeling, and a Fijian-style picnic lunch on the beach. These excursions cost F$89 ($40) per person. Water-skiing is extra. The boat runs Tuesday through Friday and on Sunday.

FLIGHTSEEING   Island Hoppers Fiji (© **672 0410**), **Turtle Airways** (© **672 2389**), and **Pacific Islands Seaplanes** (© **672 5643**) all offer sightseeing flights over Denarau Island, Nadi Bay, the Mamanucas, and Vuda Point north of Nadi between Viseisei village and Lautoka. Call them or inquire at any hotel activities desk for prices and reservations.

GARDEN OF THE SLEEPING GIANT ✮✮✮   This lovely, 50-acre orchid range was started in 1977 by the late Raymond Burr, star of TVs *Perry Mason* and *Ironside,* to house his private collection of tropical orchids (he once also owned Naitoba, a small island in the Lau Group). There's much more here than orchids, however, and the guides will describe a variety of local plants and their uses. You can get here on a tour or on your own by rental car or taxi. Look for the sign at Wailoko Road off the Queen's Road between Nadi and Lautoka. It's open Monday to Saturday from 9am to 5pm. Entrance fees are F$10 ($4.50) for adults, F$5 ($2.25) for children, including guided tour and a fruit drink. Burr's former home in the hills overlooking Saweni Bay north of Nadi is now owned by Don and Aileen Burness, who have a collection of Fijian artifacts. Call them for information about touring the home (© **666 2206**).

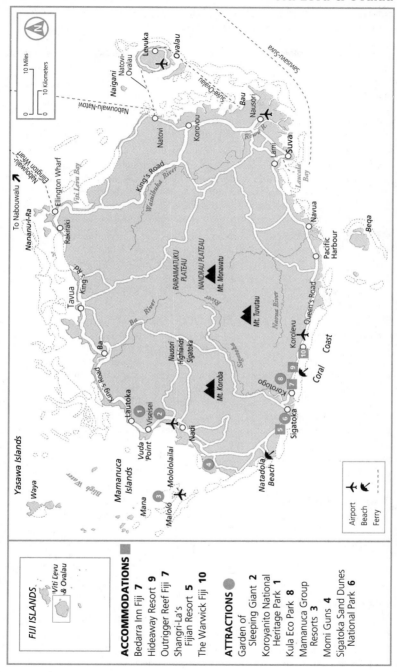

Viti Levu & Ovalau

FIJI ISLANDS

Viti Levu & Ovalau

ACCOMMODATIONS
Bedarra Inn Fiji **7**
Hideaway Resort **9**
Outrigger Reef Fiji **7**
Shangri-La's
Fijian Resort **5**
The Warwick Fiji **10**

ATTRACTIONS
Garden of
Sleeping Giant **2**
Koroyanito National
Heritage Park **1**
Kula Eco Park **8**
Mamanuca Group
Resorts **3**
Momi Guns **4**
Sigatoka Sand Dunes
National Park **6**

Airport
Beach
Ferry

NADI AREA   Several companies have half-day tours of the Nadi area, including the Nadi Town market, an Indo-Fijian sugar cane farm, a Fijian village, a Muslim mosque and a Hindu temple, and the orchid range at Garden of the Sleeping Giant (see above). Another version of this tour goes to Lautoka instead of Nadi Town, with a stop at the Garden of the Sleeping Giant on the way. Many of these tours include **Viseisei Village,** on the Queen's Road about halfway between Nadi and Lautoka. One legend says that the first Fijians settled here. Today it's a typical, fairly prosperous Fijian village, with some modern houses and some shacks of concrete block and tin, a small handcraft shop, and the usual road humps that bring traffic to a crawl. These trips usually cost about F$50 ($22.50).

NAUSORI HIGHLANDS   Several road tours go through the sugar cane fields to the steep, grass-covered hills of the Nausori Highlands, a cool 750m (2,500 ft.) above Nadi. There are some fine vistas from up there, including many out to sea. These tours include brief visits to Fijian villages and Muslim mosques, but they are primarily sightseeing excursions. Cost is about F$45 ($20) per adult.

SIGATOKA HIGHLANDS   For a variation of the Sigatoka Valley trip (see below), this one goes up the valley and then on forestry roads across the steep hills of the scenic Nausori Highlands to Nadi. The full-day trip includes information about Fiji's pre-European days. The price is about F$75 ($33.75), including lunch in a Fijian village. See "The Coral Coast," below, for more information about the highlands.

SIGATOKA VALLEY & KULA ECO PARK   Another full-day tour goes to the town of Sigatoka on the Coral Coast and the meandering river and fertile valley of the same name. The valley has so many market gardens that it is known as "Fiji's Salad Bowl." The tour usually includes a stop at **Nakabuta** or **Nadroga,** small villages in the valley where Fijians still make pottery in the traditional way of their ancestors. You will have time for lunch and some shopping in Sigatoka. The best part of this trip for animal lovers is **Kula Eco Park** ★★. Opposite the Outrigger Reef Fiji, the country's only wildlife park has a fine collection of tropical birds, whose feathers have the colors of a rainbow, and an aquarium stocked with examples of local sea life. You can visit Kula Bird Park (© **650 0505**) on your own. It's open daily 10am to 4:30pm. Admission is F$11 ($5) for adults, free for children under 12. See "The Coral Coast," below, for more information about Sigatoka.

SUVA DAY TOUR   The three major tour companies all have buses that leave Nadi about 8am Monday to Saturday for the 4-hour drive to Suva, picking up passengers at the Coral Coast hotels and stopping for a tour of Pacific Harbour Cultural Centre (see "Pacific Harbour," below). Guests have lunch on their own in Suva, then are escorted on a guided tour of the city. The buses leave Suva about 4pm for the return trip. You'll pay about F$70 ($31.50) per person from Nadi, less from the Coral Coast hotels.

CULTURAL TOURS ★★
Several tours include brief visits to Fijian villages; the ones described here give an in-depth look at Fijian culture.

KOROYANITU NATIONAL HERITAGE PARK   In the mountains above Lautoka, the **Koroyanitu National Heritage Park** is an ecotourism project operated by Abaca ("Ambartha") village and funded by the Native Land Trust Board, the South Pacific Regional Environment Programme, and the New

Fun Fact **The Dreaded Degei**

The tour guides like to point out that **Viseisei** village between Nadi and Lautoka is where the great canoe *Kaunitoni* came out of the west and deposited the first Fijians some 3,000 years ago. From there, the legend goes, they dispersed all over the islands. The yarn is helped by the local district name Vuda, which means "our origin" in Fijian, and Viseisei, which means "to scatter."

Although it's clear today that the Fijians did indeed migrate from the west, no one knows for sure whether they landed first at Viseisei, for like all Pacific islanders, the Fijians had no written language until the missionaries arrived in the mid–19th century.

The most common oral legend has the great chiefs Lutunasobasoba and Degei arriving in the *Kaunitoni* on the northwest coast of Viti Levu. From there they moved inland along the Nakauvadra Range in Northern Viti Levu. Lutunasobasoba died on this trip, but Degei lived on to become a combination man, ancestor, and spirit—and an angry spirit at that, for he is blamed for causing wars and a great flood that washed the Fijians to all parts of the islands.

The dreaded Degei supposedly still inhabits a mysterious cave in the mountains above Rakiraki, but no one is about to go in there to find out.

Zealand government. The park includes native forests, grasslands, waterfalls, and magnificent mountain vistas. Admission is F$5 ($2.25). Fijian villagers guide half-day walks to the Savuione waterfall for F$5 ($2.25) per person and, during the dry season, all-day treks up Mount Batilamu for F$10 ($4.50) a head. Wear comfortable walking shoes! Nase Lodge has basic accommodation for F$15 ($7) per person per night and serves Fijian-style meals. You can also camp at the lodge for F$10 ($4.50) per site or stay in a village for F$30 ($13.50) a night, including meals. This is not a national park in the American sense, so before you set out call the **Ambaca Visitor Center** (© 666 6644 and dial 1234 after the second ring). For transportation to the park call © **666 6590.** It's about a 50-minute ride from Nadi.

NAVUA RIVER TOUR ★★   This full-day trip goes by bus to Navua, a rice-growing town near the mouth of the Navua River on Viti Levu's south coast. You will then travel by outrigger canoe past waterfalls and through forests to Namua-mua, a Fijian village that puts on a yaqona ceremony, a lunch of local-style foods, and a traditional dance show. Price is about F$135 ($61) from the Nadi hotels, less from those on the Coral Coast. UTC calls this its Jewel of Fiji tour; others call it Namuamua Inland Tour. A variation includes a ride down the river on a *bilibili* (bamboo raft; see "River Rafting" under "Boating, Golf, Hiking & Other Outdoor Activities," below).

WATERFALLS & CAVES ★★   Two of the most informative outings are the waterfall and cave tours offered by **Adventures in Paradise** (© **652 0833;** wfall@is.com.fj), on the Coral Coast near the Outrigger Reef Fiji. Led by ener-getic Fijian Rusi Brown, the waterfall tour goes to Biausevu village in the Korolevu Valley. A tour bus takes you to the village, where you'll be welcomed

A Side Trip to Lautoka

Most visitors stay in Nadi and come to Lautoka, Fiji's second-largest town (pop. 30,000) and second major seaport, to board Blue Lagoon Cruises or the boats heading to Beachcomber and Treasure Island Resorts and to the Yasawa Islands. Those who spend a few hours looking around this pleasant town of broad avenues and shady sidewalks are greeted by towering royal palms marching in a long, orderly row down the middle of **Vitogo Parade,** the main drag running from the harbor to the heart of town.

The duty-free shops and other stores along Vitogo Parade mark the boundary of Lautoka's business district; behind them are several blocks of stores and the lively **Lautoka Market,** which doubles as the bus station and is second in size only to Suva's Municipal Market. Handcraft stalls at the front of the market offer a variety of goods, especially when cruise ships are in port. Shady residential streets trail off beyond the playing fields of **Churchill Park** on the other side of Vitogo Parade. The Hare Krishnas have their most important temple in the South Pacific on Tavewa Avenue.

Tourism may rule Nadi, but sugar is king in Lautoka. The **Fiji Sugar Corporation's** huge mill was built in 1903 and is one of the largest crushing operations in the southern hemisphere. If you pass the industrial port, you'll also see a mountain of wood chips ready for export; the chips are a prime product of the country's pine plantations.

Local buses leave the market in Nadi Town every half hour for the Lautoka Market from Monday to Saturday between 6am and 8pm. The fare is no more than F$1.50 (70¢), depending on where you get on. The one-way taxi fare to Lautoka is about F$25 ($11.25) from Nadi.

If you're driving yourself from Nadi, you will come to two traffic circles on the outskirts of Lautoka. Take the second exit off the first one and the first exit off the second. That will take you directly to the post office and the southern end of Vitogo Parade.

---

at a traditional yaqona ceremony. Then comes a 30-minute hike along a rocky stream to the falls, with Rusi explaining the local fauna on the way. A picnic lunch is served at the falls, which plunge straight over a cliff into a swimming hole. The sometimes slippery trail fords the stream seven times, so wear canvas shoes or a pair of strap-on sandals for the hike, and wear a bathing suit and bring a towel if you want to take a very cool and refreshing dip after the sweaty hike.

On Rusi's other excursion, you'll spend 45 minutes inside the Naihehe Cave, which was used as a fortress by Fiji's last cannibal tribe, and then return via a *bilibili* raft on the Sigatoka River (the cave is an hour's drive up the Sigatoka Valley). A yaqona ceremony will welcome you to the village, and you'll have a picnic lunch before the raft ride.

Rusi charges F$109 ($49) per person for the waterfall tour, F$99 ($44.50) for the cave trip, including lunch and transfers. Subtract F$20 ($9) if he picks you up at a Coral Coast hotel. Book at any hotel activities desk.

BOATING, GOLF, HIKING & OTHER OUTDOOR ACTIVITIES

The Nadi area offers a host of sporting and outdoor activities to suit almost every interest. Most of these are near Nadi, but some require a boat trip to the Mamanuca Islands or a bus ride to other locations on Viti Levu. The Sheraton resorts on Denarau Island both have watersports equipment and activities.

FISHING ★★ The best fishing boat here is American Tyson Johnson's *Sundancer* (© **672 0786** or 992 0044; sundancer@is.com.fj), based at Port Denarau. This custom-designed 13m (43-ft.) boat sleeps up to six persons and does both 1-day trips to the Mamanucas and extended cruises to the northern Yasawas, site of Fiji's best fishing. Fees are F$900 ($405) for half a day, F$1,500 ($675) for a full day. Inquire about prices for the extended cruises.

The two Sheraton hotels and all the resorts in the Mamanucas offer sportfishing as a pay-extra activity for their guests. On the mainland, **South Sea Cruises** (© **675 0500**) has a fleet of fishing boats and guides based at Port Denarau. Offshore, that same company operates under the name **Pleasure Marine** (© **675 0500**), with boats at Musket Cove Resort and Mana Island Resort.

GOLF & TENNIS The 18-hole, 7,150-yard, par-72 resort course of **Denarau Golf & Racquet Club** ★★ (© **675 0477**) occupies most of Denarau Island, with the club house opposite the Sheraton resorts. It has a restaurant that serves breakfast, lunch, and dinner at moderate prices, a bar, and locker rooms with showers. Greens fees are F$90 ($40.50) for guests of the two big resorts and F$95 ($43) for those of us who can't afford to stay there. The course is open daily from 7am to dark.

The club's six Wimbledon-standard grass tennis courts are open daily from 7am to dark, and its four all-weather courts stay open until 10pm. Fees are F$20 ($9) per person per hour on grass, F$15 ($7) per hour on the hard courts. Lessons are available, and proper tennis attire is required.

The **Fiji Mocambo** hotel (© **672 2000**) has a 9-hole executive course, and the hotel tour desks can arrange for you to play at the 18-hole **Nadi Airport Golf Club** (© **672 2148**) near Newtown Beach, behind the airport. The latter is a 5,882-yard, par-70 course which isn't particularly challenging, but the setting, on the shores of Nadi Bay, is attractive.

HIKING In addition to the guided walks in the Koroyanitu National Heritage Park and Adventures in Paradise's waterfall hikes on the Coral Coast (see "Cultural Tours," above), **Adventures Fiji** (© **672 2935;** fax 672 4970; rosiefiji@is.com.fj), an arm of Rosie the Travel Service, offers trekkers (as hikers are known in these parts) the chance to make a 1-day walk some 600m (2,000 ft.) up into the Nausori Highlands above Nadi. I found this walk to be strenuous but fascinating; you have to be under 45 to sign up unless you're in good physical condition. Wear walking shoes with excellent traction and that you don't mind getting wet, for the sandy trail goes into and out of steep valleys and crosses streams. Also wear sunscreen, for most of this walk is through grasslands

---

Tips **Don't Get Blistered!**

Whatever you do outdoors in Fiji, don't forget to take your hat and powerful sunblock—and use them! The sun can blister you quickly at these latitudes, even on a cloudy day.

with no shade. We had a long midday break in a Fijian village, where we shared a local-style lunch sitting cross-legged in a simple Fijian home, then took a 45-minute side excursion up a narrow valley to a waterfall. The cost is F$69 ($31) per person. The company also has 4-, 6- and 10-day hikes across central Viti Levu, ranging in price from about F$500 to F$1,200 ($225–$540), including transfers, guide, accommodation, and meals provided by Fijian villagers along the way.

HORSEBACK RIDING   A 20-minute drive and short boat ride south of Nadi Town, **Sonaisali Island Resort** (© **670 6011**) has guided horseback rides through the tropical vegetation on its 105-acre private island. A 1-hour ride costs F$26 ($11.50) for adults, F$13 ($5.75) for children under 12. Riders must be at least 8 years and not weigh over 138 kilograms (275 lb.). Reservations are required.

JET BOATS   For a thrill-a-minute carnival ride afloat, **Shotover Jet Fiji** (© **675 0400**) will take you twisting and turning through the mangrove-lined creeks behind Denarau Island. This is the company that pioneered jet-boating on the Shotover River in New Zealand, and its speedy "Big Red" boats go roaring around these Fijian waterways. Heart-stopping 360° turns are guaranteed to get the adrenaline flowing and the clothes wet. The half-hour rides depart every 30 minutes daily from Port Denarau. A shuttle connects the nearby Sheratons; there are scheduled pickups from other Nadi area hotels, so call for reservations. Price is F$69 ($31) for adults and F$25 ($11) for children.

RIVER RAFTING   Travel videos and brochures seem to always feature tourists lazily floating down a Fijian river on a raft made of bamboo poles lashed together. In the old days, mountain-dwelling Fijians really did use *bilibilis*—long, flimsy bamboo rafts—to float their crops down river to market. They would discard the rafts and walk home. Today you can ride your own *bilibili* down the Navua River, between Pacific Harbour and Suva. Several companies have cultural tours up the river to picturesque Namuamua village (see "Cultural Tours," above), but **Discover Fiji Tours** (© **345 0180;** discoverfiji@is.com.fj) not only takes you upriver by motorized canoe, it usually brings you back on a *bilibili* (make sure the *bilibili* is included before you sign up). The river itself is a scenic delight as it cuts a gorge through the foothills. Depending on how much it has rained recently, you'll have a few gentle rapids to negotiate, and you'll stop for dips in waterfalls that tumble right into the river. Wear swimsuits and sandals, but bring a sarong to wear in the village, where you'll be welcomed at a yoga ceremony. Namuamua is much like any other modern Fijian village, with tin roofs on plywood or concrete block houses, and it has glorious mountain views from a fork in the river.

These full-day trips cost about F$100 ($45) from the Nadi hotels, F$90 to F$95 ($40.50–$43) from the Coral Coast. Children pay about half fare. A minimum of two passengers is required.

If you're into serious white-water rafting, your best bet is **Rivers Fiji** ✦✦ (© **800/346-6277** in the U.S., or 345 0147; fax 345 0148; www.riversfiji.com). This American-owned outfit uses modern inflatable rafts and kayaks for trips through the Upper Navua River Gorge. These are long day trips but worth it for rafting and kayak fans. The kayak adventures cost F$175 ($79) from Nadi, F$160 ($72) from the Coral Coast, Pacific Harbour, and Suva. They don't go every day, and 24 hours advance reservations are required, so call ahead for more information.

Fun Fact **Dust to Dust**

The late actor Gardner McKay, who sailed around on the M. V. *Seaspray* while starring as Capt. Adam Troy, walked away from the boob tube after the popular TV series *Adventures in Paradise* bit the dust in the 1960s. At first he opted for real dust—as in riding across the Sahara Desert with the Egyptian Camel Corps. He went on to crew on yachts in the Caribbean and hike the Amazonian jungles before settling down as a novelist, poet, playwright, and newspaper drama critic. Despite his drop-dead good looks, he never acted again.

SAILING   The *Whale's Tale* ★★ (© **672 2455;** funcruises@is.com.fj), a luxury, 30m (100-ft.) auxiliary sailboat owned by American Paul Myers, takes no more than 12 guests on day cruises from Port Denarau through the Mamanucas. The F$180 ($80) per person cost includes a continental breakfast with champagne on departure; a buffet lunch prepared on board; and all beverages, including beer, wine, and liquor, and sunset cocktails. The *Whale's Tale* is also available for charters ranging from 1 day in the Mamanucas to 3 days and 2 nights in the Yasawas. Rates depend on the length of trip.

South Sea Cruises (© **675 0500;** southsea@is.com.fj) has day sails aboard the **MV *Seaspray,*** a 25m (83-ft.) schooner that starred in the 1960s TV series *Adventures in Paradise,* based on James A. Michener's short stories. These trips stop at Monoriki Island, where Tom Hanks filmed the movie *Cast Away*—Hanks did *not* live on the islet all by himself during production. The cruises cost F$120 to F$160 ($54–$72) for adults, half fare for kids, depending on where you board, including morning tea, lunch, beer, wine, and soft drinks. You pay more to get on at Port Denarau, less at the Mamanuca resorts.

Because of Fiji's reef-strewn waters, the government will not permit strictly "bareboat" yacht charters, but you can rent both boat and skipper or local guide for extended cruises through the islands. **Fiji Yacht Charters,** Private Bag 0352, Nadi Airport (© **666 2215;** fax 6662633; www.fijiyachting.com), acts as an agent for several boats based at Musket Cove Resort in the Mamanucas. These include the *Hobo,* an 11m (37-ft.) ketch, and *La Violente,* a 32m (106-ft.) boat built for French royalty. Both have day cruises for about F$100 ($45) an hour and are available for longer cruises. Musket Cove's marina is a mecca for cruising yachts such as these, some of whose skippers hang around and take charters for a living.

SCUBA DIVING & SNORKELING   Dive operators in the Nadi area include the American firm **Aqua-Trek,** which has an office in Nadi Town opposite the Mobil station (© **800/541-4334** or 670 2413) and dive bases at Mana and Matamanoa resorts in the Mamanucas (see "Island Escapes from Nadi," below). Aqua-Trek also has a base at Pacific Harbour (see "Pacific Harbour," below), and it owns the Garden Island Resort on Taveuni (see chapter 11). Both Sheraton resorts have dive operators on premises. **Inner Space Adventures** (© **672 3883**) at Newtown on Wailoaloa Beach caters primarily to backpackers. All have dive guides and teach courses. The price is about F$100 ($45) for a two-tank dive.

SHOPPING IN NADI

Haggling is not considered to be polite when dealing with Fijians, and the better stores now have fixed prices. Bargaining is still acceptable, however, when

---

Tips **Beware of "Sword Sellers"**

Fijians are normally extremely friendly people, but beware of so-called **sword sellers.** These are Fijian men who carry bags under their arms and approach you on the street. "Where you from, States?" will be their opening line, followed quickly by, "What's your name?" If you respond, they will quickly inscribe your name on a sloppily carved wooden sword carried in the bag. They expect you to buy the sword, whether you want it or not. They are especially numerous in Suva, but they will likely come up to you in Nadi, too. The Fiji government discourages this practice but has had only limited success in stopping it. The easiest way to avoid this scam is not tell any stranger your name and walk away as soon as you see the bag.

---

dealing with Indo-Fijian merchants in many small shops. They will start high, you will start low, and somewhere in between you will find a mutually agreeable price. I usually knock 40% off the asking price as an initial counteroffer and then suffer the merchants' indignant snickers, secure in the knowledge that they aren't about to kick me out of the store. After all, the fun has just begun.

You'll have innumerable choices of tropical clothing here, but for the most unusual items in the entire South Pacific, head out to **Michoutouchkine Creations** ★★★ at the Sheraton Fiji (✆ **675 0518**). This little shop carries the colorful creations of Nicolai Michoutouchkine and Aloi Pilioki, two noted Vanuatu artists whose unique squiggly swirls and swooshes distinguish each of their shirts, blouses, pants suits, and beach towels.

DUTY-FREE SHOPPING

Fiji has the most developed duty-free shopping industry in the South Pacific, as will be very obvious when you walk along the main thoroughfare in Nadi Town. One shop after another offers brand-name perfume, jewelry, watches, electronic equipment, cameras, liquor, cigarettes, and a plethora of other items.

The Fiji government charges a flat 10% import tax on merchandise brought into the country, so the stores aren't exactly "duty free." Check around carefully before leaving home if you are thinking of buying an expensive watch or camera. You will likely find better prices and selections at the large-volume dealers at home, especially in the United States, Canada, Australia, and New Zealand. Find the item at home first so that you can compare the price in Fiji. Also compare the models offered in the duty-free shops with those available at home. Those sold in Fiji may not be the latest editions.

If you decide to make a purchase, follow this advice from the Fiji National Duty Free Merchants Association: Request receipts that accurately describe your purchases. Make sure all guarantee and warranty cards are properly completed and stamped by the merchant. Examine all items before making payment. If you later find that the item is not what you expected, return to the shop immediately with the item and your receipt. As a general rule, purchases are not returnable and deposits are not refundable.

Always pay for your duty-free purchases by credit card. That way, if something goes wrong after you're back home, you can call for help from the large financial institution that issued the card.

To avoid the hassles of bargaining, visit **Jack's Handicrafts, Prouds,** and **Tappoo,** the largest and most reputable merchants. They have well-stocked shops on

Queen's Road in Nadi Town as well as in the shopping arcades of the larger hotels. They are also in Sigatoka and downtown Suva. The upstairs rooms in Jack's Handicrafts stores are filled with clothing and leather goods. Tappoo carries a broad range of merchandise, including electronics, cameras, and sporting goods. Prouds concentrates on jewelry, perfumes, and watches.

If you missed anything, you'll get one last chance at the huge shops in the departure lounge at Nadi airport.

HANDCRAFTS

Fijians produce a wide variety of handcrafts, such as carved *tanoa* (kava) bowls, war clubs, and cannibal forks; woven baskets and mats; pottery (which has seen a renaissance of late); and *masi* (tapa) cloth. Although generally not of the quality of those produced in Tonga, they are made in prolific quantities. Be careful when buying some woodcarvings, however, for many of today's items are machine-made, and many smaller items are imported from Asia. Only with *masi* can you be sure of getting a genuine Fijian handcraft.

The larger shops now sell some very fine face masks and *nguzunguzus* ("noozoo noozoos"), the inlaid canoe prows carved in the Solomon Islands, and some primitive art from Papua New Guinea. (Although you will see plenty hanging in the shops, the Fijians never carved masks in the old days.)

The largest and best-stocked shop on Queen's Road is **Jack's Handicrafts** ★★ (✆ 670 0744). It has a wide selection of handcrafts, jewelry, T-shirts, clothing, and paintings by local artists. The prices are reasonable and the staff is helpful rather than pushy. The Chefs The Restaurant complex is on premises (see "Where to Dine in Nadi," below). Jack's Handicrafts also has an outlet in the shopping arcade of the Sheraton Fiji Resort (✆ 670 1777) and in Sigatoka (✆ 650 0810).

Other places to look are **Nadi Handicraft Center** (✆ 670 2357), opposite the Bank of Hawaii on the other side of Queen's Road, and **Nad's Handicrafts** (✆ 670 3588), near the north end of town. Nadi Handicraft Center has an upstairs room that carries clothing, leather goods, jewelry, and black pearls from Tahiti. Nad's usually has the best selection of Fijian pottery.

In the Sheraton Denarau Villas arcade on Denarau Island, **Sogo Fiji** (✆ 675 0000, ext. 2317) has an excellent selection of handcrafts, including some from the Solomon Islands and Papua New Guinea (the Sogo Fiji outlet on Queen's Rd. in Nadi Town doesn't carry handcrafts). The Sheraton's shops are open daily 9am to 9pm.

Nadi Handicraft Market (no phone) is a collection of stalls on the Queen's Road near the south end of Nadi Town. The best stalls are operated by Fijian women who sell baskets and other goods woven of pandanus. But note that Jack's and the other large stores buy the best items directly from the makers, so the choices at the market are primarily of the souvenir variety.

Tips **Wait Until You Visit Suva**

If you're going to Suva, wait until you visit the **Government Handicraft Centre** to buy handcrafts. There you will see authentic items made in Fiji and get a firm idea of the going prices. See "Shopping in Suva," below.

WHERE TO STAY IN NADI

Most Nadi-area hotels are on or near the Queen's Road, either near the airport or in the suburban area known as **Martintar** between the airport and Nadi Town. Except for backpacker-oriented hostels in Newtown on Wailoaloa Beach, none of these establishments are on a beach, and even if they were, runoff from the mountains, hills, cane fields, and coastal mangrove swamps perpetually leaves **Nadi Bay** murky, sometimes for several miles offshore.

About 7km (4⅓ miles) to the west of Nadi Town, pancake-flat **Denarau Island** is home to a huge real estate project known in its entirety as Denarau Island Resort. It includes the two Sheraton hotels (and more under construction), an adjacent 150-unit time-share complex, an 18-hole golf course, Port Denarau marina, where most of the area's cruises are based, and room for much more. Denarau is only technically an island, for a narrow, winding creek through a mangrove forest is all that separates it from the mainland. If you stay on Denarau, you will have to take a taxi to get anywhere else after 6:30pm, when the only bus stops running between there and Nadi Town. See "Getting There & Getting Around" in chapter 9 for taxi fares.

Fiji's other big resort, the 400-room **Shangri-La's Fijian Resort,** 45 minutes south of Nadi (see the section "The Coral Coast," below), has a whiter beach and clearer lagoon than those at Denarau, but it lacks the convenience of having so many activities on its doorstep.

IN THE AIRPORT AREA

Fiji Mocambo   This sprawling hotel atop a hill south of the airport was about to get some much-needed renovation during my recent visit, for it suffered more than most hotels from the drop-off in tourism following the coup in 2000. I found soiled and torn carpets, aging furniture, and several other shortcomings, such as empty liquid soap dispensers (instead of bar soap) in the bathrooms. Once the best airport hotel, it had fallen several notches below its rival, the nearby Tanoa International Hotel (see below). Also, the main lounge is a popular spot for dancing after 9pm, and its live music can be heard in some rooms. Don't hesitate to ask for another room if the noise bothers you. If you do stay here, opt for a "superior" room on the top floor. The peaked ceilings in these rooms give them the feel of individual bungalows, and some of their bathrooms have both tubs and walk-in showers.

P.O. Box 9195, Nadi Airport (Votualevu Rd., 2km/1 mile south of airport). (C) **800/942-5050** or 672 2000. Fax 672 0324. www.shangri-la.com. 127 units. F$270–F$277 ($121.50–$124.50) double. AE, DC, MC, V. **Amenities:** 2 restaurants (regional), 2 bars; outdoor pool; 9-hole golf course; 2 tennis courts; activities desk; business center; shopping arcade; 24-hr. room service; babysitting; laundry service. *In room:* A/C, TV, fridge, coffeemaker, hair dryer, iron.

Raffle's Gateway Hotel   Along with the more modern and entertaining Tokatoka Resort Hotel next door, this older property (no connection to Singapore's famous Raffles Hotel) is Nadi's most convenient place to wait for a flight at the airport just across Queen's Road. And as at the Tokatoka, you can slip down a water slide into a swimming pool, this one shaped like a figure 8. A plantation theme dominates the property, with the main building somewhat reminiscent of a colonial planter's home. Medium-size rooms are in two-story buildings on either side of a courtyard and a second, older swimming pool with its own thatch-roof bar. The rooms are modest but nicely appointed with coconut wood furniture. The more expensive units have sitting areas. The roadside main building houses a 24-hour coffee shop.

Nadi

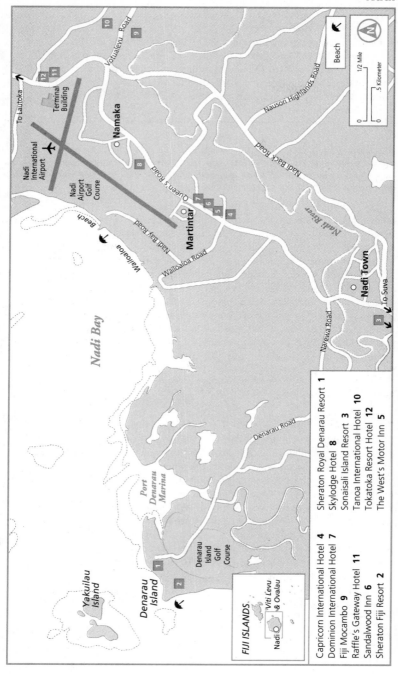

Beach

0 1/2 Mile
0 .5 Kilometer

FIJI ISLANDS

Viti Levu & Ovalau
Nadi

To Lautoka

Terminal Building

Nadi International Airport

Nadi Airport Golf Course

Voualevu Road

Namaka

Nausori Highlands Road

Nadi Back Road

Queen's Road

Martintar

Nadi Bay Road

Waqadra

Beach

Wailoaloa Road

Nadi River

Nadi Town

To Suva

Nadi Bay

Naisali Road

Narewa Road

Port Denarau Marina

Denarau Road

Denarau Island

Denarau Island Golf Course

Yakuilau Island

Capricorn International Hotel **4**
Dominion International Hotel **7**
Fiji Mocambo **9**
Raffle's Gateway Hotel **11**
Sandalwood Inn **6**
Sheraton Fiji Resort **2**

Sheraton Royal Denarau Resort **1**
Skylodge Hotel **8**
Sonaisali Island Resort **3**
Tanoa International Hotel **10**
Tokatoka Resort Hotel **12**
The West's Motor Inn **5**

271

> ## *Tips*   Last-Minute Plans
>
> If you're making last-minute plans, talk to **Impulse Trips Fiji,** P.O. Box 1000, Nadi Airport (© **672 3952;** fax 672 5064; www.impulsefiji.com), which sells "unused" hotel rooms at reduced rates. It saves you the trouble of asking the front desk for a discount on rooms that would otherwise would go unused. You can also get discounts if you book in advance on the company's website.

P.O. Box 9891, Nadi Airport (Queen's Rd., directly opposite airport). © **672 2444.** Fax 672 0620. rafflesres@ is.com.fj. 93 units. F$117–$161 ($52.50–$72.50) double. AE, DC, MC, V. **Amenities:** 2 restaurants (regional), 1 bar; 2 outdoor pools; tennis court; Jacuzzi; game room; activities desk; 24-hr. room service; babysitting; laundry service. *In room:* A/C, TV, fridge, coffeemaker, hair dryer.

Tanoa International Hotel ★★   One of the few properties to be upgraded following the 2000 coup, this well-managed motel is the top place to stay near the airport. The bright public areas open onto a lush garden with a waterfall splashing into a swimming pool. Thatch-covered walkways lead to medium-size, motel-style rooms in white, two-story blocks. Most units have cool tile floors, bright spreads, tropical furniture, a double and a single bed, combination tub-and-shower bathrooms, and balconies or patios. Each executive room has a king-size bed, a large desk, and a sofa; these rooms are Nadi's best for business travelers. Two luxurious one-bedroom suites are often taken by dignitaries. Dining facilities include an open-air restaurant by the pool and a 24-hour air-conditioned coffee shop, a delightful respite in these humid climes.

P.O. Box 9203, Nadi Airport (Votualevu Rd., 2km/1¼ miles south of airport). © **800/835-7742** or 672 0277. Fax 672 0191. www.tanoahotels.com. 135 units. F$190–F$210 ($85.50–$94.50) double; F$220–F$400 ($99–$180) suite. AE, DC, MC, V. **Amenities:** 2 restaurants (regional), 1 bar; outdoor pool; 2 tennis courts; exercise room; Jacuzzi; sauna; activities desk; salon; 24-hr. room service; massage; babysitting; laundry service; coin-op washers and dryers. *In room:* A/C, TV, dataport, fridge, coffeemaker, hair dryer, iron.

Tokatoka Resort Hotel ★ *Kids*   The highlight at this modern complex is an unusual swimming pool–restaurant-bar at the rear of the property, which makes it a favorite of families with children. The youngsters can play to their hearts' content on an S-shaped water slide that streams down into the angular pool, which is partially under the same steel-beam- and brick-supported roof that covers the restaurant and bar. Indeed, this is the best place in Nadi to kill time while waiting for a flight home. You'll also find Nadi's most varied mix of accommodations here, from hotel rooms to apartments to two-bedroom bungalows, many of them equipped with cooking facilities. The poolside restaurant is open 24 hours a day for snacks and a blackboard meal menu, and a jazz group plays every evening from an island in the pool. Tokatoka has a tour desk, a grocery store, and a boutique. Some units are equipped for guests with disabilities.

P.O. Box 9305, Nadi Airport (Queen's Rd., opposite airport). © **672 0222.** Fax 672 0400. tokatokaresort@ is.com.fj. 112 units. F$144–$178 ($65–$80) double; F$160–F$322 ($72–$145) bungalow. AE, DC, MC, V. **Amenities:** 1 restaurant (regional), 1 bar; outdoor pool; playground; activities desk; shopping arcade; tour desk; salon; 24-hr. room service; massage; babysitting; laundry service; coin-op washers and dryers. *In room:* A/C, TV, kitchen (in deluxe units), fridge, coffeemaker.

IN THE MARTINTAR AREA

Capricorn International Hotel   You won't enjoy luxuries at this simple motel-style hostelry, but you will get a clean room and a very firm mattress—both trademarks here and at its equally spotless sister in Suva, the Capricorn

Apartment Hotel (see "Where to Stay in Suva," below). Each smallish room is simply furnished with a blonde wood desk, wicker chairs and a wicker coffee table, and both a double and a single bed. Top picks are rooms with balconies or patios overlooking a lush tropical courtyard with pool. These more spacious units have glass shower stalls with doors, and the others have French-style showers, which can result in wet tile floors. Least expensive are the standard rooms, which are entered from the rear and have window walls instead of balconies overlooking the courtyard. This is often the lowest priced Nadi property offered on package tours.

P.O. Box 9043, Nadi Airport (Queen's Rd., at Wailoaloa Rd, 5km/3 miles south of airport). *C* **672 0088.** Fax 672 0522. capricorn@is.com.fj. 62 units. F$85–$110 ($38–$49.50) double. AE, DC, MC, V. **Amenities:** 1 restaurant (Indian), 1 bar; outdoor pool; activities desk; car-rental desk; limited room service; massage; babysitting; laundry service. *In room:* A/C, TV, fridge, coffeemaker.

Dominion International Hotel   This aging but well-maintained motel is one of the few establishments in Fiji at which you can park a car right next to your door or the stairs leading to your room. The units are in two white, three-story buildings that flank a tropical garden surrounding a swimming pool. A central building with a restaurant and bar sits at the Queen's Road end, completing the hotel's U shape. Bands play here at night in the open-air lounge, so request a unit away from the action. The spacious rooms have white tile floors, tub-and-shower bathrooms, and glass doors that slide open to patios or bougainvillea-draped balconies. A few units are equipped for guests with disabilities.

P.O. Box 9178, Nadi Airport (Queen's Rd., 5km/3 miles south of airport). *C* 800/448-8355 or 672 2255. Fax 672 0187. www.dominion-international.com. 85 units. F$130–F$174 ($58.50–$78.50) double. AE, DC, MC, V. **Amenities:** 1 restaurant (regional), 1 bar; outdoor pool; tennis court; game room; activities desk; salon; limited room service; massage; babysitting; laundry service. *In room:* A/C, TV, fridge, coffeemaker, hair dryer.

Sandalwood Lodge *Value*   "Clean and comfortable at a sensible price" is the appropriate motto at John and Ana Birch's establishment, which makes it especially popular with New Zealanders (John's a Kiwi; Ana is a friendly Fijian). About 200 yards off the Queen's Road, their spacious New Zealand–style motel units enjoy a quiet residential setting. The three two-story buildings flank a nicely landscaped lawn with a rock-bordered pool. Units in the Orchid Wing are somewhat larger than the others and have a queen-size beds instead of a double. There's no dining room on site, but it's a manageable walk to the Bounty Bar & Restaurant (see "Where to Dine in Nadi," below).

P.O. Box 9454, Nadi Airport (Martintar, near Queen's Road, 5km/3 miles south of airport). *C* **672 2044.** Fax 672 0103. sandalwood@is.com.fj. 34 units. F$77–F$90 ($34.50–$40.50) double. AE, DC, MC, V. **Amenities:** Outdoor pool; babysitting; laundry service. *In room:* A/C, TV, kitchen, coffeemaker, iron (in Orchid Wing).

Skylodge Hotel *★* *Value*   The eclectic Skylodge was built as a crew base for Qantas Airways in the early 1960s, but it has been remodeled and upgraded over the years and is a very good value today. The preferable rooms are in four-unit bungalows scattered through 11 acres of lawns and tropical trees; some have cooking facilities. Rooms in the original wooden lodge range from cramped to spacious, and some are next to the bar and swimming pool, beside which you can dine outdoors under a steel roof. There's a Jacuzzi and a little "beach" next to the pool, and the games room here is open-air in a big steel pavilion. The manager and veteran staff provide friendly and efficient service.

P.O. Box 9222, Nadi Airport (Namaka, on Queen's Rd., 3.5km/2 miles south of airport). *C* 800/448-8355 or 672 2200. Fax 672 4330. www.tanoahotels.com. 53 units. F$121–$132 ($54.50–59.50) double. AE, DC, MC, V. **Amenities:** 1 restaurant (regional), 1 bar; outdoor pool; Jacuzzi; game room; activities desk; limited room service; babysitting; laundry service; coin-op washers and dryers. *In room:* A/C, TV, kitchen (bungalows only), fridge, coffeemaker.

The West's Motor Inn This gay-friendly but not exclusively gay establishment is more like a Key West inn than a motel. Lending charm, a courtyard swimming pool partially wraps around—and is shaded by—an ancient mango tree. The rooms are comfortably furnished, although their shower-only bathrooms are cramped. Most have wooden louvered windows and doors that swing open to this vista, either directly to the courtyard or to balconies above. Although they have no view, the least expensive rooms in the rear appeal to backpackers and other cost-conscious travelers. Opening to the pool and tree, the cafe turns into a lively piano bar at night (see "Island Nights in Nadi," below).

P.O. Box 10097, Nadi Airport (Queen's Rd., 5km/3 miles south of airport). *©* **672 0044.** Fax 672 0071. west motorinn@is.com.fj. 62 units. F$44–F$129 ($20–$58) double. AE, DC, MC, V. **Amenities:** 1 restaurant (regional), 1 bar; outdoor pool; activities desk; massage; babysitting; laundry service. *In room:* A/C, TV, dataport, fridge, coffeemaker, hair dryer (in deluxe units).

ON DENARAU ISLAND

A free "Bula Bus" shuttles between the two Sheraton hotels and the Denarau Golf & Racquet Club on this sprawling resort complex, but it does not go to the Port Denarau marina.

Sheraton Fiji Resort ★★★ Although the Denarau beach is not nearly as good as the one at Shangri-la's Fijian Resort on the Coral Coast (see "The Coral Coast," below), this 1987-vintage property is the most luxurious of Fiji's three big resorts. Contrasting sharply with the dark-wood, handcraft-accented public areas of Sheraton Denarau Villas next door, the white marble lobby is strongly reminiscent of a U.S. shopping mall (it does indeed have some very fine shops). In other words, this Sheraton could be put down in any tropical resort location, not necessarily in the South Seas. Its large, bright, spacious, and tropically decorated rooms have ocean views from their private terraces or balconies.

The resort also manages the 164 adjacent condos known as the **Sheraton Denarau Villas.** Built in 1999 around a courtyard, one end of which opens to a beachside swimming pool and bar, these are Nadi's best digs. They come in various sizes, ranging from a single room to a three-bedroom apartment, and are appointed with all the comforts of home, including full kitchens and washers and dryers.

The four food choices here (none of them inexpensive) include fine dining in the swanky Ports O' Call. Planters Bar is a dimly lit pub with disco dancing after 9pm. There's a private island across the lagoon where guests can swim, snorkel, and sunbathe.

P.O. Box 9761, Nadi (Denarau Island, 7km/4.5 miles west of Nadi Town). *©* **800/325-3535** or 675 0777. Fax 675 0818. www.sheraton.com. 456 units. F$548–F$765 ($247–$344) double; F$770–F$1,557 ($347–$700) condo. AE, DC, MC, V. **Amenities:** 4 restaurants (international), 3 bars; outdoor pool; golf course; tennis courts; exercise room; watersports equipment rentals; bike rentals; children's programs; concierge; activities desk; car-rental desk; business center; shopping arcade; salon; 24-hr. room service; massage; babysitting; laundry service. *In room:* A/C, TV, dataport, minibar, kitchen (in condos), coffeemaker, hair dryer, iron, safe.

Sheraton Royal Denarau Resort ★★★ Once known as The Regent of Fiji, this venerable establishment has been one of the finest hotels in the South Pacific since 1972, and although not as luxurious, it has considerably more Fijian charms than the Sheraton Fiji Resort. Covered by a peaked wooden roof, a dark, breezy foyer opens to an irregularly shaped pool with thatch-covered, swim-up bar on one end (something the Sheraton Fiji's rectangular pool lacks). A grassy berm, built after cyclones damaged the beach, separates the pool from the gray beach. Like those at the Sheraton Fiji, the rooms here are in a series of two-story, motel-style blocks grouped in "villages" surrounded by thick, lush tropical gardens and linked by covered walkways to the central building. With lots of varnished wood trim, exposed timbers, and *masi* cloth accents, the spacious units also have more tropical charm than those at the Sheraton Fiji, although you will have to pay extra for a TV here. The five food outlets here include a steakhouse. Guests can use the private island shared with the Sheraton Fiji.

P.O. Box 9761, Nadi Airport (Denarau Island, 7km/4.5 miles west of Nadi Town). ℂ 800/325-3535 or 675 0000. Fax 675 0259. www.sheraton.com. 273 units. F$440–F$650 ($198–$293) double. AE, DC, MC, V. **Amenities:** 5 restaurants (international/steaks), 4 bars; outdoor pool; golf course; tennis courts; exercise room; watersports equipment rentals; bike rentals; children's programs; game room; concierge; activities desk; car-rental desk; shopping arcade; 24-hr. room service; massage; babysitting; laundry service. *In room:* A/C, dataport, minibar, coffeemaker, hair dryer, safe.

SOUTH OF NADI

Sonaisali Island Resort   You drive down a dirt road through cane fields and ride a boat across a narrow muddy channel to this modern resort set on a flat, 105-acre island. There is no beach here, only imported sand held in place by a seawall, and Nadi Bay becomes a broad mud flat at low tide. Nevertheless, there are Windsurfers and other toys to play with, the resort organizes diving trips to the Mamanuca reefs, and you can frolic in an attractive rock-lined pool, complete with fountain, whirlpool, kiddie area, and swim-up bar. A big shingle roof covers all other common facilities, including an air-conditioned fine-dining restaurant and a cafe that opens to the pool. A variety of guest quarters includes 32 spacious, air-conditioned hotel rooms, but the top choice are the 69 units in duplex bungalows out in the lush gardens. Some of these have air conditioners in their bedrooms, some face the beach, and some have Jacuzzi tubs on their front porches. Three of the units have two bedrooms each and are attractive to families. I wouldn't spend a week here, but this is a reasonable and less expensive alternative to the Sheratons for a short bay-side stopover.

P.O. Box 2544, Nadi (Sonaisali Island, 20 min. south of Nadi Town). (ℂ 670 6011. Fax 670 6092. www.sonaisali.com. 101 units. F$320–F$495 ($144–$223) double. Rates include breakfast. AE, DC, MC, V. **Amenities:** 2 restaurants (international), 3 bars; outdoor pool; tennis court; Jacuzzi; watersports equipment rentals; game room; activities desk; car-rental desk; business center; salon; 24-hr. room service; massage; babysitting; laundry service. *In room:* A/C (in rooms and beachfront units), minibar, coffeemaker, hair dryer, iron.

HOSTELS

Touts bombard backpackers arriving at Nadi airport with offers of cheap accommodation, for this area has a host of hostels, all of them in fierce competition with each other. The most luxurious backpacker's accommodation is at **Nadi Bay Hotel** (ℂ **672 3599;** fax 672 0092; www.fijinadibayhotel.com), an Australian-owned motel on Wailoaloa Road just off the Queen's Road in Martintar. Its concrete-and-steel building appears nondescript from the outside, but inside you'll find a courtyard with pool and a sophisticated bar and a restaurant serving reasonably priced meals. There's dining out on the patio, too. In addition to the dorm rooms, there are standard motel rooms and apartments. The property is directly under Nadi airport's flight path, however, so be prepared for the roar of jets overhead. Dorm beds go for F$15 ($7) a night. Rooms and apartments range from F$44 to F$77 ($20–$34.50) double. American Express, MasterCard, and Visa cards are accepted.

The Fijian-run **Sunview Motel and Hostel,** P.O. Box 9103, Nadi Airport (ℂ **672 4994**), on Gray Road off the Queen's Road behind the Bounty Bar &

> **Tips   Don't Miss a *Meke***
>
> Like most South Pacific islanders, the Fijians in pre-European days steamed their food in an earth oven, known here as a *lovo*. They would use their fingers to eat the huge feasts (*mekes*) that emerged, then settle down to watch traditional dancing and perhaps polish off a few cups of yaqona.
>
> The ingredients of a lovo meal are *buaka* (pig), *doa* (chicken), *ika* (fish), *mana* (lobster), *moci* (river shrimp), *kai* (freshwater mussels), and various vegetables, such as dense *dalo* (taro root), spinachlike *rourou* (taro leaves), and *lumi* (seaweed). Most dishes are cooked in sweet *lolo* (coconut milk). The most plentiful fish is the *walu*, or Spanish mackerel.
>
> Fijians also make delicious *kokoda* ("ko-kon-da"), their version of fresh fish marinated in lime juice and mixed with fresh vegetables and coconut milk. Another Fijian specialty is *palusami,* a rich combination of corned beef or fish baked in banana leaves or foil with onions, taro leaves, and coconut milk.
>
> Several Nadi hotels have *mekes* on their schedule of weekly events. The foods are cooked in a *lovo* on the hotel grounds and served buffet style, often beside the swimming pool if weather permits. Traditional Fijian dance shows follow the meals. *Spotlight on Nadi* and *Fiji Magic* both list the schedules; you can also phone the hotels to find out.

Restaurant in Martintar, has rooms in a modern building. Four are air-conditioned, two have fans. They cost F$35 ($16) per double, and a dorm bed goes for F$12 ($5.50). All include breakfast. Credit cards are not accepted.

The best of the beachside hostels is **Horizon Beach Resort** (© **672 2832;** fax 672 0662; horizon@is.com.fj), in Newtown, a compound of suburban homes and budget hostels on Wailoaloa Beach 1.5km (1 mile) west of Queen's Road. It has 14 rooms (six of them air-conditioned, all with private bathroom) and 15 dorm beds. There's a pool and an open-air restaurant-bar that serves good, inexpensive meals and cold beer. Inner Space Adventures scuba diving base is across the street. Rooms cost F$38.50 to F$60 ($17.50–$27) double, dorm beds F$10 ($4.50) each. Dorm rates include breakfast. American Express, MasterCard, and Visa credit cards are accepted.

WHERE TO DINE IN NADI

You will see Fijian-style dishes on many menus, as well as at least one Indian curry. Most curries in Fiji are prepared on the mild side, but you can ask for it extraspicy and get it so hot you can't eat it. Curries are easy to figure out from the menu: lamb, goat, beef, chicken, vegetarian. If in doubt, ask the waiter or waitress. *Roti* is the round, lightly fried bread normally used to pick up your food (it is a hybrid of the round breads of India and Pakistan). *Puri* is a soft, puffy bread, and *papadam* is round, crispy, and chiplike. The entire meal may come on a round steel plate, with the curries, condiments, and rice in their own dishes arranged on the larger plate. The authentic method of dining is to dump the rice in the middle of the plate, add the smaller portions around it, and then mix them all together.

You'll find the local **McDonald's** on the Queen's Road about 1km (½ mile) north of Nadi Town. You can get a Big Mac here, but the most interesting items are the vegetable McNuggets and the McVegetable burger, a tasty fried vegetable curry patty.

IN THE AIRPORT AREA

Maharaja's Restaurant INDIAN/EUROPEAN/CHINESE   Local expatriates flock to this storefront establishment, the best place in Nadi to sample authentic curries in a more refined setting than you'll get at other so-called curry houses. They are well seasoned here—either mild, medium, or so hot you'll want to grab a fire extinguisher. There's a selection of European dishes, which lean toward plain but hearty grilled steaks, fish, and pork and lamb chops. You can also order Chinese dishes prepared in the Cantonese style.

Queen's Rd., in K. Nataly & Sons Building near Skylodge Hotel. © **672 2962.** Reservations not accepted. Main courses F$4–F$21 ($1.80–$9.50). MC, V. Mon–Sat 9am–10pm, Sun 5–10pm.

IN THE MARTINTAR AREA

The Bounty Bar & Restaurant ★★★ *Value* INTERNATIONAL/FIJIAN   If I'm in Nadi, you will find me here, at Brian and Veronika Smith's joint, one of my favorite South Pacific pubs. Their regular menu stars grilled steaks that are just as tender but cost less than half those out at the Sheraton resorts. You will get the best hamburger in town here, too, and there's always a daily Fijian special, often including that luscious South Pacific dish known as *palusami* (fish or pork steamed with coconut milk inside taro leaves). You can order breakfast anytime. Candles and subdued lighting add a romantic atmosphere to the dining area during the evening, but a TV and two New Zealand–style drinking tables back in a corner make this the nearest thing in Fiji to a sports bar (American games come on live in the mornings and afternoons out here). You'll find a mixed clientele of tourists, resident expatriates, Air Pacific pilots, and parliamentarians enjoying the coldest draft beers in the Southern Hemisphere. There might even be live music on weekends.

Queen's Rd., Martintar. © **672 0840.** Breakfast F$4.50–F$10 ($2–$4.50); lunch F$4–F$15 ($1.80–$6.75); main courses F$12–F$20 ($5.50–$9). AE, MC, V. Daily 9am–10pm.

IN NADI TOWN

Chefs The Restaurant ★★★ *Value* INTERNATIONAL   Chef Eugene Gomes, who left the Sheraton Fiji to open the dining complexes at Jack's Handicrafts here and in Suva (see The Edge and The Corner, below), shows off his culinary skill in one of the South Pacific's handful of exquisite restaurants. Given the favorable exchange rate of the U.S. dollar against its Fijian counterpart, dining here is also one great bargain—and you get another 10% discount if you purchase F$100 ($45) worth of merchandise from Jack's (bring your receipt). A large, Sphinx-like rock wall with a waterfall and an aqua-and-coral color scheme dominate the urban-style dining room. The service is extraordinarily attentive, and the cuisine is very well presented. The menu varies with the season. You may find wonderful panfried *paka o paka* (snapper) under a sweet brown apple sauce or king prawns perfectly chargrilled and served with a salad of Boston lettuce and a slightly Roquefort dressing. Eugene also has grilled beef tenderloin and rack of lamb to satisfy his Australian and New Zealand patrons.

Sangayam Rd. (behind Jack's Handicrafts). © **670 3131.** Reservations recommended. Main courses F$26–F$49 ($11.50–$22). AE, DC, MC, V. Mon–Sat 11am–2pm and 6–10pm.

Continental Cakes BAKERY/PIZZA Master baker Dietmar Leuke supplies the major hotels with bread, cakes, and pastries from this storefront restaurant, the top place in town for a morning coffee and one of the best croissants in the South Pacific (and that includes Tahiti). Later on you can order thin-crust pizzas and deli sandwiches on fresh bread. For an afternoon sugar high, try a slice of Dietmar's authentic German black forest cake.

Queen's Rd. (opposite Mobil station). ✆ **670 3595.** Reservations not accepted. Breakfast F$6–F$8 ($2.50–$3.50), cakes and pastries F$3.50 ($1.50); sandwiches and pizzas F$7–F$19 ($3–$8.50). MC, V. Mon–Sat 8am–9pm, Sun 10am–9pm.

The Corner ★ *Value* CAFETERIA One of chef Eugene Gomes's operations, this pleasant cafeteria has an ice cream bar at the entrance offering tropical fruit selections in freshly baked cones. The cafeteria menu is varied: pastries and coffee (you can get a latte here), hot dogs and hamburgers, sandwiches and salads, roast chicken, and fish and chips. Most meals are Cantonese stir-fries, but a highlight here is a luscious creamy Thai curry chicken. From Thursday to Saturday nights the menu turns to tandoori-style and other northern Indian meals.

Queen's Rd. (opposite Jack's Handicrafts). Reservations not accepted. ✆ **670 3131.** Sandwiches, burgers, and hot dogs F$2.50–F$6.50 ($1–$3); meals F$5.50–F$10 ($2.50–$4.50). AE, DC, MC, V. Mon–Wed 8am–5pm, Thurs–Sat 8am–9pm.

Daikoku ★★ JAPANESE There are three dining areas at this fine restaurant, whose walls and ceilings are made of imported Japanese pine burned slightly to accent the grain. You can elect either the sushi bar, which uses only the freshest salmon, tuna, and lobster; the teppanyaki room, where the chef will stir-fry vegetables, shrimp, chicken, or extraordinarily tender beef as you watch; or the main dining room, which offers sukiyaki, udon, and other traditional Japanese dishes. You can pay a bundle here, but you'll get top-flight Japanese cuisine.

Queen's Rd. (near the bridge). ✆ **670 3622.** Reservations recommended weekends and holidays. Sushi F$5–F$7 ($2.25–$3); main courses F$18–F$48 ($8–$21.50). AE, DC, MC, V. Mon–Sat 11:30am–2pm and 6–10pm; Sun 6–10pm.

The Edge ★★ INTERNATIONAL The third dining establishment of chef Eugene Gomes, this air-conditioned cafe is a more comfortable, sophisticated version of The Corner. The Edge has an ice cream bar, a variety of hamburgers, and many of the same Asian stir-fries and Thai curry chicken offered at The Corner, but here they are served at your table. The dinner menu features a few simple but tasty selections, such as seafood lasagna, chicken enchiladas, and stir-fried beef. Cool and casual, The Edge is a fine place to take a shopping break over a cup of cappuccino, espresso, or herbal tea.

Sagayam Rd. (behind Jack's Handicrafts). ✆ **670 3131.** Reservations not accepted. Salads, sandwiches, burgers F$7.50 ($3.50); main courses F$10–F$15 ($4.50–$7). AE, DC, MC, V. Mon–Sat 11am–3pm and 6–9pm.

Mama's Pizza Inn ITALIAN If you need a tomato sauce fix, follow the aroma of garlic to Robin O'Donnell's cozy establishment. Her pizzas range from a small plain model to a large deluxe version with all the toppings. She also has spaghetti (under both meat and vegetarian tomato sauces), lasagna, and fresh salads. You order at a bar and take your meal at one of the picnic-style tables. There's a suburban Mama's with the same menu, prices, and hours in the Colonial Plaza shopping mall on the Queen's Road in Namaka (✆ **720922**).

Queen's Rd., Nadi Town, opposite Mobil Station. ✆ **670 1221.** Reservations not accepted. Pizzas F$6.50–F$23 ($3–$10.50); pastas F$6 ($2.50). MC, V. Mon–Sat 10am–11pm, Sun 10am–11pm.

ON DENARAU ISLAND

Cardo's Steakhouse & Bar ⭐ STEAKS/SEAFOOD   Occupying a colonial-style building beside the narrow muddy waterway at Port Denarau, this sister of Cardo's in Suva (see "Where to Dine in Suva," below) is the best place outside the Sheratons to dine with a view. Choice tables are on the wraparound porch, which catches the breeze and offers a view across the water and cane fields to the green mountains rising beyond. This vista is especially gorgeous on a moonlit night, but bring insect repellent. You can avoid the mosquitoes (and sacrifice the view) inside the air-conditioned, nonsmoking dining room. Owner Cardo is known throughout Fiji for providing quality chargrilled steaks and fish, and they're his best offerings here. This is a pleasant spot to relax after a cruise or a hair-raising ride on a Shotover Jet, and it's an inexpensive escape from the high-priced Sheraton dining rooms.

Port Denarau Marina. ⓒ **992 6460.** Reservations recommended for dinner. Main courses F$16.50–F$37 ($7.50–$16.50). AE, MC, V. Daily 9am–2:30pm and 5–10:30pm.

SPECIAL DINING EXPERIENCES

You can dine out on the lagoon on a **Starlight Dinner Cruise,** offered by Captain Cook Cruises (ⓒ **670 1823**). The boat departs from Port Denarau daily at 5:30pm and returns at 8:30pm. You'll have a choice of three main courses such as steak or a whole coral trout on a sizzling platter. Fijians serenade with island music. Call or check with any hotel activities desk for current prices and reservations, which are required.

On Nadi Bay about halfway between the airport and Lautoka, **First Landing Resort & Seafood Restaurant** (ⓒ **666 6171**) often offers a "lobster on the beach" special for F$99 ($44.50) per person, including transportation (by boat from Denarau Island). The three-course meal is served in a pleasant grove of palms beside the bay, which turns into a mud flat at low tide.

ISLAND NIGHTS IN NADI

The large hotels usually have something going on every night. As noted in the "Don't Miss a *Meke*" box, above, this might be a special meal followed by a Fijian *meke* dance show. The large hotels also frequently have live entertainment in their bars during the cocktail hour. Check with any hotel activities desk to see what's happening.

Unlike the fast, hip-swinging, suggestive dancing of Tahiti and the Cook Islands, Fijians follow the custom of the Samoas and Tonga, with gentle movements taking second place to the harmony of their voices. Only in the spear-waving war dances do you see much action. Nevertheless, taking in a *meke* is a popular way to spend at least one evening in Nadi.

The most popular watering hole here is **The Bounty Bar & Restaurant,** on the Queen's Road in Martintar (ⓒ **672 0840**), which draws many expatriate residents to its sports TV and icy draft beer (see "Where to Dine in Nadi," above).

For live music, head to the main dining room and bar in the **Fiji Mocambo Hotel** (ⓒ **672 2000**), where one of Fiji's top rock band plays for dancing after 9pm Tuesday to Saturday. The cafe at **The West's Motor Inn,** on the Queen's Road in Martintar (ⓒ **672 0044**), becomes a pleasant, gay-friendly piano bar from Monday to Saturday. See "Where to Stay in Nadi," above.

2 Island Escapes from Nadi

Offshore resorts are great places to relax or engage in romance or watersports, but they are not in themselves bases from which to explore Fiji.

Most of the resorts off Nadi are in the Mamanuca Islands, a chain of small flat atolls and hilly islands ranging from 8km to 32km (4–20 miles) west of Nadi. Others are in the Yasawa Islands, a similar but much less developed chain as much as 100km (60 miles) northwest of Nadi. Another is on Vatulele, a flat, raised coral island 48km (30 miles) south of Viti Levu but serviced from Nadi Airport.

The climate on all these islands is semiarid. Coupled with their proximity to Nadi Airport, this consistent sunshine made the Mamanuca Islands the first in Fiji to be opened to tourists back in the early 1960s. They are still very popular with Australians and New Zealanders on 1- or 2-week holidays.

GETTING TO RESORTS OFFSHORE FROM NADI

The resorts arrange transfers for their guests (reservations are required at all these resorts), so you'll probably do as you're told. How much it costs depends on whether you take a boat or fly.

South Sea Cruises (© 675 0500; southsea@is.com.fj) provides ferry service from Port Denarau to most of the Mamanuca resorts three times daily on the speedy catamaran *Tiger IV.* One-way fares are F$55 ($25). You'll have to transfer from Mana Island to Matamanoa and Tokoriki resorts by speedboat. For backpackers, this company also runs the MV *Treasure Flyer* from Port Denarau to Tavewa Island in the Yasawa Islands (call for fares). At press time it had just introduced an "Awesome Adventures Fiji" pass that allows unlimited island-hopping in the Yasawas for 21 days, at a cost of F$240 ($108).

Beachcomber Island Resort has its own fast catamarans from Denarau Island and the much slower sailing ship *Tui Tai* from Lautoka (© 666 1500 for both).

Another fast catamaran, the *Malolo Cat* (© 672 0774) runs from Denarau to Plantation Island and Musket Cove resorts on Malololailai Island. Round trips cost F$75 ($34) per person.

The quickest and easiest way to the islands is via **Sun Air** (© 672 3016) and **Air Fiji** (© 672 2521), which fly several times a day from Nadi Airport to both Mana Island and Malololailai, home of Plantation and Musket Cove resorts. **Turtle Airways** (© 672 2988) and **Pacific Island Seaplanes** (© 672 5643) both provide seaplane service to most of the islands. Turtle has a special F$79 ($35.50) one-way fare for backpackers headed to the Yasawas. It's much more expensive, but **Island Hoppers** (© 672 0140) flies its helicopters to Plantation, Musket Cove, Mana Island, Treasure Island, Tokoriki, and Castaway Island resorts. **Pleasure Marine** (© 675 0500) provides water taxi service to the islands from Port Denarau.

See "Getting There & Getting Around" in chapter 9 for more information.

DAY TRIPS TO OFFSHORE ISLANDS

The Great Sea Reef off northwest Viti Levu in effect encloses a huge lagoon whose usually calm waters surround the nearby Mamanuca and Yasawa island groups with speckled shades of yellow, green, and blue as the sea changes from shallow to deep. It's a fine place to escape to a small island for a day or longer. Most of the day trips mentioned below depart from **Port Denarau,** the marina facility on Denarau Island. Bus transportation from the Nadi area hotels is included in their prices. Book at your hotel activities desk.

Beachcomber Day Cruises ★★★ (© 666 1500; www.beachcomberfiji. com) sail from both Port Denarau and Lautoka to youth-oriented Beachcomber Island Resort (see "Where to Stay in the Mamanuca Islands," below). It's my favorite way to spend a day with the young folks frolicking in the sun, but beware if you have sensitive eyes: European women have been known to drop

> **Moments   Sand Between My Toes**
>
> Nothing relaxes me more than running sand between my toes at one of Fiji's small get-away-from-it-all resorts. If I have a day to spare in Nadi, I head out to Beachcomber Island Resort, where the floor of the bar and dining room is nothing but sand. And with all those young folks running around out on the beach, I feel like I'm 25 again.

their tops at Beachcomber. You'll pay F$69 ($31) for bus transportation, the cruise, and an all-you-can-eat buffet lunch on Beachcomber Island. Add F$20 ($9) from the Coral Coast. Swimming is free but snorkeling gear, scuba diving, and other activities cost extra. Transfers are made from Port Denarau via a speedy catamaran or from Lautoka on the *Tui Tai,* a much slower sailboat.

Captain Cook Cruises (© 670 1823; www.captaincook.com.au) uses the *Ra Marama,* a 33m (110-ft.) square-rigged brigantine built in Singapore during the 1950s and once the official yacht of Fiji's colonial governors-general, for day cruises out to Tivua Island, an uninhabited 4-acre islet in the Mamanucas. The sail takes 1 hour each way. A traditional Fijian welcoming ceremony greets guests at the island, where they can swim, snorkel, and canoe over 500 acres of surrounding coral gardens (or see the colors from a glass-bottom boat). Drinks on board the *Ra Marama* and a barbecue lunch on the beach are included in the F$73 ($33) per person cost.

Malamala Island (© 670 2433) is a 6-acre islet studded with palm trees and circled with white-sand beaches. The only inhabitants will be you and your fellow passengers, who will use Malamala's only building, a thatch bure, for a barbecue lunch. Guests are taken to the island on the glass-bottom boat *Tropic Sea.* The F$69 ($31) price includes lunch, drinks, and coral viewing.

Malololailai Island, home of Plantation Island and Musket Cove resorts, can be visited by plane as well as on a day cruise via the *Malololo Cat* (© 672 0744), a speedy catamaran that takes 50 minutes to roar between Port Denarau and the island. The *Malololo Cat* charges F$75 ($34) for adults, half that for children, for round-trip transportation and lunch at Musket Cove Resort. **Sun Air** (© 672 3016; www.fiji.to) has frequent flights from Nadi Airport to the little gravel strip that separates the two resorts for F$28 ($12.50) each way. Once on Malololailai, you can hang out at the resorts, shop at Louis and Georgie Czukelter's **Art Gallery** on the hill above Musket Cove (no phone), and dine at **Anandas Restaurant and Bar** (© 672 2333) by the airstrip. You can book at the restaurant to play the island's short nine-hole golf course; fees are F$20 ($9).

South Sea Cruises (© 675 0500; southsea@is.com.fj) runs the fast, diesel-powered catamaran *Tiger IV* three times a day through the Mamanucas. It primarily serves as a ferry for visitors who have too much luggage to fly to the Mamanucas. It departs on its 3-hour loops from Port Denarau daily at 9am, 12:15pm, and 3:15pm. You can ride along and sightsee through the islands for about F$50 ($22.50) per person, but you won't be able to luxuriate on any beaches, as the boat stops at each resort only long enough to put off and pick up passengers and their luggage. Your best bet is to take the morning voyage, get off at **Mana Island Resort** or **Castaway Island Resort** (see "Where to Stay in the Mamanuca Islands," below), have a buffet lunch, swim and sunbathe, and catch the afternoon boat back to Denarau Island. The Mana and Castaway excursions cost F$95 ($42.50) and F$99 ($44.50), respectively, including buffet lunch.

Seafari Cruise is what South Sea Cruises (© **675 0500**) calls its rent-a-boat service at Port Denarau. You design your own cruise to the Mamanuca Islands, such as picnicking at a deserted beach or picking your own snorkeling spots. Prices depend on the size of the boat. The largest can hold up to 20 passengers.

CRUISING IN THE YASAWA ISLANDS

Lt. Charles Wilkes, commander of the U.S. exploring expedition that charted Fiji in 1840, said the Yasawa Islands reminded him of "a string of blue beads lying along the horizon," and they haven't changed much over the intervening century and a half. Fijians still live in small villages huddled among the curving coconut palms beside some of the South Pacific's most awesomely beautiful beaches.

The Yasawas have a few resorts ranging from rock-bottom to luxury (see "Where to Stay in the Yasawa Islands," below), but you can't just grab a plane or a boat and go up there for a look around. The only easy way to see more than one of them is on a cruise ship that stops at several during the day and anchors off a different island each night.

BLUE LAGOON CRUISES ★★★   Started with a converted American crash vessel in the 1950s, the locally owned **Blue Lagoon Cruises** (© **666 1622;** fax 666 4098; www.bluelagooncruises.com) are so popular that they're often booked solid more than 2 months in advance of each daily departure from Lautoka.

Two of Blue Lagoon's vessels are 38m (126-ft.) -long ships capable of carrying 54 passengers in 22 air-conditioned cabins. Two others, the 54m (181-ft.) *Yasawa Princess* and the 47m (155-ft.) *Nanuya Princess,* carry up to 66 passengers each, in 33 staterooms. The newest vessel, the sleek 56m (185-ft.) *Mystique Princess,* looks as if she should belong to a Greek shipping magnate, and her 35 staterooms do indeed approach tycoon standards.

Most cruises range from 2 to 6 nights through the Yasawas, with one of the 7-day voyages designed especially for scuba divers. They depart Lautoka and arrive in the Yasawas in time for a welcoming cocktail party and dinner on board. They then proceed to explore the islands, stopping in little bays for snorkeling, picnics or lovo feasts on sandy beaches, and visits with the Yasawans in their villages. The ships anchor in peaceful coves at night, and even when they cruise from island to island, the water is usually so calm that only incurable landlubbers get seasick. In the one major variation from this theme, the *Mystique Princess* makes week-long cruises to Northern Fiji, with stops at Levuka, Savusavu, Taveuni, and several remote islands.

Rates range from F$1,000 to F$7,500 ($450–$3,375) per person double occupancy, depending on the length of the voyage, the season, and the type of cabin. All meals, activities, and taxes are included. Singles pay a hefty supplement, and children pay from F$150 to F$450 ($67.50–$202.50).

CAPTAIN COOK CRUISES   The Australian-based **Captain Cook Cruises** (© **670 1823;** fax 670 2045; www.captaincook.com.au) has 4- and 7-night cruises from Port Denarau through the Yasawas in the *Reef Escape,* a four-deck ship that carries up to 120 passengers in 60 air-conditioned staterooms and cabins. The *Reef Escape* is not as cozy as Blue Lagoon's ships, but it has a swimming pool on the top deck. Another difference is that it stops at the intriguing, grotto-like Sawa-i-lau Caves, which were featured in the *Blue Lagoon* movie starring Brooke Shields. You can take a chilly swim in a freshwater pool in the caves. Otherwise, the trips are pretty much like Blue Lagoon's, with stops at beaches for swimming, snorkeling and picnicking. Cruise prices range from F$1,200 to F$5,100 ($540–$2,300) per person double occupancy, including meals.

For the more adventurous, Captain Cook Cruises also has 3- and 4-day "Fiji Sailing Safaris" to Waya Island in the Yasawas on the square-rigged, 32m (108-ft.) *Spirit of the Pacific*. You sail up to and among the islands, and you can choose to stay on board or ashore in thatch bures beside an otherwise deserted beach. The bures have communal toilets and showers. Days are spent examining Fijian gardens, boating over to a deserted island, visiting a village for a *meke* island feast and dance show, and lots of swimming and snorkeling. The cost ranges from F$540 to F$648 ($243–$291.50) per person double occupancy, including meals.

WHERE TO STAY OFFSHORE FROM NADI

You won't get a television in your bungalow at Fiji's offshore resorts, and with a few exceptions, you won't get a telephone, either. If you really must be in touch with the world every minute of every day, stay on the "mainland" of Viti Levu. Come out here with one goal in mind: relaxation.

WHERE TO STAY IN THE MAMANUCA ISLANDS

Beachcomber Island Resort ★★ *Value*   Back in 1963, Fiji-born Dan Costello bought an old Colonial Sugar Refining Company tugboat, converted it into a day cruiser, and started carrying tourists on day trips out to a little atoll known then as Tai Island. The visitors liked it so much that some of them didn't want to leave. Recognizing the market, Costello built a few rustic bures, a dining area, and a bar, and gave the little dot of sand and palm trees a new name: Beachcomber Island. Today it still packs in the young and young-at-heart on a "deserted" island—deserted, that is, except for other like-minded souls in search of fun, members of the opposite sex, and a relatively inexpensive vacation (considering that three all-you-can-eat meals per day are included in the rates). The youngest-at-heart cram into the coed dormitories. If you want more room, you can have or share a semiprivate lodge. And if you want your own bure, you can have that, too—just don't expect luxury. Three "family" bures can sleep up to six persons, and they have outdoor showers. Rates also include snorkeling gear, coral viewing in glass-bottomed boats, volleyball, and minigolf; you pay extra for sailboats, canoes, windsurfing, scuba diving, water-skiing, and fishing trips.

P.O. Box 364, Lautoka (Tai Island, 19km/12 miles off Lautoka). © **800/521-7242** or 666 1500. Fax 666 4496. www.beachcomberfiji.com. 34 units, 100 dorm beds. F$360 ($162) double bure; F$238 ($107) double lodge; F$75 ($34) dorm bed. Rates include all meals. AE, DC, MC, V. **Amenities:** 1 restaurant (buffet), 1 bar; outdoor pool; miniature golf; watersports equipment rentals; massage; laundry service. *In room:* Fridge, coffeemaker, no phone.

Castaway Island Resort ★★ *Kids*   Built in the mid-1960s of logs and thatch, without the use of heavy equipment, Castaway maintains its rustic, Fijian-style charm despite many improvements over the years. The central activities building, perched on a point with white beaches on either side, still has a thatch roof, and the ceilings of the bures are still lined with genuine *masi* cloth. Although the guest bures sit relatively close together in a coconut grove, their roofs sweep low enough to provide some privacy. In addition to the central lounge-dining-bar building, a beachside watersports shack has a Sundowner Bar upstairs, appropriately facing west toward the Great Sea Reef. Guests dine in the central building, usually at umbrella tables on a stone beachside patio, or grab a wood-fired pizza at the Sundowner Bar. This is a very good family resort, with

---

Tips **Keeping You Entertained**

Don't worry about staying busy at the offshore resorts. You can do as much or as little as you like. All the resorts have canoes, kayaks, sailboards, snorkeling gear, and other watersports equipment for your use, and each has a scuba diving operation. In addition, Fijians make music most evenings and stage *meke* feasts at least 1 night a week at all the resorts.

---

a nurse on duty and the staff providing a wide range of activities, from learning Fijian to sack races. Consequently, couples seeking a quiet romantic retreat should look elsewhere during school holiday periods. Australian restaurateur Geoff Shaw owns both this resort and the Outrigger Reef Fiji on the Coral Coast (see "The Coral Coast," below), and the two often have attractive joint packages including helicopter transfers between them.

Private Mail Bag, Nadi Airport (Qalito Island, 21km/13 miles off Nadi). ✆ 800/888-0120 or 666 1233. Fax 666 5753. www.castawayfiji.com. 66 units. F$510–F$610 ($230–$275) double. AE, DC, MC, V. **Amenities:** 2 restaurants (international/pizza); 3 bars; outdoor pool; tennis court; watersports equipment rentals; children's programs; game room; activities desk; massage; babysitting; laundry service. *In room:* Minibar, coffeemaker, hair dryer, iron, safe, no phone.

Malolo Island Fiji (Kids) Formerly known as Naitasi Resort, this family-oriented hotel recently got a name change and a facelift. It's a good choice for families with children, and among adults it's notable primarily for having one of the best beachside bars in Fiji—a thatch-roof building with a lagoon-side deck and a lunchtime dining area under a sprawling shade tree. Unfortunately, however, storms have washed much of the sand away from the beach. Two other restaurants and bars are in a two-story building at the base of a hill at the rear of the property. They open to two swimming pools, one for children with a walk-in sand bottom under a tarp to provide shade. Painted yellow with bright blue trim, most of the guest bungalows are duplexes. Of these, 30 have separate bedrooms; the others are studios. There's also an upstairs family unit capable of sleeping 10 persons.

P.O. Box 10044, Nadi Airport (Malolo Island, 25km/15 miles off Nadi). ✆ 666 9192. Fax 666 9197. www.maloloisland.com. 51 units. F$440–F$498 ($198–$224) double; F$990 ($445) family unit. AE, DC, MC, V. **Amenities:** 3 restaurants (regional); 3 bars; 2 outdoor pools; watersports equipment rentals; children's programs; game room; activities desk; salon; massage; babysitting; laundry service. *In room:* A/C, fridge, coffeemaker, hair dryer, iron, no phone.

Mana Island Resort The largest resort off Nadi, this lively, Japanese-owned property attracts Japanese singles and honeymooners, plus Australian and New Zealand couples and families. Because it has the only pier long enough to land the interisland ferries, Mana is a popular day-trip destination from Nadi (see "Day Trips to Offshore Islands," above). Seaplanes, planes, and helicopters also land here, and Pleasure Marine has its water taxi base at Mana, so this is also the major transfer point for the outer Mamanuca islands. In other words, you'll have a *lot* of company on Mana. If you decide to brave the crowds and stay here, accommodation is in a variety of bungalows, all of European construction. The Garden units have been around a long time; they have ceiling fans but not air conditioners and can be quite warm at midday. There are a variety of newer and more comfortable air-conditioned units from which to choose, including seven honeymoon models that sit by themselves on the beach north of the airstrip (many young Japanese couples get married in Mana's wedding chapel and promptly disappear into these private, superluxe units). In addition, a block of 32 spacious hotel rooms faces the beach. The excellent U.S. firm **Aqua-Trek** has a diving operation here (© **800/541-4334** or 702413; www.aquatrek.com).

P.O. Box 610, Lautoka (Mana Island, 32km/20 miles off Nadi). © **665 0423.** Fax 665 0788. www.manafiji. com. 160 units. F$300–F$900 ($135–$405) double. Rates include buffet breakfast. AE, DC, MC, V. **Amenities:** 3 restaurants (international), 2 bar; outdoor pool; 2 tennis courts; watersports equipment rentals; children's programs; game room; activities desk; massage; babysitting; laundry service; coin-op washers and dryers. *In room:* A/C (except in Garden units), kitchen (in honeymoon units), minibar (in deluxe and honeymoon units), fridge, coffeemaker, hair dryer.

Matamanoa Island Resort ★★ The farthest of all Mamanuca resorts off Nadi, this intimate, adults-oriented complex (no kids under 12 can stay here) sits on a small island that consists of one steep hill. The bungalows, a motel-like block of rooms, and a central building with bar and open-air dining room occupy a small flat shelf on one end of the island. The shelf falls away steeply to a beach of deep white sand, which lacks shade but has great snorkeling even at low tide over a reef drop-off near the shore. Each of the spacious, rectangular bungalows faces the beach; a divider separates the sleeping area from the bungalow's lounge with wet bar. Sliding doors open to covered porches with sea views. The 13 motel rooms sit at the base of the hill; they are much smaller than the bungalows but are air-conditioned (the bures have two ceiling fans). For scuba divers, this is the closest of all Mamanuca resorts to the outer reef, and Aqua-Trek has one of its dive bases here. This well-managed resort attracts primarily European and American couples.

P.O. Box 9729, Nadi Airport (Matamanoa Island, 33km/21 miles off Nadi). © **666 0511.** Fax 666 0069. http:// matamanoa.bulafiji.com. 33 units. F$275 ($124) double; F$440 ($198) bungalow. Rates include breakfast. Children under 12 not accepted. AE, DC, MC, V. **Amenities:** 1 restaurant (regional), 1 bar; outdoor pool; tennis court; watersports equipment rentals; activities desk; massage; laundry service. *In room:* A/C (in rooms), fridge, coffeemaker, hair dryer.

Musket Cove Resort One of three Australians who own Malololailai Island, Dick Smith founded this retreat in 1977. It has grown considerably since then, and it now has a marina where cruising yachties call from June to September. The yachties congregate at the "$2.50 Bar," under a thatch roof out on a tiny man-made island reached by the marina's pontoons. Musket Cove hosts the annual Fiji Regatta Week in September, when it's the starting line for the yacht race from Musket Cove to Port Vila in Vanuatu. "Dick's Place" has been retained as the name of the pleasant open-air bar and restaurant next to two swimming pools, one with a real yacht protruding from its side, as if it has run aground. There's another cafe and a grocery store next to the marina. Although a broad mud bank appears here at low tide, Dick dredged out a swimming beach area when he built the marina. It has sailboats, Windsurfers, and rowboats. For a fee, guests can go scuba diving, rent motorboats, and make excursions to other islands.

Accommodations range from air-conditioned hotel rooms to luxury villas with living rooms, full kitchens, and master bedrooms downstairs and two bedrooms upstairs, each with its own private bathroom. Musket Cove also manages Armstrong Villas at Musket Cove, a group of two-bedroom condo bungalows that sit on a man-made island. These have kitchens and phones. You should consult with the reservationist when booking your unit to make sure you'll have the in-room amenities you desire.

Private Mail Bag, Nadi Airport (Malololailai Island, 14km/9 miles off Nadi). © **877/313-1464** or 672 2371. Fax 672 0378. www.musketcovefiji.com. 52 units. F$240 ($108) double; F$300–F$440 ($135–$198) bungalow;

F$530–F$550 ($239–$248) villa. AE, DC, MC, V. **Amenities:** 2 restaurants (regional), 2 bars; 2 outdoor pools; 9-hole golf course; tennis court; watersports equipment rentals; bike rentals; activities desk; massage; babysitting; laundry service; coin-op washers and dryers. *In room:* A/C (rooms only), kitchen (villas and some rooms), fridge, coffeemaker, hair dryer, no phone (in villas and bungalows).

Plantation Island Resort *(Kids)*   One of the oldest, largest, and most diverse of the Mamanuca resorts, Plantation primarily attracts Australian couples and families, plus day-trippers from Nadi. Like Mana Island, it has a Club Med–style atmosphere of nonstop activity. It shares Malololailai island with Musket Cove Resort, but this end boasts one of the South Pacific's most picturesque palm-draped beaches, shallow though the lagoon may be at low tide. The resort has four types of accommodations: duplex bures suitable for singles or couples, two-bedroom bungalows for families, and hotel rooms in a two-story building next to the beach. All units have phones, but only the hotel rooms are air-conditioned. A large central building beside the beach has a bar, dance floor, lounge area, coffee shop, and restaurant. Guests can also wander over to Ananda's, a barbecue-oriented restaurant near the airport, or to Musket Cove for a meal. There's a children's playroom with a full-time baby-sitter, making this a good choice for families—though not as good as Castaway Island Resort.

P.O. Box 9176, Nadi Airport (Malololailai Island, 14km/9 miles off Nadi). © **666 9333.** Fax 666 9200. www.plantationisland.com. 140 units. F$190–F$260 ($85.50–$117) double; F$260–F$420 ($117–$189) bungalow. AE, DC, MC, V. **Amenities:** 2 restaurants (regional), 2 bars; 2 outdoor pools; golf course; tennis courts; watersports equipment rentals; children's programs; game room; activities desk; salon; massage; babysitting; laundry service; coin-op washers and dryers. *In room:* A/C (in hotel rooms), fridge, coffeemaker.

Tokoriki Island Resort *(★)*   Almost as far away from Nadi as its nearest neighbor, Matamanoa Island Resort, this property sits beside a wide beach that stretches 1.5km (1 mile) along the western shore of hilly Tokoriki Island—thus rendering unimpeded sunset views. Although it doesn't have Matamanoa's deep sand, once you get past rock shelves along the shoreline, the bottom slopes gradually into a safe lagoon with colorful coral gardens protected by a barrier reef. The resort itself sits on a flat shelf of land backed by a steep hill (a 4km/2½-mile hiking trail leads up to the ridgeline). Bungalows lined up along the beach flank the huge central building here. Most of these spacious units are virtually identical to Matamanoa's, except that louvered walls separate the sleeping areas from wet-bar-equipped lounges, and they have outdoor showers. Sliding doors open from them to covered porches that overlook the beach. At the far end of the property, three honeymoon bures are perched up on a hillside, ensuring privacy

---

Tips **Making Your Choice**

Although I have placed Fiji's offshore resorts in this book according to their jumping-off points, you should review each of them carefully before making a choice. In particular, see The Wakaya Club in "Where to Stay in Suva," below, and Moody's Namena, Matangi Island Resort, and Qamea Beach Club in chapter 11.

Also note that meals are included in some room rates, but not in others. Except on Malololailai, you won't be able to walk down the road to a nearby restaurant, so that's a very important consideration in making your choice. If food is not included in the rates, ask if there is a meal plan and how much it costs. You can expect to pay about F$60 ($27) per adult per day for a meal plan, less for children.

---

and lagoon views from their decks. A central thatch-topped bar divides the long central building into lounge and dining areas. The latter opens to a swimming pool, and guests can take their excellent meals al fresco during fair weather. You pay extra for scuba diving, but a wide range of other watersports activities are included in the room rates here.

P.O. Box 10547, Nadi Airport (Tokoriki Island, 32km/20 miles off Nadi). ℭ **666 1999.** Fax 666 5295. www. tokoriki.com. 29 units. F$420–F$630 ($189–$283) bungalow. AE, DC, MC, V. **Amenities:** 1 restaurant (international), 1 bar; outdoor pool; tennis court; watersports equipment rentals; children's programs; game room; activities desk; massage; babysitting; laundry service. *In room:* A/C, fridge, coffeemaker, hair dryer, safe, no phone.

WHERE TO STAY IN THE YASAWA ISLANDS

Oarsman's Bay Lodge ★ *Value*   Sitting beside the finest beach in Fiji, this is best of several new backpackers' retreats that have sprung up in the Yasawas (see "Hostels Offshore from Nadi," below). It was designed and built by Richard Evanson of Turtle Island Resort (see below), and his company is promoting it and assisting in its management until it becomes profitable for its Fijian owners. A live tree helps support the central building with sand-floor dining room and bar. There is no communal kitchen, but you can get three meals per day for F$30 ($13.50). Steep stairs lead upstairs to a one-room coed dorm, whose residents share toilets and warm-water showers with guest camping on the grounds. Although the six tin-roof guest bungalows are a bit cramped, they are nicely appointed with wooden cabinets, full-length mirrors, reading lights over their double beds, porches with hammocks and chairs, screened louvered windows, and bathrooms with solar-heated showers. Paddle boats and canoes are available, plus gear for fabulous snorkeling. Backpacking or not, you'll find this no-frills resort to be an extraordinary bargain.

P.O. Box 9317, Nadi Airport (Nacula Island, 85km/52 miles north of Nadi, a 30-min. seaplane ride). ℭ **800/ 826-3083** or 672 2921. Fax 672 0007. nacula@hotmail.com. 6 units, 13 dorm beds. F$99 ($44.50) double; F$25 ($11) dorm bed; F$25 ($11) per person campsite with tent rental; F$10 ($4.50) per person campsite without tent. MC, V. **Amenities:** 1 restaurant (regional), 1 bar; watersports equipment rentals. *In room:* No phone.

Turtle Island Resort ★★★   Enjoying the most picturesque setting of any resort in Fiji, this famous little getaway is nestled beside an idyllic, half-moon-shaped beach and looks out on a nearly landlocked body of water, which American owner Richard Evanson (see the box "Turtle Time for *The Blue Lagoon,*" below) has dubbed "the Blue Lagoon." The beachside central building is not as impressive as those at Fiji's other high-end resorts, but it's comfortable and charming nevertheless. Beside it, ceiling fans whirl under the sprawling branches of a *baka* tree, which shades an outdoor dining and entertainment area. Supplied by the resort's own garden, the kitchen serves excellent-quality meals dinner-party fashion at a long, polished table in the beachside dining room. (This style of dining, practiced here and at Vatulele Island Resort, is a major difference from other deluxe resorts such as The Wakaya Club and Yasawa Island Resort, where guests are left more to themselves.) If you don't want company, however, you can dine alone on the beach or on a pontoon floating on the lagoon. Once a week all guests have dinner at the top of a 150m (500-ft.) peak with a panoramic vista. Staff members strumming guitars, fashion shows, and Fijian *mekes* are staged some evenings.

The beach turns into a sand bar at low tide, but you can swim and snorkel then off a long pier over the blue lagoon. Other activities include diving, canoeing, kayaking, diving, fishing, horseback riding, hiking the island's 13km (8 miles) of

---

Fun Fact Turtle Time for *The Blue Lagoon*

San Franciscan Richard Evanson graduated from Harvard Business School, made a bundle in cable television, got divorced, ran away to Fiji, and in 1972 bought Nanuya Levu, one of the few privately owned islands in the Yasawas. Growing lonely and bored, he decided to build Turtle Island, a small resort, on his hilly, 500-acre retreat. By 1980 he had completed three bures. Then a Hollywood producer leased the entire island as a set for a second version of *The Blue Lagoon*, starring the then-teenage Brooke Shields. Clocks were set ahead 1 hour to maximize daylight, and the resort still operates on "Turtle Time," an hour ahead of the rest of Fiji. The movie's most familiar scenes were shot on Devil's Beach, one of Nanuya Levu's dozen gorgeous little stretches of sand wedged between rocky headlands.

---

trails, visiting other islands, and sunset cruising. Everything is included in the rates except Hawaiian-style therapeutic massage.

Standing in a grove of trees beside the beach, a dozen of the superluxe, widely spaced bungalows have two-person spa tubs embedded in the floors of their enormous bedrooms or bathrooms. Separate sitting areas have sofas, wet bars, and remote-controlled CD players. Much of the furniture is constructed of tree limbs, including writing tables and four-poster king-size beds equipped with mosquito netting. Bathrooms have walk-in showers with his-and-her heads, his-and-her toilets, and his-and-her lavatories, plus robes, slippers, and exquisite toiletries. In a few bungalows, the front porch has a lily pond on one side and a queen-size bed under a roof on the other. A few bungalows are more modest (no spa tubs), but one of these, on a headland with a 360° view of the lagoon and surrounding islands, is the most private of all. Every unit has its own kayaks and a hammock strung between shade trees by the beach.

Only couples and singles are accepted here, except during certain family weeks in July and at Christmas, and if you do bring the kids, they will be consigned to a mandatory children's program. You won't have a phone in your bungalow, but you will have a two-way radio to call for room service.

P.O. Box 9317, Nadi Airport (Nanuya Levu Island, 80km/50 miles north of Nadi, a 30-min. seaplane ride). ℂ 800/826-3083 or 672 2921. Fax 672 0007. www.turtlefiji.com. 14 units. US$1,450 per couple. Rates include meals, drinks, all activities including game fishing and one scuba dive per day, round-trip seaplane transfers. 6-night stay required. Children under 12 not accepted except during family weeks in July and at Christmas. AE, DE, MC, V. **Amenities:** 1 restaurant (international), 1 bar; limited room service; massage; babysitting; laundry service. *In room:* Minibar, coffeemaker, hair dryer, iron, safe, no phone.

Yasawa Island Resort ★★★   This luxurious resort sits in a small indention among steep cliffs that line the west coast of skinny, relatively dry Yasawa Island, northernmost of the chain. Owner Garth Downey prices it below Turtle and Vatulele, even though the bungalows here are just as big, the food is just as good, and there's a swimming pool, which the others don't have. The Great Sea Reef is far enough offshore here that surf can slap against shelves of black rock just off a nearby beach of deep white sand. The large, air-conditioned guest bures come in two types. Most are long, 305 square-km (1,000-sq.-foot) rectangular models with thatch roofs over white stucco walls (the style makes this resort physically reminiscent of Vatulele Island Resort). A door leads from the bathroom, which has a shower, to another outdoor shower to a private sun-bathing patio. A few other one- and two-bedroom models are less appealing but are better arranged for families (children under 12 are allowed here during Jan) and have fine views from the side of the hill backing the property. Most expensive is the remote, extremely private Lomolagi honeymoon bure, which has its own beach. Guests all dine together for twice-weekly Fijian-style *lovos*, but otherwise they can choose their own spacious seating arrangements.

P.O. Box 10128, Nadi Airport (Yasawa Island, 100km/60 miles north of Nadi, 35 min. by charter flight). © **672 2266.** Fax 672 4456. www.yasawaislandresort.com. 16 units. US$750–US$1,050 double. Rates include room and all meals and nonmotorized watersports but no drinks. Round-trip transfers US$310 per person. Children under 12 not accepted except in Jan. AE, DC, MC, V. **Amenities:** 1 restaurant (international), 1 bar; outdoor pool; tennis court; limited room service; massage; babysitting; laundry service. *In room:* A/C, kitchen (2 units), minibar, coffeemaker, hair dryer, iron, safe.

WHERE TO STAY ON VATULELE ISLAND

Vatulele Island Resort ★★★   When Australian TV producer Henry Crawford *(A Town Like Alice)* turned 40 in the late 1980s, he decided to build the ultimate hideaway resort. He chose a gorgeous, 1km (½-mile) beach on Vatulele, a relatively flat island off the Coral Coast, known for its unique red prawns. With an eye on the environment, he cleared just enough thick native brush to build 18 spacious *bures* (bungalows) and a central dining room–bar-lounge complex. Each bure faces the beach but is separated from its companions by lots of privacy-providing foliage and distance. In a fascinating blend of Santa Fe and Fijian native architectural styles, the bures and main building have thick adobe walls supporting tall Fijian thatch roofs. Each L-shaped bure has a lounge and raised sleeping areas under one roof, plus another roof covering an enormous bathroom that can be entered both from the bed/dressing area and from a private, hammock-swung patio. Each unit has a king-size bed with mosquito net suspended from the rafters. Although benchlike seats in the lounge can double as beds for children, kids under 12 are allowed only during certain weeks, usually coinciding with Australian school holidays in July and September. The Point, a huge new villa that sits on a headland, should be available by the time you arrive—at a cost of US$2,200 per night.

Most meals here are dinner parties inside the main building or, weather permitting, on the adjacent patio. You can dine anytime and anyplace you want, however, including in your bure, out on the beach, or in The Folly, a cabana that sits all by itself on a headland at one end of the beach. You can even take a picnic lunch to a private beach or out to a tiny nearby islet. Although staff members play guitars and sing island songs, the nightly dinner parties *are* the entertainment at Vatulele, and they can go into the wee hours.

Guests can escape to a tiny islet for secluded picnics, and they get free use of a wide array of nonmotorized watersports equipment. They pay extra only for scuba diving and deep-sea fishing.

P.O. Box 9936, Nadi Airport (Vatulele Island, 50km/30 miles south of Viti Levu, a 30-min. flight from Nadi). © **800/828-9146** or 672 0300. Fax 672 0062. www.vatulele.com. 19 units. US$1,100 double. Rates includes room, food, bar, all activities except sport fishing and scuba diving. 4-night minimum stay required. Round-trip transfers US$330 per person (free with stays of 8 nights or longer). Children under 12 not accepted except during certain weeks. AE, DC, MC, V. **Amenities:** 1 restaurant (international), 1 bar; tennis court; 24-hr. room service; massage; laundry service. *In room:* Minibar, coffeemaker, hair dryer, safe, no phone.

HOSTELS OFFSHORE FROM NADI

HOSTELS IN THE YASAWAS   An active program since the 2000 coup has fostered the development of several village-owned backpacker accommodations in the central Yasawas near Turtle Island. Several of them have banded together in an organization known as **Nacula Tikina** (© 877/733-3454 or 672 2921; www.fijibudget.com), which promotes them and handles their bookings. Both Coral Sea Cruises and Turtle Airways also have special backpacker fares to Tavewa Island in the Yasawas (see "Getting to Resorts Offshore from Nadi," above). Once you get to Tavewa, boat rides to the other islands cost F$10 ($4.50) each way.

The best of the hostels is **Oarsman's Bay Lodge** on Nacula Island (see "Where to Stay in the Yasawa Islands," above). Also check on **Sunset Beach Resort,** a property similar to Oarsman's Bay, which was under construction on Matacawaleva Island during my recent visit. Tavewa Island has several more basic properties, including two that have been around since the 1980s: **David's Place** and **Coral View Resort,** both beside a long, gorgeous beach. Each charges F$47 ($21) per person in a simple, Fijian-style bure, F$20 ($9) for a dorm bed or camp site. Meal packages are just F$15 ($7) a day.

West Side Waters Sports (© 666 14962; westside@is.com.fj) provides daily dive trips for all the central Yasawa retreats and teaches introductory and PADI certification courses.

On picturesque Waya Island in the southern Yasawas, **Octopus Resort** (© 666 6337; fax 66210; www.octopusresort.com) also has diving, with accommodation in Fijian-style bures with showers and toilets. Rates range from F$99 to F$120 ($44.50–$54) double in bures, F$35 ($16) per dorm bed, including breakfast and dinner.

HOSTELS IN THE MAMANUCAS   Much closer to Nadi in the Mamanucas, **Ratu Kini's Resort** on Mana Island (he's Mana's friendly chief) welcomes young backpackers to stay in dormitories or simple houses for F$35 ($16) per person a day in dorms, F$73 to F$85 ($33–$38), including all meals. Round-trip transfers cost F$70 ($31.50) per person. Guests are not allowed to use the facilities at Mana Island Resort, however. Book at Ratu Kini's office on the upper level of the Nadi airport arrivals concourse (© 672 1959; fax 672 0552; ratukinihostel@is.com.fj).

3 The Coral Coast

Long before big jets began bringing loads of visitors to Fiji, many affluent local residents built cottages on the dry southwestern shore of Viti Levu as sunny retreats from the frequent rain and high humidity of Suva. When visitors started arriving in big numbers during the early 1960s, resorts sprang up among the cottages, and promoters gave a new, more appealing name to the 50km (30-mile) stretch of beaches and reef on either side of the town of Sigatoka: the Coral Coast.

The appellation was apt, for coral reefs jut out like wide shelves from the white beaches that run between mountain ridges all along this picturesque coastline. In most spots the lagoon just reaches snorkeling depth at high tide, and when the water retreats, you can put on your reef sandals or a pair of old sneakers and walk out nearly to the surf pounding on the outer edge of the shelf.

Frankly, the Coral Coast is now overshadowed by other parts of Fiji. Its large hotels host groups of tourists. Nevertheless, it does have some dramatic scenery, and it's a central location from which to see both the Suva and Nadi sides of Viti Levu.

GETTING TO THE CORAL COAST: THE QUEEN'S ROAD

Visitors can reach the Coral Coast from Nadi International Airport by taxi, bus, or rental car along the Queen's Road (see "Getting There & Getting Around" in chapter 9).

After a sharp right turn at the south end of Nadi Town, the highway runs well inland, first through sugar cane fields undulating in the wind and then past acre after acre of pine trees planted in orderly rows, part of Fiji's national forestry program. The blue-green mountains lie off to the left; the deep-blue sea occasionally comes into view off to the right.

MOMI BAY & NATADOLA BEACH

The Old Queen's Road branches off toward the coast and Momi Bay, 16km (10 miles) south of Nadi Town. This graded dirt road leads to the **Momi Guns,** the World War II naval batteries now maintained as a historical park by the National Trust of Fiji. To make this side trip, turn at the Momi intersection and follow the dirt road for 5km (3 miles) through the cane fields to a school, then turn right and drive another 4km (2½ miles) to the concrete bunkers. They command a splendid view over the water to the west. The park has toilets and drinking water.

Maro Road branches off the Queen's Road 35km (21 miles) south of Nadi and runs down to **Natadola Beach** ★★★, the only exceptionally beautiful beach on Viti Levu. It's so nice, in fact, that a project has been approved to build a big resort hotel here (don't cringe if you see construction cranes at work). A sign for Tuva Indian School marks Maro Road, which turns off the Queen's Road between a mosque and Gosai & Sons store. Turn right on Maro Road and right again at the first intersection almost immediately after leaving the Queen's Road. This dirt track leads another 8km (5 miles) to a T-intersection. Turn left, cross a one-lane railroad bridge, and you'll arrive at the beach. Natadola has a grassy, parklike area all along it. A break in the reef allows some surf to break here, especially on the south end. Here're you'll find **Natadola Beach Resort** (© **672 1000**), a small, Mediterranean-style hotel with a dining room and bar in a shady courtyard. The *Fijian Princess,* a refurbished train that comes here daily from Shangri-La's Fijian Resort (see "Sightseeing & Cultural Tours," earlier in this chapter), stops just outside the hotel, which has changing rooms and welcomes daytime guests for lunch.

SIGATOKA SAND DUNES NATIONAL PARK

The pine forests on either side of the Queen's Road soon give way to rolling fields of mission grass before the sea suddenly emerges at a viewpoint above Shangri-La's Fijian Resort on Yanuca Island. After you pass the resort, watch on the right for the visitor center for **Sigatoka Sand Dunes National Park** (© **652 0343**). Fiji's first national park protects high sand hills, which extend for several miles along the coast. About two-thirds of them are stabilized with grass, but some along the shore are still shifting sand (the surf crashing on them is dangerous). Ancient burial grounds and pieces of pottery dating from 5 B.C. to A.D. 240 have been found among the dunes, but be warned: Removing them is against the law. Exhibits in the visitor center explain the dunes and their history. Rangers are on duty daily from 7am to sunset. Admission to the visitors center is free, but you pay F$5 ($2.25) to actually visit the dunes. Call ahead for a guided tour, which costs F$3 ($1.35) per person. (*Note:* You must go to the visitors center before visiting the dunes, which are not accessible from Club Masa, about 1km/½ mile toward Sigatoka.)

SIGATOKA TOWN

About 3km (2 miles) from the park visitor center, the Queen's Road enters **Sigatoka** (pop. 2,000), a quiet, predominantly Indo-Fijian town perched along the west bank of the **Sigatoka River,** Fiji's longest waterway. The broad, muddy river lies on one side of the main street; on the other is a row of duty-free and other shops. The river is crossed by the Melrose Bridge, named in honor of Fiji's winning the Melrose Cup at the Hong Kong Sevens rugby matches in 1997.

While here, you can do some serious shopping at **Jack's Handicrafts** and **Sigatoka Handicraft Centre,** both on the main street facing the river. **Prouds** and **Tappoo** also have large stores on the waterfront, as does **Sogo Fiji,** purveyor of upmarket resort- and beachwear. The street next to Westpac Bank will take you to the active **Sigatoka Municipal Market.**

WHERE TO DINE IN SIGATOKA   Next to Jack's Handicrafts, Roshni and Jean-Pierre Gerber's clean but not air-conditioned **Le Cafe** (© **652 0668**) offers a mixed menu of sandwiches, salads, curries, spaghetti, pizzas, fish and chips, banana fritters, and other snacks. Prices range from F$5.50 to $F12 ($2.50–$5.50). Credit cards are not accepted. Le Cafe is open Monday to Saturday from 8am to 5pm. The Gerbers—she's from Fiji, he's a Swiss chef—also serve dinners at Le Cafe on the Queen's Road in Korotogo, west of the Outrigger Reef Fiji (see "Where to Dine on the Coral Coast," below).

SIGATOKA VALLEY

From Sigatoka, you can go inland along the west bank of the meandering river, flanked on both sides by a patchwork of flat green fields of vegetables that give the **Sigatoka Valley** its nickname: "Fiji's Salad Bowl." The pavement ends about 1km (½ mile) from the town; after that, the road surface is poorly graded and covered with loose stones.

The residents of **Lawai** village at 1.5km (1 mile) from town offer Fijian handcrafts for sale. Two kilometers (1¼ miles) farther on, a small dirt track branches off to the left and runs down a hill to **Nakabuta,** the "Pottery Village," where the residents make and sell authentic Fijian pottery. This art has seen a renaissance of late, and you will find bowls, plates, and other items in handcraft shops elsewhere. Tour buses from Nadi and the Coral Coast stop there most days.

If you're not subject to vertigo, you can look forward to driving past Nakabuta: the road climbs steeply along a narrow ridge, commanding panoramic views across the large Sigatoka Valley with its quiltlike fields to the right and much smaller, more rugged ravine to the left. It then winds its way down to the valley floor and the **Sigatoka Agricultural Research Station,** on whose shady grounds some tour groups stop for picnic lunches. The road climbs into the interior and eventually to Ba on the northwest coast; it intersects the **Nausori Highlands** road leading back to Nadi, but it can be rough or even washed out during periods of heavy rain. Unless they have a four-wheel-drive vehicle or are on an organized tour with a guide, most visitors turn around at the research station and head back to Sigatoka.

TAVUNI HILL FORTIFICATION

A sign on the east end of the old Sigatoka River bridge in town (turn right at the stoplight) points left to the **Tavuni Hill Fortification,** built by an exiled Tongan chief as a safe haven from the ferocious Fijian hill tribes living up the valley. Those highlanders constantly fought wars with the coastal Fijians, and they were the last to give up cannibalism and convert to Christianity. When they rebelled against the Deed of Cession to Great Britain in 1875, the colonial administration sent a force of 1,000 men up the Sigatoka River. They destroyed all the hill forts lining the river, including Tavuni. Today the fort is a Fiji Heritage Project that's open to the public. There's a reception bure, with toilets and a refreshment stand, which has brochures and exhibits. Admission is F$6 ($2.70) for adults and F$3 ($1.35) for children.

GETTING AROUND THE CORAL COAST

The large hotels have car-rental desks as well as taxis hanging around their main entrances. Express buses between Nadi and Suva stop at Shangri-La's Fijian Resort, the Outrigger Reef Fiji, the Hideaway Resort, and the Warwick Fiji. Local buses ply the Queen's Road and will stop for anyone who flags them down. See "Getting There & Getting Around" in chapter 9 for more information.

FAST FACTS: The Coral Coast

The following information applies to the Coral Coast. If you don't see an item here, see "Fast Facts: Nadi," earlier in this chapter, and "Fast Facts: Fiji" in chapter 9.

Camera/Film **Caines Photofast** has a shop on Market Road in Sigatoka (© 500877). Most hotel boutiques sell color print film and provide 1-day processing.

Currency Exchange **ANZ Bank** and **Westpac Bank** have branches on the riverfront in Sigatoka. The hotel desks will cash traveler's checks.

Drugstores **Patel Pharmacy** (© 650 0213) is on Market Road in Sigatoka.

E-mail **Adventures in Paradise,** on the Queen's Road adjacent to the Outrigger Reef Fiji (© 652 0833), has computer terminals for e-mail and web surfing.

Emergencies The emergency phone number for **police** is © 917; for **fire** and **ambulance** dial © 911. The Fiji **police** has posts at Sigatoka (© 650 0222) and at Korolevu (653 0322).

Healthcare The government-run **Sigatoka Hospital** (© 650 0455) can handle minor problems.

Post Office Post offices are in Sigatoka and Korolevu.

Telephone/Telegrams/Fax You can make long-distance telephone calls and send telegrams and faxes at the post offices in Sigatoka and Korolevu. Coral Coast telephone numbers are listed under "Sigatoka" in the Fiji directory.

WHAT TO SEE & DO ON THE CORAL COAST

Hotel reception or tour desks can make reservations for many of the activities mentioned in the "Nadi" section in this chapter. These include tours of the Sigatoka Valley and day trips to Pacific Harbour and Suva. From the Coral Coast, you may have to pay more for Nadi-based activities such as cruises and island excursions than if you were staying on the west coast. On the other hand, you are closer to Coral Coast activities, such as the *Fijian Princess* railroad trips to Natadola Beach (© 652 0434), the cave and waterfall tours offered by

Adventures in Paradise (© **652 0833**), and the rafting trips on the Navua River. The **Kula Eco Park** is just east of the Outrigger Reef Fiji (© **650 0505**).

Although not as informative as the Pacific Harbour Cultural Center (see "Pacific Harbour," below), **The Kalevu Cultural Museum,** opposite Shangri-la's Fijian Resort (© **652 0200**), has authentic traditional bures and presents demonstrations of kava processing, handcraft making, cooking, and fishing. Admission is F$15 ($7). It's open daily from 10am to 5pm. You can also get refreshment here at Gecko's Restaurant (see "Where to Dine on the Coral Coast," below).

From here you can easily take advantage of the golf, fishing, and diving at Pacific Harbour and see the sights in Suva.

WATERSPORTS & OTHER OUTDOOR ACTIVITIES   Most hotels have abundant sports facilities, including diving, for their guests (see "Where to Stay on the Coral Coast," below).

Mike's Divers, on the Queen's Road near the Warwick Fiji (© **650/ 879-0421** in the U.S., or 653 0222; www.dive-fiji.com), provides scuba diving at F$110 ($49.50) for two tanks, and it teaches PADI certification courses. The base is a short boat ride to the outer reef and Morgan's Wall, one of the Coral Coast's most famous sites. Mike's Divers is a joint project between an American couple and Votua village.

SHOPPING   The large hotels have shopping arcades with duty-free shops and clothing and handcraft boutiques, and Fiji's major handcraft and duty-free dealers have stores in Sigatoka (see "Sigatoka Town," above). Prices at relaxed **Baravi Handicrafts** (© **652 0364**), in Vatukarasa village 13km (8 miles) east of Sigatoka, are somewhat lower than you'll find at the larger stores, and it has a snack bar that sells excellent coffee made from Fijian-grown beans. The owners actively promote Fijian handcraft making and buy directly from village artisans. It's open Monday to Saturday 7:30am to 6pm, Sunday 8:30am to 5pm. Vatukarasa also has two roadside stalls where you might find unusual seashells.

WHERE TO STAY ON THE CORAL COAST
EXPENSIVE
Outrigger Reef Fiji ★★ *Kids*   This new lagoon-side resort almost ranks with Shangri-la's Fijian Resort and the two Sheratons as Fiji's best hotels, but alas, Mother Nature has robbed the beach here of most of its sand. You can still go kayaking, spy-boarding and snorkeling at high tide, but the gorgeous, brick-fringed swimming pool—the most attractive such facility in Fiji—is the center of attention here.

In a way, the Outrigger is two hotels in one, for most of the accommodation is in modern five-story hillside buildings at the rear of the property, while the 47 thatch-roof guest bungalows and restaurants look like a traditional Fijian village in a coconut grove down by the lagoon. A few other hotel rooms are in a three-story lagoon-side building, the last remnant of The Reef Resort, which once stood here. Although of moderate size and furnished with contemporary pieces like a big-city hotel, the rooms are equipped with most modern amenities, and all have balconies (with spectacular views from the upper floors). The tropics prevail in the comfortable guest bungalows, which have *masi*-lined peaked ceilings. These also are moderate sized, and they are cooled by ceiling fans, not air conditioners. The six beachfront bungalows are the pick of the litter. A few bungalows are joined together to make family units.

Australian restaurateur Geoff Shaw, who owns both this resort and Castaway Island Resort in the Mamanucas (see "Island Escapes from Nadi," above), sees to it that everyone is well fed in an intimate fine-dining restaurant, a large open-air dining room, and a midday grill by the pool.

P.O. Box 173, Sigatoka (Queen's Rd., 78km/49 miles from Nadi Airport, 8km/5 miles east of Sigatoka). ℂ 800/688-7444 or 650 0044. Fax 652 0074. www.outrigger.com. 254 units. F$410–F$495 ($185–$223) double; F$625–F$1,150 ($281–$518) bungalow. AE, DC, MC, V. **Amenities:** 3 restaurants (regional), 4 bars; outdoor pool; 2 tennis courts; exercise room; Jacuzzi; watersports equipment rentals; children's programs; game room; activities desk; car-rental desk; business center; shopping arcade; salon; massage; babysitting; laundry service; coin-op washers and dryers. *In room:* A/C (in hotel rooms), TV, dataport, fridge, coffeemaker, hair dryer, iron, safe.

Shangri-La's Fijian Resort ★★★ Fiji's largest hotel, "The Fijian" occupies all 105 acres of flat Yanuca Island, which is joined to the mainland by a short, one-lane causeway. The ocean side of Yanuca is lined with a coral-colored sand beach that is superior to those at the two Sheratons on Denarau Island near Nadi. Needless to say, there are a host of watersports activities here, including diving, or you can play tennis or knock around the nine-hole golf course. Covered walkways wander through thick tropical foliage to link the hotel blocks to three main restaurant-and-bar buildings, both adjacent to swimming pools. The Fijian is so spread out that a shuttle constantly runs around the property, and like a Good Humor ice cream wagon for adults, a mobile bar trolls along the beach. There's a real ice cream bar here, too.

The spacious rooms and suites occupy two- and three-story buildings, all on the shore of the island, so each room has a view of the lagoon and sea from its own private balcony or patio. The suites have separate bedrooms and two bathroom sinks. Ocean view units have TVs and bathrooms with heated towel racks and combination tub-and-shower bathrooms (other units have walk-in showers). A few beachside bungalows can sleep up to six persons. The Fijian's restaurants have something for everyone's taste, if not necessarily for everyone's pocketbook, and four bars are ready to quench any thirst. Evening entertainment features traditional Fijian fire walking.

Private Mail Bag NAPO353, Nadi Airport (Yanuca Island, 60km/36 miles from Nadi Airport, 10km/6 miles west of Sigatoka). ℂ 800/942-5050 or 652 0155. Fax 652 0402. www.shangri-la.com. 436 units. F$370–F$680 ($166–$306) double. AE, DC, MC, V. **Amenities:** 4 restaurants (regional/Asian), 4 bars; 3 outdoor pools; 9-hole golf course; 4 tennis courts; health club; watersports equipment rentals; bike rentals; children's programs; game room; concierge; activities desk; car-rental desk; business center; shopping arcade; salon; 24-hr. room service; massage; babysitting; laundry service; coin-op washers and dryers. *In room:* A/C, TV (in ocean view units), dataport, fridge, coffeemaker, hair dryer, iron, safe.

MODERATE

Hideaway Resort ★★ (Value Brothers Robert and Kelvin Wade bought this beachside property in the 1980s and have been enlarging and improving it ever since. During their early years it was famous as a young persons' hangout, with a large dormitory and mile-a-minute entertainment. The dormitory belongs to history now, but the Hideaway still attracts an active clientele of all ages, both married and single, and children are welcome, too.

The Wades have added accommodations laterally along their narrow strip of land between the Queen's Road and the beach. Near the main building, the 16 original, A-frame bungalows have been brought up to speed but lack air conditioners. Most of their other units are in modern, duplex bungalows with tropical furnishings and shower-only bathrooms, but the crown jewels here are new "deluxe villas" at the far, private end of the property. With pastel stucco walls, trim of local timber antiqued with mud, curved dividers separating sleeping areas from vanities, and both indoor and outdoor showers, they are like smaller and much less expensive versions of the bungalows at Vatulele Island Resort (see "Island Escapes from Nadi," above). A few larger family units here can sleep up to five persons.

The main building—with dining, bar, and entertainment areas—opens to a beachside pool with a waterfall, a water slide, and a special area for training scuba divers. This vista is especially appealing at night, when underwater lights illuminate the pool and a flame shoots from the top of the water slide. Meals feature buffets, barbecues, and Fijian *lovo* feasts several nights a week, followed by Fijian *meke* dancing and Club Med–style cabaret shows.

As has happened at the Outrigger Reef Fiji (see above), the beach here has mostly eroded away, but you can still enjoy snorkeling, kayaking, and windsurfing at high tide, plus good scuba diving and surfing out on the reef. You can keep busy ashore with tennis, horseback tours, trips to the mountains and waterfalls, minigolf, Fijian fish-drives, and pumping iron in an exercise room under its own thatch roof (where you can catch the news on TV).

P.O. Box 233, Sigatoka (Queen's Rd., 92km/55 miles from Nadi Airport, 21km/13 miles east of Sigatoka). (©) **650 0177.** Fax 652 0025. www.hideawayfiji.com. 100 units. F$235–F$410 ($106–$185) bungalow. Rates include full breakfast. AE, DC, MC, V. **Amenities:** 1 restaurant (European/Indian/Fijian), 1 bar; outdoor pool; tennis court; miniature golf; exercise room; watersports equipment rentals; children's programs; game room; concierge; activities desk; car-rental desk; salon; massage; babysitting; laundry service; coin-op washers and dryers. *In room:* A/C, dataport, fridge, coffeemaker, hair dryer, iron.

The Warwick Fiji   Sitting on a palm-fringed beach with a bit more sand than you'll find at Outrigger Reef or the Hideaway, this complex appears to be little different from other tropical resorts when seen from the road. The interior of the central building, however, clearly reflects a legacy of distinctive architecture from its origins as the Hyatt Regency Fiji. A sweeping roof supported by natural wood beams covers a wide reception and lobby area bordered on either end by huge carved murals depicting Capt. James Cook's discovery of Fiji in 1779. A curving staircase descends from the center of the lobby into a large square well, giving access to the dining and recreation areas on the lagoon level. The medium-size guest rooms are in two- and three-story blocks that flank the central building. Each room has its own balcony or patio with a view of the sea or the tropical gardens surrounding the complex. The most expensive units are suites, which directly face the lagoon from the ends of the buildings. The sand-floored Wicked Walu, under a thatch roof on a tiny island offshore, is the choice dining spot here.

P.O. Box 100, Korolevu (104km/62 miles from Nadi Airport, 32km/20 miles east of Sigatoka). (©) **800/448-8355** or 653 0555. Fax 653 0010. Fax 520010. www.warwickfiji.com. 250 units. F$286–F$450 ($129–$203) double; F$600 ($270) suite. AE, DC, MC, V. **Amenities:** 4 restaurants (seafood/Japanese/Italian), 5 bars; 2 outdoor pools; 4 tennis courts; exercise room; Jacuzzi; watersports equipment rentals; children's programs; activities desk; car-rental desk; business center; shopping arcade; salon; 24-hr. room service; massage; babysitting; laundry service; coin-op washers and dryers; concierge-level rooms. *In room:* A/C, TV, dataport, minibar, coffeemaker, hair dryer, iron.

INEXPENSIVE

Bedarra Inn Fjiji *Value*   This comfortable inn began life as a private home with bedrooms on either end of a great, two-story central hall, which opened to a veranda overlooking a swimming pool and, through the trees, the lagoon. The beach is across a dead-end road known as Sunset Strip, which was the main drag before the Queen's Road was diverted around the new Outrigger Reef Fiji resort, a short walk from here. Today a square bar and lounge furniture occupy the great hall, and a romantic restaurant has taken over the veranda (see "Where to Dine on the Coral Coast," below). Upstairs, another veranda wraps around the house.

Inside the house, guests can opt for two-bedroom suites capable of sleeping up to four persons, or hotel-style rooms, each equipped with a double bed. These may someday be air-conditioned; in the meantime, fans kick up a breeze. Out back, a two-room bure can accommodate four persons. And to the side of the house, a two-story motel block holds 16 air-conditioned rooms, all with traditional oak furniture and large bathrooms with walk-in showers. Four of these also have cooking facilities.

P.O. Box 1213, Sigatoka (Sunset Strip, 78km/47 miles from Nadi Airport, 8km/5 miles east of Sigatoka). © **650 0476.** Fax 652 0166. bedarrahouse@is.com.fj. 21 units. F$90 ($40.50 double). AE, DC, MC, V. **Amenities:** 1 restaurant (regional), 1 bar; outdoor pool; games room; laundry service. *In room:* A/C (in motel rooms), TV, dataport, kitchen (in 4 units), fridge, coffeemaker, hair dryer, no phone.

HOSTELS

The Beachouse ★ Andrew Waldken-Brown, a European who was born in Fiji, and his Australian wife, Jessica, have turned his family's old beachside vacation cottage into one of the South Pacific's best backpacker resorts. Built in the old South Seas style of tin roof, clapboard sides, and big windows with push-out, prop-up shutters, the charming cottage serves as lounge, bar, and dining room, where guests (but not outsiders) can order inexpensive meals. Andrew and Jessica built their airy, two-story dorms from scratch and gave them the ultimate in luxuries—well, at least as far as backpackers are concerned. Downstairs is divided into quadrangles, each with its own ceiling fan, and each of the five beds in each section has reading lights. Upstairs is aimed at couples, with partitions separating roomettes with ceiling fans and mosquito netted double beds, but the walls don't reach the ceiling, so you can easily be overheard. Much better for couples are 12 garden rooms in a separate building; each has a double bed and two settees for lounging. All beds here have reading lights, and the windows are screened. All guests, including campers who can pitch their tents on the spacious lawn, share clean toilets and a modern communal kitchen. The beach here is one of the finest on the Coral Coast.

P.O. Box 68, Korolevu (105km/65 miles from Nadi Airport, 37km/23 miles east of Sigatoka). © **0800/653 0530** toll-free in Fiji, or 653 0500. Fax 345 0400. www.fijibeachouse.8m.com. 12 units (none with bathroom), 40 dorm beds. F$40–F$46 ($18–$20.50) double; F$16.50 ($7.50) dorm bed; F$8.80 ($4) per person camping. MC, V. **Amenities:** 1 restaurant (regional), 1 bar; free use of canoes, paddle boards, and bikes. *In room:* No phone.

Tubakula Beach Bungalows *Value* This simple establishment (whose name is pronounced " *Toomb*-a-koola") sits almost next door to the Outrigger Reef Fiji than at The Beachouse, in a lagoon-side coconut grove. The bungalows are A-frame cottages with simple furnishings. The downstairs of each bungalow has a lounge, kitchen, bathroom, and bedroom; upstairs is a sleeping loft. Each can sleep six persons, so sharing one represents good value. The dorms are in European-style houses. No more than four beds are in any one room, and guests share communal kitchens, showers, and toilets. A minimart sells beer, soft drinks, and basic groceries.

P.O. Box 2, Sigatoka (Queen's Rd., 79km/49 miles from Nadi Airport, 13km/7 miles east of Sigatoka). © **650 0097.** Fax 334 0236. 23 units, 24 dorm beds. F$50–F$86 ($22.50–$38.50) bungalow; F$15 ($6.75) dorm bed. AE, DC, MC, V. **Amenities:** 1 restaurant (Indian/Chinese), 1 bar; outdoor pool; game room. *In room:* Kitchen, no phone.

WHERE TO DINE ON THE CORAL COAST

Many Coral Coast hotels have special nights, such as *meke* feasts of Fijian foods cooked in a *lovo*, served buffet style, and followed by traditional dancing.

Bedarra Inn Restaurant INTERNATIONAL   Overlooking a lush tropical garden surrounding a swimming pool, the veranda of the Bedarra Inn Fiji (see "Where to Stay on the Coral Coast," above) is the most romantic place to dine here. The menu offers an uninspired but varied selection, including tender steaks under peppercorn or red wine sauce, fresh local fish panfried with lemon caper sauce, crumbed veal slices topped with asparagus, a vegetarian pasta, and spicy version of spaghetti carbonara. You can also try Fijian dishes such as palusami and *ika vakalolo* (fish steamed in coconut milk). Stop in for breakfast, lunch, or afternoon Devonshire tea.

Sunset Strip, Korotogo, west of the Outrigger Reef Fiji. ℂ **650 0476.** Reservations recommended. Main courses F$14–F$26.50 ($6.50–$12). AE, DC, MC, V. Daily 7am–10pm.

Gecko's Restaurant REGIONAL   Occupying the veranda of one of the Western-style buildings at The Kalevu Cultural Museum, this pleasant restaurant offers a more affordable if not-as-good alternative to the dining rooms at Shangri-la's Fijian Resort across the Queen's Road. You can have a breakfast of omelets and other egg dishes all day here. Lunch features a choice of sandwiches, burgers, fish and chips, curry, stir-fries, and other local favorites. Dinner sees a wide-ranging menu, which includes the house specialty, mud crabs with coconut cream, chili, or Chinese-style black bean. There's live music nightly here, and the cultural center has Fijian *mekes,* kava ceremonies, and classical Indian dancing (call to see what's on).

Queen's Rd., in Kalevu Cultural Museum opposite Shangri-la's Fijian Resort. ℂ **652 0200.** Reservations accepted. Breakfast F$5–F$8 ($2.25–$3.50); lunch F$5–F$11 ($2.25–$5); main courses F$14–F$30 ($6.50–$13.50). AE, MC, V. Daily 10am–10pm.

Le Cafe ★★ INTERNATIONAL   After they've served breakfast and lunch at Le Cafe in Sigatoka (see "Sigatoka Town," above), Roshni and Jean-Pierre Gerber turn their attention to this little establishment, where they display their culinary skills on fish and chips, Indian curries, Italian pastas, and some of Fiji's best pizzas. You can also opt for chicken cordon bleu, fresh fish filet with drawn lemon butter sauce, pepper or garlic steak, garlic prawns, or local lobster with Mornay sauce. Facing the sea, the thatch-topped bar out front is a great place for a sunset cocktail.

Sunset Strip, Korotogo, west of the Outrigger Reef Fiji. ℂ **652 0877.** Reservations accepted. Pizzas and main courses F$5.50–F$14.50 ($2.50–$6.50). No credit cards. Daily 4–10pm.

Vilisite's Seafood Restaurant ★★ (Value) SEAFOOD/INDIAN/CHINESE   Vilisite (sounds like "Felicity"), a friendly Fijian who lived in Australia, operates one of the few places in Fiji where you can dine right by the lagoon's edge. Come in time for a sunset drink and bring a camera, for the westward view from Vilisite's veranda—albeit through a fishnet to keep the mynah birds from stealing your lunch—belongs on a postcard. Her well-prepared cuisine is predominately fresh local seafood—fish, shrimp, lobster, octopus—in curry, garlic, and butter, or coconut milk (the Fijian way). She offers only five full seafood meals at dinner, or you can choose from chop suey, curry, and shrimp, or fish and chips. Vilisite will arrange rides for dinner parties of four or more from as far away as the Outrigger Reef Fiji, but be sure to ask about the cost. You won't soon forget the view or this extraordinarily friendly Fijian, who certainly knows how to cook.

Queen's Road, Korolevu, between the Warwick and the Naviti. ℂ **653 0054.** Reservations recommended. Lunch F$6.50–F$14 ($3–$6.50); full dinners F$7–F$39 ($3–$17.50). MC, V. Daily 8am–10pm.

ISLAND NIGHTS ON THE CORAL COAST

Coral Coast nightlife centers around the hotels and whatever Fiji *meke* shows they are sponsoring. The famous **Fijian fire walkers** from Beqa, an island off the south coast (remember, it's pronounced "Mbengga," not "Beck-a"), parade across the steaming stones to the incantations of "witch doctors" at various hotels on the Coral Coast and at Nadi. The **Outrigger Reef Fiji** (✆ **500044**) and the **Warwick Fiji** (✆ **530010**) usually sponsor fire-walking shows at least once a week. Call them or ask at your hotel for the schedule.

4 Pacific Harbour

Although it never has reached its potential, Pacific Harbour was begun in the early 1970s as a recreation-oriented, luxury residential community and resort (translated: a real estate development). Although a number of expatriates have built homes here (they have their own tourist information website at **www.pacificharbour-fiji.com**), Pacific Harbour is known today primarily for its excellent golf course, great deep-sea fishing, and the diving in the beautiful Beqa Lagoon offshore. Given the heat, humidity, and amount of rain it gets, however, Pacific Harbour is not the place to come for a typical beach vacation.

Sitting on the Queen's Road, the somewhat shopworn **Pacific Harbour Cultural Centre & Market Place** was designed to serve both tourists and residents of the real estate development. The market place consists of colonial-style clapboard buildings joined by covered walkways. In addition to the grocery store, you can wander through its boutiques and handcraft shops.

Definitely worth seeing here is the **Pacific Harbour Cultural Centre** ★★ (✆ **345 0095**; www.pacific-harbour.com). This replica of an ancient Fijian village sits on "Sacred Island," in a lake behind the market place. You get over there on boats paddled by muscular young Fijian men dressed in traditional costumes. A tall *burekalou* ("spirit house") dominates the other thatch-roofed buildings in the village. There's even an enclosure where the high chiefs kept their concubines. Fijians demonstrate age-old skills such as cooking, pottery making, wood carving, and boat building. Beqa Islanders perform their fire-walking ceremony here, and you'll see one of the country's best dance troupes perform. The cultural center is open only on Tuesday and Thursday from 9:30am to 1:30pm, with the fire-walking and dance performances at 2:30pm, but you should call ahead for the current schedule. Admission is F$18 ($8).

GETTING TO PACIFIC HARBOUR & GETTING AROUND

Pacific Harbour is on the Queen's Road, 30km (50 miles) west of Suva. All buses that run between Nadi and Suva stop at the Centra Resort Pacific Harbour, where you'll also find taxis waiting in the parking lot. See "Getting There & Getting Around" in chapter 9 for more information.

FISHING, GOLF & SCUBA DIVING

FISHING   The waters off southern Viti Levu are renowned for their big game fish, especially when the tuna and mahimahi are running from January to May and when big wahoos pass by in June and July. The women's world records for wahoo and travelli were set here.

Baywater Charters (✆ **345 0573;** fax 345 0606) will tailor an excursion to your liking—be it going for the big ones offshore or trolling for smaller but exciting catch inshore. Fishing costs about F$600 ($270) for half a day, F$1,000

($450) for a full day (the boat is equipped with sleeping quarters and showers, so longer trips are possible). It's also available for picnic trips over to Beqa, or sunset cruises.

GOLF   One of the South Pacific's finest, the course at **Centra Resort Pacific Harbour** (© **345 0048**) is the centerpiece of the planned resort community on the north side of the Queen's Road, opposite the resort hotel. The clubhouse needs serious refurbishment, but the 18-hole, par-72 course designed by Robert Trent Jones Jr. is worth playing despite the heat, humidity, and frequent rain here. Some of the fairways cross lakes; others cut their way through narrow valleys surrounded by jungle-clad hills. Visitors are welcome to use the links; greens fees are F$30 ($13.50). A full range of equipment can be rented at the pro shop.

SCUBA DIVING & SNORKELING 🐠🐠   San Francisco–based **Aqua-Trek** (© **800/541-4334** or 345 0324; fax 345 0324; www.aquatrek.com) has expeditions to Beqa Lagoon, a 30-minute boat ride across an open water channel from the Centra Resort Pacific Harbour. Aqua-Trek also teaches resort and a full range of PADI courses.

WHERE TO STAY IN PACIFIC HARBOUR

Centra Resort Pacific Harbour   Built in 1972, this beachside hotel attracts primarily divers, fishers, and serious golfers. The complex sits beside a long gray-sand surf beach with a terrific view of Beqa across the channel. You enter an open lobby upstairs, where there's a restaurant, a bar, and a gift shop. Steps lead down to a kid's club play area, an irregular-shaped pool, and the beach. The spacious hotel-style rooms are in two-story wings to either side. Each has tile floors, one queen or two double beds, a tub-and-shower bathroom, and a door that opens to a balcony or patio facing the sea.

P.O. Box 144, Pacific Harbour (142km/88 miles from Nadi Airport, 48km/30 miles west of Suva). © **800/835-7742** or 345 0022. Fax 345 0262. www.sphc.com.au. 83 units. F$158 ($71) double. AE, DC, MC, V. **Amenities:** 1 restaurant (regional), 1 bar; outdoor pool; golf course; 3 tennis courts; watersports equipment rentals; children's programs; game room; activities desk; limited room service; massage; babysitting; laundry service; coin-op washers and dryers. *In room:* A/C, TV, dataport, fridge, coffeemaker, hair dryer, iron.

WHERE TO DINE IN PACIFIC HARBOUR

Oasis Restaurant REGIONAL   Owned by English expatriates Monica Vine and Colin Head, this airy dining room with widely spaced tables makes an excellent pit stop if you're driving between Nadi and Suva. The house specialty is authentic London-style fish and chips, often using flaky red snapper fresh from the sea. You can get tasty burgers, sandwiches, salads, curries, omelets, and English-style breakfasts all day. Evening sees a blackboard dinner menu with the likes of panfried mahimahi, perhaps caught by one of the charter boat skippers having a cold one and throwing darts at Colin's friendly corner bar. Monica and Colin will let you use their computer with Internet access for F40¢ (18¢) per minute.

Queen's Rd., in Pacific Harbour Marketplace. © **345 0617**. Reservations accepted. Snacks, sandwiches, and lunch F$5–F$15 ($2.25–$6.50); main courses F$15–F$35 ($6.50–$15.50). MC, V. Daily 9:30am–3pm and 6–9:30pm (bar to 11pm).

5 Suva

Neither the likelihood of frequent showers nor an occasional deluge should discourage you from visiting Suva, Fiji's vibrant, sophisticated capital city. Grab your umbrella and wander along its broad avenues lined with grand colonial buildings and orderly parks left over from the British Empire. Its streets will be

---

Impressions

The English, with a mania for wrong decisions in Fiji, built their capital at Suva, smack in the middle of the heaviest rainfall. . . . Yet Suva is a superb tropical city.

—James A. Michener, Return to Paradise, 1951

---

crowded with Fijians, Indians, Chinese, Europeans, Polynesians, and people of various other ancestries.

Suva sprawls over a hilly, 16 square-km (10-sq.-mile) peninsula that juts like a thumb from southeastern Viti Levu. To the east lies windswept **Laucala Bay** and to the west, Suva's busy harbor and the suburbs of **Lami Town** and **Walu Bay.** Jungle-draped mountains rise to heights of more than 1,200m (4,000 ft.) on the "mainland" to the north, high enough to condense moisture from the prevailing southeast trade winds and create the damp climate that cloaks the city in lush green foliage all year round.

Suva was a typical Fijian village in 1870, when the Polynesia Company sent a group of Australians to settle the land it bought in exchange for paying Chief Cakobau's foreign debts. The Aussies established a camp on the flat, swampy, mosquito-infested banks of **Nubukalou Creek,** on the western shore of the peninsula. When they failed to grow first cotton and then sugar, speculators obtained the land and in 1875 convinced the new British colonial administration to move the capital from Levuka in 1882.

The business heart of the city still sits near Nubukalou Creek, and visitors can see most of the city's sights and find most of its shops, interesting restaurants, and lively nightspots along historic **Victoria Parade,** the main drag.

On the beautiful island of Ovalau, some 32km (20 miles) east of Viti Levu, the old town of Levuka still looks very much as it did during its heydays before the government moved to Suva. In marked contrast to Suva, never-changing Levuka remains a charming example of what South Pacific towns were like in the 1870s. Levuka makes a good day trip from Suva—if you don't mind the risk of not getting back on the same day—or longer if you don't need accommodations with modern amenities.

GETTING TO SUVA & GETTING AROUND
GETTING TO SUVA

Suva is served by **Nausori Airport,** 19km (12 miles) northeast of downtown near the Rewa River town of Nausori. Taxis between there and Suva cost F$20 ($9) each way. Allow at least 30 minutes for the ride during midday, an hour during morning and evening rush hours. See "Getting There & Getting Around" in chapter 9 for more information.

If you're driving from the Nadi side of Viti Levu, don't leave without a good map of Suva, whose maze of streets can be confusing, especially at night (I try never to drive in Suva after dark).

GETTING AROUND SUVA

Hundreds of **taxis** prowl the streets of Suva. Some have meters, but don't count on it. As a rule of thumb, F$2 to F$3.50 (90¢–$1.50) will get you to the sites of interest, F$7 ($3) to the Raintree Lodge. If he has a meter, make sure the driver drops the flag. The main **taxi stand** is on Central Street, behind the Air Pacific office in the CML Building on Victoria Parade (© **331 2266**), and on

Victoria Parade at Sukuna Park (no phone). I have been very satisfied with **Black Arrow Taxis** (© **330 0541** or 330 0139 in Suva, or 347 7071 in Nausori) and **Nausori Taxi & Bus Service** (© **347 7583** in Nausori, or 330 4178 in Suva), which is based at the Centra Suva parking lot. Other taxis gather at the Suva Municipal Market.

Usually crowded, local **buses** fan out from the municipal market from before daybreak to midnight Monday to Saturday (they have limited schedules on Sunday). The fares vary but should be no more than F90¢ (41¢) to most destinations in and around Suva. If you're going to ride the bus for the fun of it, do it in Nadi, where you won't get lost and aren't as likely to be robbed.

See "Getting There & Getting Around" in chapter 9 for the phone numbers of the major **car rental** firms.

 FAST FACTS: Suva

The following facts apply to Suva. If you don't see an item here, see "Fast Facts: Fiji" in chapter 9.

American Express **Tapa International Ltd.** (© **330 2333**) has an office on the fourth floor of the FNPF Building, on Downtown Boulevard at Victoria Parade. Hours are Monday to Friday from 8:30am to 5pm, Saturday from 9am to noon. Personal check cashing is available only from 9:30am to 3pm weekdays, since you have to take your approved check to an ANZ Bank. The mailing address is G.P.O. Box 654, Suva.

Bookstores **Dominion Book Centre,** in Dominion Arcade on Thomson Street behind the Fiji Visitors Bureau © **330 4334**), has the latest newsmagazines, local and Australian newspapers, and books on the South Pacific.

Camera/Film **Caines Photofast,** corner of Victoria Parade and Pratt Street (© **331 3211**), sells a wide range of film and provides 1-hour processing of color-print film.

Currency Exchange **ANZ Bank** and **Westpac Bank** have offices on Victoria Parade, south of the Fiji Visitors Bureau. Both have ATM machines. **Thomas Cook Travel Service,** on Victoria Parade near the Fiji Visitors Bureau (© **330 1603**), cashes travelers checks Monday to Friday from 9am to 4pm and Saturday from 9:30am to noon.

Drugstores **Gordon Street Medical Centre** (see "Healthcare," below) has a pharmacy.

E-mail **Republic of Cappuccino,** in the Dolphins Food Court, Victoria Parade at Loftus Street (© **330 0333**), has Internet terminals. It's open Monday to Friday 7am to 11pm, Saturday 8am to 11pm, Sunday 10am to 7pm (see "Where to Dine in Suva," below). **Telecom Fiji** has less noisy terminals at its customer service office in Ganilau House, on Scott Street (Victoria Parade extended) at Edward Street (© **321 0335**), where you also can sign up for temporary Internet access if you brought your laptop. Telecom is open Monday to Thursday 8am to 4:30pm, Friday 8am to 4pm. Both charge F22¢ (10¢) a minute for access.

Emergencies/Police The emergency phone number for **police** is © **917.** For **fire** and **ambulance** dial © **911.** Fiji Police's **central station** is on Joske Street, between Pratt and Gordon streets (© **331 1222**).

Eyeglasses **Asgar & Co. Ltd.,** Queensland Insurance Centre, Victoria Parade (© **330 0433**), sells a complete line of eyewear, including contact lenses.

Hairdressers/Barbers **Cut Above Salon,** Honson Arcade, Thomson Street, is next to Canadian Airlines International (© **330 4553**).

Healthcare Most expatriate residents go to the private **Gordon Street Medical Centre,** 98–100 Gordon St. (© **331 3355**). It's open 24 hours a day. The clinic has Fiji's only recompression chamber facility. Ask your hotel staff to recommend a **dentist** if you need one. **Colonial War Memorial Hospital,** end of Ratu Mara Road at Brown Street, is the public hospital but go to Gordon Street Medical Centre if at all possible.

Information The **Fiji Visitors Bureau** (© **330 2433**) has its headquarters in a restored colonial house at the corner of Thomson and Scott Streets, in the heart of Suva. It's open Monday to Thursday from 8am to 4:30pm, Friday from 8am to 4pm, and Saturday from 8am to noon.

Laundry/Dry Cleaning **White & Brite Selfservice Laundry,** 177 Meade Rd. (© **338 4333**), in the Nabua suburb, has coin-operated washers and dryers; it's a $6 ($4.20) round-trip taxi ride from downtown. **Flagstaff Laundry & Drycleaners,** 62 Bau St. (© **330 1214**), has full 1-day service.

Libraries **Suva City Library** on Victoria Parade (© **331 3433**) has a small collection of books on the South Pacific. It's open Monday, Tuesday, Thursday, and Friday from 9:30am to 6pm; Wednesday from noon to 6pm; and Saturday from 9am to 1pm. The library at the **University of the South Pacific** (© **331 3900**) has one of the largest collections in the South Pacific. The university is on Laucala Bay Road.

Maps The Fiji Visitors Bureau has maps (see "Information," above). The excellent *Suva and Lami Town* is published by the **Department of Lands & Surveys,** whose main sales office is in the Government Buildings on Victoria Parade (© **321 1395**).

Post Office Fiji Post's General Post Office is on Thomson Street, opposite the Fiji Visitor's Bureau. It's open Monday to Friday from 8am to 4:30pm, Saturday from 9am to noon.

Restrooms **Sukuna Park,** on Victoria Parade, has attended (and therefore reasonably clean) public restrooms, on the side next to McDonald's. You must pay F24¢ (11¢) to use the toilets, or F61¢ (28¢) for a shower.

Safety The busy blocks along Victoria Parade are relatively safe during the evenings, but the same cannot be said for the rest of Suva. Don't wander off Victoria Parade at any time; take a taxi. See "Safety" under "Fast Facts: Fiji" in chapter 9.

Telephone/Telegrams/Fax The easiest way to call overseas is by using a prepaid Phonecard (see "Fast Facts: Fiji" in chapter 9). Edward Street next to the General Post Office has several Phonecard public telephones. International phone, telegram, fax, and telex service are provided by **Fiji International Telecommunications Ltd. (FINTEL)** at its colonial-style building on Victoria Parade. It's open Monday to Saturday from 8am to 8pm.

Water The tap water is safe to drink.

EXPLORING SUVA

Although you could easily spend several days poking around the capital, most visitors come here for only a day, usually on one of the guided tours from Nadi or the Coral Coast. That's enough time to see the city's highlights, particularly if you make the walking tour described below.

The easiest way to see the residential suburbs as well as downtown Suva is on a guided tour. **United Touring Fiji (UTC),** which has a tour desk in the lobby of the Holiday Inn Suva (© **331 2287**), charges F$30 ($13.50) per person for the 2-hour tour.

THE TOP ATTRACTIONS

Fiji Museum ★★★   You'll see a marvelous collection of war clubs, cannibal forks, tanoa bowls, shell jewelry, and other Fijian relics here, in one of the South Pacific's finest museums. Although some artifacts were damaged by Suva's humidity while they were hidden away during World War II, much remains. Later additions include the rudder and other relics of HMS *Bounty,* burned and sunk at Pitcairn Island by Fletcher Christian and the other mutineers in 1789 but recovered by the National Geographic Society in the 1950s. Exhibits in the rear of the building explain Fiji's history.

In Thurston Gardens, Ratu Cakobau Rd. off Victoria Parade. © **331 5944.** www.fijimuseum.org.fj. Admission F$3.30 ($1.50), free for school-age children. Guided tours F$3 ($1.35). Mon–Thurs and Sat 9:30am–4:30pm, Fri 9:30am–4pm.

Parliament of Fiji   Sitting on a ridge about 1km (½ mile) southeast of downtown, Fiji's new parliament building resides under a modern shingle-covered version of a traditional Fijian roof. Large *masi* cloth banners hang in the chamber, in which both houses meet. There are no organized tours, but if there isn't a coup in progress, you can watch the debates from the visitors' gallery or just stroll along the outside walkways and peer in through floor-to-ceilings windows. The entry is on Battery Road, which runs off Vuya Road, which in turn makes an arc uphill from Ratu Sukuna Road off Queen Elizabeth Drive. It's about 1km (½ mile) uphill from Queen Elizabeth Drive, but the easiest way to get here is by taxi. Call the main number or check with the Fiji Visitors Bureau to find out when parliament meets.

Battery Road, off Vuya Rd. © **330 5811.** Free admission. Mon–Fri 8am–1pm and 2–4:30pm.

Suva Municipal Market ★★★   A vast array of tropical produce is offered for sale at Suva's main supply of food, the largest and most lively market in the South Pacific. If they aren't too busy, the merchants will appreciate your interest and answer your questions about the names and uses of the various fruits and vegetables. The market teems on Saturday morning, when, it seems, the entire population of Suva shows up to shop and select television programs for the weekend's viewing. Few sights say as much about urban life in the modern South Pacific as does that of a Fijian carrying home in one hand a bunch of taro roots tied together with pandanus, and in the other a collection of rented videocassettes stuffed into a plastic bag. The bus station is behind the market on Rodwell Road; on the other side of this busy street is the **Suva Flea Market,** where other vendors sell mostly clothing and a few handcrafts.

Usher St. at Rodwell Road. No phone. Free admission. Mon–Fri 5am–6pm, Sat 5am–1pm.

Start:	The Triangle.
Finish:	Government House.
Time:	2½ hours.
Best Time:	Early morning or late afternoon.
Worst Time:	Midday, or Saturday afternoon and Sunday, when the market and shops are closed and downtown is deserted.

Begin at the four-way intersection of Victoria Parade, Renwick Road, and Thomson and Central streets. This little island in the middle of heavy traffic is called The Triangle.

❶ The Triangle

Now the center of Suva, in the late 1800s this spot was a lagoon fed by a stream that flowed along what is now Pratt Street. A marker in the park commemorates Suva's becoming the capital, the arrival of Fiji's first missionaries, the first public land sales, and Fiji's becoming a colony. Three of the four dates are slightly wrong.

From The Triangle, head north on Thomson Street, bearing right between the Fiji Visitors Bureau and the old Garrick Hotel (now the Sichuan Pavilion Restaurant), whose wrought-iron balconies recall a more genteel but non-air-conditioned era. Continue on Thomson Street to Nubukalou Creek.

❷ Nubukalou Creek

The Polynesia Company's settlers made camp beside this stream and presumably drank from it. A sign on the bridge warns against eating fish from it today—with good reason, as you will see and smell. Across the bridge, smiling Fijian women wait under a flame tree in a shady little park to offer grass skirts and other handcraft items for sale.

Pass to the left of the Fijian women across the bridge for now, and head down narrow Cumming Street.

❸ Cumming Street

This area, also on reclaimed land, was home of the Suva market until the 1940s. Cumming Street was lined with saloons, yaqona "grog" shops, and curry houses known as "lodges."

It became a tourist-oriented shopping mecca when World War II Allied servicemen created a market for curios. When import taxes were lifted from electronic equipment and cameras in the 1960s, Cumming Street merchants quickly added the plethora of duty-free items you'll find there today. Browse for a while.

Return to Thomson Street, turn right, and then turn left on Usher Street. Follow Usher Street past the intersection at Rodwell Road and Scott Street to the Suva Municipal Market.

❹ Suva Municipal Market

This market is a beehive of activity, especially on Saturday mornings (see "The Top Attractions," above). Big ships from overseas and small boats from the other islands dock at Princes Wharf and Kings Wharf beyond the market on Usher Street.

Head south along wide Stinson Parade, back across Nubukalou Creek and along the edge of Suva's waterfront to Edward Street and the gray tin roofs of the Municipal Curio and Handicraft Centre.

❺ Municipal Curio and Handicraft Centre

In yet another bit of cultural diversity, you can haggle over the price of handcrafts at stalls run by Indians. (Don't try to haggle at those operated by Fijians.) It's best to wait until you have visited the Government Handicraft Centre, however, before making a purchase (see "Shopping in Suva," below).

Continue on Stinson Parade past Central Street. The gray concrete building on the corner is the YWCA. When you get there, cut diagonally under the palms and flame trees across Sukuna Park.

⑥ Sukuna Park

This park is named for Ratu Sir Lala Sukuna, founding father of independent Fiji. This shady waterfront park is a favorite brown-bag lunch spot for Suva's office workers. On the west side is the harbor and on the east, Victoria Parade. For many years only a row of flame trees separated this broad avenue from the harbor, but the shallows have been filled and the land has been extended into the harbor by the width of a city block. The large, nondescript auditorium that stands south of the park is the Suva Civic Centre.

Head south on the seaward side of Victoria Parade, and pass the cream-colored colonial-style headquarters of FINTEL, the country's electronic link to the world. You'll come to the old Town Hall.

⑦ Old Town Hall

This is a picturesque Victorian-era building with an intricate, ornamental wrought-iron portico and a sign proclaiming it now to be the Ming Palace Restaurant. Built as an auditorium in the early 1900s and named Queen Victoria Memorial Hall, this lovely structure was later used as the Suva Town Hall (city offices are now in the modern Suva City Hall adjacent to the Civic Centre on the waterfront). The stage still stands at the rear of the restaurant.

Continue south on Victoria Parade until you come to the Suva City Library.

⑧ Suva City Library

The U.S. industrialist and philanthropist Andrew Carnegie gave Fiji £1,500 sterling to build this structure. The central portion of the colonnaded building opened in 1909, with an initial collection of 4,200 books. The wings were added in 1929. Books on Fiji and the South Pacific are shelved to the left of the main entrance. (See "Fast Facts: Suva," above, for the library's hours.)

Keep going along Victoria Parade, past Loftus Street, to the corner of Gladstone Road, where sits the Native Land Trust Board Building.

⑨ Native Land Trust Board Building

This site is known locally as Naiqaqi (The Crusher) because a sugar-crushing mill sat here during Suva's brief and unsuccessful career as a cane-growing area in the 1870s. Ratu Sir Lala Sukuna, who prepared his people for independence (see "History 101," in chapter 9), served as chairman of the Native Land Trust Board, whose main job is to collect and distribute rents on the 80% of the country that is owned by the Fijians.

Across Gladstone Road you can't miss the imposing gray edifice and clock tower of the Government Buildings.

⑩ Government Buildings

Erected between 1937 and 1939 (although they look much older), these British-style gray stone buildings house the High Court, the prime minister's office, and several government ministries. Parliament met here until 1987, when Colonel Rabuka and gang marched in and arrested its leaders; Parliament now meets in a new complex on Ratu Sukuna Road in the Muanikau suburb. The clock tower is known as "Fiji's Big Ben." When it works, it chimes every 15 minutes from 6am to midnight.

Walk past the large open field on the south side of the building; this is Albert Park.

⑪ Albert Park

This park is named for Queen Victoria's consort, Prince Albert. The pavilion opposite the Government Buildings, however, is named for Charles Kingsford Smith, the Australian aviator and first person to fly across the Pacific. Smith was unaware that a row of palm trees stretched across the middle of Albert Park, his intended landing place. A local radio operator figured out Smith's predicament, and the colonial governor ordered the trees cut down immediately. The resulting "runway" across Albert Park was barely

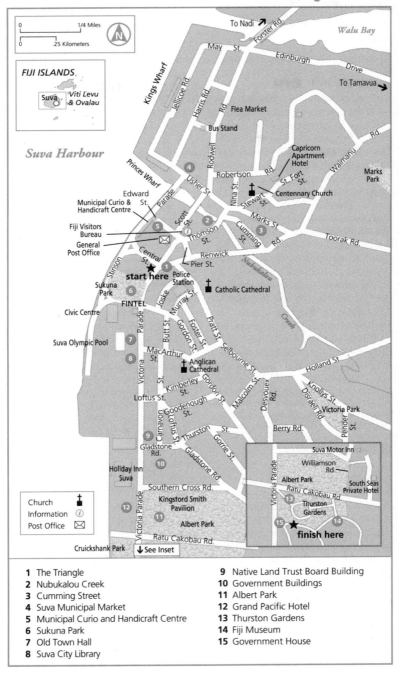

1 The Triangle
2 Nubukalou Creek
3 Cumming Street
4 Suva Municipal Market
5 Municipal Curio and Handicraft Centre
6 Sukuna Park
7 Old Town Hall
8 Suva City Library

9 Native Land Trust Board Building
10 Government Buildings
11 Albert Park
12 Grand Pacific Hotel
13 Thurston Gardens
14 Fiji Museum
15 Government House

long enough, but Smith managed to stop his plane within a few feet of its end on June 6, 1928.

Opposite the park on Victoria Parade stands the Grand Pacific Hotel.

⑫ Grand Pacific Hotel

This thoroughly dilapidated hotel has been the subject of many a delayed restoration project. The Union Steamship Company built the Grand Pacific in 1914, to house its transpacific passengers during their stopovers in Fiji. The idea was to make them think they had never gone ashore, for rooms in the GPH were designed like first-class staterooms, complete with saltwater bathrooms and plumbing fixtures identical to those on an ocean liner. All rooms were on the second floor, and guests could step outside on a 15-foot-wide veranda overlooking the harbor and walk completely around the building—as if they were walking on the deck. When members of the British royal family visited Fiji, they stood atop the wrought-iron portico, the "bow" of the Grand Pacific, and addressed their subjects massed across Victoria Parade in Albert Park.

Continue south on Victoria Parade to the corner of Ratu Cakobau Road, and enter Thurston Gardens.

⑬ Thurston Gardens

Originally known as the Botanical Gardens, this cool, English-like park is named for its founder, the amateur botanist Sir John Bates Thurston, who started the gardens in 1881. Henry Marks, scion of a family who owned a local trading company, presented the drinking fountain in 1914. After G. J. Marks, a relative and lord mayor of Suva, was drowned that same year in the sinking of the SS *Empress* in the St. Lawrence River in Canada, the Marks family erected the bandstand in his memory. Children can climb aboard

the stationary *Thurston Express,* a narrow-gauge locomotive once used to pull harvested cane to the crushing mill.

Walk to the southeast corner of the gardens, where you will find the Fiji Museum.

⑭ Fiji Museum

At this fascinating museum, you can see relics and artifacts of Fiji's history (see "The Top Attractions," above). After touring the complex, take a break at the museum's cafe, under a lean-to roof on one side of the main building; it serves soft drinks, snacks, and curries.

Backtrack through the gardens to Victoria Parade and head south again until, just past the manicured greens of the Suva Bowling Club on the harbor, you arrive at the big iron gates of Government House.

⑮ Government House

This is the home of Fiji's president, which is guarded like Buckingham Palace by spit-and-polish, *sulu*-clad Fijian soldiers. The original house, built in 1882 as the residence of the colonial governor, was struck by lightning and burned to the ground in 1921. The present rambling mansion was completed in 1928 and opened with great fanfare. It is closed to the public, but a colorful military ceremony marks the changing of the guard during the first week of each month. Ask the Fiji Visitors Bureau whether a ceremony will take place while you're there.

From this point, Victoria Parade becomes Queen Elizabeth Drive, which skirts the peninsula to Laucala Bay. With homes and gardens on one side and the lagoon on the other, it's a lovely walk or drive. The manicured residential area in the rolling hills behind Government House is known as The Domain; an enclave of British civil servants in colonial times, it is now home to the Fiji parliament, government officials, diplomats, and affluent private citizens.

SHOPPING IN SUVA

If you took the walking tour of Suva, you already have a good idea of where to shop for handcrafts and duty-free merchandise. Most of the city's best shops are

---

Fun Fact **My Word!**

Before the Government Buildings on Victoria Parade were erected between 1937 and 1939, the land under them was a swampy area called Naiqaqi, or Crusher, for the sugar mill that operated from 1873 to 1875 where the Native Lands Trust Board Building now stands. Naiqaqi was populated by shacks, some of them houses of ill-repute.

Local residents tell of a sailor who often visited the shacks while his ship was in port. He left Suva in 1931 for a long voyage, carrying with him fond memories of Naiqaqi—and, in particular, of one of its residents, a beautiful young woman named Annie.

The sailor's next visit to Suva happened in 1940. Instead of a swamp, he found an imposing gray stone building standing where the old, familiar shacks had been.

"My word!" he exclaimed upon seeing the great new structures, "Annie has done well!"

---

along **Victoria Parade** and on **Cumming Street.** The largest and most reliable merchants are **Jack's Handicrafts,** at Thomson and Pier streets, opposite the Fiji Visitors Bureau; **Prouds,** at the Triangle near the Fiji Visitors Bureau and at the corner of Thomson and Cumming Streets; and **Tappoo,** which has a large store at the corner of Thomson and Usher streets. But note that Jack's has a very small handcraft section here; it's mostly a clothing and accessories outlet. The prices are fixed in these stores, but bargaining is the order of the day in Suva's so-called duty-free shops. Before you buy at the small stores, read the discussion of duty-free shopping in "Shopping in Nadi," above.

Suva has some fine tropical clothing outlets, several of them on Victoria Parade near the Regal Theatre. The upmarket resort- and beachwear specialist **Sogo Fiji** is on Victoria Parade, opposite the theater.

Stamp collectors will find colorful first-day covers from Fiji and other South Pacific island countries at the **Philatelic Bureau,** on the first floor of the General Post Office. It's open Monday to Thursday from 8am to 1pm and 2 to 4pm, Friday to 3:30pm. American Express, Diner's Club, MasterCard, and Visa cards are accepted.

HANDCRAFTS

Government Handicraft Centre *Value*   Before buying Fijian handcrafts elsewhere, you should browse through the authentic merchandise here (no war clubs carved in Asia are sold in this shop). The center was founded in 1974 to continue and promote Fiji's handcrafts. Special attention is given to rural artisans who cannot easily market their works. You will see fine woodcarvings, woven goods, pottery, and *masi* cloth, and you will learn from the fixed prices just how much the really good items are worth. The Fijian staff is friendly and helpful.

Corner of Victoria Parade and MacArthur St., in rear of Ratu Sukuna House. © 321 1306. Mon–Thurs 8am–4:30pm, Fri 8am–4pm, Sat 8am–12:30pm.

Municipal Curio and Handicraft Centre   Having checked out the government center, you can visit these stalls and bargain with the Indian merchants (but not with the Fijians) from a position of knowledge, if not strength. Be careful, however, for some of the work here is mass produced and aimed at cruise-ship passengers who have only a few hours to do their shopping in Fiji.

Tips Sword Sellers Are in Suva, Too

Suva is crawling with the **sword sellers** I warned you about under "Shopping in Nadi," above. The government requires these scam artists to stay in Thurston Park near the Fiji Museum, but you could be approached anywhere. Avoid them!

Municipal Car Park, Stinson Parade, on the waterfront. © **331 3433.** Mon–Thurs 8am–4:30pm, Fri 8am–4pm, Sat 8am–noon.

WHERE TO STAY IN SUVA
MODERATE

Holiday Inn Suva   Formerly the Centra Suva and before that the Suva Travelodge, this is the unofficial gathering place for the city's movers and shakers. It's also the top hotel in town, although it leaves a bit to be desired. The waterfront location couldn't be better, however, for Suva Harbour laps one side, the stately Government Buildings sit across Victoria Parade on the other, and the business district is a 3-block walk away. The best units are the 55 "superior" rooms in the north wing. These were upgraded a few years ago and now have tile floors instead of carpeting, which helps reduce but not entirely eliminate the heavy-duty mustiness you'll find in the other 75 rooms, which have carpets and other original late-1960s equipment. The Holiday Inn has nonsmoking rooms, and one room is equipped for guests with disabilities.

P.O. Box 1357, Suva (Victoria Parade, opposite Government Buildings). © **800/835-7742** or 330 1600. Fax 330 0251. www.holiday-inn.com. 130 units. F$240 ($108) double. AE, DC, MC, V. **Amenities:** 1 restaurant (regional), 1 bar; outdoor pool; access to nearby health club; activities desk; business center; 24-hr. room service; babysitting; laundry service; coin-op washers and dryers. *In room:* A/C, TV, dataport, minibar, coffeemaker, hair dryer, iron.

INEXPENSIVE

Capricorn Apartment Hotel *Value*   Although it's a steep, 2-block walk uphill from Cumming Street, Mulchand Patel's establishment is popular with Australians and New Zealanders who like to do their own cooking. The three-story, L-shaped building looks out on Suva Harbour and down the mountainous coast. Private balconies off each apartment share the view, as does a pear-shaped swimming pool on the Capricorn's grounds. Except for cane and wicker chairs and coffee tables, furniture in the older, inexpensive units is on the plain side, but the mattresses here are new and among the firmest in Fiji. Mulchand and his friendly staff make sure these roomy efficiencies are kept spotless. A dozen modern, condolike units are luxuriously furnished and much better outfitted than the older apartments. Each unit has an air conditioner, although windows on both sides of the building let the cooling trade winds blow through. Continental breakfasts are available on premises, and the reception staff will sell you canned goods from its small on-premises store or have "Dial-A-Meal" deliver to your room.

P.O. Box 1261, Suva (top end of St. Fort St.). © **330 3732.** Fax 330 3069. capricornsuva@is.com.fj. 34 units. F$85–F$115 ($38–$52) double. AE, DC, MC, V. **Amenities:** 1 bar (evenings only); outdoor pool; babysitting; laundry service. *In room:* A/C, TV, kitchen, coffeemaker.

Homestay Suva ★★★ *Value*   One of the few genuine bed-and-breakfasts in the South Pacific islands, Bruce and Lesley Phillip's gorgeous 1920s-vintage colonial home sits atop a ridge in the expensive Tamavua suburb. The view from up here is stunning, for their expansive covered veranda looks out over a ridge-top swimming pool, across a steep valley, down to Walu Bay, and along the south coast of Viti Levu. The choice room (it's their most expensive, too) is appropriately named Harbor View, for it also looks out over this vista. Another upstairs room, the Nukulau, looks eastward across Laucala Bay and out to little Nukulau Island on the far-off reef, where coup-maker George Spaight was being held prisoner at press time. Three more rooms in the main house lack a view. Bruce and Lesley recently added three "lodge" units in another building a few steps from the main house. In addition to their own private entries, these more private and spacious rooms have kitchens and balconies overlooking Walu Bay. Every room here is quite comfortably furnished with a mix of tropical and traditional pieces, and you get thick, fluffy towels and other luxurious amenities, too.

Lesley serves extensive breakfasts on the veranda, and she will prepare moderately priced gourmet dinners on request. Many guests here are business types, including women traveling alone, and Lesley's dinners often turn into full-fledged parties. New Zealanders by birth, Bruce and Lesley settled here in the mid-1970s after wandering the world and chartering a sailboat in the Caribbean. Call them for directions if you're driving, or take a taxi from downtown for F$3.50 ($1.50). They charge small fees to take you on Friday evening or Sunday harbor cruises.

265 Prince's Rd. (P.O. Box 16172, Suva). ⓒ **337 0395.** Fax 337 0947. bulafiji.com/web/homestay. 8 units. F$135–F$165 ($61–$52) double. Rates include full breakfast. AE, MC, V. **Amenities:** Outdoor pool; laundry service. *In room:* A/C, TV, kitchen (in lodge units), no phone.

Raintree Lodge   Not for everyone, this rustic lodge sits beside a nearly round, quarry-turned-lake high in the hills above Suva. The climes are cool up here, and as the name indicates, it rains a lot in this forest. It's also very quiet up here, and except for the vehicles passing on Prince's Road, you'll hear very little except the songs of tropical birds. Built of pine and overlooking the lake, the five bungalows are spacious, and their beds have mosquito nets, which are much needed because the windows are not screened. All have ceiling fans and bathrooms with hot-water showers, and one large family size unit has a kitchen. Dormitories range in size from four private rooms with double beds to a hall with 20 bunk beds. Their occupants and those camping out on the lawn share toilets, showers, and a kitchen.

Although it's open all day, locals love to drive up here for lunch, especially the island-style Sunday buffet, at the rustic and inexpensive **Raintree Restaurant,** where they vie for tables on the lakeside veranda. The regular menu emphasizes both local cooking and more sophisticated treatments of fresh fish, vegetables, and fruits. The lodge is F$7 ($3) by taxi or F90¢ (40¢) by public bus from downtown Suva.

P.O. Box 16655, Suva (Prince's Rd., Colo-i-Suva, opposite post office). ⓒ **332 0562.** Fax 332 0113. www. raintreelodge.com. 5 units, 32 dorm beds. F$110–F$165 ($49.50–$74) bungalow; F$55 ($25) double dorm room; F$16.50–F$20 ($7.50–$9) dorm bed; F$5 ($2.50) per person camping. AE, MC, V. **Amenities:** 1 restaurant (regional), 1 bar; laundry service. *In room:* Kitchen (1 unit only), fridge, coffeemaker, no phone.

Suva Motor Inn ⓚ *Value*   This three-story hotel is popular with business travelers who can't afford the rates—or stand the mustiness—at the Holiday Inn Suva. It's a good bet for budget-minded couples and families, too. Just uphill from Albert Park near the Government Buildings, the L-shaped structure bends around a lush tropical courtyard with a two-level swimming pool with a Jacuzzi and a water slide. Opening to this vista is a small restaurant and a bar, which attracts business types after work. Accommodation is in spacious studios and two-bedroom apartments. The studios are fully air-conditioned, but only the master bedrooms of the apartments are cooled. All units are equipped with tropical cane-and-wicker furniture. Apartments have full kitchens; studios have refrigerators, toasters, coffeemakers, and microwave ovens. The staff will assist in arranging activities and excursions.

P.O. Box 2500, Government Bldgs., Suva (corner of Mitchell and Gorrie sts.). ℂ **331 3973**. Fax 330 0381. suvamotorinn@is.com.fj. 45 units. F$100 ($45) double; F$170 ($76.50) apt. AE, DC, MC, V. **Amenities:** 1 restaurant (international/Japanese), 1 bar; outdoor pool; laundry service; coin-op washers and dryers. *In room:* A/C, TV, kitchen, coffeemaker, no phone.

HOSTELS

Many backpackers like to spend a night or two up at the Raintree Lodge (see above).

South Seas Private Hotel   This large barrackslike wooden structure with a long sunroom across the front (it can get hot in the afternoons) could be cleaner, but it's a friendly establishment and is usually is packed with young people on the go. It has dormitories, basic rooms, a rudimentary communal kitchen, a TV lounge, and hand-wash laundry facilities. Bed linen is provided, but bring your own towel or pay a F$3 ($1.35) deposit to use one of theirs. There's a F$5 ($2.25) refundable key deposit, too. Showers have both hot and cold water. The rooms have fans, but they operate only from 4pm to 7am.

P.O. Box 2086, Government Bldgs., Suva (Williamson Rd. off Ratu Cakobau Rd., behind Albert Park). ℂ **331 2296**. Fax 330 8646. 34 units (one with bathroom), 42 dorm beds. F$24 ($11) double room without bathroom; F$36 ($16) double room with bathroom; F$9.90 ($4.50) dorm bed. No credit cards. *In room:* No phone.

A LUXURY RESORT OFF SUVA

The Wakaya Club, Fiji's most luxurious and exclusive resort, is on Wakaya Island, an uplifted, tilted coral atoll out in the Koro Sea. Beaches fringe Wakaya's north and east coasts, and tall cliffs fall into the sea on its western side. There are still relics of a Fijian fort on the cliffs. Legend says a chief and all his men leaped off the cliff to their deaths from there rather than be roasted by a rival tribe. The spot is known as Chieftain's Leap.

The Wakaya Club 🏵🏵🏵   A 20-minute flight by private plane from Nausori Airport, 50 minutes from Nadi, this superdeluxe beachside facility belongs to Canadian entrepreneur David Gilmour, who acquired the island in the 1970s. He had an interest in the Pacific Harbour development back then (see "Pacific Harbour," above). As he did there, Gilmour has sold off pieces of Wakaya for deluxe getaway homes. For a small fortune you can rent one of these villas, including Gilmore's own Japanese-influenced mansion high on a ridge overlooking the resort (it's the largest private residence in Fiji). Hollywood and Beverly Hills types who don't own—or can't borrow a friend's—private villa on the island feel right at home in the club's 457-square-km (1,500-sq.-ft.), deluxe rectangular bungalows. One end of each of these houses is a large living room with a wet bar. On the other end is a bathroom with an oversized tub, a separate shower stall, three sinks, a toilets, a bidet, and Crabtree & Evelyn toiletries imported from England. The large bedrooms with canopied king-size beds are in between.

The food here is of gourmet quality and outstandingly presented. Guests dine in a huge thatch-roofed beachside building or outside, either on a patio or under two gazebo-like shelters on a deck surrounding a pool with its own waterfall. Compared to Turtle and Vatulele, where a party atmosphere often prevails, here the management and excellent and unobtrusive Fijian staff leave the guests alone here. They will also perform just about any service that you can imagine.

P.O. Box 15424, Suva (Wakaya Island, Lomaviti Group). © **970/920-1244** or 344 0128. Fax 970/920-1225 or 344 0406. www.wakaya.com. 9 units. US$1,445–US$1,875 double. Rates include meals, bar, all activities except deep-sea fishing and scuba diving courses. Round-trip transfers U.S. $830 per couple from Nadi, U.S. $450 from Suva. AE, DC, MC, V. **Amenities:** 1 restaurant (regional), 1 bar; outdoor pool; 9-hole golf course; tennis courts; 24-hr. room service; massage; babysitting; laundry service. *In room:* Minibar, coffeemaker, hair dryer.

WHERE TO DINE IN SUVA

For the city's finest dining, head for the Suva edition of **Chefs The Restaurant** ★★★ (© **330 8556**), upstairs in the Jack's Handicrafts building at the corner of Thomson and Pier streets, opposite the Fiji Visitors Bureau. The menu here is geared slightly toward local tastes, with more Asian and less European influences. It's also a tad less expensive than the Nadi version. It's open Monday to Saturday 11am to 2pm and 6 to 10pm. Reservations are recommended for dinner.

Chef Eugene Gomes also has local versions of the less expensive **The Edge** (© **330 8566**) and the inexpensive **The Corner** (© **330 8566**) in the Jack's complex here, too.

There's also a branch of Nadi's **Daikoku** Japanese restaurant, in the FNPF Plaza building on Victoria Parade at Loftus Street (© **330 8968**). It has the same menu as the original, but the prices are lower. It's open Monday to Saturday noon to 2:30pm and 6 to 10pm, and reservations are recommended.

See "Where to Dine in Nadi," above, for more information about these restaurants.

Ashiyana ★★ INDIAN   The best Indian restaurant in Fiji, this cramped little place specializes in authentic dishes from all over the subcontinent. You can choose fiery vegetable curries from Madras, tasty tandoori lamb from the Punjab, filling basmati rice dishes from the Himalayas, or that old British Raj standby, roghan josh (lamb simmered in yogurt and tomato). They're not so spicy as to turn away the expatriates who love this place, but they will let you know this is real Indian food. Feel free to dispense with forks and pick up your food with pieces of delightful naan or roti bread (use you right hand only, as is the custom in India and Pakistan).

Victoria Parade, in Old Town Hall. © **331 3000.** Reservations recommended on weekends. Main courses F$4.50–F$13.50 ($2–$6). AE, MC, V. Mon–Fri 11:30am–2:30pm and 6–10pm, Sat–Sun 6–9:30pm.

Cardo's ★ STEAKS/SEAFOOD   You can clog your arteries on the best steaks in town at this hip upstairs restaurant, or you can opt for chicken or fresh fish singed over the charcoal grill. Among it's nongrilled items, the menu offers prawns served with broth in a cast-iron pot, Cajun-style chicken, spaghetti with eggplant, and a tasty veal parmigiana. Many of the town's young professionals will be here, enjoying both the food and a relaxed, sophisticated atmosphere enhanced by progressive jazz from the sound system. The decor is a modern version of Art Deco, with forest green walls and curving dividers separating knotty pine, picnic-style tables along big window walls looking over a parking lot to the harbor.

Regal Lane, off Victoria Parade behind McDonald's. © **331 4330.** Reservations recommended. Main courses F$13–F$33 ($6–$15). AE, MC, V. Mon–Fri noon–2:30pm; daily 5–10pm.

Hare Krishna Restaurant ★ *Value* VEGETARIAN INDIAN   This very popular casual restaurant specializes in a wide range of very good vegetarian curries—eggplant, cabbage, potatoes and peas, okra, and papaya to name a few—each seasoned delicately and differently from the others. Interesting pastries, breads, side dishes, and salads (such as cucumbers and carrots in yogurt) cool off the fire set by some of the curries. If you can't decide what to order, check the items on display in a cafeteria-like steam table near the entrance to the second-floor dining room, or get the all-you-can-eat *thali* sampler and try a little of everything—it's the most expensive item on the menu and will tingle your taste buds. Downstairs has an excellent yogurt and ice cream bar; climb the spiral stairs to reach the dining rooms. The Hare Krishnas allow no alcoholic beverages or smoking.

16 Pratt St. ⓒ 331 4154. Reservations not accepted. Curries F$2–F$7.50 (90¢–$3.50). No credit cards. Dining room Mon–Sat 11am–2:30pm; downstairs snack bar Mon–Thurs 9am–8pm, Fri 9am–9pm, Sat 9am–3:30pm.

Old Mill Cottage ★★★ *Value* FIJIAN/INDIAN/EUROPEAN   One of the few remaining late-19th-century homes left in Suva's diplomatic-government section, these adjoining two-room clapboard cottages are one of the best places in the South Pacific to get consistently good home cooking. You'll order at the cafeteria-like counters, one for breakfast, one for lunch. You'll have a choice of daily specials such as Fijian palusami, mild Indian curries, or European-style mustard-baked chicken with real mashed potatoes and peas. Diplomats (the U.S. Embassy is out the back door) and government executives pack the place at midday. Saturday's menu is geared toward Fijian seafood dishes.

47–49 Carnavon St., near corner of Loftus St. ⓒ 331 2134. Reservations not accepted. Breakfasts F$3–F$5 ($1.35–$2.25); meals F$4.50–F$8 ($2–$3.50). No credit cards. Mon–Fri 7am–6pm, Sat 7am–5pm.

Pizza Hut PIZZA/PASTA   This is not related to the U.S. chain by either quality or ownership (the proprietor of the Pizza Hut, the Bad Dog Cafe, O'Reilly's, and a nightclub on this corner building is Irishman Liam Hindle). Nevertheless, it still has reasonably good pizza and pasta. Pies range from small and plain ones to large ones with prawns. Also on the menu: salads, spaghetti, and lasagna. You can dine in a cozy, brick-accented dining room or eat and drink in a comfy bar while listening to the music of blues stars whose photos hang on the walls.

207 Victoria Parade, at MacArthur St. ⓒ 331 1825. Reservations recommended on weekends. Pizzas F$6–F$22 ($2.50–$5); pastas F$6–F$7 ($2.50–$3). AE, DC, MC, V. Mon–Thurs 10am–9:30pm, Fri–Sat 10am–10pm, Sun 4–10pm.

Tiko's Floating Restaurant SEAFOOD/STEAKS   Locals like to take out-of-town guests to dinner at this floating restaurant, which served time years ago with Blue Lagoon Cruises. One hopes they don't lean to seasickness, for the old craft does tend to roll a bit when freighters kick up a wake going in and out of the harbor. Your best bets here are the nightly seafood specials, such as *walu* (Spanish mackerel) and *pakapaka* (snapper). It's not the best in town, but the fish is fresh, the service is attentive, and a terrific jazz musician-singer usually provides dinner music—all of which makes for a pleasant night out.

Stinson Parade at Sukuna Park. ⓒ 331 3626. Reservations recommended. Main courses F$9.50–F$35 ($4.50–$16). AE, DC, MC, V. Mon–Fri noon–2pm; Mon–Sat 6–10pm.

FOOD COURTS & COFFEE SHOPS

The modern and clean **Dolphins Food Court,** in the high-rise FNPC Place building on Victoria Parade at Loftus St. (ⓒ 330 7811), has stalls that offer good European, Chinese, and Indian fare at prices ranging from F$3 to F$6 ($1.35–$2.50), plus ice cream and other goodies. The vegetarian Hare Krishna Restaurant (see above) has an outlet here. Most stalls are open daily from 11am to 10pm, although some take a break from 3 to 5pm. It's the place everyone heads on Sunday, when most other snack bars are closed. It will remind you of the food courts at most shopping malls back home.

If you're hankering for a Big Mac, head for the **McDonald's** on Victoria Parade at the northern edge of Sukuna Park.

Republic of Cappuccino ✿ COFFEE BAR "The Rock" to trendy locals, this Starbucks-style coffee shop (the U.S. chain hasn't arrived yet) occupies the triangular corner of FNPF Place, on the Victoria Parade side of Dolphins Food Court. You can listen to recorded jazz while drinking your latte or cappuccino and eating your brownie, cake, or quiche at the tall tables by the big storefront windows. You can get your e-mail here, too (see "Fast Facts: Suva," above).

Victoria Parade at Loftus St., in FNPF Place bldg. ✆ 330 0333. Reservations not accepted. Coffee F$2.50–F$3.50 ($1–$1.50); pastries and sandwiches F$1–F$5 (45¢–$2.25). No credit cards. Mon–Fri 7am–11pm, Sat 8am–11pm, Sun 10am–7pm.

ISLAND NIGHTS IN SUVA

Fijian-style *meke* feast-and-dance nights are scarce in Suva. The Centra Suva, Victoria Parade (✆ **330 1600**), usually has one a week. Otherwise, nocturnal activities in Suva revolve around going to the movies and then hitting the bars—until the wee hours on Friday, the biggest night out.

Movies are a big deal here, especially the first-run flicks playing at **Village 6 Cinemas,** on Scott Street at Nubukalou Creek, a modern, American-style emporium with six screens and a large games arcade upstairs. Check the daily newspapers for what's playing and show times. You can pig out on popcorn, candy, and soft drinks. Locals flock here on Sunday afternoon, when these plush, air-conditioned theaters offer a comfortable escape from Suva's daytime heat and humidity.

After a nighttime movie, locals head for their favorite bars. Blues and jazz fans gravitate to **Birdland,** a basement pub at 6 Carnavon St., east of Loftus Street (✆ **330 3833**), which has live music Thursday to Saturday nights. A few doors down Carnavon Street, the waiters and bouncers wear cowboy hats and other Western garb at **The Barn,** where you can line dance to tunes by country-and-western bands (✆ **330 7845**). **Trap's Bar,** 305 Victoria Parade, 2 blocks south of the Pizza Hut (✆ **331 2922**), is the most popular watering hole where you're not likely to witness a fight. A band usually plays in the back room on weekends.

O'Reilly's, on MacArthur Street just off Victoria Parade (✆ **331 2968**), is an Irish-style pub that serves Guinness stout and sports on TVs (as the bouncers on MacArthur Street will attest, it can get a bit rough, depending on who's winning the rugby matches).

Victoria Parade has a number of loud discotheques frequented by the young, noisy crowd. Just walk along; you'll hear them.

6 A Side Trip to Levuka ✦✦

You might think you've slipped into *The Twilight Zone* as you stroll down historic Beach Street in Levuka, Fiji's first capital on the ruggedly beautiful island of Ovalau. Everything here seems to be from a century earlier: ramshackle dry-goods stores with false fronts, clapboard houses with tin roofs to keep them dry and shaded verandas to keep them cool, and round clocks in the baroque tower of Sacred Heart Catholic Church. Where the regular streets end, "step streets" climb to more houses up near the base of the jagged cliffs towering over the town.

Not that Levuka hasn't changed at all since its 19th-century days as one of the South Pacific's most notorious seaports. All but one of the 50 or more hotels and saloons that dispensed rum and other pleasures disappeared long ago. The sole survivor—the Royal Hotel—is now a quiet, family run establishment. The fist-fighting whalers and drifting beach bums went the way of the square-rigged ships that once crowded the blue-green harbor beyond the row of glistening ficus trees and park benches along Beach Street. Gone, too, are the pioneering merchants and copra (dried coconut meat) planters who established Levuka as Fiji's first European-style town in the 1830s and who for years carried guns to protect themselves from its ruffians.

But Levuka still looks about the same as it did in 1882, when the colonial administration moved to Suva. The 360m (1,200-ft.) walls of basalt, which caused the demise of Levuka by preventing expansion, create a soaring backdrop that puts Ovalau in the big leagues of dramatic tropical beauty.

Despite its history, beauty, and extremely hospitable residents, Levuka is relatively off the beaten tourist track. The volcano that created Ovalau has eroded into such rugged formations that it has very little flat land and no decent beach; therefore, the island has not attracted resort or hotel development. All of Levuka's accommodations are basic and fall in the low-budget, basic category. But this is a great place to meet people and learn about Fiji's history and culture.

GETTING TO LEVUKA & GETTING AROUND

GETTING THERE **Air Fiji** (© 888/354-3454 in the U.S., 331 3666 in Suva, or 672 2251 in Nadi; www.airfiji.net) has early morning and late-afternoon flights to Ovalau's unpaved airstrip at Bureta, on the island's west coast. The excursion fare from Suva is about F$65 ($29) round-trip. Levuka is halfway around Ovalau on the east coast. An unpaved road circles the island along its shoreline and makes the bus ride from airport to town a sightseeing excursion in its own right. Airport bus transfers cost F$3.60 ($1.60) each way.

More adventurous souls can watch Ovalau's jagged green peaks go by from one of the **ferries** that run between Viti Levu and Levuka. Most boats land on the northwest coast, a 30-minute bus or taxi ride from Levuka. For more information, see "Getting There & Getting Around" in chapter 9.

GETTING AROUND Levuka is a small town, and your feet can get you to most places in 25 minutes.

For **taxis,** call **Vuniba Taxis** (© 344 0322), **Levuka Taxis** (© 344 0147), or **B. Murgan Transport Co.** (© 344 0180). Be sure you and the driver agree on a fare before departing. Local **buses** depart for the outlying villages from Beach Street about four times a day. They don't run after dark, so make sure you find out from the driver when—and whether—he returns to Levuka at the end of the day.

Tips **Bring Your Toothbrush**

You can see the prime sites in old Levuka in a day. The airstrip on Ovalau is not lighted, however, and rainy weather or delays can cause the one late afternoon flight to be canceled. If you do come over here on a day trip, bring your toothbrush and a change of clothes. If the flight doesn't happen, Air Fiji will put you up at the Royal Hotel.

Impressions

There appeared to be a rowdy devil-may-care sort of look about the whole of them; and the great part of the day, and the night too, seemed to be spent in tippling in public house bars. I dare say that of the row of houses that make Levuka, fully half are hotels or public houses. The amount of gin and water which is consumed must be amazing, for the bars are always crowded, and the representatives of white civilization always at it.

—Robert Philp, 1872

EXPLORING LEVUKA
A WALKING TOUR OF TOWN

LEVUKA COMMUNITY CENTRE   A walking tour of Levuka should take about 2 hours. Begin at the **Levuka Community Centre,** across the street from the Air Fiji office, which occupies the quaint old **Morris Hedstrom** store built by Levukans Percy Morris and Maynard Hedstrom in 1878. The trading company they founded, now one of the South Pacific's largest department store chains, pulled out of Levuka entirely a century later. The company donated the dilapidated structure to the National Trust of Fiji. The Levuka Historical and Cultural Society raised money throughout the country to restore it and install a small branch of the Fiji Museum, a public library, a meeting hall, a crafts and recreational center, and a small garden. The furniture is made of timbers salvaged from the rotting floor. Mrs. Dora Patterson, matriarch of the Patterson Brothers Shipping Company family, donated the museum's waterside garden; she could oversee the project from her colonial-style mansion on the hill above Levuka. From the Community Centre head south.

NASOVA & THE DEED OF CESSION   South of the Levuka Community Centre, the post office stands at the entrance to the **Queens Wharf.** The drinking fountain in front marks the site of a carrier-pigeon service that linked Suva and Levuka in the late 1800s. The Queens Wharf is one of Fiji's four ports of entry (Suva, Lautoka, and Savusavu are the others), but along with domestic cargo, it now primarily handles exports from the Pacific Fishing Company's **tuna cannery,** established by a Japanese firm in 1964. You can follow your nose to the cannery in the industrial buildings south of the pier.

Keep going to **Nasova,** a village on the shore of the little bay about 1km (½ mile) south of the cannery. Chief Cakobau signed the deed that ceded Fiji to Great Britain here. The site is now marked by 3 stones in the center of a grassy park at the water's edge. Plaques commemorate the signing ceremony on October 10, 1874, Fiji's independence exactly 96 years later, and the 1974 centennial celebration of the Deed of Cession. A Fijian-style thatch meeting house stands across the road.

South of Nasova, the **Old Levuka Cemetery** is tended to perfection by prison inmates. Tombstones bear the names of many Europeans who settled here in the 19th century—and some who met their demise without settling down first.

BEACH STREET   Backtrack to the weathered storefronts of Levuka's 3-block-long business district along **Beach Street.** Saloons no longer line Beach Street; instead, the Indian- and Chinese-owned stores now dispense a variety of dry goods and groceries. On the horizon beyond the ficus trees and park benches

---

Moments Traveling Back in Time

Having grown up in Edenton, which still looks very much like it did as North Carolina's colonial capital in the 1700s, I feel almost nostalgic in Levuka, which hasn't changed much since it played the same role in Fiji.

---

lie the smoky-blue outlines of Wakaya, Makogai, and other members of the Lomaiviti ("Central Fiji") group of islands. The green cliffs still reach skyward behind the stores, hemming in Levuka and its narrow valley. Walk along the waterfront, and don't hesitate to stick your head into the dry-goods stores.

After the last store stands the **Church of the Sacred Heart,** a wooden building fronted by a baroque stone tower. It was built by the Marist Brothers who came to Levuka in 1858. In case you missed the number of chimes marking the time, the clock in the tower strikes once on the hour and again, for good measure, one minute later. Across Beach Street stands a **World War I monument** to the Fijian members of the Fiji Labour Corps who were killed assisting the British in Europe.

Walk on across Totoga Creek to low **Niukaubi Hill,** on top of which is another World War I monument, this one to Levukans of English ancestry who died fighting as British soldiers in that conflict. Parliament House and the Supreme Court building sat on this little knoll before the capital was moved to Suva. They had a nice view across the town, the waterfront, and the reef and islands offshore. At the bottom of the hill is the **Levuka Club,** a colonial-era drinking establishment.

Keep going north on Beach Street, which soon passes the 1904-vintage Anglican church before arriving in the original Fijian village known as **Levuka.** The Tui Levuka who lived here befriended the early European settlers. Later, Chief Cakobau worshipped in the Methodist church built on the south side of the creek in 1869. John Brown Williams, the American consul, is buried in the village's Old Cemetery near the church. (Remember, good manners dictate that you have permission before entering a Fijian village.)

To the north, **Gun Rock** towers over Levuka village. In order to show the chiefs just how much firepower it packed, a British warship in 1849 used this steep headland for target practice. Beach Street now runs under the overhang of Gun Rock, where the Marist Brothers said their first mass. There was no road then, only a shingly beach where the sea had worn away the base of the cliff.

INLAND Beyond Gun Rock lies the village of **Vagadaci,** where the duke of York—later King George V—and his brother, the duke of Clarence, once played cricket (the field is now covered by a housing project), but I usually turn around at Gun Rock and return to the first street inland south of the hospital. It leads to the **199 steps** that climb Mission Hill from the Methodist church to the collection of buildings that comprise **Delana Methodist School.** For the energetic, the view from the 199th step is worth the climb.

From the church, cut down Chapel Hill Road and Langham Street past the Royal, the South Pacific's oldest operating hotel. Keep going south along the banks of Togoga Creek to the Roman-style **Polynesia Masonic Lodge,** which was founded in 1875. The **Town Hall,** next door, was built in 1898 in honor of Queen Victoria's 50 years on the British throne; it still houses most of Levuka's city offices. The nearby **Ovalau Club** is the oldest drinking club in the South

Pacific, a reminder of the social clubs where the Old Boys of the British Empire gathered to escape the heat, drink gin, and play snooker (billiards). The Ovalau Club today has a racially diverse membership that welcomes clean-cut visitors from overseas. Behind the lodge, club, and Town Hall, **Nasau Park** provides the town's rugby and cricket field, bowling green, and tennis courts.

Now head uphill along the creek until you get to the lovely white Victorian buildings with broad verandas of **Levuka Public School,** Fiji's first educational institution (opened in 1879) and still one of its best. A row of mango and sweet-smelling frangipani trees shade the sidewalk known as Bath Road between the school and the rushing creek. Walk up Bath Road, which soon turns into a "step street" as it climbs to a waterfall and concrete-lined swimming hole known as The Bath. Cool off at this refreshing spot before heading back down the steps to Beach Street.

ATTRACTIONS BEYOND LEVUKA

St. John's College, in the village of Cawaci north of Levuka, was founded by the Marist Brothers in 1884, primarily to educate the sons of ranking Fijian chiefs. The school sits on the grounds of **St. John's Church,** a Gothic Revival building typical of Catholic missions in the South Pacific. On a bluff overlooking the sea, the **Bishop's Tomb** holds the remains of Dr. Julian Vidal, the first Catholic bishop of Fiji.

Yavu, south of Levuka, is a hilltop overlooking the sea where, according to legend, a newly arrived chief lit a fire, which caught the attention of a chief who was already here. The two met at Yavu and agreed that one would be chief of the interior and the other would rule the coastline. They placed two sacred stones at the spot to mark their agreement. The hilltop isn't marked, so go there with a guide.

Lovoni, a picturesque Fijian village in the crater of Ovalau's extinct volcano, was the home of ferocious warriors who stormed down to the coast and attacked Levuka on several occasions. Chief Cakobau settled that problem by luring them into town to talk peace; instead, he captured them all and deported them to other parts of Fiji. Today's Lovonians have seen so many travelers wandering around their village that most are adept at pleasantly smiling while ignoring you. The houses are of wood with corrugated iron roofs.

Waitovu, about a 50-minute walk north of town (look for its mosque), has the nearest waterfall to town. Ask permission, and ask the residents to show the way. You can dive into the top pool from the rocks above.

Rukuruku village on the northwest shore has a waterfall and Ovalau's sole swimming beach.

DIVING, SNORKELING & KAYAKING

Ovalau Watersports, P.O. Box 149, Levuka, Ovalau (© **3440611;** fax 3440405; www.owlfiji.com), on Beach Street next to the Community Centre, offers scuba diving, teaches PADI courses, and has kayak tours. Dive sites include several shipwrecks in and near Levuka, plus soft-coral spots on the Wakaya Reef.

WHERE TO STAY IN LEVUKA

Mavida Guest House   These two late-19th-century clapboard cottages have charming, enclosed-veranda rooms with long rows of double-hung windows facing the lagoon across Beach Street. There's a covered patio between them for lounging. One house has private rooms, some with antique beds whose mosquito nets sweep down from 2m (7-ft.) headboards. The other has 21 beds jammed into every possible position in its rooms, none of them private. All guests share bathrooms and a communal kitchen. Inexpensive dinners are available.

P.O. Box 4, Levuka, Ovalau (Beach St.). © **344 0477.** 5 units (none with bathroom), 21 dorm beds. F$12–F$15 ($5.50–$7) per person in rooms; F$10 ($4.50) dorm bed. Rates include cooked breakfast. No credit cards.

Royal Hotel   This ancient establishment is as much an attraction as it is accommodation. Even if you don't stay at the South Pacific's oldest operating hotel, have a look at its public rooms. It was built about 1852 and "modernized" in the 1890s (except for stringing an electric light to each room and installing toilets and showers, little has been done to it since). Not much imagination is required to picture W. Somerset Maugham or Robert Louis Stevenson relaxing in the comfortable rattan chairs of the Royal's charming lounge, slowly sipping gin-and-tonics at its polished bar, or playing a game of snooker at its antique billiard table. One of Levuka's fine old families, the Ashleys, has run the Royal for more than half a century with such attentive care that it seems more like a pension full of antiques than a hotel. The 14 rooms in the original building are extremely basic, each with two cotlike single beds, a shower stall, and toilet. In contrast, four Western-style cottages between the old structure and Beach Road were built in 1998 and have more modern amenities (they are the pick of Levuka's lodgings). Two of the hotel's three older but still comfortable cottages are the island's only air-conditioned digs. The Ashleys serve three meals per day in the dining room, but book in advance.

P.O Box 47, Levuka, Ovalau (Beach St.). © **344 0024.** Fax 440174. royal@is.com.fj. 21 units. F$33 ($15) double; F$55–F$77 ($25–$34.50) cottage. No credit cards. **Amenities:** 1 restaurant (regional), 1 bar. *In room:* A/C (in 2 units).

WHERE TO DINE IN LEVUKA

Whale's Tale Restaurant REGIONAL   Australian Julia Ditrich, daughter Liza, and their Fijian partner Susana Rakala renovated one of Beach Street's old storefronts and opened this cramped but pleasant eatery. You can get a late breakfast or a lunch from a menu of sandwiches, burgers, omelets, quiches, and daily specials. At night they put cloths on the tables and offer three-course meals from a chalkboard menu, which always includes a vegetarian selection.

Beach St., middle of town. © **344 0235.** Reservations not accepted. Breakfast F$5–F$6.50 ($2.25–$3); sandwiches and snacks F$3.50–F$6.50 ($1.50–$3); dinner F$7–F$13 ($3–$6). No credit cards. Mon–Sat 11am–3pm and 5–8pm.

7 Northern Viti Levu

Few travelers will be disappointed by the scenic wonders on the northern side of Viti Levu. Cane fields climb hilly valleys to towering green mountain ridges. Cowpokes round up cattle on vast ranches. A stunning bay is bounded by dramatic cliffs and spires. A narrow mountain road winds along the rushing Wainibuka River, once called the "Banana Highway" because in preroad days Fijians used it to float their crop downs to Suva on disposable *bilibili* rafts made of bamboo. A relatively dry climate beckons anyone who wants to catch a few rays, and there's great diving on the reefs off Viti Levu's northernmost point.

THE KING'S ROAD IN NORTHERN VITI LEVU

The only way to get to northern Viti Levu is via the **King's Road,** which runs for 290km (180 miles) from Nadi Airport around the island's northern side to Suva—93km (57½ miles) longer than the Queen's Road to the south. All but a short stretch of the King's Road along the Wainibuka River Valley through the central mountains is paved. Because the mountainous portion is slow going, most visitors who drive the King's Road spend at least a night in Rakiraki, about halfway between Nadi and Suva.

Scheduled local and express buses run the entire length of the King's Road, as do unscheduled share taxis (see "Getting There & Getting Around" in chapter 9). From the Nadi side, the buses depart from the Lautoka Market. The hotels and backpackers' resorts provide their guests with transportation from Nadi (see "Where to Stay in Northern Viti Levu," below).

The King's Road officially begins at Lautoka. To reach it by car from Nadi, follow the Queen's Road north and take the second exits off both traffic circles in Lautoka.

The fast catamaran ferry *Lagilagi*, operated by **Beachcomber Cruises** (© **661500**), will drop you at Ellington Wharf on its twice-weekly runs between Nadi and Savusavu. (See "Getting There & Getting Around" in chapter 9.)

BA & TAVUA

From Lautoka, the King's Road first crosses a fertile plain and then ascends into hills dotted with cattle ranches before dropping to the coast and entering the gorgeous **Ba Valley,** Fiji's most productive sugar-growing area. With some 65,000 residents, most of them Indo-Fijians, this valley of steep hills is second only to Suva in both population and economic importance. Many of the country's most successful Indo-Fijian-owned businesses are headquartered in the town of **Ba,** a prosperous farming community on the banks of the muddy Ba River. Indeed, most Fiji towns have the air of the British Raj or Australia, but the commercial center of Ba is a mirror image of many towns in India. Ba has one of Fiji's five sugar mills. Gravel roads twisting off from town into the valley offer some spectacular vistas. One of these roads follows a tributary into the central highlands and then along the Sigatoka River down to the Coral Coast. You can explore the Ba Valley roads in a rental car, but take the cross-island route only if you have a four-wheel-drive vehicle and a good map.

From Ba, the King's Road continues to **Tavua,** another predominately Indo-Fijian sugar town backed by its own much smaller valley that reaches up to the mountains.

RAKIRAKI

The enchanting peaks of the **Nakauvadra Range** keep getting closer to the sea as you proceed eastward toward Rakiraki. Legend says the mountains are home to Degei, the prolific spiritual leader who arrived with the first Fijians and later populated the country. As the flat land is squeezed between foothills and sea, cane fields give way to the grasslands and mesas of the 17,000-acre Yaqara Estate, Fiji's largest cattle ranch. Offshore, conelike islands begin to dot the aquamarine lagoon.

Although everyone calls this area Rakiraki, the chief commercial town is actually **Vaileka,** about 1km (½ mile) off the King's Road.

Vaileka itself is home to the **Penang Mill,** the only one of Fiji's five sugar mills that produces solely for domestic consumption (the others export all their sugar). There also is a nine-hole **Penang Golf Course** near the mill, which visitors may play (arrange at the Rakiraki Hotel; see "Where to Stay in Northern Viti Levu," below).

Rakiraki itself is a Fijian village (with the usual car-destroying road humps) on the King's Road, about 1km (½ mile) past the Vaileka junction. It's home of

---

Fun Fact 900 Men for Dinner

Just before you reach the well-marked junction of the King's Road and the Vaileka cut-off, look on the right for the **Grave of Udre Udre.** Legend says the stones at the base of the tombstone represent every one of the 900 men this renowned cannibal chief had for dinner.

---

the *Tui Ra,* the high Fijian chief of Ra district, which encompasses all of northern Viti Levu. He likes to stroll over to the Rakiraki Hotel, on the village's eastern boundary.

After the village, a paved road leads to **Ellington Wharf,** the jumping-off point for **Nananu-I-Ra,** a semiarid island about 15 minutes offshore, which has four backpackers' retreats (see "Where to Stay in Northern Viti Levu," below).

RAKIRAKI TO SUVA

From Ellington Wharf, the King's Road rounds the island's northern point into **Viti Levu Bay,** whose surrounding mountains topped with basaltic cliffs, thumbs, and spires give it a tropical splendor similar to Moorea's. About 15km (9½ miles) from Rakiraki stands **St. Francis Xavier Church,** home of the unique *Naiserelagi,* or Black Christ mural painted by artist Jean Charlot in 1963.

From the head of the bay, the road begins to climb through rice paddies and more cattle country, to the head of the winding **Wainibuka River.** This "Banana Highway" is a major tributary of the mighty Rewa River that eventually flows into the sea through a broad, flat delta northeast of Suva. The cool, often cloudy highlands of the Wainibuka Valley is old Fiji, a land of few Indo-Fijians and many traditional Fijian villages perched on the slopes along the river. *Note:* If you're driving, be careful on the many switchback curves above the river. There are no shoulders to pull off on, and you suddenly come upon several one-lane wooden bridges that can be icy slick during frequent rains. And watch out for the huge buses that regularly ply this route, taking up the entire road as they rumble along at breakneck speeds.

You leave the Wainibuka and enter the dairy-farming region of eastern Fiji, source of the country's fresh milk and cheeses (be alert for cows on the road!). The small town of **Korovou,** 107km (66 miles) from Rakiraki, is the major junction in these parts. Turn right for Nausori and Suva at the dead end (a left turn will take you to Natovi Wharf).

From Korovou, the King's Road goes directly south for 25km (15½ miles) until it joins the **Rewa River,** now a meandering coastal stream. You soon come to bustling Nausori, the delta's main town. Turn right and cross the steel-girdered bridge to reach Suva.

WHERE TO STAY IN NORTHERN VITI LEVU

The area's most modern accommodation is at **Wananavu Beach Resort,** P.O. Box 305, Rakiraki (© **669 4433;** fax 669 4499; wananavuresort@is.com.fj), on Viti Levu's northernmost point. Substituting for a beach, the resort's marina is the launching pad for diving trips to the colorful reefs offshore. The dining room, bar, three villas (one with kitchen), and most of the 15 guest bungalows have great ocean views from their hillside perches. Rates range from F$198 to F$320 ($89–$144).

Hilly, anvil-shaped Nananu-I-Ra island, a 15-minute boat ride from Ellington Wharf, has long been popular as a sunny retreat for local Europeans who own beach cottages there (the island is all freehold land). Today young backpackers like to stop off for a few days here on their way by bus and ferry from Nadi to Savusavu and Taveuni. All that sunshine has a price, for Nananu-I-Ra is semiarid between May and September, when water shortages can occur. Accordingly, backpackers usually bring extra drinking water as well as their own groceries.

Of the backpackers' resorts, **Kon Tiki Island Lodge,** P.O. Box 340, Rakiraki (© **669 4290**), on the island's isolated western end, and **Charlie's Place,** P.O. Box 407 Rakiraki (© **669 4676**), near the other two on the more developed south end, are less restrained. **Betham's Beach Cottages,** P.O. Box 5, Rakiraki (© and fax **669 4132**), and **Nananu Beach Cottages,** P.O. Box 140, Rakiraki (© **669 4633**), have more the flavor of a relaxing but polite visit to grandma's (translated: no loud parties or topless sunbathing). All have dorm beds for about F$16.50 ($7.50) per person and cottages ranging from about F$40 to F$75 ($18–$34) single or double. These properties promote heavily at Nadi's inexpensive hotels and hostels, so you will have no trouble getting the full details.

Rakiraki Hotel ★   This venerable establishment is one of the few remaining colonial-era hotels in Fiji, and that means lots of charm unhurried by the pace of modern tourism. The two clapboard roadside buildings were built as guesthouses when U.S. soldiers were stationed nearby during World War II. One houses a tongue-and-groove-paneled bar and dining room, where guests enjoy home-cooked meals. The other has an old-fashioned hall down the middle with five rooms to either side. Two are air-conditioned, the others have ceiling fans, all have private bathrooms, but none have a phone. Two of these rooms have four beds each, which are rented on a dormitory basis. Out in the back yard, three modern two-story motel blocks have 36 rooms outfitted to international standards, with quiet air-conditioning units, phones, and tiled shower-only bathrooms. These rooms flank a pool, a tennis court, a games area under a thatch roof, and a championship-caliber bowling green. Behind all is an extensive garden full of tropical fruits and vegetables, which the chef raids daily. The friendly staff will arrange excursions to Vaileka and to Fijian villages, horseback riding, golfing, scuba diving, and treks into the highlands.

P.O. Box 31, Rakiraki (Rakiraki village, on King's Rd., 2.5km/1½ miles east of Vaileka, 132km/82 miles from Nadi Airport). © **800/448-8355** or 669 4101. Fax 669 4545. www.tanoahotels.com. 41 units. F$79–F$99 ($34.50–$44.50) double. AE, DC, MC, V. **Amenities:** 1 restaurant (regional); 1 bar; outdoor pool; tennis court; babysitting; laundry service. *In room:* A/C (in most units), TV, fridge, coffeemaker.

11

Northern Fiji

The pristine islands of northern Fiji are what the old South Seas are all about. Compared to relatively developed Viti Levu, Vanua Levu and Taveuni take us back to the old days of copra (dried coconut meat) planters, of Fijians living in small villages in the hills or beside crystal-clear lagoons.

The rolling plains of northern Vanua Levu, the country's second-largest island, are devoted to sugarcane and are of little interest to anyone who has visited Nadi. But on Vanua Levu's south side, rugged mountains drop to coconut plantations, to an old trading town with the singsong name Savusavu, and to villages where smiling people go about life at the ageless pace of tropical islands everywhere. And on Taveuni, Fiji's lush "Garden Isle," with the country's largest population of indigenous plants and animals, things are even more like they used to be.

The north is where you come to experience the natural wonders of Fiji—to "ecotour" in today's vogue terminology. It's also where you'll find some of the world's best scuba diving, for the strong currents in and around the Somosomo Strait between Vanua Levu and Taveuni feed a vast collection of colorful soft corals. Other South Pacific locations have more abundant sea life, but northern Fiji is unsurpassed for coral viewing.

1 Savusavu

A spine of volcanic mountains runs lengthwise down the center of Vanua Levu, trapping moisture from the southeast trade winds and giving the rolling hills and deltas of the north shore an ideal climate for growing sugarcane. Consequently, the area around the predominately Indo-Fijian town of **Labasa** is one of Fiji's prime sugar-producing regions.

On the south coast, the usually cloud-topped mountains quickly give way to narrow, well-watered coastal plains, ideal for copra plantations. Until the Great Depression of the 1930s, copra production made picturesque **Savusavu** a thriving European settlement. Savusavu is Vanua Levu's major sightseeing attraction, primarily because of its volcanic hot springs and magnificent scenic harbor—a bay so large and well protected by surrounding mountains that the U.S. Navy chose it as a possible "hurricane hole" for the Pacific Fleet during World War II.

The town of Savusavu sits snugly behind a small island in the southeastern corner of Savusavu Bay. The paved Cross-Island Road from Labasa runs along the eastern shore, through town, and out to **Lesiaceva Point** at the end of a peninsula that forms the southern side of the bay and protects it from the Koro Sea. The **Hibiscus Highway** starts at Savusavu and cuts south across the hilly peninsula to the airport before continuing along the south shore to Buca Bay. Although it is being paved, this road is neither a highway nor lined with hibiscus (cows grazing beneath the palms ate them all), but it does run along a

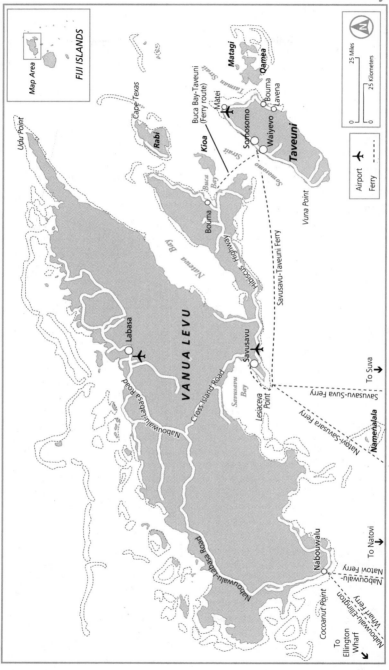

Moments The Way It Used to Be

The old South Pacific of copra plantation and trading boat days still lives in Savusavu and Taveuni. It rains more in Fiji's north, but that makes the steep hills lushly green. The diving and snorkeling here are world class.

---

picturesque, island-dotted lagoon through the heart of Vanua Levu's copra region. The coastal plain here is primarily a raised limestone shelf, which means that the reef is shallow and that the beaches pale in comparison to the magnificent white sands on Taveuni (see "Taveuni," later in this chapter).

Vanua Levu's southern coast has Fiji's largest concentration of freehold land, which Americans have been buying in recent years. Consequently, you're likely to meet more Yanks here than in any other part of Fiji.

GETTING TO SAVUSAVU

Air Fiji and **Sun Air** fly from both Nadi and Suva to Savusavu. Their flights between Nadi and Taveuni usually stop here briefly in each direction. The tiny Savusavu airport is on Vanua Levu's south coast. The hotels send buses to meet guests who have reservations.

Ferries also come up here, including the fast catamaran *Lagilagi,* which takes only half a day to reach Savusavu from Nadi. From Savusavu, a bus goes to Buca Bay on Vanua Levu's eastern end, where a small ferry crosses the Somosomo Strait to Waiyevo on Taveuni.

See "Getting There & Getting Around" in chapter 9 for more information.

GETTING AROUND SAVUSAVU

Some 30 **taxis**—an incredible number for such a small place—gather by the market in Savusavu when they're not hauling passengers. The cars of **Paradise Cab** (© 885 0018 or 956026) and **Michael's Taxi** (© 995 5727) are air-conditioned. Fares from Savusavu are F$4.50 ($2) to the airport, F$7 ($3) to Namale Resort, F$12 ($5.50) to Koro Sun Resort, and F$6 ($2.75) to the Jean-Michel Cousteau Fiji Islands Resort on Lesiaceva Point.

Local buses fan out from the Savusavu market to various points on the island. Most of them make three or four runs a day to outlying destinations, but ask the drivers when they will return to town. The longest runs should cost no more than F$6 ($2.75), with local routes in the F55¢ to F$1 (25¢–45¢) range.

You can rent **mountain bikes** from **Eco Divers-Tours** (© 885 0122), in the Copra Shed. They cost F$10 ($4.50) for a half day, F$20 ($9) for a full day.

 FAST FACTS: Savusavu

The following facts apply to Savusavu. If you don't see an item here, check "Fast Facts: Fiji" in chapter 9.

Currency Exchange **Westpac Bank** and **ANZ Bank** have offices on the main street. ANZ Bank has an ATM.

Drugstores There is a pharmacy at the government hospital. See "Healthcare," below.

E-mail **Savusavu Real Estate & Internet Centre,** in the Copra Shed (© **885 0929**), charges F35¢ (16¢) per minute for Internet access. Open Monday to Friday 8am to 5pm, Saturday 8am to 1pm.

Emergencies In an emergency phone © **917** for police, © **911** for fire or ambulance. The **police station** (© **885 0222**) is east of town.

Healthcare The **government hospital** (© **885 0800**) is east of town, in the government compound. **Dr. Joeli Taoi** has an office in town (© **885 0721**).

Information Visitors' information is posted on the walls of the Copra Shed on the main street. You can find information on the Web at **www.savu savufiji.com.**

Post Office The post office is on the main street near the east of the downtown commercial district. It's open Monday to Friday 8am to 1pm and 2 to 5pm.

Safety Savusavu generally is a safe place to visit, but don't tempt the mortals. Keep an eye on your personal property.

Telephone/Telegrams/Telex Go to the post office. There's a Phonecard public phone in the Copra Shed.

Water The tap water is safe to drink throughout Fiji.

EXPLORING SAVUSAVU

For practical purposes, Savusavu has only one street, and that runs along the shore for about 1.5km (1 mile). The modern **Copra Shed,** an old warehouse that has been turned into modern shops and a cafe, stands about midway along the shore. It and the **market** are the centers of activity.

Highlights of a stroll along the bay-hugging avenue are the gorgeous scenery and the volcanic **hot springs.** Steam from underground rises eerily from the rocky beach on the west end of town, and you can see more white clouds floating up from the ground between the sports field and the school, both behind the Shell station. A concrete pot has been built to make a natural stove in which local residents place meals to cook slowly all day. Overlooking the springs and bay, the **Savusavu Hot Springs Hotel** has great views (see "Where to Stay in Savusavu," below).

Curly and Liz Carswell of **Eco Divers-Tours** ⚓, P.O. Box 264, Savusavu (© **800/599-5507** or 885 0122; fax 885 0344; www.bulafiji.com/web/ecodiver), whose office is in the Copra Shed, arrange not only diving (see "Diving, Kayaking & Other Watersports," below) but accommodations and excursions on Vanua Levu. Originally from New Zealand, Curly and Liz have lived in Savusavu for many years and are now Fiji citizens. They have put their knowledge of the area to work on a series of tours and excursions. One goes to Naidi village, on the Hibiscus Highway, for a look at traditional Fijian lifestyles, and another takes you to a copra and beef plantation, where you can see the modern-day version of the old South Seas coconut plantation. Either of these costs F$20 ($9) per person. Another trip goes to Waisali Rainforest Reserve, a 116-hectare (290-acre) national forest up in the central mountains, which includes a visit to a waterfall. It costs F$40 ($18). They have a full-day tour to Labasa for F$90 ($40.50) per person.

Tips   **When to Go Diving in Northern Fiji**

Diving in northern Fiji is best from late May through October, when visibility reaches 120 feet and more. Because of the strong currents, however, dives to such outer reef sites as the Great White Wall and Rainbow Reef can be strenuous any time of year.

DIVING, KAYAKING & OTHER WATERSPORTS

Most of the resorts have complete diving facilities, as noted in "Where to Stay in Savusavu," below. A very long boat ride is required to dive on the Rainbow Reef and Great White wall, which are more easily reached from Taveuni than from Savusavu. But that's not to say that there aren't plenty of colorful reefs near here, including the wonderful barrier formation that nearly encircles Moody's Namena (see "A Resort off Savusavu," below).

Your one-stop shop here is the environmentally conscious **Eco Divers-Tours,** P.O. Box 264, Savusavu (© **800/599-5507** or 885 0122; fax 885 0344; www. bulafiji.com/web/ecodiver), in the Copra Shed. In addition to their land-based excursions (see "Exploring Savusavu," above), Curly and Liz Carswell offer diving, kayak rentals and trips, and sailboat rentals. Two-tank dives cost F$130 ($58.50), with a third dive of the day for F$84 ($38). They use many of the same buoyed sites as the Jean-Michel Cousteau Fiji Islands Resort. Full equipment rental is available, and they teach PADI certification courses. Snorkeling trips to colorful reefs offshore start at F$15 ($7) per person if four or more people go. The price goes up to F$25 ($11) per person for only two people. For kayakers, they offer 6-day paddling excursions to Fijian villages along the northern and western coasts of Savusavu Bay. You'll stay in the villages and dine with the villagers, so consider these to be "soft adventure" excursions. The trips cost about F$700 ($315) per person, based on groups of six paddlers. You can rent the single and double ocean kayaks when they aren't on expedition, starting at F$10 ($4.50) and F$15 ($7), respectively, per hour. The Carswells also will arrange water-skiing.

There are usually several sailboats doing day cruises and longer charters here. Check with Eco Divers for information and reservations.

You can also contact the Savusavu Hotsprings Hotel (see "Where to Stay in Savusavu," below) for deep-sea fishing, which costs about US$400 for half a day, US$600 for a full day.

The gray-sand beaches around Savusavu aren't the reason to come here. The nearest beach to town is a shady stretch on Lesiaceva Point just outside the Jean-Michel Cousteau Fiji Islands Resort, about 5km (3 miles) west of town, which is the end of the line for westbound buses leaving Savusavu market. There also is a half-moon beach at Naidi Bay, an extinct volcanic crater, just west of Namale Resort on the Hibiscus Highway. The road skirts the bay, but the beach is not easy to see. Take a taxi or ask the bus driver to let you off at Naidi Bay—not Naidi village or nearby Namale Resort. The bar and restaurant at Namale Resort are not open to walk-in customers, so bring something to drink and eat.

WHERE TO STAY IN SAVUSAVU
RESORTS

Jean-Michel Cousteau Fiji Islands Resort ★★★ *Kids*   This joint venture between the deluxe Post Ranch Inn of Big Sur, California, and Jean-Michel

Cousteau, son of the late Jacques Cousteau, looks like an old-time Fijian village set in a flat palm grove beside the bay on Lesiaceva Point. This "environmentally correct" resort is one of the best places in the South Pacific to bring young children because kids under 12 years old are *required* to participate in a "Bula Camp" educational activities program that will keep them busy during most of their waking moments.

Reception and the resort's bar are under a large roof built like a chief's *bure* (bungalow), and the dining room is covered by a taller roof, constructed to resemble a priest's bure. These impressive buildings sit next to a deck-surrounded pool just steps from one of the better beaches in the area. The large, luxurious thatch-roof guest bungalows have ceiling fans to augment the natural breezes flowing through floor-to-ceiling wooden jalousie windows that make up the front and rear walls. Most have porches strung with hammocks. Some newer, split-level units are more spacious and better equipped for families; you can pull a curtain to separate two daybeds from the regular king.

A host of watersports are available here, including snorkeling, kayaking, sailing, and scuba diving. The resort also offers environmentally oriented activities such as visits to rain and mangrove forests. An on-site marine biologist gives lectures and leads bird-watching expeditions and visits to Fijian villages. You can scuba dive with guides skilled in marine biology. The resort has a custom-built dive boat that's capable of reaching the famous Namena Reef, which surrounds Moody's Namena (see "A Resort off Savusavu," below), in about 1 hour.

Post Office, Savusavu (Lesiaceva Point, 5km/3 miles west of town). ✆ 800/246-3454 or 885 0188. Fax 885 0430. www.fijiresort.com. 25 units. US$425–US$655 double. Rates include meals, airport transfers, and all activities except scuba diving. AE, MC, V. **Amenities:** 1 restaurant (international); 1 bar; outdoor pool; tennis court; exercise room; watersports; scuba diving; children's program; activities desk; limited room service; massage; babysitting; laundry service. *In room:* Minibar, coffeemaker, hair dryer, no phone.

Koro Sun Resort   Originally known as Kontiki Resort, this property on Vanua Levu's southern coast has been considerably upgraded in recent years by its American owners. It is attractive primarily to serious divers, fishing enthusiasts, and golfers because it has no beach on the premises. It does sport a marina blasted into the reef and a 9-hole, par-3 golf course beneath the coconut palms of an old plantation. A dirt track leads around the golf course and through a rain forest to the resort's own refreshing cascades, where there's a spa in two screen bungalows (you can easily work up a sweat just getting a treatment in this humid climate).

The Hibiscus Highway runs along the shoreline, separating the property from the lagoon. The land turns quickly from flat coastal shelf to hills, where most of the guest bungalows are perched, thus commanding views through the palms to the sea. All these hillside units have screened porches, and one has two bedrooms. Down at sea level, the more spacious garden units lack views but have small front yards behind picket fences. All bungalows have ceiling fans hanging from peaked roofs, and some have outdoor showers behind high rock walls. Guests can pay to go horseback riding, game fishing, and scuba diving (which is expertly handled here by Jean-Michel Cousteau Fiji Islands Resort).

Private Bag, Savusavu (Hibiscus Hwy., 16km/10 miles east of town). ✆ 877/567-6786 or 885 0262. Fax 885 0355. www.korosunresort.com. 17 units. US$470 double. Rates include meals, nonmotorized watersports. AE, MC, V. **Amenities:** 1 restaurant (regional); 1 bar; outdoor pool; 9-hole golf course; 2 tennis courts; spa; free use of mountain bikes; free use of snorkeling gear; free use of sea kayaks; scuba diving; children's programs; massage; babysitting; laundry service. *In room:* Fridge, coffeemaker.

Lomalagi Resort   *Lomalagi* means "Heaven" in Fijian, and in one way that's an apt description for American Collin McKenny's little resort, for it sits high up on a hill overlooking Natewa Bay, a 30-minute drive east of Savusavu. One of her first guests was the late Beatle George Harrison, who was drawn to the resort's remoteness. A trail leads downhill to the shoreline, and there's a fine beach a short walk away, but the center of attention is a kidney-shaped seawater swimming pool with two waterfalls. It, the dining room, bar, and guest bungalows are spread out in a lawn under coconut trees on top of the hill. Each spacious, plantation-style tin-roof bure has a kitchen and a two-person soaking tub as well as a shower. All have decks with stunning views. The honeymoon unit is more private than the others. You can pay for village visits, horseback riding, and trips to see red prawns in a nearby salt lake. Collin will arrange scuba diving (the Cousteau-operated dive base at Koro Sun Resort is the nearest facility).

P.O. Box 200, Savusavu (Hibiscus Hwy. at Natewa Bay). © **881 6098.** Fax 881 6099. www.lomalagi.com. 6 units. US$400–US$500 double. AE, MC, V. No children accepted. **Amenities:** 1 restaurant (regional), 1 bar; outdoor saltwater pool; free use of bikes; free use of sea kayaks; game room; laundry service. *In room:* TV (videos only), CD player, kitchen, coffeemaker, hair dryer, no phone.

Namale Resort ★★★   This luxurious resort is owned by toothy American motivational author and speaker Anthony Robbins, who visits several times a year. Robbins obviously finds any dull moment distasteful, for he has built an air-conditioned gym and basketball court, an electronic golf simulator, and full-size bowling alley (I kid you not). These indoor toys will come in handy, since the climate here is borderline rain forest and the pebbly beaches are not reason alone to spend your entire vacation here. This area has been geologically uplifted, so all buildings are on a shelf 10 to 20 feet above sea level. Nevertheless, Namale has excellent scuba diving and deep-sea fishing (the only two activities demanding an extra fee) plus windsurfing, horseback riding, and hiking.

The guest quarters are widely scattered in the blooming tropical gardens surrounding the main building, thus affording honeymoon-like privacy if not a setting directly on the ocean. Crown jewels here are two houses. The "Dream House" is a two-bedroom, two-bathroom minimansion with a kitchen, its own small pool, a whirlpool bathtub, and indoor and outdoor showers. Similarly equipped, the "Bula House" has only one bedroom, but there are two guest bungalows outside (one with a queen bed, the other with two twins), and it has a Jacuzzi on its deck. Both the Dream and Bula houses have drop-down movie screens with wraparound sound systems (again, I kid you not). Your children can stay with you in the houses, but only if they're at least 12 years old (they are not allowed in the other bungalows unless you rent one just for them). There's also a deluxe honeymoon bure with its own swimming pool plus a sunken bathtub and two-person shower.

Four more honeymoon bures have bathrooms with Jacuzzi tubs, separate showers with indoor and outdoor entrances, and their own ceiling fans. Six older bures are much less spectacular, but they are attractively appointed nonetheless. If you're traveling by yourself, you can stay in one of these, but not in the larger units. Although the windows in all units are screened, the staff drops romantic mosquito nets over the beds at turndown.

Fun Fact **Do I Have a Deal for You**

Namale Resort has been a working copra plantation since the 1860s, when an Englishman bought it from the local chief for 10 rifles.

The property sits on a narrow headland jutting out into Naidi Bay, upon whose point sits the main building, with a soaring Fijian-style thatch roof. Although you can dine inside, the choice tables are on four decks commanding excellent views from the point. Reflecting Robbins's culinary likes, the chef prepares vegetarian as well as fish and meat dishes.

P.O. Box 244, Savusavu (Hibiscus Hwy., 11km/7 miles east of town). (C) **800/727-3454** or 885 0435. Fax 885 0400 or 619/535-6385 in the U.S. www.namalefiji.com. 15 units. US$675–US$900 double, US$1,500–US$1,800 house. Rates include meals, drinks, all activities except scuba diving. No children under 12 accepted. AE, MC, V. **Amenities:** 1 restaurant (international/vegetarian), 2 bars; 2 outdoor pools; tennis court; exercise room; basketball court; Jacuzzi; watersports; bike rentals; children's programs; game room; massage; laundry service. *In room:* Kitchen (in houses), minibar, coffeemaker, hair dryer, no phone.

Savusavu Hot Springs Hotel (*Value*) Once a Travelodge motel, this three-story structure overlooking Savusavu Bay has been completely renovated by Tim and Lorna Eden, who were born and bred in Fiji (he's a former Air Pacific pilot; she's related to the Douglases of Matangi Island Resort off Taveuni). The structure sits on a hill in town, and its motel-style rooms take advantage of the view by having sliding glass doors that open to balconies. The more expensive units on the third and fourth floors have the view, and the less expensive rooms on the second floor are equipped with ceiling fans but lack air conditioners. This isn't a fancy establishment, but it's clean, comfortable, friendly, and a very good value.

P.O. Box 208, Savusavu (in town). (C) **714/840-1250** or 885 0195. Fax 885 0430. hotspringshotel@is.com.fj. 48 units. F$90–F$155 ($40.50–$70) double. AE, DC, MC, V. **Amenities:** 1 restaurant (regional), 1 bar; outdoor pool; exercise room; salon; limited room service; massage; babysitting; laundry service. *In room:* A/C, TV, dataport, fridge, coffeemaker.

HOSTELS

Beachcomber Driftwood Village (*★*) Dan Costello has juxtaposed this former church camp into a Savusavu version of his rollicking Beachcomber Island Resort off Nadi (see "Where to Stay Offshore from Nadi" in chapter 10, "Viti Levu"). Granted, it doesn't have a gorgeous beach (the shoreline across the road needs sand), but you can go swimming, snorkeling, canoeing, kayaking, and windsurfing, and Jean-Michel Cousteau Fiji Islands Resort is in charge of diving here. And you'll find plenty of young company around the pool and in the big main building, where the staff dishes up Beachcomber-style all-you-can-eat buffets. Five guest bungalows are simple but comfortable, with ceiling fans, shower-only bathrooms, and screened windows on all four sides. There also are two houses with two bedrooms each. The dorms are comfortable and airy. Guests here get discounted fares on the *Lagilagi* ferry.

P.O. Box 18, Savusavu (1km/½ mile west of town toward Lesiaceva Point). (C) **885 0046.** Fax 885 0344. driftwood@is.com.fj. 7 units, 60 dorm beds. F$90 ($40.50) double, F$185 ($83) family unit, F$39 ($17.50) dorm bed. Rates include breakfast. AE, MC, V. **Amenities:** 1 restaurant (regional), 1 bar; outdoor pool; watersports equipment rentals; scuba diving; laundry service. *In room:* Fridge, coffeemaker, no phone.

WHERE TO DINE IN SAVUSAVU

Captain's Cafe SANDWICHES/PIZZA With seating inside or outside on a deck over the bay, this cafe is a pleasant place for an outdoor lunch. The name and nautical decor might be misleading, however, for only fish and chips come from the briny deep. Other offerings are sandwiches, burgers, side salads, garlic bread, and reasonably good pizzas.

Main street, in the Copra Shed. (C) **885 0511.** Reservations not accepted. Fish, burgers, and sandwiches F$3–F$5.50 ($1.35–$2.50); pizza F$6–F$20 ($2.75–$9). No credit cards. Mon–Sat 8am–8:30pm, Sun 11am–9pm.

Fale Tau's Daily Grind ⭐ *Finds* COFFEE SHOP/REGIONAL   Annabelle Faletau uses filtered water and Fiji-grown beans to make her lattes, cappuccinos, and espressos at this local version of Starbucks. You can sip away on the sofas in the front or wander in the back for fresh fruit smoothies, sweet cakes and pies, sandwiches, burgers, hot dogs, and daily specials such as Indian curries, grilled fish, chow mein, steak, garlic chicken, and beef stew served with cassava or rice. Her coffees are rich and her food good, especially for the prices she charges.

Main street, between the Copra Shed and Municipal Market. ② **885 0710.** Reservations not accepted. Breakfast F$2.50–F$6 ($1–$2.75); sandwiches, burgers, hot dogs F$2–F$4.50 (90¢–$2); main courses F$5–F$9 ($2.25–$4). No credit cards. Mon–Sat 7am–9pm.

ISLAND NIGHTS IN SAVUSAVU

The expensive resorts provide nightly entertainment for their guests. On Saturday night the locals head up the Savusavu Hot Springs Hotel for disco dancing. Otherwise, there's not much going on in Savusavu after dark except at the two local drinking establishments. The **Planter's Club** ⭐ (② **885 0233**), in an ancient clapboard building near the western end of town, is a friendly holdover from the colonial era. It has a snooker table and a pleasant bar, where you can order a cold young coconut (add gin or rum, and you've got a genuine island cocktail). It's open Monday to Thursday from 10am to 10pm, Friday and Saturday 10am to 11pm, Sunday 11am to 8pm. You'll be asked to sign the club's register. Yachties and the numerous American and other expatriates who live here congregate at the wharf-side bar of the **Savusavu Yacht Club,** in the Copra Shed (② **885 0685**). You can grab a bite at the Captain's Cafe next door and eat at the club's picnic tables. It's open Monday to Saturday from 10am to 10pm and Sunday from noon to 10pm.

2 A Resort off Savusavu

Back in the 1970s, Pennsylvanians Tom and Joan Moody (she pronounces her name "Joanne") opened a small, isolated resort in Panama's San Blas Islands, catering to serious scuba divers and others who just wanted a total escape. Terrorists attacked their peaceful outpost in 1981, however, shooting and nearly killing Tom and tying up Joan. Fortunately, they both survived, but they soon sold their place and left Panama. After searching the South Pacific, they settled on dragon-shaped Namenalala, little more than a rocky ridge protruding from the Koro Sea about 32km (20 miles) south of Vanua Levu and covered with dense native forest and bush. The huge Namena barrier reef sweeps down from Vanua Levu and creates a gorgeous lagoon. The Moodys have designated most of Namenalala as a nature preserve in order to protect a large colony of boobies that nest on the island, and sea turtles that climb onto some of the South Pacific's most gorgeous **beaches** to lay their eggs from November through February. In other words, the setting is remote and fascinating. So is their unique little resort:

Moody's Namena ⭐⭐ *Value*   The Moodys perched all but one of their comfortable bungalows up on the ridge so that each has a commanding view of the ocean but not of one another. Each of the hexagonal structures resembles a treehouse; in fact, the huge trunk of a tree grows right through the balcony surrounding one of the bures. Surely this was how Robinson Crusoe would have preferred to live. A lack of fresh groundwater adds to the effect. The "his and hers" toilets in each bungalow are flushed with seawater, and rainwater takes care of drinking and bathing. The walls of the bungalows slide back to render both views and cooling breezes, so you will sleep under a mosquito net. Instead of treading sandy paths among palm trees, you climb rocky pathways along the wooded ridge to the central building, where the Moodys provide excellent meals and ice upon which to pour the booze you bought at the duty-free store. They serve wine with dinner and can sell beer and wine at their cost, but they do not have a liquor license. After you spend 1 day in their care, these "hardships" matter not at all.

Lazing on the beaches (OCCUPIED/UNOCCUPIED signs warn guests that someone else is already cavorting on four of the island's five private beaches), hiking, kayaking, swimming, snorkeling, deep-sea fishing, and scuba diving among the colorful reefs and sea turtles are the main activities here. The Moodys do not teach scuba diving, so you must be certified in advance. The Moodys will have you brought out from Savusavu on a fast fishing boat, a voyage of 1½ hours, or arrange to charter a seaplane for the 1-hour flight from Nadi.

Private Mail Bag, Savusavu. © **881 3764.** Fax 881 2366. moodysnamena@is.com.fj. 6 units. US$177 per person. Rates include meals, wine at dinner, snacks, nonalcoholic beverages, all activities except scuba diving. MC, V. Closed Mar–Apr. **Amenities:** 1 restaurant (regional), 1 bar; game room; massage; laundry service. *In room:* Coffeemaker, no phone.

3 Taveuni ★★

Cigar-shaped Taveuni, Fiji's third-largest island, lies just 6.5km (4 miles) from Vanua Levu's eastern peninsula across the Somosomo Strait, one of the world's most famous scuba-diving spots. Although the island is only 9.5km (6 miles) wide, a volcanic ridge down Taveuni's 40km (25-mile) length soars to more than 1,200m (4,000 ft.), blocking the southeast trade winds and pouring as much as 30 feet of rain a year on the mountaintops and the island's rugged eastern side. Consequently, Taveuni's 9,000 residents (three-fourths of them Fijians) live in a string of villages along the gently sloping, less rainy but still lush western side. They own some of the country's most fertile and well-watered soil—hence Taveuni's nickname: "The Garden Isle."

Thanks to limited land clearance and the absence of the mongoose, Taveuni still has all the plants and animals indigenous to Fiji, including the unique Fiji fruit bat, the Taveuni silktail bird, land crabs, and some species of palm that have only recently been identified. The **Ravilevu Nature Preserve** on the east coast and the **Taveuni Forest Preserve** in the middle of the island are designed to protect these rare creatures.

Taveuni's most famous sight is **Lake Tagimaucia,** home of the rare *tagimaucia* flower that bears red blooms with white centers. A shallow lake whose sides are ringed with mud flats and thick vegetation, it sits among the clouds in a volcanic crater at an altitude of more than 800m (2,700 ft.).

Bouma Falls ★★★ are among Fiji's finest and most accessible waterfalls, and the area around them is now an environmental park. Past Bouma at the end of the road, a coastal hiking track begins at **Lavena** village and runs through the Ravilevu Nature Reserve.

By tradition, Taveuni's **Somosomo** village is Fiji's most "chiefly" village; that is, it's chief is the highest ranking in all of Fiji, and the big meeting house here is the prime gathering place of Fiji's influential Great Council of Chiefs.

The main village of **Waiyevo** sits halfway down the west coast. A kilometer (½ mile) south, a brass plaque marks the **180th Meridian** of longitude. This would have been the international date line were it not for its slicing of the Aleutians and Fiji in two and for Tonga's wish to be on the same day as Australia. The

---

Tips Don't Rent a Car

Taveuni's only road, which runs along the west and north coasts, is in the long process of being paved between Waiyevo and the airport. Elsewhere it's rough, winding, narrow, and at places carved into sheer cliffs above the sea. Also, many local drivers—including bus drivers—roar along at top speed. There can be very little room to get off the road to avoid them. Therefore, you should forget renting a vehicle here; hire a taxi and driver.

---

village of **Waikiki** sports both the Meridian Cinema and a lovely 19th-century Catholic mission built to reward a French missionary for helping the locals defeat a band of invading Tongans.

In stark contrast to the rest of unspoiled Taveuni, the paved roads, uninhabited condominiums, and often shaggy golf course of **Soqulu Plantation** south of Waikiki stand as a reminder that not all real estate developments work. A few expatriates have homes here, but the project has never really gotten off the ground since its conception in the 1980s.

Off Taveuni's northeastern end are the small, rugged islands of **Qamea** and **Matagi,** homes of two very fine little offshore resorts (see "Resorts Offshore from Taveuni," later).

GETTING TO TAVEUNI & GETTING AROUND

Both **Air Fiji** and **Sun Air** fly to Taveuni from Nadi, and Air Fiji has nonstop service from Nausori Airport near Suva. Taveuni's airport is at its northern tip. The hotels send buses or hire taxis to pick up their guests.

The ferries land—and most commerce takes place—at Waiyevo. Two small ferries run across the Somosomo Strait between Waiyevo and Buca Bay on Vanua Levu. They depart from the New Wharf at 8am daily. A bus connects Savusavu to the ferry wharf at Buca Bay.

For more information, see "Getting There & Getting Around" in chapter 9.

Taxis don't regularly ply the roads. The only taxi stand is outside Lesuma Supermarket in Waiyevo. Your hotel staff can hail one within a few minutes, or you can phone ⓒ **888 0705,** 888 0442, or 888 0424. Negotiate for a round-trip price if you're going out into the villages and having the driver wait for you. None of the taxis have meters, but the fare from the airport should be F$2 (90¢) to Maravu Plantation and Taveuni Island resorts and F$18 ($8) to Navakoca (Qamea) Landing, Waiyevo, or Bouma Falls. Taxis will take you anywhere for about F$30 ($13.50) an hour.

Local **buses** fan out from Waiyevo to the outlying villages about three times a day from Monday to Saturday. For example, a bus leaves Waiyevo for Bouma at 8:30am, 12:15pm, and 4:30pm. The one-way fare to Bouma is no more than F$4 ($1.80). Contact **Pacific Transport** (ⓒ **888 0278**) opposite Kaba's Supermarket in Nagara, the predominately Indian village next to Somosomo.

 FAST FACTS: Taveuni

The following facts apply to Taveuni. If you don't see an item here, see "Fast Facts: Fiji" in chapter 9.

Currency Exchange **Colonial National Bank** has an office at Waiyevo (© **888 0433**), but it does not have an ATM. This bank and the hotels will cash traveler's checks.

Emergencies In an emergency phone © **917** for the police, © **911** for fire or ambulance. The police station (© **888 0222**) is in the government compound.

Healthcare The **government hospital** (© **888 0222**) is in the government compound in the hills above Waiyevo. To get there, go uphill on the road opposite the Garden Island Resort, then take the right fork.

Post Office The post office is in the government compound (see "Health-care," above). It's open Monday to Friday 8am to 5pm.

Safety Taveuni is relatively safe, but exercise caution if you're out late at night.

Telegrams/Telex See "Post Office," above. There are Phonecard public phones at the market in Waiyevo, opposite the Garden Island Resort (see "Where to Stay on Taveuni," below), and at Bhula Bhai Store in Matei, east of the airport.

Water The tap water is safe to drink throughout Fiji.

FISHING, HIKING, DIVING & OTHER OUTDOOR ACTIVITIES

The hotels and resorts can arrange sightseeing tours to all of the sights mentioned in the introduction to this section, including the beautiful Bouma Falls, but tourism here is devoted primarily to outdoor activities.

FISHING   New Zealander Geoffrey Amos of **Matei Game Fishing** (© **888 0371**) will take you deep-sea fishing on his 36-foot *Lucky Strike,* based opposite Maravu Plantation Resort (see "Where to Stay on Taveuni," below). Call for rates and reservations.

HIKING   One attraction on everyone's list is **Bouma Falls** ★★★. They are in the Bouma Environmental Tourism Project on Taveuni's northeastern end, 18km (11 miles) from the airport, 37km (23 miles) from Waiyevo. The government of New Zealand provided funds for the village of Bouma to build trails to the three levels of the falls. It's a flat, 15-minute walk along an old road from the visitors center to the lower falls, which plunge some 180m (600 ft.) into a broad pool. From there, a trail climbs sharply to a lookout with a fine view of Qamea and as far offshore as the Kaibu and Naitoba islands east of Taveuni. The trail then enters a rain forest to a second set of falls, which are not as impressive as the lower cascade. Hikers ford slippery rocks across a swift-flowing creek while holding onto a rope (a sign says BEST WAIT FOR FLOOD—it means don't cross during a flood). This 30-minute muddy climb can be made in shower sandals, but be careful of your footing. A more difficult track ascends to yet a third falls, but I've never followed it, and people who did have told me it isn't worth the effort.

Another trail, the **Vidawa Forest Walk,** leads to historic hill fortifications and more great views. Guides lead full-day treks through the Vidawa Forest on Friday, but you'll need to book at your hotel activities desk or call the visitor center (© **880390**) at least a day in advance. The guided treks cost F$60 ($27) per person, including transfers to the park, juice, lunch, and afternoon tea. The park is

---

> **Tips** It All Depends on the Tides
>
> Because of the strong currents in the Somosomo Strait, dives on Taveuni's most famous sites must be timed according to the tides. You can't count on making the dives you would like if the tides are wrong when you're here. A very good friend of mine spent 10 days in the area and never did get out to the Rainbow Reef.

---

open daily from 8am to 5pm. Admission is F$5 ($2.25) per person. See "Getting to Taveuni & Getting Around," above, for information about how to get here.

At the end of the road past Bouma, the village of Lavena is on one of Taveuni's best beaches. From there, the **Lavena Coastal Walk** runs for 5km (3 miles) along the coast, then climbs to **Wainibau Falls.** The last 20 minutes or so of this track are spent walking up a creek bed, which can be flooded during heavy rains. The creek water is safe to drink, but you might want to bring your own supplies. Admission to the village and walking track is F$5 ($2.25) per person.

Another track leads to **Lake Tagimaucia,** home of the famous flower that blooms from the end of September to the end of December. This crater lake is surrounded by mud flats and filled with floating vegetation. Beginning at Somosomo village, the hike to the lake takes about 8 hours round-trip. The trail is often muddy and slippery, and given the usual cloud cover hanging over the mountains by midmorning, you're not likely to see much when you reach the top. Only hikers who are in shape should make this full-day trek, and then only with a guide. An alternative is to take a four-wheel-drive vehicle up Des Voeux Peak for a look down at the lake. The drive is best done early in the morning, when the mountain is least likely to be shrouded in clouds. The Garden Island Resort (see "Where to Stay on Taveuni," below) will make arrangements for a guide or vehicle.

SCUBA DIVING ★★★   The swift currents of the Somosomo Strait feed the corals on the Rainbow Reef and the White Wall between Taveuni and Vanua Levu, making them two of the world's most colorful and famous scuba-diving sites. The Rainbow Reef is only 4 miles off Waiyevo, so the Garden Island Resort is the closest dive base. In addition to the operators mentioned here, Matangi Island Resort and Qamea Beach Club (see "Resorts Offshore from Taveuni," below) specialize in diving equally great locations off Taveuni's eastern end.

The closest operator to the Rainbow Reef and Great White Wall, both a 20-minute boat ride across the Somosomo Strait from Waiyevo, is **Aqua-Trek** (© 800/541-4334 or 888 0286; fax 888 0288; www.aquatrek.com), the U.S. firm that owns the Garden Island Resort (see "Where to Stay on Taveuni," below). This five-star PADI operation has full equipment rental, E-6 film processing, NITROX, and teaches courses from beginner to dive master. Aqua-Trek's prices start at US$82 for a two-dive excursion. PADI learn-to-dive courses cost US$330.

Farther away but still in easy range at the northern end of Taveuni are **Swiss Divers Fiji** (© 885 0586; www.swissfijidivers.com), where Dominique Edgerter runs two dives a day, and **Aquaventure Taveuni** (© and fax 888 0381; www.aquaventure.org), where New Zealander Tania de Hoon does the same. Both charge about US$65 for a two-tank dive and both teach PADI certification courses. Bring your own regulators, wetsuits, masks, fins, and snorkels. They supply the weight belts, backpacks, and tanks.

SWIMMING, SNORKELING & KAYAKING Because Taveuni is a relatively new island in geological terms, it doesn't have a great number of good swimming beaches. But the few it has are first rate. The best is at Lavena village at the far end of the north shore road (see "Hiking," above). More convenient places to swim and snorkel are **Prince Charles Beach** and the lovely, tree-draped **Beverly Beach,** both south of the airport.

Aqua-Trek (see "Scuba Diving," above) has snorkeling trips to Korolevu, a rocky islet off Waiyevo, daily at 10am and 2pm for F$10 ($4.50) per person, plus F$11 ($5) for gear rental. The company will even take you snorkeling out to the Rainbow Reef, but book these trips well in advance.

One of the most popular things to do on Taveuni is rent a kayak and paddle out to the three little rocky islets that sit off the north shore, near the airport. The reefs here are great to snorkel over, provided that kelp from the nearby seaweed farms isn't drifting by. You can land on the islands for a picnic. **Coconut Grove Beachfront Cottages & Restaurant** (© 888 0328), opposite the airport, rents two-person ocean kayaks for F$30 ($13.50) per half day, F$55 ($25) all day. Owner Ronna Goldstein will prepare a picnic lunch if you give her advance notice. You can also rent kayaks at **Beverly Campground** (© 888 0381), from where Kenny Madden leads paddling excursions.

At Waiyevo, the **Garden Island Resort** (see "Where to Stay on Taveuni," below) rents kayaks for F$11 ($5) per hour or F$44 ($20) per day. From there, you can paddle out to Korolevu, a rocky islet off Waiyevo.

WHERE TO STAY ON TAVEUNI
RESORTS

Coconut Grove Beachfront Cottages ★★ *Value* Ronna Goldstein, who named this place not for the palm trees growing all around it but for her hometown in Florida, has two bures set above a fine little beach next to her restaurant (see "Where to Dine on Taveuni," below). Ronna lives here, and the restaurant is on her big, breezy front porch overlooking the sea. Next door, her "Mango" cottage has interior walls made of rough-hewn mango timber. It has a small kitchen, its bathroom opens to an outdoor shower, and it has a terrific view of the sea and offshore islet from its front porch. Actually in front of the restaurant and almost on the beach, the smaller "Papaya" bure lacks a kitchen but has a sea view. Inside Ronna's house, the "Guava" room has a king-size bed and two twin beds and a ceiling fan. Gracie, Ronna's friendly Doberman, is in charge of guest relations.

Postal Agency, Matei, Taveuni (opposite airport). © and fax 888 0328. www.coconutgrovefiji.com. 3 units. US$50–US$85 per person. Rates include breakfast and dinner. MC, V. **Amenities:** 1 restaurant (international); massage; babysitting; laundry service. *In room:* Kitchen (in 1 unit), fridge, coffeemaker, no phone.

Garden Island Resort ★ *Value* Built as a Travelodge motel in the 1960s, this waterside hotel has been renovated by its owners, the San Francisco–based dive company Aqua-Trek, which has its Taveuni base here. Most of the clientele are

---

Tips **Beware of "Jaws"**

Ancient legend says that Taveuni's paramount chief is Fiji's highest ranking because sharks protect the island from enemies. True or not, shark attacks are frequent here, so be extremely careful when you're swimming and snorkeling, and don't under any circumstances swim out to the edge of the reef.

divers, since this is the closest hotel to the White Wall and Rainbow Reef, but the friendly staff and managers welcome everyone. There is no beach, but there is a fine view over the Somosomo Strait to Vanua Levu, and all the rooms face it. Each medium-size unit has a queen and a single bed, tropical-style chairs, a desk, and a tub-and-shower combo bathroom. All but the two rooms used as dormitories are air-conditioned (the dorms have ceiling fans).

Opening to a strait-side pool, the dining room serves meals, which always include vegetarian selections, at reasonable prices. Guests and nonguests can rent kayaks and go on snorkeling trips to Korolevu islet offshore and even to the Rainbow Reef with Aqua-Trek. The hotel also arranges hiking trips and other excursions.

P.O. Box 1, Waiyevo, Taveuni (Waiyevo village, 11km/7 miles south of airport). © 800/541-4334 or 888 0286. Fax 888 0288. www.aquatrek.com. 28 units, 8 dorm beds. US$92 double room, US$16.50 dorm bed. AE, MC, V. **Amenities:** 1 restaurant (regional), 1 bar; outdoor pool; watersports; bike rentals; limited room service; massage babysitting; laundry service. *In room:* A/C (except in dorms), fridge, coffeemaker, safe.

Maravu Plantation Resort ☆ Although it has its own beach across the road (a 5-min. downhill walk), this unusual retreat is set among the palms of a working copra plantation (with some cocoa, coffee, and vanilla thrown in for diversification). Only two of the guest bungalows have ocean views, and those are through the palm trees. The bures are laid out among grounds that are carefully planted with bananas, papayas, and a plethora of ginger plants and wild orchids brought down from the mountains. This plantation setting means the property can get warm and humid during the day. The guest bungalows have ceiling fans and front porches but not air conditioners. Built like old-fashioned planters' houses rather than as Fijian bures, they have thatch-covered tin roofs and reed or mat accents that lend a tropical ambience. Three units have outdoor showers and sun decks surrounded by rock walls. With an emphasis on "nouvelle Fijian" cuisine, the dining room is under the high thatch roof and looks out to the lawns and a pool that's surrounded by an expansive deck. Wine lovers are in for a treat here, for owner Jochen Kiess, a former German lawyer, has accumulated one of the finest lists in Fiji.

Postal Agency, Matei, Taveuni (1km/½ mile south of airport). © 888/FIJI-NOW or 888 0555. Fax 888 0600. www.maravu.net. 10 units. US$160–US$190 per person double occupancy. Rates include meals, airport transfers, and most activities. AE, DC, MC, V. **Amenities:** 1 restaurant (regional), 1 bar; outdoor pool; children's programs; activities desk; limited room service; massage; babysitting; laundry service. *In room:* Minibar, coffeemaker, hair dryer, no phone.

Taveuni Island Resort Formerly known as Dive Taveuni, one of the best diving operations in Fiji, this resort has given up the tanks and weight belts and turned to honeymooners for the bulk of its business (no kids under 15 here). If you are among these romantic souls, you had best not want to step out of your bungalow onto the beach, for this property sits high on a bluff overlooking Somosomo Strait, and you will have to climb down it to reach the sand. (Lomalagi Resort in Savusavu and Maravu Plantation across the road here are in the same situation.) To compensate, there's a hilltop pool, which commands a magnificent view over the strait, as do the central building and the seven guest bungalows here. Six of the units are hexagonal models built of pine with side wall windows that let in the view and the breeze. The most stunning view of all is from the spacious deck of the honeymoon bure—or you can sit up and take in the vista from its king-size bed. One deluxe unit has a separate bedroom. All units have outdoor showers.

Postal Agency, Matei, Taveuni (1.5km/1 mile south of airport). *C* **877/828-3864** or 888 0441. Fax 888 0466. www.taveuniislandresort.com. 7 units. US$261–US$308 per person. Rates include meals, transfers, and non-alcoholic beverages. AE, MC, V. Children under 15 not accepted. **Amenities:** 1 restaurant (regional), 1 bar; outdoor pool; limited room service; massage; laundry service. *In room:* A/C, minibar, coffeemaker, hair dryer, no phone.

HOSTELS

Don't forget the dormitory at the Garden Island Resort (see above).

Tovu Tovu Resort   Spread out over a lawn across the road from the lagoon, Alan Petersen's simple bungalows have front porches, reed exterior walls, tile floors, ceiling fans, and bathrooms with hot-water showers. Three of them also have cooking facilities. The dorm building sits on a hill, but a fine sea view from up there is your compensation for not being steps from the beach. The Vunibokoi Restaurant is here (see "Where to Dine on Taveuni," below).

Postal Agency, Matei, Taveuni (1km/½ mile east of airport). *C* **888 0560.** Fax 888 0722. tovutovu@is.com.fj. 5 bungalows, 8 dorm beds. F$65–F$75 ($29–$34) bungalow, F$15 ($7) dorm bed. AE, MC, V. **Amenities:** 1 restaurant (regional), 1 bar; bike rentals; laundry service. *In room:* Kitchen (in 3 units).

COTTAGE RENTALS

In addition to Coconut Grove Beachfront Cottages (see above), you can rent a Western-style, hexagonal bungalow from American Audrey Brown of **Audrey's By the Sea** (*C* **888 0039**). The cottage sits next to her own home on 14 acres of tropical gardens across the road from the lagoon. It has a kitchenette, a separate bedroom, and a bathroom with hot-water shower. Audrey charges F$105 ($47) per night but does not accept credit cards. Her mailing address is Postal Agency, Matei, Taveuni.

CAMPING

You'll get the most fabulous view of any campground in Fiji from **Todranisiga** ★★ (*C* and fax **888 0381**), about .5km (⅓ mile) south of the airport, where owner May Goulding has four large "permanent" tents sitting on a lawn overlooking the Somosomo Strait. *Todranisiga* means "Blaze of Sun" in Fijian, and you'll see great sunsets from up here, too. May is a native of Fiji and a hospitality industry veteran. Her tents have white sand foundations, big screened windows, and double-size inflatable beds. Guests share showers, toilets, and a kitchen. Guests pay F$12.50 per ($6) person, and May does not accept credit cards. Like everyone else's here, May's address is Postal Agency, Matei, Taveuni.

WHERE TO DINE ON TAVEUNI

The best place to dine here is the Coconut Grove Restaurant (see below), opposite the airport. East of there, **Audrey's Sweet Somethings** (*C* **888 0039**) really isn't a restaurant, it's American Audrey Brown's front porch. Audrey is known as Taveuni's best baker, and she offers her pastries, cakes, and Fiji coffees for F$6 ($2.75) per serving. Audrey's is open daily from 10am to 6pm, and it doesn't accept credit cards.

Vunibokoi Restaurant (*C* **888 0560**), on the front porch of the main house at Alan Petersen's Tovu Tovu Resort (see above), serves breakfast, lunch, and dinner, with a blackboard menu that features good Fijian and Western fare. Main courses run F$7.50 to F$15 ($3.50–$7). It's open daily from 8am to 2pm and 6 to 9pm. American Express, MasterCard, and Visa cards are accepted. There's a Friday night buffet here, followed by live music.

In Waiyevo just south of the Garden Island Resort (see "Where to Stay on Taveuni," above), the **Cannibal Cafe** (*C* **888 0382**) is a great place to sit and have a cold beer under a thatch roof beside the Somosomo Strait. The food is plain local fare—curry, chop suey, fish and chips—at F$4 to F$5.50 ($1.80–$2.50) a plate. Go through Wathi Pokee Restaurant to reach the cafe. It's open Monday to Saturday 7:30am to 8pm, Sunday 11am to 8pm. Credit cards are not accepted.

Coconut Grove Restaurant ★★ INTERNATIONAL American Ronna Goldstein offers a variety of fare at her little enclave, where she also rents cottages (see "Where to Stay on Taveuni," above). She offers breakfasts (her banana bread is fabulous) and salads, soups, burgers, sandwiches, and grilled lamb chops for lunch. Dinner sees a variety of local seafood dishes, spicy Thai and mild Fijian curries (I love the Thai fish), and homemade pastas. Dining is on Ronna's veranda, which has a great view of the little islands off Taveuni, making it a fine place not just for lunch or dinner but to wait for your flight.

Matei, opposite airport. © **888 0328.** Reservations recommended for dinner. Main courses F$15–F$22 ($7–$10). MC, V. Daily 8am–5pm and 6–9pm.

4 Resorts Offshore from Taveuni

The northern end of Taveuni gives way to a chain of small, rugged islands that are as beautiful as any in Fiji. Their steep, jungle-clad hills drop to rocky shorelines in most places, but here and there little shelves of land and narrow valleys are bordered by beautiful beaches. The sheltered waters between the islands cover colorful reefs, making the area a hotbed for scuba diving and snorkeling. Except for a few Fijian villages and the two resorts described below, these little gems are undeveloped and unspoiled.

Matangi Island Resort ★★★ (Kids) It's unfortunate that geography places this resort next to last in my coverage of Fiji, for Matangi is one of the best values in the South Pacific—which is one reason it's also one of the most popular (book early, for it's usually full). Another reason is owners Noel and Flo Douglas. Of English-Fijian descent, Flo's family owns all of hilly, 260-acre Matagi Island, a horseshoe-shaped remnant of a volcanic cone, where in 1987 they built their resort in a beachside coconut grove on the western shore (expect gorgeous sunset views of Qamea and Taveuni). At first they catered to low-budget Australian divers, but as their business grew, their clientele shifted to a mix of diving and nondiving Americans, plus a few Australians and Europeans. For divers who bring their children, the Douglases send the grown-ups out in the boats for two morning dives, while the staff keeps the kids busy building sand castles on the shady beach. This arrangement makes Matangi one of the South Pacific's top family resorts. But by the same token, honeymooners can escape to 3 romantic bures 20 feet up in the air, one of them actually in a shady Pacific almond tree. These units all have outdoor showers. You can also be taken to the spectacular half-moon beach in aptly named Horseshoe Bay and be left alone for a secluded picnic. Other nondiving activities include hiking, kayaking, bird-watching, sailing, windsurfing, and sportfishing.

Except for the honeymoon bures, Matangi's bungalows are round, in the Polynesian-influenced style of eastern Fiji. Umbrella-like spokes radiating from hand-hewn central poles support reed-lined conical roofs. Reed dividers separate sitting areas with single-bed settees from sleeping areas to the rear of the units. Although somewhat small, their tiled shower-only bathrooms are adequate. One bure is equipped for disabled guests. There's a Phonecard unit outside the office.

P.O. Box 83, Waiyevo, Taveuni (Matagi Island, 20 min. by boat from Taveuni). *C* **888/MATANGI** or 888 0260. Fax 888 0274. www.matangiisland.com. 14 units. US$152–US$268 per person. Rates include all meals, non-alcoholic beverages, and all excursions and activities except scuba diving, water-skiing, and sportfishing. Family rates available. Round-trip transfers from Taveuni airport US$60 per person. AE, DC, MC, V. **Amenities:** 1 restaurant (regional); 2 bars; children's programs; watersports; limited room service; massage; babysitting; laundry service. *In room:* Minibar, coffeemaker, hair dryer, no phone.

Qamea Beach Club ★★★ *Value*   This is another property I regret having to list last, for American Jo Kloss has some of the most stunning bures and main building of any resort in Fiji, and the value for dollar here is excellent. In the proverbial lagoon-side coconut grove, this entire property shows remarkable attention to American-style comfort and Fijian detail. Qamea's centerpiece is a soaring, 16m (52-ft.) high priest's bure supported by two huge tree trunks. Rope made of coconut fiber and some well-disguised nuts and bolts hold the poles and sweeping thatch roof together. Orange light from kerosene lanterns hung high under the roof lends incredibly romantic charm at twilight. That's when you wash your bare feet in giant clamshells and sit on the surrounding veranda to sip cocktails and recap your days of scuba diving, snorkeling, visiting Fijian villages, trekking to Bouma Falls on Taveuni, or doing absolutely nothing except sleep in your own hammock.

You will relive the old South Seas days and nights in the most charming of all Fijian bures. If I were to build a set for a South Seas movie, it would feature these bungalows covered by a foot-thick Fijian thatch. Spacious and rectangular, each has an old-fashioned screen door that leads out to a porch that's complete with a hammock strung between two posts. Each bure is reed lined and large enough to swallow the king-size bed, two oversize bamboo sitting chairs, a coffee table, and several other pieces of island-style furniture exquisitely handcrafted by the staff. If you need more space, you can rent the split-level villa, which is twice the size of the regular bures, with a living room, separate bedroom, a huge bathroom with sunken shower, and a front porch with a lagoon view.

Gourmet-quality meals are served in the big central bure, as is silver-service afternoon tea. Three tables are set aside for honeymooners to dine in relative privacy. There is no children's menu because no kids under 13 are accepted here.

P.O. Matei, Taveuni (Qamea Island, 15 min. by boat from Taveuni). *C* **800/392-8213** or 888 0220. Fax 888 0092. www.qamea.com. 12 units. US$550–US$700 bungalow. Rates include meals, airport transfers, all activities except diving and sportfishing. AE, DC, MC, V. Children under 13 not accepted. **Amenities:** 1 restaurant (regional), 1 bar; outdoor pool; laundry service. *In room:* Minibar, coffeemaker, hair dryer, no phone.

12

Samoa

The scenic 31km (19-mile) drive from Faleolo Airport into the historic capital of Apia provides a fitting introduction to Samoa. Here in this cultural storehouse, which until 1997 was officially known as Western Samoa, the old Polynesian lifestyle known as *fa'a Samoa*—"The Samoan Way"—remains very much alive and well. On one side of the road lies an aquamarine lagoon; on the other, coconut plantations climb gentle slopes to the volcanic ridge along the middle of Upolu, the main island.

Along the shore sit hundreds of Samoan *fales* (houses), their big turtle-shaped roofs resting on poles, their sides open to the breeze and to the view of passersby. Their grass carefully trimmed and their borders marked with boulders painted white, expansive village lawns make the entire route seem like an unending park. Samoans wrapped in *lavalavas* shower under outdoor faucets and sit together in their fales. Only the dim glow of television screens coming from beneath tin roofs rather than thatch remind us that a century has passed since Robert Louis Stevenson lived, wrote, and died here in Samoa.

Even the town of Apia harkens back to those bygone South Seas days. While landfills have extended the shoreline, government high-rises now stand on the waterfront, and traffic lights blink at several corners, many old white clapboard buildings still sleep along Beach Road, just as they did when Stevenson stepped ashore here in 1889. Compared with the hustle and bustle of Papeete in French Polynesia, or with the congestion and tuna canneries of Pago Pago in nearby American Samoa, life in Apia is slow and easy.

If you go with an eye to exploring the culture as well as visiting some of the South Pacific's most beautiful and undeveloped beaches, Samoa will enchant you just as it did Stevenson, W. Somerset Maugham, and Margaret Mead, all of whom found plenty here to write home about.

Tips **Make This Your Base in the Samoas**

Although American ways have made a serious impact in neighboring American Samoa (see chapter 13), the people there share *fa'a Samoa* with their relatives here in Samoa. Much of the background information in this chapter, therefore, applies equally to both countries. American Samoa suffers a serious lack of accommodations, whereas Samoa is blessed with comfortable hotels and beach resorts. Even if you plan to visit American Samoa, I recommend that you stay here and treat American Samoa as a day trip from Apia.

1 Samoa Today

The Samoa Islands, which include the independent nation of Samoa and the territory of American Samoa, stretch for some 480km (300 miles) across the central South Pacific, some 2,000km (1,200 miles) west of Tahiti and 4,000km (2,600 miles) southwest of Hawaii. Samoa has the nine western islands; the others are in American Samoa.

Independent Samoa, which many people still call Western Samoa, much to the disgust of its citizens, has a land area of 2,800 sq. km. (1,090 square miles), two-thirds of which are on **Savai'i,** the largest Polynesian island outside Hawaii and New Zealand. A series of volcanoes on a line running roughly east to west formed **Upolu,** which is about 63km (39 miles) long and 21km (13 miles) wide, about the size of Tahiti. Although it's considerably smaller than Savai'i, 21km (13 miles) to the west, some 75% of Samoa's population lives on Upolu. On the other hand, Savai'i in many ways is the most "old Polynesia" of any island covered in this book; there are no towns there, and the villagers live very much by *fa'a Samoa.*

The tops of two small volcanoes, **Apolima** and **Manono** islands sit in the Apolima Strait between the two main islands. Locals like to claim that James A. Michener was inspired by Apolima and Manono to create the mysteriously romantic island of "Bali Ha'i" in his *Tales of the South Pacific.* Michener once said in a television interview, however, that he got the idea from a cloud-draped island off Espiritu Santo in Vanuatu, where he spent much of World War II.

GEOGRAPHY   With few exceptions, all of the Samoa Islands are high and volcanic, lush, and well watered. Geologically they are younger than the islands in French Polynesia—volcanoes on Savai'i erupted as recently as 1911. Consequently, the coral reefs fringing the islands have not had time to enclose deep lagoons, and the surf pounds directly on black volcanic rocks in many places. In other places in the Samoas there are small bays with some of the most picturesque beaches in the South Pacific.

GOVERNMENT   An independent nation since 1962, Samoa is ruled by a Parliament made up of 47 members, of whom 45 are *matais,* or chiefs. Only *matais* could vote for candidates for these seats until 1991, when universal suffrage was enacted. Part-Samoan and non-Samoan citizens elect the two non-*matai* members. There are two political parties: the Human Rights Protection party and the Christian Democratic party.

The titular head of state is Malietoa Tanumafili II, one of Samoa's four paramount chiefs and a descendant of the Malietoa who sided with the Germans in 1887–89 during the lead-up to Western Samoa's becoming a German colony in 1890 (see "History 101," below). Malietoa Tanumafili II, now in his 80s, will hold the job for the rest of his life. Under the constitution, Parliament will

---

Impressions

Imagine an island with the most perfect climate in the world, tropical yet almost always cooled by a breeze from the sea. No malaria or other fevers. No dangerous snakes or insects. Fish for the catching, and fruits for the plucking. And an earth and sky and sea of immortal loveliness. What more could civilization give?

—Rupert Brooke, 1914

choose his successor from among Samoa's four paramount chiefs. That person will serve not for life but for a term of 5 years.

ECONOMY   Samoa exports copra (dried coconut meat), coconut cream, kava, fresh fish, beer (try a German-style Vailima brew while you're here), and some fresh fruits and vegetables, primarily to the other South Pacific islands. There is some light manufacturing, including cigarettes and garments. The country's exclusive fishing zone is one of the smallest in the Pacific. Although there has been significant economic growth and development in recent years, mainly in and around Apia, foreign aid and remittances sent home by Samoans living in American Samoa or overseas keep the country out of bankruptcy.

As a consequence, Samoa's currency (the *tala*) remains seriously devalued. Local hotels, car-rental firms, and some tour operators quote their rates in U.S. dollars to avoid the "price shocks" if their prices were quoted in local currency. Although high by local standards, most prices here are among the lowest in the South Pacific for travelers using U.S. dollars.

A majority of the Samoan workforce is employed by the government. Even in those jobs, wages are so low that several thousand Samoans regularly live and work in the much more prosperous American Samoa.

2 History 101

Archaeologists believe that Polynesians from Southeast Asia settled in the Samoa Islands about 3,000 years ago. Their great migration halted here for some 1,000 years before voyagers went on to colonize the Marquesas, Society Islands, and other island groups farther east, in the great triangle known today as Polynesia. Thus the Samoas are known as the "Cradle of Polynesia."

The universe known by the early Samoans included Tonga and Fiji, to which they regularly journeyed, often waging war. Tongan invaders ruled the Samoas for some 300 years, between A.D. 950 and 1250.

The first European to see the Samoas was Dutchman Jacob Roggeveen, who in 1722 sighted the Manu'a Islands in what is now American Samoa. After visiting Tahiti in 1768, the Frenchman Antoine de Bougainville sailed through the Samoas and named them the Navigator Islands because of the natives he saw in canoes chasing tuna far offshore. The first Europeans to land in Samoa were part of a French expedition under Jean La Pérouse in 1787.

Dateline

- 3,000 B.C. Polynesians arrive from the west, settle the Samoa Islands.
- 2,000 B.C. Samoans venture south and west, colonize Tonga, the Marquesas, the Society Islands, and other island groups.
- A.D. 950 Tongans invade, conquer Samoans, and rule until 1250.
- 1722 Dutch explorer Jacob Roggeveen is the first European to sight the Samoa Islands.
- 1768 After finding Tahiti, de Bougainville sails through the Samoas but does not land; he names them the Navigator Islands.
- 1787 Thirty-nine Samoans and 12 members of a French exploring team under Jean La Pérouse are killed during a skirmish at Massacre Bay on Tutuila in American Samoa.
- 1830 Rev. John Williams lands the first missionaries at Leone on Tutuila, American Samoa. European-style settlements are soon established at Apia and Pago Pago.
- 1850s Germans start plantations on Upolu.
- 1872 The U.S. Navy negotiates a treaty with Tutuila chiefs for a U.S. coaling station at Pago Pago.

continues

They came ashore on the north coast of Tutuila in American Samoa and were promptly attacked by Samoan warriors. Twelve members of the landing party and 39 Samoans were killed during the skirmish.

To the Samoans, the great ships with their white sails seemed to have come through the slit that separated the sky from the sea, and they named the strange people sailing them *papalagi,* "sky busters." Shortened to *palagi,* the name now means any Westerner with white skin.

The Rev. John Williams, who roamed the South Pacific in *The Messenger of Peace,* discovering islands and preaching the Gospel, landed the first missionaries in Samoa in 1830. Shortly afterward came traders—including John Williams Jr., the missionary's son. European-style settlements soon grew up at Apia on Upolu and on the shores of Pago Pago Bay on Tutuila. By the late 1850s German businessmen had established large copra plantations on Upolu. When steamships started plying the route between San Francisco and Sydney in the 1870s, American businessmen cast an eye on Pago Pago. The U.S. Navy negotiated a treaty with the chiefs of Tutuila in 1872 to permit the United States to use Pago Pago as a coaling station. The U.S. Congress never ratified this document, but it served to keep the Germans from penetrating into Eastern Samoa, as present-day American Samoa was then known.

THE GERMANS TAKE OVER

Germans, Brits, and Americans jockeyed for position among the rival Samoan chiefs on Upolu, with the Germans gaining the upper hand over today's independent Samoa when they staged a coup in 1887, backed up (unofficially) by German naval gunboats. They governed through Malietoa, one of the islands' four paramount chiefs, who had thrown in

- 1887 German residents on Upolu stage a coup, set off an argument between the United States Britain, and Germany.
- 1888 Ousted chief Mataafa leads bloody rebellion at Apia but loses to German-backed chief Malietoa.
- 1889 Warships arrive at Apia to back claims of Western powers; hurricane sinks four, drives two aground, kills 146 sailors. Treaty of Berlin is negotiated and signed. Robert Louis Stevenson settles in Apia.
- 1890 Treaty goes into effect, giving Samoa to Germany, Eastern Samoa to the United States, free hand in Tonga to Britain.
- 1894 Robert Louis Stevenson dies at Vailima, his home above Apia, and is buried at the end of the "Road of the Loving Hearts."
- 1900 Germany officially establishes the colony of Samoa and raises its flag at Apia. The United States negotiates a treaty with Tutuila chiefs to cede their island; the U.S. flag is raised at Pago Pago.
- 1905 The chief of Manu'a finally cedes his islands to the United States, completing American possession of Eastern Samoa.
- 1914 A New Zealand expeditionary force seizes Samoa from Germany at the outbreak of World War I and confiscates German lands.
- 1920 The League of Nations establishes New Zealand trusteeship over Samoa.
- 1929 New Zealand constables put down Mau rebellion, killing nine Samoans. U.S. Senate ratifies treaties of 1900 and 1905, turning Eastern Samoa over to the United States.
- 1942–45 Allied troops use both Samoas as training bases for World War II battles in the central and southwestern Pacific. Aggie Grey starts her hot dog and hamburger business in Apia.
- 1949 New Zealand creates a local legislative assembly in Apia and grants Samoa limited internal self-government.
- 1951 U.S. government transfers administration of American Samoa

continues

his lot with them. One of his rivals, Mataafa, lost a bloody rebellion in 1888, during which heads were taken in Samoan style. Mataafa was subsequently exiled to the German Marshall Islands.

Continuing unrest turned into a major international incident—fiasco is a better word—when the United States, Britain, and Germany all sent warships to Apia. Seven vessels arrived, anchored in the small and relatively unprotected harbor, and proceeded to stare down each other's gun barrels. It was March 16, 1889, near the end of the hurricane season. When one of the monster storms blew up unexpectedly, only the captain of the British warship *Calliope* got his ship under way. It was the sole vessel to escape. In all, four ships were sunk, two others were washed ashore, and 146 lives were lost, despite heroic efforts by the Samoans on Upolu, who stopped their feuding long enough to pull the survivors through the roaring surf. Of the three American warships present, the *Trenton* and the *Vandalia* were sunk, and the *Nipsic* was beached. Another beached ship, the Germans' *Adler*, rested half exposed until the reef was covered by landfill 70 years later. (A newspaper story of the time is mounted in the lounge of Aggie Grey's Hotel in Apia.)

- from the navy to the Department of the Interior.
- **1960** The Samoas vote for independence, draft a constitution.
- **1961** *Reader's Digest* criticizes American Samoa as "America's Shame in the South Seas." U.S. aid starts flowing to Pago Pago.
- **1962** Samoa becomes the first South Pacific colony to gain independence.
- **1977** American Samoans choose first locally elected governor.
- **1990** The first of two hurricanes devastate crops, destroy roads.
- **1991** A second hurricane hits; universal suffrage comes to Samoa after 30 years of only chiefs voting for Parliament.
- **1997** Nation's name changed from Western Samoa to Samoa.
- **1999** Government changes policy, encourages economic development; small building boom commences in Apia.

Cooler heads prevailed after the disaster, and in December 1889 an agreement was signed in Berlin. Germany was given what is today Samoa. The United States was handed the seven islands to the east, in what is now American Samoa. And Britain was left to do what it pleased in Tonga (it created a protectorate). After many years of turmoil, the two Samoas were split apart and swept into the colonial system.

The German flag was raised in Apia on March 1, 1900, after which several stern governors sent more of Mataafa's followers and other resisters into exile. Malietoa remained as the chosen chief, and the Germans residing in Samoa proceeded to make fortunes from their huge, orderly copra plantations.

A KIWI BACKWATER   German rule came to an abrupt end with the outbreak of World War I in 1914, when New Zealand sent an expeditionary force to Apia and the German governor surrendered without a fight. The Germans in Samoa were interned for the duration of the war, and their huge land holdings were confiscated. The plantations are still owned by the Samoa Trust Estates Corporation (STEC), a government body whose name you see all over the country.

New Zealand remained in charge until 1962, first as warlord, then after World War I as trustee, initially under the League of Nations and then under the United Nations. The New Zealand administrators did relatively little in the islands except keep the lid on unrest, at which they were generally successful. In 1929, however, the Mau Movement under Tupua Tamasese Lealofi III created an uprising. The movement was crushed when the New Zealand constables fired

The Teller of Tales

The salvage crews were still working on the hulks of the British, American, and German warships sunk in Apia's harbor by a hurricane in 1889 when a thin, tubercular writer arrived from Scotland.

Not yet 40 years old, Robert Louis Stevenson was already famous—and wealthy—for such novels as *Treasure Island* and *Dr. Jekyll and Mr. Hyde*. He arrived in Samoa after traveling across the United States and a good part of the South Pacific, in search of a climate more suitable to his ravaged lungs. With him were his wife, Fanny (an American divorcée 11 years his senior), his stepmother, and his stepson. His mother joined them later.

Stevenson intended to remain in Apia for only a few weeks while he caught up on a series of newspaper columns he was writing. He and his entourage stayed to build a mansion known as Vailima on the slopes of Mount Vaea, overlooking Apia, where he lived lavishly and wrote more than 750,000 published words. He learned the Samoan language and translated "The Bottle Imp," his story about a genie, into it. It was the first work of fiction translated into Samoan.

Stevenson loved Samoa, and the Samoans loved him. Great orators and storytellers in their own right, they called him *Tusitala*, the "Teller of Tales."

On December 3, 1894, almost 5 years to the day after he arrived in Apia, Stevenson was writing a story about a son who had escaped a death sentence handed down by his own father and had sailed away to join his lover. Leaving the couple embraced, Stevenson stopped to answer letters, play some cards, and fix dinner. While preparing mayonnaise on his back porch, he suddenly clasped his hands to his head and collapsed. He died not of tuberculosis but of a cerebral hemorrhage.

More than 200 grieving Samoans hacked a "Road of the Loving Hearts" up Mount Vaea to a little knoll below the summit, where they placed him in a grave with a perpetual view overlooking Vailima, the mountains, the town, the reef, and the sea he loved. Carved on his grave is his famous requiem:

> *This be the verse you grave for me:*
> *Here he lies where he longed to be;*
> *Home is the sailor, home from the sea,*
> *And the hunter home from the hill.*

on Tamasese and a crowd of his followers gathered outside the government building in Apia, killing him and eight others.

Twenty years later, after opposition to colonialism flared up in the United Nations, a Legislative Assembly of *matais* was established to exercise a limited degree of internal self-government. A constitution was drafted in 1960, and the people approved it and their own independence a year later by referendum (the only time until 1991 that all Samoans could vote). On January 1, 1962, Samoa became the first South Pacific colony to regain its independence from the Western powers.

The new nation was known as Western Samoa until 1997, when its citizens voted to change its name to simply Samoa. In doing so, they expressed their pride in being Samoan, ridded themselves of a last vestige of colonialism, and distinguished themselves from their American Samoan cousins, who immediately took offense that their independent relatives were usurping the name of their islands. Many Samoans bristle at the fact that the international telephone companies still say they live in Western Samoa. So don't go around telling everyone how much you like it here in "Western Samoa."

For most of its life as a colony and trusteeship territory, Samoa remained in the backwaters of the South Pacific. Only during World War II did it appear on the world stage, and then solely as a training base for thousands of Allied servicemen on their way to fight the Japanese in the islands farther west and north. Tourism increased after the big jets started landing at Pago Pago in the early 1960s, but significant numbers of visitors started arriving only after Faleolo Airport was upgraded to handle large aircraft in the 1980s.

3 The Samoan People

About 174,000 people live in independent Samoa, the vast majority of them full-blooded Samoans. They are the second-largest group of pure Polynesians in the world, behind only the Maoris of New Zealand.

Although divided politically in their home islands, the people of both Samoas share the same culture, heritage, and, in many cases, family lineage. Despite the inroads that Western influences have made—especially in American Samoa—they are a proud people who fiercely protect their old ways.

"Catch the bird but watch for the wave" is an old Samoan proverb that expresses the basically cautious approach followed in the islands. This conservative attitude is perhaps responsible for the extraordinary degree to which Samoans have preserved *fa'a Samoa* while adapting it to the modern world. Even in American Samoa, where most of the old turtle-shaped thatch fales have been replaced with structures of plywood and tin, the firmament of the Samoan way lies just under the trappings of the territory's commercialized surface.

The showing of respect permeates Samoans' lives. They are by tradition extremely polite to guests, so much so that some of them tend to answer in the affirmative all questions posed by a stranger. The Samoans are not lying when they answer wrongly; they are merely being polite. Therefore, visitors who really need information should avoid asking questions that call for a yes or no answer.

THE *AIGA*

The foundation of Samoan society is the extended family unit, or *aiga* (pronounced "ah-*eeng*-ah"). Unlike the Western nuclear family, an *aiga* can include thousands of relatives and in-laws. In this basically communal system, everything is owned collectively by the *aiga;* that is, the individual has a right to use that property but does not personally own it. As stated in a briefing paper

---

(*Tips*   **Keep an Eye on Your Camera**

As is the case throughout the South Pacific islands, traditional Samoan custom is at odds with Western concepts of property ownership. You may notice the difference directly when a camera or other item left unattended suddenly disappears.

Tips How to Drink Kava

During a Samoan kava ceremony, coconut shells are scooped into a large wooden bowl of the gray liquid, which looks like mud and tastes like sawdust. The host passes a cup to one person at a time. When you get yours, hold the cup straight out with both hands, and say *"Manuia"* ("Good health") before gulping most of it down in one swallow. Save a little to toss on the floor mats before handing the cup back to your host.

---

prepared for the government of American Samoa by the Pacific Basin Development Council, "the [Samoan] attitude toward property is: if you need something which you don't have, there is always someone else who has what you need."

At the head of each of more than 10,000 *aigas* is a *matai* ("mah-tie"), a chief who is responsible for the welfare of each member of the clan. The *matai* settles family disputes, parcels out the family's land, and sees that everyone has enough to eat and a roof over his or her head. Although the title *matai* usually follows bloodlines, the family can choose another person—man or woman—if the incumbent proves incapable of handling the job.

Strictly speaking, Samoans turn all money they earn over to their *matai,* to be used in the best interest of the entire clan. The system is being threatened, however, as more and more young Samoans move to the United States or New Zealand, earn wages in their own right, and spend them as they see fit. Nevertheless, the system is still remarkably intact in both Samoas. Even in Samoan outposts in Hawaii, California, Texas, and Auckland (which collectively have a larger Samoan population than do the islands), the people still rally around their *aiga,* and *matais* play an important role in daily life.

Land ownership is a touchy subject here. About 11% of the land here is freehold, which Samoan citizens can buy and sell. Non-Samoans can lease freehold and communal property, but they cannot buy it.

ORGANIZATION & RITUAL

Above the *aiga,* Samoan life is ruled by a hierarchy of *matais* known in English as high talking chiefs, high chiefs, and paramount chiefs, in ascending order of importance. The high talking chiefs do just that: talk on behalf of the high chiefs, usually expressing themselves in great oratorical flourishes in a formal version of Samoan reserved for use among the chiefs. The high chiefs are senior *matais* at the village or district level, and the paramount chiefs can rule over entire island groups. The chiefly symbol, worn over the shoulder, is a short broom that resembles a horse's tail.

The conduct and relations between chiefs are governed by strict rules of protocol. Nowhere is ritual more obvious or observed than during a kava (pronounced *'ava* in Samoan) ceremony. The slightly narcotic kava brew is made by crushing the roots of the pepper plant *Piper methysticum* (see "A Bowl of Grog" in chapter 9). In the old days the roots were chewed and spit into the bowl by the virgin daughter of a chief. That method of kava preparation has disappeared in the face of modern notions of disease control.

MISSIONARIES & MINISTERS

Like other Polynesians, the Samoans in pre-European days worshiped a hierarchy of gods under one supreme being, whom they called Le Tagaloa. When the

---

Tips **Wonderful Harmony**

Even if you can't understand the sermon, the sound of Samoans singing hymns in harmony makes going to church here a rewarding experience.

London Missionary Society's Rev. John Williams arrived in 1830, he found the Samoans willing to convert to the Christian God. He and his Tahitian teachers brought a strict, puritanical version of Christianity. His legacy can be seen both in the large white churches that dominate every settlement in all the Samoa Islands and in the fervor with which the Samoans practice religion today.

The majority of Samoans are members of the Congregational Christian Church, a Protestant denomination that grew out of the London Missionary Society's work. Independent Samoa almost closes down on Sunday, and things come to a crawl on the Sabbath even in more Westernized American Samoa. Swimming on Sunday is tolerated in both countries only at the hotels and, after church, at beaches frequented by overseas visitors.

Christianity has become an integral part of *fa'a Samoa,* and every day at about 6:30pm each village observes *sa,* 10 minutes of devotional time during which everyone goes inside to pray, read Scripture, and perhaps sing hymns. A gong (usually an empty acetylene tank hung from a tree) is struck once to announce it's time to get ready, a second time to announce the beginning of *sa,* and a third time to announce that all's clear. It is permissible to drive on the main road during *sa,* but it's not all right to turn off into a village or to walk around.

MISS MEAD STUDIES SAMOAN SEX

Despite their ready acceptance of much of the missionaries' teaching, the Samoans no more took to heart their puritanical sexual mores than did any other group of Polynesians. In 1928 anthropologist Margaret Mead published her famous *Coming of Age in Samoa,* which was based on her research in American Samoa. She described the Samoans as a peaceable people who showed no guilt in connection with ample sex during adolescence, a view that was in keeping with practices of Polynesian societies elsewhere. Some 55 years later, New Zealand anthropologist Derek Freeman published *Margaret Mead and Samoa: The Making and Unmaking of an Anthropological Myth,* in which he took issue with Mead's conclusions and argued instead that Samoans are jealous, violent, and not above committing rape. The truth may lie somewhere in between.

The Samoans share with other Polynesians the practice of raising some boys as girls, especially in families short of household help. These young boys dress as girls, do a girl's chores around the home, and often grow up to be transvestites. They are known in Samoan as *fa'afafines.*

RULES OF CONDUCT

You should be aware of several customs of this conservative society. A briefing paper prepared by the Pacific Basin Development Council for the American Samoan Office of Tourism gives some guidelines that may be helpful:

- In a Samoan home, don't talk to people while standing, and don't eat while walking around a village.
- Avoid stretching your legs straight out in front of you while sitting. If you can't fold them beneath you, then pull one of the floor mats over them.

Tips   Don't Wear Skimpy Clothing

Don't wear bathing suits, short shorts, halter tops, or other skimpy clothing away from the beach or hotel pool. Although shorts of respectable
length are worn by an increasing number of young Samoan men and
women in Apia and Pago Pago, it is considered very bad form for a
Samoan to display his or her traditional tattoos, which cover many of
them from knee to waist. Even though Samoan women went bare-
breasted before the coming of Christianity, going topless is definitely forbidden today. Traditional Samoan dress is a wraparound *lavalava* (sarong)
that reaches below the knee on men and to the ankles on women.

- If you are driving through a village and spot a group of middle-aged or
elderly men sitting around a fale with their legs folded, it's probably a gathering of *matais* to discuss business. It's polite not to drive past the meeting
place. If going past on foot, don't carry a load on your shoulders or an open
umbrella (even if several of Pago Pago's 500 centimeters (200 in.) of annual
rainfall are pouring on you).
- If you arrive at a Samoan home during a prayer session, wait outside until
the family is finished with its devotions. If you are already inside, you will
be expected to share in the service. If you go to church, don't wear flowers.
- If you are invited to participate in a kava ceremony, hold the cup out in front
of you, spill a few drops on the mat, say "Manuia," and take a sip. In Samoa
you do not bolt down the entire cup in one gulp as you would in Fiji; instead,
you save a little to pour on the floor before handing back the empty cup. And
remember, this is a solemn occasion—not a few rounds at the local bar.
- Whenever possible, consult Samoans about appropriate behavior and practices. They will appreciate your interest in *fa'a Samoa* and will take great
pleasure in explaining their unique way of life.

Finally, should you be invited to stay overnight in a Samoan home, let them
know at the beginning how long you will stay. Upon leaving, it's customary to
give a small gift known as a *mea alofa*. This can be money—between $5 and $10
a day per person—but make sure your hosts understand that it is a gift, not a
payment.

Most Samoan villages charge small "custom fees" to visitors who want to use
their beaches or swim under their waterfalls. These usually are a dollar or two
and are paid by local residents from other villages as well as by tourists.

In all cases, remember that almost everything and every place in the Samoas
is owned by an *aiga*, and it's polite to ask permission of the nearby *matai* before
crossing the property, using the beach, or visiting the waterfall. They will appreciate your courtesy in doing so.

4 The Samoan Language

Although English is an official language in both Samoa and American Samoa and
is widely spoken, Samoan shares equal billing and is used by most people for
everyday conversation. It is a Polynesian language that's somewhat similar to
Tahitian, Tongan, and Cook Islands Maori, but with some important differences.

The vowels are pronounced not as in English (*ay, ee, eye, oh,* and *you*) but in
the Roman fashion: *ah, ay, ee, oh,* and *oo* (as in kanga*roo*). All vowels are

sounded, even if several of them appear next to each other. The village of Nu'u-uli in American Samoa, for example, is pronounced "New-u-u-lee." The apostrophe that appears between the vowels indicates a glottal stop—a slight pause similar to the tiny break between "Oh-oh!" in English. The consonants *f, g, l, m, n, p, s, t,* and *v* are pronounced as in English, with one major exception: The letter *g* is pronounced like "ng." Therefore, *aiga* is pronounced "ah-eeng-ah." Pago Pago is pronounced "Pango Pango" as in "pong."

Here are some words that may help you win friends and influence your hosts:

English	Samoan	Pronunciation
hello	**talofa**	tah-*low*-fah
welcome	**afio mai**	ah-*fee*-oh my
good-bye	**tofa**	tow-*fah*
good health	**manuia**	mah-*new*-yah
please	**fa'amolemole**	fah-ah-*moly*-moly
man	**tamaloa**	tah-mah-*low*-ah
woman	**fafine**	fah-*fini*
transvestite	**fa'afafine**	fah-fah-*fini*
thank you	**fa'afetai**	fah-*fee*-tie
kava bowl	**tanoa**	tah-*no*-ah
good	**lelei**	lay-*lay*
bad	**leaga**	lay-*ang*-ah
happy/feast	**fiafia**	fee-ah-*fee*-ah
house	**fale**	fah-*lay*
wraparound skirt	**lavalava**	lava-lava
dollar	**tala**	tah-*lah*
cent	**sene**	say-nay
high chief	**ali'i**	ah-*lee*-ee
small island	**motu**	mo-*too*
white person	**palagi**	pah-*lahng*-ee

Many words in Samoan—as in most modern Polynesian languages—have European roots. Take the word for corned beef, *pisupo* ("pee-*soo*-poh"). The first Western canned food to reach Samoa was pea soup. *Pisupo,* the Samoan version of pea soup, was adopted as the word for corned beef, which also came in cans. It was and still is much more popular than pea soup.

5 Visitor Information & Entry Requirements

VISITOR INFORMATION

The friendly staff of the **Samoa Visitors Bureau,** P.O. Box 2272, Apia, Samoa (© **63-500;** fax 20-886; www.visitsamoa.ws), have free brochures, maps, and other publications available at their office in a handsome Samoan fale on the harbor side of Beach Road, east of the Town Clock. The bureau is open Monday through Friday from 8am to noon and from 1 to 4:30pm, Saturday from 8am to 12:30pm.

The visitors bureau has offices in:

- **Australia:** P. O. Box 361, Minto Mall, Minto, NSW 2566 (© **02/9324-5050;** fax 02/9824-5678; samoa@ozemail.com.au)

- **Germany:** Franziskanerstr. 15, 81669 Muenchen (© **89/746625-10;** fax 89/746625-910; samoa@kiwitours.com)
- **New Zealand:** Level 1, Samoa House, 283 Karangahape Rd. (P.O. Box 68423), Newton, Auckland (© **09/379-6138;** fax 09/379-8154; samoa@samoa.co.nz)

The bell captain's desk at **Aggie Grey's Hotel** (see "Where to Stay on Upolu," below) also has brochures and other information.

ENTRY REQUIREMENTS

No **visa** or entry permit is required for visitors who intend to stay 30 days or less and who have a valid passport, a return or ongoing airline ticket, and a place to stay in Samoa. As a practical matter, however, your passport will be stamped for the length of stay you request, up to 30 days or the date of your flight out, whichever is earlier. Those who want to stay longer must apply, before arrival, to the Immigration Office, Government of Samoa, P.O. Box 1861, Apia, Samoa (© **20-291**).

Vaccinations are not necessary unless you're arriving within 6 days of being in an infected area.

Customs exemptions for visitors are 200 cigarettes, 1 liter of liquor, and their personal effects. Firearms, ammunition, illegal drugs, and indecent publications are prohibited. Plants, live animals, or products of that nature, including fruits, seeds, and soil, will be confiscated unless you have obtained prior permission from the Samoa government's Department of Agriculture and Forest.

6 Money

Samoa uses the *tala* (the Samoans' way of saying "dollar"), which is broken down into 100 *sene* ("cents"). Although most people will refer to them as dollars and cents when speaking to visitors, you can avoid potential confusion by making sure they mean dollars and not *talas*. The official abbreviation for the currency is SAT, but I have used **S$** in this chapter. Samoa's major hotels and most car-rental firms quote prices in U.S. dollars. Their U.S. dollar prices are given in this chapter as **US$**.

At press time the **exchange rate** was about S$3.50 for each US$1 (that is, S$1 equaled US28¢). The rate is not published in major newspapers, but you can find it on currency conversion sites such as **www.xe.com**.

HOW TO GET LOCAL CURRENCY   ANZ Bank, Pacific Commercial Bank, and **National Bank of Samoa** have offices on Beach Road in Apia. ANZ Bank has an ATM. Banking hours are Monday to Wednesday from 9am to 3pm, Thursday and Friday from 8:30am to 3pm. National Bank of Samoa's small agency near the new market also is open Saturday from 8:30am to noon. No bank fees are charged to exchange foreign currency or traveler's checks, but you will have a few *seni* deducted for stamp tax. The banks also have offices in the

---

Tips Get Rid of Your *Talas*

Since the Samoan *tala* is worthless outside the independent nation of Samoa (and that includes American Samoa), you won't be able to buy any before arriving here. Remember, too, to change your *talas* back to another currency before leaving Samoa. You can change them at the airports.

The Tala & U.S. Dollar

At this writing, S$1 = approximately US28¢ (or US$1 = approximately S$3.50), the rate of exchange used to calculate the U.S. dollar prices given in this chapter. This rate may change by the time you visit, so use the following table only as a guide:

S$	US$	S$	US$
.25	.07	15.00	4.20
.50	.14	20.00	5.60
.75	.21	25.00	7.00
1.00	.28	30.00	8.40
2.00	.56	35.00	9.80
3.00	.84	40.00	11.20
4.00	1.12	45.00	12.60
5.00	1.40	50.00	14.00
6.00	1.68	75.00	21.00
7.00	1.96	100.00	28.00
8.00	2.24	125.00	35.00
9.00	2.52	150.00	42.00
10.00	2.80	200.00	56.00

baggage claim area at Faleolo Airport, which are open when international flights arrive and depart.

CREDIT CARDS   American Express, Visa, MasterCard, and Diner's Club credit cards are accepted by the major hotels and car-rental firms, and many restaurants accept MasterCard and Visa. Discover cards are not accepted. When traveling outside Apia and to Savai'i, you should carry enough cash to cover your anticipated expenses.

7 When to Go

THE CLIMATE

The Samoas enjoy a humid tropical climate, with lots of very intense sunshine, even during the wet season (Dec–May). Average daily high temperatures range from 83°F (28°C) in the drier and somewhat cooler months of June through September to 86°F (30°C) from December to April, when midday can be hot and sticky. Evenings are usually in the comfortable 70s (21°C–26°C) all year-round.

EVENTS

Duffers from around the South Pacific descend on Apia in early January for the **Head of State's Birthday Golf Tournament.** The **Arts and Crafts Fair** during the third week in March is dedicated to reviving the ancient handcrafts. **Easter Week** sees various religious observances, including hymn singing and dramas. **Independence Day** 🌺🌺 in early June is the biggest event here, featuring dances, outrigger-canoe races, marching competitions, and horse racing. The **Teuila Tourism Festival** during the first week of September involves a variety of entertainment, including canoe races, dance competitions, and traditional games. The **Miss Samoa Pageant** in early September crowns the country's top beauty.

Impressions

Day after day the sun flamed; night after night the moon beaconed, or the stars paraded their lustrous regimen. I was aware of a spiritual change, or perhaps rather a molecular reconstitution. My bones were sweeter to me. I had come home to my own climate, and looked back with pity on those damp and wintry zones, miscalled the temperate. . . . I am browner than the berry: only my trunk and the aristocratic spot on which I sit retain the vile whiteness of the north.

—Robert Louis Stevenson, 1891

The second Sunday in October is observed as **White Sunday,** during which children go to church dressed in white, lead the services, and are honored at family feasts. **Christmas week** is celebrated with great gusto.

Late October or early November see hundreds if not thousands of Samoans out on the reefs with lanterns and nets to snare the wiggly *palolo,* a coral worm that comes out to mate on the seventh day after the full moon. *Palolo* are considered by Pacific islanders to be the caviar of their region.

The **Samoa Visitors Bureau** posts the precise dates and the schedules for these events on its website, **www.visitsamoa.ws**.

HOLIDAYS

Offices and schools are closed both January 1 and January 2 for New Year's; Good Friday and Easter Monday; April 25 as Anzac Day, to remember those who died in the two World Wars; the Monday after the second Sunday in May as Mothers' Day of Samoa; June 1 through June 3, for the annual Independence Celebrations; the first Friday in August as Labour Day; the Monday after the second Sunday in October, in honor of the preceding White Sunday; the first Friday in November as Arbor Day, to encourage the planting of trees and appreciation of conservation; Christmas Day; and December 26 as Boxing Day.

8 Getting There & Getting Around

GETTING THERE

Air New Zealand has nonstop flights between Los Angeles and Apia. It also has service from Auckland, with a brief stop in Tonga. **Polynesian Airlines** connects the country with Honolulu, Sydney, Melbourne, Auckland, Wellington, Nadi, and Tonga. **Air Pacific** has service between Apia and Fiji. See "Getting There & Getting Around" in chapter 2 for details.

A less desirable way to get to Apia is on **Hawaiian Airlines,** which flies between several West Coast cities and Honolulu, thence to Pago Pago in American Samoa. Connections to Samoa can then be made on **Polynesian Airlines** or **Samoa Air** (© 22-321 in Apia, or 633-4331 in American Samoa; www.samoaair.com). **Samoa Air** also flies nonstop between Pago Pago and Maota Airstrip on Savai'i.

Flights into and out of the Samoas are often packed with Samoans leaving and returning to the islands, so reserve a seat as soon as possible.

ARRIVING

Unless you're coming from Pago Pago, your flight will arrive at **Faleolo Airport,** on the northwest corner of Upolu about 32km (19 miles) from Apia. **Fagali'i**

Airport near Apia is used only for flights between Samoa and Pago Pago and between Apia and Savai'i.

There are duty-free shops and two currency exchange windows in the baggage claim area at Faleolo Airport, so you can shop and change money while waiting for your luggage. Once you've cleared Customs, you can use ANZ Bank's ATM in the main concourse. There's a currency exchange window and a small duty-free shop at Fagali'i.

Transportation from the Faleolo Airport is by taxi or by a relatively small Polynesian Airlines bus that meets all international flights (you will be astounded by how many passengers and their baggage can be crammed into one of these vehicles). The bus ride costs S$10 ($2.80) each way. The government-regulated taxi fare into town is S$35 ($10).

Transportation from Fagali'i Airstrip is by taxi only. The fare into downtown Apia is S$5 ($1.40).

The airline buses also transport passengers from the Apia hotels to Faleolo Airport for departing international flights. They arrive at the hotels at least 2 hours before departure time. Be sure to tell your hotel what flight you are leaving on; otherwise, the bus could leave you behind.

When leaving the country, get your boarding pass and then pay S$30 ($8.40) **departure tax** at one of the banks in the main concourses at Faleolo and Fagali'i airports.

There is no bank in the departure lounges of either airport, so change your leftover talas before clearing Immigration. Remember, Samoan currency cannot be exchanged outside the country, even in American Samoa.

GETTING AROUND
BY PLANE
Polynesian Airlines (© 800/264-0823 or 22-737; www.polynesianairlines.com) flies several times a day between Fagali'i Airstrip near Apia and Maota Airstrip, near Salelologa on the southeast corner of Savai'i, less frequently between Faleolo and Maota. The round-trip Fagali'I–Savai'i fares is about S$67 ($19).

BY FERRY
The *Lady Samoa,* a passenger and automobile ferry, operates three times daily between Mulifanua Wharf on Upolu and Salelologa on Savai'i. The one-way fare is S$7 ($2). Local buses leave regularly from the Apia market and pass Mulifanua Wharf on their way to Pasi O Le Vaa. Taxi fare to the wharf is S$40 ($11.25); bus fare is S$2 (55¢). For more information, ask at the visitors bureau or contact the **Samoa Shipping Corporation** (© 20-935), on Beach Road opposite the main wharf.

BY RENTAL CAR
The car-rental firms will arrange to pick you up at the airport if you have reservations. Most of them quote their rates in U.S. dollars and accept American Express, Diner's Club, MasterCard, and Visa credit cards. Insurance policies do not cover damage to the vehicles' undercarriages, which may occur on some rocky, unpaved roads. Depending on your own insurance policies, you might also want to buy optional personal accident coverage, which covers you and your passengers.

The main roads on both islands are paved and in good condition, but none of Apia's car-rental firms will allow you to drive on unpaved roads or take a rented vehicle on the ferry to Savai'i. Don't count on buying gasoline outside Apia.

The Samoa Islands

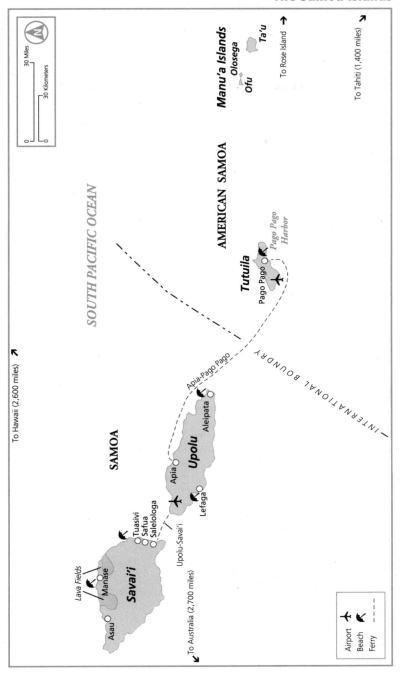

Tips **Watch Out for Dogs, Chickens & Pigs**

Samoans and their dogs, chickens, and pigs have a habit of walking in the middle of the roads that pass through their villages, so proceed with care when driving here. Even if the way is clear, local courtesy dictates that you slow down when going through the villages so as not to kick up a lot of dust. Special care is required on Sundays, when Samoans usually lounge around the village after going to church.

The largest and best rental firm here is **Funway Rentals,** which has a modern depot on Beach Road opposite the main wharf (© **22-045;** fax 25-008; funwayrentals@samoa.ws). It rents Suzuki four-wheel-drive vehicles starting at S$110 ($31) a day, plus S$20 ($5.60) per day for insurance. MasterCard and Visa credit cards are accepted.

Both **Budget Rent-A-Car** (© **800/527-0700** or 20-561; hhtps://rent.drive budget.com) and **Avis** (© **800/831-2847** or 20-486; www.avis.com) have agencies here. Avis also has an agency in American Samoa and will reserve a car for you in Pago Pago, but give them a day's notice.

DRIVING RULES You **drive on the right-hand side of the road.** You must stop for pedestrians in crosswalks and not exceed the speed limits of 35 mph on the open road or 25 mph in Apia and the villages.

Visitors are technically required to get a local **driver's license** from the police department traffic office on Ifi'ifi Street. You neglect this cumbersome procedure at your own risk; that having been said, I've never bothered to get one, nor do I know anyone who has. The car-rental firms will ask to see your home driver's license.

BY BUS

Samoa has a system of "*aiga* buses" (similar to those in American Samoa), most of which have wooden passenger compartments built on the back of flatbed trucks. The main **bus station** is behind the Old Apia Market on Beach Road, but the buses stop at the New Market before leaving town. They have the names of their villages written on the front. The first buses usually leave their villages between 5 and 7am, with the last departure between 2 and 2:30pm. They turn around in Apia and go back to the villages. The last departure from town is about 4:30pm. They do not run on Saturday afternoon or Sunday. The buses are always crowded.

The Samoa Visitors Bureau has the schedules and fares. Here are the destinations most often visited, followed by the names of the village buses that go there:

To Robert Louis Stevenson Museum: Vaoala, Si'umu.
To Sinalei and Coconut Beach resorts: Si'umu.
To Fagali'i Airport: Fagali'i-uta.
To Piula Cave Pool: Falefa or Saoluafata.
To Return to Paradise Beach: Lefaga.
To Papase'a Sliding Rocks: Se'ese'e.
To Faleolo Airport: Faleolo, Pasi o le Vaa.
To Muliafanua Wharf: Pasi o le Vaa.

The Si'umu bus is the only one that goes all the way to the south coast via the Cross Island Road.

In general, 50 sene (17¢) will take you around Apia and into the hills above the town. The maximum fare is about S$4 ($1.12) to the most distant villages and to Mulifanua Wharf, where the Savai'i ferries land on Upolu's western end (see "Savai'i," later in this chapter).

BY TAXI

Central Taxi (*(C)* 23-600), **Silver Star Taxis** (*(C)* 21-770), **Marlboro Taxis** (*(C)* 20-808), **Vailima Taxis** (*(C)* 22-380), **Heini Taxis** (*(C)* 24-431), and **Town Taxis** (*(C)* 21-600) all provide taxi service in Apia. They have stands at the Town Clock on Beach Road and nearby on Vaea Street. **Town Taxis** also has a stand at the airport.

The cabs do not have meters, but **fares** are set by the government. A pamphlet listing them is available at the visitors bureau and at the Ministry of Transport. In general, S$2 (55¢) will take you around Apia and its hotels. One-way fares are S$5 ($1.40) from Apia to Vailima; S$5 ($1.40) to Fagali'i Airstrip; S$35 ($10) to Faleolo Airport; S$35 ($10) to Coconuts Beach Club & Resort; S$45 ($12.60) to Lefaga and Return to Paradise Beach; and S$25 ($7) to Piula College and Cave Pool.

 FAST FACTS: **Samoa**

American Express There is no American Express representative in Samoa.

Babysitters Your hotel can arrange for qualified a babysitter.

Baggage Storage The hotels will store your extra gear for free.

Bookstores **Aggie's Gift Shop** (*(C)* 22-880), next to Aggie Grey's Hotel on Beach Road, carries books on Samoa and the South Pacific and a few paperback novels. **Le Moana Cafe** (*(C)* 24-828), in the Lotemau Centre at Vaea and Convent streets, has the latest editions of *Time* and *Newsweek,* the latter in *The Bulletin.*

Business Hours Most shops and government offices are open Monday to Friday from 8am to noon and 1:30 to 4:30pm, Saturday from 8am to noon. Except for the major hotels, the only businesses open on Sunday are the scores of mom-and-pop grocery shops in Apia and some villages.

Camera/Film **Photomart Camerahouse**, in the first block of Vaea Street off Beach Road (*(C)* 22-868), carries a wide range of color print film and has 1-hour processing.

Clothing Lightweight, informal summer clothing is best throughout the year, although a light sweater or wrap could come in handy for evening wear from June through September. Men can wear shorts and shirts almost anywhere, but women should stick to modest, knee- and shoulder-covering dresses away from the hotels and should never wear bathing suits or skimpy clothing away from the beach or pool. Topless or nude bathing is outlawed. Outside Apia most Samoans still wear wraparound *lavalavas,* which come well below the knees of men and to the ankles on women.

Currency Exchange See "Money," above.

Drugstores **Samoa Pharmacy** (*(C)* 22-595) and **Apia Pharmacy** (*(C)* 22-703) are both on Beach Road west of the Town Clock. They carry cosmetics, nonprescription remedies, and prescription drugs—most of New Zealand or Australian manufacture.

Electricity Electricity in Samoa is 240 volts, 50 cycles, and most plugs have angled prongs like those used in New Zealand and Australia. Aggie Grey's Hotel and the Kitano Tusitala Hotel supply 110-volt current for electric shavers only; you need a converter and adapter plugs for other American appliances.

Embassies/Consulates The **U.S. Embassy** (© 21-631) is in the John Williams Building on Beach Road at Falealili Street (the Cross Island Rd.). Hours are Monday to Friday from 9:30am to 12:30pm. New Zealand and Australia both have high commissions here.

E-mail **Cappuccino Vineyard,** on Beach Road in the ABC House mall (© 22-049), has Internet access. It's open Monday to Saturday from 7am to 10pm. See "Where to Dine in Apia," below, for more about this terrific coffeehouse and cafe. **CSL Internet Cafe,** in the Lotemanu Centre, corner of Vaea and Convent streets (© 20-926), also has Internet access. It's open Monday to Friday 8am to 4:30pm, Saturday 8am to noon. Despite its name, CSL is a computer shop, not a cafe. Both charge S$5 ($1.40) for 5 minutes.

Emergencies/Police The emergency phone numbers are © 995 for police, © 994 for fire, and © 996 for an ambulance. The **police station** (© 22-222) is on Ifi'ifi Street, inland from the prime minister's office.

Eyeglasses Try the **National Hospital** (see "Healthcare," below).

Gambling There are no casinos in Samoa, but you can play the local lottery at its office on Vaea Street.

Hairdressers/Barbers **Aggie Grey's Hotel** has a salon (© 23-277).

Healthcare The best doctors are at the **MedCen Private Hospital,** a modern facility on the Cross Island Road (© 26-519). The government-run **National Hospital,** on Ifi'ifi Street in Apia (© 21-212), has an outpatient clinic open daily from 8am to noon and from 1 to 4:30pm. Ask your hotel staff to recommend a dentist if you need one.

Insects There are no dangerous insects in Samoa, and the plentiful mosquitoes do not carry malaria. Bring a good insect repellent with you, and consider burning mosquito coils at night.

Liquor Laws The legal drinking age is 18. Except for a prohibition of Sunday sale of alcoholic beverages outside the hotels or licensed restaurants, the laws are fairly liberal. Bars outside the hotels can stay open Monday to Saturday to midnight. Spirits, wine, and beer are sold at private liquor stores.

Maps The **Samoa Visitors Bureau** distributes a one-sheet collection of maps of Upolu, Savai'i, and Apia town. See "Visitor Information & Entry Requirements," above.

Newspapers/Magazines The daily *Samoa Observer* (www.samoaobserver. ws) carries local and world news. **Le Moana Cafe,** in the Lotemau Centre at Vaea and Convent streets (© 24-828), sells *Time* and *Newsweek.*

Post Office The chief post office is on Beach Road, east of the Town Clock (© 23-480). Hours are Monday to Friday from 9am to 4:30pm.

Radio/TV Samoa has two broadcast television stations, one owned by the government and one by a Christian religious organization. The government channel has New Zealand programming daily from 5 to 11pm (earlier or later if there's a rugby game on). Many homes on Upolu's north shore can receive the American Samoan channels, one of which has commercial shows, the other Public Broadcasting System programs and live news from the United States. The government also operates two AM radio stations, on which most programming is in Samoan. The world news is rebroadcast from Radio Australia and Radio New Zealand several times a day. A privately owned FM station broadcasts lots of music on FM 98.8.

Safety Remember that the communal property system still prevails in the Samoas, and items such as cameras and bags left unattended may disappear. Street crime has not been a serious problem, but be on the alert if you walk down dark streets at night. Women should not wander alone on deserted beaches. Samoans take the Sabbath seriously, and there have been reports of local residents tossing stones at tourists who drive through some villages on Sunday. If you plan to tour by rental car, do it during the week.

Taxes Samoa imposes a 10% General Services Tax, which is included in restaurant and bar bills and is added to the cost of some other items, including rental cars, but be sure to ask if your hotel has included the tax in its room rates. Also, an airport departure tax of S$30 ($8.40) is levied on all passengers leaving Samoa at both Faleolo and Fagali'i airports. No such tax is imposed on domestic flights or on the ferry to Pago Pago.

Telephone/Fax International calls can be directly dialed into Samoa from most parts of the world. The international country code is **685.**

The easiest way to call home is via a Phonecard public telephone, which you will find at post offices as well as other places. You buy the cards at the post office. Station-to-station calls to North America cost S$13.50 ($3.75) per minute. Calls to Australia and New Zealand cost about half that amount.

Pay telephones are in post offices in the villages. Phonecard phones have replaced most coin phones. On a card phone, lift the handset, insert the Phonecard, and dial the number. A digital readout will tell you how much money you have left on your card. Old-fashion coin phones require a 20-sene coin.

Domestic long-distance and international calls can also be placed at the **Samoa Communications Ltd.,** inside the chief post office on Beach Road, but be prepared for long lines, since most Samoans do not have telephones and come here to do their calling. The corporation does not accept credit cards, so you must reverse the charges or pay cash in advance of having your call placed. The bureau is open Monday to Saturday from 8am to 10pm, but fax services are available Monday to Friday from 8am to 4:30pm.

The number for directory assistance is © **933;** for the international operator, © **900;** for international directory assistance, © **910;** and for the domestic long-distance operator, © **920.**

Time Local time in Samoa is 11 hours behind GMT. That means it's 3 hours behind Pacific standard time (4 hr. behind during daylight saving time). If it's noon standard time in California and 3pm in New York, it's 9am in Apia. During daylight saving time in California and New York, it's 8am in Samoa.

Samoa is east of the international date line; therefore, it shares the same date with North America and is one day behind Tonga, Fiji, Australia, and New Zealand. That's worth remembering if you are going on to those countries or will be arriving in Samoa from one of them.

Tipping Tipping is discouraged as being contrary to the traditional way of life. One exception is the practice of throwing money on the dance floor to show appreciation of a show well performed.

Water All tap water should be boiled before drinking. Safe bottled water is produced locally and is available at most grocery stores.

Weights/Measures Samoa is officially on the metric system, but in their everyday lives, most residents still calculate distances by the British system used in American Samoa and in the United States. Speed limits are posted in miles per hour, and the speedometers of many local vehicles (all of which have the steering wheels on the left side, in the American and European fashion) show units of miles per hour.

9 Exploring Apia & the Rest of Upolu

The town of Apia sits midway along the north coast of Upolu, which makes it a centrally located base from which to explore the main island. The Cross Island Road runs 23km (14 miles) from town, across the range of extinct volcanoes that form Upolu, thereby bringing the south coast within easy reach of town.

THE TOP ATTRACTION

Robert Louis Stevenson Museum & Grave ★★★ When Robert Louis Stevenson and his wife, Fanny, decided to stay in Samoa in 1889 (see "The Teller of Tales" box, above), they bought 314 acres of virgin land on the slopes of Mount Vaea above Apia and named the estate **Vailima**—or "Five Waters"—because five streams crossed the property. They cleared about 8 acres and lived there in a small shack for nearly a year. The U.S. historian Henry Adams dropped in unannounced one day in 1890 and found them dressed in *lavalavas* and doing dirty work about their hovel. To Adams, the couple's living conditions were repugnant. Their Rousseauian existence didn't last long, however, for in 1891 they built the first part of a mansion that was to become famous through the South Pacific.

When it was completed, the big house had five bedrooms, a library, a ballroom large enough to accommodate 100 dancers, and the only fireplace in Samoa. The Stevensons shipped 72 tons of furniture from England, all of which was hauled the 3 miles from Apia on sleds pulled by bullocks. A piano sat in one corner of the great hall, in a glass case to protect it from Samoa's humidity. Among their possessions were a Rodin nude presented to Stevenson by the sculptor himself, a damask tablecloth that was a gift from Queen Victoria, and a sugar bowl that had been used by both Robert Burns and Sir Walter Scott.

The Stevensons' lifestyle matched their surroundings. Oysters were shipped on ice from New Zealand, Bordeaux wine was brought by the cask from France and bottled at Vailima, and 1840 vintage Madeira was poured on special occasions.

Moments Expecting R. L. S. to Walk In

Anyone who has ever put words on paper or a computer screen will feel a sense of awe when reading Robert Louis Stevenson's requiem carved on his grave up on Mount Vaea overlooking Apia. The climb isn't easy, but it's worth it if you have a single literary bone in your body. The museum is one of the finest literary shrines I've ever seen: You almost expect Stevenson to walk in at any second, so much does Vailima look like it did when he was alive.

They dressed formally for dinner every evening—except for their bare feet—and were served by Samoans dressed in tartan _lavalavas,_ in honor of the great author's Scottish origins.

Vailima and this lavish lifestyle baffled the Samoans. As far as they could tell, writing was not labor; therefore, Stevenson had no visible way of earning a living. Yet all this money rolled in, which meant to them that Stevenson must be a man of much _mana._ He was also a master at one of their favorite pastimes—storytelling—and he took much interest in their own stories, as well as their customs, language, and politics. When the followers of the defeated Mataafa were released from prison, they built a road from Apia to Vailima in appreciation for Stevenson's support of their unsuccessful struggle against the Germans. And when he died in 1894, they cut the "Road of the Loving Hearts" to his grave on Mount Vaea overlooking Vailima.

Stevenson's wife, Fanny, died in California in 1914, and her ashes were brought back to Vailima and buried at the foot of Robert's grave. Her Samoan name, Aolele, is engraved on a bronze plaque.

Samoa's head of state lived in Vailima until hurricanes severely damaged the mansion in 1990 and 1991. Since then, an extraordinary renovation has turned it into the **Robert Louis Stevenson Museum.** It now appears as it did when Stevenson lived here—without the Rodin. A sitting room matches exactly that seen in a photo made of Fanny on a chair. Another photo of Stevenson dictating is hung in his library, where he stood at the time.

The "Road of the Loving Hearts" leading to **Stevenson's Grave** passes a lovely cascade that Stevenson turned into a swimming pool. A short, rather steep walking track to the grave takes about 30 strenuous minutes; a longer but easier path takes about an hour. Mount Vaea is best climbed in the cool of early morning.

Vailima, on the Cross Island Rd., 5km/3 miles south of Apia. © 20-798. Admission S$15 ($4.20) adults, S$5 ($1.40) children under 11. Mon–Fri 9am–4pm, Sat 8am–noon. Guided tours Mon–Fri 1pm.

A STROLL THROUGH APIA

Like most South Pacific towns, Samoa's capital and only town has expanded from one small Samoan village to include adjacent settlements and an area of several square miles, all of which is now known collectively as Apia (the name of the village where Europeans first settled). The town now has a population approaching 50,000. Most points of interest lie along **Beach Road,** the broad avenue that curves along the harbor, a waterfront promenade on one side and churches, government buildings, and businesses on the other.

Apia can be brutally hot at midday, so the best time to make the following walk is right after the **Samoa Police Brass Band** marches along Beach Road to Government House, where they raise the national flag daily at 8am. It's worth

Impressions
Our place is in a deep cleft of Vaea Mountain, some six hundred feet
above the sea, embowered in a forest, which is our strangling enemy,
and which we combat with axes and dollars.
                                        —Robert Louis Stevenson, 1890

watching the cops in their white helmets, light blue uniforms, and *lavalavas,*
even if you don't make the walking tour. If you take photos, don't get between
the band and the flagpole.

We start our walking tour of downtown at **Aggie Grey's Hotel,** on the banks
of the Vaisigano River. This famous hotel and its founder are stories unto themselves, which are recounted in "Where to Stay on Upolu," below. From Aggie's,
head west, or to the left as you face the harbor.

The two large churches on the left are both Protestant, legacies of the Rev.
John Williams, for whom the modern high-rise office building at the corner of
Falealili Road is named. On the waterfront across Beach Road stands the **John
Williams Memorial** to this missionary who brought Christianity to Samoa and
many more South Pacific islands. Williams's bones are reputedly buried beneath
the clapboard **Congregational Christian Church,** directly across Beach Road
from the memorial. The missionary was eaten after the natives did him in on
Erromango in what now is Vanuatu; the story has it that his bones were recovered and brought to Apia.

During business hours there's usually a line outside the **New Zealand High
Commission** office, just beyond the church, as Samoans wait to apply for visas.
Like their American Samoan cousins who flock to the United States, they
migrate to Auckland for better jobs and higher pay. Unlike them, however,
Samoans do not have unrestricted access to the larger country and must apply
for visas to enter New Zealand, their former "Mother Country."

The clapboard, colonial-style **Courthouse** on the next corner formerly
housed the Supreme Court and Prime Minister's office, before they moved into
the big high-rise buildings across the road. In colonial times, it was headquarters
of the New Zealand trusteeship administration and site of the Mau Movement
demonstration and shootings in 1929.

The Marist Brothers' Primary School is on the banks of Mulivai Stream. Across
the bridge stands **Mulivai Catholic Cathedral,** begun in 1885 and completed
some 20 years later. Farther along, the imposing **Matafele Methodist Church**
abuts the shops in the **Wesley Arcade.** According to a monument across Beach
Road, Chief Saivaaia of Tafua in Tonga brought Methodism to Samoa in 1835.

The remains of the German warship *Adler* are buried under the reclaimed
land, now the site of two huge, fale-topped government office buildings. Built
in the mid-1990s with foreign aid from China, the huge structures house the
prime minister's offices, government departments, and the central bank. On the
water side of Beach Road stands a memorial to the Samoans who fought alongside the New Zealanders during World War II.

The center of modern Apia's business district is the **Town Clock,** the World
War I memorial at the foot of Vaea Street. Across the street, the **Chan Mow &
Co.** building, formerly the home of Burns Philp trading corporation, is a fine
example of late South Seas colonial architecture; its arches and red tile roof make
it look almost Spanish. Between the clock and the water stands a large Samoan

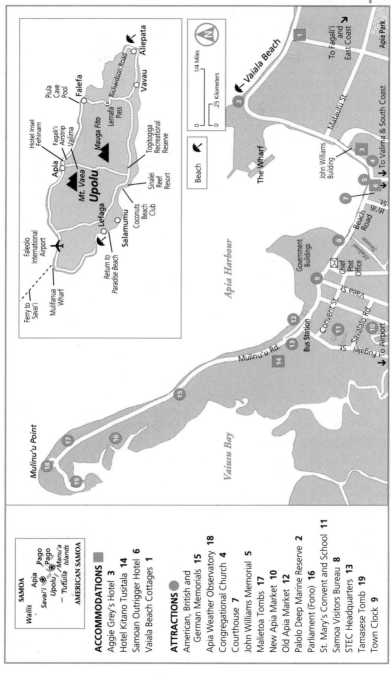

Apia

To Fagali'i and East Coast

Apia Park

Vaiala Beach

Malauu St

To Valima & South Coast

John Williams Building

The Wharf

Beach Road

Fa'atoia St

Government Buildings

Chief Post Office

Apia Harbour

Vaea St.

Convent St.

Savalalo Rd.

To Airport

Fugalei St.

Bus Station

Mulinu'u Rd.

Mulinu'u Point

Vaisu Bay

SAMOA

Wallis

Savai'i • Apia
Upolu • Pago Pago
Tutuila • Manu'a Islands

AMERICAN SAMOA

ACCOMMODATIONS

Aggie Grey's Hotel **3**
Hotel Kitano Tusitala **14**
Samoan Outrigger Hotel **6**
Vaiala Beach Cottages **1**

ATTRACTIONS

American, British and
 German Memorials **15**
Apia Weather Observatory **18**
Congregational Church **4**
Courthouse **7**
John Williams Memorial **5**
Malietoa Tombs **17**
New Apia Market **10**
Old Apia Market **12**
Palolo Deep Marine Reserve **2**
Parliament (Fono) **16**
St. Mary's Convent and School **11**
Samoa Visitors Bureau **8**
STEC Headquarters **13**
Tamasese Tomb **19**
Town Clock **9**

Upolu (inset)

Faleolo International Airport

Mulifanua Wharf

Ferry to Savai'i

Return to Paradise Beach

Lefaga

Mt. Vaea

Hotel Insel Fehmarn

Fagali'i Airstrip

Vailima

Apia

Mauga Fito

Lemafa Pass

Richardson Road

Piula Cave Pool

Falefa

Vavau

Aliepata

Togitogiga Recreational Reserve

Sinalei Reef Resort

Salamumu

Coconuts Beach Club

Beach

N

0   1/4 Miles

0   25 Kilometers

fale known as **Pulenu'u House,** where local residents can be seen lounging or eating their lunches. Next to the clock on the water side is **Nelson Memorial Public Library,** which has a collection of South Pacific literature in the Pacific Room, to the right after you enter. The clock and library were gifts from the family of Olaf Nelson, a Swede who arrived in 1868 and built a sizable trading empire.

Continuing west on Beach Road, you come to the sprawling **Old Apia Market.** Once the vegetable market, this large covered space is now home to flea-market stalls where you can find a wide range of items, from sandals to toothpaste. One area is devoted to handcraft vendors, and you can stop and watch local women weaving *pandanus* mats, hats, and handbags. This is a good place to shop for woodcarvings and *tapa* cloth (called *siapo* here; see "Shopping," below). I haven't had the stomach for such local fare since my days as a young backpacker, but the food stalls along the market's water side are the cheapest (and dirtiest) places in town to get a meal.

Fugalei Street, which leaves Beach Road across from the market, goes to the airport and the west coast. Walk down it a block, and turn left and go east on Convent Street past picturesque **St. Mary's Convent and School.** At the next corner, turn right on Saleufi Street and walk inland 2 blocks to the **New Apia Market,** a modern, tin-roofed pavilion where Samoan families sell a wide variety of tropical fruits and vegetables, all of which have the prices clearly marked (there is no bargaining). Like everywhere else in the islands, the market is busiest on Saturday morning.

THE MULINU'U PENINSULA

Beyond the market, Beach Road becomes Mulinu'u Road, which runs about a mile to the end of **Mulinu'u Peninsula,** a low arm that separates Apia Harbour to the east from shallow Vaiusu Bay on the west.

Just beyond the market on the left is the **Samoan Trust Estates Corporation (STEC) Headquarters.** STEC took over the copra plantations after New Zealand kicked the Germans out of the islands during World War I. The STEC building was originally headquarters of the German firms that owned and managed the plantations. The Kitano Tusitala Hotel just up the way was built where once stood a boarding house for the German employees of the original company.

About halfway out on the peninsula stand the **American, British, and German Memorials,** one dedicated to the German sailors who died in the 1889 hurricane, one dedicated to the British and American sailors who were drowned during that fiasco, and one to commemorate the raising of the German flag in 1900.

The Mulinu'u Peninsula is home of the **Fono,** Samoa's parliament. The new Fono building sits opposite a memorial to Samoa's independence, the two separated by a wide lawn. The Fono's old home is next to the road in the same park. A tomb on the lawn holds the remains of Iosefa Mataafa, one of the paramount chiefs.

Beyond the Apia Yacht Club stand the tombs of the Malietoa family of paramount chiefs, which makes this the **burial grounds** of Samoa's incumbent "royalty." At the end of the paved road, a dirt path goes left past a gravel quarry to the **tombs** of Tuimalaeali'ifano and Tupua Tamasese, two other paramount chiefs.

At the end of the peninsula you'll find the **Apia Weather Observatory,** originally built by the Germans in 1902 (they apparently learned a costly lesson from the unpredicted, disastrous hurricane of Mar 1889).

EXPLORING UPOLU

To travel along the roads of Upolu away from Apia is to see Polynesia relatively unchanged from the days before the Europeans arrived in the islands. Bring your swimming gear, for you'll also visit some of the South Pacific's most stunningly beautiful beaches.

If you're driving, be sure to buy a map from the visitors bureau (see "Visitor Information & Entry Requirements," above).

THE NORTHEAST COAST: APIA TO ALEIPATA

One of the most popular sightseeing tours makes a loop from Apia to the long, magnificent white beaches of Aleipata District on Upolu's eastern end. Most of Upolu is a volcanic shield that slopes gently to the sea, but because the east is older—and therefore more eroded and rugged than the central and western portions—this area has the island's most dramatic scenery. Serrated ridges come down to the sea, giving the eastern third of the island a tropical beauty reminiscent of Moorea in French Polynesia.

The East Coast Road follows the shore for 26km (16 miles) to the village of Falefa, skirting the lagoon and black-sand surf beaches at Lauli'i and Solosolo. Look for **Piula College,** a Methodist school on a promontory overlooking the sea about 3.25km (2 miles) before Falefa, turn in at the playing field, and drive around to the school on the right. Park there and follow the steps down to the freshwater **Piula Cave Pool** ★★. Bring snorkeling gear to swim through an underwater opening at the back of the pool into a second chamber. The cave pool is open from 8am to 4:30pm Monday through Saturday; admission is S$2 (55¢). There is a rudimentary changing room for visitors. No alcoholic beverages are allowed on the grounds.

To the left of the bridge beyond Falefa village lie **Falefa Falls,** which are especially impressive during the rainy season. The road then slowly climbs toward 285m (950-ft.) **Le Mafa Pass** in the center of the island, with some great views back toward the sea. Another rugged, winding road to the left just before the pass dead ends at picturesque **Fagaloa Bay,** once a volcanic crater that exploded to seaward, leaving a mountain-clad bay cutting deep into the island. The Fagaloa road should be traveled only in a four-wheel-drive vehicle—and even then with the utmost caution.

Once you're over the pass, the main paved road crosses a bridge. Just beyond, an unpaved and unmarked road goes to the right and cuts through the forests down to the south coast. We will come back this way, road conditions permitting, but for now go straight ahead on the **Richardson Road.** Once a bush path, this paved road crosses a refreshingly cool high plateau and skirts **Afulilo Lake,** formed by the country's hydroelectric dam.

ALEIPATA ★★★

From Afulilo Lake, the road gently descends into **Aleipata,** an enormously picturesque district whose villages sit beside **Aleipata Beach** ★★★, one of the most

> **Moments** A Day on a Beautiful Beach
>
> A Sunday afternoon at one of the South Pacific's most beautiful beaches is on my agenda every time I come here. Return to Paradise Beach, where Gary Cooper filed *Return to Paradise,* is what all beaches should be like: surf breaking around black rock outcrops, palm trees draped over white sand. But I'm also enamored of Aiepata Beach, where a clifflike mountain provides a backdrop and offshore islands enhance the sea view.

gorgeous white-sand beaches in the South Pacific. Four small islands offshore enliven the view, and on a clear day you can see the jagged blue outline of American Samoa on the horizon.

As you turn the corner to the south coast, stop at the overlook. The villagers may ask for S$5 ($1.40) for the privilege, but your photos from here should be among the best you'll take in Samoa, for the view includes the clifflike escarpment that leaves a narrow shelf of land bordered by a long, white-sand beach. There's not enough space here for villages, but on these sands stands a collection of rustic **beach fales** available for camping (see "Where to Stay on Upolu," below). You can refuel your body at **Boomerang Creek** (© **40-3580**), where the Kangarumu Restaurant and Harro's Bar offer inexpensive meals and libation.

Keep going along the southeast shore to Vavau village, where the paved Le Mafa Pass Road begins (don't take the unpaved road to the left; it dead-ends at a river). Le Mafa Pass Road climbs steadily uphill to a viewpoint overlooking 53m (175-ft.) **Sopo'aga Falls** 🎄. The villagers have built a small park on a cliff overlooking the deep and narrow gorge, complete with picnic tables and toilets. They charge S$3 (85¢) per vehicle, but that's a small price to pay for this view.

THE CROSS ISLAND ROAD

The Cross Island road runs for 23km (14 miles) from the John Williams Building on Beach Road in Apia to the village of Si'umu on the south coast. Along the way it passes first the Robert Louis Stevenson Museum at Vailima and then the **Malololeilei Scenic View,** a park on the eastern side of the road. Pull off here and take the short walks to views over Apia, the sea, and a waterfall. Back on the road, you'll later pass the modern, nine-sided **House of Worship,** one of six Baha'i Faith temples in the world. Open for meditation and worship, the temple was dedicated in 1984. An information center outside the temple makes available materials about the Baha'i Faith.

After passing the temple, the road winds through cool, rolling pastures and then starts its descent to the east coast. Watch on the right for a parking area overlooking **Papapai-tai Waterfalls,** which plunge 90m (300 ft.) into one of the gorges that streams have cut into central Upolu's volcanic shield. Of the many waterfalls on Upolu, Papapai-tai is the most easily seen.

THE SOUTHWEST COAST 🎄🎄

A left turn at the end of the Cross Island Road in Si'umu village on the south coast leads to **O Le Pupu-Pue National Park** and the **Togitogiga National Forest** 🎄. The park contains the best remaining tropical rain forest on Upolu, but you'll have to hike into the valley to reach it. Some 51 species of wildlife live in the park: 42 species of birds, 5 of mammals, and 4 of lizards. Lovely **Togitogiga Falls** are a short walk from the entrance, from where a trail to **Peapea Cave** also begins. It's a 2-hour round-trip hike to the cave. Another walking trail leads seaward to arches cut by the surf into the south coast. **Mount Le Pu'e,** in the northwest corner of the park, is a well-preserved volcanic cinder cone. The park and reserve are open during the daylight hours seven days a week, and there's no admission fee.

Heading west from Si'umu, the road soon passes the Coconuts Beach Club & Resort and then the nearby **Togo Mangrove Estuary,** a tidal waterway that's alive with birds, flowers, bees, and other wildlife. **Pacific Quest Marine Adventures,** based at Sinalei Reef Resort, rents kayaks for exploring the waterways through this enchanting, swamplike preserve (see "Watersports, Golf & Other Outdoor Activities," below).

Some of Upolu's most beautiful beaches are on the southwest coast, particularly in the Lefaga district. One of these is at the village of **Salamumu.** Farther on the south coast road, Matautu village boasts **Return to Paradise Beach** ★★★. Palms hang over this marvelous sandy beach punctuated by large boulders that confront the breaking surf. It gets its name from the movie starring Gary Cooper that was filmed here in 1951. The S$5 ($1.40) per-person custom fee charged by Matautu village is well worth it.

From Matautu the main road winds across the center of the island to the north coast.

ORGANIZED TOURS

Based at Aggie Grey's Hotel, **Samoa Scenic Tours** (© 22-880) offers a variety of tours that stop for photographs and a swim at beautiful beaches and water-falls. The Apia and surroundings tour includes a stop at the Robert Louis Stevenson Museum. A morning excursion goes to Piula Cave Pool and Falefa Falls. They both run Monday to Saturday and cost S$38 ($10.50) per person. One full-day trip goes to Lefaga and Matareva village, with a swim at Return to Paradise Beach when you get there. Another takes in Aleipata and the northeast coast, including Togitogiga Falls. These cost S$100 ($28) per person. Another full-day excursion goes out to Manono Island, for about S$120 ($33.50). The full-day trips usually go twice a week. Full-day tours include a beachside barbe-cue lunch (including beer and soft drinks). On Sunday there's a beach outing to the southwest coast, with juice and towels included for S$100 ($28) per person. Each day's offerings are written on a notice board in the lobby at Aggie's.

Oceania Travel & Tours (© 24-443; www.oceania-travel.ws) at the Hotel Kitano Tusitala has similar outings.

Outrigger Adventure Tours, based at The Samoan Outrigger Hotel (© 20-042; fax 23-880; outrigger@samoa.ws), has excursions to Aleipata on Sundays, and to Paradise and Matareva beaches and Togitogiga Falls on Wednesdays. Both cost S$65 ($18.20) per person, including lunch. Bring your bathing suit, towel, and snorkeling gear.

ENVIRONMENTAL TOURS

The sightseeing tours don't go to the remote areas visited by Dr. Steve Brown and his Samoan wife, Funealii Sooaemalelagi, of **Ecotour Samoa,** P.O. Box 4609, Matautu-uta (© and fax **22-144** or 25-993; www.ecotoursamoa.com). Leading proponents of nature-sensitive "sustainable tourism," the Browns have a number of 2- to 6-day tours that explore the wildlife and fauna of such places as the Mount Vaea rain forest, remote Fagaloa Bay, the south coast estuaries and wet-lands, Monono Island, and Lake Lanotoo (a crater lake in the center of Upolu that should be seen only with a guide). They also have expeditions to Savai'i.

10 Watersports, Golf & Other Outdoor Activities

You'll soon get to know American Roger Christman of **Pacific Quest Marine Adventures** (© 24-728 or 70-509; fax 20-285; www.dive.ws), who offers not just scuba diving but a host of activities, including fishing charters, snorkeling trips, kayak rentals and guided kayak tours of the Togo Mangrove Estuary on the south coast, and sunset cruises. He has an office at Samoa Marine, opposite the main wharf on Beach Road, and at Sinalei Reef Resort (see "Where to Stay on Upolu," below).

FISHING   Pacific Quest Marine Adventures (© 24-728 or 70-509; fax 20-285; www.dive.ws) has sport fishing charters, and **Samoa Marine** (© 22-271) does deep-sea fishing. Both are near Apia's main wharf. You can also go game fishing with Peter Merideth of **Sau'la Charters** (© 23-898 or 70-001). Expect to pay about US$300 for a half day, US$500 for a full day's fishing.

GOLF   The **Royal Samoan Golf Club** (© 20-120) has a nine-hole course at Fagali'i, on the eastern side of Apia, and visitors are welcome to use the facilities. Call the club's secretary for information and starting times.

KAYAKING   Kayak rentals are available from **Pacific Quest Marine Adventures** (© 24-728 or 70-509; fax 20-285; www.dive.ws). A self-guided tour goes through the Togo Mangrove Estuary, whose entrance is a short paddle west of Coconuts Beach Club & Resort. Another goes east to lava walls and arches along the coast near the Togitogiga National Forest. Kayaks cost S$12 ($3.50) per person per hour.

As part of his **Ecotour Samoa** (© and fax 22-144 or 25-993; www.ecotour samoa.com), Dr. Steve Brown will take you sea kayaking to Manono Island. These trips are usually part of his environmentally friendly tour packages (see "Environmental Tours," above).

You can also go on guided day tours or overnight expeditions to Manono Island with **Island Explorer** (© 22-401 or 71-814; www.islandexplorer.ws). This company is operated by Mats Arvidsson, a Swede who has lived in Samoa for several years. He needs one day advance notice.

SCUBA DIVING   Pacific Quest Marine Adventures (© 24-728 or 70-509; fax 20-285; www.dive.ws) will pick you up in Apia for dives on the south coast rocks and reefs. A two-tank dive costs about US$64 plus equipment rental if needed. Pacific Quest also does a short resort course and teaches PADI certification courses.

Claus Hermansen of **Outrigger Adventure Tours,** at The Samoan Outrigger Hotel (© 20-042; fax 23-880; outrigger@samoa.ws), takes his divers to a turtle nesting area on the southeast coast. He charges S$220 ($61.50) for a two-tank dive. He also teaches IDEA (European) certification courses.

SWIMMING & SNORKELING   The best swimming and snorkeling is on the beaches of Aleipata and the southwest coast (see "Exploring Upolu," above). In town, just east of the main wharf, canyons in the reef at **Palolo Deep Marine Reserve** ✦ (no phone) make for good snorkeling without having to leave town. The snorkeling is best at high tide, when you can swim rather than walk across the reef to the deep-water canyons. The small sandy beach is good for sunning at any tide. This city park has changing rooms, and it rents snorkeling gear. Admission is of S$2 (55¢). The reserve is open daily from 8am to 6pm.

On the south coast, **Pacific Quest Divers** (© 24-728) has guided snorkeling expeditions for US$25, including gear.

Some people think a trip to **Papase'a Sliding Rocks** is a highlight of a trip to Apia. You of strong bottom can slide down this waterfall into a dark pool. Take a taxi or the Se'ese'e village bus. The rocks are about 2 kilometers (1¼ miles) from the paved road; the bus driver may go out of his way to take you there, but you will have to walk back to the bus route. The villagers extract a S$2 (55¢) custom fee per person.

Another popular outing away from Apia is to **Piula Cave Pool** and the out-lying beaches. See "Exploring Upolu," above, for details.

11 Shopping

Although not in the quantity you'll find in Tonga, Samoans turn out excellent handmade baskets, sewing trays, purses, floor mats, napkin rings, place mats, and fans woven from *pandanus* and other local materials, plus some woodcarvings.

Except for the Old Apia Market, which is open all day, the stores below observe regular business hours (see "Fast Facts: Samoa," above).

Aggie's Store   This hotel gift shop has Apia's best selection of handcrafts and Samoan products such as sandalwood soap, small bags of kava, and watercolors by local artists. The handcrafts include shell and black coral jewelry and *siapo* cloth, carved wooden war clubs, ceremonial kava bowls, and high talking chiefs' staffs (known as *tootoo*). Among clothing items are hand-screened *lavalavas*, T-shirts, shorts, and dresses. The shop also carries books about the Samoas and has a snack bar just inside the front door. Beach Rd., next to Aggie Grey's Hotel. © **22-880.**

Kava Kavings Handicraft   Harry Paul has been encouraging Samoans to resume making handcrafts, and he carries some of the resulting works: bone fish-hooks, carved war clubs, spears, and orators' staffs and "horses' tails" of the type carried by high talking chiefs, hair clasps and ukuleles made from coconut shells, and many other items. He also has imported handcrafts from Tonga, Fiji, and other South Pacific islands. Fungulei Rd., 3 blocks south of Beach Rd. © **25-080.**

Old Apia Market   Once the town's vegetable market, this giant shed is now a crowded and very active flea market, with vendors selling everything from cos-metics to shoes (local wags say it's better stocked than Apia's regular stores because some goods may have been slipped past Customs on their way from American Samoa). Your best buys here are fine mats and other Samoan hand-crafts; in fact, you can even watch local women at work in their stalls. The other handcraft shops usually have better-quality pieces, but you might find an excep-tional one here. Especially look for the merchant who sells intricately carved *tanoa* (kava) bowls. Beach Rd., west of Town Clock. No phone.

12 Where to Stay on Upolu

IN APIA

Aggie Grey's Hotel ★★★   The son of the late Aggie Grey, Alan Grey, his wife Marina, and their son and daughter, Fred and Tonya, are making sure that the hotel has the same warm, family feeling instilled by Aggie when she opened it in 1943 (see the "Hot Dogs & Hamburgers" box, below). Aggie's Store next door will show you what this venerable hotel looked like in those days. Now a modern but Victorian-style building fronting Beach Road houses the reception area, the air-conditioned Le Tamarina restaurant (see "Where to Dine in Apia," below), an open-air bar facing the harbor, and two floors of modern rooms and suites with private verandas overlooking Apia Harbour. The new facility hasn't

Hot Dogs & Hamburgers

Back in 1919, a young woman of British and Samoan descent named Agnes Genevieve Grey started the Cosmopolitan Club on a point of land where the Vaisigano River flows into Apia Harbour. It was just a small pub, catering to local businessmen and the occasional tourists who climbed off the transpacific steamers stopping in Apia.

And then the U.S. Marines landed.

That was in 1942, when thousands of American servicemen arrived in Samoa to train for the South Pacific campaigns against the Japanese. Aggie Grey started selling them much-appreciated hot dogs and hamburgers. Quickly her little enterprise expanded into a three-story clapboard hotel, with a bar at ground level, a dining room on the next, and rooms to rent on the third. Many of those young marines, including future U.S. Secretary of State George Shultz, left Samoa with fond memories of Aggie Grey and her hotel.

Another serviceman who came to Aggie's was a U.S. naval historian named James A. Michener. Everyone in Samoa believes Michener used Aggie as the role model for Bloody Mary, the Tonkinese woman who provided U.S. servicemen with wine, song, and other diversions in his *Tales of the South Pacific.*

Although her hotel grew after the war to include more than 150 rooms, Aggie always circulated among her guests, making them feel at home. Everyone sat down family style when taking a meal in the old clapboard building on Beach Road, and afterward they all moseyed over for coffee in the lounge. Afternoon tea was a time for socializing and swapping gossip from places far away. And on *fiafia* nights, when the feasts were laid out, Aggie herself would dance the graceful Samoan *siva.*

Like Robert Louis Stevenson before her, Aggie Grey was revered by the locals. They made her the only commoner ever to appear on a Samoan postage stamp. And when she died in 1988 at the age of 90, Head of State Malietoa Tanufafili II and hundreds of other mourners escorted her to her final resting place in the hills above Apia.

changed the relaxed atmosphere back in the large, exquisite fale beside the swimming pool that has a palm tree growing in the middle. Guests can still take their meals under the great turtle-shaped roof or wander over to the bar for a cold Vailima beer and a chat with friendly strangers. The efficient staff prepares feasts and barbecues in which the quantity of food dished out is, as it was in Aggie's day, astounding. Marina Grey now dances the siva during the weekly *fiafias* (see "Island Nights on Upolu," below).

In addition to the hotel units in the new building, other hotel rooms are housed in modern, stone-accented, two-story buildings that ramble through a garden so thick with tropical vegetation that it's easy to get lost trying to find your way from one unit to another. They are all comfortable and have both air conditioners and good natural ventilation. Each has a veranda or balcony. My favorites are the less modern but much more charming individual "VIP fale suites," which are bungalows topped by turtle-shaped roofs. Each of these enormous units bears the name of one of Aggie's famous past guests, such as actors Gary Cooper, William Holden, and Marlon Brando. They have old-fashioned touches like fold-down ironing boards and irons mounted in their own wooden holders.

P.O. Box 67, Apia (Beach Rd., on the waterfront). ℂ 800/448-8355 or 22-880. Fax 23-626. www.aggiegreys. com. 181 units. US$100–$145 double. AE, DC, MC, V. **Amenities:** 3 restaurants (regional), 3 bars; outdoor pool; exercise room; children's programs; concierge; activities desk; business center; salon; 24-hr. room service; babysitting; laundry service. *In room:* A/C, TV, fridge, coffeemaker, hair dryer, iron.

Hotel Insel Fehmarn   This modern, well-kept establishment sits on the side of the hill above Apia, affording some of its motel-style rooms with views of town and the offshore reef from their balconies, especially those on the third (top) floor. Each identical room in this beige concrete block structure has two double beds, chairs, table, tiled shower-only bathroom, and kitchenette. There is a dining room and bar on the premises, as well as a convenience store, two tennis courts, and a pool. It's popular with business travelers looking for kitchen-equipped accommodations. Giodanno's Cafe & Pizzeria is across the road (see "Where to Dine in Apia," below).

P.O. Box 3272, Apia (on Cross Island Rd., 2km/1¼ miles uphill from Beach Rd.). ℂ 23-301. Fax 22-204. insel@samoa.ws. 54 units. US$85 double. AE, DC, MC, V. **Amenities:** 1 restaurant (regional), 1 bar; outdoor pool; 2 tennis courts; laundry service; coin-op washers and dryers. *In room:* A/C, TV, kitchen, coffeemaker.

Hotel Kitano Tusitala   Built in 1974 by the government and named the Tusitala in honor of Robert Louis Stevenson, this hotel is now owned by Kitano, a Japanese construction company. The public areas are in three Samoan-style fales with huge turtle-shaped roofs. They ring a tropical garden featuring a children's wading pool, from which water falls down two levels into a larger adult swimming pool. The rooms are all in five two-story motel-style buildings grouped beyond the swimming pools. "Superior" units facing the pool have been refurbished and are in much better condition than the "standard" rooms, which have been repainted but still show their age. All have sliding glass door opening onto either a private patio or balcony. They are air-conditioned, but you won't feel any cross-ventilation unless you leave the back door open.

A bar and lounge in one of the open-air fales stands next to the pool, as does a daytime snack bar. Another of the three big common buildings houses Stevenson's Restaurant (with portraits of R. L. S. himself). The hotel's Seaview Restaurant, across the main driveway, proffers both Western and Japanese fare.

P.O. Box 101, Apia (Beach Rd., Mulinu'u Peninsula). ℂ 800/448-8355 or 21-122. Fax 23-652. www.kitano.ws. 94 units. S$234–S$359 ($65.50–100.50) double. AE, DC, MC, V. **Amenities:** 4 restaurants (regional/Japanese), 3 bars; outdoor pool; 2 tennis courts; bike rentals; children's programs; activities desk; business center; limited room service; babysitting; laundry service; coin-op washers and dryers. *In room:* A/C, TV, fridge, coffeemaker, hair dryer (in superior rooms).

Vaiala Beach Cottages *Value*   These comfortable, modern, and airy bungalows share a yard with frangipani, crotons, and other tropical plants, across the street from Vaiala Beach. Except for the tropical furnishings and decor, such as cane furniture and woven floor mats, the bungalows are all identical: a full kitchen with stainless-steel sink, a bedroom with either one double or two twin beds, a spacious bathroom with a shower that dispenses hot water, and a narrow balcony off a bright living room. They are built of pine, including the varnished interior walls. The living rooms have ceiling fans hanging over the sitting area, but the large, screened, louvered windows and sliding doors leading to the balconies usually allow the trade winds to cool the house without such assistance. Reservations are advised.

P.O. Box 2025, Apia (Vaiala Beach, 1.5km/1 mile east of Main Wharf). © **22-202**. Fax 22-008. vaialabeach@ samoa.ws. 7 units. US$75 double. MC, V. **Amenities:** Laundry service. *In room:* Kitchen, coffeemaker, no phone.

ON THE SOUTH COAST

Coconuts Beach Club & Resort   Former Hollywood show-biz lawyers Barry and Jennifer Rose developed this funky resort on a piece of land abutting the Togo Mangrove Estuary (mosquitoes can be plentiful here at times). They chopped down enough of this dense growth for seven lagoon-facing bungalows and a two-story, motel-style block of eight rooms reached by treehouselike stairs. Later they added two luxuriously appointed hexagonal cottages out over the lagoon, Samoa's only overwater bungalows. By far the best units here, the overwaters have floor-to-ceiling glass walls and coffee tables with see-through tops for looking into the lagoon. Use of a four-wheel-drive vehicle is included in the rates. Ashore, the spacious thatch-roofed, clapboard-sided bungalows (one has two bedrooms) have a rustic look without giving up luxuries. They have outdoorsy screened bathrooms with showers pouring down rock walls into sunken tubs. In the rooms, you can step from oval bathtubs directly onto 7m (24-ft.) covered patios or balconies. Lots of natural wood creates unusual accents, such as tree limbs used as posts for the king-size beds, towel racks in the baths, and legs for coffee tables. Another European-style building holds seven standard units with mat-lined walls and air-conditioned bedrooms.

A bearded restaurateur named Mika, who formerly lived in Hawaii, holds forth under an open-sided thatch pavilion with a friendly beachfront bar—although I must say that service here was nonchalant during my recent visit. Mika specializes in fresh seafood, especially local lobster and mud crabs from the nearby mangrove estuary.

Erosion has wiped away the beach here, and now there is a rock breakwater across most of the property. You can walk around the breakwater, however, and swim out to a lava wall, which creates a good snorkeling area. A gecko-shaped pool with a gecko tile mosaic bottom sits just behind the breakwater but away from the main building.

P.O. Box 3684, Apia (in Si'umu, 30 min. south of Apia; turn right at end of Cross Island Rd.). © **24-849**. Fax 20-071. www.coconutsbeachclubsamoa.com. 24 units. US$99–US$149 double; US$199–US$299 bungalow. Rates for overwater bungalows include user of a car. AE, MC, V. **Amenities:** 1 restaurant (regional); 2 bars; outdoor pool; watersports equipment rentals; bike rentals; activities desk; massage; babysitting; laundry service. *In room:* A/C, dataport, minibar, coffeemaker, safe, no phone.

Sinalei Reef Resort 🌟🌟   More formal and reserved than Coconuts Beach Club, this fine resort sits on a rise overlooking the lagoon, but it has a path down to its end of a magnificent crescent-shaped beach—backed by the proverbial palm grove—which separates it from Coconuts. There's also a second, more private, beach area here, with beach fales for lounging or escaping the sun. A group of three open, Samoan-style thatch-roof buildings comprise the central complex, one each covering reception and gift shop, dining room, and bar. The bar opens to lovely hilltop pool with a waterfall and huge lava rocks at its edge.

Twenty of the guest bungalows flank the central buildings, which gives some of them fine sea views. They are of European construction, with peaked shingle roofs and glass walls across the front. Some also have ceiling fans and separate bedrooms. Ventilation is at a premium, but they are all air-conditioned. Five honeymoon fales lack air conditioners (they do have ceiling fans) but are down by a small beach instead of up on the hill. They have wraparound beachside verandas and large outdoor bathrooms equipped with Jacuzzis.

With a view down over the sea, the dining room provides European and Polynesian fare, and Samoans strum guitars for evening entertainment. A bar provides wood-fired pizzas from a perch overlooking freshwater welling up from a spring beneath the lagoon. Guests can use nonmotorized watersports equipment for free, and they pay extra for village visits and excursions to the mangrove swamp and freshwater springs. Pacific Quest Marine Adventures has a scuba diving and watersports base here.

P.O. Box 1510, Apia (in Si'umu, 30 min. south of Apia). © 25-191. Fax 20-285. www.sinalei.com. 25 units. US$180–US$300 bungalow. Rates include tropical breakfast, afternoon tea, town shuttle daily. AE, MC, V. **Amenities:** 1 restaurant (regional), 2 bars; outdoor pool; 9-hole golf course; 2 tennis courts; free use of non-motorized watersports equipment; scuba; bike rentals; activities desk; limited room service; massage; baby-sitting; laundry service. *In room:* A/C (except in honeymoon units), fridge, coffeemaker, hair dryer, iron.

HOSTELS

The Samoan Outrigger Hotel   Claus Hermansen liked what he saw so much during a visit to Samoa that he gave up a banking career in Denmark to live here. In addition to diving, he operates this backpackers' hostel, one of the best in the South Pacific. There's a reading room and TV lounge with billiards table, and to the rear is a pleasant communal kitchen and dining area. The best rooms have their own toilets and cold-water showers. Other guests share five showers, four toilets, and laundry facilities. All rooms have fans as well as mosquito nets over their beds. Claus's hostel has been spotlessly clean throughout my recent visits. Guests get free use of 15-speed bikes. Outrigger Adventure Tours is based here (see "Exploring Upolu," above), and Claus will take you diving or teach you to scuba (see "Watersports, Golf & Other Outdoor Activities," above).

P.O. Box 4074, Apia (Cross Island Rd., 1km/½ mile south of Beach Rd). © 20-042. Fax 23-880. outrigger@ samoa.ws. 13 units (5 without bathroom), 12 dorm beds. S$65–S$95 ($18–$26.50) double; S$35 ($10) dorm bed. Rates include continental breakfast. MC, V. *In room:* No phone.

BEACH FALES AT ALEIPATA

Samoa has seen an explosion of **beach fales** in recent years. Although included in many accommodation listings, these rustic little structures belong in the camping category. They are miniature Samoan fales, with oval thatch roofs covering open-air platforms, and most provide mosquito nets, foam mattresses, and pull-down canvas or colorful plastic sides to afford some privacy and protection against the elements. Guests share communal toilets and showers in separate buildings.

Far and away the most popular of these is **Tanu Beach Fales** on Savai'i (see "Savai'i," below). The best of Upolu's lot are on the great beach of Aleipata, 1 hour by car from Apia on Upolu's southeastern corner (see "Exploring Upolu," earlier in this chapter). Directly on that beach, **Litia Sini's Beach Fales** (© 24-327) actually has wood sides on some of its fales and is the most popular. **Tafua Beach Fales** (© 20-180) has a restaurant and bar across the road. **Boomerang Creek** (© 40-358; boomerangcreek@yahoo.com) is on the mountain side of the road, thus defeating the *beach* in *beach fale,* but it has the pleasant Kangarumu Restaurant, where you can order sandwiches, steaks, local lobster, and other simply prepared fare from a blackboard menu, and Harro's Bar dispensing libation.

Namu'a Beach Fales (ⓒ **20-566** or 41-079), are on Namu'a, one of the rocky islets off Aleipata Beach. A boat ferries guests from Mutiatele village to a deep-sand beach on the island. From there you have a splendid view back to Upolu. It's very rustic, with no electricity, but owner Tuisala (he's the high chief of this district) and his family will make you feel at home despite the inconveniences.

All the fales have cold-water showers and charges S$50 ($14) per person, including breakfast and dinner (except on Namu'a, where you get lunch, too). None of them accept credit cards, so bring cash.

13 Where to Dine in Apia

Start thinking seafood here, for a small but thriving local fishing industry means Apia is one of the best places in the South Pacific to dine on fresh yellowfin tuna (great for sashimi) and light, flaky mahimahi (known here as *masi masi*). Tropical lobsters are available here, too, although not in the numbers harvested in Tonga.

The local **McDonald's** is on Vaea Street, a block inland from the Town Clock.

Cappuccino Vineyard ★★ COFFEE HOUSE/SNACKS   The most recent creation of Sails Restaurant and Bar owners Ian and Lyvia Black (see below), this chic sidewalk cafe—it would be at home in New York or Sydney—is the best place in Apia to stop in for a cappuccino, an espresso, or a latte made from freshly roasted Fijian beans. For breakfast you can accompany it with yogurt or a freshly baked pastry. Sashimi, steamed oysters, spicy Buffalo wings, Chinese dim sum, Australian meat pies, and big American burgers appear in the cafeteria-style cases about midday. Hang around during the evening for live jazz and island music. The best tables are under umbrellas out on the pedestrian mall beside the high-rise ACB House on Beach Road.

Beach Rd., in ACB House mall west of Town Clock. ⓒ **22-049.** Reservations not accepted. Snacks S$6–S$12 ($1.50–$3.50). No credit cards. Mon–Sat 7am–10pm.

Giodanno's Cafe & Pizzeria ★ (Value) PIZZA/PASTA   Follow your nose around the take-out counter to Alex Stanley's romantic courtyard, where patio tables with candles sit under a breadfruit and other tropical trees. Small- or large-size pizzas come with a choice of several toppings. Pasta dishes, which all cost the same, consist of lasagna with beef sauce or spaghetti under Bolognese, marinara, carbonara, or a spicy vegetarian sauce. With jazz on the speaker system, this is a very popular establishment with local expatriate residents.

Cross Island Rd., opposite Hotel Insel Fehmarn. ⓒ **25-985.** Reservations recommended. Pizzas S$10–S$27 ($2.80–$7.50); pasta S$18–S$28 ($5–$8). MC, V. Tues–Sat 3–10pm, Sun 5–9pm.

Gourmet Seafood & Grille (Value) SEAFOOD/STEAKS   You can start your day with fresh fruit pies and muffins at this popular local establishment, which would win all awards for charm in the inexpensive-restaurant category anywhere. Large tree trunks hold up the roof, under which fishnets form a ceiling. Buoys and other nautical items add to the atmosphere. There's nothing gourmet here, but the hallmark is fresh fish. You'll get a monstrous slab of grilled mahimahi, most likely caught earlier in the day, served with french fries and a salad. You can also get fish and chips, New Zealand steaks, and Apia's best *oka* (marinated raw fish with coconut cream and vegetables). Order at the counter; they will call your number.

Convent St., 1 block behind Central Post Office. ⓒ **24-625.** Breakfast S$2.50–S$10 (70¢–2.80); sandwiches and burgers S$2.50–S$10 (70¢–$2.80); main courses S$9–S$22 ($2.50–$6). No credit cards. Mon–Sat 7am–10pm.

Tips   Don't Miss a *Fiafia*

Like other islanders, the Samoans gave up the use of pottery at least 1,000 years before the Europeans arrived in the South Pacific. As did their fellow Polynesians, they cooked their foods in a pit of hot stones, which the Samoans call an *umu*. When it had all steamed for several hours, they threw back the dirt, unwrapped the delicacies, and sat down to a **fiafia**.

Favorite side dishes were fresh fruit and *ota* (fish marinated with lime juice and served with vegetables in coconut milk, in a fashion similar to poisson cru in Tahiti). If you happen to be in Samoa on the seventh day after the full moon in late October or early November, the meal may include the coral worm known as *palolo*.

Aggie Grey's Hotel (✆ 22-880) has the best fiafia, traditionally on Wednesday night. The **Hotel Kitano Tusitala** (✆ 21-122), **Coconuts Beach Club** (✆ 24-849), and **Sinalei Reef Resort** (✆ 25-191) also have at least one fiafia a week. Check with them to find out when they have their fiafia nights. Expect to pay about S$45 ($12.50) per person. You'll pass a long buffet table loaded with European, Chinese, and Samoan dishes. After stuffing down the food, you get to watch a show of traditional Samoan dancing.

Le Tamarina Restaurant ★★ INTERNATIONAL   Tropical plants and furnishings lend appropriate atmosphere to this elegant, air-conditioned dining room with a view of Apia from the ground floor of Aggie's. Guests can wear shorts for buffet lunches, but slacks and dresses are required for evening meals, which feature local and New Zealand produce in a variety of preparations. Fresh lobster comes grilled with garlicky greens, and prime New Zealand steak in a pastry puff also appears here. Saturday evenings usually see an extensive seafood buffet laid out.

Beach Rd., in Aggie Grey's Hotel. ✆ 23-626. Reservations recommended. Main courses S$33–S$48 ($9.25–$13.50). AE, DC, MC, V. Mon–Sat noon–2pm and 7–10pm.

Sails Restaurant and Bar ★★★ SEAFOOD/STEAKS   I first met Ian and Lyvia Black, a charming Australian-Samoan couple, when they were expertly managing hotels in Fiji. In 1996 they returned to Samoa and turned the second floor of this historic clapboard store—the first place Robert Louis Stevenson lived when he arrived here in 1889—into one of the South Pacific's best and most charming restaurants. Be sure to reserve a table out on the front porch above Beach Road, where you'll get a view over the white-and-blue railing of Apia Harbour. And by all means start with Sail's signature dish, Commodore Sashimi, a lightly seared tenderloin-size cut of fresh yellowfin tuna rolled in Jamaican jerk and other spices. You won't find anything quite like it in these islands. The creamy lobster bisque loaded with chunks of lobster is out of this world, too. For a main course, move on to a daily special, such as mahimahi in a luscious cream, lemon, and fruit juice sauce. If you're a meat eater, opt for the tender New Zealand filet in chili and ginger sauce (it starts out gingery but leaves a spicy bite). You can order a breakfast of eggs and bacon all day. Lunch features salads, sandwiches, and burgers, and Ian and Lyvia keep the bar open all day for drinks, the second best cappuccino in town, and snacks (including Commodore Sashimi). Nautical decor and jazz on the speakers add to the relaxed, friendly atmosphere.

Beach Rd., between Ifiifi St. and Mulivai Stream. ℂ **20-628**. Reservations recommended for dinner. Breakfast S$15 ($4); lunch S$12.50–S$25 ($3.50–$7); main courses S$24.50–S$49 ($7–$13.75). AE, DC, MC, V. Mon–Sat 9am–11pm, Sun 6–11pm.

14 Island Nights on Upolu

SAMOAN DANCE SHOWS ★★★ Samoa is no different from the other Polynesian countries in that watching a traditional dance show as part of a feast night (in Samoa called a *fiafia*) is a highlight of any visit. Samoan dance movements are graceful and emphasize the hands more than the hips; the costumes feature more *siapo* cloth and fine mats than flowers. While the dances are not as lively nor the costumes as colorful as those in Tahiti and the Cook Islands, they are definitely worth seeing.

Aggie Grey's Hotel ★★★ (ℂ **22-880**) consistently has the best *fiafia* night in town, usually on Wednesday, and the show just keeps getting better. This isn't a Las Vegas floor show, but the fire dance around the pool is nothing short of spectacular for these parts. Aggie's *fiafia* night is traditionally on Wednesday at 6:45pm. But don't be late, for the show starts promptly at 6:45pm, and dinner is served afterward.

Hotel Kitano Tusitala (ℂ **21-122**) usually has its show in one of its huge fales on Friday at 7pm.

On the south coast, **Sinalei Reef Resort** (ℂ **25-191**) puts on its *fiafia* on Friday nights, and **Coconuts Beach Club** (ℂ **24-849**) does its on Saturday.

The dinners and shows cost about S$45 ($12.50) at all the hotels. Compared to what you'll pay elsewhere in the South Pacific, that's a steal.

CABARET SHOWS Set aside Saturday night to join the crowd at **Cindy's Cabaret Show,** starting at 8:30pm at the Hotel Kitano Tusitala (ℂ **21-122**). Cindy's drag show is so entertaining that he (or is it she?) has taken it to Auckland (and San Francisco could be next). The troupe lip-syncs to recorded popular tunes, but there's definitely a Samoan influence in their colorful costumes, elegant dance steps, and satirical humor. The dinner and show costs about S$55 ($15.50).

PUB CRAWLING Nights are quiet in Apia from Sunday to Thursday. Then everyone heads down Beach Road, hitting one pub after another. Most of these have live bands on Friday (the biggest night) and Saturday. Thanks largely to citizens outraged by bars opening in residential neighborhoods, pubs legally must close at midnight throughout the week (none are open on Sun). As a practical matter, some of them keep right on going into the wee hours, especially on Friday night.

Moments **A Spectacular Fire Dance**

The dancing is more suggestive in French Polynesia and the Cook Islands than in Samoa, but there is a warmth and charm to the *fiafia* nights at Aggie's Grey's Hotel that no other establishment comes close to matching. Even if I have been out reviewing restaurants on Wednesday night, I always get back to Aggie's in time for a spectacular fire dance around the pool.

Tips Don't Sit Near the Door

When pub crawling along Beach Road, don't sit near the door. This is where fights are most likely to erupt as bouncers evict drunken and unruly customers who don't want to leave.

Start at Aggie Grey's Hotel, where you can start off with a cocktail or cold Vailima beer, and head west along Beach Road. You'll come to the slapped-together facade and worse-than-plain furniture at **Otto's Reef** (*Ⓒ* **22-691**), the most popular bar in town with both locals and expatriate residents. You can look right into this open-air establishment. Next door is **The Coast** (*Ⓒ* **26-669**) and two doors down is the air-conditioned **On the Rocks** (*Ⓒ* 20-093), Apia's only real cocktail bar (it often has good live music on Thurs night). The crawl then skips past the Town Clock to **Cappuccino Vineyard** (*Ⓒ* **22-049**), Ian and Lyvia Black's sophisticated coffeehouse where musicians make jazz and island music.

The young set end their night at the **Mount Vaea Club** (*Ⓒ* **21-627**) on Vaitele Street near Tofafuafua Road. Don't expect much charm here, just loud music, much talk, a packed house of young Samoans, and an occasional fight around midnight on Friday and Saturday. Women should exercise caution if visiting this old-time South Seas joint alone.

15 Savai'i ★ ★

You might wish you had stayed longer on Savai'i, whose green mountains rise out of the sea and into the clouds across the 21km (13-mile) -wide Apolima Strait. Savai'i is half again as large as Upolu, yet it has only a third as many people as its smaller and more prosperous sister, and they live in villages mainly along the east and south coasts. Elsewhere, Savai'i is made up of practically deserted lava fields and forests. Its 470 volcanic craters are considered to be dormant (the last major eruption occurred in 1911).

On Savai'i, rural Samoan life is very much like it always has been. You'll see one picturesque traditional village after another, sitting on the edge of the lagoon.

On the trip over, you will pass the small islands of **Manono** and **Apolima,** which sit in the Apolima Strait between Upolu and Savai'i. Apolima is a small volcanic crater. The beachside village of Apolima-tui sits on the shore where the crater collapsed on one side. Small boats shuttle between Apolima Island and the village of Apolima-uta on Upolu's western end. Boats to Manono leave from Mulifanua Wharf. **Samoa Scenic Tours** (*Ⓒ* **22-880**) at Aggie Grey's Hotel operates popular day trips to Manono and its beautiful surrounding reef, and Dr. Steve Brown of **Ecotour Samoa** (*Ⓒ* and fax **22-144** or 25-993; www.ecotour samoa.com) has sea kayaking expeditions to Manono (see "Exploring Apia & the Rest of Upolu," earlier in this chapter).

GETTING THERE & GETTING AROUND

Air services to Savai'i are provided by **Polynesian Airlines** and **Samoa Air,** and the *Lady Samoa* ferry service between Upolu and Savai'i. See "Getting There & Getting Around," earlier in this chapter.

You can organize a trip to Savai'i yourself, but the easiest way is to contact one of the tour operators in Apia (see "Organized Tours," earlier in this chapter). For example, **Oceania Travel & Tours** (℃ **24-443;** www.oceania-travel.ws) has a 2-day, 1-night package for about US$160; it includes accommodation, round-trip transportation, transfers, and a half-day tour of Savai'i. Oceania's day trips to Savai'i cost about US$110 per person.

Ecotour Samoa (℃ and fax **22-144** or 25-993; www.ecotoursamoa.com) has 2- and 3-day expeditions around Savai'i, with an emphasis on exploring the volcanic craters, lava fields, wetlands, and rain forests. See "Environmental Tours," above, for more information about this company.

Taxis meet the planes and ferry. One-way fare from Maota Airstrip to Safua on the east coast is S$15 ($4.20). From the ferry wharf to the east-coast hotels costs S$8 ($2.25) one way. The one-way fare is F$60 ($17) to Stevenson's at Manase and Tanu Beach Fales, and S$100 ($28) to Asau village, 89km (55 miles) away on the opposite side of Savai'i.

Local **buses** primarily take passengers to and from the ferry. In other words, they arrive at Salelologa wharf in time for their passengers to catch the ferry to Upolu, and they depart on their return trips to the villages shortly after each ferry arrival. Those headed to Puapua and Tuasivi villages pass the hotels. The fare is S60¢ (15¢).

Savai'i Car Rentals (℃ **51-392;** fax 51-291; cars@samoa.ws), rents Jeeps for S$110 to S$140 ($31–$39) per day. A deposit of S$250 ($70) is required, or you can pay by MasterCard or Visa. It is part of **Savai'i Travel & Tours** (℃ **51-206**), at the intersection of the wharf and main roads in Salelologa, which can assist with reconfirming your return flight on Polynesian Airlines or Samoa Air. If you rent a vehicle in Apia, be sure to ask if you can bring it to Savai'i on the ferry.

The round-island road is completely paved.

EXPLORING SAVAI'I

Unless you have a week or more and plenty of energy, you should take a guided tour of this large and sparsely populated island with so little public transport and few road signs. Even then, you'll need 3 days to see all of the readily accessible sights and have no time for the beach.

Based at the Safua Hotel, **Safua Tours** ✮✮✮ (℃ **51-271;** fax 51-272) offers excursions guided by Warren Jopling, a retired Australian geologist who has lived on the island for many years. Warren is a font of information, especially about the desertlike lava fields. He will tailor any tour to suit your interests. It will take a full day to see most of the sights, with half the day spent going along the east and north coasts, the other half along the south shore. His full-day excursions cost US$45 per person if you book directly and not through a travel agent. Reservations are required.

THE EAST & NORTH COASTS

Leaving the Safua Hotel, the east-coast road soon passes a memorial to the Rev. John Williams, then goes up a rise to **Tuasivi,** the administrative center of the island and site of the hospital and police station. From there it drops down to **Faga** and **Siufaga,** two long, gorgeous beaches. Many villages along this stretch have bathing pools fed by freshwater that runs underground down from the mountains. Only the south side of Savai'i has rivers and streams. Rainwater seeps into the porous volcanic rock elsewhere and reappears as springs along the shoreline.

Mount Matavanu last erupted between 1905 and 1911, when it sent a long lava flow down to the northeast coast, burying villages and gardens before backing up

---

Moments **Browsing Through a Living Museum**

You won't believe your eyes when you tour the desolate lava fields of Savai'i with retired Australian geologist Warren Jopling. Having lived on Savai'i for many years, Warren also is an expert on Samoan customs and lifestyles (as you will see, everyone on the island knows him). Touring with Warren is like browsing through a living geological and cultural museum.

---

behind the reef. Today the desertlike **Matavanu lava field** is populated primarily by primitive ferns. The flow very nearly inundated the village of **Mauga,** which sits along the rim of an extinct volcano's cone. The villagers play cricket on the crater floor. Past Mauga is the **Virgin's Grave,** a hole left around a grave when the lava almost covered a nearby church. The steeple still sticks out of the twisted black mass. The villagers charge S$2 (55¢) to visit the grave.

The north-coast road past the lava fields is picturesque but holds little of interest other than gorgeous tropical scenery. A drink at **Le Lagoto Bar,** between Fagamalo and Lelepa, or lunch at **Stevenson's at Manase,** just west of Manase village, makes a nice refueling stop if you get that far (see "Where to Stay & Dine," below).

THE SOUTH COAST

On the south coast near Vailoa, on the Letolo Plantation, stands the ancient **Pulemelei Mound,** a collection of rocks similar to the ceremonial temples, or *maraes,* in French Polynesia and the Cook Islands. It's the largest archaeological ruin in Polynesia: A two-tiered pyramid 72m (240 ft.) long, 58km (193 ft.) wide, and 14m (48 ft.) high. This one is so old, however, that the Samoans no longer have legends explaining their original function. A New Zealand–funded project is under way to clear the ruins and improve access. The side road, which passes Afu'a'au Waterfall, ends some 2.5km (1½ miles) from the mound. A steep and often muddy track leads down to the waterfall.

From the mounds, the south-coast road continues to Gautavai Waterfall, a lovely black-sand beach at Nu'u, and geyserlike blowholes at Taga on the island's southernmost point.

WHERE TO STAY & DINE ON SAVAI'I

Le Lagoto Beach Resort ✪   Kuki and Sara Retzlaff have five cottagelike fales and three rooms in a two-story, European-style house at the end of their shady property, which has a beautiful sunset view from its lovely beachside perch (*lagoto* means "sunset" in Samoan). One fale has a separate bedroom and a great view from its front porch. Each unit is equipped with a queen-size bed with a mosquito net, a kitchenette, a fan, a TV, and a shower-only bathroom. The Retzlaffs also serve breakfast, lunch, and dinner in a screened Samoan-style fale with a beachside deck, or you can do your own cooking in the two-story house. They provide complimentary snorkeling gear and canoes for guests to explore a marine reserve offshore.

P.O. Box 34, Fagamalo, Manase (between Fagamalo and Lelepa villages, 45km/28 miles north of ferry wharf). (© **58-189.** Fax 58-249. 8 units. US$99 double. MC, V. **Amenities:** 1 restaurant (regional), 1 bar; free use of snorkeling equipment and canoes. *In room:* TV, kitchen.

Safua Hotel   This rustic hotel is known not so much for the quality of its accommodations as for its owner, Moelagi Jackson, who holds two chiefly titles.

Her main fale holds a bar and dining room, where family style meals feature Samoan favorites such as chicken curry and whole fish in ginger. The fales scattered about her lawn are of clapboard construction, with front porches, screened windows, basic electric lights, and bathrooms with cold-water showers. Don't be surprised to hear a catfight or the grunts of pigs running loose at night. The Safua will arrange village accommodation for US$35 per person, including meals.

Private Bag, Salelologa, Savai'i (in Safua village, 6.5km/4 miles north of wharf). ☎ **51-271.** Fax 51-272. safuahotel@lesamoa.net. 12 units. US$70 fale. Rates include all meals. AE, MC, V. **Amenities:** 1 restaurant (regional), 1 bar. *In room:* No phone.

The Savaiian Hotel   This lagoon-side motel is the most modern and up-to-date accommodation on Savai'i. There's no beach here, only a breakwater, but the property has a wonderful view of the Apolima Straight and Upolu's northern coast. A restaurant that serves breakfast, lunch, and dinner is in large main building, which often hosts official functions on weekend evenings. The six identical motel rooms are in three duplex, concrete block structures that sit in a large lawn. They all have sliding doors that open to porches, four of them with a view. Away from the shore, four much more basic Samoan-style bungalows have real thatch roofs, screened windows, cold-water showers, and ceiling fans but not air conditioners.

P.O. Box 5082, Salelologa, Savai'i (in Lalomalava village, 6.5km/4 miles north of ferry wharf). ☎ **51-296.** Fax 51-439 or 51-291. savaiian@lesamoa.net. 10 units. S$135 ($38) double; S$66 ($18.50) bungalow. MC, V. **Amenities:** 1 restaurant (regional), 1 bar; laundry service. *In room:* A/C, kitchen, minibar, coffeemaker, no phone.

Siufaga Beach Resort   Dr. Peter Cafarelli, an Italian who has lived on Savai'i since the late 1960s, actually owns the 7 acres of lawn under his six Samoan-style fales facing Faga Beach and an emerald lagoon speckled with coral heads. Two fales are equipped with front porches, full kitchens, and hot-water showers. They are much larger than the other, somewhat basic, tin-roofed fales, which have small refrigerators, hot plates, and cold-water showers. All units are cooled by the trade winds but have electric fans just in case. Also on the premises, the upstairs Parenzo's Bar/Restaurant (same phone number) offers inexpensive Italian fare. You can dine at tables inside or outside on a porch with lagoon views.

P.O. Box 8002, Tuasive, Savai'i (in Faga village, 13km/8 miles north of ferry wharf). ☎ **53-518.** Fax 53-535. siufaga@lesamoa.net. 8 units. S$120–S$210 ($33.50–$59) double. MC, V. **Amenities:** 1 restaurant (regional), 1 bar. *In room:* Kitchen, no phone.

Stevenson's at Manase   The best features of this eclectic resort, on a lovely beach just west of Manase village, are two stunning thatch-roofed, sawdust-floored buildings that hold Fanny's Restaurant and the Admiral Benbow Bar. Near them, 19 smallish, motel-style rooms occupy what appear to be converted shipping containers; some but not all of these plain rooms have much-needed air conditioners. Far better choices are five bungalows (they call them "villas" here) across the road on the beach. Leaf exteriors and *siapo*-lined ceilings make these houses look rustic, but inside they are relatively modern, with air conditioners, televisions, and outdoor hot-water showers enclosed by rock walls. Backpackers can share beach fales. Stevenson's is a popular local beach on weekends, when a bar opens in a beachside pavilion. Guests have free use of paddle boats, canoes, and snorkeling gear, but at low tide the lagoon is too shallow for such diversions.

P.O. Box 210, Apia (at Manase village, 48km/30 miles north of ferry wharf). ☎ **58-219.** Fax 58-219. 33 units (10 without bathroom). S$88 ($24.50) double; S$220 ($61.50) bungalow; S$22 ($6) per person in beach fales. MC, V. **Amenities:** 1 restaurant (regional), 2 bars; watersports. *In room:* A/C (villas and some rooms), TV (villas only), no phone.

BEACH FALES AT MANASE

Like Upolu, Savai'i has scores of beach fales. The most popular is **Tanu Beach Fales,** Post Office, Fagamalo (☎ and fax **54-050**), which shares a north-shore beach with Stevenson's at Manase (see above). A majority of its 26 fales sit right by the lagoon, and the others are in a grove of tropical trees. They all have electric lights, mosquito nets, linen, mattresses, pillows and pull-down side mats for privacy. A central, European-style building provides a lounge and dining area, and guests can also wander into the owner's traditional Samoan fale. Guests share cold-water showers. There's a communal kitchen and grocery shop, or you can walk along the beach to Stevenson's for lunch or dinner. Musicians entertain several nights a week here, and Tanu has island tours in its own bus (which will meet guests at the ferry). Rates are S$50 ($14) per person, including breakfast and dinner. MasterCard and Visa are accepted.

On the same beach but in the middle of Manase village, **Jane's Beach Fales,** Post Office, Fagamalo (☎ **54-066;** sbec@samoa.ws), is a bit more luxurious—if that word can be applied to these rustic accommodations. Her 12 fales are larger than Tanu's, and each is about half front porch, half bedroom. One actually has a kitchen and its own bathroom, and the others share toilets, cold-water showers, and a communal kitchen. The fales sit among palms and breadfruit trees on a lawn of grass, as opposed to sand at Tanu. A restaurant here serves simple local-style meals daily and stages a *fiafia* on Saturday nights. Jane charges S$50 ($14) per person per night, including breakfast and dinner, but she does not accept credit cards.

13

American Samoa

The main reason to visit American Samoa is to see its incredible beauty, and you'll get an eyeful of that on the 11km (7-mile) ride from the airport at Tafuna into the legendary port of Pago Pago. Instead of following a gentle shoreline like the west coast road does in independent Samoa, this road twists and turns along the gorgeous rocky coastline of Tutuila, one of the South Pacific's most dramatically beautiful islands. At places it rounds the cliffs of headlands that drop down to the sea; at others it curves along beaches in small bays backed by narrow valleys. All the way, the surf pounds on the reef. When you make the last turn at Blount's Point, there before you are the green walls dropping precipitously into Pago Pago Harbor. If you ignore the mountain of rusting shipping containers and the two smelly tuna canneries on the shore of the harbor, the physical beauty of this little island competes with the splendor of Moorea and Bora Bora in French Polynesia.

You will see the effects of American dollars when you pass through Nu'uli,

once a sleepy Samoan village but now a bustling suburb with shopping centers and a modern multiscreen cinema. You will discover that the roads here are crowded with automobiles and buses and are patrolled by policemen bedecked with revolvers in big American-style cruisers. It's little wonder, therefore, that many visitors see American Samoa as ruined by modern commercialism, crowded, littered, and run-down.

Yet despite the obvious inroads of Western ways and American loot, the local residents still cling to *fa'a Samoa,* the ancient Samoan way of life (see "The Samoan People" in chapter 12). While many young American Samoans wear Western clothes and speak only English, often with a pronounced Hawaiian or Californian accent, in the villages the older folk still converse in Samoan and abide by the old ways.

Nevertheless, Samoan culture is best experienced in independent Samoa. I like to stay in Apia and make a day trip from there to Pago Pago.

1 American Samoa Today

The seven islands of American Samoa are on the eastern end of the 483km (300-mile)-long Samoa Archipelago. Together they comprise a land area of 124 square km (77 square miles), 53 of which belong to **Tutuila,** the slender remains of an ancient volcano. One side of Tutuila's crater apparently blew away, almost cutting the island in two. Thus was created the long, bent arm of **Pago Pago Harbor,** one of the South Pacific's most dramatically scenic spots.

American Samoa is the only U.S. territory south of the equator. American Samoans are nationals, not citizens, of the United States. They often refer to the islands—not to the United States—as their "country." Although they carry

American passports, have unrestricted entry into the United States, and can serve in the U.S. armed forces, they cannot vote in U.S. presidential elections.

Only half as many American Samoans live in their home islands as reside in the United States, where a number of them have made names for themselves as college and pro football players. The expatriate American Samoans have been replaced at home by their kindred from independent Samoa and by some Tongans, who have swelled the population to some 57,000, up from 30,000 in the early 1990s.

GOVERNMENT   The U.S. Department of the Interior in Washington, D.C., has jurisdiction over American Samoa, but the territory has considerable say over its local affairs. The territorial government is patterned on that of the United States, with some important local wrinkles. American Samoans elect their own governor, who's head of the executive branch, and they choose members of their House of Representatives, the lower house of the bicameral legislature known as the Fono. In the upper house, senators are picked by the chiefs in accordance with Samoan custom. The Fono has authority over the budget and local affairs, although both the governor and the U.S. Department of the Interior can veto the laws it passes. A political appointee from Washington, D.C., heads the third branch of government, the High Court of American Samoa. The court has a special department that deals exclusively with land ownership and *matai* titles.

American Samoans also elect a nonvoting delegate to the U.S. House of Representatives in Washington.

The territorial government's annual budget is considerably larger than that of independent Samoa, which has a population some three times larger. Washington provides about half the government's revenue. Some 80% of the taxes raised locally go to pay more than 40% of the local workforce.

ECONOMY   The American Samoa islands are small, rugged, and relatively unproductive. Money from Washington and the tuna canneries are the major sources of income. The canneries employ around 4,000 workers. Most other workers are employed by retail establishments, a few small manufacturers, and service businesses, especially shipping companies, which have made Pago Pago a major transshipment point (the American-brewed Budweiser beer sold in Samoa and Tonga is shipped through Pago Pago). Tourism is a very small part of the economy; in fact, the overwhelming number of tourists who visit are on large cruise ships that put into Pago Pago for a day.

2 History 101

As friendly as American Samoans are today, their ancestors did anything but warmly welcome a French expedition under Jean La Pérouse, which came ashore in 1787 on the north coast of Tutuila. Samoan warriors promptly attacked, killing 12 members of the landing party, which in turn killed 39 Samoans. The site of the battle is known as **Massacre Bay.** La Pérouse survived that incident, but he and his entire expedition later disappeared in what is now the Solomon Islands.

U.S. businessmen cast an eye on Pago Pago in the mid-1800s, and in 1872, the U.S. Navy negotiated a treaty with the chiefs of Tutuila to permit it to use Pago Pago as a coaling station. The U.S. Congress never ratified this document, but it helped keep the Germans out of Eastern Samoa, as present-day American Samoa was then known.

In 1900 the chiefs on Tutuila ceded control of their island to the United States, and the paramount chief of the Manu'a Group of islands east of Tutuila did

> **Fun Fact**   Unfriendly Fire
>
> During World War II a Japanese submarine surfaced off Tutuila and lobbed a few shells ashore. Ironically, their target was a store owned by Frank Shimasaki, the island's only resident of Japanese descent.

likewise in 1905. Finally ratified by the U.S. Senate in 1929, those treaties are the legal foundation for the U.S. presence in American Samoa. *Presence* is the accurate term, for under those treaties the United States does not "possess" American Samoa. Instead, the arrangement is subject to the treaties, which require the United States to preserve the system of chiefs and to retain the traditional ways of *fa'a Samoa,* including the communal ownership of Samoan land.

ON THE DOLE   From 1900 until 1951, U.S. authority in Samoa rested with the U.S. Navy, which maintained the refueling station at Pago Pago and for the most part let the local chiefs conduct their own affairs. Tutuila became a training base for U.S. servicemen during World War II, but things quickly returned to normal after 1945. Because Samoa had little military value, control of the territory was shifted from the navy to the U.S. Department of the Interior in 1951.

The Department of the Interior did little in the islands until 1961, when *Reader's Digest* magazine ran an article about "America's shame in the South Seas." The story took great offense at the lack of roads and adequate schools, medical care, water and sewer service, and housing. The U.S. federal government reacted by building sealed roads, an international airport, water and electrical systems, the then-modern Rainmaker Hotel, and a convention center. A 1.5km (½ mile) -long cable was strung across Pago Pago Harbor to build a television transmitter atop 480m (1,610-ft.) Mount Alava, from which education programming was beamed into the schools. The territory's duty-free status and relatively low wages enticed U.S. firms to build the two tuna canneries.

For fear of losing all that federal money, American Samoans were reluctant to tinker with their political relationship with Washington during the 1960s and 1970s, when other South Pacific colonies were becoming independent. The United States offered to let them have local autonomy, but they refused. That attitude finally changed in the mid-1970s, when an appointed governor was very unpopular. After twice turning down the proposal, American Samoans voted in 1976 to elect their own governor, and they did so for the first time in 1977.

3 Visitor Information & Entry Requirements

VISITOR INFORMATION

The **American Samoa Office of Tourism,** P.O. Box 1147, Pago Pago, AS 96799 (© **633-2092;** fax 633-1094; www.amsamoa.com), has offices in Utulei, next to the yacht club. The office is open Monday to Friday 7:30am to 4pm.

The **Delegate from American Samoa to the U.S. Congress** also dispenses some tourist information. The address is U.S. House of Representatives, Washington, D.C. 20515 (© **202/225-8577**).

ENTRY REQUIREMENTS

Visas are not required for stays of up to 30 days. Technically, U.S. citizens need only proof of citizenship (such as a birth certificate) to enter American Samoa.

They need valid passports to enter independent Samoa, however, and having one speeds entry here and back into the United States (entry into American Samoa is not the same as entering the U.S.). Citizens of other nations must have passports to enter American Samoa. Everyone must possess a ticket for onward passage.

Immunizations are required only if a person has been in an infected yellow fever or cholera area within 14 days of arrival at Pago Pago.

Customs allowances are 1 liter of liquor or wine and one carton of cigarettes. Illegal drugs and firearms are prohibited, and pets are quarantined. Returning U.S. citizens get larger customs allowances for purchases made in American Samoa than they do elsewhere in the South Pacific, provided that they have been in the territory for at least 48 hours (see "What You Can Take Home" in chapter 2).

4 Money

U.S. bank notes and coins are used in American Samoa. Samoan currency is not accepted, nor can it be exchanged in American Samoa. There is no bargaining over prices here.

HOW TO GET LOCAL CURRENCY   The **Bank of Hawaii** and the **ANZ/Amerika Samoa Bank,** both in Fagatogo, are open Monday to Friday from 9am to 3pm. Both have ATMs.

CREDIT CARDS   American Express, Visa, MasterCard, and Diners Club are accepted by the hotels, car-rental firms, and airlines. Otherwise, it's best to carry enough cash to cover your anticipated expenses. No one here accepts Discover.

5 When to Go

CLIMATE
"It did not pour, it flowed," wrote W. Somerset Maugham in his 1921 short story "Rain," the famous tale of prostitute Sadie Thompson, who seduces a puritanical missionary while stranded in American Samoa. This description, however, applies mainly to Pago Pago, which, because of its location behind appropriately named Rainmaker Mountain, gets an average of over 500 centimeters (200 in.) of rain per year. For the most part, American Samoa enjoys a typically tropical climate, with lots of very intense sunshine even during the wet season, from December to April. Average daily high temperatures range from 83°F (28°C) in the drier and somewhat cooler months of June through September to 86°F (30°C) from December to April, when midday can be hot and sticky. Evenings are usually in the comfortable 70s (21°C–26°C) all year-round.

EVENTS & HOLIDAYS
The biggest celebration is on April 17, when **American Samoa Flag Day** commemorates the raising of the Stars and Stripes over Tutuila in 1900. The second Sunday in October is observed as **White Sunday;** children attend church dressed in white and are later honored at family feasts.

Public holidays are New Year's Day, Martin Luther King Jr. Day (third Mon in Jan), President's Day (third Mon in Feb), Good Friday, American Samoa Flag Day (Apr 17), Memorial Day (last Mon in May), the Fourth of July, Labor Day (first Mon in Sept), Columbus Day (second Mon in Oct), Veteran's Day (Nov 11), Thanksgiving (fourth Thurs of Nov), and Christmas Day.

6 Getting There & Getting Around

GETTING THERE

FROM SAMOA **Polynesian Airlines** (© **800/644-7659,** 22-737 in Apia, or 633-4331 in Pago Pago; www.polynesianairlines.com) and **Samoa Air** (© **22-321** in Apia, or 699-9126 in Pago Pago; www.samoaair.com) both shuttle back and forth between Fagali'i Airstrip near Apia and Pago Pago several times a day. Round-trip fares on both airlines are S$256 ($71.50) if purchased in Apia, US$122 if bought in American Samoa. The savings is one more reason to make your Samoan base in Apia.

For the adventurous, a relatively modern ferry, the *Lady Naomi,* makes the 8-hour voyage between Pago Pago and Apia once a week, usually leaving the main wharf in Apia at 11pm on Wednesday and departing Pago Pago's marine terminal at 4pm Thursday for the return voyage. Tickets should be bought at least a day ahead of time. One-way tickets purchased in Apia cost S$50 ($14) for a seat, S$70 ($19.50) for a bunk. One-way fares purchased in Pago Pago are $40 and $50, respectively. The *Lady Naomi* is operated by the **Western Samoa Shipping Corporation,** whose ticket office is on Beach Road, opposite the main wharf in Apia (© **20-935**). The American Samoa agent is **Polynesia Shipping Services** (© **633-1211**). Because the trade winds prevail from the southeast, the trip going west with the wind toward Apia is usually somewhat smoother.

FROM OTHER COUNTRIES The only international carrier that serves American Samoa is **Hawaiian Airlines,** which flies from several U.S. West Coast cities to Pago Pago, with a change of planes at its base at Honolulu. Otherwise, you can fly to Faleolo Airport in Samoa on **Air New Zealand, Air Pacific,** or **Polynesian Airlines,** and then connect to Pago Pago. For more information, see "Getting There & Getting Around" in chapter 2.

ARRIVING & DEPARTING The runways at **Pago Pago** International Airport extend for half their length on landfills over the reef near the village of Tafuna, about 11km (7 miles) west of The Rainmaker Hotel. Taxi fare is about $10 from the airport to Pago Pago. There is no departure tax on passengers leaving Pago Pago.

GETTING AROUND

BY RENTAL CAR The only international car-rental firm in American Samoa is **Avis** (© **800/331-1212** or 699-4408; www.avis.com), which rents air-conditioned models for $55 to $65 per day, including unlimited mileage, plus an optional $10 for insurance. The Avis office in Apia (© **20-486**) will reserve a car in Pago Pago for you. Local firms include **Royal Samoan Car Rental** (© **633-2017** or 633-4545) and **Pavitt's U-Drive** (© **633-1456**).

Your valid home driver's license will be honored in American Samoa. **Driving is on the right-hand side of the road,** and traffic signs are the same as those used in the United States. The speed limit is 15 mph in the built-up areas and 25 mph on the open road.

Tips **Reconfirm Your Return Flight at the Airport**

Right after you land at Pago Pago, go to the airline's office and reconfirm your return flight. This is especially important if you're flying back to Apia on the last flight of the day.

BY BUS   It sometimes seems that every extended family on Tutuila owns an "*aiga* bus," since so many of these gaily painted vehicles prowl the roads from early in the morning until sunset every day except Sunday, when they are put to use to haul the family to church. Basically they run from the villages to the market in Pago Pago and back, picking up anyone who waves along the way. To get off, push the button for the bell as you approach your destination. Some buses leave the market and run to Fagasa on the north coast or to the east end of the island; others go from the market to the west. None goes from one end of the island to the other, so you'll have to change at the market in order to do a stem-to-stern tour of Tutuila. The drivers are friendly and helpful, so just ask how far they go in each direction. Fares are between 50¢ and $1 per ride.

BY TAXI   There are **taxi stands** at the **airport** (© 699-1179) and at the **Pago Pago market** (no phone). The taxi companies are **Aeto Cab** (© 633-2366), **Black Ace** (© 633-5445), **Island Taxi** (© 633-5645), and **Samoa Cab Service** (© 633-5870 or 633-5871). None of the taxis have meters, so be sure to negotiate the fare before driving off. The fares should be about $1 per mile.

 FAST FACTS: **American Samoa**

American Express   There is no American Express representative in American Samoa.

Baggage Storage   The hotels will store your extra gear for free.

Bookstores   **Polynesian Picks,** the gift shop in the Rainmaker Hotel (© 633-2366), carries some paperback books and has current U.S. magazines.

Business Hours   Normal shopping hours are Monday to Friday from 9am to 6pm and Saturday from 9am to 2. Government offices are open Monday to Friday from 7:30am to 4pm.

Camera/Film   A wide variety of film is available at reasonable prices. **Samoa Photo Express,** opposite the Fono building in Fagatogo (© 633-2374), has 1-hour developing of color print film.

Clothing   Lightweight, informal summer clothing is appropriate all year, with a light sweater or wrap for evenings from June through September. I always carry a folding umbrella or plastic raincoat because it can rain any time of the day or night in Pago Pago. Young American Samoans have adopted Western-style dress, including blue jeans and shorts of respectable length, although the traditional wraparound *lavalava* is still worn by many older men and women. In keeping with Samoan custom regarding modesty, visitors should not wear bathing suits or other skimpy clothing away from the hotels. Women must wear their bikini tops on the beach.

Drugstores   See "Healthcare," below.

Electricity   American Samoa uses 110-volt electric current and plugs identical to those in the United States.

Embassies/Consulates   The governor of American Samoa is a consular official of the U.S. federal government and can issue temporary passports to U.S. citizens and nationals who lose theirs, provided that they have some other proof of citizenship. Applications should be made to the **Immigration Office** (© 633-4203), in the Department of Legal Affairs. The Republic of

Korea has a consulate, and the Republic of China (Taiwan) maintains a liaison office in Pago Pago, primarily to assist the Korean and Taiwanese crews of the tuna boats unloading their catches at the tuna canneries.

Emergencies The emergency telephone number for the **police, fire department,** and **ambulance** is 🕻 **911.** In a medical emergency, you can call or go to **Lyndon B. Johnson Tropical Medical Center (🕻 633-5555)** in Faga'alu, which is open 24 hours a day. The **police station (🕻 633-1111)** is in Fagatogo, across the *malae* (open field) from the Fono.

E-mail **DDW Internet Cafe,** in Pago Plaza at the head of the bay **(🕻 633-5297),** has Internet access for $3 for 15 minutes, $5 for 30 minutes, $10 for an hour. It's open Monday to Friday 7am to 6pm, Saturday 7am to noon. You can get breakfast and lunch here, too.

Eyeglasses Try the **Lyndon B. Johnson Tropical Medical Center** (see "Healthcare," below).

Firearms Guns are tightly controlled, and permits are required.

Gambling There are no casinos or other organized forms of gambling in American Samoa, except for slot machines in some stores and private clubs. Money is also wagered at very popular bingo games.

Healthcare The **Lyndon B. Johnson Tropical Medical Center (🕻 633-5555** for emergencies, or 633-1222) in Faga'alu west of Pago Pago (turn off the main road at Tom Ho Chung's store) is a classic example of socialized medicine, providing all of the territory's medical, dental, and eyeglasses services. The outpatient clinic is open 24 hours daily.

Insects There are no dangerous insects in American Samoa, and the plentiful mosquitoes do not carry malaria.

Liquor Laws There are no unusual laws to worry about. Most of the beer consumed is imported from the United States.

Maps The American Samoa Office of Tourism distributes a sheet of maps (see "Visitor Information & Entry Requirements," above).

Newspapers/Magazines The daily *Samoa News* (www.samoanews.com) carries world news and colorful coverage of local events.

Post Office The U.S. Postal Service's main post office is in Fagatogo. Regular U.S. postage rates apply, and first-class and priority letters and packages go by air between American Samoa and the United States. Unless you pay the first-class or priority mail rate, however, parcel post is sent by ship and will take several weeks to reach the United States. The main post office is open Monday to Friday from 7:30am to 3:30pm and Saturday from 7:30am to 1pm. The zip code for all of American Samoa is **96799.**

Radio/TV The transmitters atop Mount Alava are used during the day to send educational TV programs to the territory's public schools and to transmit CNN and live sporting events. At night they broadcast two channels of U.S. network entertainment programs. The broadcasts can be seen 129km (80 miles) away, in Samoa. Many homes in American Samoa also have cable television.

The territory has three FM radio stations, which transmit American network news broadcasts on the hour.

Safety Street crime is not a serious problem in American Samoa except at night around Pago Pago Harbor. Fa'a Samoa and its rules of communal ownership are still in effect, however, so it's wise not to leave cameras, watches, or other valuables lying around unattended.

Taxes There is no airport departure tax, and there is no sales tax. However, an import tax of 5% is imposed on most merchandise (it's much stiffer on tobacco and alcoholic beverages).

Telephone/Fax Telephone calls can be dialed directly into American Samoa from most parts of the world. The territory's international country code has been **684**, but plans were under way at press time to make 684 a domestic U.S. area code. When this happens, the country code for American Samoa will be **1**. When the change goes into effect, American Samoa will be a regular long-distance call from the United States; that is, you dial **1** followed by the **684** area code and the local number.

The easiest way to call home from here is to buy a prepaid **Blue Sky card**, available at many shops. You can use these cards from any phone as you would a prepaid card at home. You can also use MCI calling cards by dialing ✆ **633-2624** from a pay phone.

Visitors can also place overseas calls at **American Samoa Telecommunications Authority**, diagonally across the Fagatogo *malae* from the Fono building. The office is open 24 hours daily.

The local phone system is identical to that in the United States, and the pay phones are the same type used throughout the United States. The number for directory assistance is ✆ **411**. For emergencies, dial ✆ **911**.

Time The local time in American Samoa is the same as in independent Samoa: 11 hours behind Greenwich mean time. That's 3 hours behind Pacific standard time (4 hr. behind during daylight saving time). In other words, if it's noon standard time in California and 3pm in New York, it's 9am in Pago Pago. If daylight saving time is in effect in the United States, it's 8am in American Samoa.

American Samoa is east of the international date line and shares the same date with North America, 1 day behind Tonga, Fiji, Australia, and New Zealand.

Tipping Although this is a U.S. territory, officially there is no tipping in American Samoa. A lot of American Samoans have lived in the United States, however, so the practice is not exactly uncommon.

Water The tap water is treated and is safe to drink except during periods of heavy rain.

Weights/Measures American Samoa is the only country or territory in the South Pacific whose official system of weights and measures is the same as that used in the United States—the British system of pounds and miles, not the metric system of kilograms and kilometers.

7 Exploring American Samoa

A STROLL THROUGH PAGO PAGO

Although the actual village of Pago Pago sits at the head of the harbor, everyone refers to the built-up area on the south shore of the harbor, including Fagatogo,

Tips Seeing American Samoa as a Day Trip from Apia

The easiest way to see American Samoa as a 1-day side trip from independent Samoa is to buy a package from **Oceania Travel & Tours,** at the Kitano Tusitala Hotel in Apia (✆ **24-443;** fax 22-255; www.oceania-travel.ws). The $150 per-person fee includes round-trip airfare, a guided tour of the island, and lunch.

To do it yourself, fly early in the morning from Apia to Pago Pago. Go immediately to the airline offices and reconfirm your afternoon return flight, and then take a taxi to The Rainmaker Hotel. Stroll through Pago Pago as described in "Exploring American Samoa," below, and then stop for lunch. Grab an *aiga* bus at the market for a ride to the east end, and then take another bus ride to the west end. On the way back, you can get off and call a taxi, catch an *aiga* bus, or walk the 2.5km (1½ miles) from the main road to the airport for your late-afternoon return flight to Apia.

the government and business center, as Pago Pago. The harbor is also called the Bay Area. Despite development that has come with economic growth of the territory, Pago Pago still has much of the old South Seas atmosphere that captivated W. Somerset Maugham when he visited and wrote "Rain" in the 1920s.

A stroll through the Pago Pago area should take about 2 hours. Begin at **The Rainmaker Hotel** on the east end of the inner harbor, actually in the village of Utulei. Just across the main road from the hotel, a set of concrete steps climbs to **Government House,** the clapboard mansion built in 1903 to house the governor of American Samoa. Unless you have business with the governor, the mansion is not open to the public. There is a nice view, however, from the top of the steps looking back over the hotel and across the harbor to flat-top Rainmaker Mountain.

Back on the main road heading north toward town, you walk pass a mountain of shipping containers that stand idle on the main wharf. In front of them is the **Feleti Pacific Library,** which has a good collection of books on the South Pacific. Beyond the busy port terminal is the **Jean P. Haydon Museum** (✆ **633-4347**), in an old iron-roofed building that was once the U.S. Navy's commissary. The museum features exhibits on Samoan history, sea life, canoes, kava making, and traditional tools and handcrafts, including the finely woven mats that have such great value in Samoa and Tonga. The museum has been undergoing a lengthy renovation, so it might not be open when you arrive. If it is, normal hours are Monday to Friday from 9am to 3pm, except on holidays. Admission has been free in the past, but donations are accepted.

Every Samoan village has a ***malae,*** or open field, and the area across from the museum is Fagatogo's. The chiefs of Tutuila met on this *malae* in 1900 to sign the treaty that officially established the United States in Samoa. The round modern building across the road beside the harbor is the **Fono,** American Samoa's legislature; the visitors' galleries are open to the public. The ramshackle stores along the narrow streets on the other side of the *malae* were for half a century Pago Pago's "downtown," although like any other place under the Stars and Stripes, much business is now conducted in suburban shopping centers. On the

Pago Pago

ACCOMMODATIONS

Pago Airport Inn **10**
Rainmaker Hotel **1**

ATTRACTIONS

Feleti Pacific Library **3**
Fono (Legislature) **5**
Government House **2**
Jean P. Haydon Museum **4**
High Court **6**
Markets **7**
Pago Plaza **9**
Sadie Thompson Building **8**

To East Coast

Tuna Canneries

Ronald Reagan Shipyard

Pago Pago Harbor

Small Boat Harbor

Goat Island Point

Lee Auditorium

Tourism Office

Utulei

To Airport & West Coast

Container Dock

Ferry Dock

Main Post Office

Police

Malae

Fagatogo

Communications Office

Bus Station

SAMOA
Wallis
Apia
Savai'i
Upolu
Pago Pago
Manu'a Islands
Tutuila
AMERICAN SAMOA

Malaloa

Happy Valley

Pago Pago Park

Pago Pago

To Fagasa

Tutuila

Tula
Aoa Bay
Alao
Vatia
Mt. Alava
Pago Pago
Pago Pago Harbor
Pago Pago International Airport
Nu'uli
Vaitogi
Aoloaufou
Massacre Bay
Leone
Fagasa (Forbidden Bay)

Beach
Post Office
Information

0   2 Miles
0   2 Kilometers

N

malae, the **American Samoa Archives Office** occupies the old stone jail that was built in 1911.

Just beyond the *malae* on the main road stands the **Judicial Building,** home of the **High Court** of American Samoa (everyone calls it the Court House). The big white clapboard building with columns looks as if it should be in South Carolina rather than the South Pacific. Across the road on the waterfront stands **Fagatogo Plaza,** a modern shopping center. You can take a refreshment break here, at **Billy's,** on the water side of the center (see "Where to Dine," below).

In marked contrast to Fagatogo Plaza are the **produce and fish markets** a few yards farther on. They are usually poorly stocked, and when they do have produce, it most likely comes by ferry from Samoa. The markets also serve as the bus terminal.

Continuing north along the harbor, you soon come to the **Sadie Thompson Building.** This large wooden structure, which was recently renovated, was the rooming house where W. Somerset Maugham was marooned during a measles epidemic in the early 1920s. It provided the grist for his famous short story "Rain."

A TOUR OF TUTUILA
THE NORTH COAST OF TUTUILA

A paved road turns off the main highway at Spenser's Store in Pago Pago village and leads up **Vaipito Valley,** across a ridge, and down to Fagasa, a village huddled beside picturesque Fagasa, or **Forbidden Bay,** on Tutuila's north shore. The road is steep but paved all the way, and the view from atop the ridge is excellent. The track up Mount Alava begins on the saddle (see "National Park of American Samoa," below). Legend says that porpoises long ago led a group of three men and three women to safety in Fagasa Bay, which has long been a porpoise sanctuary.

THE EAST SIDE OF TUTUILA

The 29km (18-mile) drive from Pago Pago to the east end of Tutuila skirts along the harbor, past the canneries and their fishy odor, and then winds around one headland after another into small bays, many of them with sandy beaches and good swimming holes over the reef. Watch particularly for **Pyramid Rock** and the **Lion's Head,** where you can wade out to a small beach.

From Aua, at the foot of Rainmaker Mountain, a switch-backing road runs across Rainmaker Pass (great views from up there) to the lovely north-shore village of **Vatia,** on a bay of the same name. World War II pillboxes still dot the beach here. At the north end of Vatia Bay sits the skinny, offshore rock formation known as **The Cockscomb,** one of Tutuila's trademarks.

Another paved road leaves Faga'itua village and climbs to a saddle in the ridge, where it divides. The left fork goes down to Masefau Bay; the right goes to Masausi and Sa'ilele villages. Near the east end, a road from Amouli village cuts across Lemafa Saddle to **Aoa Bay** on the north coast.

Aunu'u Island will be visible from the main road as you near the east end of Tutuila. Aunu'u is the top of a small volcanic crater and has a village near a famous quicksand pit. Motorboats leave for it from the small-boat harbor at Au'asi on the southeast coast.

Alao and **Tula** villages on the east end of Tutuila are the oldest settlements in American Samoa. They have long, gorgeous surf beaches, but be careful of the undertow from waves driven by the prevailing southeast trade winds.

THE WEST SIDE OF TUTUILA

You saw some of Tutuila's rugged coast on the drive in from the airport west of Pago Pago, including the **Flower Pot,** a tall rock with coconut palms growing on

> **Tips A Fascinating Pit Stop**
>
> Ramshackle bars by the beach are part of the South Seas lore, but few of these establishments actually exist these days. One that does is **Tisa's Barefoot Bar** on Alega Beach (© 622-7447). This funky joint looks slapped together because it actually is. The owners put it together from driftwood, scrap lumber, well-worn tables, and whatever else they could find lying around. Libation is served daily from 11am to 7pm, with seafood dinners afterward by advance reservation only. You can go snorkeling and swimming here at high tide, and you can pay your bill at any tide with your American Express, MasterCard, or Visa.

its top sitting in the lagoon. About halfway from the airport to The Rainmaker Hotel is a road inland (at Tom Ho Chung's store) that leads to the **Lyndon B. Johnson Tropical Medical Center** in the Faga'alu Valley. If you feel like taking a hike, take the left fork in the road past the medical center, and when the pavement ends, follow the track to **Virgin Falls.** It's not the easiest walk, but the falls have a nice pool beneath them. Give yourself several hours for this sweaty outing.

The **airport** sits on the island's only sizable parcel of relatively flat land, and the main road west from there cuts through rolling hills and shopping centers until emerging on the rugged west end.

At Pava'ia'i village a road goes inland and climbs to the village of A'oloaufou, high on a central plateau. A hiking trail leads from the village down the ridges to the north coast; from here it drops to A'asutuai on **Massacre Bay,** where Samoans attacked the La Pérouse expedition in 1787. The French have put a monument there to the members of the expedition who were slain by Samoan warriors.

Back on the main road, head west and watch for a sign on the left that marks the turn to the villages of Illi'ili and Vaitogi. Follow the signs to **Vaitogi,** and when you're in the village, bear right at the fork to the beach. Take the one-lane track to the right along the beach, past some graves and the stone remains of an old church, and up a rocky headland through pandanus groves. When you reach the first clearing on the left, stop the car and walk over to the cliff. According to legend, Vaitogi once experienced such a severe famine that an old blind woman and her granddaughter jumped off this cliff and were turned into a shark and a turtle. Today the villagers can reputedly chant their names, and the turtle and the shark will appear. The view of the south coast from **Turtle and Shark Point,** with the surf pounding the rocks below you, is superb.

The Rev. John Williams chose the picturesque village of **Leone,** which sits on a white-sand beach in a small bay, as his landing place on Tutuila in 1830, and it became the cradle of Christianity in what is now American Samoa. There is a monument to Williams in the village. The road beside the Catholic church leads about 2.5km (1½ miles) to **Leone Falls,** which has a freshwater pool for swimming (but as in the equally religious Samoa, never on Sun).

The road from Leone to the western end of the island is scenic; it winds in and out of small bays with sandy beaches and climbs spectacularly across a ridge to Poloa village on the northwest coast.

8 National Park of American Samoa

The **National Park of American Samoa** was authorized by the U.S. Congress in 1988, and although its facilities have been slow in coming (little has been developed except a few rough hiking trails), the park has amassed some 10,000 pristine acres—3,000 of them on Tutuila and another 6,000 in the Manu'a Islands. In all, they protect some extraordinarily beautiful shoreline, magnificent beaches, cliffs dropping into the sea, colorful reefs, and rain forest reaching up to serrated, mist-shrouded mountain peaks.

Because development is ongoing, you should stop by the **Park Visitors Center,** in the Pago Plaza shopping center at the head of the bay, or contact them at NPAS, Pago Pago, AS 96799 (© **633-7082;** fax 633-7085; www.nps.gov). The center has exhibits that explain Samoa's prehistory.

On Tutuila, the park essentially starts along the ridge atop Mount Alava and drops down sharp ridges and steep valleys to the north coast. It includes The Cockscomb off the north coast and the scenic Amalau Valley, near the picturesque north shore village of Vatia, where you can see many of Samoa's native bird species, as well as flying foxes (fruit bats). See "A Tour of Tutuila," above, for directions to Vatia.

Hikers can scale 480m (1,600-ft.) Mount Alava via a trail that beings in the Fagasa Pass and ascends steeply through the rain forest. It's a 3-hour walk uphill along a seldom used four-wheel-drive track, and it takes about 2 hours to get back down, but you'll be rewarded with a view straight down over the entirety of Pago Pago Harbor and most of Tutuila Island. It's one of the most spectacular vistas in the South Pacific, if not the world. Be sure to take plenty of water.

Rory West of **North Shore Tours** (© **644-1416** or 733-3047) has various expeditions to the north coast, including hiking, camping, and fishing trips. Prices start at $25.

Unlike other U.S. National Parks, in which the federal government buys property outright, here the National Park Service has leased the land from the villages for 50 years, thereby protecting both the natural environment and traditional Samoan ownership customs.

9 Where to Stay

Most package tours put visitors up at **The Rainmaker Hotel,** P.O. Box 996, Pago Pago, AS 96799 (© **633-4241;** fax 633-5959). This establishment was built with government backing in the 1960s, and under government management it has gone steadily downhill. At press time efforts were being made to sell it, but until new owners infuse a mountain of cash into it, it's best to avoid this hotel. The Rainmaker originally had 184 rooms; no more than 40 were serviceable during my recent visit. If you must stay here, demand an upstairs room in the Beach Wing. Avoid any attempt to put you in the Harbor Wing or in a downstairs room in the Beach Wing. And inspect your room thoroughly before moving in. Make sure that the air conditioner works, the night latches engage properly, the plumbing actually does what it's supposed to do, and the sheets and towels are clean. Leave absolutely no valuables in your room, and lock the safety latch when you're inside. A restaurant, snack bar, salon, and tour desks are on the premises. Upstairs rooms in the Beach Wing cost $85 (an exorbitant amount compared to what you get at Aggie Grey's Hotel or the Hotel Kitano Tusitala in Apia for only slightly more).

The best alternatives are out by the airport, including the **Pago Airport Inn** (see below). In Vaitogi village beyond the airport, **Tessarea's,** P.O. Box 2551, Pago Pago, AS 96799 (© **699-5396;** fax 699-7790; tessa@samoatelco.com), has eight hotel rooms and five apartments, all air-conditioned, with phones, televisions, and private bathrooms. It also has a pool and laundry facilities. Rooms cost $85 per double, apartments are $100 to $145. MasterCard and Visa are accepted.

The National Park of American Samoa (see above) operates a **homestay program** known as Fale, Fala Ma Ti, in which it matches visitors seeking inexpensive accommodation with local families that are willing to take in paying guests. Prices are $45 per person a night, including meals. Some are Western-style houses; others are Samoan fales. All of them have modern toilets and showers. Some homes in the Manu'a Islands also have space for campers who bring their own tents. The Samoan hospitality will more than make up for the simple accommodation. Prior arrangements are required.

Pago Airport Inn   In a village setting, this two-story motel was built in 1997 and was the pick of the litter during my last visit. The motel-style rooms open to veranda-like walkways across the front of the white stucco building. The units are simple but clean and each is equipped with a double or two single beds, cable-fed TV mounted on the wall, a desk and chairs, and a tiled shower-only bathroom. Coffee is supplied in the morning, and there's a free shuttle to restaurants within a 8km (5-mile) radius (nevertheless, you'll want to consider renting a car).

P.O. Box 783, Pago Pago, AS 96799 (Tafuna, 3 min. from airport). ✆ **699-6333.** Fax 699-6336. pagoinn@blueskynet.as. 20 units. $90 double. AE, MC, V. **Amenities:** Laundry service. *In room:* A/C, TV, fridge.

10 Where to Dine

Billy's PIZZA/SNACK BAR   A decent place to stop for refreshment during a walking tour of Pago Pago, this waterfront establishment offers pizzas, fried chicken, sandwiches, hamburgers, hot dogs, nachos, fish and chips, and daily specials such as corned beef and cabbage. It's not as fast as it could be because all items are cooked to order. Even if you don't eat here, stop by for a cold soda and enjoy the magnificent view of the harbor.

Fagatogo, in Fagatoga Square behind Tedi of Samoa. ✆ **633-1199.** Reservations not accepted. Fried chicken, sandwiches, burgers, and hot dogs $1.50–$6. No credit cards. Mon–Sat 7am–9pm, Sun 9am–4pm.

DeLuxe Cafe ✦ AMERICAN   I always stop for breakfast at this modern, American-style cafe complete with Leatherette booths. The walls are adorned with large paintings of Samoan wildlife both in and out of the sea, which adds a touch of sophistication. Among the eye-openers are eggs Benedict, fresh fruit plates, and banana pancakes. Lunch sees a collection of American-style soups, salads, sandwiches, burgers, and fried chicken, shrimp, and fish.

Nu'uli, on main rd. east of airport. ✆ **699-4000.** Reservations not accepted. Breakfast $8–$8; lunch $5–$12. MC, V. Tues–Sat 7am–2pm, Sun 9am–2pm.

Rubbles Tavern AMERICAN/MEXICAN   It's a long way from town, but this friendly air-conditioned pub is a good place to cool off while you're waiting for the last plane back to Apia. Except for the bamboo lining the walls of one dining room and the mat panels and huge Samoan war canoe rudder adorning the other, Rubbles could be in any Western city. You can even watch live contests on the two TVs that show sporting events behind the long bar. The fare includes salads, nachos, burgers, sandwiches, chicken wings, and grilled steaks and fish.

Main rd., in Nu'uli Shopping Center (east of airport turnoff). ✆ **633-4403.** Reservations not accepted. Burgers, sandwiches, and salads $5.50–$9; main courses $8–$23. MC, V. Mon–Sat 11am–11pm (bar open later).

14

The Kingdom of Tonga

Thanks to a quirk of humankind and not of nature, the international date line swings eastward from its north-south path down the middle of the Pacific Ocean just enough to make the last Polynesian monarch the first sovereign to see the light of each new day. When the king of Tonga greets the dawn and looks out on his realm from the veranda of his whitewashed Victorian palace, he sees a country of low but extremely fertile islands, of gorgeous sandy beaches, and of colorful coral reefs waiting to be explored.

His is a nation protected but never ruled by a Western power. Like Samoa to the north, Tonga has managed to maintain its Polynesian culture in the face of modern change. The Tonga Visitors Bureau is spot on when it says the kingdom "still remains far away from it all; still different, still alone, and to the joy of those who find their way to her—essentially unspoiled."

While this description is true of the perfectly flat main island Tongatapu, it is even more applicable to Vava'u and Ha'apai. Vava'u is a group of hilly islands whose fjordlike harbor makes it one of the South Pacific's most popular yachting destinations, and the low islands of the Ha'apai group seem to have changed little since the crew of HMS *Bounty* staged their mutiny just offshore in 1789. Visiting Vava'u is extremely pleasant to the eyes, and taking a trip to Ha'apai is like traveling back in time to the old South Seas.

Bring a taste for adventure and your sense of humor to Tonga, for this is the poorest country in the South Pacific. The electricity might quit working, and the tap water might be turned off (not that you can drink it when it's running). You'll see multitudes of dogs, chickens, and even pigs almost everywhere, even wandering the streets of Nuku'alofa, the capital. And with a few exceptions, you'll stay in accommodations that make a Motel 6 seem luxurious. But if you can do without many comforts of home, you'll get a most fascinating glimpse into the way things used to be out here.

1 Tonga Today

In other Polynesian languages, the word *tonga* means "south." It stands to reason that Tonga would be so named because the kingdom lies south of Samoa, the first islands permanently settled by Polynesians and presumably the launching site for the colonization of Tonga and the rest of Polynesia. But to the Tongans the name means "garden," and when you drive from the airport into **Nuku'alofa,** the nation's capital, you can see why. It seems that every square yard of the main island of **Tongatapu** ("Sacred Garden") not occupied by a building or by the road is either under cultivation with bananas, tapioca, taro, yams, watermelons, tomatoes, squash, and a plethora of other fruits and vegetables. Crops grow in small plots under towering coconut palms so numerous that this flat island appears to be one huge copra plantation.

Impressions
Nature, assisted by a little art, no where appears in a more flourishing
state than at this Isle.
                                                    —Capt. James Cook, 1773

The Tongans might be generally poor in terms of material wealth, but they own some of the South Pacific's most fertile and productive land. There just isn't much of it. The kingdom consists of 170 islands, 36 of them inhabited, scattered over an area of about 160,934 square km (100,000 sq. miles), an area about the size of Colorado. The amount of dry land, however, is only 700 square km (269 sq. miles). That's smaller than New York City.

The largest island in the kingdom, Tongatapu, has about a third of the country's land area and about two-thirds of its population. It's a flat, raised atoll about 65km (40 miles) across from east to west and 32km (20 miles) across from north to south at its longest and widest points. In the center is a sparkling lagoon that's now unfortunately void of most sea life.

The government and most businesses and tourist activities are in Nuku'alofa (pop. 22,000), but there is much to see outside town, including some of the South Pacific's most important and impressive archaeological sites.

There are three major island groups in the country. Tongatapu and its neighbor, the smaller **'Eua,** comprise the southernmost group. About 155km (96 miles) north are the islands of **Ha'apai,** where Fletcher Christian led the mutiny on the *Bounty.* About 108km (67 miles) beyond Ha'apai is the beautiful **Vava'u,** the kingdom's sailing mecca. Even farther north are the remote **Niuas Islands,** but you won't be going up there.

THE NATURAL ENVIRONMENT   Tonga lies roughly north-south along the edge of the Indo-Australian Plate. The Tonga Trench, one of the deepest parts of the Pacific Ocean, parallels the islands to the east, where the Pacific Plate dips down and then under the Indo-Australian Plate. The resulting geological activity puts Tonga on the Ring of Fire that encircles the Pacific Ocean. One of Tonga's islands, **Tofua** in the Ha'apai group, is an active volcano.

Most of the islands are raised coral atolls. The exceptions are the Niuas and, in Ha'apai, the active volcano Tofua and its sister volcanic cone, Kao. Geologists say that the weight of the growing Ha'apai volcanoes has caused the Indo-Australian Plate to sag like a hammock, thereby raising Tongatapu and 'Eua on the south end of the Tongan chain and Vava'u on the north end. As a result, the sides of Tongatapu and Vava'u facing Ha'apai slope gently to the sea, and the sides facing away from Ha'apai end in cliffs that fall into the ocean.

GOVERNMENT   Although Tonga technically is a constitutional monarchy, the king in reality is head of a system of hereditary Polynesian chiefs who happen to have titles derived from England. The present king, Taufa'ahau Tupou IV, picks his own Privy Council of advisors and appoints nine cabinet members and the governors of Ha'apai and Vava'u. With a few exceptions they are nobles. The cabinet members and the governors hold 11 of the 30 seats in the Legislative Assembly. Of the 19 other members of the assembly, the nobles choose 10 from among their ranks, leaving 9 to be elected by the taxpaying commoners.

It would be an understatement to say that the royal family has a hand in every important decision made in Tonga; in fact, very little gets done without the royal family's outright or tacit approval or involvement.

Fun Fact   Stop It!

Legend says that Tonga's frequent earth tremors are caused when the Polynesian goddess Havea Hikule'o moves around in her underground lair. Tongans customarily stomp the shaking ground to get her to stop whatever she's doing down there.

With more and more Tongans living abroad, and those at home being exposed more and more to news of the world, the monarchy has been under increasing pressure to move to a democracy. This is not likely to happen as long as King Taufa'ahau Tupou IV—now in his 80s—is on the throne. What happens after he dies was very much up in the air during my recent visit (see "History 101," below).

ECONOMY   Tonga has few natural resources other than its fertile soil and the fish in the sea within its exclusive economic zone. The world markets for its major exports—vanilla, kava, bananas, coconut oil, pineapples, watermelons, tomatoes, squash, and other vegetables—has been unstable and even depressed at times in recent years. The country imports far more than it exports.

In addition, the kingdom has run out of land to apportion under the rule that gives each adult male 8¼ acres for growing crops. Given this lack of land, plus little chance of upward economic or social mobility, many thousands of Tongans have left the country and now live in Australia, New Zealand, and the United States. Money sent home by them is a major source of foreign exchange for the country.

For the commoners who remain behind, labor unions are illegal, and the primary chance for economic advancement is in small businesses. Although some of these are flourishing compared to those of other South Pacific island countries, the royal family can get involved when leases or permits are required from the government. The royals are partners in many businesses operated here by both Tongans and expatriate residents, and they reportedly own majority interests in the corporations that control Tonga's communications satellite slot above the Pacific and the allocation of Internet addresses that use its extension "to."

2 History 101

Legend has it that the great Polynesian god Maui threw a fishhook into the sea from Samoa and brought up the islands of Tonga. He then stepped on some of his catch, flattening them for gardens. Tofua and Kao in the Ha'apai group and some of the Niuas were left standing as volcanic cones.

Polynesians found and settled these gardens sometime around 500 B.C. on their long migration across the South Pacific. Around A.D. 950, according to another myth, the supreme Polynesian god (known here as Tangaloa) came down to Tongatapu and fathered a son

Dateline

- 500 B.C. Polynesians from Samoa settle in Tonga.
- A.D. 950 By legend, supreme god Tangaloa comes to earth and fathers a son by a beautiful virgin, thus founding the Tui Tonga dynasty.
- 1642 Dutchman Abel Tasman is the first European to set foot in Tonga.
- 1777 Captain Cook is feted by Finau I in the Ha'apai group, names them "The Friendly Islands," and leaves as Finau plans to kill him.
- 1781 Spaniard Francisco Mourelle "discovers" Vava'u.

continues

by a lovely Tongan maiden. Their son, Aho'eitu, thus became the first Tui Tonga—king of Tonga—and launched one of the world's longest-running dynasties. Under subsequent tuis, Tonga became a power in Polynesia; its large war canoes loaded with fierce warriors conquered and dominated the Samoas and the eastern islands of present-day Fiji.

The first tuis ruled from Niutoua village on the northwest corner of Tongatapu. They moved to Lapaha on the shore of the island's interior lagoon about 800 years ago, apparently to take advantage of a safer anchorage for the large, double-hulled war canoes they used to extend their empire as far as Fiji and Samoa. At that time, a deep passage linked the lagoon to the sea; it has been slowly closing as geological forces raise the island and reduce the entrance to the present shallow bank.

Over time, the tui became more of a figurehead, and his power was dispersed among several chiefs, all of them descendants of the original tui. For centuries the rival chiefs seemed to stop warring among themselves only long enough to make war on Fiji and Samoa. One of the domestic wars was in full swing when missionaries from the London Missionary Society arrived in 1798 and landed on Lifuka in Ha'apai. Two of the missionaries were killed. The rest fled to Sydney, leaving Tonga to the warring heathens.

EUROPEANS ARRIVE   Tongatapu and Ha'apai had been sighted by the Dutch explorers Schouten and Lemaire in 1616, and the Dutchman Abel Tasman had landed on them during his voyage of discovery in 1643. The missionaries knew of the islands, however, from the visits of British Captains Samuel Wallis, James Cook, and William Bligh in the late 1700s. During his third voyage in 1777, Captain Cook was feted lavishly on Lifuka by a powerful chief named Finau I.

- 1789 Mutiny on the *Bounty* takes place off Ha'afeva in the Ha'apai group.
- 1798 The first missionaries land in Ha'apai during Tongan wars; two are killed, and the rest flee to Australia.
- 1806 Chief Finau II captures the *Port au Prince* and slays all its crew except young Will Mariner, who becomes the chief's favorite and later writes a book about his adventures.
- 1823 Wesleyan missionaries settle on Lifuka in Ha'apai; Chief Taufa'ahau begins his rise to power.
- 1831 Taufa'ahau converts to Christianity, names himself George, and with missionary help launches wars against his rivals.
- 1845 Taufa'ahau conquers all of Tonga and proclaims himself King George.
- 1860 Rev. Shirley Baker arrives and exercises influence over Tonga for next 30 years.
- 1862 King George I frees commoners, makes his chiefs "Nobles of the Realm," establishes Privy Council, and gives land to every male.
- 1875 King George I adopts Constitution, including "Sabbath-is-sacred" clause, essentially shutting down Tonga on Sundays.
- 1890 Under Treaty of Berlin, Great Britain establishes protectorate over Tonga, kicks out Reverend Baker, and straightens out the kingdom's finances.
- 1893 King George I dies, ending reign of 48 years. King George II assumes the throne.
- 1900 King George II turns Tonga's foreign affairs over to Great Britain, preventing further colonial encroachments.
- 1918 King George II dies, Queen Salote begins 47-year reign during which Tonga remains a backwater.
- 1953 Queen Salote comes to world attention by going bareheaded during a rainstorm at the coronation of Queen Elizabeth II in London.
- 1965 Queen Salote dies, and the new King Taufa'ahau Tupou IV begins opening Tonga to tourists.
- 1967 King Taufa'ahau Tupou IV is crowned among pomp and circumstance; International Dateline Hotel opens.

continues

Cook was so impressed by this show of hospitality that he named the Ha'apai group "The Friendly Islands." Unbeknownst to Cook, however, Finau I and his associates apparently plotted to murder him and his crew, but they couldn't agree among themselves how to do it before the great explorer sailed away. The name he gave the islands stuck, and today Tonga uses "The Friendly Islands" as its motto.

- **1970** King ends treaty with Great Britain; Tonga resumes its own foreign affairs.
- **1989** Commoner members of Parliament begin to push for more accountability from the king's government.
- **1990** Passport scandal rocks the government.
- **1992** Prodemocracy conference calls for new elections.
- **1993** New elections bring the same old results.

Captain Bligh and HMS *Bounty* visited Lifuka in 1789 after gathering breadfruit in Tahiti. Before he could leave Tongan waters, however, the famous mutiny took place near the island of Ha'afeva in the Ha'apai group.

Some 20 years later Chief Finau II of Lifuka captured a British ship named the *Port au Prince,* brutally slaughtering all but one member of its crew, stealing all of its muskets and ammunition, and setting it on fire. The survivor was a 15-year-old Londoner named Will Mariner. He became a favorite of the chief, spent several years living among the Tongans, and was made a chief. Mariner later wrote an extensive account of his experiences, telling in one of the four volumes how the Tongans mistook 12,000 silver coins on the *Port au Prince* for gaming pieces they called *pa'angas.* The national currency today is known as the pa'anga.

The arrival of the Wesleyan missionaries on Lifuka in the 1820s coincided with the rise of Taufa'ahau, a powerful chief they converted to Christianity in 1831. With their help, he won a series of domestic wars and by 1845 had conquered all of Tonga. He made peace with Fiji, took a wife of the incumbent Tui Tonga as his own, and declared himself to be the new Tui Tonga. The deposed tui, last of the direct descendants of the original Tui Tonga, lived on until 1865.

ROYALTY ARRIVES   Taufa'ahau took a Christian name and became King George I of Tonga. In 1862 he made his subordinate chiefs "nobles," but he also freed the commoners from forced labor on their estates and instituted the policy of granting each adult male a garden plot in the countryside and a house lot in town. He created a Privy Council of his own choosing and established a legislative assembly made up of representatives of both the nobles and commoners. This system was committed to writing in the Constitution of 1875, which still is in effect today, including its "Sabbath-is-sacred" clause. The legislative assembly is known now as Parliament.

King George I was dominated during his later years by the Rev. Shirley W. Baker, a missionary who came to Tonga from Sydney in 1860 under the auspices of the Wesleyan Church. Over the next 30 years Baker held almost every important post in the king's government. When the British established their protectorate over Tonga according to the terms of the 1889 Berlin treaty, which also

---

Impressions

The good natured old Chief interduced me to a woman and gave me to understand that I might retire with her, she was next offered to Captain Furneaux but met with a refusal from both, tho she was neither old nor ugly, our stay here was but short.

—Capt. James Cook, 1773

A clause in Tonga's constitution declares, "The Sabbath Day shall be sacred in Tonga forever and it shall not be lawful to work, artifice, or play games, or trade on the Sabbath." The penalty for breaking this stricture is a T$10 ($4.50) fine or 3 months in the slammer at hard labor. Although there is now some flexibility that allows hotels to cater to their guests on Sunday, almost everything else comes to a screeching halt on the Sabbath. Taxis don't run, airplanes don't fly, and most restaurants other than those in the hotels don't open. Tongans by the thousands go to church and then enjoy family feasts and a day of lounging around in true Polynesian style.

---

divided the Samoas between Germany and the United States, they found the kingdom's finances to be in a shambles. In cleaning up the mess, they arranged to have Baker deported to New Zealand, where he stayed for 10 years. Baker returned to Tonga in 1900 as a lay reader licensed by the Anglican church and died in 1903. His children erected a large statue of his likeness at his grave on Lifuka, in Ha'apai.

King George I died in 1893 at the age of 97, thus ending a reign of 48 years. His great-grandson, King George II, ruled for the next 25 years and is best remembered for signing a treaty with Great Britain in 1900. The agreement turned Tonga's foreign affairs over to the British and prevented any further encroachments on Tonga by the Western colonial powers. Thus was the Kingdom of Tonga never colonized.

King George II died in 1918 and was succeeded by his daughter, the 6-foot-2-inch Queen Salote (her name is the Tongan transliteration of "Charlotte"). For the next 47 years Queen Salote carefully protected her people from Western influence, even to the extent of not allowing a modern hotel to be built in the kingdom. She did, however, come to the world's attention in 1953, when she rode bareheaded in the cold, torrential rain that drenched the coronation parade of Queen Elizabeth II in London (she was merely following Tongan custom of showing respect to royalty by appearing uncovered in their presence).

KING TAUFA'AHAU TUPOU IV   Queen Salote died in 1965 and was succeeded by her son, the present King Taufa'ahau Tupou IV. Trained in law at Sydney University in Australia, the new king—then in his late 40s—set about bringing Tonga into the modern world. On the pretext of accommodating the important guests invited to his elaborate coronation scheduled for July 4, 1967, the then-modern International Dateline Hotel was built on Nuku'alofa's waterfront, and Fua'amotu Airport on Tongatapu was upgraded to handle jet aircraft. Tourism, albeit on a modest scale, arrived in Tonga.

The king ended the treaty of protection with Great Britain, and in 1970 Tonga reassumed her small role on the world's stage. This enabled her to acquire aid from other countries with which to make further improvements.

Although not as tall as his mother, the king stands above 6 feet and once weighed on the order of 460 pounds (the large statue of him beside the old terminal at Fua'amotu Airport is only a slight exaggeration of his former size). He has slimmed down in recent years to just over 300 pounds. I have seen him wearing ski goggles and a motorbike helmet when flying from island to island. Watching him arrive at an airport should not be missed.

> **Moments** Seeing His Highness Arrive
>
> Being an American and therefore not particularly enamored of royalty, I nevertheless enjoy watching King Taufa'ahau Tupou IV being chauffeured around his kingdom in the back seat of his big black SUV and being given the royal treatment whenever he arrives somewhere.

DEMOCRACY DOESN'T ARRIVE   The king and his government have had their problems, thanks to more and more of his commoner subjects going overseas to work in the Western democracies, and to those at home becoming better educated and more aware of what's going on both in Tonga and in the rest of the world. In the late 1980s a group of commoners founded *Kele'a*, a newspaper published without the king's input. The paper created a ruckus almost from its first issue by revealing that some government ministers had rung up excessive travel expenses on trips abroad.

Then came news that the government had stashed millions of dollars in U.S. banks, money earned from selling Tongan passports to overseas nationals (most of them Chinese but including Imelda Marcos, wife of the deposed Philippine dictator). For $20,000 the buyers received a passport declaring them to be "Tongan protected persons." The documents didn't allow the person to live in Tonga, however, so other nations refused to recognize them. To compound the problem, the Tongan High Court ruled the sales to be unconstitutional. Rather than refund the money, Parliament held a special session in 1991 and amended the constitution—a document that had not been significantly changed since 1875. It also raised the price of the passports to $50,000. The new passports also allow the holders to live in Tonga. An influx of Chinese immigrants has caused racial animosity in the kingdom in recent years.

Incensed, several hundred Tongans marched down Nuku'alofa's main street in a peaceful protest. Nothing like that had ever happened in Tonga before, but it was just the beginning. When the king kept on selling passports, the leaders held a prodemocracy conference in late 1992. That led to fresh elections in 1993—with the same old results. As late as 2001 the government refused to recognize the Tonga Human Rights Democracy Movement. Recent scandals such as the loss of some $20 million of Tonga's overseas trust fund through a questionable investment by the official Court Jester (actually an American businessman) have exacerbated the kingdom's problems.

It is difficult at press time to predict what future course Tongan politics will take. Most observers believe the monarchical system will stay intact as long as King Taufa'ahau Tupou is on the throne. His second son, Prime Minister Prince 'Ulukalala Lavaka Ata, has already instituted some minor reforms, and his older brother, Crown Prince Tupuoto'a, has indicated that more will come when he becomes king.

3 The Tongans

The population of Tonga is estimated at somewhere around 100,000 (no one knows for sure). Approximately 98% of the inhabitants are pure Polynesians, closely akin to the Samoans in physical appearance, language, and culture.

As in Samoa, the bedrock of the Tongan social structure is the traditional way of life—*faka Tonga*—and the extended family. Parents, grandparents, children, aunts, uncles, cousins, nieces, and nephews all have the same sense of obligation to each other as is felt in Western nuclear families. The extended-family system makes sure that no one ever goes hungry or without a place to live.

THE TONGAN SYSTEM   The extended family aside, some striking differences exist between Tonga, Samoa, and the other Polynesian islands. Unlike the others, in which there is a certain degree of upward mobility, Tonga has a rigid two-tier caste system. The king and 33 "Nobles of the Realm"—plus their families—make up a privileged class at the top of society. Everyone else is a commoner, and although commoners can hold positions in the government, it's impossible for them to move up into the nobility even by marriage. Titles of the nobility are inherited, but the king can strip members of the nobility of their positions if they fail to live up to their obligations (presumably including loyalty to the royal family).

Technically the king owns all the land in Tonga, which makes the country his feudal estate. Tonga isn't exactly like the old European feudal system, however, for although the nobles each rule over a section of the kingdom, they have an obligation to provide for the welfare of the serfs rather than the other way around. The nobles administer the villages, look after the people's welfare, and apportion the land among the commoners.

As noted above, each adult male is entitled to a garden plot of 8¼ acres and a site for a house in the village. Although the population has outstripped the amount of available land, this system is primarily responsible for the intensely cultivated condition of Tongatapu and the other islands and for the abundance of food in the country.

Foreigners are absolutely forbidden to own land in Tonga, and leases require approval of the cabinet, which for all practical purposes means the royal family.

TONGAN DRESS   Even traditional dress reflects the Tongan social structure. Western-style clothes have made deep inroads in recent years, especially among young persons, but many Tongans still wear wraparound skirts known as *valas*. These come to well below the knee on men and to the ankles on women. To show their respect for the royal family and to each other, traditional men and women wear finely woven mats known as *ta'ovalas* over their *valas*. Men hold these up with waistbands of coconut fiber; women wear decorative waistbands known as *kiekies*. Tongans have *ta'ovalas* for everyday wear, but on special occasions they break out mats that are family heirlooms, some of them tattered and worn. The king owns *ta'ovalas* that have been in his family for more than 500 years.

Tongan custom is to wear black for months to mourn the death of a relative or close friend. Since Tongan extended families are large and friends numerous, the black of mourning is seen frequently in the kingdom.

In keeping with Tonga's conservatism, it's against the law for men as well as women to appear shirtless in public. While Western men can swim and sunbathe shirtless at the hotel pools and beaches frequented by visitors, you will see most Tongans swimming in a full set of clothes.

RELIGION   Wesleyan missionaries gained a foothold in Tonga during the early 1820s, and by 1831 had converted Taufa'ahau, the high chief of Ha'apai. As happened with the converted chief Pomare in Tahiti, Taufa'ahau then used missionary support—and guns from other sources—to win a series of wars and become king of Tonga. Tonga quickly became a predominantly Christian nation—apparently an easy transition, as Tongan legend holds that their own king is a descendant of a supreme Polynesian god and a beautiful earthly virgin.

About half of all Tongans belong to the Free Wesleyan Church of Tonga, founded by the early Methodist missionaries and headed by the king. The Free

---

Fun Fact What Day Is It?

Tonga was the first nation to welcome the new millennium because of a capricious quirk in the international date line. Established in 1884, this imaginary line marks the start of each calendar day. Theoretically, it should run for its _entire length_ along the 180th meridian, halfway around the world from the prime meridian, the starting point for measuring international time.

If it followed the 180th meridian precisely, however, most of the Aleutian Islands would be a day ahead of the rest of Alaska, and Fiji would be split into 2 days. To solve these problems, the date line swings west around the Aleutians, leaving them in the same day as Alaska. In the South Pacific, it swerves east between Fiji and Samoa, leaving all of Fiji a day ahead of the Samoas.

Since Tonga and Samoa lie east of the 180th meridian, both countries should logically be in the same day. But Tonga wanted to have the same date as Australia and New Zealand, so the line was drawn arbitrarily east of Tonga, putting it 1 day ahead of Samoa.

To travelers, it's even more confusing because Tonga and Samoa are in the same time zone. When traveling from one to the other, therefore, only the date changes, not the time of day. For example, if everyone is going to church at 10am on Sunday in Tonga, everyone's at work on Saturday in Samoa.

Tonga's Seventh-Day Adventists, who celebrate the Sabbath on Saturday but work on Sunday, have taken advantage of this abnormality to avoid running afoul of Tonga's tough Sunday blue laws. In God's eyes, they say, Sunday in Tonga really is Saturday. Accordingly, Tonga is the only place in the world where Seventh-Day Adventists observe their Sabbath on Sunday.

Church of Tonga is an offshoot that is still allied with the Methodist synods in Australia and New Zealand. There are also considerable numbers of Roman Catholics, Anglicans, Seventh-Day Adventists, and Mormons. Church services are usually held at 10am on Sunday, but very few of them are conducted in English. St. Paul's Anglican Church, on the corner of Fafatehi and Wellington roads, usually has communion in English on Sunday at 8am. The royal family worships at 10am in Centenary Church, the Free Wesleyan Church on Wellington Road, a block behind the Royal Palace.

The red national flag has a cross on a white field in its upper corner to signify the country's strong Christian foundation.

The Mormon church has made inroads in Tonga. Gleaming white Mormon temples have popped up in many Tongan villages, along with modern schools that offer quality education and the chance for students to go on to Mormon colleges in Hawaii and Utah. Many Tongans have joined the church, reportedly for this very reason, and there are now sizable Tongan communities in Honolulu and around Salt Lake City, headquarters of the Mormon church. Unlike the Samoans and Cook Islanders, Tongans do not have unlimited access to a larger Western country such as the United States and New Zealand, and the promise

---

(Fun Fact Buried with Beer Bottles

Tongans of all religions bury their dead in unique cemeteries set in groves of frangipani trees. The graves are sandy mounds decorated with flags, banners, artificial flowers, stones, and seashells. Many of them are for some reason bordered by brown beer bottles.

---

of Mormon help in settling in America is an appealing prospect in light of the population pressures at home.

As was the case throughout Polynesia, the Tongans accepted most of the puritanical beliefs taught by the early missionaries but stopped short of adopting their strict sexual mores. Today Tongan society is very conservative in outlook and practice in almost every aspect of life except the sexual activities of unmarried young men and women.

As is true elsewhere in Polynesia, Tongan families without enough female offspring will raise boys as they would girls. They are known in Tongan as *fakaleitis* ("like a woman") and live lives similar to those of the *mahus* in Tahiti and the *fa'afafines* in the Samoas. In Tonga they have a reputation for sexual promiscuity and for persistently approaching Western male visitors in search of sexual liaisons.

4 Language

The official language in Tonga is Tongan, but English is taught in the schools and is widely spoken in the main towns.

Tongan is a Polynesian language that's similar to Samoan. One major difference between them is the enormous number of glottal stops (represented by an apostrophe in writing) in the Tongan tongue. These are short stops similar to the break between "Oh-oh" in English.

Every vowel is pronounced in the Latin fashion: *ah, ay, ee, oh,* and *oo* (as in kangar*oo*) instead of *ay, ee, eye, oh,* and *you* as in English. The consonants are sounded as they are in English.

An extensive knowledge of Tongan will not be necessary for English-speakers to get around and enjoy the kingdom, but here are a few words you can use to elicit smiles from your hosts and to avoid the embarrassment of entering the wrong restroom:

English	Tongan	Pronunciation
hello	**malo e lelei**	*mah*-low ay *lay*-lay
welcome	**talitali fiefia**	tah-lay-*tah*-lay fee-ay-*fee*-ah
how do you do?	**fefe hake?**	*fay*-fay *hah*-kay?
fine, thank you	**sai pe, malo**	*sah*-ee pay, *mah*-low
good-bye	**'alu a**	ah-*loo* ah
thank you	**malo**	*mah*-low
how much?	**'oku fiha?**	*oh*-koo *fee*-hah?
good	**lelei**	lay-*lay*-ee
bad	**kovi**	*koh*-vee
woman	**fefine**	fay-*feen*-ay
man	**tangata**	tahn-*got*-ah
house	**fale**	*fah*-lay
transvestite	**fakaleiti**	fah-ka-*lay*-tee

The Friendly Islands Bookshop on Taufa'ahau Road carries language books, and the Tonga Visitors Bureau on Vuna Road distributes a brochure of Tongan phrases.

5 Visitor Information & Entry Requirements

VISITOR INFORMATION

The friendly staff has many brochures, maps, and other materials available at the **Tonga Visitors Bureau (TVB),** P.O. Box 37, Nuku'alofa, Kingdom of Tonga (© **21-733;** fax 23-507; www.tongaholiday.com or www.vacations.tvb.gov.to). The office is on Vuna Road near the International Dateline Hotel. Especially good are the bureau's brochures on Tongan dancing, handcrafts, archaeology, construction skills, and a walking tour of central Nuku'alofa. A stop by the "TVB" is a must before setting out to see the country. Hours are Monday to Friday from 8am to 5pm and Saturday from 8am to 2pm.

Other sources of information are:

- **North America:** Tonga Consulate, 360 Post St., Suite 604, San Francisco, CA 94108 (© **415/781-0365;** fax 415/781-3964)
- **Australia:** Tonga Visitors Bureau, 642 King St., Newton, NSW 2042 (© **02/9519-97009;** fax 02/9519-9419)
- **New Zealand:** Tonga Visitors Bureau, P.O. Box 24-054, Royal Oak, Auckland (© **09/634-1519;** fax 09/636-8973)
- **United Kingdom:** Tonga High Commission, 36 Molyneux St., London W1H 6AB (© **724-5828;** fax 723-9074)

Once you're in Nuku'alofa, **Friends Tourist Center,** on Taufa'ahau Road between Wellington and Salote roads (© **26-323**), is another good source of information. Owned by Paul Johansson, a Tongan who lived overseas for many years, it arranges tours of the islands and has Internet access (see "Fast Facts: Tonga," below).

Also be on the lookout for *'Eva: Your Holiday Guide to Tonga,* a slick bimonthly tabloid that's full of news about Tongan tourism and advertisements for the hotels, restaurants, and nightclubs. It's carried as a supplement in *Matagi Tonga,* an excellent local magazine.

ENTRY REQUIREMENTS

Visas are not required for bona fide visitors to enter Tonga, who are permitted to stay for up to 30 days, provided they have a valid passport, an onward air or sea ticket, proof of adequate funds, and relevant health certificates. As a practical matter, your initial permit will likely be limited to the number of days you request on your entry form or the date of your return or onward ticket, whichever is earlier. Expect to have your tickets examined.

Applications for stays of longer than 30 days must be made to the principal immigration officer in Nuku'alofa.

Vaccinations are required only if a traveler has been in a yellow fever or cholera area within two weeks prior to arrival in Tonga.

CUSTOMS   Visitors are allowed to bring in 200 cigarettes and 1 liter of alcoholic beverage, as well as personal belongings in use at the time of arrival. Pets, dangerous drugs, firearms, and ammunition are prohibited, and foodstuffs must be declared and inspected. Arriving visitors can buy duty-free merchandise at Fua'amotu Airport after clearing Immigration but before going through Customs.

6 Money

The Tongan unit of currency is the **pa'anga,** which is divided into 100 **seniti.** The pa'anga is abbreviated in this book as **T$.** Most Tongans refer to "dollars" and "cents" when doing business with visitors, meaning pa'angas and senitis.

The value of the pa'anga is determined by a basket of currencies. At the time of writing, T$1 was worth about US45¢. The equivalent U.S. dollar prices given in parentheses are based on this rate of exchange. The rate is not published in major newspapers, but it is usually within a few cents of the Australian dollar's worth against the U.S. dollar. You can find the pa'anga exchange on currency conversion sites such as www.xe.com.

Tongan coins bear the likeness of the king on one side and such items as bananas, chickens, and pigs on the other.

HOW TO GET LOCAL CURRENCY   The easiest way to get local currency is to use the ATM at **ANZ Bank,** at the corner of Railway and Salote roads near the market. ANZ's offices are open Monday to Friday from 9am to 4pm and Saturday from 8:30 to 11:30am. The **Bank of Tonga** has an office at the waterfront end of Taufa'ahau Road, Nuku'alofa's main street. It is open Monday to Friday from 9am to 3:30pm and Saturday from 8:30 to 11:30am.

CREDIT CARDS   The major hotels, car-rental firms, travel agencies, and Royal Tongan Airlines accept American Express, Diners Club, MasterCard, and Visa credit cards. Some restaurants and other businesses accept MasterCard or Visa; those that do may add 4% or 5% to your bill for doing so. It's a good idea to ask first if you want to put your purchases on plastic. Leave your Discover card at home.

The Pa'anga & the U.S. Dollar

At this writing, T$1 = approximately US45¢ (or US$1 = approximately T$2.22), the rate of exchange used to calculate the U.S. dollar prices given in this chapter. This rate may change by the time you visit, so use the following table only as a guide.

T$	US$	T$	US$
.25	.11	15	6.75
.50	.23	20	9.00
.75	.34	25	11.25
1	.45	30	13.50
2	.90	35	15.75
3	1.35	40	18.00
4	1.80	45	20.25
5	2.25	50	22.50
6	2.70	75	33.75
7	3.15	100	45.00
8	3.60	125	56.25
9	4.05	150	67.50
10	4.50	200	90.00

7 When to Go

THE CLIMATE

Like Rarotonga in the Cook Islands to the east, Tongatapu is far enough south of the equator to have cool, dry, and quite pleasant weather during the austral winter months (July–Sept), when temperatures range between 60°F and 70°F (15.5°C–21°C). However, the ends of occasional cold fronts from the Antarctic and periods of stiff southeast trade winds can make it seem even cooler during this period. During the summer (Dec–Mar), the high temperatures can reach above 90°F (32°C), with evenings in the comfortable 70s (21°C–26°C). A sweater, jacket, or wrap will come in handy for evening wear at any time of the year.

The islands get about 180 centimeters (70 in.) of rainfall a year (compared to 500cm/200 in. in Pago Pago, American Samoa), the majority of it falling during the summer months. Vava'u to the north tends to be somewhat warmer and slightly wetter than Tongatapu.

Tonga is in the southwestern Pacific cyclone belt, and hurricanes are possible from November to April. In fact, one severely damaged Vava'u early in 2002. Rest assured, however, that there will be ample warning if one bears down on the islands while you're there. The Tongans have seen enough hurricanes to know how to ensure their guests' safety.

FESTIVALS & EVENTS

The largest annual festival is **Heilala,** which coincides with the King's Birthday on July 4. Nuku'alofa goes all out for a week of dance and beauty competitions, parades, sporting matches, band concerts, marching contests, yacht regattas, parties, and the lovely Night of Torches on the waterfront. Tongans living overseas like to come home for Heilala, so hotel reservations should be made well in advance. Vava'u stages its own version of Heilala early in May.

The Tonga Visitors Bureau keeps track of when the festivals will occur each year.

HOLIDAYS

Public holidays in Tonga are New Year's Day, Good Friday and Easter Monday, Anzac (Memorial) Day (Apr 25), Crown Prince Tupouto'a's birthday (May 4), Emancipation Day (in honor of King George I, June 4), the King's Birthday (July 4), Constitution Day (Nov 4), King Tupou I Day (Dec 4), Christmas Day, and Boxing Day (Dec 26).

8 Getting to Tonga & Getting Around

GETTING THERE

Air New Zealand flies between Los Angeles and Tonga at least once a week, with brief stops in Honolulu and Samoa. Those flights go on to Auckland and return over the same route. **Air Pacific** connects Tonga to its flights to Fiji from Los

---

Tips **Avoid Royal Funerals**

There's no way to plan for it, but you do not want to be in Tonga if a key member of the royal family dies. The entire country virtually shuts down for a lengthy period of mourning.

Nuku'alofa

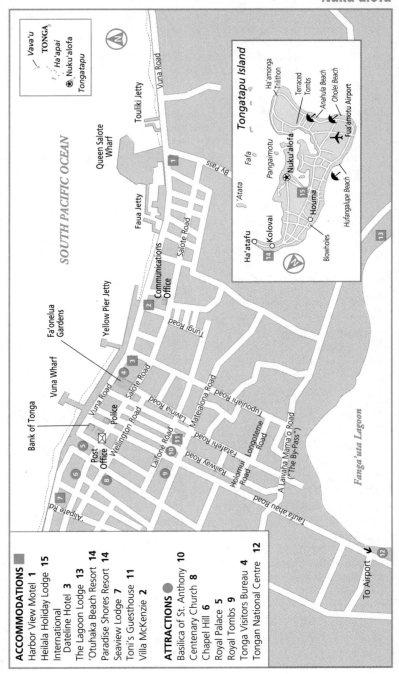

ACCOMMODATIONS ▪
Harbor View Motel **1**
Heilala Holiday Lodge **15**
International
 Dateline Hotel **3**
The Lagoon Lodge **13**
'Otuhaka Beach Resort **14**
Paradise Shores Resort **14**
Seaview Lodge **7**
Toni's Guesthouse **11**
Villa McKenzie **2**

ATTRACTIONS ●
Basilica of St. Anthony **10**
Centenary Church **8**
Chapel Hill **6**
Royal Palace **5**
Royal Tombs **9**
Tonga Visitors Bureau **4**
Tongan National Centre **12**

Angeles, Australia, and New Zealand. **Polynesian Airlines** also flies to Tonga from Auckland, Sydney, and Samoa. **Royal Tongan Airlines** flies between Tongatapu and Auckland, Wellington, Sydney, and Apia. **Samoa Air,** based in American Samoa, flies its small planes between Pago Pago and Vava'u.

There are no flights into, out of, or in Tonga on Sunday, when the local airports are closed.

For more information, see "Getting There & Getting Around" in chapter 2.

ARRIVING & DEPARTING   Except for the few international flights destined for Vava'u, most land at **Fua'amotu Airport** on Tongatapu, 24km (14 miles) from Nuku'alofa. The terminal has currency exchange counters, a duty-free shop, a snack bar, and a small handcraft outlet. International passengers can purchase duty-free liquor and cigarettes after clearing Immigration but before going through Customs.

Transportation from the airport into Nuku'alofa is by hotel minibuses or taxi. The bus ride to town costs T$6 ($2.70). The one-way taxi fare into Nuku'alofa is about T$12 ($5.50); the drivers will be happy to take U.S., New Zealand, or Australian currency.

A **departure tax** of T$25 ($11.25) is charged of all passengers leaving on international flights. You pay it in Tongan currency at Fua'amotu Airport, at a separate booth outside Immigration. There is no departure tax for domestic flights.

There is no currency exchange facility in the departure lounge, so swap your money before clearing Immigration.

GETTING AROUND
BY PLANE
Royal Tongan Airlines, in the Royco Building on Fatafehi Road at Wellington Road (© **800/486-6426** or 23-414; www.flyroyaltongan.com), has a monopoly on air travel within the country. It provides at least two round-trip flights per day between Tongatapu and Vava'u. Daily service is also provided between Tongatapu, 'Eua, and Ha'apai. The round-trip fare from Tongatapu to Vava'u is about T$261 ($117.50); to 'Eua, T$38 ($17); and to Ha'apai, T$131 ($59).

Royal Tongan can be unreliable. It has few planes, and if one of them needs unexpected maintenance, it can throw the entire schedule out of whack. And when a royal or a noble wants to fly someplace, all other Tongans and you will have to wait. It's always a good idea to book your flights as far in advance as you can.

BY RENTAL CAR
Avis (© **800/331-1212** or 21-179; www.avis.com) has an office upstairs in the Tungi Arcade on Taufa'ahau Road. Rates start at T$70 ($31.50) per day, including unlimited kilometers. **E.M. Jones Travel** (© **23-422** or 29-858), also on Taufa'ahau Road, rents cars starting at T$50 ($22.50) per day, including unlimited mileage and insurance.

Tips   Don't Miss Your Flight Home

Given the unreliability of Royal Tongan Airlines, it's a good idea not to plan on flying back from Vava'u or Ha'apai to Nuku'alofa on the day your international flight is scheduled to take you home. Give yourself at least a day's cushion. And remember to always reconfirm your return flight as soon as possible after arriving on an outer island.

Tips **Watch Out for the Crown**

When driving in Tonga, be alert for pigs, dogs, horses, and chickens, and pull over for policemen on motorcycles escorting the king in his big black sport utility vehicle bearing license plates with no numbers, only a crown.

Gasoline (petrol) is available only at stations in Nuku'alofa, so fill up before leaving town. It costs about double what you pay in the United States.

Before you can officially drive in Tonga you must obtain a **local driver's license** from the central police station (© 21-222), on Wellington Road just off Taufa'ahau Road in Nuku'alofa. You will need your home driver's license and T$15 ($6.75). First fill out the forms at the police counter, then go pay the cashier, and then go back to the police counter with your receipt. It's a cumbersome process, so bring your sense of humor.

Driving in Tonga is on the left-hand side of the road. Speed limits are 65kmph (39 mph) on the open road and 40kmph (24 mph) in the towns and villages.

BY TAXI

Taxis usually gather near Maketi Talamahu at the corner of Salote and Railway roads in Nuku'alofa. The largest firm is **Five Star Taxis** (© 21-595 or 21-429). **Nuku'alofa Taxis** (© 22-624) are radio dispatched. Others are **Holiday Taxis** (© 21-858), **One-Way Taxis** (© 21-741), **Malolala Taxis** (© 22-500), and **City Taxis** (© 24-666).

Fares are T$1 (45¢) in town. Longer distances cost T$1.50 (70¢) for the first kilometer plus T30¢ (15¢) for each additional kilometer, but since the taxis have no meters, make sure you and the driver agree on just how much the fare will be. The fares are doubled on Sundays, when taxis are officially permitted only to take passengers to church and back (some of them will carry tourists from their hotels or guesthouses to the wharf in order for them to get to the offshore islands).

BY BUS

Buses use the **Vuna Road waterfront** as their terminal. Town buses stop in front of the Tonga Visitors Bureau; long-distance ones stop in front of the government buildings. They fan out from there to all parts of Tongatapu, but there are no reliable schedules. Simply ask the bus drivers at the market where they are going. If you take one into the countryside, remember that they make their last runs back to Nuku'alofa at about 3pm daily, in time to pick up passengers who are just getting off work. Once they make their last runs to the villages, they don't come back to town until the next morning. About T$2 (90¢) will take you to the end of the island in either direction.

BY BICYCLE

Tongatapu is virtually flat, making it an ideal island on which to ride a bicycle. "Pushbikes" can be rented from **Niko's Bike Rental** (no phone) on the Vuna waterfront near the International Dateline Hotel. One-speed models cost T$2 (90¢) per hour, T$8 ($3.60) for a full day.

BY FERRY

It's not for everyone, but the **Shipping Corporation of Polynesia** (© 21-699) operates weekly ferry service from Nuku'alofa to Ha'apai and Vava'u, using the

MV *Olovaha*, a car-ferry with a few passenger cabins. It usually leaves Nuku'alofa 1 day a week at 5:30pm and takes about 16 hours to make the 262km (163-mile) trip to Vava'u, stopping at Lifuka in the Ha'apai group on the way. The ship then turns around and arrives back in Nuku'alofa late the next afternoon. The one-way fare between Nuku'alofa and Vava'u is T$45 ($20.25) for deck passage.

 FAST FACTS: Tonga

American Express American Express has no representative in Tonga.

Bookstores **Friendly Islands Bookshop,** on Taufa'ahau Road near the Pacific Royale Hotel (© 23-787), carries greeting cards made from *tapa* cloth, paperback books, postcards, international news magazines, week-old Australian newspapers, books about Tonga and the rest of the South Pacific, and a sheet of maps of Tonga.

Business Hours In general, Tonga's shops are open Monday to Friday from 8am to 1pm and 2 to 5pm, Saturday from 8am to noon. Government offices are open Monday to Friday from 8:30am to 12:30pm and 1:30 to 4:30pm.

Camera/Film **Foto Fix,** on Taufa'ahau Road south of Wellington Road (© 23-466), sells Kodak and Fuji film and provides 1-hour color film processing.

Clothing Summer clothing is in order during most of the year, but a sweater, jacket, or wrap should be taken for evening wear throughout the year. Tongans are very conservative, and visitors should not wear bathing suits or skimpy attire away from the hotel pools or beaches frequented by foreigners. In fact, appearing in public without a shirt is a punishable offense for both men and women, as is nudity of any degree.

Currency Exchange See "Money," above.

Drug Laws A drug-sniffing dog roams the baggage claim area at the airport, so don't even think about bringing illegal narcotics or dangerous drugs into Tonga.

Drugstores See "Healthcare," below.

Electricity Electricity in Tonga is 240 volts, 50 cycles, and the plugs are the heavy, angled type used in Australia and New Zealand. You will need a converter and adapter plug to operate American appliances.

E-mail **Friends Tourist Center** (© 26-323), on Taufa'ahau Road between Salote and Wellington roads, has a computer with Internet access. It charges T$4 ($1.80) for the first 15 minutes. **Comput@Cafe** (© 26-798), upstairs in the TCF Supermarket Building on Wellington Road (you can see across the parking lot on Taufa'ahau Road), has access at T15¢ (5¢) a minute. Both are open Monday to Friday 9am to 4:30pm, Saturday 9am to 2pm.

Tonga Communications Corp. (© 23-499), on Salote Road at Takaunove Road, also has terminals at T$2 (90¢) per minute online. If you brought your laptop, you can apply there for a temporary Internet access account. There's a T$30 ($13.50) setup fee plus T$10 ($4.50) for every hour spent online, all chargeable to your MasterCard or Visa card. Go into the accounting office, which is open Monday to Friday from 8:30am to 12:30pm and 1:30 to 4pm. See the "Getting Online" box in chapter 3 for information on how to configure your computer.

Embassies/Consulates The nearest U.S. embassy is in Suva, Fiji. Consular offices in Tonga are the **Australian High Commission** (© 21-244), the **British High Commission** (© 21-021), the **New Zealand High Commission** (© 21-122), and the **People's Republic of China Embassy** (© 24-554).

Emergencies/Police The emergency telephone number for the **police, fire department,** and **hospital** is © 911. The main **police station** (© 21-222) is on Salote Road at Railway Road.

Eyeglasses **Vaiola Hospital** (© 21-200) is the only place to get glasses fixed or replaced. See "Healthcare," below.

Firearms Guns are illegal in Tonga.

Gambling There is no casino or other form of organized gambling in Tonga.

Healthcare **Vaiola Hospital** (© 21-200) provides medical, dental, and optical service, but it's considerably below the standards you're used to. The outpatient clinics are open from 8:30am to 4:30pm daily. German-trained Dr. Heinz Betz practices at the **German Clinic & Pharmacy,** on Vahiaholo Road at Uelingitoni Road, 1 block behind the Royal Palace (© 22-736). **Vaiola Hospital** provides dental service in Nuku'alofa; the outpatient clinics are open from 8:30am to 4:30pm daily.

Hitchhiking It's not against the law, but Tongans are not particularly accustomed to picking up strangers.

Insects There are no dangerous insects in Tonga, and the mosquitoes do not carry malaria. Vava'u, warmer and more humid than Tongatapu, tends to have more mosquitoes and has tropical centipedes that can inflict painful stings if touched; watch your step if walking around with bare feet.

Library **'Utue'a Public Library,** on the ground floor of Basilica of St. Anthony of Padua on Taufa'ahau Road, is usually open Monday to Friday from 3 to 9pm and Saturday from 10am to 3pm.

Laundry/Dry Cleaning **Savoy Dry Cleaners,** on Fatefehi Road (© 23-314), has 1-day laundry and dry cleaning service. Open Monday to Friday 7:30am to 6pm, Saturday 7:30am to 3pm.

Liquor Laws The legal drinking age is 18. Licensed hotels can sell alcoholic beverages to their guests 7 days a week; otherwise, sale is prohibited from midnight Saturday to midnight Sunday. Royal beer is brewed here (Ikale is the higher-quality export brand).

Maps Free maps of Nuku'alofa, Tongatapu, and Vava'u are available at the Tonga Visitors Bureau.

Newspapers/Magazines The *Tonga Chronicle* is a government-owned weekly newspaper. It carries local news in both Tongan and English, but there are so many stories about the king and his family that many locals facetiously call it the "Royal Diary." For a different view, look for *Matangi Tonga,* a fine monthly magazine edited by the noted Tongan writer and publisher Pesi Fonua. It carries features about the kingdom and its people.

Post Office The **Nuku'alofa Post Office** is at the corner of Taufa'ahau and Salote roads. It's open Monday to Friday from 8:30am to 4pm. Tongan stamps, some of which are in the shape of bananas and pineapples, are collectors' items.

Radio/TV The government-owned radio station, A3Z ("Radio Tonga"), broadcasts in both the AM and FM bands. Most programming on the AM station is in Tongan, although the music played is mostly U.S., Australian, or British popular tunes. The news in English is relayed from the BBC or Radio Australia several times a day. Four privately owned FM stations in Nuku'alofa play popular music.

Tonga has one television channel, which carries predominately Christian programming with CNN International on and off during the day. It can be received only on Tongatapu and 'Eua.

Safety Although crimes against tourists have been rare in Tonga, remember that the communal property system still prevails in the kingdom. Items such as cameras and bags left unattended might disappear, so take the proper precautions. Street crime is not a problem, but it's a good idea to be on the alert if you walk down dark streets at night. Women should not wander alone on deserted beaches.

Taxes The government imposes a 5% sales tax on all items purchased in Tonga, 7½% on hotel rooms. The tax is added to some bills in the American fashion and included in the price in others. All passengers on international flights pay a departure tax of T$25 ($11.25).

Telephone/Fax Calls can be dialed directly into Tonga from most areas of the world. The international country code is **676**.

International calls, telegrams, and telex messages can be placed from your hotel or at Tonga Communications Corporation (TCC), on Salote Road at the corner of Takaunove Road. The office is open Monday through Saturday 7am to midnight, Sunday noon to midnight. You can pay cash or use your MasterCard or Visa credit cards Monday to Saturday 7am to midnight, Sunday 4pm to midnight. Station-to-station phone calls to the United States cost T$9.50 ($4.25) for the first 3 minutes, T$12 ($5.50) for person-to-person. The rates to Australia and New Zealand are about half those amounts.

It's less expensive to call from Cardphone public telephones at TCC, the post offices, and at the airport. These phones use plastic credit cards, which you can buy at the post offices or at TCC. Lift the receiver, insert the card in the slot, and dial your number. A digital readout tells you how much money you have left. Direct-dial calls to North America using Cardphones cost about T$3 ($1.35) a minute.

The number for directory assistance is ℂ **910** or ℂ **919** and the number for the international operator is ℂ **913**.

Time Local time in Tonga is 13 hours ahead of Greenwich mean time. It's in the same day as Australia, New Zealand, and Fiji, and a day behind the United States, the Samoas, the Cook Islands, and French Polynesia. Translated, Tonga is 3 hours behind the U.S. West Coast during standard time (4 hr. behind during daylight saving time)—and 1 day ahead. If it's noon on Tuesday in Tonga, it's 3pm Pacific standard time on Monday in Los Angeles and 6pm eastern standard time on Monday in New York.

Tipping Although it has gained a foothold, tipping is officially discouraged in Tonga because it's considered contrary to the Polynesian tradition of hospitality to guests. One time it is encouraged is during Tongan dance shows, when members of the audience rush up to the female dancers and stick notes to their well-oiled bodies.

Water Although the government proclaims the tap water in the main towns to be chlorinated and thus safe, I don't know anyone who drinks it. Because it comes from wells in the limestone bedrock, it's very hard (laden with minerals) and doesn't easily rinse off soap and shampoo. Bottled water is available at most grocery stores in Nuku'alofa.

Weights/Measures Tonga uses the metric system.

9 Exploring Tongatapu

You'll need about half a day to stroll around Nuku'alofa and see its sights and a full day to tour the island—half a day on the eastern end, another half to see the west.

THE TONGAN NATIONAL CENTRE ★★★
Make time to visit the **Tongan National Centre** (© **23-022**), one of the South Pacific's best cultural expositions. Located on Fanga'uta Lagoon about 1.5km (1 mile) south of Nuku'alofa on Taufa'ahau Road, the center's turtle-roof, Tongan fale-style buildings house displays of the kingdom's history, geology, and handcrafts. In fact, artisans work daily on their crafts and sell their wares to visitors. In other words, you can see how Tonga's remarkable handcrafts are made, which should help as you later scour the local shops for good buys. The center is open Monday to Wednesday and Friday from 8:30am to 5pm, Tuesday and Thursday from 8:30am to 9:30pm, Saturday from 8:30am to 4pm. Admission is free. A lunch of Tongan food is followed by special displays from 2 to 4pm featuring demonstrations of carving, weaving, *tapa* making, food preparation, a kava ceremony, and dance demonstration. The price is T$12 ($5.50) for lunch and a tour, T$8 ($3.60) for the tour only. A travel agent or hotel tour desk will make reservations, which are essential.

A STROLL THROUGH NUKU'ALOFA
Before you start out to see Nuku'alofa, drop by the Tonga Visitors Bureau office on Vuna Road near the International Dateline Hotel and pick up a copy of the excellent brochure "Walking Tour of Central Nuku'alofa." A morning's stroll around this interesting town will be time well spent, for in many respects it's a throwback to times gone by in the South Pacific.

Although there are no street-name posts, the visitors bureau has put up signs that give general directions to the main sights. In addition, Nuku'alofa is more or less laid out on a grid, so you shouldn't have trouble finding your way around. It's also flat, with no hills to climb.

Start at the **Tonga Visitors Bureau** and walk west along Vuna Road toward the heart of town. The park on the left as you leave the Visitors Bureau is known as **Fa'onelua Gardens.** The modern three-story building before Railway Road houses the government ministries of works, agriculture, health, education, lands and survey, and civil aviation. As a resident of the Washington, D.C., area, every time I see this building I think of my own nation's capital, where it takes several

---

Fun Fact The Queen's Robe & Tui Malila

A highlight at the Tongan National Centre is the long robe Queen Salote wore at the coronation of Queen Elizabeth II in 1953. Another is the carcass of Tui Malila, the Galapagos tortoise Capt. James Cook reputedly gave the Tui Tonga in 1777. The beast lived until 1968.

---

huge buildings and hundreds of acres of land to house that many departments of the U.S. government.

Turn left on Railway Road. The small colonial-era wooden structure on the left in the first block serves as both the **Court House** and **parliament** when it meets from June to September. Both court and parliament sessions are open to the public. Now return to Vuna Road and turn left.

Vuna Wharf, at the foot of Taufa'ahau Road, Nuku'alofa's main street, was built in 1906, and for some 60 years most visitors to Tonga debarked from ships that tied up here. It became less trafficked when Queen Salote Wharf was erected east of town in 1966 to handle large ships, and a major earthquake in 1977 damaged Vuna Wharf so extensively that it has been used since only in emergencies. A railroad once ran through town along Railway Road to transport copra and other crops to Vuna Wharf.

Directly across Vuna Road from the wharf is the low **Treasury Building.** Constructed in 1928, it's a fine example of South Pacific colonial architecture. Early in its life it housed the Tongan Customs service and the post office as well as the Treasury Department.

The field to the west of the wharf is the **Pangai,** where royal feasts, kava ceremonies, and parades are held.

Overlooking the Pangai and surrounded by towering Norfolk pines is the **Royal Palace** ★★★. The king lives in a modern mansion out on the lagoon shore these days, but he still conducts business and entertains dignitaries in this white Victorian building with gingerbread fretwork and gables under a red roof. The palace was prefabricated in New Zealand, shipped to Tonga, and erected in 1867. The second-story veranda was added in 1882. You can get a good view over the low white fence built of coral blocks (the best spot for photographs is on the east side, so save some film until we get around there). The king and queen usually live on a large spread west of town.

Now walk up Taufa'ahau Road past the huge rain tree in front of the modern Bank of Tonga (a local gathering place). Across the street stands the colonial-style **Prime Minister's Office** with its quaint tower.

Turn right at the post office on Salote Road. The **Nuku'alofa Club** on the left, about halfway down the block, is another holdover from the old South Pacific: It's a private club where Tonga's elite males gather to relax over a game of snooker and a few Australian beers. The next block of Salote Road runs behind the Royal Palace. You can look over the backyard fence and observe the royal geese. Turn right on Vaha'akolo Road and walk along the west side of the palace toward the sea. The highest point on Tongatapu, **Chapel Hill** (or Zion Hill) to the left, part of the Royal Estate, was a Tongan fort during the 18th century and the site of a missionary school opened in 1830 and a large Wesleyan church built in 1865. The school is now located 6.5km (4 miles) west of Nuku'alofa and is known as **Sia'atoutai Theological College.** The church has long since been torn down.

When you get to the water, look back and take your photos of the palace framed by the Norfolk pines.

Picturesque **Vuna Road** runs west from the palace, with the sea and reef on one side and stately old colonial homes on the other. The house at the end of the first block was the home of a Tongan noble who on several occasions in the 1800s went to England, where he stayed with friends in Newcastle; accordingly, he named the house **Niukasa.** The British High Commissioner's residence, in the second block, sports a flagpole surrounded by four cannons from the *Port au Prince,* the ship captured and burned by the Tongans at Ha'apai in 1806 after they had clubbed to death all its crew except young Will Mariner. King George I had two wives—not concurrently—and both of them are buried in casuarina-ringed Mala'e'aloa Cemetery, whose name means "tragic field." The clapboard house in the next block is known as **Ovalau** because it was built in the 1800s at Levuka, the old capital of Fiji on the island of Ovalau, and was shipped to Tonga in the 1950s.

Turn inland at the corner, walk 2 blocks on 'Alipate Road, take a left on Wellington Road, and walk 2 blocks west to **Centenary Church.** The mansion just before the church was reputed to have been built about 1871 by the Rev. Shirley W. Baker, the missionary who had so much influence over King George I. Now it's the home of the president of the Free Wesleyan Church of Tonga. Centenary Church was built by the Free Wesleyan Church of Tonga between 1949 and 1952. Most of the construction materials and labor were donated by members of the church. While construction was going on, the town was divided into sections that fed the workers three meals a day on a rotating basis. The amount of money spent on the building was about T$80,000 ($36,000); the actual value of the materials and labor was many times that amount. The church seats about 2,000 persons, including the king and queen, who worship there on Sunday mornings.

Turn right past the church and proceed inland on Vaha'akolo Road. On the right behind the Centenary Church is the old **Free Wesleyan Church of Tonga,** built in 1888 and an example of early Tongan church architecture. Past the old church is **Queen Salote College,** a girls' school named for a wife of King George I and not for his great-great-granddaughter, the famous Queen Salote.

Turn left at the first street, known as Laifone Road, and walk along a large open space to your right. Since 1893 this area has been known as the **Royal Tombs** ★★. King George I, King George II, Queen Salote, and most of their various wives and husbands are buried at the center of the field. For many years

---

Tips **Surviving Sunday in Tonga**

This quaint little kingdom has a lot for visitors to see and do 6 days a week. Sunday in Tonga is more of a challenge. Planes don't fly, ships don't sail, shops don't open, and taxis run only to carry everyone to church. You can worship with the royal family at 10am in the Centenary Church on Wellington Road. Tongan men wear neckties, but tourists get by without if they're neatly dressed. Women should wear dresses that cover the shoulders and knees. After church, many of us visitors—and many a Westernized Tongan, too—head for one of the offshore resorts, where we can get a meal, some libation, and a legal swim. See "Island Excursions, Watersports & Other Outdoor Activities," below.

the rest of the area was used as a golf course; today, however, the king's cattle keep the grass mowed. On Taufa'ahau Road, behind this open expanse stands the modern **Queen Salote Memorial Hall,** the country's national auditorium, which opened in 1994.

On the other side of Taufa'ahau Road, opposite the Royal Tombs, rises the tent-shaped **Basilica of St. Anthony of Padua,** the first basilica built in the South Pacific islands. On the ground level are the Loki Kai Cafeteria (more commonly known as Akiko's Restaurant; see "Where to Dine on Tongatapu," below) and the 'Utue'a Public Library.

Now follow **Taufa'ahau Road** toward the waterfront. On this main street, you'll pass shop after shop, some of them carrying handcrafts and clothing. Between Wellington Road and Salote Road is an old house that is now the home of the **Langafonua Women's Association Handicraft Center** (see "Shopping on Tongatapu," below). The clapboard house was built by William Cocker, a local merchant, for his five daughters, who lived in New Zealand but spent each winter in Nuku'alofa.

Turn right on the next street—Salote Road—and walk past the police station on the left to **Maketi Talamahu** in the second block, the lively produce market where vendors sell a great variety of fresh produce, ranging from huge taro roots and watermelons to string beans and bananas. Tongatapu's climate is just cool enough during the winter months that both European and tropical fruits and vegetables grow in great bounty. Upstairs, several stalls carry handcraft items, such as *tapa* cloth and straw baskets and mats.

After looking around the market and perhaps munching on a banana or sipping a fresh young coconut, continue walking east. In the next block is Fa'onelua Gardens; walk through it to the Tonga Visitors Bureau, where you began our tour and can end it.

TOURING TONGATAPU

Most visitors see Tonga's main island in two parts: first the eastern side and its ancient archaeological sites, and then the western side for its natural spectacles. You can do these on your own via rental car or go with one of the local tour operators (see "Organized Tours," below). Either way, pick up a copy of the visitors bureau's "The Capital Places Tour," which covers the entire island.

THE EASTERN TOUR

Take Taufa'ahau Road out of Nuku'alofa, making sure to bear left on the paved road. If you want to see tropical birds in captivity, watch for the signs on the right-hand side of the road directing you to the **Bird Park** and follow the dirt track about 3km (1¾ miles). There you will find the **Tongan Wildlife Centre** ★★ (© 29-449), which has a fine collection of colorful tropical birds from Tonga and other South Pacific islands. They are kept in cages carefully planted with native vegetation. A star is the Tongan megapode, a native only of Niuafo'ou in the Niuas islands; it buries its eggs in volcanic vents where the temperature is a constant 35°C (95°F), and then flies away, never to see its offspring. Admission is T$3 ($1.35). The center is open daily 9am to 5pm.

Now backtrack to the main road and turn right toward the airport. Keep left, especially at Malapo (where the road to the airport goes to the right), and follow the Tonga Visitors Bureau's excellent signs, which will show you the way to **Mu'a.** When the road skirts the lagoon just before the village, watch for the stone-and-brass monument marking **Captain Cook's Landing Place** ★★. The great British explorer landed and rested under a large banyan tree here when he came ashore in 1777 to meet with Pau, the reigning Tui Tonga. He attended the traditional presentation of first fruits marking the beginning of the harvest season. The banyan tree is long gone.

The next village is **Lapaha** ★★, seat of the Tui Tonga for 6 centuries, beginning about A.D. 1200. All that remains of the royal compound is a series of *langa,* or ancient terraced tombs, some of which are visible from the road. A large sign explains how the supreme Polynesian god Tangaloa came down from the sky about A.D. 950 and sired the first Tui Tonga. The last Tui Tonga, who died in 1865, after being deposed by King George I in 1862, is buried in one of the tombs. The 28 tombs around Lapaha and Mu'a are among the most important archaeological sites in Polynesia, but none of them have been excavated. Walk down the dirt road near the sign to see more of the tombs.

From Lapaha, follow the scenic paved road along the coast until reaching the **Ha'amonga Trilithon** ★★★, near the village of Niutoua on the island's northeast point, 32km (19 miles) from Nuku'alofa. This huge archway, whose lintel stone is estimated to weigh 35 tons, is 4.75m (16 ft.) high and 5.75m (19 ft.) wide. Tradition says it was built by the 11th Tui Tonga about A.D. 1200, long before the wheel was introduced to Tonga, as the gateway to the royal compound. The present King Taufa'ahau Tupou IV advanced a theory that it was used not only as a gateway but also for measuring the seasons. He found a secret mark on top of the lintel stone and at dawn on June 21, 1967, proved his point. The mark pointed to the exact spot on the horizon from which the sun rose on the shortest day of the year. You can stand under this imposing archway and ponder just how the ancient Tongans got the lintel stone on top of its two supports; it's the same sense of mysterious wonderment you feel while looking at Stonehenge in England or contemplating the great long-nosed heads that were carved and somehow erected by those other Polynesians far to the east of Tonga, on Easter Island.

The paved road ends at **Niutoua,** but a narrow dirt track proceeds down the east coast. **Anahulu Beach** has a cave with limestone stalactites near the village of Haveluliku. A gorgeous sand beach begins here and runs to **Oholei Beach.** 'Eua Island is visible on the horizon.

On the way back to Nuku'alofa you can take a detour to **Hufangalupe Beach** on the south coast for a look at a large natural bridge carved out of coral and limestone by the sea.

THE WESTERN TOUR

Proceed out of Nuku'alofa on Mateialona Road and follow the Visitors Bureau signs to the **Blowholes** ★★ near the village of Houma on the southwest coast. At high tide the surf pounds under shelves, sending geysers of seawater through holes in the coral. These are the most impressive blowholes in the South Pacific, and on a windy day the coast for miles is shrouded in mist thrown into the air

---

⌒Moments High & Dry Above the Blowholes

Having crossed the Pacific several times in U.S. Navy ships and sailed across it once in a small boat, I am acutely aware of the power of the sea. It's strangely comforting to watch it explode through the Blowholes on Tongatapu's south coast. Maybe it's because I know those waves can't get me up there on dry land.

> (*Fun Fact* **Tap-Tap-Tap**
>
> That tap-tap-tap sound you hear in many villages is the tattoo of hammers
> flattening the bark of the paper mulberry tree into Tongan *tapa* cloth.

---

by hundreds of them working at once. They perform best on a day when the surf
is medium—that is, just high enough to pound under the shelves and send water
exploding up through holes in them. Lime sediments have built up terraces of circles, like rice paddies, around each hole, and the local women come just before
dusk to gather clams in the shallow pools formed by the rings. There is a park with
benches and a parking area at the end of the road near the blowholes, but you'll
need shoes with good soles to walk across the sharp edges of the top shelf to get
the best views. This area once was an underwater reef, and corals are still very
much visible, all of them now more than 15m (50 ft.) above sea level. (Look for
what appear to be fossilized brains; they are appropriately named brain corals.)
The blowholes are known in Tongan as *Mapu'a a Vaea,* "the chief's whistle."

From Houma, proceed west to the village of Kolovai and watch for the trees
with strange-looking fruit. The sounds you hear and the odors in the air are
coming from what appear to be black fruit hanging on the trees. In reality, these
are the **Flying Foxes of Kolovai** ✿, a bat with a foxlike head found on many
islands in the Pacific. They are nocturnal creatures who spend their days hanging upside down from the branches of trees like a thousand little Draculas awaiting the dark, their wings like black capes pulled tightly around their bodies.
They don't feed on blood but on fruit; hence they are known as fruit bats. On
some islands they are considered a delicacy. In Tonga, however, where they live
in trees throughout the villages of Kolovai and Ha'avakatolo, they are thought
to be sacred, and only members of the royal family can shoot them. Legend says
that a Samoan princess gave the first bats to a Tongan navigator.

Near the end of the island is **Ha'atafu,** site of an offshore reef preserve. The
first missionaries to land in Tonga came ashore at the end of the peninsula on
the northwest coast, and a sign now marks the spot at the end of the road. They
obviously got their feet wet—if they were not inadvertently "baptized"—
wading across the shallow bank just offshore.

You've now toured Tongatapu from one end to the other. Turn around and
head back to town.

ORGANIZED TOURS

Several companies have half- and full-day tours around Nuku'alofa and the rest
of the island. *Note:* You should reserve any of these tours at least a day in advance.

The **Tongan National Centre** ✿✿✿ (✆ **23-022**) has informative half- and
whole-day island tours on Friday. Make your reservations well in advance.

The most fun is a 45-minute town tour in a *tuk-tuk*—an open-air tricycle taxi
from Thailand—offered by **Friends Tourist Center,** on Taufa'ahau Road
between Wellington and Salote roads (✆ **26-323**). These breezy runs around
town cost T$12 ($5.50) per person. Island tours in a regular van cost T$34
($15.25) for half a day (that is, half the island), T$64 ($29) for a whole
day/whole island tour.

Kingdom Tours, in the Air New Zealand office on Taufa'ahau Road (✆ **25-
200**), has a full-day town tour that's divided into two parts: sightseeing in the
morning for T$17 ($7.50) per person and a cultural tour of the Royal Palace and

Tongan National Centre in the afternoon for T$20 ($9). Its history tour to the east end of the island takes 2 to 3 hours and costs T$25 ($11.25). Its west-end tour takes 4 hours and costs T$53 ($24), including lunch.

Backpackers especially like **Toni's Tours** (© 21-049). Englishman Toni Matthias of Toni's Guesthouse (see "Where to Stay on Tongatapu," below) leads the tour and stops at Anahulu Beach, where you can swim inside the cave.

10 Island Excursions, Watersports & Other Outdoor Activities

ISLAND EXCURSIONS ★★★   Watersports activities are concentrated in the huge lagoon on Tongatapu's north shore, especially at resorts on the small islets off Nuku'alofa. In fact, the most popular way to spend a day—particularly a very slow Sunday in Tonga—is swimming, snorkeling, sunbathing, dining, or just hanging out at the flat, small islands of Pangaimotu, Fafa, or 'Atata, each of which has a resort just a few miles off Nuku'alofa. These little beachside establishments have restaurants and bars, too.

Tongan Beachcomber Island Village ★★ (© 23-759) on Pangaimotu is the oldest and closest of the offshore resorts, and it's also the most popular. Virtually hanging over a lovely beach, its main building oozes slapped-together, old South Seas charm. Its boat usually leaves Faua Jetty on Vuna Road at 10 and 11am Monday to Saturday, and at 10, 11am, noon, and 1pm on Sunday. They return at 4 and 5pm Monday to Saturday, and at 3, 4, 5, and 6pm on Sunday. Round-trip fare is T$12 ($5.50). Once there, a chalkboard menu offers burgers and sandwiches, and owner Earle Emberson serves icy cold brews from a giant ice box behind the bar. There's a children's playground.

Royal Sunset Island Resort ★ (© 21-155) on 'Atata, the most modern and comfortable of the resorts, welcomes day-trippers only on Sunday. Cost there is T$35 ($15.75), including transfers and lunch.

Fafa Island Resort (© 22-800), a German-owned Robinson Crusoe–like establishment, operates its own sailboat from Faua Jetty daily at 11am. Round-trip transfers and lunch cost T$35 ($15.75).

See "Where to Stay on Tongatapu," below, for more information about these offshore resorts.

FISHING   You can go game and deep-sea fishing with **Royal Sunset Charters,** based at Royal Sunset Island Resort on 'Atata Island (© 21-254); and with **Deep Blue Watersports** (© 25-392) and **Atiu Charters** (© 26-019) in Nuku'alofa.

GOLF   You won't be playing any golf on Sunday, but you can every other day at the flat nine-hole **Manamo'ui Golf Course,** home of the Tonga Golf Club. The tour desk at the International Dateline Hotel (© 21-411) can arrange equipment rentals and tee times on this somewhat-less-than-challenging course, which is on the main road between the airport and town.

SAILING   In addition to the charter yachts based in Vava'u (see "Vava'u," below), **Royal Sunset Cruising** ★★★, based at Royal Sunset Island Resort on 'Atata Island (© 21-254), has the 15m (51-ft.) yacht *Impetuous* that's available for charter anywhere in Tonga. It's one of the best ways to explore the more remote islands in the Ha'apai group. This crewed craft has three cabins, each with its own head (restroom) with shower. Cost is T$503 ($226) per person per day if two people go, T$208 ($94) per person if more than two go. The skipper, cook, and provisions are included.

> **Moments Lazing Away Sunday on an Islet**
>
> I usually stay very busy when I'm in Tonga, to revise this guide, but I am forced by law to put it aside and relax on Sunday in Tonga. I like to spend my day doing nothing except eating, drinking, and lazing in the sun at one of the little resorts off Nuku'alofa.

SCUBA DIVING & SNORKELING   Although diving off Tongatapu plays second fiddle to diving off Vava'u, the reefs offshore have some colorful coral and a great variety of sea life. Herbert Keller's **Deep Blue Diving Centre,** on Vuna Road at Faua Jetty (② and fax **23-576;** www.deep-blue-diving.to), has dives to Hakaumana'o and Malinoa Reef Reserves, two protected underwater parks, and to nearby 'Eua island, which has one of the largest underwater caves in the South Pacific (the entry is 28m/85 ft. deep). A two-tank dive costs T$120 ($54), including all equipment. Nondivers can go on many of his diving trips for T$35 ($15.75), including equipment. Herbert also has 2- and 3-day diving, snorkeling, hiking, and horseback riding safaris to 'Eua. On Sundays he takes both divers and nondivers out to Tau, an islet off Nuku'alofa. These outings cost T$100 ($45) for divers, T$65 ($29) nondivers, including lunch, soft drinks, and diving and snorkeling gear.

11 Shopping on Tongatapu

Tonga is the best place in the South Pacific to shop for extraordinary Polynesian handcrafts, such as *tapa* cloth, mats, carvings, shell jewelry, and other exquisite items. Your large laundry basket will take at least 3 months to get home via ship if you don't send it by air freight or check it as baggage on your return flight, but the quality of its craftsmanship will be worth the wait.

Tapa cloth and finely woven *pandanus* mats are traditional items of clothing and gifts in Tonga, and the women of the kingdom have carried on the ancient skills, not only out of economic necessity but also out of pride in their craft. Collectively they produce thousands of items each day, every one made by hand and no two exactly alike.

For an excellent description of how *tapa* cloth is made and the process by which the women weave baskets, mats, and other items from natural materials, pick up a copy of the Tonga Visitors Bureau's brochure "Tongan Handicrafts."

It's fun to browse around the handcraft stalls on the second level of **Maketi Talamahu** on Salote Road, where you can occasionally find an excellent basket or other item.

Except for tobacco products and liquor, Tonga has little to offer in the way of duty-free shopping. Get your booze and smokes at the airport, or order them at least one day prior to departure at Leiola Duty Free Shop in the International Dateline Hotel.

Kalia Handicrafts (FIMCO)   This retail outlet of the Friendly Islands Marketing Cooperative (FIMCO) gets a large variety of baskets, mats, *tapa,* shell jewelry, and other handcrafts. You can pay with American Express, MasterCard, and Visa credit cards, and the staff will pack and ship your purchases home. Taufa'ahau Rd., opposite Air New Zealand. ② **23-155.** Mon–Fri 8am–5pm, Sat 8am–noon.

Langafonua Women's Association Handicraft Center *Finds*   This terrific shop in the colonial house on Taufa'ahau Road was founded by Queen Salote in

---

Tips Buy It Ready-Made

To make sure you get what you paid for, purchase handcraft items already made and on display rather than ordering for future production and delivery after you have left Tonga.

1953 in order to preserve the old crafts and provide a market. It has an excellent collection, and some items may be priced somewhat lower than elsewhere. It does not accept credit cards, nor will it pack and ship your purchases. Taufa'ahau Rd, second block inland. ✆ **21-014.** Mon–Fri 8:30am–4:30pm, Sat 8:30am–noon.

Miki's Curio Shop   This small emporium is run by veteran carver Mickey Guttenbeil and his family, who export their black coral, mother-of-pearl, wood, bone carvings, and scrimshaw to other South Pacific and Hawaiian shops. Vuna Rd., next to the International Dateline Hotel. ✆ **32-083.** Mon–Fri 9:30am–4:30pm, Sat 9am–noon.

12 Where to Stay on Tongatapu

Let's put it this way: If an expensive, superluxurious vacation or honeymoon is your primary reason for coming to the South Pacific, go to Fiji or French Polynesia, not to Tonga. There are no luxury resorts at all in Tonga, although there are comfortable hotels and island hideaways from which to choose. Tonga is more of a developing nation than any other South Pacific country or territory, so don't set your expectations too high.

That's not to say that some establishments here don't have considerable charm, especially Tonga's offshore resorts, those little hideaways that sit all by themselves on small islands off Tongatapu's north shore. Go there to rest, relax, sunbathe, swim, snorkel, dive, dine, get drunk, or do whatever comes naturally in a romantic South Seas bungalow. On the other hand, don't spend your entire holiday at an offshore resort if you want to see much of the country or to sample exciting nightlife, because to get anywhere else requires a rather lengthy boat ride. Consider spending a weekend out in the islands, since everyone else will be there on Sunday anyway.

HOTELS

Harbor View Motel   Built in 1997, this three-story concrete building offers a variety of simple but clean rooms. The location on the waterfront is convenient if not particularly quiet, since the town's commercial wharf is across the road in front and the Billfish Bar and Restaurant is one door removed. The choice place to stay here is the huge executive suite, which occupies all of the third floor; its has windows on three sides, a TV, both a queen and a double bed, and a large bathroom with a Jacuzzi tub. On the second floor, spacious deluxe rooms are equipped with TVs, refrigerators, sofas, and their own bathrooms. Seven budget rooms share five bathrooms; four of these have a double bed each, but one has only a single (it's the least expensive room here), and none of them has a TV or air conditioner. This is a walk-up establishment with external stairways that lead to verandas on each floor.

P.O. Box 83, Nuku'alofa (Vuna Rd.), opposite Queen Salote Wharf). ✆ **25-488.** Fax 25-490. harbvmtl@ kalianet.to. 12 units (7 without bathroom). T$60–T$170 ($27–$76.50) double. Rates include continental breakfast. MC, V. **Amenities:** 1 bar; laundry service; coin-op washers and dryers. *In room:* A/C (in some units), TV (in some units), fridge (in some units), no phone.

International Dateline Hotel   As we went to press a major and much-needed renovation project was set to upgrade Tonga's flagship hotel, so I can't tell you what you'll find here when you arrive. Built by the government before the king's coronation in 1967, it is Tonga's most widely known place to stay, and most tour packages put you here. I would book here with caution, however, since it was far from international standard during my last visit. Renovated or not, the Dateline will remain Nuku'alofa's prime place for meetings, conventions, and other functions. The property enjoys a choice location facing the harbor across Vuna Road on Nuku'alofa's waterfront, a few blocks from downtown, and it's the only hotel on Tongatapu with spacious grounds featuring a swimming pool.

P.O. Box 39, Nuku'alofa (Vuna Rd. at Tupoulahi Rd., on the waterfront). © 23-411. Fax 23-410. idh@ kalianet.to. 76 units. T$115–T$154 ($52–$69 double). AE, DC, MC, V. **Amenities:** 2 restaurants (regional), 1 bar; outdoor pool; activities desk; limited room service; babysitting; laundry service. *In room:* A/C, TV, mini-bar, coffeemaker.

The Lagoon Lodge   Built in 2000 on the shores of Fanga'uta Lagoon, which is suitable for boating but not for swimming, these apartments are Nuku'alofa's newest and most spacious digs. They occupy a modern three-story building set perpendicular to the lagoon. The bottom two stories hold 10 townhouse-style apartments, with living room and kitchen downstairs and somewhat steep steps leading to a bedroom and shower-only bathroom upstairs. The top floor holds four one-bedroom suites and a two-bedroom, one-bathroom penthouse. Each unit has a balcony with at least a partial lagoon view. A landfill in front of the property has thatch cabanas and chairs for lagoon-side lounging. There's a boat for sunset cruises, and plans were to add kayaks, canoes, and sailboats. The front desk is open only on weekdays, and you get maid service only twice a week here. The noisy Blue Pacific Club is nearby, so this is not a good choice for Friday and Saturday nights.

P.O. Box 51, Nuku'alofa (on Fanga'uta Lagoon, 5km/3 miles east of Taufa'ahau Rd.). © 26-515. Fax 24-059. lagoon.lodge@kalianet.to. 15 units. T$115–T$250 ($52–$112.50) double. AE, MC, V. **Amenities:** Laundry service; coin-op washers and dryers. *In room:* Kitchen, coffeemaker.

Seaview Lodge ★★   Pending the International Dateline Hotel's being seriously upgraded, Nuku'alofa's best rooms are upstairs over the fine Seaview Restaurant (see "Where to Dine on Tongatapu," below). Three of these spacious, light, and airy units have balconies with fine views across Vuna Road to the lagoon and are the choice here. Two others face inland over the gardens. Each is equipped with a TV and a VCR, a ceiling fan over a queen-size bed, and a spacious bathroom with European-style, glass-enclosed showers with large heads. Six other less attractive but still comfortable units are in another building next door (only three of these are air-conditioned). Business travelers keep this place busy, so book as early as possible. The Seaview Restaurant is open to lodge guests for breakfast.

P.O. Box 268, Nuku'alofa (Vuna Rd. west of Royal Palace). © 23-709. Fax 26-906. www.tongaholiday.com/ seaview.htm. 11 units. T$85–T$155 ($38–$70) double. MC, V. **Amenities:** 1 restaurant (international), 1 bar; laundry service. *In room:* A/C (in 8 units), TV, dataport, minibar, coffeemaker.

Villa McKenzie ★★   This charming one-story colonial clapboard home on the waterfront is one of the South Pacific's few real bed-and-breakfasts. A central hallway is flanked on one side by a large lounge room (equipped with TV and VCR), an old-fashioned dining room with chintz curtains, and a huge country kitchen. To the other side, the four rooms all have tongue-in-groove walls, mosquito nets over their beds (doubles in two rooms, twins in the others), and tiny, closetlike bathrooms with shower stalls, sinks, and toilets. Tea, coffee, and soft drinks are available around the clock in the kitchen. The town's expatriate movers and shakers turn up here for snacks and kava in the rear garden Wednesday to Friday evenings. This clean and comfortable choice is the only one in town with old South Seas charm, so book several months in advance.

P.O. Box 1892, Nuku'alofa (Vuna Rd., at Tungi Rd.). © and fax **24-998**. villamac@kalianet.to. 4 units. T$120 ($54) double. Rates include full breakfast. MC, V. **Amenities:** Rental car; laundry service. *In room:* A/C, no phone.

HOSTELS

Heilala Holiday Lodge   Waltrand Quick and her son Sven Quick, both natives of Germany, operate this hostel set among garden plots, coconut palms, and fruit trees (you'll hear the neighborhood roosters before dawn). The best units are three bungalows with private bathrooms, ceiling fans, and big verandas with hammocks. In the original house, five upstairs rooms share two bathrooms with hot-water showers, a communal kitchen, and a second-story porch (where smokers can light up). These simple rooms have table fans, platform twin beds that can be pushed together, and screened windows with Venetian blinds. Complimentary breakfast is served in a single-roof restaurant, which is open for weeknight dinners by reservation only, Saturday and Sunday nights without reservation. The Quicks provide a shuttle to the beach and a free introductory tour of Nuku'alofa. They also operate Quick Tours, which provides low-budget island tours in both German and English.

P.O. Box 1698, Nuku'alofa (3km/2 miles south of town). © **29-910**. Fax 29-410. www.kalianet.to/quick. 8 units (5 without bathroom). T$38 ($17) double; T$85 ($38) double bungalow. Rates include breakfast. AE, DC, MC, V. **Amenities:** 1 restaurant (regional), 1 bar; outdoor pool; bike rentals; laundry service. *In room:* No phone.

'Otuhaka Beach Resort   This attractive, Tongan-operated hostel sits on a section of Ha'atafu Beach that is wider and has more sand than at Paradise Shores Resort (see below). Unfortunately, however, the sand all along Ha'atafu Beach ends abruptly in a coral ledge at the lagoon's edge, so it's better for sunning than swimming. The best units here are four bungalows built of plywood and equipped with fans, screen windows, and hot-water showers in their private bathrooms. Four smaller bungalows are built of thatch and other natural materials; although charming, they rely on mosquito nets instead of screens to keep the insects away, and they share toilets and cold-water showers. The most expensive but far less charming unit is a two-bedroom apartment in a Western-style house; it has a kitchen and private bathroom. A tin-roofed central building houses a bar and restaurant that serves inexpensive fare.

P.O. Box 374, Nuku'alofa (Kanokupolu village, 45km/27 miles west of town). © **41-599**. Fax 24-266. www. tongaholiday.com/otuhaka.htm. 9 units (5 with bathroom). T$35–T$125 ($15.75–$56) double. Rates include breakfast. MC, V. **Amenities:** 1 restaurant (regional), 1 bar; laundry service. *In room:* No phone.

Paradise Shores Resort   Operated by American Dave Bergeron, this friendly backpackers' resort sits on Ha'atafu Beach, one of the island's best. A Western-style house with a big veranda holds a restaurant and bar that looks across a lawn, upon which stands an outdoor Jacuzzi tub under the palm trees. The basic but charming guest fales are made of natural materials, and each has a double bed or two single beds with mosquito nets, ceiling fans, tables, a chair, and a dresser. Guests share toilets and showers in a rustic communal building. A free shuttle goes to town once a day. Tongans and local expatriate residents like to spend Sunday afternoons here, having lunch, drinking at the bar, and going for a swim.

P.O. Box 976, Nuku'alofa (Ha'atafu Beach, 48km/30 miles west of town). © **41-158.** Fax 41-158 or 24-868. paradise-shores@kalianet.to. 12 units (none with bathroom). T$40 ($18) double; T$10 ($4.50) dorm bed. MC, V. **Amenities:** 1 restaurant (regional), 1 bar; Jacuzzi; laundry service. *In room:* No phone.

Toni's Guesthouse   Englishman Toni Matthias has managed this basic but clean establishment, the most popular backpacker accommodation in town, since 1986. The rooms are in a long, Day-Glo green building fronted by a communal kitchen and covered gathering area on the carport. Toni does a kava ceremony some evenings and runs all-day island tours in his own truck for T$20 ($9) per person.

P.O. Box 3084, Nuku'alofa (corner of Railway and Mateialona rds.). © **21-049.** Fax 22-970. 8 units (none with bathroom). T$10.75 ($5) per person. Rates include tax. No credit cards. *In room:* No phone.

OFFSHORE RESORTS

Fafa Island Resort   German Rainer Urtel has stocked his little resort, on a 17-acre atoll-like island studded with coconut palms, with bungalows made entirely of coconut timbers and thatch. Although rustic and definitely not for anyone looking for all the comforts of home, they have Robinson Crusoe charm that has attracted a largely European clientele. An unusual feature has the toilets and lavatories on rear porches and showers actually sitting in the middle of fenced-enclosed courtyards. The push-out windows aren't screened, so each of the platform beds has a mosquito net. The bungalows all have front porches, over two of which are romantic "honeymoon" sleeping lofts with lagoon views.

Early morning coffee and tea are delivered to the units, and the dining room in a beachside central building features excellent seafood specialties. Guests can use snorkeling gear for free; they pay extra for Windsurfers, Hobie Cats, and trips to an uninhabited island for snorkeling.

P.O. Box 1444, Nuku'alofa (Fafa Island, 10km/6 miles off Nuku'alofa). © **22-800.** Fax 23-592. www.kalianet. to/fafa. 12 units. T$180 ($81) double. Meal plans T$70 ($31.50) per person per day. Round-trip transfers T$20 ($9) per person. AE, DC, MC, V. **Amenities:** 1 restaurant (regional), 1 bar; watersports; limited room service; massage; babysitting; laundry service. *In room:* No phone.

Royal Sunset Island Resort ★★   New Zealanders David and Terry Hunt's resort shares small, tadpole-shaped 'Atata Island with a native Tongan village. One of the South Pacific's finest beaches swings around their end, the "tail" of the tadpole, and the surrounding lagoon attracts swimmers, snorkelers, scuba divers, and anyone who loves to fish. Two large shingle-roofed fales house a dining room that serves fine meals and a triangular sunken bar, which opens to a pool surrounded by a deck that's dotted with lawn tables and umbrellas.

Each of the basic but comfortable guest bungalows sits behind privacy-providing foliage just off the shoreline. About half face the prevailing southeast trade winds; these can be chilly from June to August but provide nature's air-conditioning during the warmer months of December to March. You pay more for the other units, which face the lagoon, but they have a much better beach, plus views of the royal sunsets. Of modern construction, they have spacious shower-only bathrooms with hot and cold water, kitchenettes, ceiling fans in both rooms, and large, fully screened windows. A few bungalows are "minisuites"—one room with sitting areas and tea-and-coffee facilities but no kitchens.

Guests can use snorkeling gear, kayaks, sailboats, and Windsurfers for free, and they can pay to water-ski, sport fish, and scuba dive (you must be certified in advance).

P.O. Box 960, Nuku'alofa ('Atata Island, 10km/6 miles off Nuku'alofa). © **800/227-5317** or 24-923. Fax 21-254. royalsun@kalianet.to. 26 units. T$120–T$170 ($54–$77) double. Meals T$45 ($20.25) per person per day. Round-trip transfers T$40 ($18) per person. AE, DC, MC, V. **Amenities:** 1 restaurant (regional), 1 bar; outdoor pool; babysitting; laundry service. *In room:* Kitchen (in some units), fridge, coffeemaker, no phone.

Tongan Beachcomber Island Village   Unless I were backpacking, I wouldn't want to stay at Earle Emberson's lively little joint, usually referred to as "Pangaimotu Island Resort," but you will find me out here on Sunday afternoons, when it's packed with tourists, local expatriate residents, and Westernized Tongans. Wait until you see the rickety lagoon-side shack where Earle plays jazz compact discs and serves up ice-cold beer from a huge chiller behind the bar. It's one of the South Pacific's most charming pubs. Meanwhile, his staff whips up full meals or burgers and sandwiches served on an adjacent sundeck hanging over a lovely beach. You can swim and snorkel here, in one of the safest lagoons in Tonga.

Earle's four basic guest fales are built of natural materials. Each has separate sitting and sleeping areas, a platform double bed with a mosquito net, and a simple bathroom with a cold-water shower. All the fales face the beach. Dorm beds are in a larger communal fale, and campers can pitch tents on the lawns. Dorm dwellers and campers share communal cold-water showers, toilets, and kitchen facilities. There's a small store that dispenses groceries.

Private Bag 49, Nuku'alofa (Pangaimotu Island, 3km/2 miles off Nuku'alofa). © 11-236. Fax 23-759. 4 units, 12 dorm beds. T$50 ($22.50) bungalow; T$15 ($6.75) dorm bed; camping T$10 ($4.50) per person. Round-trip transfers T$12 ($5.50). MC, V. **Amenities:** 1 restaurant (regional), 1 bar. *In room:* No phone.

13 Where to Dine on Tongatapu

Nuku'alofa is blessed with a few restaurants that serve Continental cuisine of remarkably high quality for such a small and unsophisticated town. Most are operated by expatriates, especially from Germany and Italy. This also means a high turnover factor because not all expatriates stay in the islands forever. The establishments listed below were open when I was here recently. There may be more by the time you arrive—or these may be gone.

There's no McDonalds here yet, but you can get inexpensive burgers, fish and chips, sandwiches, and other quick fare at **The Grill,** on Taufa'ahau Road, between Wellington and Laifone roads (© 26-874). This upstairs joint is open Monday to Wednesday from 8am to 11pm, Thursday 8am to midnight, Friday from 8am to 2am, and Saturday 10am to midnight. MasterCard and Visa cards are accepted.

MODERATE

Billfish Bar and Restaurant INTERNATIONAL   This is primarily a socializing and drinking spot (see "Island Nights on Tongatapu," below), so dine at the Billfish after you've exhausted the other options here. It serves meals under its thatch-lined, lean-to roof. A floor of crushed coral and white picnic tables also help create a tropical ambience. Look for spicy Thai-style chicken curry, pepper steaks, and fresh fish steamed with fresh herbs and coconut milk. For lunch you can opt for burgers, sandwiches, fish and chips, grilled chops, and curries.

Vuna Rd., opposite Queen Salote Wharf. © 24-084. Reservations recommended for dinner. Lunch T$7–T$22 ($3–$10); main courses T$18–T$22 ($8–$10). MC, V. Mon–Fri noon–2pm and 6–10:30pm, Sat 6pm–midnight. Bar open Mon–Thurs noon–10:30pm, Fri noon–2am, Sat 6pm–midnight.

Davina's Harbourside Bar & Restaurant ✦ REGIONAL   Englishman David Foy has operated this pleasant restaurant in a pink stucco-over-cinder-block house since 1989. He keeps it open all day for breakfast, lunch, afternoon snacks, and dinners, but it's best known for the long front porch bar,

> **Tips** **Dine Like a Tongan**
>
> Like most Polynesians, the Tongans in the old days cooked their food over hot rocks in a pit—an *umu*—for several hours. Today they roast whole suckling pigs on a spit over coals for several hours (larger pigs still go into the *umu*). The dishes that emerge from the *umu* are similar to those found elsewhere in Polynesia: pig, chicken, lobster, fish, octopus, taro, taro leaves cooked with meat and onions, breadfruit, bananas, and a sweet breadfruit pudding known as *faikakai-lolo*, all of it cooked with ample amounts of coconut cream. Served on the side are fish *(ota ika)* and clams *(vasuva)*, both marinated in lime juice.
>
> The best place to sample Tongan food is during the evening buffets and dance shows at the **Tongan National Centre** (① 23-022). Others are the **International Dateline Hotel** (① 23-411) and the **Good Samaritan Inn** (① 41-022). See "Island Nights on Tongatapu," below, for details.

a favorite drinking spot for expatriate residents and Tongan businessmen. Meals are eaten in a dining room attractively furnished with cane. Ceiling fans whirring overhead add to the tropical atmosphere. The main courses feature the best steaks in town, plus fish, chicken, and local lobsters.

Vuna Rd., at Faua Jetty. ① 23-385. Reservations recommended at dinner. Breakfast T$5–T$12.50 ($2.25–$5.50); sandwiches and snacks T$7.50–T$12.50 ($3.50–$5.50); main courses T$12.50–T$26 ($5.50–$11.75). MC, V. Mon–Sat 9am–11pm (breakfast all day, lunch noon–3pm, snacks 3–6pm, dinner 6–11pm).

Seaview Restaurant ✩✩✩ CONTINENTAL   Offering the best cuisine in Tonga, this pleasant establishment is tastefully decorated inside with *tapa* cloth and mats to give the dining room an appropriately tropical atmosphere, but the best seats are on the screened porch, which has a sea view. Featured are fresh lobster from Tonga and quality meats imported from New Zealand. Some items that might appear are filet mignon wrapped in bacon and grilled, pepper steak, and fresh lobster or fish "Polynesia" (made sweet with papaya and other tropical fruits). Start with a chilled seafood cocktail and finish with homemade German pastries for dessert.

Vuna Rd., 3 blocks west of Royal Palace. ① 23-709. Reservations recommended. Main courses T$21.50–T$43 ($9.50–$19.50). MC, V. Mon–Fri 6–10pm.

Waterfront Cafe ✩✩ INTERNATIONAL   Under a big tin roof, this open-air creation of Daniella Orbessano, an Italian who once worked on Princess Cruises's ships, is the next best place to dine here after the Seaview. It's also another popular watering hole, but unlike the Billfish (see above), the products of Daniella's kitchen are reason enough to come here. Her menu changes every month, but you can always choose from homemade pastas, freshly caught red snapper, and tender steaks. If they're available, start with New Zealand mussels steamed with coconut cream and onions and laced with red chilies. Of several treatments of snapper, an islandy version is steamed in parchment paper with coconut cream and taro leaves. Many wines from Australia, New Zealand, and Italy are available by the glass.

Vuna Rd., opposite Faua Jetty. ① 24-962. Reservations recommended Thurs and Fri. Snacks T$7–T$8 ($3–$3.50); main courses T$12–T$30 ($5.50–$13.50). MC, V. Mon–Sat 10:30am–10:30pm, Sun 6–9pm.

INEXPENSIVE

Akiko's Restaurant (Loki Kai) *Value* EUROPEAN/CHINESE   Known as Akiko's in honor of its former Japanese owner, this plain but spotlessly clean establishment provides sandwiches and a selection of plain and simple European and Chinese selections that are marvelous bargains. No alcoholic beverages are served here.

Taufa'ahau Rd., in Basilica of St. Anthony of Padua. No phone. Reservations not accepted. Sandwiches T$1.50 (70¢); meals T$2–T$4.50 (90¢–$2). No credit cards. Mon–Fri 11:30am–2pm.

Friends Cafe ★★ COFFEE HOUSE/CAFE   This sophisticated coffee shop and cafe provides a delightful oasis in Taufa'ahau Road's dusty business scene. The cappuccino, espresso, and latte here are first rate (they aren't kidding when they say they have the best coffee in the kingdom). You can also eat the town's best cakes and pastries, luscious fruit plates, and made-to-order sandwiches at the counter, then sip or dine at the round wooden tables while listening to jazz or classical music on the sound system. A blackboard menu offers specials such as quiche and salad, braised lamb shanks in tomato sauce, and a sweet, New Orleans–style gumbo over rice.

Taufa'ahau Rd., between Salote and Wellington rds. © 21-284. Reservations not accepted. Breakfast T$4.50–T$8.50 ($2–$3.75); lunch T$5–T$12 ($2.25–$5.50). No credit cards. Mon–Fri 8am–4pm, Sat 8:30am–2pm.

Pizzeria Little Italy ★★ *Value* SOUTHERN ITALIAN   Angelo Crapanzano, who learned his trade as a pizza chef in Milan, Italy, now scurries around the open kitchen in this unusual restaurant: It's a genuine, thatch-roofed Tongan fale, but empty Ruffino wine bottles dangle from the support posts, and hats of every imaginable description adorn the walls. Don't be in a hurry, for Angelo makes everything from scratch, including the pizza dough and pasta. I started with a focaccia of thin, crispy pizza crust, and went on to an Italian-style side salad with virgin olive oil, oregano, and salt. My main course was a delicious helping of penne pasta in a medium-thick cream sauce accented with smoked salmon. I finished with a cup of real cappuccino. You can also choose from a limited list of Italian wines.

Vuna Rd., 5 blocks west of Royal Palace. © 21-053. Reservations recommended. Pizzas T$8–T$13.50 ($3.50–$6); pastas T$9.50–T$12 ($4.25–$5.50); main courses T$16–T$21 ($7–$9.50). MC, V. Mon–Fri noon–2pm and 6:30–11pm, Sat 6:30–10:30pm.

14 Island Nights on Tongatapu

TONGAN DANCE SHOWS ★★★   As in Samoa, traditional **Tongan dancing** emphasizes fluid movements of the hands and feet instead of gyrating hips, as is the case in French Polynesia and the Cook Islands. There is also less emphasis on drums and more on the stamping, clapping, and singing of the participants. The dances most often performed for tourists are the *tau'olunga,* in which one young woman dances solo, her body glistening with coconut oil; the *ma'ulu'ulu,* performed sitting down by groups ranging from 20 members to as many as 900 for very important occasions; the *laklaka,* in which rows of dancers sing and dance in unison; and the *kailao,* or war dance, in which men stamp the ground and wave war clubs at each other in mock battle.

The best place to see it is at **Tongan National Centre** ★★★ (© **23-022**), which stages a full Tongan-style feast complete with a traditional kava welcoming ceremony and dance show Tuesday and Thursday evenings. What makes the evening special is an explanation, in English, of what each dance represents. Cost is T$21 ($9.50). Book by 4:30pm.

Another good choice is the Friday night feasts at the **Good Samaritan Inn** (© **41-022**), on the beach 18km (11 miles) west of Nuku'alofa. Good Samaritan has an extensive buffet of Tongan and Western foods, followed by a dance show beside the lagoon. The meal and show costs T$20 ($9.50), plus T$5 ($2.25) for round-trip transportation from town if you need it. Reservations are advised.

You'll also have a chance to see Tongan dancing in Nuku'alofa at the **International Dateline Hotel** (© **23-411**), where floor shows start about 9pm after buffet-style dinners (the nights and prices change, so check with the hotel).

PUB CRAWLING   Because all pubs and nightclubs must close at the stroke of midnight Saturday, Friday is the busiest and longest night of the week in Tonga. That's when some establishments stay open until 2am or even 5am. Many Tongans start their weekends at one of the local bars and then adjourn to a nightclub for heavy-duty revelry.

Clubs change in popularity quickly, so it's best to ask around to learn which ones are drawing the crowds. During my recent visit, everyone started the Friday revelry with drinks at either **Davina's Restaurant** or the **Billfish Bar and Restaurant,** both on Vuna Road opposite Queen Salote Wharf (see "Where to Dine on Tongatapu," above). They then adjourned for late-night dancing at the **Blue Pacific Club,** on the Fanga'uta Lagoon east of town (access is by dirt road, so take a taxi).

15 Vava'u ★★★

Approximately 260km (163 miles) north of Tongatapu lies enchanting Vava'u, the second-most-visited group of islands in the kingdom, one of the South Pacific's great yachting meccas, and one of this region's most unusual destinations.

Often mispronounced "Va-vow" (it's "Va-*va*-oo"), the group consists of one large, hilly island shaped like a jellyfish, its tentacles trailing off in a myriad of waterways and small, sand-ringed islets. In the middle is the magnificent fjord-like harbor known as **Port of Refuge,** one of the finest anchorages in the South Pacific. From its picturesque perch above the harbor, the main village of **Neiafu** (pop. 5,000) evokes scenes from the South Seas of yesteryear.

To the south of Neiafu, the reef is speckled with 33 small islands, 21 of them inhabited. The others are spectacularly beautiful little dots of land that fall into the Robinson Crusoe category of places to escape from it all for a day. The white beaches and emerald surrounding lagoon are unsurpassed in their beauty.

When you see these protected waterways, you'll know why cruising sailors love Vava'u. But this is heaven not just to sailors but to any watersports enthusiast. Getting out on the water for a day is easy. If you like walking on unspoiled white sandy beaches on uninhabited islands, swimming in crystal-clear water, and taking boat rides into mysterious caves cut into cliffs, you'll like Vava'u, too.

Vava'u is the most seasonal destination in the South Pacific. Virtually asleep for 6 months of the year, it comes alive during the yachting season from May to October, when more than 250 boats can be in port at any one time. This is also the time of year when humpback whales migrate from the Antarctic to frolic in Tongan waters. You can often see them close inshore at Vava'u.

As with Savai'i in Samoa, you will wish you had stayed longer in this most beautiful and enchanting part of Tonga.

> **Tips** **Don't Forget to Reconfirm**
>
> It's imperative to reconfirm your return flight to Tongatapu as soon as possible after arriving on Vava'u. The staff at your hotel can take care of this for you, or you can visit the office of Royal Tongan Airlines, on the main street in Neiafu (© **70-149**).

HISTORY 101

Vava'u has its own unique history. The first European visitor was Spanish explorer Francisco Antonio Mourelle, who happened upon the islands in 1781 on his way to the Philippines from Mexico. He gave Port of Refuge its name. At the time, Vava'u was the seat of one of three chiefdoms fighting for control of Tonga. Finau II, who captured the *Port au Prince* in 1806, built a fortress at Neiafu and kept Will Mariner captive there until the young Englishman became one of his favorites. Two years later the brutal Finau won a major victory by faking a peace agreement with rival chiefs. He then tied them up and let them slowly sink to their deaths in a leaky canoe.

Finau II's successor, Finau 'Ulukalala III, converted to Christianity but died while his son was too young to rule. Before dying he asked George Taufa'ahau, who was then chief of Ha'apai, to look after the throne until the young boy was old enough. George did more than that; he took over Vava'u in 1833. Twelve years later he conquered Tongatapu and became King George I, ruler of Tonga.

GETTING TO VAVA'U & GETTING AROUND
GETTING THERE

Royal Tongan Airlines (© **800/486-6426** or 23-414 in Nuku'alofa, 70-149 in Vava'u; www.flyroyaltongan.com) has at least two flights a day between Tongatapu to Vava'u. **Samoa Air** flies very small planes between Pago Pago and Vava'u once a week.

Lupepa'u International Airport is on the north side of Vauau'u, about 7km (4 miles) from Neiafu. The Paradise International Hotel's bus provides airport transfers to its guests for free and T$4 ($1.75) to anyone else, or you can take one of the island's few taxis to Neiafu for about T$7 ($3).

The ferries from Nuku'alofa land in Neiafu at Uafu Lahi, which everyone calls the "Big Wharf." From there you can walk or take a taxi ride to your hotel or guesthouse. If you're on foot, turn right on the main street to reach the center of town and the accommodations.

The road from the airport dead-ends at a T-intersection atop the hill above the wharf. The main street runs from there in both directions along the water, with most of the town's stores and government offices flanking it.

GETTING AROUND

You can explore all of Neiafu on foot, but public transportation to the outlying areas of Vava'u is limited. If you book an excursion, ask about the availability of transportation to and from the event.

Sailing Safaris, a yacht chartering and watersports operation on the waterfront (© **70-650**), rents four-wheel-drive vehicles for T$100 ($45) per day and scooters for T$30 ($13.50) per day.

Adventure Backpackers (© **70-955;** backpackers@kalianet.to) rents mountain bikes for T$15 ($6.75) a day. See "Where to Stay on Vava'u," below.

> **Fun Fact** The Road of the Doves
>
> The government used convicted adulteresses to help build the main road in Neiafu; hence, its Tongan name is Hale Lupe—"The Road of the Doves." There are no street signs, but the Tonga Visitors Bureau's helpful signs point the way to most establishments and points of interest.

Taxis are not metered, so be sure you determine the fare before getting in. **Falepiu Taxi** (✆ 70-671) has a stand opposite the Bank of Tonga; **Liviela Taxi** (✆ 70-240) is opposite the big Frisco store; **Hamana Taxi** (✆ 70-257 or 70-157) is near the market; and **Lopaukamea Taxi** (✆ 70-153) is opposite the market. Fares are T$2 (90¢) in town, or you can hire one for about T$10 ($4.50) per hour, but be sure to negotiate a fare in advance.

Buses and pickup trucks fan out from the market in Neiafu to various villages, but they have no fixed schedule and are not a reliable means of transport. If you take one, make sure you know when and whether it's coming back to town.

 FAST FACTS: Vava'u

If you don't see an item here, check "Fast Facts: Tonga," earlier in this chapter, or just ask around. Vava'u is a very small place where nearly everyone knows everything.

Currency Exchange **ANZ Bank,** on the main street in Neiafu, has an ATM that is open during business hours. The **Bank of Tonga** is nearby. Banking hours are Monday to Friday from 9am to 3:30pm, Saturday 9:30am to noon. You can cash small-denomination traveler's checks at **Paradise International Hotel** when the banks are closed.

E-mail **Sailing Safaris,** on the waterfront (✆ 70-650), will send and receive e-mail (you can't surf the Web here). They charge T$8 ($3.60) to send messages, T$2 (90¢) to receive.

Emergencies/Police The telephone number for the **police** is **70-234.**

Healthcare **Dr. Alfredo Carafa** (✆ 70-607), an engaging Italian, has a private clinic with two doctors and a dentist next to the Bank of Tonga. The clinic is open Monday to Friday 9am to 2pm. The government has a **small hospital** in Neiafu, but I recommend that you call Dr. Alfredo at his clinic instead.

Information The **Tonga Visitors Bureau** (✆ 70-115; fax 70-666; tvbvv@ kalianet.to) has an office on the main road in Neiafu. Check there for lists of local activities while you're in town. The staff can also help arrange road tours of the island and boat tours of the lagoon. The office is open Monday to Friday from 8:30am to 4:30pm, Saturday from 8:30am to noon. The address is P.O. Box 18, Neiafu, Vava'u.

Laundry **Sailing Safaris,** on the waterfront (✆ 70-650), has commercial-size coin-operated washers and dryers. A wash-dry-fold load costs T$5 ($2.25).

Post Office The post office opposite the wharf is open Monday to Friday from 8:30am to 4pm.

Telephone Tonga Communications Corporation next to the post office is open 24 hours a day, 7 days a week for domestic and long-distance calls. It also has a card phone (there's one next to the Bank of Tonga, too).

Time Tonga observes "standard time" from the last Sunday in January until the first Sunday in November, when local time is 13 hours ahead of Greenwich mean time. The clocks are moved ahead 1 hour from the first Sunday in November until the last Sunday in January during Tonga's daylight saving time, when local time is 14 hours ahead of Greenwich mean time. Tonga is in the same day as Australia, New Zealand, and Fiji, and a day behind the United States, the Samoas, the Cook Islands, and French Polynesia.

Water Don't drink the tap water.

EXPLORING VAVA'U

Be sure to take a walk along Port of Refuge from Paradise International Hotel into town, a stroll of about 15 minutes.

The flat-top mountain across the harbor is **Mo'unga Talau,** at 204m (675 ft.) the tallest point on Vava'u. A hike to the top takes about 2 hours round-trip. To get there, turn inland a block past the Bank of Tonga on the airport road, and then turn left at the Old Market. This street continues through the residential area and then becomes a track. The turnoff to the summit starts as the track begins to head downhill. It's a steep climb and can be slippery in wet weather.

The **Tonga Visitors Bureau** (© 70-115) will arrange **sightseeing tours** of the island. Cost is about T$25 ($11.25) per person, with a minimum of three persons required. You will see lovely scenery of the fingerlike bays that cut into the island, visit some beautiful beaches, and take in the sweet smell of vanilla—the principal cash crop on Vava'u—drying in sheds or in the sun.

BOAT TOURS ✸✸✸

The absolute best thing to do in Vava'u is to take a boat tour out on the fabulous fjords for a day of swimming, snorkeling, and exploring of the caves and uninhabited islands.

The typical tour follows Port of Refuge to **Swallows Cave** on Kapa Island and then to **Mariner's Cave** (named for Will Mariner, the young Englishman captured with the *Port au Prince* in 1806) on Nuapapu Island. Both of these have been carved out of cliffs by erosion. Boats can go right into Swallows Cave for a look at the swallows flying in and out of a hole in the cave's top. Swimmers with snorkeling gear and a guide can dive into Mariner's Cave. Both caves face west and are best visited in the afternoon, when the maximum amount of natural light gets into them. Most trips also include a stop at one of the small islands for some time at a sparkling beach and a swim over the reefs in crystal-clear water.

Every hotel and guest house here can arrange boat tours, or you can drop by **Sailing Safaris** (© 70-650; sailingsafaris@kalianet.to), which has all-day snorkeling trips to the caves and islets for T$50 ($22.50) per person. They sometimes use longboats, which have no cover to protect you from the sun, so if you're sunsensitive, ask what type of craft will be used before going on these trips. Or you can rent a powerboat or sailboat and go where you please. Boats cost T$80 ($36) a day, T$120 ($54) with a skipper. The skipper is worth having on a day trip, since he will take you to the caves and then stand by the boat while you explore.

(**Moments** The Ghost of Will Mariner

Every time I pop my head out of the water in Mariner's Cave, I swear I can see the ghost of the young Englishman Will Mariner, who wrote a best-selling book about being held captive here in the early 19th century.

SAILING ★★

The waterfront at the base of the hill in Neiafu is home to more than 30 charter yachts that you can rent for as many days as you can afford. Most Americans who visit Tonga, in fact, come here to explore Vava'u in a chartered yacht. You can spend your time sailing from one tiny islet to another in these calm waters. There are dozens of gorgeous beaches off which to anchor, and there are several restaurants to visit at night.

The best of the charter companies is **The Moorings** ★★★ (© 800/534-7289 or 70-016; www.moorings.com), the Florida-based pioneer of chartering sailboats in the Caribbean. The Moorings requires that you be qualified to handle sailboats of the size it charters, and the staff will check out your skills before turning you loose. If you don't qualify, you can hire a skipper or guide at extra cost. Boats range in length from 11m to 15m (36 ft.–51 ft.) and in price from US$390 to US$745 a day per boat for bareboat charters (that is, you hire the "bare" boat and provide your own skipper and crew). A skipper will cost another US$132 per day. The Moorings will do your shopping and have the boat provisioned with food and drink when you arrive.

Also on the waterfront is the New Zealand–based **Sunsail Yacht Charters** (© and fax **70-646;** www.sunsail.co.nz). Its boats range from 9.5m to 15m (32 ft.–51 ft.) in length and cost from US$545 to US$1,300 per day.

If you want smaller craft, try **Sailing Safaris** (© and fax **70-650;** sailingsafaris@kalianet.to), whose headquarters is next to The Moorings. It has 4.75m to 8.5m (16-ft.–28-ft.) sailboats available from T$80 to T$220 ($36–$99) per day. This company also acts as a booking agent for larger boats.

WHALE-WATCHING ★★★

Humpback whales breed in the waters off Vava'u from June to October, and going out to see them is a highlight of a visit here during the season. Other whale-watching destinations such as Hawaii won't allow you to swim with the whales, but that's not the case here. Local operators say there's a 50% to 60% chance you'll get to snorkel among the whales and a 90% chance of seeing them during the season.

Both **Whale Watch Vava'u** (© **70-493;** mounu@kalianet.to) and **Sailing Safaris** (© **70-650;** sailingsafaris@kalianet.to) take guests out to snorkel among these huge animals for T$65 ($29) per person. They ordinarily use boats with shade canopies and toilets for these trips, but don't go if it's in an uncovered longboat. These are all-day voyages, and the sun can be brutal. Book Whale Watch Vava'u at the Bounty Bar & Cafe in Neiafu (see "Where to Dine on Vava'u," below). Sailing Safaris has its office on the waterfront.

FISHING, KAYAKING & SCUBA DIVING

As noted above, Vava'u has a very busy yachting and whale-watching season from May to October. Some of the activities mentioned below operate only during this period and then clear out of Tonga entirely during the hurricane season from November to April. It's best to ask in advance whether any particular activity is available when you will be here.

FISHING   The waters off Vava'u hold a large number of sizable blue marlin, sailfish, yellowfin and dogtooth tuna, mahimahi, and other species, and you can charter one of several boats here to go get 'em.

New Zealanders Keith and Pat McKee of *Kiwi Magic* (© and fax **70-441;** kiwifish@kalianet.to) take visitors offshore for a full day of sports fishing, and snorkelers can go along by arrangement. The McKees operate year-round, as do their fellow Kiwis, Henk and Sandra Gross of **Target One** (© and fax **70-647;** www.invited.to/target1) and Geoff and Janine Le Strange of the *Hakula* (© **70-872;** fax 70-875; fishtonga@kalianet.to). They all charge about US$90 per person per day, including bait, tackle, and lunch. A minimum of three persons must be on board.

KAYAKING   Yachties aren't the only ones who can enjoy the multitude of protected waterways here. Kayakers can, too. **Friendly Islands Kayak Company** (© **70-173;** fax 70-173 or 22-970; www.fikco.com), a New Zealand firm based south of the Paradise International Hotel from May to January, rents sea kayaks and conducts guided tours. It has scheduled 4-, 10-, and 12-day trips through the islands, using double- and single-seat kayaks. The tours range from US$550 to US$1,350 per person. These should be arranged in advance. Or you can call when you get here for a guided day trip, which costs about US$50, including kayak, snorkeling gear, and lunch. You can contact the company during the off-season at P.O. Box 142, Waitati, Otago, New Zealand (© and fax **3/482-1202**).

Do-it-yourselfers can rent kayaks from **Sailing Safaris** (© **70-650;** sailing safaris@kalianet.to) on the waterfront for T$25 ($11.25) for single- or double-seated craft.

SCUBA DIVING ★★   There's good diving in these clear waters, especially since you don't have to ride on a boat for several hours just to get to a spot with colorful coral and bountiful sea life. In Port of Refuge, divers can explore the wreck of the copra schooner *Clan McWilliam,* sunk in 1906.

The Dutch–New Zealander couple Huib and Sybil Kuilboer of **Beluga Diving** (© and fax **70-087;** www.belugadivingvavau.com) offers a variety of diving

---

The Easy Way to Go

If you don't want to haul lines and raise sails, try **Coral Island Cruises** ★★★ (© **24-923;** fax 21-254; www.coralislandcruises.com), which uses the diesel-powered MV *Oleanda,* a former member of the Blue Lagoon Cruises fleet in Fiji (see chapter 10), to explore both Vava'u and Ha'apai. This comfortable, 39m (120-ft.) craft has 18 cabins and a suite, all of them air-conditioned and all of them with private bathrooms.

During its 4-day Vava'u cruise, the *Oleanda* stops at remote beaches for swimming and snorkeling, at islands for village visits, and at a restaurant for an on-shore dinner. These 4-day cruises cost T$1,050 to T$1,560 ($473–$702) per person double occupancy, including all meals and activities.

A 6-day "Discover Tonga" cruise spends 2 days in Vava'u, 2 days in the Ha'apai Group, and 2 days in the lagoon off northern Tongatapu. You can get on either in Vava'u and work south or in Nuku'alofa and cruise north to Vava'u. These voyages cost T$1,615 to T$2,660 ($727–$1,197) per person double occupancy.

excursions as well as parasailing and Windsurfer rentals. Two-tank dives cost T$95 ($43), including equipment, and Huib teaches PADI open-water courses for T$350 ($158). The Kuilboers also offer parasailing for T$40 ($18) for a 20-minute ride, and they rent Windsurfers for T$30 ($13.50) for half a day.

Dolphin Pacific Diving (℃ and fax **70-292;** dive-adi@wave.co.nz) offers two-tank dives for T$95 ($43), including tanks and weight belts. They teach PADI courses from open-water to dive master.

SHOPPING

If you depart Vava'u directly for Pago Pago or Nadi, you can buy some duty-free merchandise at **Leiola Duty Free Shop,** which has shops in the Paradise International Hotel and next door to the Tonga Visitors Bureau on the main street.

As noted earlier in this chapter, Vava'u produces some of the finest handcrafts in Tonga. The establishments listed below will pack and ship your purchases home. Also look in the small jewelry shops along the main street for items of black coral and shell.

Friendly Islands Marketing Cooperative (FIMCO)   The Vava'u branch of FIMCO has some good items, but most of the best is shipped to the main store in Nuku'alofa for sale (see "Shopping on Tongatapu," above). Main st., opposite Tong Visitors Bureau. ℃ **70-142.** Mon–Fri 8:30am–4:30pm (to 5pm June–Nov), Sat 8:30am–noon.

Langafonua Handicrafts   The Vava'u branch of Langafonua, the women's handcraft organization founded by Queen Salote (see "Shopping on Tongatapu," above), has a shop in a Tongan fale adjacent to the Tonga Visitors Bureau. It has a good variety of baskets, mats, wood carvings, and other items at reasonable prices. Main st., in Tonga Visitors Bureau. ℃ **70-356.** Mon–Sat 8:30am–4pm; Sat 8:30am–noon.

WHERE TO STAY ON VAVA'U
HOTELS & RESORTS

Hilltop Hotel ⚲   Sitting on a hill with a view of Port of Refuge, this recently renovated and upgraded hotel has the most modern and comfortable accommodations on Vava'u—if you don't mind the steep climb to get here. Two Western-style houses each hold four of the rooms, the pick of which are the four "sea-view" units with verandas overlooking the port. The four "standard" units face away from the water; they have neither verandas nor air conditioners. All are moderately spacious and have cool terra-cotta tile floors, pine furniture imported from Italy (from whence the owners hail), and ample private bathrooms with hot-water showers. The Sunset Restaurant is on the premises (see "Where to Dine on Vava'u," below).

Private Bag, Neiafu, Vava'u (off the airport rd.; follow TVB signs). ℃ and fax **70-209.** sunset@kalianet.to. 8 units. T$75–T$100 ($34–$45) double. MC, V. **Amenities:** 1 restaurant (regional), 1 bar; laundry service; coin-op washers and dryers. In room: A/C (in 4 units), no phone.

Mounu Island Resort ⚲⚲   The long-time dream of New Zealanders Allan and Lyn Bowe, this little resort sits beside a wraparound beach of deep white sand on Mounu ("Bait Fish" in Tongan), an atoll-like, 6-acre islet near the southern end of Vava'u's outer islands. Cruising yachties moor their boats over the colorful corals and row their dinghies ashore to imbibe and dine on freshly caught seafood in the Bowes' main building, a lovely mat-lined Tongan fale right on the beach. Their three widely spaced guest fales are rustic but charming, with futon beds covered with mosquito nets (which are necessary because the windows aren't screened), rattan easy chairs and glass-topped coffee tables, bathrooms with hot-water showers, and front porches facing the lagoon. Solar power generates the electricity, and rain provides all the fresh water here. You can swim, snorkel, kayak, fish, go on village visits, and observe seabirds at a nearby breeding colony. This is a very popular retreat during the June-to-October whale-watching season, when Allan operates Whale Watch Vava'u (see "Whale Watching," above). It's a fine place to unwind after a week or two on a charter yacht any time of year.

Private Box 7, Neiafu (Mounu Island, 25 min. by speedboat from Neiafu). (C) **70-747**. Fax 70-493. www. mounu.com. 3 units. T$200 ($90) double. Meals T$65 ($29) per person per day. Transfers T$50 ($22.50) per person. MC, V. **Amenities:** 1 restaurant (regional), 1 bar; watersports; laundry service. *In room:* No phone.

Paradise International Hotel   Perched on a grassy ridge overlooking Port of Refuge and a short walk from Neiafu, this is one of the most comfortable hotels in Tonga, although it's in need of some refurbishment. A large central building houses the reception area, a gift shop, bar, restaurant, and TV lounge. Next to it on a grassy lawn is a pool with a panoramic view of the harbor below. A path leads down to the water's edge, where the hotel has its own pier and kayaks for rent. The large rooms, in one- and two-story buildings, are devoid of any tropical charms except the views from their balconies (the most expensive units have unimpeded views of Port of Refuge). They have various bed combinations, recliner chairs, coffee tables, and ample bathrooms with tub-and-shower combos. A few older "economy" rooms have ceiling fans but neither air conditioners, tea- and coffee-making facilities, hot water, nor harbor views.

P.O. Box 11, Neiafu, Vava'u, Tonga (east end of Neiafu). (C) **70-211**. Fax 70-184. www.kalianet.to/paradise. 48 units. T$89–T$169 ($40–$76) double. AE, DC, MC, V. **Amenities:** 1 restaurant (regional), 1 bar; outdoor pool; watersports; limited room service; babysitting; laundry service. *In room:* A/C (in most units), fridge, coffeemaker.

Tongan Beach Resort   This isolated resort sits beside a lovely narrow channel south of Port of Refuge, giving guests their own swimming beach and jumping-off point for scuba diving, kayaking, and other watersports. The main building here is an open Tongan fale that houses a restaurant whose menu varies each day, depending on the catch, the emphasis being on fresh seafood. A sand-floored bar is in its own fale next door. The star accommodations here are two overwater bungalows with thatch-covered tin roofs and steps down into the shallow lagoon (these are not nearly as luxurious as overwater units found elsewhere in the South Pacific). Ashore, comfortable, motel-like guest rooms flank the main complex. They are of New Zealand–style construction and furnishings. Each has tile floors, ceiling fans, a dressing area, one queen and one single bed, and shower-only bathrooms.

P.O. Box 104, Neiafu, Vava'u (on 'Utungake Island, 8.8km/5½ miles from Neiafu, 14.5km/9½ miles from airport via dirt rd. and causeway). (C) and fax **70-380**. www.thetongan.com. 12 units. US$85 double, US$165 bungalow. Meals US$40 per day adults, US $10 per day children under 10. Meals T$60 ($27) per person per day. Round-trip airport transfers T$25 ($11.25). MC, V. **Amenities:** 1 restaurant (regional), 1 bar; free use of kayaks and snorkeling gear; laundry service. *In room:* Fridge, coffeemaker, no phone.

Twin View Motel   The best thing about this simple but clean motel is its spectacular views of both Port of Refuge and the Old Harbor. Built in 1999 atop a ridge between the two harbors, it is little more than three blocks of spacious apartments. Four of them have two bedrooms, two have a single bedroom, and the sixth is a studio unit. All have bright tile floors, peaked ceilings, doors that open to long porches across the fronts of the buildings, and shower-only bathrooms. Only two units have hot water. None of them have air conditioners, but the trade winds can blow with ferocity up here.

Private Bag, Neiafu, Vava'u (opposite Paradise International Hotel). ℂ **70-597**. Fax 70-622. 6 units. T$45–T$100 ($20–$45) double. MC, V. **Amenities:** Laundry service. *In room:* Kitchen, coffeemaker, no phone.

HOSTELS

Adventure Backpackers   In the center of Neiafu's commercial strip, this excellent backpackers' hostel has a marvelous view of Port of Refuge from its communal kitchen and lounge with TV. Six of the nine rooms have private bathrooms. Two of these are in a separate building and are much more private. One is a family size unit with a double bed and two twins. Everyone else shares four toilets and four showers.

Private Bag 3, Neiafu, Vava'u (main st. next to Royal Tongan Airlines). ℂ **70-955**. Fax 70-647. backpackers@kalianet.to. 9 units (3 without bathroom), 16 dorm beds. T$50–T$60 ($22.50–$27) double; T$15–T$18 ($6.75–$8) dorm bed. MC, V. *In room:* No phone.

WHERE TO DINE ON VAVA'U

'Ana's Waterfront Cafe BREAKFAST/SNACKS   Go down the steep steps next to The Moorings to reach this friendly cafe on a covered dock by the bay. While you're sitting on the dock, notice the lighted cave in the cliff that drops from the main road to the harbor ('Ana is not a woman's name; it means "cave" in Tongan). The Moorings owns this restaurant, which explains the "Eggs McMoorings" on the breakfast menu—along with fruit plates, omelets, sandwiches, and pancakes. The rest of the day sees big burgers, fish and chips, and the like. If they're not over at The Mermaid Bar & Grill next door, you'll find all the town's expatriate residents and most of the yachties here.

Neiafu, main st. next to The Moorings. ℂ **70-664**. Reservations not accepted. Breakfast, salads, sandwiches, and burgers T$4.50–T$12.50 ($2–$5.50). MC, V. Mon–Sat 8am–10pm.

Bounty Bar & Cafe SNACKS/REGIONAL   With its great view overlooking Port of Refuge, the Bounty Bar is primarily a popular spot for morning tea or coffee and an afternoon beer or soft drink. The view is much better than at either 'Ana's or The Mermaid Bar & Grill, but the food is not. You can order cooked breakfasts, burgers and sandwiches, and meals of fried rice and fresh local fish.

Neiafu, main st. in heart of town. ℂ **70-576**. Reservations recommended for dinner July–Aug. Breakfast T$3–T$15 ($1.35–$6.75); snacks and meals T$4–T$15 ($1.75–$6.75). No credit cards. Sept–May, Mon–Fri 8:30am–7pm; June–Aug, Mon–Fri 8:30am–10pm.

Mermaid Bar & Grill SNACKS/SEAFOOD   Operated by Sailing Safaris, this open-air restaurant beside the harbor serves breakfast, sandwiches, burgers, salads, and dinner choices, including grilled lobster and fish, seafood curry, and chicken in a spicy Thai curry sauce. For lunch try the lobster salad. Along with 'Ana's next door (see above), this is a popular hangout for local expatriates and passing yachties, especially during happy hour from 5 to 7pm.

Neiafu, main st. on the water next to Sailing Safaris Marine Center. ℂ **70-730**. Reservations recommended for dinner July–Aug. Breakfast T$3–T$12 ($1.35–5.50); salads, sandwiches, and burgers T$5–T$15 ($2.25–$6.75); main courses T$18–T$28 ($8–$12.50). MC, V. Mon–Sat 8am–9pm (bar to midnight).

Ocean Breeze Restaurant ⭐⭐ REGIONAL   Born in Tonga, Amelia Dale lived for 15 years in England, where she met and married her husband, John. In 1988 she and John converted their living room and veranda overlooking the Old Harbour into a restaurant and have been serving the best food on the island ever since. I love the curries, which are right up there with any curry I've had anywhere, and that includes India and Pakistan. Ask Amelia to turn down the chilis if you have a tender tongue! You can have a drink out in the Bistro Bar on the

---

Tips **A Tongan Feast at the Beach**

If you missed a Tongan feast in Nuku'alofa or you just liked it so much you want to go to another, head for **Hinakauea Beach Feast,** which takes place Thursday on lovely Lisa Beach. It costs T$20 ($9) per person. Inquire at the Paradise International Hotel or the Tonga Visitors Bureau.

---

lawn. The trail across the peninsula from Port of Refuge and the Paradise International Hotel is narrow and can be muddy. Take a cab for T$2 (90¢) each way.

Neiafu, on the Old Harbor. ℭ **70-582.** Reservations required. Main courses T$11.50–T$29.50 ($5–$13.25). MC, V. Mon–Sat noon–2pm and 6–10pm, Sun by prior arrangement only.

Sunset Restaurant ITALIAN   Italians own both this restaurant and the Hilltop Hotel (see "Where to Stay on Vava'u," above), and here they serve genuine wood-fired pizzas and bowls of pasta under authentic old-country sauces. The pizzas are of the thin-crust variety, and the sauces include many southern Italian favorites plus a delightful smoked salmon in cream. Main courses emphasize steaks and fresh local lobster and fish. Like the hotel, the thatch-lined restaurant has a fine view over Port of Refuge.

In Hilltop Hotel, off the airport rd. ℭ **70-838.** Reservations recommended June–Aug. Breakfast T$7–T$10 ($3–$4.50); pizza T$6–T$15 ($2.75–$6.75); main courses T$17–T$22 ($7.50–$10). MC, V. Daily 8–9:30am and 6–9:30pm.

ISLAND NIGHTS ON VAVA'U

Bands play from June through August at the **Paradise International Hotel** (ℭ 70-211), and Tongans entertain at **The Mermaid Bar & Grill** (ℭ 70-730). Otherwise, there's not much to do except hang out with all the expatriates and yachties down at The Mermaid and 'Ana's Waterfront Cafe on the waterfront (see "Where to Dine on Vava'u," above).

16 Ha'apai

Off the beaten path but easily accessible, Ha'apai is central in both Tonga's geography and history. In the middle of the kingdom, 155km (96 miles) north of Nuku'alofa and 108km (67 miles) south of Vava'u, Ha'apai consists of numerous small, atoll-like islands scattered across the sea. The largest and most often visited, **Lifuka** and **Foa,** are linked by a causeway. On the horizon to their west sits the active volcano **Tofua,** where puffs of steam spew from the rim above its crater lake, and the perfectly shaped cone of its inactive neighbor, **Kao.**

The Dutchman Abel Tasman landed on one of the islands in 1643. Capt. James Cook was so impressed with the Tongans' hospitality when he visited Lifuka in 1773 and 1777 that he named the group the "Friendly Islands" (he sailed away unaware that the local chief had plotted to do him in). Fletcher Christian and the *Bounty* mutineers cast Capt. William Bligh adrift in a longboat off Tofua in 1789. In 1806 the locals ransacked the British privateer *Port-au-Prince,* killing all of its crew except the young Will Mariner, who lived to write about his adventure. Tonga's first Wesleyan missionaries arrived here in the 1820s. With their help, the converted local chief Taufa'ahau captured the rest of Tonga, changed his name to King George I, and in 1845 created the realm we visit today. The Rev. Shirley Baker, who dominated King George during his later years, is buried on Lifuka in **Pangai,** Ha'apai's only town.

Today Lifuka and the other islands seem much as they must have been when King George moved his capital to Tongatapu. You'll find some great beaches and fine scuba diving here, but there's not much else to do except relax, explore Pangai's historical sights, and go diving. In other words, it's a fine place to get away from it all.

GETTING TO HA'APAI & GETTING AROUND

Royal Tongan Airlines (© 800/486-6426 or 23-414; www.flyroyaltongan.com) flies from Tongatapu and Vava'u to **Salote Pilolevu Airport,** on Lifuka's northern end, at least once every day except Sunday. The airline's bus will take you from the airport 5km (3 miles) south to Pangai. The **Shipping Corporation of Polynesia** (© 21-699 in Nuku'alofa) operates weekly MV *Olovaha* ferry service from Nuku'alofa to Ha'apai. For details see "Getting to Tonga & Getting Around," above.

EXPLORING LIFUKA

Begin your visit at the local **Tonga Visitors Bureau (TVB)** branch, in the government compound on Palace Road (© 60-733), which distributes free maps of the island and a very helpful "Strolling Through Lifuka" brochure (you can pick these up at the TVB in Nuku'alofa, too). The post office, infirmary, Tonga Communications Corporation, and other offices are in the compound.

Check with Australian **Trevor Gregory,** owner of Mariner's Bar & Cafe (© 60-374), about guided walking tours of town. See "Where to Dine on Ha'apai," below.

Easily explored on foot, the town of Pangai spreads out from **Taufa'ahau Wharf,** on the western, lagoon side of Lifuka. Europeans settled north of the wharf and built colonial-style houses, a clapboard hotel, and a cemetery, where the **Rev. Shirley Baker Monument** is a major site today. In those days, the king resided in an impressive palace that stood at the inland end of Palace Road. The incumbent king stays at a much more modest **Royal Palace** on the lagoon, south of the wharf.

Billed as "The Smallest Museum in the World," the **Afa Eli Historical Museum & Research Library,** inland near the old palace site (no phone), is the creation of Virginia Watkins, a Vermont native who has lived in Tonga since 1981. The museum actually resides in a window, in which Mrs. Watkins displays small exhibits of Tongan culture and lore. She lives across the road and is always happy to show the 3,000-year-old pottery shards and other items she has collected. Admission is free but donations are appreciated.

South of town, the tiered **Olovehi Tomb** was constructed of limestone in the late 1700s for the eldest sister of the high chief. The chiefly **Bathing Well at 'Ahau** nearby was dug as an inverted cone to stabilize the porous bedrock. Trees in the bottom provided privacy.

Captain Cook sailed past the **Huluipaongo Tomb,** built on the southern end of Lifuka by harsh chiefs who were notorious for making their subjects work on this and other mounds. Stones for those projects were taken from the **Holopeka Beach Quarry,** northeast of town on Lifuka's ocean side.

SCUBA DIVING ⭐⭐ & OTHER WATERSPORTS

The largest underwater caves and canyons in the South Pacific beckon divers to the fish-filled seas surrounding these islands. **Happy Ha'apai Divers** (© and fax 60-600; sandybch@kalianet.to), at Sandy Beach Resort (see "Where to Stay on

Ha'apai," below), charges about T$95 ($43) for a two-tank dive, including tanks and weights. It operates from April through November.

WHERE TO STAY ON HA'APAI

The pick of the basic, low-budget accommodations here is **Fifita Guesthouse** (✆ **60-213;** fax 60-374; mariners@kalianet.to), over Mariner's Bar & Cafe in the middle of Pangai (see "Where to Dine on Ha'apai," below). A simple, shared-bathroom double room costs about T$25 ($11.25). No credit cards.

Resort at Billy's Place   Tongan Billy Hu'akau and his American wife, Sandy, operate this basic but friendly and clean little resort on a nearly deserted beach on Lifuka's ocean side. You won't be able to swim here, however, for the waves crash on a shallow coral shelf. Wooden walkways run through a thick tropical forest to their bungalows, which are made of timber over concrete floors. Each has two single beds that can be pushed together. Guests share communal toilets and showers (don't expect hot water). Inexpensive meals are served under a tent next to a central building.

P.O. Box 66, Pangai, Ha'apai (1km/½ mile northeast of Pangai). ✆ **60-336.** Fax 60-200. 5 units (none with bathroom). T$55–T$65 ($25–$29) double. Rates include breakfast. No credit cards. **Amenities:** 1 restaurant (regional), 1 bar. *In room:* No phone.

Sandy Beach Resort ✰✰   Sigrid ("Siggy") and Juergen Stavenow's resort is aptly named, for it sits beside one of the South Pacific's great beaches, a glorious curving stretch of white sand that faces west, toward Tofua and Kao on the horizon. And unlike so many beaches in the islands, at this one you can swim and snorkel at all tides. You can have a meal or a cold drink while taking in this view from the central building's big concrete veranda. Of modern construction but with Tongan style, each light, airy bungalow has a porch facing the beach and is equipped with a cool tile floor, either a double or two single beds, and an ample bathroom with a tiled hot-water shower. Each bungalow also has its own hammock and a thatch cabana out by the beach. To provide privacy, the bungalows are staggered and have a solid wall on the side facing their nearest neighbor. Guests can take nature walks (Juergen's specialty), watch a culture show, and catch a daily shuttle to Pangai. You'll pay extra for diving, horseback riding, boat trips, and tennis at the local Mormon church (bring your own racquet and balls).

P.O. Box 61, Pangai, Ha'apai (north end of Foa island). ✆ and fax **60-600.** www.tongaholiday.com/sandy-beach.htm. 12 units. T$160 ($72) bungalow. Rates include airport transfers. Breakfast and dinner T$51 ($23) per person per day. AE, MC, V. Children under 16 accepted on request only. Closed Dec 1–Feb 1. **Amenities:** 1 restaurant (regional); 1 bar; free use of snorkeling gear, kayaks, and bikes; laundry service. *In room:* Fridge, coffeemaker, no phone.

WHERE TO DINE ON HA'APAI

Mariner's Bar & Cafe REGIONAL   Australian Trevor Gregory sailed to Ha'apai on a yacht and like it so much he returned to open the town's only restaurant. A tin roof covers the wooden tables and white plastic tables. There's nothing fancy here—burgers, curries, steaks, chops, stir fries, and fish and chips—but the company's friendly and informative.

Fau Rd., Pangai. ✆ **60-374.** Reservations not accepted. Lunch T$2–T$5 (90¢–$2.25); dinner T$5–T$10 ($2.25–$4.50). MC, V. Mon–Sat 8am–8pm.

Appendix:
The South Pacific in Depth

The South Pacific islands have romantically affected the Western imagination since Tahitians gave a roaring, bare-breasted welcome to an English sea captain and his crew in 1767. To European minds back then, the Pacific islanders seemed to be Rousseau's "noble savages," living guilt-free lives beside crystal-clear lagoons. Fletcher Christian committed the world's most famous mutiny, in part because of his obsession for a Tahitian *vahine*. Missionaries soon arrived to save these heathen souls, and traders came to sell them whiskey and guns in exchange for sea cucumbers, coconuts, and land. Literary giants such as Herman Melville, Robert Louis Stevenson, W. Somerset Maugham, and James A. Michener spun great yarns about the islands, and actors like Clark Gable and Mel Gibson (both portraying Christian) brought colorful island characters to life on the silver screen.

Despite the inroads of modern materialism and the moral fervor of Christian fundamentalism instilled by the missionaries, today's travel posters don't lie about these languid islands. Palm-draped beaches beckon us to get away from it all. Blue lagoons and colorful reefs offer some of the world's best diving and snorkeling. Steep mountain valleys await hikers to visit islanders who live much as their ancestors did centuries ago. And uninhabited islets beg to be explored under sail.

Best of all, the proud and friendly Pacific Islanders stand ready to welcome you to their shores and explain their ancient customs and traditions. If the enormous beauty of their islands doesn't charm you, their highly infectious smiles surely will.

1 History 101

Islanders had been living on their tiny outposts for thousands of years before Europeans had the foggiest notion that the Pacific Ocean existed. Even after Vasco Nuñez de Balboa crossed the Isthmus of Panama and discovered this largest of oceans in 1513, and Ferdinand Magellan sailed across it in 1521, more than 250 years went by before Europeans paid much attention to the islands that lay upon it.

For most of that time, the Pacific was the domain of a Spanish sea captains, whose job was not discovery but bringing loot from the rich Spice Islands (now Indonesia and the Philippines) to Peru. Magellan stumbled upon few Pacific islands, none of which were below the equator. Alvaro de Medaña discovered some of the Solomon, Cook, and Marquesas islands in 1568 and 1595, and in 1606 Pedro Fernández de Quirós happened upon some of the Tuamotu, Cook, and New Hebrides (now Vanuatu) islands. Otherwise, the Spanish missed the South Pacific islands. Dutchman Abel Tasman discovered and explored much of Australia, New Zealand, Tonga, and Fiji in 1642, but the Dutch did nothing to exploit his discoveries, nor did they follow up on those of Jacob Roggeveen, who arrived at Easter Island and Samoa in 1722.

VENUS IN A GRASS SKIRT

The South Pacific came to Europe's attention during the latter half of the 18th century, when a theory came into vogue that an unknown southern land—a *terra australis incognita*—lay somewhere in the southern hemisphere. It had to exist, the theory went, for otherwise the unbalanced earth would wobble off into space. King George III of Great Britain took interest in the idea and in 1764 sent Capt. John Byron (the poet's grandfather) to the Pacific in HMS *Dolphin*. Although Byron came home empty-handed, King George immediately dispatched Capt. Samuel Wallis in the *Dolphin*. Wallis had no luck finding the unknown continent, but in 1767 he stumbled upon a high, lush island known as Tahiti. Canoeloads of Tahitians, including multitudes of young women clad only in grass skirts, paddled out to give him a rousing welcome.

Less than a year later, the Tahitians similarly welcomed French explorer Louis Antoine de Bougainville. So enchanted was Bougainville by the Venus-like quality of Tahiti's women that he named their island New Cythère—after the Greek island of Cythera, associated with the goddess Aphrodite (Venus).

Bougainville continued west, discovering several islands in Samoa and exploring the Solomon Islands, of which the island of Bougainville—now part of Papua New Guinea—still bears his name. So does the bright tropical shrub known as bougainvillea. He was the first Frenchman to circumnavigate the globe and was treated to a warm reception when he returned home in 1769. He brought with him a young Tahitian, whom the Parisians saw as living proof of Rousseau's theory that man at his best lived an uninhibited life as a noble savage.

CAPTAIN COOK'S TOURS

After Wallis arrived back in England, the

Dateline

- **30,000 B.C.** Australoid peoples settle in Southwest Pacific.
- **7,000–3,500 B.C.** Papuans arrive from Southeast Asia.
- **3,000–1,000 B.C.** Austronesians arrive from Asia, push eastward.
- **1,000 B.C.** Polynesians migrate eastward to Samoa and Tonga.
- **A.D. 1513** Balboa is the first European to see the Pacific Ocean.
- **1521** Magellan crosses the Pacific.
- **1568** Medaña discovers the Marquesas and some of Cook and Solomon islands.
- **1606** De Quirós "discovers" islands in the Tuamotus, the Cooks, and the New Hebrides (Vanuatu).
- **1642** Abel Tasman explores the western Pacific and finds Tonga and Fiji.
- **1722** Roggeveen happens upon Easter Island and Samoa.
- **1764** Byron fails to find terra australis incognita.
- **1767** Wallis discovers Tahiti.
- **1768** Bougainville also discovers Tahiti.
- **1769–71** Captain Cook observes the transit of Venus from Tahiti, explores the South Pacific.
- **1772–74** On his second voyage, Cook finds New Caledonia, Norfolk Island, more of the Cook Islands, and Fiji.
- **1778–79** Cook explores northwest America, dies in Hawaii.
- **1789** Fletcher Christian leads the mutiny on the *Bounty*.
- **1797** The first missionaries arrive in Tahiti.
- **1800–10** Whalers, merchants, and sandalwood traders flock to the islands, bring guns and whiskey.
- **1808** The last *Bounty* mutineer is discovered on Pitcairn.
- **1820–50** *Bêche-de-mer* (sea cucumber) trade flourishes; Western-style towns are founded in Tahiti, Samoa, Tonga, and Fiji.
- **1842** France annexes Tahiti; Herman Melville arrives in Papeete the same day.
- **1848** Tonga captures eastern Fiji.
- **1858** Fiji asks to become a British colony.

continues

Lords of the Admiralty put a young lieutenant named James Cook in command of a converted collier and sent him to Tahiti. A product of the Age of Enlightenment, Cook was a master navigator, a mathematician, an astronomer, and a practical physician who became the first captain of any ship to prevent scurvy among his crewmen by feeding them fresh fruits and vegetables. His ostensible mission was to observe the transit of Venus—the planet, that is—across the sun, an astronomical event that would not occur again until 1874, but which, if measured from widely separated points on the globe, would enable scientists for the first time to determine longitude on the earth's surface. Cook's second, highly secret mission was to find the elusive southern continent.

Cook's measurements of Venus were somewhat less than useful, but his observations of Tahiti, made during a stay of 6 months, were of immense importance in understanding the "noble savages" who lived there.

Cook then sailed southeast to carry out the secret part of his mission. He discovered the Society Islands northwest of Tahiti and the Australs to the south, and then he fully explored the coasts of New Zealand and eastern Australia, neither of which had been visited by Europeans since Tasman's voyage in 1642. After nearly sinking his ship on the Great Barrier Reef, he left the South Pacific through the strait between Australia and Papua New Guinea, which he named for his converted collier, the *Endeavor*. He returned to London in 1771.

During two subsequent voyages, Cook visited Tonga and discovered several other islands, among them what are now Fiji, the Cook Islands, Niue, New Caledonia, and Norfolk Island. His ships were the first to sail below the Antarctic Circle; although

- 1865 First Chinese are brought to Tahiti to harvest cotton.
- 1874 Britain accepts Fiji as a colony.
- 1879 First Indians are brought to Fiji.
- 1884 International Dateline established.
- 1888 Britain, foiling France, declares protectorate over the Cook Islands.
- 1889 Unrest in Western Samoa; hurricane destroys U.S., British, and German warships at Apia. Robert Louis Stevenson settles in Apia.
- 1890 Germany takes western Samoa, United States gets eastern Samoa, Britain claims protectorate over Tonga.
- 1891 Painter Paul Gauguin arrives in Tahiti.
- 1894 Robert Louis Stevenson dies in Samoa.
- 1901 Paul Gauguin dies in the Marquesas Islands of French Polynesia.
- 1915 During World War I, German Admiral von Spee shells Papeete.
- 1917 Count von Luckner is captured in Fiji after his German raider runs aground in the Cook Islands.
- 1933 Charles Nordhoff and James Norman Hall publish *Mutiny on the Bounty*, which becomes a bestseller.
- 1935 *Mutiny on the Bounty*, starring Clark Gable and Charles Laughton, is a smash box-office hit.
- 1941 Japanese bomb Pearl Harbor in Hawaii and begin advance into the South Pacific.
- 1942–44 Allied forces strike Guadalcanal in the Solomon Islands and use other islands as bases for attacks on the Japanese.
- 1947 James A. Michener's *Tales of the South Pacific* is published and gives rise to the musical and movie *South Pacific*.
- 1959–60 International airports open at Tahiti and Fiji.
- 1960 MGM remakes *Mutiny on the Bounty*, starring Marlon Brando.
- 1962 Western Samoa becomes independent.
- 1965 The Cook Islands gain local autonomy in association with New Zealand.
- 1966 France explodes its first nuclear bomb in the Tuamotus.

continues

he failed to sight Antarctica, he put to rest the theory that a large land mass lay in the tropical South Pacific. On his third voyage in 1778–79, he traveled to the Hawaiian Islands and explored the northwest coast of North America until ice in the Bering Strait turned him back. He returned to the Big Island of Hawaii, where, on February 14, 1779, he was killed during a petty skirmish with the islanders.

With the exception of the Hawaiians who smashed his skull, Captain Cook was revered throughout the Pacific. Although he claimed many of the islands for Britain, he hoped they would never be colonized. He treated the islanders fairly and respected their traditions. The Polynesian chiefs looked upon him as one of their own. (So revered was Capt. James Cook that today you'll find Cook's Bay, Cooktown, Cook Strait, any number of Captain Cook's Landing Places, and an entire island nation named for this giant of an explorer.)

- 1970 Fiji gains independence from Britain.
- 1985 The Treaty of Rarotonga declares the South Pacific to be a nuclear-free zone.
- 1987 Fiji's military overthrows the elected government.
- 1992 France halts nuclear testing in the Tuamotus; Fiji elects civilian government.
- 1995 France resumes limited nuclear testing, protesters riot in Papeete.
- 1996 France ends nuclear testing program.
- 1997 Western Samoa officially changes its name to Samoa; French Polynesia embarks on hotel-building campaign.
- 1998 Fiji adopts multiracial constitution.
- 1999 Fiji elects its first Indo-Fijian prime minister.
- 2000 Insurrection overthrows government in Fiji.
- 2001 Indigenous Fijians win elections, return to power.

MUTINY ON THE *BOUNTY*   Based on reports by Cook and others about the abundance of breadfruit, a head-size, potato-like fruit that grows on trees throughout the islands, a group of West Indian planters asked King George III if he would be so kind as to transport the trees from Tahiti to Jamaica as a cheap source of food for the slaves. The king dispatched Capt. William Bligh, who had been one of Cook's navigators, in command of HMS *Bounty* in 1787. One of Bligh's officers was a former shipmate named Fletcher Christian.

Their story is one of history's great sea yarns. The *Bounty* was late arriving in Tahiti, so Christian and the crew frolicked on Tahiti for 6 months, waiting for the next breadfruit season. They obviously enjoyed the affections of young Tahitian women as well as the balmy climate, for on April 28, 1789, on the way home, they overpowered Bligh off Tonga. After setting the captain and his loyalists adrift, Christian and eight other mutineers, along with their Tahitian wives and six Tahitian men, disappeared with the ship. Bligh and his men miraculously rowed the *Bounty's* longboat some 4,830km (3,000) miles to the Dutch East Indies, where they hitched a ride back to England. The Royal Navy then rounded up the *Bounty* crewmen left on Tahiti, and three of them were later hanged.

Fun Fact **Recovering the *Bounty's* Rudder**

Sunk by the mutineers in 1789, HMS *Bounty* remained in its watery grave until it was discovered by a *National Geographic* expedition in the 1950s. The *Bounty's* rudder is now on display at the Fiji Museum in Suva.

Christian's whereabouts remained a mystery until 1808, when a U.S. whaling ship discovered the last surviving mutineer on remote Pitcairn Island. The mutineers, after landing there in 1789, had burned and sunk the *Bounty*. Their descendants still live on Pitcairn and elsewhere in the South Pacific.

See "History 101" in chapter 3 for more about the mutiny.

GUNS & WHISKEY   The U.S. ship that found the mutineers' retreat at Pitcairn was one of many whalers roaming the South Pacific in the early 1800s. Their ruffian crews made dens of iniquity of many ports, such as Lahaina and Honolulu in Hawaii, Papeete and Nuku Hiva in what is now French Polynesia, and Levuka in Fiji. Many crewmen jumped ship and lived on the islands, some of them even casting their lots—and their guns—with rival chiefs during tribal wars. With their assistance, some chiefs were able to extend their power over entire islands or groups of islands.

Along with the whalers came traders. Some of them sailed from island to island in search of sandalwood, pearls, shells, and the sea cucumbers known as *bêches-de-mer*, which they traded for beads, cloth, whiskey, and guns and then sold at high prices in China. Others established stores that became the catalysts for Western-style trading towns. The merchants brought more guns and alcohol to people who had never used them before. They also put pressure on local leaders to coin money, which introduced a cash economy where none had existed before. Guns, alcohol, and money had far-reaching effects on the easygoing, communal traditions of the Pacific Islanders.

Diseases brought by the Europeans and Americans were even more devastating. The Polynesians had little, if any, resistance to such ailments as measles, influenza, tuberculosis, pneumonia, typhoid fever, and venereal disease. Epidemics swept the islands and killed the majority of their inhabitants.

While the traders were building towns, other arrivals were turning the bush country into plantations: cotton in Tahiti, sugar in Fiji, coconuts everywhere. With the native islanders either disinclined to work or unable to do so, Chinese indentured laborers were brought to a cotton plantation in Tahiti in the 1860s. After it failed, some of the Chinese stayed and became farmers and merchants. Their descendants now form the merchant class of French Polynesia. Something similar happened in Fiji, where East Indians were brought to work the sugar plantations.

BRINGING THE WORD OF GOD   The reports of the islands by Cook and Bougainville may have brought word of noble savages living in paradise to some people in Europe; to others, they heralded heathens to be rescued from hell. So while alcohol and diseases were destroying the islanders' bodies, a stream of missionaries arrived on the scene to save their souls.

The "opening" of the South Pacific coincided with a fundamentalist religious revival in England, and it wasn't long before the London Missionary Society (LMS) was on the scene in Tahiti. Its first missionaries, who arrived in the LMS

⌜Fun Fact First Novels

One deserter who jumped ship in the Marquesas Islands and later went to Tahiti, in the early 1820s, was Herman Melville. He returned to New England and wrote two books, *Typee* and *Omoo*, based on his South Pacific exploits. They were the start of his literary career.

Impressions

It would have been far better for these people never to have known us.
                                                            —Capt. James Cook, 1769

ship *Duff* in 1797, were the first Protestant missionaries to leave England for a foreign country. They chose Tahiti because there "the difficulties were least."

Polynesians, already believing in a supreme being at the head of a hierarchy of lesser gods, quickly converted to Christianity in large numbers. As an act of faith, the puritanical missionaries demanded the destruction of all *tikis,* which they regarded as idols. (As a result, today most Polynesian tikis carved for the tourist souvenir trade resemble those of New Zealand, where the more liberal Anglican missionaries were less demanding.) The missionaries in Polynesia also insisted that the heathen temples (known as *maraes*) be torn down. Many have now been restored, however, and can be visited in the islands.

Roman Catholic missionaries made less puritanical progress in Tahiti after the French took over in the early 1840s, but for the most part the South Pacific was the domain of rock-ribbed Protestants. The LMS extended its influence west through the Cook Islands and the Samoas, and the Wesleyans had luck in Tonga and Fiji. Today, thanks to those early missionaries, Sunday is a very quiet day throughout the islands.

COLONIALS TAKE CHARGE   Although Captain Cook laid claim to many islands, Britain was reluctant to burden itself with such far-flung colonies, beyond those it already had—Australia and New Zealand. Accordingly, colonialism was not a significant factor in the history of the South Pacific islands until the late 19th century. The one exception was France's declaring a protectorate over Tahiti in 1842.

This situation changed half a century later, when imperial Germany colonized the western islands of Samoa in the 1890s (at the same time that novelist Robert Louis Stevenson arrived to live there). Britain took over Fiji and agreed to protect the Kingdom of Tonga from takeover by another foreign power; France moved into New Caledonia; and the United States stepped into the eastern Samoan islands, which became known as American Samoa. Britain also claimed the Cook Islands, but they were later annexed by newly independent New Zealand. Thus, within a period of 30 years, every South Pacific island group except Tonga became a colony.

After World War I, when Germany was stripped of its colonies, New Zealand took over in Western Samoa. Otherwise, the colonial structure in the South Pacific remained the same, politically, until the 1960s.

Economically, the islands came under the sphere of Australia and New Zealand. Large Australian companies, such as Burns Philp and Carpenters, built up trading and shipping empires based on the exchange of retail goods for copra and other local produce, and Australian and New Zealand banks came to dominate finance in most islands outside the French and U.S. territories.

THE COUNT & THE CONSTABLES   Although thousands of Pacific islanders went off to fight with their colonial rulers during World War I, the islands themselves escaped action, with two exceptions.

First, a small German naval force under Adm. Graf von Spee sped across the Pacific during 1915, sinking Allied merchant ships and shelling the town of Papeete.

Two years later, the colorful Count von Luckner brought his German raider *Seeadler* into the Pacific to hunt for merchant prey. After 3 months' prowling, which netted only three small sailing vessels, the *Seeadler* was swept onto the reef at Mopelia atoll in the remote northern Cook Islands. Von Luckner and five crewmen set out in the ship's launch for Rarotonga to commandeer another ship. He could have captured the town of Avarua but steered away when he saw a "ship" in port—in reality, a wreck sitting upright on the reef. He then headed for Fiji, where, deceived as to the actual British force on the island, he surrendered to one armed policeman and five unarmed constables sent to investigate.

BASES, ROADS & AIRSTRIPS   The South Pacific leaped onto the front pages in World War II. Within weeks after the bombing of Pearl Harbor, in December 1941, the Japanese drove south to Papua New Guinea and the Solomon Islands, where, in July 1942, they began constructing an airfield on Guadalcanal. The U.S. Marines invaded Guadalcanal and nearby Tulagi on August 8, and during the next 6 months one bloody jungle skirmish and sea battle after another took place. By February 1943, with Guadalcanal entirely in U.S. hands, the Japanese advance in the southwestern Pacific had been stopped. The stage was soon set for the Allied counteroffensive that would island-hop its way toward Japan.

Although the South Pacific fighting took place only in Papua New Guinea and the Solomon Islands, many other islands played significant supporting roles. Airstrips and training bases were built all over the South Pacific; many of the airfields are still in use today. Out-of-the-way islands, such as Bora Bora and Aitutaki, became refueling stops on transpacific flights, and the Samoas and Fiji were invaded by thousands of U.S. Marines and GIs preparing for the fighting farther west and north. Entire communities with modern infrastructures were built in weeks—only to be abandoned almost overnight when the war ended.

The war's effect on the islanders was profound. The profusion of new things that arrived on their islands, and the wages paid them for working on the Allied bases, brought a wave of Western influence. The experience was so overwhelming on some Melanesian islands that local "cargo cults" began worshipping Americans or the airplanes with which they brought "mana from heaven."

The soldiers, sailors, and marines also left behind another legacy: thousands of mixed-race children.

CHIEFS, MINISTERS & NUCLEAR BOMBS   Colonialism began to crumble in the South Pacific when New Zealand granted independence to Western Samoa in 1962 and, 3 years later, gave complete local autonomy to the Cook Islands. Fiji became independent of Great Britain in 1970. Elsewhere, Britain left the Solomon Islands in 1978, and in 1980 Britain and France gave up their condominium government in the New Hebrides, which became the independent Republic of Vanuatu.

All these young nations have governments based on the Westminster parliamentary system, with wrinkles tailored to fit their citizens' traditions. Almost everywhere there is a council of chiefs to advise the modern-style ministers on custom and tradition. In a modern vestige of the old chiefly system, the national governments tend to have strong individuals at the helm. Elections in these small countries, where everyone seems to know everyone else, often are hard fought and sometimes bitter. Usually, the victors take office and the vanquished keep on grouching until the polls open again. Fiji's bloodless military coups of 1987, which overthrew that country's first Indo-Fijian-dominated government, was a shock to observers because it was directly opposed to this democratic tradition. Fiji has since adopted a constitution that provides for an elected parliament.

Of the old colonial powers, only the United States and France remain.

As American nationals, American Samoans are eligible for most U.S. federal aid programs and U.S. passports (about two-thirds of all American Samoas reside on Hawaii or the U.S. mainland). Moreover, except for Washington's control of their budget, they already have almost complete say over their domestic affairs. They are not clamoring for independence.

The problems facing French Polynesia are a good deal thornier. Many Tahitians would like to see their islands free of France and actively campaign for independence, but the majority keep voting not to turn off the money coming their way from Paris.

Between 1966 and 1992, the French exploded 210 nuclear weapons in the Tuamotu Archipelago, about 1,208km (750 miles) southeast of Tahiti, first in the air and then underground. Led by New Zealand, where French secret agents sank the Greenpeace protest ship *Rainbow Warrior* in 1985, many South Pacific island nations vociferously complained about the blasts. That same year, the regional heads of government, including the prime ministers of New Zealand and Australia, adopted the Treaty of Rarotonga, calling for the South Pacific to become a nuclear-free zone. After a lull, French Pres. Jacques Chirac decided in 1995 to resume nuclear testing, a move that set off worldwide protests, a day of rioting in Papeete, and a Japanese tourist boycott of French Polynesia. After six underground explosions, the French halted further tests, announced plans to close the testing facility, and in 1996 signed the Treaty of Rarotonga. To help the territory make up for the tons of francs France was spending on the testing program, Paris is providing French Polynesia with an "economic restructuring fund" until 2006. Meanwhile, French Polynesia's status has shifted from a French "territory" to a "country of France"—whatever that means. The local government has assumed more powers over its affairs, although France still retains control over law enforcement, defense, foreign affairs, and a few other crucial matters.

THIS LAND IS OUR LAND   Underlying many political issues in the South Pacific is the fundamental question of land rights. There simply isn't much land in these islands, and the indigenous peoples want to maintain their customary ownership of it. Thus, when Vanuatu became independent in 1980, it abolished freehold property and returned all land to its customary owners. Similarly, in 1987, when it appeared in Fiji that a government dominated by Indo-Fijians would rewrite the laws protecting Fijian land rights, the military staged two coups. Fiji has since returned to civilian control, despite an insurrection in 2000 that was spurred by fears of Indo-Fijian economic power.

Despite an occasional riot in Tahiti, the coups in Fiji, and the usual fisticuffs after too many beers on a Friday night, violence is not the usual way by which islanders solve their problems, whether political or personal. They prefer what they call the "Pacific way": discussion, compromise, and consensus, often achieved during all-night sessions over a bowl of kava, the slightly narcotic drink much favored in the islands for ceremonial as well as pleasurable purposes.

The islanders are protective of their land, and they're also concerned about the surrounding ocean. The Pacific island states have opposed drift-net fishing; it not only kills dolphins and other sealife unnecessarily, they argue, but it also strips them of a vital natural resource. The islanders are also involved in efforts to reduce pollution of the oceans. Many of them see a looming threat in the greenhouse effect: An increase in world temperatures could raise the world's sea level by melting part of the polar ice caps, endangering many of the low-lying islands.

2 The Islanders

The early European explorers were astounded to find the far-flung South Pacific islands inhabited by peoples who shared similar physical characteristics, languages, and cultures. How had these people—who lived a late Stone Age existence and had no written languages—crossed the vast Pacific to these remote islands long before Europeans had had the courage to sail out of sight of land on the Atlantic? Where had they come from? Those questions baffled the early European explorers, and they continue to intrigue scientists and scholars today.

THE FIRST SETTLERS

Thor Heyerdahl drifted in his raft *Kon Tiki* from South America to French Polynesia in 1947, to prove his theory that the Polynesians came from the Americas, but most experts now believe that the Pacific islanders have their roots in Southeast Asia. The generally accepted view is that during the Ice Age a race of early humans known as Australoids migrated from Southeast Asia to Papua New Guinea and Australia, when those two countries were joined as one land mass. Another group, the Papuans, arrived from Southeast Asia between 5,000 and 10,000 years ago. Several thousands of years later, a lighter-skinned race known as Austronesians pushed the Papuans inland and out into the more eastern South Pacific islands.

The most tangible remains of the early Austronesians are remnants of pottery, the first shards of which were found during the 1970s in Lapita, a village in New Caledonia. Probably originating in Papua New Guinea, Lapita pottery spread as far east as Tonga. Throughout the area it was decorated with geometric designs similar to those used today on Tongan tapa cloth.

Lapita was the only type of pottery in the South Pacific for a millennium. Apparently, however, the Lapita culture died out some 2,500 years ago. By the time European explorers arrived in the 1770s, gourds and coconut shells were the only crockery used by the Polynesians, who cooked their meals underground and ate with their fingers off banana leaves. Of the islanders covered in this book, only the Fijians still make pottery using Lapita methods.

MELANESIANS

The islands settled by the Papuans and Austronesians are known collectively as *Melanesia*, which includes Papua New Guinea, the Solomon Islands, Vanuatu, and New Caledonia. Fiji is the melting pot of the Melanesians to the west and the Polynesians to the east.

The name Melanesia is derived from the Greek words *melas*, "black," and *nesos*, "island." The Melanesians in general have negroid features—brown-to-black skin, flat or hooked noses, full lips, and wiry hair—but the interbreeding among the successive waves of migrants resulted in many subgroups with varying physical characteristics. That's why the Fijians look more African American than Polynesian. Their culture, on the other hand, has many Polynesian elements, brought by interbreeding and conquest.

Impressions
You who like handsome men would find no shortage of them here; they are taller than I, and have limbs like Hercules.
—Paul Gauguin, 1891

POLYNESIANS

The Polynesians' ancestors stopped in Fiji on their migration from Southeast Asia but later pushed on into the eastern South Pacific. Archaeologists now believe that they settled in Tonga and Samoa more than 3,000 years ago and then slowly fanned out to colonize the vast Polynesian triangle.

These extraordinary mariners crossed thousands of miles of ocean in large, double-hulled canoes capable of carrying hundreds of people, animals, and plants. They navigated by the stars, the wind, the clouds, the shape of the waves, and the flight pattern of birds—a remarkable achievement for a people who on land used no metal tools and had given up the use of pottery of any kind thousands of years before.

Most Polynesians have copper skin and black hair that is straight or wavy rather than fuzzy. A well-built, athletic people, many have become professional football and rugby players in the United States, Australia, and New Zealand. Their ancestors fought each other with war clubs for thousands of years, and it stands to reason that the biggest, strongest, and quickest survived. The notion that all Polynesians are fat is incorrect. In the old days, body size did indeed denote wealth and status, but obesity today is more likely attributable to poor diet. On the other hand, village chiefs are still expected to partake of food and drink with anyone who visits to discuss a problem; hence, great weight remains an unofficial marker of social status.

POLYNESIAN SOCIETY   Although Polynesians frequently experienced wars among their various tribes, generally their conflicts were not as bloody as those in Fiji. Nor were they followed as often by a cannibalistic orgy at the expense of the losers.

Polynesians developed highly structured societies, and to this day they place great emphasis on hereditary bloodline when choosing leaders. Strong and sometimes despotic chiefdoms developed on many islands. The present king of Tonga carries on a line of central leaders who were so powerful in the 1700s that they conquered much of Fiji, where they installed many Polynesian customs, including their hereditary chiefly system. Just to make sure, the victorious Tongans forced the conquered Fijian chiefs to take Tongan wives. As a result, today Tongan blood flows in the veins of many Fijian chiefs, some whom have the Polynesian title *tui*.

In some places, such as Tahiti, the Polynesians developed a rigid class system of chiefs, priests, nobility, commoners, and slaves. Their societies emphasized elaborate formalities, and even today ceremonies featuring kava—a slightly narcotic drink—play important roles in Samoa, Tonga, and Fiji. Everyday life was governed by a system based on *tabu*, a rigid list of things a person could or could not do, depending on his or her status in life. *Tabu* and its variants *(tapu, tambu)* are used throughout the South Pacific to mean "do not enter"; from them derives the English word *taboo*.

Western principles of ownership have made inroads, but by and large everything in both Polynesia and Fiji—especially land—is owned communally by families. In effect, the system is pure communism at the family level. If your brother has a crop of taro and you're hungry, then some of that taro belongs to you. The same principle applies to a can of corned beef sitting on a shelf in a store, which helps explain why islander-owned grocery shops often teeter on the edge of bankruptcy.

Although many islanders would be considered poor by Western standards, no one in the villages goes hungry or sleeps without a roof over his or her head. Most of the thatch roofs in Polynesia today are actually bungalows at the resort hotels; nearly everyone else sleeps under tin. It's little wonder, therefore, that visitors are greeted throughout the islands by friendly, peaceable, and extraordinarily courteous people.

THE OLD GODS   Before the coming of Christian missionaries in the 1800s, the Fijians believed in many spirits in the animist traditions of Melanesia. The Polynesians, however, subscribed to the idea of a supreme spirit, who ruled over a plethora of lesser deities who in turn governed the sun, fire, volcanoes, sea, war, and fertility. *Tikis* were carved of stone or wood to give each god a home (but not a permanent residence) during religious ceremonies, and great stone *maraes* were built as temples and meeting places for the chiefs. Sacrifices—sometimes human—were offered to the gods, and cannibalism was not unknown in Polynesia, although it was not as widely practiced there as it was in Fiji and Melanesia.

LANGUAGES

Traced by linguists to present-day Taiwan, the Austronesian family of languages are spoken across a wide area, extending from Madagascar, off the coast of Africa, through Indonesia, Malaysia, the Philippines, and parts of Vietnam, to the South Pacific as far as Easter Island, off the coast of South America. No other group of ancient languages spread to so much of the earth's surface.

Today, the Polynesian islanders still speak similar languages from one major island group to another. For example, the word for "house" is *fale* in Tongan and Samoan, *fare* in Tahitian, '*are* in Cook Islands Maori, *hale* in Hawaiian, and *vale* in Fijian. Without ever having heard the other's language, Cook Islanders say they can understand about 60% of Tahitian, and Tongans and Samoans can get the gist of each others' conversations.

Thanks to the American, British, New Zealand, and Australian colonial regimes, English is an official language in the Cook Islands, both Samoas, and Fiji. It is spoken widely in Tonga. French is spoken alongside Tahitian in French Polynesia, although English is understood among most hotel and many restaurant staffs.

FEASTS FROM UNDERGROUND OVENS

Before the Europeans arrived, the typical South Pacific diet consisted of bananas, coconuts, and other fruits. Staples were starchy breadfruit and root crops, such as taro, arrowroot, yams, and sweet potatoes. The reefs and lagoons provided abundant fish, lobsters, and clams to augment the meats provided by domesticated pigs, dogs, and chickens. Taro leaves and coconut cream served as complements. Corned beef has replaced dog on today's menu; otherwise, these same ingredients still make up what is commonly called an "island feast."

Like their ancestors, today's islanders still prepare their major meals in an earth oven, known as *himaa* in Tahiti, *lovo* in Fiji, and *imu* or *umu* elsewhere.

Individual food items are wrapped in leaves, placed in the pit on a bed of heated stones, covered with more leaves and earth, and left to steam for several hours. The results are quite tasty, with the steam spreading the aroma of one ingredient to the others.

When the meal has finished cooking, the islanders uncover the oven, unwrap the food, and, using their fingers, set about eating their feast of *umukai* (island food) in a leisurely and convivial manner. Then they dance the night away.

The underground oven still is widely used on special occasions and for big family meals after church on Sunday. If you're lucky enough to be invited, don't miss a family feast. Otherwise, many restaurants, especially those at the resort hotels, prepare traditional "island night" feasts for their guests. Don't worry: You can use knives and forks instead of your fingers.

3 The Islands & the Sea

A somewhat less-than-pious wag once remarked that God made the South Pacific islands on the sixth day of creation so He would have an extraordinarily beautiful place to relax on the seventh day. Modern geologists have a different view, but the fact remains that the islands and the surrounding sea are possessed of heavenly beauty and a plethora of life forms.

HIGH, LOW & IN BETWEEN

The Polynesian islands were formed by molten lava escaping upward through cracks in the earth's crust as it has crept slowly northwestward over the eons, thus building great seamounts. Many of these—called "high islands"—have mountains soaring into the clouds. In contrast, pancake-flat atolls were formed when the islands sank back into the sea, leaving only a thin necklace of coral islets to circumscribe their lagoons and mark their original boundaries. In some cases, geologic forces have once again lifted the atolls, forming "raised" islands whose sides drop precipitously into the sea. Still other, partially sunken islands, are left with the remnants of mountains sticking up in their lagoons.

The islands of Tonga and Fiji, on the other hand, were created by volcanic eruptions along the collision of the Indo-Australian and Pacific tectonic plates. Although the main islands are quiet today, they are part of the volcanically active and earthquake-prone "Ring of Fire" around the Pacific Ocean.

FLORA & FAUNA

Most species of plants and animals native to the South Pacific originated in Southeast Asia and worked their way eastward across the Pacific, by natural distribution or in the company of humans. The number of native species diminishes the farther east one goes. Very few local plants or animals came from the Americas, the one notable exception being the sweet potato, which may have been brought back from South America by voyaging Polynesians.

PLANTS   In addition to the west-to-east differences, flora changes according to each island's topography. The mountainous islands make rain from the moist tradewinds and thus possess a greater variety of plants. Their interior highlands are covered with ferns, native bush, or grass. The low atolls, on the other hand, get sparse rainfall and support little other than scrub bush and coconut palms.

Ancient settlers brought coconut palms, breadfruit, taro, paper mulberry, pepper (kava), and bananas to the isolated midocean islands because of their usefulness as food or fiber. Accordingly, they are generally found in the inhabited areas of the islands and not so often in the interior bush.

With a few indigenous exceptions, such as the *tiare Tahiti* gardenia and Fiji's *tagimaucia,* tropical flowers also worked their way east in the company of humans. Bougainvillea, hibiscus, allamanda, poinsettia, poinciana (the flame tree), croton, frangipani (plumeria), ixora, canna, and water lilies all give colorful testament to the islanders' love for flowers of every hue in the rainbow. The aroma of the white, yellow, or pink frangipani is so sweet it's used as perfume on many islands.

ANIMALS & BIRDS   The fruit bat, or "flying fox," and some species of insect-eating bats are the only mammals native to the South Pacific islands. Dogs, chickens, pigs, rats, and mice were introduced by early settlers. There are few land snakes or other reptiles in the islands. The notable exceptions are geckos and skinks, those little lizards that seem to be everywhere. Don't go berserk when a gecko walks upside-down across the ceiling of your bungalow. They are harmless and actually perform a valuable service by eating mosquitoes and other insects.

The number and variety of species of bird life also diminishes as you go eastward. Most land birds live in the bush away from settlements and the accompanying cats, dogs, and rats. For this reason the birds most likely to be seen are terns, boobies, herons, petrels, noddies, and others that earn their livelihoods from the sea. Of the introduced birds, the Indian myna exists in the greatest numbers. Brought to the South Pacific early in the 20th century to control insects, the myna quickly became a noisy nuisance in its own right.

THE SEA

The tropical South Pacific Ocean virtually teems with sea life, from colorful reef fish to the horrific Great White sharks featured in *Jaws,* from the paua clams that make tasty chowders in the Cook Islands to the deep-sea tuna that keep the canneries going at Pago Pago.

More than 600 species of coral—10 times the number found in the Caribbean—form the great reefs that make the South Pacific a divers' mecca. Billions of tiny coral polyps build their own skeletons on top of those left by their ancestors, until they reach the level of low tide. Then they grow outward, extending the edge of the reef. The old skeletons are white, and the living polyps present a rainbow of colors; they grow best and are most colorful in the clear, salty water on the outer edge or in channels, where the tides and waves wash fresh seawater along and across the reef. A reef can grow as much as 2 inches a year in ideal conditions. Although pollution, rising seawater temperature, and a proliferation of crown-of-thorns starfish have greatly hampered reef growth—and beauty—in parts of the South Pacific, there still are many areas where the color and variety of corals are unmatched.

The lagoons formed by the reefs are like gigantic aquariums filled with a plethora of tropical fish and other marine life, including whales, which migrate to Tonga and Fiji from June to October, and sea turtles, which lay their eggs on some beaches from November through February. Nearly every main town has a bookstore with pamphlets that contain photographs and descriptions of the creatures that will peer into your face mask.

Most South Pacific countries restrict the use of spearguns, so ask before you go in search of the catch of your life. Sea turtles and whales are on the list of endangered species, and the importation of their shells, bones, and teeth is prohibited by many countries, including the United States.

> ### *Tips* Be Careful What You Touch
>
> Most island countries have tough laws protecting their environment, so *don't deface the reef.* You could land in the slammer for breaking off a gorgeous chunk of live coral to take home as a souvenir. The locals know what they can and cannot legally take from under the water, so buy your souvenir coral in a handcraft shop.

SOME WARNINGS   By and large, the South Pacific's marine creatures are harmless to humans, but there are some to avoid. Always **seek local advice** before snorkeling or swimming in a lagoon away from the hotel beaches. Many diving operators conduct snorkeling tours. If you don't know what you're doing, go with them.

Wash and apply a good antiseptic or antibacterial ointment to all **coral cuts and scrapes** as soon as possible.

Because coral cannot grow in fresh water, the flow of rivers and streams into the lagoon creates narrow channels known as **passes** through the reef. Currents can be very strong in the passes, so stay in the protected, shallow water of the inner lagoons.

Sharks are curious beasts that are attracted by bright objects such as watches and knives, so be careful what you wear in the water. Don't swim in areas where sewage or edible wastes are dumped, and never swim alone if you have any suspicion that sharks might be present. If you do see a shark, don't splash in the water or urinate. Calmly retreat and get out of the water as quickly as you can, without creating a disturbance.

Those round things on the rocks and reefs that look like pin cushions are **sea urchins,** and their calcium spikes can be more painful than needles. A sea-urchin puncture can result in burning, aching, swelling, and discoloration (black or purple) around the area where the spines entered your skin. The best thing to do is to pull any protruding spines out. The body will absorb the spines within 24 hours to 3 weeks, or the remainder of the spines will work themselves out. Again, contrary to poplar wisdom, do not urinate or pour vinegar on the embedded spines—this will not help.

Jellyfish stings can hurt like the devil but are seldom life threatening. You need to get any visible tentacles off your body right away, but not with your hands, unless you are wearing gloves. Use a stick or anything else that is handy. Then rinse the sting with salt- or freshwater, and apply ice to prevent swelling and to help control the pain. If you can find it at an island grocery store, Adolph's Meat Tenderizer is a great antidote.

The **stone fish** is so named because it looks like a piece of stone or coral as it lies buried in the sand on the lagoon bottom with only its back and 13 venomous spikes sticking out. Its venom can cause paralysis and even death. You'll know by the intense pain if you're stuck. Serum is available, so get to a hospital at once. **Sea snakes, cone shells, crown-of-thorns starfish, moray eels, lionfish,** and **demon stingers** also can be painful, if not deadly. The last thing any of these creatures wants is to tangle with a human, so keep your hands to yourself.

Index

See also Accommodations index, below.

Frommer's® Complete Travel Guides

Alaska
Alaska Cruises & Ports of Call
Amsterdam
Argentina & Chile
Arizona
Atlanta
Australia
Austria
Bahamas
Barcelona, Madrid & Seville
Beijing
Belgium, Holland & Luxembourg
Bermuda
Boston
Brazil
British Columbia & the Canadian Rockies
Budapest & the Best of Hungary
California
Canada
Cancún, Cozumel & the Yucatán
Cape Cod, Nantucket & Martha's Vineyard
Caribbean
Caribbean Cruises & Ports of Call
Caribbean Ports of Call
Carolinas & Georgia
Chicago
China
Colorado
Costa Rica
Denmark
Denver, Boulder & Colorado Springs
England
Europe
European Cruises & Ports of Call
Florida

France
Germany
Great Britain
Greece
Greek Islands
Hawaii
Hong Kong
Honolulu, Waikiki & Oahu
Ireland
Israel
Italy
Jamaica
Japan
Las Vegas
London
Los Angeles
Maryland & Delaware
Maui
Mexico
Montana & Wyoming
Montréal & Québec City
Munich & the Bavarian Alps
Nashville & Memphis
Nepal
New England
New Mexico
New Orleans
New York City
New Zealand
Northern Italy
Nova Scotia, New Brunswick & Prince Edward Island
Oregon
Paris
Philadelphia & the Amish Country
Portugal
Prague & the Best of the Czech Republic

Provence & the Riviera
Puerto Rico
Rome
San Antonio & Austin
San Diego
San Francisco
Santa Fe, Taos & Albuquerque
Scandinavia
Scotland
Seattle & Portland
Shanghai
Singapore & Malaysia
South Africa
South America
South Florida
South Pacific
Southeast Asia
Spain
Sweden
Switzerland
Texas
Thailand
Tokyo
Toronto
Tuscany & Umbria
USA
Utah
Vancouver & Victoria
Vermont, New Hampshire & Maine
Vienna & the Danube Valley
Virgin Islands
Virginia
Walt Disney World & Orlando
Washington, D.C.
Washington State

Frommer's® Dollar-a-Day Guides

Australia from $50 a Day
California from $70 a Day
Caribbean from $70 a Day
England from $75 a Day
Europe from $70 a Day

Florida from $70 a Day
Hawaii from $80 a Day
Ireland from $60 a Day
Italy from $70 a Day
London from $85 a Day

New York from $90 a Day
Paris from $80 a Day
San Francisco from $70 a Day
Washington, D.C. from $80 a Day

Frommer's® Portable Guides

Acapulco, Ixtapa & Zihuatanejo
Amsterdam
Aruba
Australia's Great Barrier Reef
Bahamas
Baja & Los Cabos
Berlin
Boston
California Wine Country
Cancún
Charleston & Savannah
Chicago
Disneyland
Dublin
Florence

Frankfurt
Hawaii: The Big Island
Hong Kong
Houston
Las Vegas
London
Los Angeles
Maine Coast
Maui
Miami
New Orleans
New York City
Paris
Phoenix & Scottsdale

Portland
Puerto Rico
Puerto Vallarta, Manzanillo & Guadalajara
Rio de Janeiro
San Diego
San Francisco
Seattle
Sydney
Tampa & St. Petersburg
Vancouver
Venice
Virgin Islands
Washington, D.C.

Frommer's® National Park Guides

Banff & Jasper
Family Vacations in the National Parks
Grand Canyon

National Parks of the American West
Rocky Mountain

Yellowstone & Grand Teton
Yosemite & Sequoia/ Kings Canyon
Zion & Bryce Canyon

FROMMER'S® MEMORABLE WALKS

Chicago	New York	San Francisco
London	Paris	

FROMMER'S® GREAT OUTDOOR GUIDES

Arizona & New Mexico	Northern California	Vermont & New Hampshire
New England	Southern New England	

SUZY GERSHMAN'S BORN TO SHOP GUIDES

Born to Shop: France	Born to Shop: Italy	Born to Shop: New York
Born to Shop: Hong Kong,	Born to Shop: London	Born to Shop: Paris
Shanghai & Beijing		

FROMMER'S® IRREVERENT GUIDES

Amsterdam	Los Angeles	San Francisco
Boston	Manhattan	Seattle & Portland
Chicago	New Orleans	Vancouver
Las Vegas	Paris	Walt Disney World
London	Rome	Washington, D.C.

FROMMER'S® BEST-LOVED DRIVING TOURS

Britain	Germany	Northern Italy
California	Ireland	Scotland
Florida	Italy	Spain
France	New England	Tuscany & Umbria

HANGING OUT™ GUIDES

Hanging Out in England	Hanging Out in France	Hanging Out in Italy
Hanging Out in Europe	Hanging Out in Ireland	Hanging Out in Spain

THE UNOFFICIAL GUIDES®

Bed & Breakfasts and Country	Southwest & South Central	Mid-Atlantic with Kids
Inns in:	Plains	Mini Las Vegas
California	U.S.A.	Mini-Mickey
Great Lakes States	Beyond Disney	New England and New York with
Mid-Atlantic	Branson, Missouri	Kids
New England	California with Kids	New Orleans
Northwest	Chicago	New York City
Rockies	Cruises	Paris
Southeast	Disneyland	San Francisco
Southwest	Florida with Kids	Skiing in the West
Best RV & Tent Campgrounds in:	Golf Vacations in the Eastern U.S.	Southeast with Kids
California & the West	Great Smoky & Blue Ridge Region	Walt Disney World
Florida & the Southeast	Inside Disney	Walt Disney World for Grown-ups
Great Lakes States	Hawaii	Walt Disney World with Kids
Mid-Atlantic	Las Vegas	Washington, D.C.
Northeast	London	World's Best Diving Vacations
Northwest & Central Plains		

SPECIAL-INTEREST TITLES

Frommer's Adventure Guide to Australia & New Zealand
Frommer's Adventure Guide to Central America
Frommer's Adventure Guide to India & Pakistan
Frommer's Adventure Guide to South America
Frommer's Adventure Guide to Southeast Asia
Frommer's Adventure Guide to Southern Africa
Frommer's Britain's Best Bed & Breakfasts and Country Inns
Frommer's Caribbean Hideaways
Frommer's Exploring America by RV
Frommer's Fly Safe, Fly Smart
Frommer's France's Best Bed & Breakfasts and Country Inns
Frommer's Gay & Lesbian Europe

Frommer's Italy's Best Bed & Breakfasts and Country Inns
Frommer's New York City with Kids
Frommer's Ottawa with Kids
Frommer's Road Atlas Britain
Frommer's Road Atlas Europe
Frommer's Road Atlas France
Frommer's Toronto with Kids
Frommer's Vancouver with Kids
Frommer's Washington, D.C., with Kids
Israel Past & Present
The New York Times' Guide to Unforgettable Weekends
Places Rated Almanac
Retirement Places Rated